Inner Development Goals

Inner Development Goals

Stories of Collective Leadership in Action,
Volume 2: From "We" to "Systems Change"

Edited by
Eleftheria Egel and Mauricio Campos Suarez

DE GRUYTER

The original version of chapter 20 was revised. Unfortunately, the author Carlos Largacha-Martinez was misspelled in the original publication. This has been corrected. We apologize for the mistake.

ISBN 978-3-11-145334-7
e-ISBN (PDF) 978-3-11-145372-9
e-ISBN (EPUB) 978-3-11-145398-9

Library of Congress Control Number: 2025931337

Bibliographic information published by the Deutsche Nationalbibliothek
The Deutsche Nationalbibliothek lists this publication in the Deutsche Nationalbibliografie; detailed bibliographic data are available on the internet at http://dnb.dnb.de.

© 2025 Walter de Gruyter GmbH, Berlin/Boston, Genthiner Straße 13, 10785 Berlin
Cover image: Ruth D Moore
Typesetting: Integra Software Services Pvt. Ltd.

www.degruyter.com
Questions about General Product Safety Regulation:
productsafety@degruyterbrill.com

Ruth D. Moore

The piece for the book cover is entitled

YUI

結

Yui (結) is a Japanese word that expresses the idea of tying together.
Related to the idea of tying together is Yui's secondary meaning of cooperation, a very powerful element of traditional Japanese culture. In the past, communities would come together to build houses or farm crops – the spirit of emotional connectedness and mutual aid underpinning these acts is Yui.

45.5 cm x 30.5 cm

Acrylics, pencil and mixed papers on 300 gm cotton paper.

The work draws inspiration from rock sculptures and ancient cairns, structures nestled within the landscape. Built to endure eternity or collapse in a strong breeze, they ask: Will we work on ourselves to thrive in the world that sustains us, or will we succumb to the next strong storm?

The artist: Ruth D Moore is a British-Trinidadian artist and systemic coach living in Switzerland, who started painting seven years ago after over 15 years as a body therapist and Shiatsu practitioner.

Foreword

I was honored by the invitation to write the preface for the second volume of the book *Inner Development Goals: Collective Leadership in Action*: *From "We" to "Systems Change"*. The editors believed that my personal journey as a social change-maker and as co-founder of the World Human Forum[1] resonate deeply with the volume's focus on exploring the broader societal shifts and systemic changes driven by collective leadership initiatives towards sustainability.

I learned the most valuable lessons about social transformation and systems change from the poorest communities in the Global South. In Indian slums and remote African villages, I met women and men who transformed their own lives, their children's futures, and their communities while promoting the implementation of the United Nations 2030 Agenda for Sustainable Development, without even knowing about it.

Coming from the Global North and having grown up in a political family and studied political science at a prestigious French university, this is not what I had learned. For me, systemic change was happening through political action. Political players were at the heart of it: political parties, in the best-case scenario of more or less functioning representative democracies, and autocrats when things didn't work as they should.

But this? This change literally happening from the bottom? How was it possible? Where did that force, that energy, come from? How was it that some people, often without any formal education, sometimes without elementary writing and budget literacy, were able to transform their lives and the lives of their communities?

Back then, on the agenda of progressive development NGOs, there was a lot of talk about the importance of social movements in systemic change. Rightly so: a lot of work was done in that direction; but I always felt that there was something missing in that analysis. The fact that the work we were doing in poor communities was more and more focused on empowerment, particularly women's empowerment, was certainly going in the right direction. And yet, we didn't seem to fully recognize the role of these individual changemakers. And something else was intriguing me. It was as if many of these individuals, transforming into emerging community leaders, were self-empowered, or as if it only required a small spark to light the fire in them to go out and make change happen. So, what did they have in common? What were their skills and qualities? And what if we finally acknowledged those skills and qualities as essential prerequisites for broader systemic change to happen? And what if more people had those skills and qualities? What if our societies recognized them, promoted them, and presented those people as role models for many more?

---

1 https://worldhumanforum.earth/

https://doi.org/10.1515/9783111453729-202

Much later on, and reflecting back on my own life, I realized that I shouldn't have been so surprised because, in a sense, this was exactly what had happened to me. It took years of inner work for me before I managed to move from being a passive observer to becoming an active agent of change. In 1998, this transformation enabled me to create what was to become the biggest Greek development organisation, ActionAid Hellas. To achieve this, I needed to develop some skills and qualities that I might have had inside me, but I certainly did not dare to use. This, I realize now, could only happen once my emotions and my inner self aligned with my actions and my logical analysis of what was happening around me.

But as rewarding as my work with ActionAid was, something was always missing. And that was exactly the fact that very few NGO decision makers seemed to seriously take into account in their theory of change those amazing people I was meeting on the ground at an individual level. Tobias, a simple yet resourceful teacher in a remote village in Kenya, literally managed to save his village from a series of disasters. Zeitouna, a beautiful, proud woman living on the border of Ethiopia and Somalia, who, having acquired elementary reading skills as an adult, had become an incredible community leader. It is those encounters that were giving me hope. Each time, they were for me a beautiful gift!

It became more and more clear that it was through the recognition of change happening from the bottom up that we could start addressing the many crises we were facing simultaneously. Simultaneously and everywhere, in the rich, developed Global North as well as in the Global South. Crises of inequality and poverty, democracy, human rights, and education but also the climate crisis, biodiversity crisis, and broader ecological sustainability, to which now we had to add a loneliness crisis in the Global North. In all those fields, people around the world were active, creative, successful, and thus inspiring many more to act.

Could technology help us in this direction? And very importantly, what was the role of the arts in this process of empowerment and effective personal transformation in order to create systemic change? Seeking answers to these questions, a small and diverse group of citizens from all walks of life and different parts of the world gathered in 2017 in the small town of Delphi, Greece. Inspired by the town's symbolic history as the navel of the world, our task was clear: imagining and building the World Human Forum, a space where personal transformation and collective action came together to drive systemic change. It was there that the Delphic Cube emerged as a sensemaking tool and pathway from "I" to "We" and from "We" to "Systems Change". The Delphic Cube, with its six interconnected sides – Sustainability & Regeneration, Democracy, Education, Inner Transformation, Science & Technology, and Art – demonstrates in a simple yet powerful way the interdependence of diverse fields. It highlights the complexity of addressing each in isolation, underscoring the need for holistic approaches that embrace their interconnected nature. In this sense, the Delphic Cube serves as both a valuable reminder and a complement to the transformative path proposed by the IDG framework as well as the comprehensive and multidisciplinary approach reflected in this book's chapters. Within each section, the individual chapters dive deeper into the intricate and diverse aspects of systemic change, examining how change is unfolding on multiple levels or in different contexts through academic insights, case studies, and artistic expressions.

I invite you, the reader, to engage with this volume, explore its ideas, and discover new knowledge and tools that will inspire and equip you to apply its insights to your own journey from "We" to "Systems Change".

Alexandra Mitsotaki
Co-founder and Chair World Human Forum

Acknowledgments

The creation of this book has been a collaborative journey, enriched by the support, encouragement and contributions of many individuals and organizations.

First and foremost, we extend our deepest gratitude to all the *authors* for their willingness and openness to co-create this work with us. Your insights, dedication, and shared vision brought this project to life.

We are profoundly thankful to our *families* for their understanding and patience as we devoted countless hours—on weekends and evenings—over many months to this endeavor. Your encouragement has been our bedrock through every step of the journey.

We wish to acknowledge *Impact Hub Basel,* whose vibrant community and innovative space provided the home where the idea for this project first took shape. Your commitment to empowering changemakers has been a constant source of inspiration and motivation.

We would also like to recognise the incredible support from our *Basel IDG community*. Your inspiration, shared commitment to fostering positive change, and support of this initiative from its inception has been invaluable. A special note of appreciation goes to our Basel IDG community member *Hape Mueller* for your pivotal role in supporting our communication efforts and website.

We deeply appreciate being part of the vibrant IDG Movement & Community, which has been instrumental in bringing this project to life. Special thanks go to Tomas Björkman for your unwavering presence and inspiration, and to Fredrik Lindencrona with the IDG Researchers Circle for your support from the beginning.

We extend our sincere thanks to Judi Neal, CEO of Edgewalkers International, for your invaluable advice in helping us identify the perfect publisher. Your guidance has been critical to our success.

Lastly, we are deeply grateful to De Gruyter Brill for your openness and partnership in making this publication a reality and for embracing this non-conventional book project. Your collaboration has allowed us to reach a broader audience and share this work in its fullest expression.

To everyone who has been part of this journey, we offer our heartfelt thanks. Your belief in our vision, your generosity, and your unwavering support have made this book possible.

— The Editors

https://doi.org/10.1515/9783111453729-203

Contents

Section 1: **Education**

Section 3: **Systems change**

Section 4: **IDG Movement**

Editor biographies

Mauricio Campos Suarez

Mauricio's journey as a transformative leader spans over 20 years, encompassing healthcare, technology, leadership development, and innovation in more than 40 countries. With a background as an engineer, MBA, and certified Integral™ (ICF PCC) and Systemic Senior Team Coach, he integrates inner development with business strategy through cultural transformation. After holding pivotal roles in large global corporations, he now collaborates with organizations and supports leaders as an independent coach and transformation catalyst. His dedication to organizational and leadership transformation fuels his drive to elevate awareness and create a better world. Deeply committed to fostering the sustainability shift needed to address humanity's most pressing challenges, he supports companies globally from his base in Switzerland, helping them expand their purpose and build their legacy. As a father of two and a long-time yoga and mindfulness practitioner, Mauricio's mission is to help organizations embrace change, enhance well-being, and drive personal and systemic transformation in a rapidly evolving world.

Dr Eleftheria Egel

Eleftheria is a scholar, board member, business mentor for female entrepreneurs and the co-founder of EOS Academy, an Edtech social startup. The focus of her work is on social sustainability. Her research and publications are in the fields of spiritual, female and sustainability leadership. She has published in academic journals and book collections and presented her work at international conferences worldwide. Eleftheria currently serves on the Executive Board of One Planet Education Networks and is a member of the Advisory Board at Ethics International Press. Previously, she was Board Member of the "Management, Spirituality & Religion" Division of the Academy of Management. Her vision is to drive positive change by challenging conventional thinking, fostering compassion and pushing the boundaries of what is possible in individual and socio-organisational contexts. A fervent community supporter, Eleftheria co-founded #SheHustlesAfrica in Nigeria together with the indigenous NGO AKAWI. Together, they empower local women entrepreneurs to tackle business challenges and grow. Close to her heart lies girls' education in developing countries. Her guiding motto is *"The phoenix cannot rise out of the ashes until the past has been laid to rest"*.

https://doi.org/10.1515/9783111453729-205

Eleftheria Egel
Introduction to Volume II

I am excited to share with you the second volume of the book, the culmination of over a year of dedicated collaboration between my co-editor, Mauricio Campos Suarez, and I. Throughout this journey, our collaboration has deepened and evolved, with discussions aimed at better understanding each other's perspectives, reconciling differing priorities and working styles, and ultimately finding common ground that would enable us to shift from an "I" to a "We" perspective. Our shared belief in the value of this book helped us to foster the collaborative mindset needed to envision the desired outcomes, agree on the approach, and complete this edition.

While collective leadership is either implied or explicitly promoted in all five dimensions of the IDG framework, bringing it to life is no easy task. Our aim with this two-volume edition was to conceptualize what collective leadership might look like if the IDG framework was employed, as well as to present real-world examples of collective leadership in action. To achieve this, we used a three-step co-creation process:

1. We urged the authors to co-create by presenting their work at a local IDG hub and incorporate audience feedback into the final chapter.
2. As editors, we collaborated closely with the authors, offering our perspectives to refine each chapter.
3. Together with our partner Sutra, we developed a digital space where authors can continue to engage and collaborate with their audience, extending the dialogue beyond the pages of the book.

I would now like to take a moment to explain how we approached the theme, selected the contributions, and structured the flow of this volume. We began with the concept of "We", which we view not as a simple aggregation of individual "I's" but as something greater that emerges when individuals come together.[1] In this context "We" represents a shared identity, a collective purpose, and a sense of mutual responsibility and ownership. The concept of systems change is the second one central to our approach. It refers to the transformation of fundamental structures, mindsets, customs, power dynamics, and policies – those that address the root causes of issues rather than just their symptoms. Achieving long-term environmental, social, and economic sustainability necessitates a fundamental shift in how systems function. Key aspects of this shift include recognizing that problems are interconnected and cannot be solved in isolation, as well as knowing that systems are dynamic, requiring adaptability and continuous learning.

---

[1] E.g., Durkheim's (2004) collective consciousness, group dynamics, system's emergent properties, Searle's (1990) collective intentionality.

https://doi.org/10.1515/9783111453729-001

To enable "We" to leverage this understanding for driving meaningful change, fostering collaboration, and acting purposefully we need to construct a new narrative, founded on two key elements: an expanded understanding of moral reasoning and a new conception of our role in this transformation. This narrative will allow us to transition from a dualistic to a more holistic worldview and become the architects of our collective future.

Our current industrial mode of meaning making promotes the myth of the market – the modern story of individual competition fueling techno-industrial progress toward a consumerist utopia. A more life-enhancing ecology, on the other hand, broadens our sense of responsibility to include nonhumans (e.g., animals), nature, future generations, and vulnerable (human) beings. We are willing and are often called upon by our institutions and organizations to make the right decisions that promote systemic change. But how do we define and agree on what the right decision is, and for whom? Our moral reasoning is largely shaped by widely accepted ethical principles which guide us in evaluating possible actions and eventually making the right decision (moral judgment). These same principles also serve as the basis for justifying our decisions (moral justification).[2] The moral reasoning we presently rely on to analyze systemic issues, evaluate consequences, and consider the rights and responsibilities of those involved is outdated. It fails to challenge the status quo or envision more equitable, sustainable, and inclusive systems. Instead, it is frequently used to justify "business as usual" and even green washing. Contemporary rule-based ethical theories – such as utilitarianism, rights/duties, reciprocity – place a premium on individual autonomous choice and equality, aiming to ensure both fairness in treatment and accountability for one's actions, by linking the outcomes people receive to the effort or ability they demonstrate. As such, they are insufficient to morally justify the rights of future human beings, nonhuman entities, and nature. As philosopher Hans Jonas (1984) eloquently describes it, future generations and nonhuman beings do not have rights. Thus, our duties to them transcend any idea of rights or reciprocity. According to him, we are bound by an "imperative of responsibility" to act in ways that protect the continuity of human life and preserve the integrity of nature.

To challenge the established narrative, we need to broaden our moral reasoning through an ethics of care. This approach embraces moral responsibility towards those who are vulnerable and in need of protection – those who have no voice to express their needs (future generations, animals, and the ecosystem) and those who have no power to negotiate their rights (e.g., marginalized groups). Care is rooted in the inherent dignity of all (human) beings and recognizes the justice of their claims, independent of their merit or ability to negotiate. An ethics of care is highly subjective and selective. Similar to virtue ethics, it highlights character traits, such as sympathy, compassion, and friendship. It also values nurturing community and connection while

---

2 E.g., Colby & Kohlberg (2011); Bandura (2002); Haidt (2001); Greene (2014).

considering the specific contexts and needs that influence moral decisions. In contrast to justice-oriented approaches which support the rights of one party only, an ethics of care looks into ways to simultaneously fulfil competing responsibilities to others (Ciulla, 2020; Gilligan, 1982).

In order for "We" to come to together to create systems change, we need to reformulate the answers to the following questions: Who is worth of our care and attention? And how can we love unconditionally?

To achieve the second key element of the transformation – reimagining our role as architects of our collective future – we need to take a quantum leap and challenge conventional thinking which sees the future as a linear progression from the past through the present. Rather than seeing ourselves as passive subjects of change, we need to embrace the possibility that the future may emerge from deeper, often unseen patterns and that multiple potential futures exist beyond a single pre-determined outcome. Being architects of our future implies acknowledging that our collective consciousness and intentions play a role in shaping the future. We should stop simply reacting to changes imposed upon us by external forces, systems, or authorities; feeling powerless and resigned in the face of challenges. We need to become proactive agents of change; be empowered by thinking out of the box, tapping into the creative power of our imagination, and crafting innovative solutions.

But how can we come together as architects to co-create our future? Renowned quantum physicist David Bohm (2013) introduced a transformative process that can help us think together in a deeper, more collaborative way, allowing us to tap into our collective intelligence and cultivate shared meaning and common consciousness. This process, called *dialogue,* is defined by Bohm as a stream of meaning flowing among and through a group of people, out of which may emerge new understanding. Unlike discussions aimed at reaching decisions or goals, Bohmian dialogue is rooted in exploration and collective learning. At its heart, the process relies on two key principles: unconditional acceptance and authentic presence. To foster these principles, participants are encouraged to cultivate qualities, such as humility, empathy, compassion, self-awareness, courage, trust, authenticity, and self-esteem. These qualities enable us to practice deep, active listening –opening space for new insights. "Listening to the whole," as Bohm describes, means becoming aware of and suspending our deeply held assumptions, beliefs, and certainties while remaining nonjudgmental and open to other perspectives, even if they differ from our own. In this space, there is no right or wrong; rather, a shared space where new potentialities can emerge. Respecting others' perspectives, however, does not mean diminishing our own expression. Authentic expression, or voicing, is equally essential to ensure inclusiveness. We are called to trust our own voice; speak from the present moment, express what is truly engaging us, rather than repeat rehearsed arguments or theories.

The IDG framework can support and enhance the practice of Bohmian dialogue in two ways. First, it can promote the same qualities essential to effective dialogue, such as empathy, self-awareness, and active listening. Second, Bohmian dialogue can gain depth when participants embody core IDG qualities like humility, authenticity, and compassion, which enable individuals to set aside their own assumptions and embrace others' perspectives. This shift from an individual "I" to a collective "We" is foundational to fostering meaningful dialogue and creating a shared understanding.

In this volume, we present a selection of theories, tools, and methods that have been developed and applied within specific organizational and institutional settings. These resources are designed to foster personal growth and align individuals toward shared objectives, ultimately enabling them to come together as a cohesive "We" with a clear, purpose-driven intention to drive systemic change.

Our invited preface contributor, Alexandra Mitsotaki, shares insights from her journey in social transformation and systems change, along with her experience in building social enterprises. Her key takeaway: we can tackle the polycrisis through change that begins from the ground up.

References

Bandura, A. (2002). Selective moral disengagement in the exercise of moral agency. Journal of Moral Education, 31(2), 101–119.

Bohm, D. (2013). *On dialogue*. Routledge.

Ciulla, J. B. (2020). *The search for ethics in leadership, business, and beyond* (Vol. 50). Springer Nature.

Colby, A., & Kohlberg, L. (2011). *The measurement of moral judgment (Vol. 1)*. Cambridge University Press.

Durkheim, E. (2004). Readings from Emile Durkheim. Psychology Press.

Gilligan, C. (1982). *In a different voice*. Harvard University Press.

Greene, J. D. (2014). Beyond point-and-shoot morality: Why cognitive (neuro) science matters for ethics. Ethics, 124(4), 695–726.

Haidt, J. (2001). The emotional dog and its rational tail: a social intuitionist approach to moral judgment. Psychological review, 108(4), 814.

Searle, J. R. (1990). Collective intentions and actions.

Jonas, Hans (1984). The imperative of responsibility: in search of an ethics for the technological age. Chicago: University of Chicago Press.

Structure of the book

Section 1: **Education** highlights the various ways the IDGs are being applied in schools, universities, and other learning spaces to reshape educational environments.

Chapter 1: **Prelude**.

Chapter 2: **Forming the Sustainable Citizenry through SEE Learning and the Inner Development Goals: Educating the heart and mind** illustrates how the IDGs can work collaboratively with a research-based program called SEE Learning in schools to build the skills and mindsets essential for navigating current and future challenges related to climate change.

Chapter 3: **Unlearning hierarchy in knowing: With IDGs towards inclusive spaces for actions of change** explores the potential of IDGs to create inclusive spaces that empower collective action, giving marginalized groups access to knowledge and a voice in decision making.

Chapter 4: **The Sustainability Mindset Indicator: A tool to assess and develop the Inner Development Goals** is a theoretical exploration of how the IDGs and their associated skills align with the Sustainability Mindset, a research-based framework for personal development and change management.

Chapter 5: **Changing business schools from within: A case study on the inner transformative potential of co-creative learning spaces** outlines a collaborative initiative at a Swiss university aimed at transforming business school education from within by focusing on community building and collective leadership, with the IDGs integrated as core principles.

Chapter 6: **What we have learned at Rflect: Catalyzing the scalable integration of the Inner Development Goals in higher education through tech** explores the development of an innovative edtech start-up in Switzerland that developed an app to support students' personal development, with the IDGs as a primary tool.

Section 2: **Interventions in organizations** highlights the transformative potential of the Inner Development Goals in helping organizations to improve their internal dynamics and strengthen their sustainability efforts.

Chapter 7: **Prelude**.

Chapter 8: **World Civility Index and Inner Development Goals: Connecting inner development to mainstream success** links the competencies of the IDGs with the inner development qualities assessed and certified by a universal standard known as the World Civility Index.

Chapter 9: **Measuring and training Inner Development Goals: Developing inner drivers for achieving sustainability goals** addresses the challenge of connecting individuals to climate change issues through the IDGs by utilizing two tools: the IDG-A questionnaire and the meaning, awareness, and purpose (MAP) model.

Chapter 10: **How to get rid of old habits: The relevance of unlearning and inner development in self-organization- experiences of a pharmaceutical service providers journey** explores the transformative journey of ten23 health, a pharmaceutical service provider, towards self-organization, unlearning, and inner development with the help of the IDGs.

Chapter 11: **Global Leadership for Sustainability (GLfS) and Inner Development Goals (IDGs): An integrated framework and roadmap to enhance leader and leadership development** presents an integrated framework that incorporates the IDGs in a model of Global Leadership for Sustainability (GLfS), along with a roadmap designed to enhance leader and leadership capacity in addressing sustainability challenges.

Section 3: **Systems change** presents a collection of case studies and research that illustrate successful examples of systemic transformation.

Chapter 12: **Prelude**.

Chapter 13: **Getting free from internalized capitalism: Inner Development Goals and narrative shift** explores the narratives and beliefs that underpin capitalism and proposes a systems change through narrative transformation, alongside the cultivation of the IDG competencies.

Chapter 14: **Keeping students in school with the Inner Development Goals framework and the Insights Finding Tool: A Thai case study** examines the application of the Insights Finding Tools program in conjunction with the IDG framework to empower changemakers with the skills and empathy needed to address student dropout rates in Phetchaburi, Thailand.

Chapter 15: **IDGs and integral politics: The marriage of depth and power** explores the interrelations between the IDG framework and an integral approach to politics.

Chapter 16: **Relating, cooperating and co-creating: The inner skills at the heart of cultural and intergenerational trauma healing and flourishing** looks into the flourishing of individuals descending from those affected by Colombia's armed conflict, proposing a healing process grounded in three IDG dimensions: relating, collaborating, and acting.

Chapter 17: **Futures Dialogues: Co-creating common good and becoming a community through the IDGs** details a two-year social improvement project in Novazzano, Switzerland, as a part of the national Future Dialogues program guided by Theory U's conscious, systemic approach and the development of inner capacities as outlined in the IDG framework.

Section 4: **The IDG movement** comprises a diverse array of narratives from the global IDG movement from around the world that reflect the diverse experiences and initiatives within the IDG movement.

Chapter 18: **Prelude**.

Chapter 19: **Lotus gardening with presence, wisdom, and inner freedom:: Co-creation of the Inner Development Goals Switzerland Center** narrates the community-building journey of IDG Switzerland, using the metaphor of a lotus flower's growth – from the introspective "mud" to the purposeful "bloom" of collective purpose within the hub's collaborative space.

Chapter 20: **How to unravel the IDGs' skills in practice: Making the IDGs work in Colombia** reflects on the ways in which Colombia's unique local context and cultural nuances shaped the founding of the national IDG Colombia Centre in 2021, influencing both its strategic focus and the approach to its initiatives.

Chapter 21: **Transforming tomorrow: The IDG Global Practitioners' Network's journey towards sustainable development – harnessing collective wisdom for global impact and personal growth** details the IDG Global Practitioners' Network, a vibrant and growing community of over 800 practitioners from more than 50 countries, founded in October 2022.

Chapter 22: **Research as co-creation: Creating a space in between for academia in the Inner Development Goals ecosystem** outlines the purpose and journey of the research circle, highlighting the potential of the IDGs as an emerging field of study by exploring various IDG-related research and publications.

Chapter 23: **Towards an increasing institutionalization of the IDGs: From individual to culture and system transformation** introduces the Global Leadership for Sustainable Development (GLSD) program, detailing its origins, outlining its evaluation process and outcomes, and highlighting key insights into how sustainability-focused leadership and education can drive transformative change.

Chapter 24: **Deep casting the IDGs: Exploring the cross-dimensional quality of coherence** presents and discusses preliminary findings from the EU-funded Cohere+ project and offers valuable insights and learnings that could benefit the IDG community.

As editors, we are grateful for the collaboration and insights shared by each contributor, whose expertise and perspective makes this work a rich resource for readers. We invite you, the reader, to engage deeply with the ideas presented, to reflect on their implications, and to consider how they may inform your own work and thinking. It is our hope that this book not only provides knowledge but also sparks dialogue and inspires action.

Thank you for joining us on this journey, and we look forward to the conversations and transformations this work may inspire.

Inner Development Goals (IDGs)

In 2015, the United Nations introduced the Sustainable Development Goals (SDGs), a comprehensive blueprint with the noble intention of achieving a sustainable world by 2030. Yet, almost a decade on, progress has been alarmingly slow, and it seems increasingly unlikely that these goals will be met on time. One critical reason for this shortfall is the lack of a fundamental inner dimension in our policy approaches, education, societal structures, economic models, and production systems. To confront and effectively address the complex challenges we face today, we must urgently enhance our collective abilities. This is where the IDGs become essential.

The IDG framework, developed with the insights and collaboration of over 4,000 scientists, experts, and practitioners, outlines the inner capabilities, qualities, and skills necessary to accelerate progress toward the SDGs. Comprising 23 specific attributes grouped into five dimensions, the framework offers a structured approach to cultivating the essential capacities of the human mind and heart – those inner qualities and abilities critical for addressing the multifaceted challenges of our time.

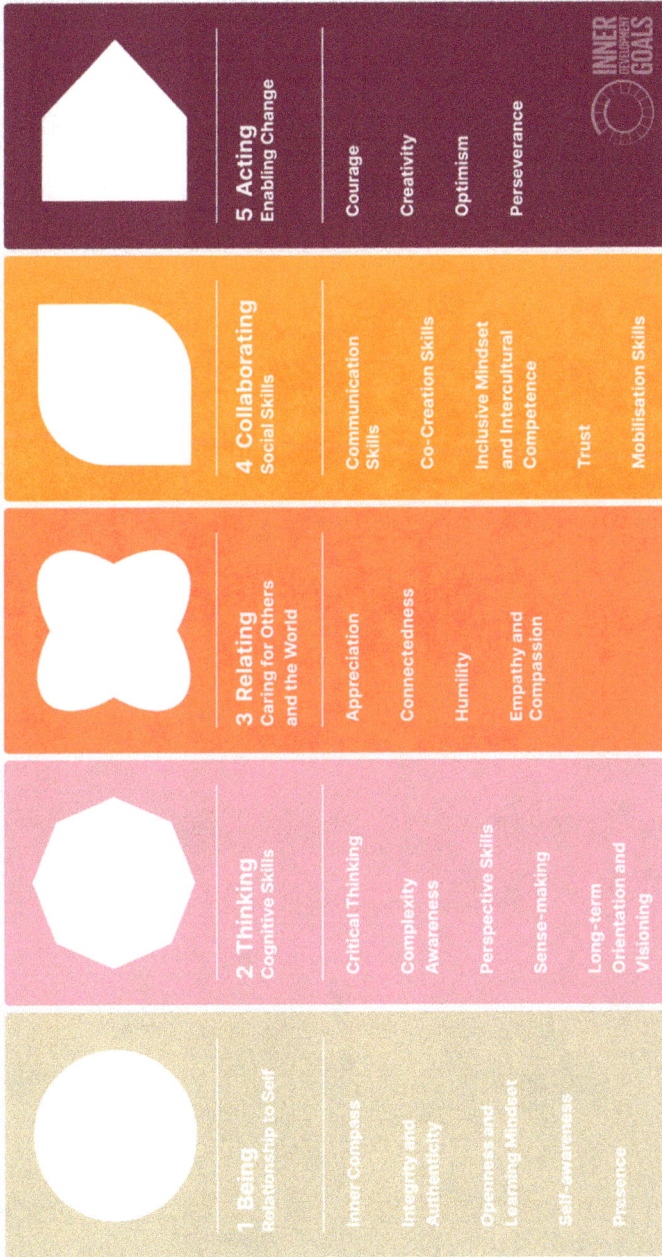

Figure 0.1: The Inner Development Goals framework.

Note: This framework outlines the 23 attributes, grouped into five dimensions, that are essential for developing the inner capacities necessary to achieve sustainable development.

Source: Inner Development Goals https://innerdevelopmentgoals.org/

Section 1: **Education**

Ana Gabriela Mata Carrera and Mauricio Campos Suarez

Chapter 1
Prelude

The United Nations Sustainable Development Goals (SDGs) present a bold vision for a better world by 2030, and Goal 4 is at the heart of this vision: "Ensure inclusive and equitable quality education and promote lifelong learning opportunities for all." (United Nations, 2015). To meet this ambitious goal, education must evolve beyond traditional paradigms, fostering skills like analytical thinking, creativity, emotional intelligence, and resilience.

In our rapidly evolving, automated world, where information is ubiquitous but wisdom is rare, education must bridge the gap between information, knowledge, and wisdom. Achieving SDG 4 demands embracing diverse and innovative learning paradigms that extend beyond conventional methods. This section delves into global approaches that nurture personal and inner development, supporting a more just and sustainable future through education.

The journey begins by illuminating the historical role of education in societal transformation, emphasizing the need for programs that integrate the Social, Emotional, and Ethical Learning (SEE Learning) framework with sustainability goals.

Building on this foundation, the next chapter addresses the systemic barriers to knowledge equity. It explores how hierarchical power systems degrade the credibility of marginalized voices and violate their capacity as knowers. By offering an IDG-based strategy, this chapter underscores the importance of empowering individuals and communities to achieve social justice.

The journey then transitions to personal development through mindset transformation. Linking the five dimensions of the IDGs with sustainability mindset principles (SMPs), this chapter introduces tools like the Sustainability Mindset Indicator (SMI) to illustrate how mindset changes can drive sustainable behaviors. Case studies, such as those from the University of Bergamo, demonstrate the transformative potential of these tools in teaching, coaching, and research.

The section proceeds with a focus on higher education, highlighting an initiative from the University of St. Gallen in Switzerland. This initiative addresses contemporary systemic crises by creating transformative learning spaces for sustainability leadership. By promoting peer-to-peer learning, critical reflection, and collaboration with stakeholders, it equips students with the skills needed to tackle complex sustainability challenges.

Finally, the section culminates by showcasing a start-up in the education technology sector. This innovative company leverages technology to convert theoretical inner development frameworks into practical strategies for students. Their solutions empower educational institutions to create environments that prioritize both personal growth and academic excellence.

https://doi.org/10.1515/9783111453729-002

Together, these chapters weave a narrative illustrating how education, when aligned with sustainability and inner development goals, can drive both personal and societal transformation.

References

United Nations. (2015). Transforming our world: The 2030 Agenda for Sustainable Development. https://sdgs.un.org/2030agenda

Figure 1.1: Camino a la vida (2021).
Photograph by A. G. Mata Carrera, Alba Adriática, Italia.
"The forest unfolds before us, a tangled maze we've navigated since youth, learning to chart our course in a complex system without maps."

Effortless
Like the cloud floating in the sky,
let the air flow through you,
like water in spring, flowing to the sea.
From the top of the mountain, melting the ice in you
no need to do anything,
everything is already there.
Our work is to stay present,
to be kind,
to notice beauty in everything and everyone.
No need to force it,
as it would become an obstacle.
Instead, open up to this moment
and observe the signals,
as subtle as the smell of rosemary in winter
Don't rush,
take one step and stop,
and then take another step or two.
Enjoy life flowing through you.
Ultimately, time is an illusion
there is no place to go.

M. Campos Suarez (2020)

Author's note. During the early days of my children's Montessori enrollment, I observed the classroom and noticed a distinct atmosphere compared to traditional education, which often focuses heavily on academic achievement. This can become a trap, stifling creativity and emotional growth. The Montessori approach made me reflect on the importance of fostering happiness, personal growth, and a love for learning in children. I realized that true fulfillment comes from enjoying the journey of life, rather than focusing solely on hitting specific milestones. These reflections inspired me to write a poem for my daughter, Lua.

Ryder Delaloye

Chapter 2
Educating the heart and mind: Forming
a sustainable citizenry through SEE Learning
and the Inner Development Goals

Abstract: Education is a tool that guides the development of future generations. A
new value set of sustainability is arising as people face unprecedented challenges associated with climate change and environmental degradation. Targets like the Sustainable Development Goals (SDGs) were created to guide policy and individual behavior. Unfortunately, the SDGs have failed to achieve their intended outcomes. The
SGDs neglect the inner transformation of values, traits, and behaviors needed for individuals to act sustainably. Education can help build the skills and mindsets needed
to navigate both current and future challenges associated with climate change. The
domains and skills contained within the Inner Development Goals (IDGs) can serve as
a lens through which education can be transformed. In collaboration with the research-based program called Social, Emotional, and Ethical Learning (SEE Learning®)
the IDGs have been introduced to students and integrated into schools. This chapter
provides a case study in Colombia of how students and their teacher have been impacted by their experience with the IDGs and SEE Learning. One student stated, "I can
practice the Inner Development Goals both in school and in my everyday life to solve
problems or find solutions to issues that may arise in the future." This case study can
serve as the basis for future work to bring the IDGs and SEE Learning to students
around the world in order to help create a sustainable citizenry capable of fulfilling
each target of the SDGs.

Keywords: education, citizen, compassion, sustainability, transformation

Introduction

Education is the vehicle for societal transformation. In order for the communities and
nations around the world to become more sustainable, education must play a role in
shaping future generations. Building the values, attitudes, and behaviors needed for a
sustainable future in which issues of equity, environmental conservation, and justice
are prioritized can be achieved through schooling and education. Many examples
exist historically of educational reform serving to build a new citizenry that was capable of addressing the needs and challenges arising from a changing society. A major
societal challenge today is the climate and environmental crisis. The outcomes needed

https://doi.org/10.1515/9783111453729-003

to achieve climate action and sustainability on the part of communities and nations have been articulated in the United Nations Sustainable Development Goals (SDGs). The SDGs outline a future vision through targets for poverty reduction, gender equality, clean water, climate action, responsible consumption, and many other key indicators of societal health. Achieving the SDGs requires nations around the world to take collective action to transform their economies and societies.

Personal transformation is the first step in creating a more sustainable future. In order to support personal transformation aimed at accomplishing a more sustainable future, the Inner Development Goals (IDGs) were created. These goals consist of five domains: *being, thinking, relating, collaborating*, and *acting*. These domains contain focused skills that individuals can develop to foster values, attitudes, and behaviors that lead to sustainability. Education has a long history of building values, attitudes, and behaviors within students. In order to cultivate competencies that lead to sustainability we need to transform education and schooling to better prepare future generations for the task of creating a more sustainable future for all.

Purpose of education

A primary goal of education is to prepare future generations to navigate the challenges associated with a changing society. Gow (1989) states that:

> in our institutions of learning we need to reemphasize the kind of education that cultivates minds and characters, that communicates and affirms ethical normality, and that helps young people develop the moral and intellectual discernment needed to distinguish between true and false, right and wrong, noble and base. (p. 545)

Evidence of this focus on the development of both mind and character can be seen in the Federal Ministry of Education and Research in Germany. It states that:

> education provides the basis for leading an autonomous, responsible and participatory life within industry and society. Education provides our children with the tools they need to meet the challenges of a changing and increasingly globalized world. (BMBF, 2024)

The German education system is seeking to prepare students for their future and provide them with the essential tools needed to live a "responsible and participatory life".

Within the Basic Act on Education in Japan, the purpose of education is intended to support the "full development of personality" and to foster the "dignity of the individual" (OECD, 2018). Included within the Japanese objectives of education are:

> fostering the values of respect for justice, responsibility, equality between men and women, and mutual respect and cooperation, as well as the value of actively participating in building our society and contributing to its development. (MEXT, 2024)

The objectives for education call for "fostering the values of respecting life, caring about nature, and desiring to contribute to the preservation of the environment" (MEXT, 2024). The holistic and citizenship development focus of the Japanese education system provides the essential tools needed for the formation of future citizens (Boyle, 1992). Countries like Japan and Germany model how traits such as caring, prepared, knowledgeable, and engaged characterize the central purpose of education.

The purpose of education at the local and national level is to create citizens that are capable of embodying the skills, habits, and dispositions needed to navigate their future. Just as numeracy and reading skills can be formed, so can skills focused on self-compassion and emotional literacy be developed. At the macro level, transforming education:

> requires educators and policymakers to take a hard look at contemporary society and to begin to construct a vision of education and society that transcends narrow utilitarianism and considers the real-world challenges that confront society in the 21st century. (Mason, 2017, p. 53)

Addressing the issue of climate change and environmental degradation requires significant innovation within education.

The role of education and schools in shaping individuals

Examples throughout history exist of how education served to create a citizenry that reflected the values and interests of a changing society. Napoleon implemented universal civic education in order to form a collective identity around the nation state. He used the institution of education to form his vision of a civil and functional society by focusing education towards science and the formation of rational thought (Williams, 1956). Education was transformed "by making the sciences a permanent part of the curriculum and by creating institutions which have influenced systems of education all over the world" (p. 369). As the modern conception of the nation state within the Napoleonic reforms took shape, the formalization of schooling also took shape. To form a consistent national identity, schools were established with a centralized curriculum and uniform approach. Language instruction was prioritized to create a national language from which communication, commerce, and mobility was made more efficient. Content was introduced to create a national identity. Educational reform had far-reaching impacts on personal and cultural identity of the French citizenry. "The effects of the Napoleonic educational reforms have entered into the very fabric of French life" (Williams, 1956, p. 381). Although it occurred long ago, the current French education system still experiences the influence of Napoleon's reforms.

In industrialized countries, the goal of education was to create a citizenry that was capable of fulfilling the needs of a changing economic and civil society. The paradigm of efficiency within the factory model that dominated society at this time was reflected in the design and running of schools. This model created "a school system that socialized youth for their new economic roles and sorted them into their appropriate niches in the expanding capitalist division of labor" (Kantor, 1986, p. 402). Schools mirrored factories in their structure; even today it is possible to see this influence in education. In most classrooms, students are arranged in rows in order to learn content that is highly segmented. Within the factory model of education, students – just like factory workers – were cued when to eat, when to sit, when to take a break, and when to work. Schools and educational institutions have traditionally served to reinforce and fulfill the objectives a society holds. The utilization of school to build employability skills was not new to the period of industrialization: "from the mid-nineteenth century on, the idea of using school to teach steady work habits and to increase the efficiency of wage earners had appealed to educational reformers" (Kantor, 1986, p. 423). This legacy continues today through initiatives like technical and vocational education and training (TVET).

Education has also served to promote peace and reconciliation. Peace education emerged from numerous efforts and initiatives to foster and sustain peace within conflict zones. Many countries that struggled with conflict adopted peace education as a formal education initiative:

> In 2015, the Colombian government mandated the inclusion of peace education across all levels of schooling. The law reflected increased attention to young people's potential development and role as peacebuilders. (Velez, 2021, p. 2)

The goal of peace education is to transform education for the purpose of addressing violence in all of its forms (direct, structural, and cultural) across society (Velez, 2021). The tenets of peace education include nonviolence, conflict resolution, communication, social justice, and intercultural awareness. Through this program, students build skills such as empathy, perspective taking, perseverance, cooperation, and compassion. The inclusion of peace education creates the seeds for conflict transformation and healing by building the inner skills needed for students and society.

Social and emotional learning (SEL) has shaped education significantly. In 1995, Daniel Goleman wrote *Emotional Intelligence* which formalized the field of SEL. Goleman synthesized insights that connected neuroscience to emotional well-being. Through science-based research he asserted that character traits such as impulse control, kindness, and perspective taking were skills that could be developed. Goleman made the case that these skill traits have far-reaching benefits for individuals and our changing society. Many policymakers and educators agreed with this assertion and began prioritizing the development of "soft skills". SEL not only promotes students' social and emotional competence, it also enhances their academic achievement (Schonert-Reichl, 2017). The meta-study of the impacts of SEL on education by Durlak et al. (2011) showed that students who received SEL programming performed 11% better on achievement tests than students who did not receive SEL programming. "The case for

SEL is stronger than ever" (Weissberg & Cascarino, 2013, p. 13). SEL is furthering the essential goal of citizen formation by helping students to develop the habits needed to be caring and engaged citizens. Schonert-Reichl (2017), states that:

> for our children and youth to achieve their full potential as productive adult citizens, parents, and volunteers in a pluralistic society, educators must focus explicitly on social and emotional competence. (p. 138)

The development of soft skills such as impulse control, empathy, perspective taking, ethical decision making, and systems thinking are needed to navigate a rapidly changing society and economy. Each of these examples of education reform – modernity, peace education, industrialization, and SEL – played a central role in the formation of citizens who were aligned and prepared to support a changing society.

Education for climate action and sustainability

The current climate crisis facing the world is causing significant instability around the world by undermining the well-being of billions of people (Sustainable Development Solutions, 2020). In order to address the climate crisis, education needs once again to be transformed. In response to the climate and environmental crisis, the concept of sustainability was developed. One of the first definitions of sustainability emerged from the World Commission on Environment and Development (1987). Sustainable development was defined as the activity that "meets the needs of the present without compromising the ability of future generations to meet their own needs" (p. 1). A lack of valuing environmental systems and the overuse of those systems is causing significant environmental collapse. The externalities created from over consumption are impacting vulnerable populations at a much higher rate than people in high-income earning countries (United Nations, 2012). To address this issue the United Nations in 2005 launched the Decade of Education for Sustainability (UNESCO, 2005). Sustainability education (or education for sustainability) focuses on building the habits of sustainability. This includes reducing consumption and waste, learning about the climate and environmental issues, and engaging in practices that foster sustainability. What has traditionally been lacking in sustainability education is the important connections that exist between behaviors, emotions, and action.

The formation of an emotional literate citizenry who embodies the knowledge, skills, and inner traits needed to address the climate and environmental crisis can be formed through education of the heart and mind. In order for this vision to be achieved, education for sustainability needs to be implemented in educational settings around the world. In 2012, the United Nations released the SDGs (United Nations, 2012). In 2015, many of the countries of the world committed themselves to fulfilling the targets contained within the SDGs. Specific targets were developed to address the systemic and far-reaching issues associated with the climate and environmental crisis. "The 17 SDGs were established in 2015 as an urgent call to action by all countries to tackle global challenges such as poverty and inequality, climate change and environmental decline" (Shih, 2023). This global initiative was designed to guide the formation of policy at all levels to fulfill the vision of sustainability. Malekpour et al. (2023) state that "without accelerated action, the ambitious plan that the world signed up to in 2015 will fail". School systems and educational institutions around the world have attempted to bring the SDGs into student learning. Approaches to teaching sustainability specific to the SDGs focus on helping learn about the values and practices associated with clean air, water and other SDGs. Unfortunately, the SDGs have fallen short within education due to competing interests and a lack of clarity as to the process and purpose of educating students in the SDGs.

The Inner Development Goals as a response to supporting the SDGs

The Inner Development Goals (IDGs) were created to foster systemic changes for people, communities, and the environment in order to fulfill the promise of the SGDs. The IDGs contains five domains (being, thinking, relating, collaborating, acting). These domains contain the skills needed to support a person's inner development. The assertion made within the IDGs is that a person who embodies the skills within the IDGs, such as having an "inner compass" or "perseverance" and a sense of "connectedness", will be better able to take steps to actualize the SDGs. The IDGs assert that there is often a divide that exists between the values individuals hold and the skills or behaviors they possess. Within the IDG domains are essential skills such as optimism, presence, and appreciation. These skills directly support and sustain activities related to sustainability and sustainability education. Many of the skills outlined within the IDGs coexist within the field of SEL. Helping to develop social and emotional competencies directly supports the cultivation of IDG domains and skills.

Many educational programs foster the social-emotional growth of students, one of which is Social, Emotional, and Ethical Learning (SEE Learning®). Daniel Goleman (2019) calls SEE Learning (2024), "SEL 2.0". SEE Learning is suited to support the fulfillment of the IDGs because it contains four key focus areas for student development: compassionate and ethical discernment; trauma- and resilience-informed practices; attention and awareness training; and systems thinking. SEE Learning is freely available and was developed to help students around the world develop competencies related to awareness, resilience, compassion for self and others, and systems thinking. Within SEE Learning students build habits through engaging and meaningful experiences that directly align with the competencies needed for both inner development and sustainability-oriented activity. To accomplish the SDGs, inner values need to be cultivated. The following framework demonstrates the alignment that exists between the SDGs, the IDGs, and SEE Learning. Through the cultivation of competencies contained within SEE Learning, the IDGs can be fulfilled and thus help individuals foster a more sustainable future for all.

An education that prioritizes ethical discernment, self-regulation, awareness, systems thinking, and compassion for self and others will require a substantive transformation of the modern school system. This transformation has already begun in many schools and communities that are seeking to build a more sustainable and compassionate future for all. The integration of SEE Learning, and programs like it, into education and schools can help fulfill the purpose of education by developing a citizenry that is capable of achieving the ambitious outcomes outlined by the SDGs. Drawing from programs like SEE Learning makes it possible to transform schools and education once again to create a citizenry that is capable of navigating the new challenges of our changing society and planet.

What is the sustainable citizenry?

The SDGs contain 17 targeted outcomes. Achieving the SDGs relies on many factors, one of which is the formation of inner tools and skills held by individuals. Combining the IDG skills and domains (being, thinking, relating, collaborating, and acting) with SEE Learning allows students to develop the underlying skills and competencies needed for individuals to act and live in a manner that fosters sustainability. Developing compassion, awareness, resilience, and systems thinking serves as the foundation for the sustainable citizenry.

The sustainable citizenry contains the values, knowledge, skills, and behaviors that will lead to the fulfillment of the SDGs. Compassion is the foremost competency held by the Sustainable Citizenry. In order to work towards achieving sustainability, a person must have the desire to act with compassion towards others and nature. Compassion is defined as the desire to alleviate the suffering of others with tenderness and care (Ash et al., 2021). According to Ash et al. (2021), compassion has both an intrapersonal component that leads to greater resilience and an interpersonal component that leads to greater compassion. The competency of compassion consists of many underlying traits that contribute to it and support it being practiced. Through an education that engages students to understand and practice compassion they can begin to embody it. In addition to being explicitly stated as a "relating" skill within the IDGs, a more expanded understanding of compassion can be seen in other IDG skills (see Figure 2.1), such as: courage, connectedness, perseverance, presence, and inner compass. A compassionate person is one that is courageous and capable of acting. The compassionate outlook developed through years of practice is not narrow or limited to a select few, rather it is expansive in its ability to recognize shared common humanity. A person with a compassionate capability has an expanding desire to alleviate the suffering of others

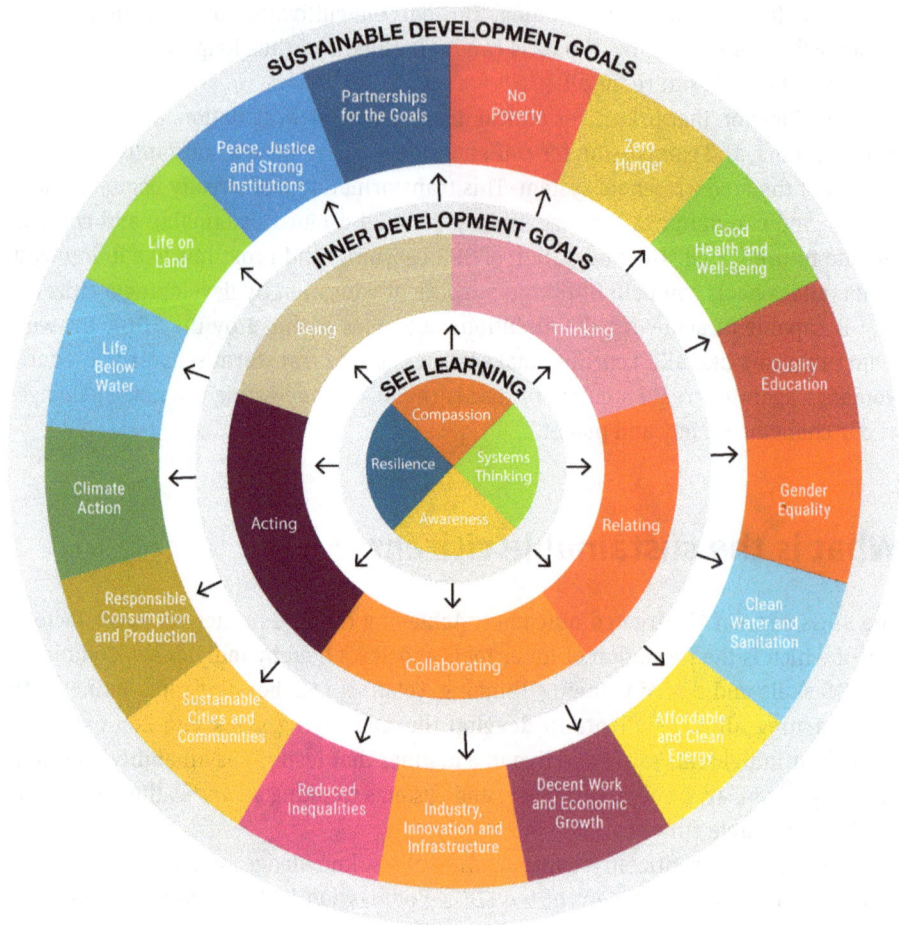

Figure 2.1: The Relationship between SEE Learning, the Inner Development Goals, and the Sustainable Development Goals. Source: SEE Learning, 15 June 2024.

across groups of people, animals, and natural systems. This degree of compassion also contains an understanding and appreciation for interdependence. By recognizing the interrelated nature of all things through discernment, a sustainable citizen can skillfully navigate adversity and apply compassion to both human and nonhuman systems. Compassion is not just limited to care for others, but also care for oneself. Self-compassion coupled with awareness and attention training become a tool for resilience in which students are capable of perspective taking, emotional regulation, attentional control, and awareness of self and others.

Compassion allows a person to apply discernment in a manner that directs their behaviors towards activities that will cause the least harm while also providing the most benefit for themselves and others. Related to discernment and systems thinking, the IDGs contain important skills: complexity awareness, sensemaking, long-term orientation, and critical thinking. Trained in the recognition of shared common humanity, a compassionate person is capable of transforming their narrow in-group bias to one that is more realistic. Instead of maintaining the view that only a limited few people are responsible for their well-being, a compassionate citizen recognizes the ways in which a huge array of people and natural systems contribute to their well-being and the well-being of others. This attunement engenders a strong feeling of appreciation and also a desire to repay the kindness of others.

Empathy plays an important role in the progression towards compassion. With empathetic concern, an individual relates to the suffering and distress of another person. Within SEE Learning, empathy is considered the foundation for compassion but does not have the important action-oriented quality that compassion has to alleviate the suffering of another. This action-oriented quality is essential for sustainable citizenry. The IDG skill of mobilization is directly aligned with the action-oriented stance of compassion. The sustainable citizenry, having trained in resilience, recognizing common humanity, and other capabilities, has the potential to transform their experience of empathic attunement into a strong motivation to help alleviate the suffering of another through the application of compassion. By attuning to the fundamental reality of interconnectedness they and others share with everyone else, the sustainable citizenry can make decisions that are more aligned with sustainability and also encourage transformation by creating opportunities for others to achieve sustainable outcomes.

The sustainable citizenry embodies competencies that foster their resilience. Resilience is the capacity to bounce back from adversity. Throughout our lives, we face challenges that undermine our well-being and erode our happiness. Within the IDGs, resilience is present in the skills of perseverance, optimism, self-awareness, and sensemaking. Given the immensity of the challenges faced related to climate change and the decline of environmental systems, resilience is recognized as a key competency needed for addressing the climate crisis. It is first and foremost a felt experience; when individuals experience stress or adversity their bodies react in a protective manner to safeguard themselves from harm. The typical response when faced with a perceived danger is to move into a fight, flight, or freeze physiological response in order to activate a nervous system response that works to protect us from harm. Unfortunately, our nervous system is not very good at distinguishing between running away from a lion or worrying about climate change. Our stress response is a basic survival strategy; however, our ability to rebound and manage it is essential for maintaining our well-being and also our capacity to act rationally. When we are distressed we lose our ability to discern clearly and make rational decisions. Cultivating resilience is essential for navigating the complex challenges of the climate crisis.

Training in resilience begins with nervous system regulation. This occurs by recognizing the connections that exist between the mind and body. Within SEE Learning, students learn strategies that help to bring the body from a dysregulated state to one that is regulated and calm. Students learn that by regulating the body it is possible to make more rational and ethical decisions. Training in resilience includes learning how to manage emotions. The skill of emotional regulation requires a person to observe the mind and identify when thoughts, feelings, and responses arise that can or are undermining one's stability and well-being. Resilience requires attentional stability and the capacity for self-awareness. Students learn to observe the mind in its natural state and become aware of the thoughts, feelings, and sensations that arise. When dealing with issues related to sustainability, climate action, and environmental justice, a person will face many challenges that are outside of their control. Learning how to foster resilience in an embodied manner not only supports their well-being as they face adversity but also enables them to make clearer, more rationale, and ultimately more effective, decisions.

Ethical discernment is an important trait of the sustainable citizenry. One of the best ways to develop discernment is to train in the habits of a systems thinker. Systems thinking is a skill set that supports an individual's capacity to examine issues from multiple perspectives. The complexity of topics related to the climate, the environment, and to sustainability is significant. Engaging in systems thinking enables a person to examine an issue from multiple perspectives in order to identify the potential impact associated with making different decisions related to the issue. Through this process of considering various short-term and long-term outcomes, a more skillful and ethical decision can be made.

Discernment occurs when a student is capable of evaluating the benefit or harm of their decisions for themselves and others. Discernment involves considering the impact of one's actions both now and into the future. Training in discernment relies on becoming aware of the multitude of ways that people and the environment are connected. The capacity to understand, and even feel, this sense of interdependence can be developed through engaging in different activities, reflections, and practices. Discernment strengthens our capacity to feel a sense of tenderness, appreciation, gratitude, and connection towards others. Having developed this far-reaching attitude, a new ethic arises within a person who has trained as a systems thinker to relate towards others with care, kindness, and compassion. Through recognizing that their happiness and well-being is directly related to the happiness and well-being of others, their behaviors shift and become more skillful. In the context of sustainability, a person capable of systems thinking is more capable of making compassionate and ethical decisions that foster collective well-being and happiness both now and into the future.

By developing resilience and discernment, a person's capacity for compassion is enhanced and strengthened. In addition to skills that promote and support compassionate responses, the IDGs contain other essential skills needed to support the sustainable citizenry. They include competencies such as co-creation skills, inclusive mindset, trust, mobilization, openness and learning mindset, integrity and authenticity, and communication skills. Like other abilities such as swimming or solving a mathematical equation, skills are formed through learning and experience. Creating a sustainable citizenry through learning and experience requires an education system that prioritizes the development of these skills within students.

The SDGs are the outcomes needed to accomplish a more sustainable future, one in which environmental, social, and economic systems are in balance and operating in a manner that ensures the welfare of future generations. Achieving the goals outlined within the SDGs requires that individuals, organizations, and institutions prioritize the development of inner skills according to the IDG domains of being, thinking, relating, collaborating, and acting. SEE Learning, as both a framework and curriculum, is capable of integrating into the existing education systems to develop the essential sustainability-related skills and competencies in students. As students grow and develop, they will form a sustainable citizenry who will be responsible for not only achieving, but also maintaining, the SDGs in the future.

Pilot case study: IDGs being implemented in schools to develop the sustainable citizenry

The IDGs are being taught to students to help them cultivate the skills they need to navigate the challenges associated with creating a more sustainable world. Through SEE Learning, students are developing enduring capabilities that can support them in fostering both personal, societal, and global well-being. In Colombia a curriculum is being implemented to introduce and engage students in the IDGs. The learning experiences contain a brief check-in, an overview of a specific IDG domain, a SEE Learning activity, and a reflection. The learning experiences enable students to explore each IDG domain and engage in a SEE Learning activity in order for that domain and the skills contained within the domains to become relevant and developmentally appropriate for students. Through their engagement in the learning experience, students are encouraged to personalize and internalize the target IDG domain.

The pedagogical model utilized in this case study guided students through three levels of understanding to support them in developing proficiency in the fundamentals of each IDG domain. In the first level (received knowledge), students learn by listening, reading, discussing, exploring, and experiencing. This level exposes students to basic information and experiences related to the competencies and helps them develop a rich understanding of each one. Students should also be encouraged to use their critical thinking to investigate the topics deeply, using many different lines of approach, and apply them to their own situations so that they can reach the second level of critical insight. This refers to "aha" moments in which students gain personal insight, connecting the knowledge they have received to their own lives and existence. At this level, the knowledge is not merely received but has led to a new perspective on the world; it has become the students' own knowledge. Each learning experience in the SEE Learning curriculum provides several "insight activities" for achieving these new perspectives over time. Through regular reinforcement of the concepts and activities, students develop embodied understanding. Critical thinking facilitates the acquisition of knowledge at each of these successive levels of understanding. This pedagogical model implies exploration by students on their own, not direct instruction. The teacher's role in the curriculum is often that of a facilitator rather than instructor. Through repeated practice and authentic personalization students develop the third level of understanding which is embodied understanding. Students are encouraged to think for themselves and embrace their questions. This is the only way to progress through the three levels of insight.

The "SEE Learning Introduction to the Inner Development Goals" curriculum IDG Introduction Curriculum draws from the SEE Learning threads: critical thinking, reflective practices, scientific perspectives, and an engaged learning pedagogy. The first of the key learning threads is critical thinking, which forms an essential part of both the IDGs and SEE Learning at every stage. Within the context of the IDGs, critical thinking can be understood as the exploration and investigation of topics and experiences through logical reasoning, multiple perspectives, dialogue, debate, and other related activities in order to reach a deeper and more nuanced understanding. Similar to the IDGs, critical thinking is essential in SEE Learning because the emotional and ethical literacy being cultivated in the program cannot be imposed from the outside in or in a top-down manner, but should arise and develop on the foundation of a firm personal understanding that is consistent with personal experience and the realities of the world. The key learning thread of critical thinking in the IDGs and SEE Learning involves encouraging students to make sound arguments and engaging in reasoning. The goal is for students to ask the right questions rather than having the right answers. Critical thinking also involves the cultivation of "epistemic humility": an openness to the possibility of being wrong; the realization that one's knowledge is always partial and limited and can be informed by other information and perspectives; and the recognition that one's views can develop and change over time. This in turn facilitates the ability to engage in dialogue, discussion, and debate without the emotional reactivity that can hinder such activities when individuals become too attached to their own positions or lose sight of the possibility of learning more.

The second key learning thread is reflective practices. Reflective practices can be seen in the inner compass, perspective skills, and sensemaking domains contained within the IDGs. These reflective practices are activities in which students direct attention toward their inner experience in a sustained and structured way in order to develop a deeper personal understanding and internalize the skills and topics covered in their learning. These are "first-person" practices in the sense that students seek direct experience of aspects of the material being covered through attention, observation, and reflective examination. This involves practices such as attending to bodily sensations, cultivating attention on the breath, noticing the momentariness of thoughts and emotions, and noticing the effects of certain thoughts and emotions on one's body and mind. The reflective practices of attention support a second category of reflective practices involving analysis and critical thinking, such as reflecting on a certain topic with sustained attention and investigating it from various angles. Reflective practices are key tools for developing a richer received knowledge and for deepening that received knowledge to the levels of critical insight and eventually embodied understanding. Some schools choose to frame these practices as focus-building experiences that support cognitive learning, based on current understandings of neuroscience and brain development.

The third key learning thread is scientific perspectives. Within the IDGs, scientific perspectives can be seen in the skills of long-term orientation and complexity awareness. Because SEE Learning approaches ethical development in large part through the cultivation of emotional literacy, it is crucial that teachers and students gradually develop an understanding of the science around emotions and other topics included in the program. In this context, "scientific perspectives" refers to modes of inquiry that depend on and are informed by prevailing scientific understandings of ourselves and the world in which we live. The program material will be better understood and students and teachers will be more motivated to engage with it if they understand some of the science informing the approaches and topics being presented. Like common experience and common sense, science helps to provide a common foundation for an approach to ethics that is impartial with regard to culture or religion. Because science is based on empirical observation and the theorizing and testing of cause and effect, the key learning thread of scientific perspectives also supports critical thinking. It also serves as the third-person complement to the first-person approach of the key learning thread of reflective practices, yielding a well-rounded and more complete understanding of the topics in SEE Learning.

The fourth and final key learning thread is engaged learning. Within the IDG skills, engaged learning can be seen within co-creation skills, mobilization skills, and connectedness. This term refers to learning strategies and methods that are active, participatory, and embodied for students, in contrast to approaches where students receive material in a passive and static way. Engaged learning involves cooperative learning (group projects, student-led discussion, collaborative games), creative expression (arts, music, writing, performance), community engagement projects (such as service projects), and ecological learning (such as engaging directly with the natural world). Engaged learning is complementary to the other key learning threads and allows students to experience and further explore what they are learning in a direct, embodied, and practical way by seeing what it is like to put into practice what they have been learning conceptually or by engaging in a practice that they can reflect on subsequently. As with the other key learning threads, engaged learning helps facilitate the movement of students through the three levels of learning: received knowledge, critical insight, and embodied understanding.

Tulua, Colombia, case study: Bringing the IDGs to the students

Students received the IDG Introduction Curriculum on a weekly basis spanning six weeks. Each week the students received a 45-minute learning experience that introduced the IDGs and each of the five domains contained within the IDGs. The introductory learning experience was titled "What are the Inner Development Goals and why do they matter?". In this learning experience students explored the purpose and benefits of the IDGs and SEE Learning. This introductory experience allowed them to personalize the benefits of both the IDGs and SEE Learning to enable them to see how developing the skills contained within the IDGs can help them promote their well-being, executive functioning skills, and relationship skills. Through a fun small-group activity, students were given the 23 skills contained within the domains of the IDGs that were randomly organized and asked to work collaboratively to order them according to the domains of being, thinking, relating, collaborating, and acting. After organizing the skills, the students were then shown how the IDGs are organized. Students were then given the opportunity to explore different connections and ways of organizing the skills by recognizing there are many ways that these skills can be structured and organized. Then students were exposed to a core foundation practice within SEE Learning to support nervous system regulation. The students were introduced to the practices of grounding and the "Help Now!" strategies. These practices are important in that they support a person's ability to cultivate well-being by allowing them to move from a dysregulated state to a more regulated and calm state of being. This essential resilience skill serves as a foundation-level competency for engaging in the work of inner development. The next five learning experiences focused on each of the IDG domains. In each learning experience, students engaged in an activity by which they explored and defined the respective domains in a manner that was developmentally appropriate and authentic. Using examples from their life experiences, students were able to connect personal meaning to each of the domain areas. Within each learning experience, the students engaged in a SEE Learning insight activity which served as an anchor experience to help them create an embodied understanding and personal connection.

Below are the responses of the students and teachers regarding their experiences in learning, exploring, and embodying the IDGs through engaging activities. Through these introductory experiences, the students and teacher developed direct experience with the IDGs and made personal and school-based connections to the IDGs. The insights shared below highlight the values and competencies needed for the sustainable citizenry. The formation of caring and engaged citizens can be achieved through the development of the skills contained within the IDGs.

In Tulua, Colombia, middle school students in 7th and 8th grade are actively learning about the IDGs (See Figure 2.2). When asked the what the student liked most about the IDG curriculum they were learning, they said:

Personally, I feel that the classes and activities we are doing during the sessions are very enjoyable and creative because I am learning new terminology and I'm expanding my vocabulary. However, what I like the most is the teamwork that takes place during this process and also our oral participation in the lessons.

I like that I'm learning new concepts that I didn't know before.

I like to discuss the Inner Development Goals with my classmates because I consider them important topics. It is also very interesting to hear different points of view and compare them with my own, knowing that there are no wrong answers.

The lessons are good. I feel comfortable and the teaching method is fun and easy to understand.

What I like the most is the teaching method provided by the teacher and the dedication to making the classes fun to impart knowledge in our minds and leave an impact on our lives.

Figure 2.2: Students in Tulua doing SEE Learning Activities. Source: Ryder Delaloye (2024).

When asked what the value and importance of the Inner Development Goals is, students reported (see Figure 2.3):

In my opinion, I feel that this has been a very wholesome journey because it has shown a correlation with the SEE Learning subject since we have covered topics about emotions, skills, and talents.

The importance of the Inner Development Goals is that I'm learning things I can put into practice in the future for my life.

I consider them important because they help us reflect on various relevant topics, such as recognizing our skills. These types of activities enhance teamwork, like when we share our points of view.

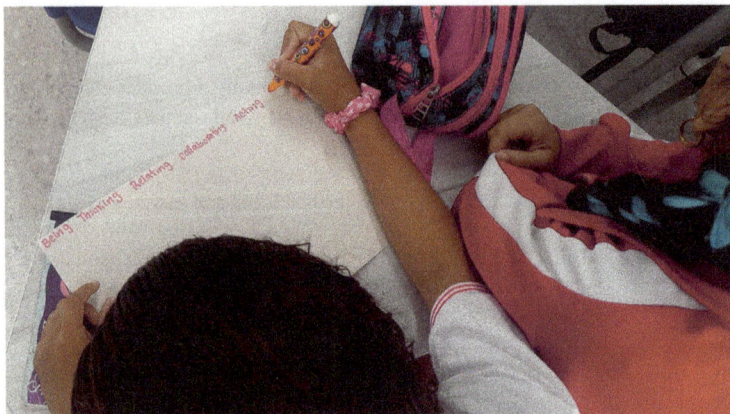

Figure 2.3: Students in Tulua, Colombia engaging in the "SEE Learning Introduction to the Inner Development Goals" curriculum. Source: Ryder Delaloye (2024).

The importance is that it helps us control ourselves, understand how we behave, and improve as individuals.

In my opinion, they are important because we can develop significant traits in our lives, communicating effectively with others and creating good memories of the moment. This seems important to me because, thanks to the teacher, we will have more knowledge about this topic. Therefore, it helps us improve as individuals in our lives.

The students were also asked to how they might apply the IDGs at school and in their personal life:

I can practice it in my daily life since it teaches us words that expand our vocabulary and help us recognize skills, talents, and virtues, which can facilitate our continuous learning and personal development.

I can practice the Inner Development Goals both in school and in my everyday life to solve problems or find solutions to issues that may arise in the future.

I can apply skills like trust when I am going to give a presentation or want to share an opinion because I trust that I will do it well, which is something we often do at school. On the other hand, at home, I can use respect and communication to talk with the people I live with and avoid conflicts.

In school, it's about knowing how to solve problems with classmates, and in my personal life, it would be the same but could involve family, friends, or people on the street.

This helps me be more empathetic with people. Some of us find it difficult to express ourselves in a positive way, which is why I believe we should know about Inner Development Goals. Understanding these can help us consider them more in how we express ourselves, think, and speak. This way, we can better appreciate and understand other people's ways of being.

When the classroom teacher was asked to respond to the three questions, they responded as follows:

What do you like most about the IDG curriculum lessons?

What I like the most about the IDG curriculum lessons is how they promote teamwork in the classroom. During the sessions, I have noticed that some students who usually do not participate in other classes become more engaged and actively share their opinions.

What is the value and importance of the Inner Development Goals?

I consider the importance of the Inner Development Goals to be closely related to teamwork and how students can transform their community through action and collaboration with others. In this sense, IDGs are also associated with the SEE Learning concept of interdependence by recognizing how each individual depends on others to some extent in a society.

How can you practice and embody the Inner Development Goals at school and in your personal life?

I can practice the Inner Development Goals at school by planning new projects and programs for my students in collaboration with other teachers. In this way, every team member contributes to the design of the activities, considering our students' needs and learning objectives. Once we have designed the project, we implement it into practice to analyze its results and the students' experiences throughout the process. On the other hand, I can apply them in my personal life by viewing my relationship with family and friends as a system in which I actively collaborate to make decisions and benefit our dynamic. This perspective helps me to foster a supportive environment for myself and others around me.

The comments provided from students and the classroom teacher highlight the profound impact that the Inner Development Goals can have on both teaching and learning. Helping to bring the IDGs into schools has the potential to not only transform individuals within a school but also the entire school community. In helping to cultivate a focus on inner development through the IDGs, it is possible to build skills in students that foster the enduring capabilities of awareness, resilience, and compassion.

Helping students to become the change they want to see in the world

Just as it has in the past, education can be transformed once again to reflect the changing needs of society. In reflecting on why education was shaped by Napoleon, Williams (1956) states that:

> the ideals of a society are often most clearly seen in the provisions made for training its future citizens, and the philosophy underlying this training reveals the values on which a particular society is built. (p. 369)

As the values of sustainability continue to strengthen within people, it is possible to shape education to build the skills needed for sustainability. The sustainable citizenry is resilient and are capable of navigating adversity with awareness, compassion, and discernment. It is a citizenry that engages in responsible decision making as they seek to understand how their actions may benefit or cause harm to others both now and in the future. The SDGs can be achieved by prioritizing within schools and systems of education the development of inner competencies within students. This will create a future generation that is capable of fulfilling all 17 of the SDGs. It is possible to not only transform future citizens but also current citizens through inner development. Teaching a child the skill of recycling requires the building of habits. Students learn by understanding the benefits recycling for themselves and others and through direct experience with the practice of recycling. Not only does recycling as a skill become an enduring competency that the student can carry with them for the rest of their lives, it can also serve to shape a family and community culture right now. The child will hold their parents and community accountable to recycling. Imagine the power of teaching a child about the values, benefits, and practice of compassion, and how that act could transform their own experience and the community they live in. We have the opportunity to truly change the future of our communities, if only we are bold enough to prioritize teaching our children the necessary skills of compassion, resilience, and systems thinking.

References

Ash, M., Harrison, T., Pinto, M., DiClemente, R., & Negi, L. T. (2021). A model for cognitively-based compassion training: Theoretical underpinnings and proposed mechanisms. *Social Theory & Health*, *19*(1), 43–67. https://doi.org/10.1057/s41285-019-00124-x.

Boyle, F. (1992). *A cross-cultural comparison of the American and Japanese educational systems*. Diane Publishing. https://doi.org/10.1080/08824090109384791.

Durlak, J. A., Weissberg, R. P., Dymnicki, A. B., Taylor, R. D., & Schellinger, K. B. (2011). The impact of enhancing students' social and emotional learning: A meta-analysis of school-based universal interventions. *Child Development*, *82*(1): 405–432. https://doi.org/10.1111/j.1467-8624.2010.01564.x.

Federal Ministry of Education and Research (BMBF). (2024). About Us: Objectives and Tasks. www.bmbf. de/bmbf/en/ministry/objectives-and-tasks/objectives-and-tasks_node.html.

Goleman, D. (1995). Emotional intelligence. *Bantam Books, Inc.*

Goleman, D. (2019) What Our Kids Need. LinkedIn. https://www.linkedin.com/pulse/what-our-kids-need-daniel-goleman/.

Gow, H. B. (1989). The true purpose of education. *The Phi Delta Kappan, 70*(7), 545–546. http://www.jstor. org/stable/20403956.

Kantor, H. (1986). Work, education, and vocational reform: The ideological origins of vocational education, 1890–1920. *American Journal of Education, 94*(4), 401–426. https://doi:10.1086/443860.

Malekpour, S., Allen, C., Sagar, A., Scholz, I., Persson, Å., Miranda, J. J., Bennich, T., Dube, O. P., Kanie, N., Madise, N., Shackell, N., Montoya, J. C., Pan, J., Hathie, I., Bobylev, S. N., Agard, J., & Al-Ghanim, K. (2023, September 13). What scientists need to do to accelerate progress on the SDGs. Nature News. https://research.monash.edu/en/publications/what-scientists-need-to-do-to-accelerate-progress-on-the-sdgs.

Mason, L. (2017). The significance of Dewey's *Democracy and Education* for 21st-century education. *Education and Culture, 33*(1), 41–57. https://doi:10.5703/educationculture.33.1.0041.

Ministry of Education, Culture, Sports, Science and Technology – Japan (MEXT). (2018). Koutoukyouiku no syuugaku shien shin seido [New Student Support in Tertiary Education].https://www.mext.go.jp/en/ policy/education/lawandplan/title01/detail01/1373798.htm.

OECD (2018). Education policy in Japan: Building bridges towards 2030, Reviews of National Policies for Education. OECD Publishing. https://www.oecd-ilibrary.org/education/education-policy-in-japan _9789264302402-en.

Schonert-Reichl, K. A. (2017). Social and emotional learning and teachers. *The Future of Children, 27*(1), 137–155. https://doi:10.1353/foc.2017.0007.

SEE Learning. (2024). *Center for Contemplative Science and Compassion-based Ethics*, Emory University. https://seelearning.emory.edu/.

Sustainable Development Solutions Network. (2020). *Sustainable development policy in crisis mode*. Sustainable Development Solutions Network. http://www.jstor.org/stable/resrep25837.

UNESCO. (2005). Draft international implementation scheme for the United Nations Decade of Education for Sustainable Development. UNESCO. https://unesdoc.unesco.org/ark:/48223/pf0000139023.lo cale=en.

United Nations. (2012). Rio+20: The future we want. Outcome document of the United Nations Conference on Sustainable Development June 2012. https://sustainabledevelopment.un.org/content/documents/ 733FutureWeWant.pdf.

Shih, I. (2023, September 14). World failing on Sustainable Development Goals. University of Sydney. Retrieved April 19, 2024. https://www.sydney.edu.au/news-opinion/news/2023/09/14/world-failing-on-sustainable-development-goals.html.

Weissberg, R. P. & Cascarino, J. (2013). Academic learning + social-emotional learning = national priority. *The Phi Delta Kappan, 95*(2), 8–13. https://doi:10.1177/003172171309500203.

Williams, L. P. (1956). Science, education and Napoleon I. *Isis, 47*(4), 369–382. https://www.jstor.org/sta ble/i302250.

World Commission on Environment and Development. (1987). *Our common future*. Oxford: Oxford University Press.https://sustainabledevelopment.un.org/content/documents/5987our-common-future.pdf.

Velez, G. (2021). Learning peace: Adolescent Colombians' interpretations of and responses to peace education curriculum. *Journal of Peace Psychology, 27*(2), 146–159. https://doi.org/10.1037/pac0000519.

Luciano Gagliardi
Chapter 3
Unlearning hierarchy in knowing: Towards inclusive spaces for actions of change with the IDGs

Abstract: Hierarchical power systems undermine the credibility and significance of marginalized people's knowing and fundamentally violate their capacity as knower. This form of everyday discrimination is a challenging starting point for the vision of the Inner Development Goals (IDGs): providing skills and capacities which empower individuals and communities to successfully face and overcome complex challenges, the IDGs envision an inner development that is equally shaped by all members of a community. Providing marginalized groups access to knowledge and decision making can foster their individual inner development, but as long as systems of oppression degrade their knowing, the violation of their right to be acknowledged as knowers and actors for change continues. This urges for a shift in system, away from oppression towards inclusive spaces. Offering an IDG-based exist strategy out of oppression, this chapter investigates on the potential IDGs provide in establishing inclusive spaces for collective actions of change.

Keywords: structural discrimination, degradation in knowing, power structures, unlearning oppressive hierarchies, liberating framework, equity

Introduction

When was the last time you felt your experience and knowledge was excluded and unheard? Think of job situations like discussions with colleagues or supervisors where you felt you were not getting enough space to present your ideas, your inputs simply got ignored, or your expertise was not asked at all. Or was it in private life, in situations with partners, friends or in public space? Do you remember the feelings which followed the exclusion you experienced and what behavior it triggered?

The last time I felt my expertise being ignored was in a situation where I was a patient. I fully acknowledged the doctor's professional opinion, but he refused to give me space to express my knowledge I gathered in living with the health issues I faced at that time. Knowing how it is to live with the limitations my health gave me, I had a sense of what I needed and my own perspective about which therapy was most compatible with my life. The doctor's denial of my knowledge about my health gave me a sense of being disenfranchised from my body. My health – one of the most personal

https://doi.org/10.1515/9783111453729-004

properties I have – became externally controlled. Acting from the privileged position I live in, I was able to change doctor and find someone who was willing to co-create my healing journey with me. I regained space for acting, felt heard, and quickly recovered.

Not sure what your story is about, but my story had a happy end, simply because I live in a privileged position and because the exclusion of my knowledge was probably more a matter of the doctor's ignorance than structural in nature. But generally speaking, we know that today's knowledge is deeply shaped by multiple structural discriminations: patriarchy marginalizes voices of women, ageism limits the participation of youth, ableism denies the self-determination of disabled persons, egoism restricts team collaboration, intellectualism ignores the power of everyday expertise by overestimating academia, and Eurocentrism denies the non-Western knowledge traditions – to name only some of the power dynamics we face today.

Recent discussions about knowledge center around *leaving no one behind* by guaranteeing access to knowledge and decision making to people who are excluded by structural discrimination. A very important approach, but my call goes far beyond providing merely access to excluded people. Based on experiences I gathered in trustful collaboration with people who are deeply affected by structural discrimination – combined with experiences arising from my own becoming – I realized that marginalized people are affected by what I call *degradation in knowing*. Degrading someone in knowing is not simply crushing a person into silencing. As we are going to see, degrading someone in knowing is destabilizing a person's credibility and life reality, resulting in violating the person's capacity as knower. This is a challenging starting point for the vision of the Inner Development Goals (IDGs). The IDGs is a framework of skills and capacities which empowers individuals and communities to successfully face and overcome complex challenges. The structural denial of knowledge, expertise, and know-how of millions of people rejects their ability to design and lead transformation processes. This is not only an injustice to millions of people, but also an injustice to humanity: If we do not break through those forms of oppression, inner development and growth will remain controlled by an elite, reproducing structural discrimination and hinder multilocal and multi-lead transformation processes.

In this chapter I do not only focus on how the violation of marginalized people's capacity as knowers hinders the vision of the IDGs. Rather, I outline how the IDGs could act as a *liberating framework*, leading towards inclusive spaces for actions of change and – as I'm going to argue – resulting in shifting systems of oppression. My discussion starts at the center of the challenge – namely the power structures that causes injustice in knowing (see Figure 3.1). Starting with the *why*, I focus on the ways power acts through rejecting the knowledge of marginalized people. I will sharpen our focus for why we must disentangle knowledge from power to achieve inclusive spaces for actions of change. Moving to the *how*, I will outline how the IDGs contribute to the disentanglement of knowledge from power. Here I will propose a revisited

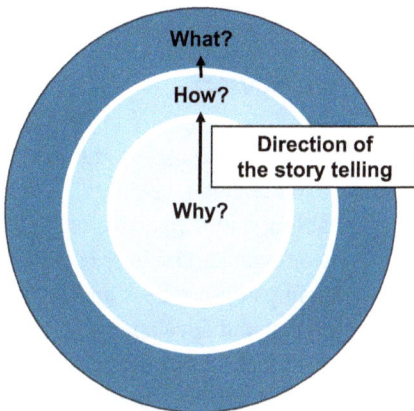

Figure 3.1: The direction of the story telling based on Simon Sinek's Golden Circle. Source: Compiled by author based on Sinek 2011.

understanding of the IDG framework as a liberating framework. Ending with the *what,* I illustrate what exactly is needed for the IDGs to shift systems of oppression.

This chapter should be read as a guide for self-reflection addressing practitioners like me: sensitive to structural discrimination, reflective about power dynamics, but still acting from a privileged position. Unlearning hierarchy is a practice of *allyship.* Allyship describes actions whereby a person in a position of privilege and power seeks to operate in solidarity with a marginalized group. It is important to distinguish allyship from saviorism: Whereas the savior reinforces power dynamics – by knowing "better" what marginalized groups need and should do – the ally seeks to challenge oppressive power structures by reevaluating their own role in perpetuating systems of oppression. An ally always acts in partnership with and under full recognition of the people the ally is in solidarity with (PeerNetBC, n.d.). In what follows, I retell stories which I retrospectively see as crucial for my own becoming as an ally, hoping those stories guide the readers' self-reflection. I am incredibly grateful to all the people who gave me access to their thoughts, experiences, and traumas caused by structural discriminations. Those stories and experiences guided my self-reflection. As my becoming journey evolves, I encounter more people who help me to develop my thinking. At this point, I would like to thank all those who participated in the collective reviewing of this chapter, contributing not only to sharpen this chapter, but also to sharpen my thoughts.[1]

---

1 On March 22 and 23, 2024, I organized open hackathon sessions in a collective reviewing of this chapter. The participants were: Ali Akdas, Jeyani Thiyagaraj, Lesli Gutierrez, and Nina Hurni based in Switzerland; Mirjam Johansson, based in Sweden; and Nodumo Ndhlovu and Tayson Mudarikiri based in Zimbabwe. The group was diverse in terms of age, professional expertise, life context, and geographical localization.

Let's dive into the why

Why should we disentangle knowledge from power?

Inner development is based on two interlinked foundational pillars: (1) on the sum a person knows – ranging from educational knowledge, to embodied knowledge, to values, memories, emotions, and so on; and (2) on an enabling and supportive community. No skills or capacities presented in the IDG framework can successfully be developed in isolation. Moreover, it is only through relationships with others and in the context of concrete actions that inner qualities are expressed and developed. This renders the inner development to a collective and cultural project that is always embedded in a community. On the other hand, this entanglement with the community exposes inner development to a community's existing values, patterns, and mindsets. Those may be enabling conditions, like a mindset open for change. But they can also be restrictive, like oppressive power structures that regulate access to knowledge and define whether a person's individual knowing gains credibility and significance in the wider community or not. This last condition is crucial: Constant degradation of someone's knowing by telling them that what someone knows is wrong or insignificant not only hinders the person from building on their own ideas but – as we are going to see – fundamentally violates the person's psychological capacities needed to act for change. This urges for a shift in system, away from oppressive spaces towards inclusive spaces.

Before we turn to the question of how to shift systems of oppression later in this chapter, I will focus on the ways those systems operate in violating marginalized people's capacity as knower. In a first step, I will have a closer look at how patterns of abusive power degrade marginalized groups in their knowing. Those patterns are the starting point to understand both the effect the violation of a marginalized person's capacity as knower has on the affected person themself, and the role this violation plays in maintaining systems of oppression.

Degrading someone in knowing as a pattern of abusive power

Classifying a person's knowing as credible and significant or not is rarely based on objective fact alone. During the time I worked with marginalized groups, I realized that stigmatized people's capacity as knowers is constantly questioned and deeply shaped by structural discrimination. The violations in knowing I noticed over the years can be summarized in two patterns. The first pattern operates by degrading a marginalized person's credibility. The second pattern functions by turning invisible a marginalized person's reality.

Pattern 1: Degrading someone's credibility

During a temporary job in an institution which offers job opportunities to people with cognitive disability, I realized for the first time how discrimination violates a stigmatized person's credibility. Shortly before I arrived, the management decided to hand over the cleaning of the factory to their own employees and not outsourcing it anymore. The new facility team was put together of employees from whom the management thought they are overchallenged by other work activities in the factory. When I arrived, the motivation of the, at that time, recently established facility team was very low. Quite understandable: the cleaning was physically demanding and – especially cleaning the toilets – was not a highly regarded task throughout the whole team. Moreover, the team members did not choose their new jobs themselves. I had the impression that the whole layout of this newly created department was very much externally determined; the people who had to carry out the task were not involved at all. We made a deal: we would spend two to three hours a day working on the transformation of everything that bothers us as a team, but by the end of the day all cleaning tasks had to be completed.

Our first transformation task was to replace the cleaning manuals and work planner which was hanging on the walls in our small team office. What surprised me the most about those documents was that they were all in written language not very accessible to people with reading and writing difficulties. My predecessor – so the team members explained me – checked the work planner every morning and read out to them their tasks and responsibilities. We decided to create a new work planner which allowed each team member – regardless of their writing and reading skills – to independently identify their daily duties. Finally, a board was created on which we assigned pictures of the tasks to photos of the team members, and on an old smartphone we recorded audio explanations of selected manuals. The daily transformative challenges served not only in changing our work conditions, but also in leading the team towards self-determined solution findings. I took on the role of a coach, primarily leading the group discussions and creating a safe space for testing the solutions proposed by the team. Acknowledging the team members as experts of their lives, it was important to me to take their expertise seriously and test their ideas. Simply because some of their ideas didn't make sense in my way of thinking didn't mean they weren't worth testing. Moreover, the testing provided us a shared reality from which we could make decisions on an equitable basis. This was crucial: Accepting everyone as expert with their own expertise connected us to a network in which everyone had a role on an equal level, but according to what was physically and cognitively possible. We created an inclusive space that allowed collective actions for change.

In that time, I noticed that the different generations of people with cognitive disabilities differed in their capabilities in developing their own ideas and taking decisions, even though the degree of their disability seemed to be similar. Whereas the older generation was less comfortable in relying on their knowing, the younger generation seemed more self-confident and more autonomous. I attribute this to the societal change in dealing with cognitive disabilities. The older generation grew up in a time where people with cognitive disabilities were discriminated against as irrational or unreasonable, incapacitated by the state, institutions, and their own families in taking their own decisions. The younger generation, on the other hand, is individually encouraged in building on their own ideas and living self-determined lives. This difference in growing up had a huge impact on the knowing and self-awareness of the people I worked with. This experience deeply sensitized me for the fact that a person's credibility is deeply affected by whether a person is perceived as rational thinking or not. Rationality, on the other hand, is negotiated and deeply informed by structural discrimination.

To sum up, a marginalized group's capacity as knowers is often distorted by deforming their rationality, resulting in questioning their credibility and leading to the denial of their knowledge. This is not only true for stigmatized persons under ableism but occurs in all forms of structural discrimination. The American writer Rebecca Solnit, for example, published in 2014 a collection of essays under the title *Men Explain Things to Me* (2014a). Her essays all sum up one key aspect of violating women's capacity as knowers under patriarchy, by questioning women's rationality: As Solnit writes, "women have been told they are delusional, confused, manipulative, malicious, conspiratorial, congenitally dishonest, often all at once" (Solnit, 2014b). The French anthropologist Philippe Descola, on the other hand, shows how the "irrationalization" of indigenous knowledge by Western societies has resulted in this body of knowledge not having the credibility and significance it deserves (Descola, 2013).

Pattern 2: Turning realities invisible

The second pattern in reinforcing the marginalization of people by degrading them in knowing is by not letting them evolve their realities. I discovered this form of injustice in 2023. At that time, I was working for a Swiss-based, but internationally operating, NGO in the field of youth work. In 2022 we started the Youth Speaks program. The aim of the program was to introduce and coach young people in self-designed and self-guided context analysis. My colleagues[2] – acting as senior coaches – trained youth facilitators in methods and supported them in designing peer-to-peer workshops in data collection, data analysis, and data reporting. The youth facilitators were empowered to design the workshops according to their life realities: From selecting the methods, to where and how to conduct it, and how to document and report the results,

---

2 I am grateful for the collaboration with you and that you always share your experiences with me. Laura Rodriguez based in El Salvador; Drucila Meireles based in Mozambique; Fernanda Cruz based in Brazil; Mlungisi Nyathi based in Zimbabwe; and Jorge Contreras based in Nicaragua.

everything was defined by the young people according to what made sense to them. We launched the first round of the researchLAB – as we called it – in Brazil, El Salvador, Mozambique, Nicaragua, South Africa, Tanzania, and Zimbabwe. In the "LABs", young people were asked to analyze their life contexts and search for fields of action for future projects. The research question was: "Which are the five most important fields of actions which, according to you, urge for project interventions? Explain why they are important and sketch out the perfect future after the project's intervention." Apart from a few challenges in the implementation – which projects of this kind always have – this first launch was a success. The young people were thrilled to get the space, not only in expressing their thoughts and needs, but also in freely designing the process and means according to their life realities. In 2023, I was invited to an online event in which the youth facilitators from Brazil presented their results and experiences.[3] The feedback of one particular youth group drew my attention to a dimension of injustice in knowing that lies much deeper than deforming one's credibility and that I had not been able to grasp properly until then: the injustice of not being able to give people, who do not share the same life realities, access to one's own interpretation of the facing reality. This inability does not arise from a lack of space for self-expression, but from a lack in having words or concepts to name the particularities of their life realities. The youth facilitator, Urubu do Quilombo, explained that in some cases he and his peer group simply did not know existing words or concepts – which is a question of having access to knowledge. But moreover – and this caught my attention – no established words or concepts which fully captured the particularity of their life realities existed. At this point I realized that Urubu do Quilombo and his peer group, who describe themselves as *pessoas negras* – the common Brazilian Portuguese expression for people of color – are so deeply marginalized as youth and people of color that their life realities do not enter mainstream language. As we know, thoughts and emotions, as well as the processes of becoming aware of one's own reality, are structured by language. The limitation described here not only erases the particularity of their life realities, it also prevents the young people from becoming aware of them. Urubu do Quilombo concluded that the research workshops created a safe space were the youth group realized for the first time the external limitation of their becoming aware of their own realities, and at the same time it opens space for confirming to each other that these realities exist and are real.

Western-based knowledge production recently became more self-critical about the fact that the realities of marginalized groups are fundamentally neglected. Regarding psychological research for example, the American journalist Helen Santoro (2023) writes that Western psychology not only has a long history of being led primarily by

3 I am grateful to all youth groups for giving me access to their realities and sharing with me their experiences. And I am grateful to Urubu do Quilombo who presented the results of his peer group. Without his reflections, it would not have been possible for me to evolve my becoming aware of the injustice in knowing.

white men, but that most findings are based on scientific research which includes mainly white study participants, although the findings are applied universally on all life realities. Gabrielle Jackson (2019) shows how centuries of exclusion of female realities in the production of Western medical knowledge led to the fact that women's diseases are often missed, misdiagnosed, or remain a total mystery – and still are today. This list of how the exclusion of marginalized realities distorts Western knowledge production can be easily continued and extended to knowledge productions in other geographical contexts.

The effects of degrading someone in knowing

Violating a marginalized person's capacity as knower is best understood as a practice of a microaggression. Microaggression describes a form of covert everyday discrimination. They occur in commonplace verbal, behavioral, or environmental slights that communicate hostile, derogatory, or negative attitudes toward individuals of marginalized groups (Sue & Spanierman, 2020). The prefix "micro" does not refer to being small or innocuous but rather underscores the interpersonal, microlevel context of the act. Whereas macroaggressions – like hate crimes for example – affect whole groups and occur often in the public sphere, microaggressions happen in everyday interactions between a perpetrator and a member of a marginalized group (Sue & Spanierman, 2020). As we are going to see in the following section, microaggressions have a huge impact in disrupting an affected person's self and their relation to the outside world. On a community level, this form of structural discrimination perpetuates systems of oppression.

Effect on individual level: Distorting the self of affected Individuals

To try a first attempt in understanding how the degradation of someone in knowing affects marginalized people, I suggest having a look at the concept of *gaslighting*. Gaslighting derives from the field of psychology and describes an intense form of psychological power abuse. A key element of gaslighting is to control and manipulate a person's knowing by systematically fed false information and telling them what the person thinks or sees is not true or does not exist. Gaslighting, as the American psychoanalyst Robin Stern who originally introduced the concept in 2007 points out, can lead to confusion, powerlessness, shame, emotional instability, low self-esteem, and even to a loss of trust in one's own memories, feelings, or senses. Gaslighted persons may genuinely believe they are mentally not well and that their memories and knowledge are inaccurate or wrong. This can go so far that they adopt the view of reality imposed on them and incorporate it as their own reality (Stern, 2018). Although Stern presents almost exclusively case studies that situate the gaslighting effect in private relationships were the man is the gaslighter and the women affected by it, I argue that this effect can be traced in every abusive power context where a person's capacity as knower is violated. This is true for the above-discussed questioning of the credibility of persons with cognitive disabilities as well as for the canceling of Urubu do Quilombo's and his peers' reality. And I dare to say, this is also true for structural forms of degrading someone in knowing like, for example, the irrationalization of indigenous knowledge by Eurocentrism (Descola, 2013), the marginalization of women under patriarchy (Solnit, 2014a), and the denial of non-binary life realities under heteronormativity (Santoro, 2023).

Effect on community level: Perpetuating hierarchies of power

It is crucial to understand that discrimination only occurs in context of power, privilege, and dominance. These contexts are deeply shaped by dynamics of oppression where a dominant group is assigned to a higher position in society, while the rest is classed into subordinated groups (see Figure 3.2). This hierarchy of dominance decides the distribution of privileges and access to power. Concerning Western societies, the highest position – and with this position the access to power and privilege – is reserved to white, heterosexual, and mentally healthy men (Etchells et al., 2017). Segregation builds the fundament of hierarchies and follows a simple – but powerful and inescapable – binary logic: you are a man or non-man, you are white or non-white, you are mentally healthy or not mentally healthy, and so on. One category is always related to the dominant group and higher ranked. Whereas the category at the other end of the spectrum relates to the oppressed groups, positioned at the bottom of the hierarchy (A or non-A, see Figure 3.2). Discrimination serves to maintain the separation: overemphasizing a specific aspect of one's appearance or identity which differs from the predominate ideal norm demarcates those individuals and groups as deviating from the norm. This can be differences in class, gender, sex, sexual orientation, race, ethnicity, mother tongue, age, body shape, disability, religion, and so on. Attributing these demarcated groups with negatively connoted characteristics pushes them to the margins of a society, exposes them to hostility, increases their invalidation, and leads to unjustified criminalization. Such push backs in subordinated positions reinforce white supremacy, patriarchy, heteronormativity, and other systems of oppression. In Western societies, the nature of separation practices has shifted over time from overt expressions – like school segregation in the United States based on students' ethnicity, for example – towards covert expressions like the here-discussed degradation in knowing. Whereas the violence that emerges from overt forms of separation is apparent, microaggressions remain subtle, the emanating violence only noticeable to affected individuals. The American psychologist Derald Wing Sue, who dedicated his research to the study of everyday microaggressions, concludes that the biggest harm and injustice doesn't come from overt forms of discrimination but rather from these subtle, everyday discriminations (Sue & Spanierman, 2020). Sue's argumentation is based on two facts. Frist, microaggressions derive often from well-intended people with egalitarian values who would never consciously discriminate. This turns everyone into a potential perpetrator in committing discriminations. Second, the fact that these subtle forms of discrimination are only noticeable to affected people not only makes it difficult for those who are affected to denounce the violence they experience, but the dominant groups perceive their societies as discrimination-free (Sue & Spanierman, 2020).

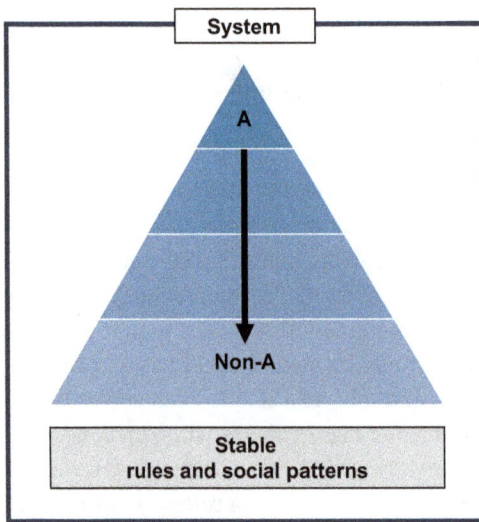

Figure 3.2: The figure shows the inner logic of the system, depicted as a hierarchy. Source: Compiled by author.

The cycle of socialization, as outlined by the American social justice educator Bobbie Harro (see Figure 3.3), helps to reflect on the way in which we are socialized into hierarchical power systems. According to Harro (2000), individuals are positioned either within the dominant norm, securing higher societal status, or among subordinates. These assigned roles determine not only if and how one experiences oppression but also whether and how one might uphold oppressive systems. For both privileged and marginalized groups, these roles are nearly inescapable. Our existence begins outside of established rules and patterns, but upon entering family life, we take the first step in our socialization into an assigned role (see Figure 3.3). As we grow, we increasingly absorb influences from the external world, entering a phase of institutional and cultural socialization through entities such as the church, school, legal system, media, and language. This leads to a lifelong phase of enforcement, where we experience sanctions or punishments that reinforce our subordinated position within the hierarchy. If we fall within a privileged group, we receive rewards and empowerment, af-

firming our alignment with societal norms. Ultimately, we reach a state of internalized reinforcement, wherein we have fully absorbed the hierarchy of power and our
role within it. At this point, power structures are unconsciously enacted in daily life,
consistently reproduced, and gradually legitimized, thereby sustaining the superiority
of the dominant norms.

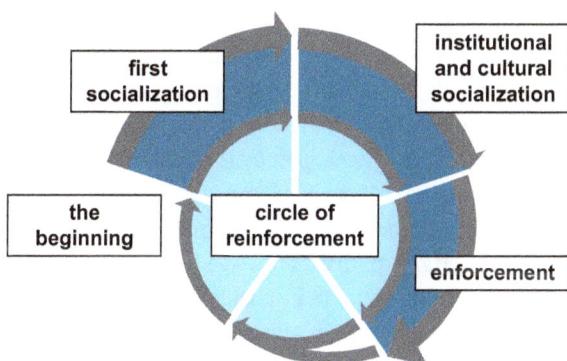

Figure 3.3: The cycle of socialization illustrates how systems perpetuate themselves through socialization.
Source: Adaptation of Harro (2000), compiled by author.

Conclusion: Call for systemic change towards unlearning hierarchies

Harro's reflection about the inescapable socialization in hierarchies of power and
Sue's highlighting that well-intentioned and egalitarian values do not prevent from
committing discrimination makes it apparent that systems which are shaped by
power hierarchies will never be just, fair, and inclusive. Reframing it in the discussion
of justice in inner development, I conclude that marginalized people can foster their
individual inner development, but as long as systems of oppression degrade the credibility and significance of their knowing, the violation of their capacity as knowers
continues. Such a power setting will never provide inclusive spaces for collective actions of change. This urges for a radical unlearning of hierarchies in knowing and a
shift in systems of oppression. The following section will explore the potential the
IDGs provide for such unlearning journeys.

Let's dive into the how

How do the IDGs contribute to unlearning hierarchies in knowing?

In 2021 I started a new position as project coach for a project named "imagine" run by the Swiss-based NGO terre des hommes schweiz. In the project, young people between 16 and 26 engage in creating more safe spaces for marginalized groups in Swiss society. Besides peer-to-peer workshops, panel discussions, or art interventions, the project group annually organizes an entry-free festival under the slogan "For Diversity. Against Discrimination". The project layout is deeply shaped by the concept of participation: a group of eight young people between the ages of 18 and 26 run the project in self-organization, supported by me as project coach. When I took over the coaching, I was confronted with a very diverse project group: diverse in age, diverse in experience they already had in project management, diverse in structural discrimination they faced, diverse in access to privileges, and diverse in emotional and psychological resilience. But they all shared a socialization in hierarchical learning settings from where they embodied that – whether as youngsters, as racially oppressed, or marginalized due to their gender identity – they cannot completely rely on what they already know, but are always dependent on someone else. Starting my work I faced one major challenge: the project group restricted themselves by waiting for orders and tasks from a senior position – like me or the management of the organization. At this point I decided to apply project-based learning (PBL) to lead the project group towards unlearning the inherited hierarchical learning settings and foster the group's self-organization. PBL – originally introduced as a teaching method – is a form of social learning oriented towards the way human beings intrinsically learn: namely, engaged in real-life contexts and in interaction with others. The layout of PBL is not only focusing on implementing projects but also on guiding the project members in their inner development and growth.

In what follows, I will share what I retrospectively think were the fundamental turning points in the unlearning hierarchy journey. I will start by outlining the two major conditions for an unlearning journey: (1) a hierarchy-free project structure; and (2) a need-oriented project coaching. I will conclude the section by discussing the five dimensions of the IDGs and how they contributed to this unlearning journey.

Condition 1: Hierarchy-free project structure

Quite simply, if hierarchy is the instrument of oppression, the anti-oppression journey should be hierarchy-free. Which doesn't mean that there are no leading dynamics at all: In hierarchy-based organizations, leading is acted by persons in higher position according to the organizational hierarchy, whereas in hierarchy-free set-ups, the organizational structure is leading, not the involved persons. To reframe it: the leading power is shifted from persons to structure. For the organization of the imagine project, we structured it according to *sociocracy* – an approach to design and lead organizations hierarchy-free and rooted in the network mindset (Bockelbrink, David, & Priest, 2024). The project's main tasks are divided into so-called circles. Every circle consists of several team members who complete the tasks the circle is assigned to. The tasks within a circle are self-organized by its members who know best how to organize and do the work. Every circle has a delegated person to be the so-called project coordination circle, which deals with the project's governance tasks like project budgeting and financing, public relations, or recruiting new project members. Whereas in hierarchical organizations the governance is assigned to higher positions with fixed responsibilities and privileges – like supervisor or management – the network-oriented sociocracy is governed by *roles*. A role consists of an area of responsibility – also known as a domain. The role keeper – to whom a certain domain is delegated – has autonomy to make decisions and take actions within the boundaries of the role's domain (Bockelbrink, David, & Priest, 2024). With regards to the imagine project, the responsibilities and boundaries of a role can be called into question by any member at any time. The ongoing negotiation of responsibilities and boundaries ensures that the decision-making power is always under critical examination, which makes it almost impossible for individual members to accumulate power. In addition, the ongoing reevaluation guarantees that the structure adapts to the changing needs and particularities of the project members. This flexibility makes the project incredibly responsive to changing circumstances and thus increases the resilience of both the project and the project members. This hierarchy-free structure, which is under ongoing negotiation and critical examination of power distribution, inscribes equity and justice into the project DNA, making it a foundational element of the imagine network.

Condition 2: Need-oriented project coaching

If we understand the above-described project structure as a network of people who interact together in achieving a common vision, my role as project coach is one element in that network. The coach's role is that of an ally: acting under full recognition of the project members, close to their needs, but still operating from a *step back* (see Figure 3.4). The *metodología del paso atrás* ('step-back approach') was developed by the Asociación Infantil Tuktan Sirpi (n.d.), an association based in Jinotega, northern Nicaragua, advocating for children's participation and rights. The approach points out that the aim of project coaching is to lead the project group towards a consolidated state. In this condition, the group acts self-guided in both implementing the project and maintaining the project structure. As the inner development of the project group evolves – from being enabled towards being consolidated – the project coach's way in

development of the project team

consolidated

strengthened

developed

enabled

encourage

accompany

advice

the step back from the project coach

Figure 3.4: The step-back approach involves gradually reducing the project coach's direct involvement, allowing team members to assume greater responsibility and autonomy. Source: Compiled by author based on Asociación Infantil Tuktan Sirpi, n.d.

supporting as well as the intensity of their interactions with the group are evolving too (see Figure 3.4).

When I started the unlearning journey, my main task was to enable the group members by encouraging them to discover their already existing personal resources which could be crucial in managing their project tasks. We focused on what they already knew and on similar experiences they already made, and – to the surprise of the group – every member could share something. This was a good starting point from which I could encourage the members to sharpen their lenses for what they additionally needed in order to act. As the project group's inner development evolved, so also did my role evolve. Whereas I started with weekly inputs or guiding group discussions, I more and more handed over those tasks to the group members, acting finally from an advisory perspective. To ensure that my role was synchronized with the needs of the project group, it was important that I remained a member of the network, with stable relationships to all members and constantly collectively reassessing of my role.

The IDGs as a liberating framework

In the following sections I will look back on the last two years and define skills and capacities which, in my opinion, were essential to the project members' unlearning journeys in overcoming hierarchies in knowing. Although the IDG framework was not developed when I started the unlearning hierarchy journey, the presented skills and capacities are deeply interlinked with the IDGs' vision. Therefore, the discussion of the skills and capacities is grounded in the IDG framework's five dimensions: *being*, *thinking, relating, collaborating*, and *acting*. Applied together, the discussed skills and capacities are so powerful in overcoming oppressive power structures that they build what I call the *liberating framework*.

Dimension 1 – being: Starting with presence

Every project member had to go on their own learning journey. Whereas the most vulnerable project members had to learn to trust more of their own capacities, the less vulnerable and more privileged project members had to learn their role as an ally and how they could contribute to a safer space that allows vulnerability without being judged and hurt.

The arriving in a state of liberated presence is only possible when the project members feel safe enough to wake up and grow, as well as to exercise their rights to challenge existing structures in the project, to share their thoughts, and to trust in their own abilities as well as in the other group members. Psychological safety was the foundation of such an enabling project environment, and therefore we invested a lot of time and energy in establishing and maintaining a psychologically safe project environment.

Dimension 2 – thinking: Changing perspectives

Perspective skills were key in the unlearning journey. Self-awareness about their own position and getting an understanding about from which position the other project members acted was crucial. When we I started the unlearning journey, I noticed a big difference in skills between the different group members. I attributed this difference primarily to the fact that, due to privileges, some members had access to experiences which enabled them to develop certain skills that others did not yet have. And I noticed that members who had had these learning experiences before were quicker to engage in learning new skills than members who had had no access to such learning experiences so far. I faced this challenge by implementing a peer-to-peer support system. Every member developed a map with strengths, naming skills and knowledge the person already had. And they made a list of growth areas, listing skills and knowledge they considered as needed to be developed. These maps gave orientation because the project members could learn about the needs of the others and knew from whom they could get support. On the other hand, every member had to discover already existing strengths and got acknowledged for them by the others. This was a key moment in awakening. First, it brought all members to the same level because everyone could contribute with their own strengths to the growth of the group's development. And second, everyone gained from the perspectives and strengths of the others.

Dimension 3 – relating: Equity-orientation as foundation

The imagine project's equity-oriented approach is caring for others by definition: Developing empathy for other lived realities, acting in accordance with their own needs and the needs of the others, being connected to the others, and appreciating every project member in their being was the foundation of the unlearning journey we started. This equity orientation is an ongoing process and needs constant reassessment: As the imagine project team evolves and new members join, the group is constantly reevaluating and negotiating the project structure. This became an institutionalized component of our inner growth. The IDG framework became our orientation matrix, guiding the group's inner development journey. Every year the project members define three skills from the IDG framework they individually would like to strengthen during an upcoming project year. Additionally, the project group defines skills they think the group as a whole should invest in growing.

Dimension 4 – collaborating: Co-creation that hurts

Collaboration in settings of different values, skills, and competencies urges for a co-creation that *hurts* – by which I mean only if all group members feel that their own ideas or thinking get remarkably challenged can real co-creation happen. If this is not the case, there are still some opinions, ideas, or ways of thinking in the group that are dominant. Such a radical approach to co-creation ensures that the spaces of collaboration are created in a shared and co-inspired mindset with a shared logic and commonly negotiated language.

Good communication builds the foundation of such a dynamic, constantly evolving collaborative network. Our aim is that the project members listen more than they speak. To achieve this form of active listening, we institutionalized different methods such as discussions in rounds, timekeeping, prototype presentations, or decision-making processes based on consent. Like this we ensure that every person in the group gets the same space to express their opinions and the same access to decisions.

Complete transparency at any time is our top priority. Project progress, obstacles, but also mistakes or difficult team dynamics, are addressed directly and at any time. Moreover, every project member has full access to all project-relevant information and decisions.

Dimension 5 – acting: Stand up for self-established realities

Establishing over the years a structure based on equity and liberated from hierarchies lets the project members experience an alternative way of societal order. This experiencing of a counter reality that differs from the system of oppression activated the project members' personal resources, providing a stable base for inner growth. As the project groups evolved towards consolidation, they started to transfer the liberating framework into the contexts of their activities and life realities. Empowered and acting as allies themselves, they provide the same space for awakening to others.

Conclusion: The liberating potential of the IDGs

The IDGs' vison of fostering inner development to face and overcome complex challenges is deeply driven by the belief that only communities which include all members in its action of change can successfully meet these challenges. Based on my experience, I argue that the IDG framework provides crucial guidance in developing the skills and capacities which are needed to build inclusive, just, and resilient communities. Applied in a context which is sensitive to structural discrimination and aims to overcome power dynamics, the IDG framework becomes, in my opinion, a powerful instrument for empowering marginalized groups to break free from the hierarchies that constrain them, while guiding privileged groups to reevaluate the hierarchies they perpetuate. This leads the community towards social justice. Here I located the IDGs' potential as a liberating framework in shifting systems of oppression. Nevertheless, the IDG framework alone does not shift systems of oppression. In the following section I outline a first attempt at what an IDG-based exit strategy could look like.

Let's dive into the what

What is needed for the IDGs to shift systems of oppression?

As we have seen, contexts of power, privilege, and dominance will always demarcate subordinated groups and violate them based on their marginalization. Even if everyone would act motivated by egalitarian values and would never consciously discriminate, the discussion of microaggressions revealed that the socialization in hierarchies of power produces inescapable biases, prejudices, and stereotypical thinking. The IDGs can intervene in such a context, maybe contributing to more fairness, but can never transform hierarchies of power into just, fair, and inclusive systems. Only a radical shift away from hierarchical systems can lead towards justice. Based on the discussion in this chapter and on my experiences in working with marginalized groups, I will outline a first attempt of what an IDG-oriented exit strategy out of oppression could look like.

The outline of an exit strategy: Fixing the system, not the marginalized groups

Whereas approaches in social work often stress working with marginalized groups in separated safe spaces, located outside the contexts of oppression, I argue for an integrated but equity-oriented approach. A one-sided focus only on the marginalized groups risks creating the impression that marginalized people are the problem and need to be fixed, failing to grasp the real source of injustice: It is always the hierarchical power system which is the problem. A lasting shift towards social justice is only achievable when we deconstruct hierarchies in our minds, everyday lives, and institutions. This is not an endeavor that only concerns marginalized groups. A real exit strategy out of systems of oppression affects the whole global community.

The presented exit strategy is based on both an individual inner development of the marginalized and privileged groups, and a change in system. My approach targets breaking the cycle which socializes us into systems of oppression (see Figure 3.5); it consists of three steps. First, by empowering marginalized groups in their knowing we irritate the existing system of oppression. Second, we stabilize the irritation by implementing networks as a counter structure. This counter structure allows a community's equity-oriented inner development which includes all forms of knowing and further paralyzes the hierarchical system. And third, the new direction is consolidated by implementing project-based learning to lead marginalized as well as privileged groups towards unlearning hierarchies.

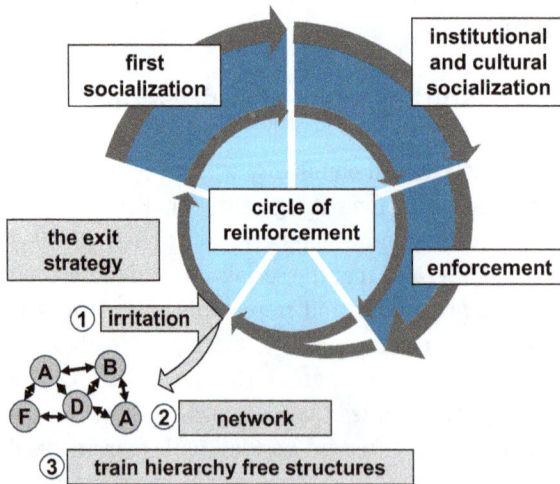

Figure 3.5: The exit strategy breaks the cycle of socialization and stabilizes the liberating counter structure. Source: Adaptation of the cycle of socialization by Harro (2000), compiled by author.

Irritation: Empowering someone in knowing as waking up

If degrading someone in knowing is the source of exclusion, empowering someone in knowing is the starting point of the exit strategy out of oppression. As the discussion of the effect degrading someone in knowing showed, these forms of structural gaslighting can lead to confusion, powerlessness, shame, emotional instability, low self-esteem, and even to a loss of trust in one's own memories, feelings, or senses. But inner development and personal growth require a certain degree of resilience, self-confidence, and trust in one's own abilities. These are personal resources which a gaslighted person hardly has. Approaches in positive psychology focus on overcoming paralyzing moments by reactivating a person's positive psychological state. This state consists of four key components: (1) self-efficacy, described as the belief in one's own abilities to achieve goals; (2) hope, understood as the persistent pursuit of goals even in challenging circumstances; (3) optimism, commonly seen as a positive outlook on the future and confidence in success; and (4) resilience, described as the ability to overcome problems and hurdles (Carr, 2022). These four elements are fundamentally based on what a person knows. Empowering a person's knowing is therefore key in activating an oppressed person's inner growth. The IDGs contribute significantly with its focus on relationship to self (Dimension 1) and developing cognitive skills (Dimension 2) to this awakening which will irritate the system of oppression.

Stabilization: Networks as counter structures to hierarchical systems

Simply empowering marginalized people in their knowing will not challenge the system of oppression. As we have seen in the discussion of the circle of socialization, systems of oppression will incorporate the empowered groups. To not risk the reintegration of an empowered person into the system of oppression, it is crucial to stabilize the irritation by establishing a counter structure. I propose networks as an alternative organizational structure. A network – as I understand it – can simply be defined as connections between people who came willingly together to form a reality. The rules and patterns which organize a network are co-created by the people in the network (see Figure 3.6). These guiding structures are not stable, but rather are constantly being negotiated by the network's members. Each member has the same space for negotiation. This ensures that as soon as a new person enters a network, the guiding rules and patterns are reevaluated. As a result, networks are adaptive to the members' particularities and needs as well as flexible and dynamic in reaction to change. This makes the network permeable for every kind of knowing and inclusive for all forms of experts, no matter if an expert is formed by a formal or academic education or by real-life experiences. Whereas in hierarchical systems the system's elements are shaped by top-down power dynamics, the members in a network are organized by the relationships they enter willingly. These relationships are co-created by the members involved and therefore established under full recognition of their needs and particularities. The network's ability to provide orientation and identity, while remaining flexible and adaptive, makes a network a powerful transformative counter structure to hierarchical systems. The IDGs' focus on caring for others and the world (Dimension 3) and the development of social skills for collaboration (Dimension 4) is fundamental in the stabilization of the network.

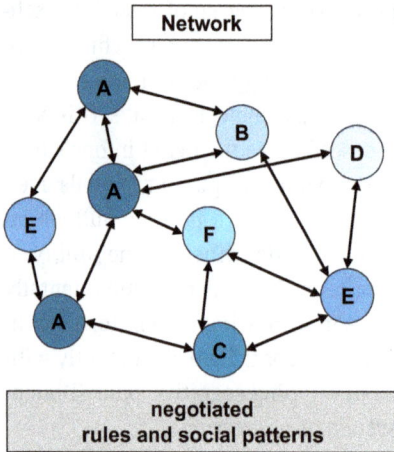

Figure 3.6: In contrast to the system, the network is characterized by a continuously negotiated structure. Source: Compiled by author.

Consolidation: Constant unlearning of inherited power patterns

Socialized power patterns are pervasive for both the perpetrators and the affected persons. An exit strategy only succeeds when socialized power patterns are detected, put into question, and activity replaced by jointly created new patterns. Those new patterns need to be trained day by day, until they get embodied and completely replace the old abusive power patterns. This final step leads to the consolidation of the established counter reality. In this step the network is able to act and foster change. PBL combined with the IDGs' orientation towards acting to enable change (Dimension 5) can be crucial in fully unleashing the transformative power in enabling systemic change.

Conclusion: With the IDGs from inner growth to outer change

Starting by individual inner development, the discussed exit strategy aims to initiate an outer change. The IDG framework – understood in its potential as a liberating framework – is key in this endeavor: The IDGs contribute to individual awakening as well as to the creation, stabilization, and consolidation of inclusive counter structures.

These counter structures create spaces for collective actions for change. This is a promising starting point for shifting systems of oppression and gives an idea of how the five dimensions of being, thinking, relating, collaborating, and acting, applied in an equity-oriented manner, become a force for transformative change.

Let's zoom out: Towards collective leadership in actions of change

Complex challenges are often found in contexts that are deeply shaped by structural discriminations like poverty, racism, or gender-based violence. In these contexts, the groups affected by discrimination are the actual experts of their lived realities, keeping the crucial contextual knowledge to produce impactful context-based solutions for overcoming these challenges. But as we have seen, structural discrimination in general, and degrading someone's knowing in particular, hinders marginalized groups in acting as local experts. Living in a context of abusive power and facing constant degradation of one's own capacity as knower violates psychological well-being and results in the loss of trust in one's own memories, capacities, feelings, or senses. This hinders stigmatized individuals from acting for change in their life contexts. Simply providing marginalized groups access to knowledge and decision making can foster their individual inner development, but as long as systems of oppression degrade the credibility and significance of their knowing and turns their life realities invisible, the violation of their right to be acknowledged as knowers and actors for change continues. This urges for a shift in system, away from oppressive spaces towards inclusive spaces for collective actions of change.

The IDG framework – revisited as a liberating framework – can be key in overcoming systems of oppression. Nevertheless, the potential of the IDG framework as a liberating framework is only released when two essential conditions are met. Frist, the IDG project is laid out as what I call an *unlearning of hierarchies towards inclusive spaces*. Intervening in contexts of oppressive power, the unlearning journey enables marginalized groups to break free from the hierarchies that constrain them, while guiding privileged groups to reevaluate the hierarchies they perpetuate. This leads the community towards social justice. As a person's individual inner development is deeply influenced by the unique cultural and societal environment, the second key condition for the IDG framework to operate as liberating framework is that the individual inner development goes in parallel with an outer development, aiming to challenge systems of oppression. This is only achievable when the unlearning journey aims to replace discriminating structures by inclusive counter structures.

Investing in local initiatives of change to become locally embedded IDG hubs and supporting them to apply the IDG framework and its liberating potential opens inclusive spaces for collective actions of change. Everyone and everywhere could become a leading figure in designing and implementing locally embedded solutions for locally embedded challenges. This collective leadership in actions of change unleashes a transformative energy we have never seen before, but which we urgently need to overcome the challenges we face today.

References

Bockelbrink, B., David, L., & Priest, J. (2024). A practical guide for evolving agile and resilient organizations with Sociocracy 3.0. Sociocracy 3.0. https://patterns.sociocracy30.org/all.html (accessed Oct. 27, 2024).

Carr, A. (2022). *Positive psychology: The science of wellbeing and human strengths* (3rd edn). Routledge.

Descola, P. (2013). *The ecology of others*. Prickly Paradigm Press.

Etchells, M. J., Deuermeyer, E., Liles, V., Meister, S., Suarez, M. I., & Chalklen, W. L. (2017). White male privilege: An intersectional deconstruction. *Journal of Ethnic and Cultural Studies*, 4(2), 13–27. https://doi.org/10.29333/ejecs/78.

Harro, B. (2000). The cycle of socialization. In M. Adams, W. J. Blumenfeld, H. W. Hackman, M. L. Peters, & X. Zuniga (eds.), *Readings for Diversity and Social Justice* (pp. 15–21). Routledge.

Jackson, G. 2019. *Pain and prejudice: A call to arms for women and their bodies*. Little, Brown Book Group.

PeerNetBC. (n.d.). *Allyship*. The Anti-Oppression Network. https://theantioppressionnetwork.com/allyship/ (accessed Mar. 30, 2024).

Santoro, H. (2023). The push for more equitable research is changing the field. American Psychologist. https://www.apa.org/monitor/2023/01/trends-inclusivity-psychological-research (accessed Oct. 27, 2024).

Sinek, S. (2011). *Start with why: How great leaders inspire everyone to take action* (2nd edn). Portfolio.

Solnit, R. (2014a). *Men explain things to me: And other essays*. Granta Books.

Solnit, R. (2014b). Cassandra among the creeps. *Harper's Magazine*, 10. https://harpers.org/archive/2014/10/cassandra-among-the-creeps/ (accessed Oct. 27, 2024).

Stern, R. (2018). *The gaslight effect: How to spot and survive the hidden manipulation others use to control your life* (2nd edn). Harmony.

Sue, D. W. & Spanierman, L. B. (2020). Microaggressions in everyday life (2nd ed.). John Wiley & Sons, Inc.

Asociación Infantil Tuktan Sirpi. (n.d.). Metodología Paso Atrás. https://unidosporlainfancia.org/wp-content/uploads/2018/06/4.-Paso-Atr%C3%A1s.pdf (accessed March 30, 2024).

Isabel Rimanoczy, Beate Klingenberg and Albachiara Boffelli

Chapter 4
The Sustainability Mindset Indicator®: A tool to assess and develop the Inner Development Goals

Abstract: This chapter presents the complementarity of the Inner Development Goals (IDGs) and their respective skills with the sustainability mindset, a research-based, personal development and change management framework. The sustainability mindset consists of 12 principles, encompassing four content areas (ecological worldview, systems perspective, emotional and spiritual intelligence) that represent paths to develop this mindset for sustainability, addressing key aspects of our thinking, doing, and being. These sustainability mindset principles (SMPs) and their cognitive, behavioral, and affective dimensions are introduced and then mapped against the five IDG dimensions and the IDG skills, illustrating how the two frameworks are mutually supportive in the development of inner dimensions. The SMI®, an online questionnaire-based tool of personal growth and change management rooted in the SMPs, is presented. Through a three-phased developmental process consisting of the experience of choosing from opposing statements that question underlying values and paradigms, a detailed personal report that encourages reflection and purposeful change, as well as a comprehensive toolkit for coaches or trainers, the SMI® supports and enables the concurrent development of IDG skills and SMPs due to their symbiotic relationships. A case study in higher education offers insights into the practical implementation of this joint learning. The chapter concludes with encouragements of reflection on the two frameworks and the personal path one may choose to further their development.

Keywords: personal development, assessment, Sustainability Mindset, IDG skills, joint learning

دیروز باهوش بودم پس می خواستم دنیا را تغییر دهم، امروز عاقل هستم، پس دارم خودم را تغییر می دهم.

Yesterday I was clever, so I wanted to change the world; today I am wise, so I am changing myself. – Rumi

https://doi.org/10.1515/9783111453729-005

Introduction

The quest for understanding the self has been the call for millennia, voiced by sha-mans, prophets, philosophers, poets, religious leaders, behavioral scientists, and common people. It is astounding that after thousands of years perfecting what we teach our children and our youth, the focus has been moving to technical skills and scientific knowledge, neglecting the basic invitation to "know thyself", which has universal application and practical implications in how we live our lives, how we interact with others, and the decisions we make. Certainly, digital intelligence has become an important competency; however, are we balancing it with comparable social and emotional learning (Yeke, 2023)? Are we in an era of pervasive technology, where digital systems will declare to know us better than we know ourselves (Andrejevic & Selwyn, 2023)?

In the dawn of a climate tipping point that has already started to impact lives in every corner of the world, we are experiencing a new and messy economic, political, environmental, and social landscape, for which we have no handbook to consult. Or do we?

With 2030 approaching and insufficient progress towards the Sustainable Development Goals (SDGs) (Partzsch, 2023), attention has increasingly been drawn to what might be holding us back, to what is in the way of achieving these valuable goals. Who doesn't want to create a world that works for all? And yet, cognitive acceptance doesn't seem to be enough to be converted into action. Pondering the obstacles, we started to hear references to the mindset, the paradigm, the narrative, the collective worldview, the inner dimensions, such as the Inner Development Goals (IDGs) (Andrejevic & Selwyn, 2023; Halle, Najam, & Beaton, 2013).

This chapter is about these inner dimensions. It argues that fostering personal growth has a transformational impact on how we see ourselves, each other, and the world. It takes the mindset as the conceptual anchor: when we accomplish a mindset shift, it has an unquestionable impact on our behaviors, with ripple effects on the people we interact with, directly and indirectly (Rimanoczy & Llamazares, 2021). We will spell this out by introducing the framework of the sustainability mindset principles (SMPs), highlighting how the development of these principles can be a path to developing the IDG skills. The SMPs focus on the development of a mindset that evolves around the objective of a sustainable lifestyle, by connecting what we know about sustainability and the consequences of unsustainable living with our inner values, anchors of identity, and ways of being, as well as with our behaviors and actions. The interconnected cognitive, affective, and behavioral dimensions of this mindset align with many of the IDG principles, as will be elaborated, thus allowing a symbiotic development of the sustainability mindset and IDG skills.

To illustrate how this path can happen, the authors will introduce in the following section the SMPs and the Sustainability Mindset Indicator (SMI®), an online questionnaire-based assessment and tool for personal development and change management rooted in the SMPs. Through opposing statements and a personal report, the individual is invited to pause and reflect on their assumptions and beliefs that have been taken for granted. This process provides an opportunity for mindset development which can go hand in hand with IDG skills development due to their complementarity, which will be discussed later in this chapter. The SMI® is an enabler of joint learning and personal growth toward the IDG skills and the sustainability mindset. Finally, a pre-post case study of students at the University of Bergamo in Italy will exemplify the development of IDG skills, using the SMPs as indicators of cognitive, affective, and behavioral changes facilitating those skills.

The sustainability mindset principles

Background

The sustainability mindset principles (SMPs) are a conceptual framework based on the doctoral work of Rimanoczy (2010) as she explored if there were any skills, competencies, or specific knowledge that could be intentionally taught or developed for a new generation of leaders. The findings of her qualitative exploratory study showed that the studied business leaders replaced their conventional business behaviors with unusual innovations that positively impacted the environment or society. They did so at a great personal cost since their ideas were not easily understood by their peers, leadership team, board, or even employees. However, their inner engagement was so strong that no obstacle stopped them in the pursuit of a new way of seeing their business's role. The new perspective they pioneered had no precedent or notes to follow, as mainstream business was set in a different approach: short-term focus, win-lose attitude, nature as a resource to exploit, and maximizing profits to stay competitive.

The research revealed that the main driver was these leaders' mindset, which had shifted from the conventional to a sustainability one. Careful consideration of their individual cases showed that this mindset had specific elements of a particular way of thinking and being that could be developed. Rimanoczy (2010) called this set of aspects the "sustainability mindset", which can be developed through 12 principles, grouped into four content areas: ecological worldview, systems perspective, emotional intelligence, and spiritual intelligence (See Figure 4.1).

The SMPs are 12 paths to develop this mindset for sustainability that address key aspects of our thinking and being, which, if unscrutinized, risk anchoring us in unintentional unsustainable behaviors (Rimanoczy, 2020). They are described in the following subsection.

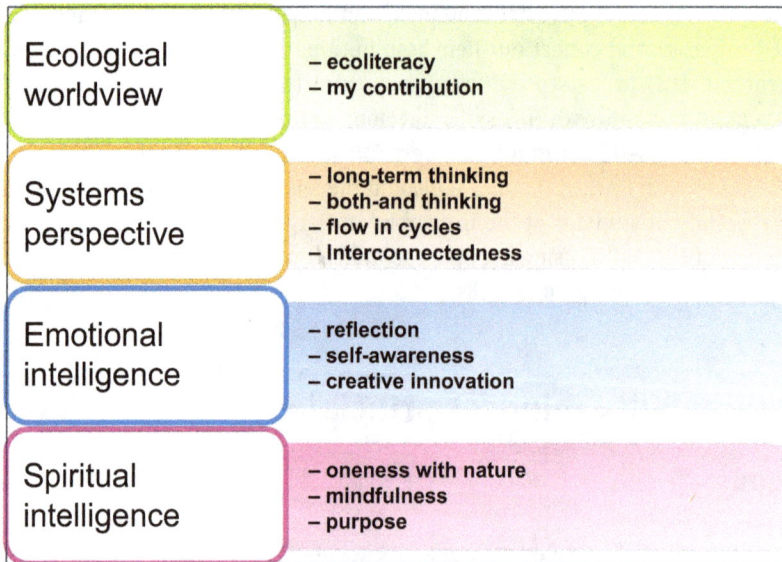

Figure 4.1: The 12 sustainability mindset principles and the four content areas.
Source: Based on authors' own figure adapted from Rimanoczy (2020).

The sustainability mindset content areas and principles (based on Rimanoczy, 2020)

In this section we introduce the four content areas and the 12 sustainability mindset principles, based on Rimanoczy, 2020.

ECOLOGICAL WORLDVIEW

1. Ecoliteracy: "Understanding the state of the planet allows us to be more fully aware of challenges, exploring the complexity of how they are linked to each other, and our feelings lead to engaged actions" (p. 27).
2. My contribution: Every person plays a role in contributing to the planetary challenges, mostly unintentionally and frequently without realizing it. "When we identify the ways in which we are unintentionally contributing to the problems, we have a chance to do something about them" (p. 37).

SYSTEMS PERSPECTIVE

3. Long-term thinking: Efficiency, speed, and habits prompt us to make decisions based on the short- or medium-term horizon. Every action, however, also has consequences that are not immediately visible. "Considering the long term when analyzing situations and making decisions has a positive impact on global sustainability" (p. 53).

4. Both+And thinking: Rational thinking and logic operates under the either/or logic, and when decisions are made solely from that perspective, they tend to create exclusion of key stakeholders, prioritizing one over other, and creating zero-sum solutions. "Both+and thinking allows us to understand paradoxes and calls for creative solutions that are inclusive of all stakeholders" (p. 64). These types of solutions are key for the health of the ecosystem and create fair and peaceful societies.

5. Flow in cycles: "There are no linear processes in Nature: everything flows in cycles of birth, growth, death, rebirth . . . Many aspects of man-created unsustainability of the planet are a result of the misconception that we are not governed by this law of Nature" (p. 80). We are excessively attached to planning, serving our desire to control, at the neglect of the flexibility required to incorporate feedback, adapt, and develop resiliency.

6. Interconnectedness: We move around in our world automatically analyzing, clustering, and differentiating ourselves and all that surrounds us. The appreciation of diversity provides richness to our life, like the different cells in our body. Yet this must be complemented by an integration, understanding the interconnectedness of all that is, like the organs in our body contributing to the functioning of the whole. When we consider both diversity and interconnectedness, our decisions and actions are more inclusive and contribute to the sustainability of the whole.

EMOTIONAL INTELLIGENCE

7. Reflection: Speed and efficiency create automated actions, which may create unwanted consequences. Reflective practices help to pause, to ponder the situation before jumping into action Also, learning is enhanced when individuals regularly pause and reflect on what happened, how this matched the expectation, and how behaviors may have impacted the results.

8. Self-awareness: Human evolution is a journey of expanding consciousness, into larger scopes of understanding and caring. Our values are anchors of our identity and exploring them helps us notice inconsistencies between what we value and what our actions express. "When we explore our personal values, beliefs, assumptions, and motivations we gain greater control over our own actions and can see new alternative behaviors" (p. 144).

9. Creative innovation: Resilience is based on constant creativity, innovation, and experimentation, capabilities that are mostly generated by our right brain hemisphere. The ancestral nonverbal wisdom of our species, the holistic and intuitive perceptions of the world are a valuable input for our survival. Our rational thinking (mostly left brain hemisphere) is meant to complement that input, analyzing and fragmenting information, clustering it, and establishing linear processes of implementation. When we neglect the nonrational wisdom we have in us, our sol-

utions are missing critical information, are poor quality and may create negative impacts on the ecosystem and society

SPIRITUAL INTELLIGENCE

10. Oneness with Nature: The materialistic, consumption-oriented society has placed nature outside the individual, as a resource to be used. The "take-make-waste" model resulted in a large part of the problems we are facing at a planetary level. Understanding that we are one with Nature, that we are a species within species, and that all Nature is in us, is a powerful spiritual experience that cannot be quantified or measured. Yet the experience of oneness can shape behaviors and decisions that lead to more satisfying lives and to a more harmonic relationship with each other and all beings.

11. Mindfulness: Our pace of life is increasingly fast, aided by technology and the growing urban concentrations. This promotes reactive and automated thoughtless behaviors. Processing information to understand what it means requires slowing down, and creating spaces to observe, notice, and connect with our feelings). These nonthinking practices integrate our spiritual dimension and help us develop mindfulness, an ancestral goal to expand consciousness.

12. Purpose: The materialistic economic paradigm focuses on consumption and profit, neglecting the higher self of the individual, our spiritual well-being, and what brings deeper fulfillment. Incorporating into our life the concept of purpose helps identifying what really matters to us personally, and what difference we want to make in the world. This is a powerful motivator to drive actions for the greater good and to shape a flourishing world.

How sustainable is our mindset and how can we develop it?

To expand the research base of the sustainability mindset, specifically how to assess and develop said mindset, in 2014 Rimanoczy convened scholars into the Working Group of the sustainability mindset, within the Principles of Responsible Management Education (PRME), the academic arm of the United Nations Global Compact. The working group is an international network of scholars from over 290 universities in 59 countries, whose members are creating an academic body of knowledge on the mindset for sustainability. These scholars provided their diverse and valuable input to the development of pedagogical interventions, but also voiced the need for a way to assess the impact of their teaching on the mindset, which resulted in the design of the Sustainability Mindset Indicator (SMI®), which was launched in 2022 (Rimanoczy & Klingenberg, 2021).

The SMI® is an assessment and tool for personal development and change management that provides the individual with pointers to reflect on their views and values, using the concepts of positive psychology (Seligman & Csikszentmihalyi, 2000) and intentional change theory (Boyatzis & Akrivou, 2006). The SMI® has been designed and validated to provide the individual with an appreciative picture of where they are in their personal journey towards a sustainability mindset, offering information about how certain paradigms play a key role in our sustainable or un-sustainable behaviors. The developmental impact of the SMI® can occur in three stages. Firstly, a user of the tool is exposed to opposing statements in the online questionnaire that require the evaluation of one's own position towards sustainability and underlying paradigms. Having to choose which statement is a closer representation of one's mindset is a process that may prompt reflection upon personal values, drivers, behaviors, and emotional positions. Secondly, upon completion, the user receives a 32-page-long, detailed personalized report that provides a qualitative assessment of this person's mindset and offers guidance for in-depth reflection, questioning, and experiencing of the SMPs and their dimensions. It highlights the up- and downsides of our automatic behavioral patterns, in addition to suggestions, questions for reflection, and developmental tips. When used in coaching or training settings, there is a third option for personal development: the SMI® provides an anonymous, aggregate group report that allows identifying strengths and weaknesses in the cognitive, behavioral, and affective expression of the sustainability mindset of this group. Based on this information, coaches or trainers can develop interventions that specifically address weaknesses while exploring strengths to encourage further development of the mindset. Besides their own experience and knowledge, coaches and trainers can also base this process on a multitude of experiences and exercises provided through sustainability mindset resource books (Rimanoczy, 2022). This three-phase process of personal development that is enabled by the SMI® is also suitable for a targeted and purposeful encouragement of IDG skills development. The following section maps the IDG skills and the SMPs, thus elaborating on how the complementarity of the two frameworks allows individuals, coaches, and trainers to work on a joint development using the various experiences and tools the SMI® offers.[1]

---

[1] The SMI® is currently available in English, French, German, Indonesian, and Spanish, to support such varied purposes as the development of K12 teachers of the 200 Indonesian Green Schools, for teaching and research projects in Mexico and Switzerland, and to support coaches working in the personal development of leaders in the financial sector. It is thus far used in higher education institutions in Australia, Austria, Canada, Germany, Indonesia, Ireland, Italy, Mexico, the Philippines, Russia, Spain, Sweden, Switzerland, United Kingdom, and the United States. Three international awards from the Wharton School and the QS World University Rankings (UK) have been awarded to the conception and development of this tool, recognizing its potential to accelerate change.

Comparing the sustainability mindset Principles and the Inner Development Goals

The sustainability mindset principles (SMPs) and the Inner Development Goals (IDGs) are two initiatives focusing on the inner dimensions. The former, as explained in the previous section, from the perspective of the mindset foundation (Rimanoczy, 2020), the latter from the perspective of skills and attitudes (Stålne & Greca, 2022).

Within the SMI®, for each SMP, the cognitive, behavioral, and affective dimension of the mindset is assessed. The reason for this approach is that individuals may know something, but not necessarily act upon that knowledge, or act but feel emotionally disengaged. To be able to identify where an individual is on their journey from these three different angles provides a subtle distinction and information, which gives the educator/coach new directions of where best to intervene. Figure 4.2 maps the connections of the five IDG dimensions and the three dimensions addressed in the SMI®.

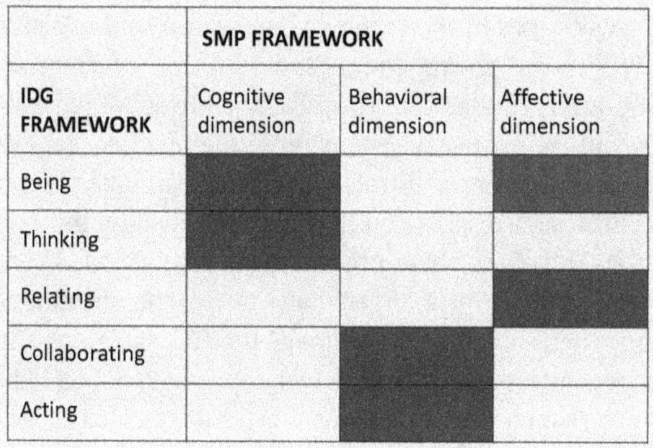

IDG FRAMEWORK	SMP FRAMEWORK		
	Cognitive dimension	Behavioral dimension	Affective dimension
Being	■		■
Thinking	■		
Relating			
Collaborating		■	
Acting		■	

Figure 4.2: IDG framework's five dimensions and the cognitive, behavioral, and affective dimensions of the SMI®.

Table 4.1 presents the proposed complementarity of the IDGs and the SMPs, indicating the skills listed in the five categories of the IDGs that are addressed or promoted within the framework of the SMP. Of the 23 IDG skills, 16 can be mapped to one or more SMPs, with critical thinking, communication skills, co-creation skills, trust, and mobilization, as well as courage and perseverance, not having a direct equivalent in the SMPs. In Rimanoczy's (2010) research, general leadership characteristics such as ability to mobilize and engage others, collaborate, communicate, or critically think were present among the individuals studied, but were not included in the framework because they were deemed very important but generic leadership aspects, and not characteristics specifically of a mindset for sustainability. Courage and perseverance were considered equally important personal characteristics, and while instrumental for championing initiatives in general, they were at the time not identified as specific to developing a mindset for sustainability. On the other hand, the SMP *Oneness with Nature* is not directly reflected in the IDG skills.

As mentioned above, considering not only the SMPs but also the underlying dimensions (cognitive, behavioral, affective) allows for a more granular complementarity of the two frameworks (also included in Table 4.1). For example, the SMP *ecoliteracy* can support the skill e*mpathy and compassion*, which belongs to *relating* and is therefore mirrored in the *affective* dimension of this principle. Ecoliteracy may also support *complexity awareness*, a *thinking* skill, thus represented through the *cognitive* dimension of this SMP.

Table 4.1: Mapping for complementarity of the 12 SMPs and their dimensions (cognitive, behavioral, affective) with 16 of the IDG skills.

Sustainability mindset principle (Rimanoczy, 2020)	IDG skills supported, IDG dimension, and SMP dimension
Ecoliteracy – Understanding the state of the planet allows us to be more fully aware of the challenges, exploring the complexity of how they are linked to each other, and our feelings, leading to engaged actions.	– empathy and compassion (Relating – Affective) – complexity awareness (thinking – cognitive)
My contribution – When we identify the ways in which we are contributing to the problems, we have a chance to do something about it.	– humility (relating – affective) – optimism (acting – behavioral)
Long-term thinking – Considering the long term when analyzing situations and making decisions has a positive impact on global sustainability.	– long-term orientation and visioning (thinking – cognitive)
Both+and thinking – Both+and thinking allows us to understand paradoxes and calls for creative solutions that are inclusive of all stakeholders.	– inclusive mindset collaborating (collaborating – behavioral) – perspective skills (thinking – cognitive)
Flow in cycles – Many aspects of man-created unsustainability of the planet are a result of the misconception that we are not governed by this law of Nature.	– sensemaking (thinking – cognitive)

Table 4.1 (continued)

Sustainability mindset principle (Rimanoczy, 2020)	IDG skills supported, IDG dimension, and SMP dimension
Interconnectedness – When we consider both diversity and interconnectedness, our decisions and actions are more inclusive and contribute to the sustainability of the whole.	– connectedness (relating – affective) – appreciation (relating – affective)
Reflection – Reflective practices help to pause, to ponder the situation before jumping into action.	– self-awareness (being – cognitive/affective) – presence (being – cognitive/affective) – openness and learning mindset (being – cognitive/affective)
Self-awareness – When we explore our personal values, beliefs, assumptions, and motivations we gain greater control over our own actions and can see new alternatives behaviors.	– integrity/authenticity (being – cognitive/affective) – openness and learning mindset (being – cognitive/affective) – self-awareness (being – cognitive/affective) – humility (relating – affective)
Creative innovation – When we neglect the non-rational wisdom we have in us, our solutions are missing critical information, are poor quality and may create negative impacts on the ecosystem and society.	– creativity (acting – behavioral)
Oneness with nature – Understanding that we are one with Nature, that we are a species within species, and that all Nature is in us, can shape behaviors and decisions that lead to more satisfying lives and to a more harmonic relationship with each other and all beings.	Not directly reflected in IDG skills.
Mindfulness – Processing information to understand what it means requires slowing down, and creating spaces to observe, notice, and connect with our feelings.	– inner compass (being – cognitive/affective) – self-awareness (being – cognitive/affective) – presence (being – cognitive/affective)
Purpose – Purpose helps identifying what really matters to us personally, and what difference we want to make in the world. This is a powerful motivator to drive actions for the greater good and to shape a flourishing world.	– inner compass (being – cognitive/affective) – self-awareness (being – cognitive/affective)

As the IDG framework proposes, "no skills or capacities in the IDG framework can successfully be developed in isolation" (Inner Development Goals, 2023). This is equally true for the SMPs (Rimanoczy & Klingenberg, 2021) and, as such, Figure 4.2 shows how different skills can be linked to various principles, and their dimensions. Taking the example of the SMPself-awareness, which has the exact counterpart in the IDG *being* dimension, Table 4.1 shows that this IDG skill is also supported by the principles of reflection, mindfulness, and purpose, which support other skills, e.g., presence and inner compass, creating a symbiotic relationship where developing a specific IDG skill or SMP supports others. Table 4.1 also reveals that some SMPs support one IDG area (e.g., self-awareness supports skills from the being dimension), while others support two. my contribution, for example, supports the *relating* skill "humility" (thus affective) and "optimism" (*acting* dimension, hence behavioral). It is proposed that other synergies exist: the affective humility skill could further behavioral adjustments, allowing for the development of optimism.

Considering the three-phase developmental process explained earlier, Table 4.1 allows to map results from the SMI® personal and aggregate group reports to receive a picture of status of IDG skills development, and to create purposeful interventions for IDG skill growth.

In the following section, a case study will exemplify how the SMPs and IDG skills could be jointly developed. This is one of the first examples of a fully integrated use of the SMI® with engineering management students.

Case study: A sustainable supply chain management course at the University of Bergamo in Italy

This chapter takes as a case study a sustainable supply chain management course that is part of the second year of the master's degree program in management engineering at the University of Bergamo in Italy. The course awards to the students six ECTS credits upon completion of the final exam that can be taken in two modes: as an attending student, which means following 48 hours of in-class activities, delivering all the intermediate assignments, and participating in two group projects; or as non-attending student, which means taking an oral exam by preparing all the material provided in class plus additional readings. The course was delivered for the first time in October to December 2022, involving three educators in the teaching activities and evaluation of the students. In total, 37 students took part in the course. The students were also assessed in terms of their proactiveness during the lectures and they were distributed as follows: 29.7% very active, 48.6% partially active, 8.1% low participation, 10.8% non-attending. The following analysis of the SMI® results only focuses on the first three categories of students.

The course design in terms of general contents and modules was initiated by one of the researchers, with the support and feedback of other colleagues, almost one year before the course started. Moreover, all the teachers had the chance to train themselves with the tools that were planned to be used along the course. Two educators received training in the SMPs (participating in the SMP Action Lab). Finally, one of the educators was one of the ideators of the SMI®, allowing a complete and rigorous interpretation of the results in real time for the students. This process of continuous learning and improvement enacted by the three educators involved in the course design resulted in an initial course structure that was dynamically adapted in terms of the activities proposed to the students (Klingenberg, Boffelli, & Madonna, 2023).

During the initial lecture, the students were asked to take the SMI® without receiving any introduction to sustainability, even if one could assume they had previously been exposed to some related content during their studies or everyday life. During the course, one module was explicitly dedicated to explaining the SMPs and to reflect on the personal report that each student received after completing the SMI®. Furthermore, throughout the course, specific exercises or activities of experiential learning were used to develop certain SMPs that appeared less developed, as shown in the aggregate results of the SMI®, such as "my contribution" and "reflection". These activities were inspired by the resource workbooks, supplement material to the SMI® (Rimanoczy, 2022). At the end of the course, the SMI® assessment was repeated to determine the changes that happened in the students' mindset. Table 4.2 shows examples of the two principles, "my contribution" and "reflection", breaking the observed changes down for those dimensions that relate to IDG skills.

Table 4.2: Assessment of SMPs, IDG skills, and their pre-post changes in scores.

Principle and dimension	IDG skill	Pre-post percentage change of sustainability mindset scores
My contribution: Behavioral	Optimism	32%
My contribution: Affective	Humility	25%
Reflection: Cognitive	Self-awareness, presence, openness and learning mindset	14%
Reflection: Affective	Self-awareness, presence, openness and learning mindset	14%
Self-awareness: Cognitive	Self-awareness, integrity/authenticity, openness and learning mindset	−7%
Self-awareness: Affective	Self-awareness, integrity/authenticity, openness and learning mindset, humility	−3%

The values of the pre-post percentage change are determined as follows. The total number of participants that expressed the sustainability mindset at the beginning of the course is compared to the total number that did the same at the end. The numbers show that, for these two exemplarily chosen SMPs, the developmental and experiential activities conducted throughout the course appear to have supported the students in furthering their sustainability mindset. Although it was not specifically measured, it is suggested that the respective IDG skills could have equally seen improvements. On the other hand, the two dimensions of self-awareness see a reduction in the expression of the sustainability mindset. Two explanations are offered: while self-awareness is cross-linked to reflection, and therefore could have seen a symbiotic joint development, the former was not the focus during the course, or. stated differently, no specific exercises or activities were dedicated to this principle. Furthermore, when looking at the details of what the participants chose instead of the sustainability mindset on the SMI® survey, it shows that they all moved from "sustainability mindset" to "neither", an option that expresses that they feel in between a sustainability and more conventional mindset. This is of interest, as it could mean that the course provided inputs that resulted in a more critical reflection of one's position towards what the SMP and IDG skill of self-awareness means.

To summarize, the exemplary SMI® shows that it allows for the measurement of mindset changes, and as such, through the mapping of the IDG skills, opens the possibility to measure developmental changes also in the latter.

Conclusion

With increasing attention given globally to the SDGs of the United Nations 2030 Agenda, and as the deadline is approaching with less than expected progress towards achieving these SDGs, attention has started to focus on the obstacles in the way, and the mindset has been noted as one key aspect that can both hinder and accelerate the transformation.

This chapter describes two initiatives, the sustainability mindset principles with its assessment tool, the SMI®, and the Inner Development Goals, and its 23 skills. These are two frameworks created to address the inner dimensions. Both initiatives have a common goal: to prompt awareness in a larger audience about the importance of the inner dimensions to enable sustainable behaviors. Furthermore, both initiatives center on the individual via the scrutiny of the personal or shared worldview/paradigm (SMPs) and via the skills associated with a satisfying life and resilient behaviors for the greater good (IDGs).

Both frameworks address the need to consider diversity of contexts and cultures: the SMPs has done so through a validation process with peer-reviewers from the Global North and Global South; the IDGs is doing it in its current iteration, reaching out to a more diverse audience for input on their one-question survey, conducted from 2023 to 2024.

The SMP framework is designed to provoke reflection and scrutiny of the unconscious paradigm, values, and worldview behind our individual actions and has informative content to show the consequences of conventional beliefs on the environment and society. This is offered through the conceptual framework presented in articles, papers, books, and training programs for educators and coaches, as well as through resources like the Sustainability Mindset Indicator® and workbooks (Rimanoczy, 2022) with specific activities/exercises to develop the cognitive, behavioral, and affective dimensions of the SMPs. The SMPs and related materials aim at expanding self-awareness, at educating and informing about the unintentional impact on the world of our adopted narratives and supporting personal development and growth. Its focus is specifically on the mindset.

The IDG framework is designed to develop awareness of the skills that can lead to a more satisfactory life and interactions, with impact on behaviors that can support a more sustainable world (i.e., achieving the SDGs and 2030 Agenda). The IDG framework is not intended to develop the particular skills for which other resources can be used. Its main aim is to expand public awareness of the importance of the inner dimensions.

The SMPs and related resources, including the Sustainability Mindset Indicator®, are a natural complement and resource to the skills listed in the IDG framework, by opening the possibility of assessing, provoking thought, and introspection, supporting educators and coaches in how to address the inner dimensions with their audiences, and operationalizing the insights via specific activities tailored and adaptable to different contexts.

In conclusion, we would like to encourage the reader to explore the complementarity of the IDG skills and the SMPs, as outlined in Figure 4.2 and Table 4.2, with reflective questioning, such as: Where am I on the path towards being, thinking, relating, collaborating, and acting? Which SMPs would I like to explore to support my IDG skills? How can I leverage my IDG skills and the development of the inner dimensions of the SMPs to support the greater good?

References

Andrejevic, M. & Selwyn, N. (2023). Education in an era of pervasive automation. *Postdigital Science and Education*, 5(1), 220–231. https://doi.org/10.1007/s42438-022-00336-x.

Boyatzis, R. E. & Akrivou, K. (2006). The ideal self as the driver of intentional change. *Journal of Management Development*, 25(7), 624–642. https://doi.org/10.1108/02621710610678454.

Halle, M., Najam, A., & Beaton, C. (2013). *The future of sustainable development: Rethinking sustainable development after Rio+ 20 and implications for UNEP*. The International Institute for Sustainable Development. https://www.iisd.org/system/files/publications/future_rethinking_sd.pdf.

Inner Development Goals. (2023). *Going deeper 2023.* https://www.samrye.xyz/content/files/2023/06/IDG-Going-Deeper-2023.pdf.

Klingenberg, B., Boffelli, A., & Madonna, A. (2023). *Innovative teaching: A case study on teaching sustainable supply chain management and a sustainability mindset.* Proceedings of the Decision Sciences Institute Annual Conference 2023, Atlanta, Georgia, November 19.

Partzsch, L. (2023). Missing the SDGs: Political accountability for insufficient environmental action. *Global Policy, 14*(3), 438–450. https://doi.org/10.1111/1758-5899.13213.

Rimanoczy, I. B. (2010). *Business leaders committing to and fostering sustainability initiatives.* Teachers College, Columbia University.

Rimanoczy, I. (2020). *The sustainability mindset principles: A guide to developing a mindset for a better world.* Routledge.

Rimanoczy I. (2022). *The resource workbook for educators, vol. 1–4.* Self-published, Amazon.com.

Rimanoczy, I. & Klingenberg, B. (2021). The Sustainability Mindset Indicator: A personal development tool. *Journal of Management for Global Sustainability, 9*(1), 43–79. https://archium.ateneo.edu/jmgs/vol9/iss1/4.

Rimanoczy, I., & Llamazares, A. M. (2021). Twelve principles to guide a long-overdue paradigm shift. *Journal of Management, Spirituality & Religion, 18*(6), 54–76. https://doi.org/10.51327/jkki4753.

Seligman, M. E. & Csikszentmihalyi, M. (2000). Positive psychology: An introduction. *The American Psychologist, 55*(1), 5–14. https://doi.org/10.1037/0003-066X.55.1.5.

Stålne, K. & Greca, S. (2022). *Inner Development Goals: Phase 2 research report.* Inner Development Goals. https://idg.tools/assets/221215_IDG_Toolkit_v1.pdf.

Yeke, S. (2023). Digital intelligence as a partner of emotional intelligence in business administration. *Asia Pacific Management Review, 28*(4), 390–400. https://doi.org/10.1016/j.apmrv.2023.01.001.

Fabio Allegrini, Monica Barroso, Rachel Brooks, Jost Hamschmidt
and Johannes Tschiderer

Chapter 5
Changing business schools from within: A case study on the inner transformative potential of co-creative learning spaces

Abstract: This case study illustrates how members of Student Impact (SI), a student-led sustainability consultancy at the University of St. Gallen in Switzerland, collaborated with faculty, students and alumni to design, deliver, and begin to scale a new type of seminar that embodies Student Impact's mantra of "Be the Change" (BTC). The collaboration marked the beginning of an exciting journey of experimentation, community building, and collective leadership with the goal of transforming business school education from within. As the initiative has grown, it has integrated the Inner Development Goals (IDGs) as guiding principles for personal development and capacity building for sustainability and societal change. This chapter explores how the BTC approach builds selected transformational skills encompassed by the IDGs by discussing two separate deliveries of BTC. We share our learnings, experiences, and emerging perspectives in co-creating and co-teaching these courses – and illuminate the methods and formats we have experimented with in enabling individuals across generations and sectors to connect, collaborate, and affect positive change. By sharing this emergent pedagogy for change, we aim to encourage educators to experiment with collaborative learning designs to foster inner and outer transformation.

Keywords: co-creativity, cross-generational learning, reflective practice, inner development

Nature is our home, and in nature we are at home. – Carlo Rovelli

Introduction

We live in a time of multiple systemic crises. Tackling the current interconnected grand challenges requires us to unlearn conventional thinking about progress, change, and innovation. We need to go beyond "business as usual" pedagogies to catalyze the necessary change (see Wamsler 2018, 2020). To do this, we need to start at the level of the individual. Business education must shift to foster and enable the curation of learning communities grounded on peer-to-peer learning and critical reflection, collective empowerment, individual self-reflection, and inner development (see Bristow et al, 2024).

https://doi.org/10.1515/9783111453729-006

Everything started with the well-known mantra "Be the Change" (BTC). Student Impact,[1] a student-led sustainability consultancy at the University of St. Gallen in Switzerland, adopted this as their slogan and rallying cry to communicate its mission of developing students to become responsible agents of change and utilize business as a force for good to transition our global society and economy towards social and ecological sustainability. And in 2021 a group of Student Impact members partnered up with educators and alumni from the University of St. Gallen to design and deliver a new type of seminar that encapsulated the "Be the Change" mantra. This marked the starting point for an exciting journey of experimentation, community building, and collective leadership with the ultimate goal of transforming business school education from within.

The strength of this cause is based on the conviction that there is an urgent need for change in the business school education system (see Hoffman, 2024; Laasch, 2024). Curricula and learning environments continue to be steeped in reductionist and mechanistic logics that prioritize narrow notions of (monetary) value, markets as supreme problem-solving mechanisms, and an unquestionable belief in human ingenuity, exceptionalism, and independence from outside forces. All of this leaves students woefully under equipped to face and navigate transformations of unprecedented scope and scale, driven by a host of wicked challenges in a world of polycrisis – despite the widespread aim of business schools that they are educating the leaders of tomorrow.

Born out of students' experiences with these dominant approaches to teaching and learning in business schools, the frustration of recognizing their shortcomings and apparent disconnect from the real world, and the contrast of empowering and effective learning experiences gained in the extracurricular context of organizations like Student Impact, BTC seminars are prototypes of new and different approaches to learning and development.

At their very core rests the conviction that students can be the principal architects of their own learning experiences and that they should sit at the heart of wider learning communities that comprise educators, fellow students, and critically also nonacademic actors including university alumni, businesses, and NGOs. The underlying vision is to create transformative learning spaces that inspire and support students in building and exercising the analytical, emotional, and collaborative skills needed for tackling complex global challenges. Transformative learning for sustainability (see Bornemann et al., 2020; De Witt et al., 2023) would also imply:

> *a shift of consciousness that dramatically and permanently alters our way of being in the world. Such a shift involves our understanding of ourselves and our self-location: our relationships with other humans and with the natural world. (Morrell & O'Connor, 2002, p. xvii)*

---

[1] https://www.studentimpact.ch/.

As such, we have seen the approach become a lever for building skills and competencies associated with inner development – and not just among students, as tomorrow's leaders, but also among the educators and practitioners that are involved. The BTC learning design aims to provide and hold space for being and relating, invites critical cognitive engagement beyond the common business school frames, and leverages collaboration as a principal means for enabling and enacting change towards social and ecological sustainability. And while the connection to inner development is apparent, the original BTC course design was conceived in 2021 – before the publication of the IDG framework. Still, the IDGs provide a valuable frame of reference to make sense of and communicate the various avenues through which BTC drives inner transformation and also to continuously tweak and adapt the BTC learning design. In applying the IDG framework, this chapter seeks to present the BTC learning design as a successful case study for the value and potential of actively using the IDGs in the context of education.

Outline

Along this chapter we aim to share experiences and emerging future perspectives of the BTC endeavor. Drawing from two successful pilots, we share our learnings to encourage students and faculty to co-develop locally adapted prototypes. This chapter is anchored by knowledge co-created with students and a growing body of BTC alumni, who we have seen leaving the courses with indications of heightened self-awareness and self-reflection, openness to approaching challenges from diverse perspectives, a greater capacity to relate to others with empathy and compassion, as well as the ability to trust their peers and act with courage, optimism, and perseverance.

We will first illustrate the general design of the BTC learning journey which unfolds as a unique blend of action and reflection, peer-to-peer dynamics and targeted expert inputs, and the formation of an open and hierarchy-free learning community. We then proceed to illustrate two specific case studies of BTC bachelor-level courses. The first case features the seminar Be the Change: Discovering Consulting and Sustainability, the pilot project that was co-designed and developed with Student Impact. It invites students on an exploratory learning journey into the consulting industry and its role and dynamics in the context of a growing momentum for sustainability. The second case study features the seminar Be the Change: Exploring Systems Leadership for Sustainability. In this course students apply a systems approach to leadership in the context of complex sustainability challenges, with consideration of the system, community, and individual levels. By collaborating in groups on real-case challenges, students identify their own resources and obstacles in the context of sustainability and systems leadership.

Finally, we will share our learnings and perspectives of the BTC course development. We illustrate the process of designing structures and spaces outside of the curriculum that are needed to effectively build and strengthen the multi-stakeholder relationships across areas of expertise, background, and age that we think are critical to the thriving of the BTC movement.

While we are still at the beginning of our journey, we are convinced that BTC presents a viable manifestation of the learning environments, principles, and process that business schools need to embrace to build urgently needed capacities for self-leadership, understanding, and collaboration as represented by the Inner Development Goals.

Introduction to BTC

The BTC learning design rests on three distinct pillars, as outlined below.

(1) Learning by doing

BTC puts a strong emphasis on providing opportunities for experiential learning by allowing students to obtain hands-on project experience working in teams on challenges provided by partner organizations. In general, these are purpose-driven organizations that are actively focused on tackling the socio-environmental crises of our times and work on issues that are closely aligned with the topical focus of the respective seminars. They can be start-ups, NGOs, or foundations.

There are three main rationales for focusing on curating practical opportunities in BTC. Firstly, from a learning perspective, it encourages students to directly experience the practical realities, challenges, and opportunities faced by organizations that represent a new and different way of doing business with a dedicated impact-first purpose. For example, they get to support start-ups grappling with the question of aligning their environmental credentials with a reliance on continued expansion or support early-stage businesses on reaching beyond a core clientele of environmentally minded early adopters. Thus, in line with the skills related to the *thinking* dimension of the IDGs, students are asked to assume different perspectives, make sense of the situation and circumstances faced by their partner organizations and related stakeholders, and become aware of the complexity faced by impact-oriented businesses with a view towards positively influencing their environment and society while having to navigate commercial realities.

Secondly, the experience of contributing to the solution of real and oftentimes pressing challenges faced by the partner organizations can instill a powerful sense of self-efficacy and agency among students. The prevailing societal and business climate rewards experience and seniority over youthful innovativeness, freshness, and drive and the reality of having to spend years progressing along the career ladder in order to have a meaningful say. This stands in stark contrast with the lived reality of students who grow up in the face of urgent socio-ecological challenges that are widely expected to worsen over the coming years and that they will have to contend with over their own lifetimes. This disconnect between having to bear the brunt of the unfolding socio-ecological crises but not being able to meaningful contribute at present can be profoundly disheartening for students, many of whom do have a strong will to make a positive difference. Yet, there are ways to contribute where students' inexperience is not a liability but an asset as the BTC consulting projects seek to showcase: from ideating new ways to bringing sustainable products to market to developing creative ways of attracting new customers for existing sustainable products, to providing clear and unbiased assessments of opportunities and risks for new business endeavors. Gaining such experiences during their studies and thereby moving into a mode of "acting" as outlined in the IDG framework can have a profound impact on students' personal and professional lives by nurturing a sense of courage and trust in their innate creativity as well as instilling a sense of optimism in light of their own agency to positively affect the future.

And thirdly, we are in times of polycrisis that call for urgent actions. Hence, from an impact perspective it seems like an unwarranted luxury to waste the creative potential and energy of students on fictitious case studies (their pedagogic quality and especially their scalability notwithstanding). Countless small organizations and initiatives within large and established players are actively trying to combat the many grand challenges we are facing, and the BTC seminars seek to support these initiatives and amplify their real-world impact potential by weaving them into the BTC action-learning design and making them the beneficiaries of students' innate drive and energy to make a positive difference.

(2) Learning from practitioners

In order to best enable students to be the change in their personal and professional lives, the BTC learning journey runs as close to the "real world" as possible. Besides the aforementioned case challenges, it also puts a strong focus on bringing diverse perspectives into the classroom and fostering generative exchange between students and practitioners. The aim behind this is twofold.

Firstly, it presents an acknowledgement of the fact that our times call for a systemic transformation of our socio-economic systems. This requires us to embrace new ways of thinking, acting, and being that focus on sensing and probing to deal with our complex, fast-moving and emergent context. Bringing in diverse perspectives of practitioners working directly on these complex challenges is therefore quintessential to offer timely and relevant perspectives to students.

And secondly, bringing practitioners into the classroom offers a different approach to learning that asks students to make sense of reality through the prism of practical realities instead of theory. The latter is still important but only in the real-world context and only to the degree that students themselves find meaning and relevance in applying theory to make sense of the perspectives shared by practitioners. This induces a much more proactive engagement with theory than what many students are used to.

(3) Learning from one another

Lastly, the BTC seminar design aims to develop the skills and qualities represented in the *collaborating* dimension of the IDGs by putting a strong emphasis on peer-to-peer learning dynamics. It rests on the conviction that everything that is needed to create transformative learning is already assembled in the group of learners in the form of the knowledge, experience, and interests among the students, lecturers, and practitioners, all of which are integral parts of the BTC learning community. The key to unlock this potential is the facilitation of spaces that build trust and inclusivity and encourage co-creative participation by all members of the learning community. Given the fast-moving context of today's world, the traditional knowledge dissemination from an expert to eager listeners is often inadequate and it is likely that the collective of assembled students holds more expertise than their teacher. Also, the complex nature of the grand challenges of our time strongly depreciates the value of expertise per se. Additionally, the peer-to-peer focus is an acknowledgement of the simple fact that the goal of this seminar is to create a valuable learning experience for its principal stakeholder, namely the students. It seems all too obvious then to also put the students in the driver's seat to design and shape their own learning experience.

These three pillars provide a common reference point for all BTC learning journeys. They are, however, not prescriptive, and every seminar may differ in how much emphasis is put on any one of them or in adding additional elements depending on the specific context, including topical focus, the experience and interest of the students and facilitators, or also logistical factors such as the length and regularity of sessions.

And overall, this basic design resonated well with students, as illustrated by the quote of Iñigo, a student participant of the very first BTC course:

> It is this change mantra that gives the course this special resonance. The change mantra is almost omnipresent; it lies within the combination of the three pillars of learning into a class, in the inspiration towards change within the student's immediate environment through real case challenges, in the experience of vivid examples of change narrating their individual change story, in the encouragement for the students to look into their inner change through the reflection exercises, or explicitly by writing it on the course description. But above all, the course itself is a change to other courses already with its existence; so the mere fact of students taking the course makes them aware, that they are being part of the change process, encouraging them to increase this change within their lives.

Cases

Be the Change: Discovering Consulting and Sustainability

The bachelor-level course Be the Change: Discovering Consulting and Sustainability seeks to take students on an exploratory learning journey into the consulting industry and its changing fortunes and potential role in the context of the systemic transition of our global socio-economic systems towards sustainability. The course was designed and piloted as a collaboration between Student Impact and the Sustainability & Responsibility team of the University of St. Gallen. It was borne out of the simple idea to translate the valuable learning experience offered to members of the student association on an extracurricular basis into a course setting. After a successful submission, the seminar was piloted in the fall semester of 2021, which marked the beginning of a success story that earned rave reviews from students and practitioners and piqued the interest of impact-oriented educators across Switzerland. The seminar was repeated every year since and in 2023 also saw the birth of a first "spin-off" course, which is introduced below.

In line with the previously introduced learning pillars, this seminar puts a strong focus on experiential and practice-oriented learning. On the one hand, students are asked to work in teams to tackle real-life consulting challenges posed by impact-oriented early-stage start-ups. In past editions of the seminar, these included companies working on innovative business propositions in diverse fields including the production of novel food ingredients derived from the upcycling of byproducts in the value chains of both cocoa processing and beer production, the development of algae-based packaging solutions, and the grading of forest projects for high-grade carbon compensation schemes. Students were asked to consult these companies on various pressing business-related challenges, including the development of market entry strategies, assessing competitive landscapes, identifying target groups, and developing tailored marketing strategies and supporting product development by gathering first-hand market intelligence.

In addition to gaining practical consulting experience, the students also hear from guest speakers working at the intersection of consulting and sustainability, who provide perspectives on the state of play in their respective fields and industries and also share valuable lessons from their own personal and professional development paths in these fields. In order to give students the broadest possible view of the field, we seek to invite a diverse array of speakers, both people who are active in consulting (and possibly have never seen anything else) and those who consciously quit the industry, hailing from large established firms or up-and-coming new players focused on various subthemes of the sustainability transition, like new work and systemic innovation.

Besides these experiential and practical elements, the learning journey of this particular BTC seminar also puts a strong emphasis on creating a learning community with strong peer-to-peer dynamics. A variety of design elements play into this. Firstly, the outsized role of Student Impact and its members. Not only did the student association play a key role in initiating and designing the basic outline of this seminar, but it is also instrumental in its planning and delivery. Members of SI, either experienced bachelor or master students, are responsible for the facilitation of the course experience throughout the semester, by working with partner companies to prepare the case studies, developing, and adapting the learning design, guiding through the sessions, and providing support outside of the classroom. They also provide mentoring on the case challenges on content-related matters as well as methodological questions or team-internal issues. Additionally, they run dedicated consulting-related input sessions ranging from presentation training to sessions on how to build and structure compelling presentations. While all these contributions are valuable in and of themselves, they also add up to something more significant: they represent learning dynamics unfolding entirely between students, seeing eye to eye, and interacting in an authentic manner which fosters a hierarchy-free, engaging, and safe atmosphere in the seminar. And by allowing students to share their co-curricular experiences, they can infuse the same level of motivation, commitment, and energy which characterizes their voluntary engagement at Student Impact into the seminar context.

Yet, the learning community does not only include the students and their peer coaches and supporters from Student Impact but also the guest speakers, which are (almost) exclusively alumni of the university. Thus, they have a shared set of experiences with the students sitting on the other side of the classroom which provides a great basis for fruitful and engaging discussion. Guest speakers are also asked to specifically talk about their own career pathways and reflect on the lessons they learned throughout and the decisions they would take if they were to be back at university. And again, the shared experience lends great credence to such considerations and makes them much more approachable and relevant for the students in the classroom. And while BTC seeks to bring in outside perspectives to contribute to the learning experience of students, these learning processes are always bilateral, and the setting also allows the guest speakers to come away with new insights and connections about what moves the new generation of students and changemakers.

Besides these design elements that hold the potential for the formation of a learning community, BTC also plays with various rituals to nurture feelings of togetherness and to release pent-up energy to further foster the community spirit. Every session opens with an energizer activity, be it a creative exercise that involves drawing or something to get participants moving or something that requires people to think collectively. And the seminar also always ends with a small ritual, a simple clap performed in unison. While these interventions seem trivial, the experience from past seminars shows that they add a lot of value to the students' experience: They provide stability and structure, and sometimes expand students' comfort zones, as this quote from Davide's reflection paper from the 2023 BTC course illustrates:

Before the course started, I felt there was a low energy in the room. Then we did something to-gether which involved moving our body. For example, we clapped around a circle or moved around the room and drew each other's faces using only one line. During those energizers, we laughed and moved and somehow broke our rigid protections surrounding us. After the energizers, there was higher energy in the room, and the mood was more excited. I use such energizers now whenever I have classes or lectures. In the end of the course, we did a ritual called clap out. Three, two, one, and we all clapped at the same time. This meant the course was finished. It helped me to finish the class. Sometimes in other courses, people start going away, and the lecturer is still talking but the time is up, and in this course, everyone was present until the clap out. I will use this as well be-cause energizers and rituals are helpful.

Beyond designing for and making such multilateral learning processes explicit, the notion of a learning community in BTC also entails students taking ownership of their own learning journey. This is most notably the case for the consulting challenges and accompanying mentoring and input sessions facilitated by Student Impact where it is ultimately upon the students themselves to experiment with tools and frameworks and modes of working and to actively make use of the offer for mentorship. However, the BTC seminar also includes other course elements that explicitly put students in the driver's seat of their own learning experience. For example, after the energizer activity, every session opens with an "open space" which allows students to bring topics into the classroom that they deem relevant in the context of the seminar and would like to discuss with their peers. The underlying intention is to create the space for dynamics to unfold that are like those random dinner-table discussions that ever so often become the most interesting conversations one has in a day. In the same vein, it is also an invitation for students to bring in topics that move them, which of-tentimes are difficult for lecturers to anticipate but are crucially important, especially for a seminar on sustainability which for many young people is a matter of deep per-sonal concern. Also, it again reflects the acknowledgement that the speed at which the sustainability field is moving makes it likely that the collective intelligence of the group is more informed about the latest news than a single lecturer could ever be. And to put learnings into perspective, the open space allows students to build connec-tions between the seminar and issues they encounter outside of it, thus seeking to break up the compartmentalization of learning processes into neatly timed slots allo-cated to specific programs of study and disciplines of thought.

Lastly, taking ownership of one's own learning not only entails various modes of absorbing input but also critically includes the sensemaking and reflection around it. In line with one of our core mantras – "It is not about what we cover in the seminar, but about what students discover through the seminar"– BTC also puts a strong em-phasis on creating space for reflection through various formats: short journaling exer-cises during various sessions, dedicated sessions focused entirely on reflection, and a reflection paper as a graded deliverable at the end of the seminar. These activities serve to nurture some of the skills entailed in the *being* and *relating* dimensions of the IDGs. They ask students to relate the insights and learnings from the seminar to their broader context, cultivate self-awareness, and provide opportunities to finetune their personal inner compasses. Thus, they hold the potential to unlock transformative processes of inner change, living up to the promise laid out in the title of the seminar, as students like Konstantin shared in their reflection papers:

> *Being the change, embodying it and reflecting on the progress has played a significant part in my life since then, and this course is the first course I have taken at the University of St. Gallen that empowered me to act towards these things.*

Or as another student put it:

> *It was the values I acquired along the way and the in-class learning laboratory that gave me the sense of fulfillment and aided in personal growth. And I wish that to any other student trying to find their place in the business world.*

A clear indication of the potential for inner transformation that lies in a co-creative, polyperspective course design; and an invitation for lecturers and future students to embrace these lessons and continue to experiment, reflect, and learn.

Be the Change: Exploring Systems Leadership for Sustainability

Our second case, Be the Change: Exploring Systems Leadership for Sustainability, strived to nurture the IDG pillars of *being* and *collaborating*. We do this in three ways: first, by course structure and activities, and connecting these activities to transformational skills emphasized in the IDGs; secondly, by bringing in students' experiences, drawing from reflection papers produced within the course; and thirdly, by summarizing key takeaways for faculty and practitioners aiming to build IDG skills related to *being* and *collaborating* in their students and teams. In alignment with ethical guidelines of the University of St. Gallen, all reflections and citations included here have provided informed consent to cite their work. Two cited students, Faith and Nikita, wished to be referenced by name, and two wished to remain unnamed. Here, we refer to them as Student A and Student C.

Based on the premise of the pilot BTC course, this second BTC course on systems leadership built on a co-creative approach with a bachelor student co-facilitator, Fabio Allegrini, and two university lecturers, Rachel Brooks and Justus von Grone. Drawing from the model of systems leadership put forth by Dreier, Nabarro and Nelson at the Harvard Kennedy School, the course aimed to empower students with the tools, skills and mindset to lead sustainability on individual, organizational, and global levels (2019). It did this in three ways: by striving to create a safe and reflective community space in the classroom, by encouraging ongoing personal reflection both with peers and individually through a digital platform, and by providing students with the opportunity to work with practice partners on real-world challenges and opportunities that required a systemic approach to problem solving and leadership.

Course facilitators understood characteristics of system leaders as defined by Senge, Hamilton, and Kania (2015):

> *Though they differ widely in personality and style, genuine system leaders have a remarkably similar impact. Over time, their profound commitment to the health of the whole radiates to nurture similar commitment in others. Their ability to see reality through the eyes of people very different from themselves encourages others to be more open as well. They build relationships based on deep listening and networks of trust and collaboration start to flourish. They are so convinced that something can be done that they do not wait for a fully developed plan, thereby freeing others to step ahead and learn by doing . . . (page 28).*

This excerpt paints system leaders as possessing many of the characteristics and skills encompassed by the Inner Development Goals. At the center of this are *being* and *collaborating*, which are the two pillars most emphasized in the course through its focus on individual-, community-, and systems-level lenses on systems leadership.

Course structure and activities

The second pilot of BTC was facilitated over the course of the fall semester of 2023 in six 4-hour sessions, which took place bi-weekly. The course sessions were thematically focused as follows: the first an introduction, the second on systems, the third on communities, the fourth on the individual, the fifth featured student presentations, and the final session was a reflection and celebration. Following the first introductory session, Fabio prepared the sessions and led the courses, with Rachel and Justus supporting when needed, including feedbacking the lesson structure in advance of classes with thematic expertise on systems leadership, with practice project and interview contacts from their business network, to co-developing topics for personal reflection, and to taking the lead on the grading and evaluation of assignments. While the facilitators leveraged several methods and formats to foster students' skills in the pillars of *being* and *collaborating*, we explore three here explicitly.

Code of conduct

In the initial sessions, our goal was to establish the tone for the upcoming sessions. We encouraged students to bring their personal perspectives to the group and emphasized we wanted them to feel comfortable voicing their opinions and feelings. We wanted to emphasize the importance of creating a space within the group where we could nurture co-creation skills as part of collaboration. We initiated the process of creating this safe space by co-creating a code of conduct. In this, our intent was to bring in all students' voices, and to build a common language for our classroom community by openly discussing personal needs and expectations for both the topic at hand and the group work.

As a first step, students took a moment individually to think about two questions: *What values are personally important to you?* and, *What do you need to feel good about yourself?*

These questions served to facilitate introspection and help students identify what they need to feel comfortable and motivated to collaborate with others. Some students struggled to answer these questions initially, so Fabio provided additional prompts: *When have you experienced successful teamwork?* and, *Why was it successful?*

By focusing on these questions, students were encouraged to shift their focus from themselves to external factors, allowing them to articulate what contributes to their well-being in both individual and group settings. They then captured their thoughts on Post-it notes for further discussion.

Next, students exchanged in the group regarding what they had written. Fabio clustered the Post-its and wrote down the topics represented by the clusters to develop a co-created, written code of conduct that provided the basis for the classroom community to refer to in case of challenges and conflicts, and to create mutual accountability for the values of the group. This activity laid the groundwork for an environment in which participants could bring forth their personal perspectives and feel comfortable expressing their opinions. In the pillar of *being*, the process of creating this shared artifact, which expressed a common language and common values for the group, fostered integrity and authenticity. Everyone's voice was brought into the room, and therefore each student was called by the resulting social contract to be present, and to invoke self-awareness in assessing their own alignment with the group's code of conduct. The clustering of thoughts on Post-its demonstrated common themes and perspectives within the group. The process also demonstrated divergence of opinions and experiences, but paired with shared values, this difference enabled students to cultivate openness and a learning mindset. In the pillar of *collaborating*, the process fostered nurtured respectful communication skills in establishing shared ownership and collective responsibility. By working together to identify shared values and priorities, the group leveraged and fostered an inclusive mindset and intercultural competence along with co-creation skills in building a group contract for how they wanted to be, relate to, and act with one another – feeding into additional IDG pillars. This contributed to a foundation of trust.

For students, this exercise was a stark contrast to collaborations in many other classes throughout their university careers. Student A wrote that:

> [in the course] I recognized a tendency towards individualism and a desire to manage every aspect of the work. With this project, I realized how these traits could impact my group work. This self-awareness highlighted the reasons why I might not have gotten the best experiences from earlier group projects. After some thought, I believe that these inclinations are partially the result of unpleasant prior experiences when differences in effort, dedication, and communication have produced less-than-ideal results. Creating a code of conduct, in my opinion, was incredibly beneficial since it helped us to stay in line with our expectations and goals for our joint presentation and work.

Opinion scale and sharing triads

The second method we used involved using an opinion scale combined with sharing triads, with the aim to guide participants toward heightened self-awareness. The opinion scale serves as an accessible tool for showing different viewpoints on a variety of topics. A key principle underlying the process is that no opinion is inherently right or wrong. The primary objective is to illustrate and engage with the diversity of perspectives on socially relevant issues.

To start, we began with simple statements such as "I grew up close by", "I love talking in front of others", or "I prefer sweet over salty". Participants were then asked to position themselves on a scale, indicating their agreement, disagreement, or varying indifference to the statement posed. Next, we introduced more controversial statements, such as, "To reduce inequality, taxes on big corporations and wealthy individuals should be increased". We instructed students not to talk to one other, but rather to observe and register where they and others positioned themselves. Afterwards, we brought students back together in groups of three. Each group member had two minutes to express their thoughts while the others listened. The discussion questions were pre-defined by us to foster a structured exchange, and included: *About which statement did you have a strong opinion, and why?* and, *About which statement did you not have a strong opinion, and why?*

After each student had the opportunity to answer one question, they rotated to the next question. These sharing triads were followed by an open exchange in the large group.

In the *being* pillar, by using an opinion scale and sharing triads, this exercise aimed to encourage students to explore their own beliefs and perspectives on various topics. This cultivates self-awareness, as the students reflect on where they stand on certain issues and confront the differences or similarities they share with others in the group. Emphasizing that there was no right or wrong answer in this exercise underscored the importance of embracing different viewpoints and being open to new ideas, that is, openness and learning mindset. It cultivated presence by encouraging students to physically position themselves in interaction with their peers. By making their position on topics visible, students needed to take ownership of their opinions, urging integrity and authenticity. In the *collaborating* pillar, this exercise provides an opportunity for participants to engage in meaningful dialogue with others on challenging and divisive topics, encouraging respectful communication. By listening to different opinions and perspectives, individuals can practice empathy and gain a deeper understanding of alternative viewpoints, building an inclusive mindset and intercultural competence. The structured format of the discussion questions encourages participants to articulate their thoughts and reasons behind their opinions, fostering a culture of openness and vulnerability, building trust.

Students found both the opinion scales and reflections in triads insightful. One student, Nikita, shared that:

[the exercise] allowed me to realize that none of the questions were unanimously clear and that each of them could be the subject of discussion. Throughout these, I observed that everyone had their own vision of things, and debating with divergent opinions allows one to broaden their horizons and move forward, which is a fundamental principle for systemic change. Moreover, engaging with people who hold different views enables the participants to perceive the issues from varied angles, enriching the debate and leading to a more effective outcome.

Nikita went on to share the impact the reflections in class, including in triads, had on his self-awareness. He wrote:

I realized that I am impatient and do not listen enough to others' standpoints. . . . Since I noticed it, I've been trying to change this and be more open, asking questions instead of telling what is right or wrong. However, I am persuaded that there is always room for improvement, and personally, the way I communicate with others is still in progress.

Another student, Student C, who wished to remain anonymous, wrote:

The "sharing triads" exercise was very helpful as it shifted our focus from conventional discussions, often resembling debates, to genuine dialogue. Often discussions are more oriented toward a debate, while this time we really had the chance to listen to others' opinions and share our own understandings without trying to convince each other. It was really refreshing and helped as a reminder that we do not always need to agree and although we might disagree, we should still respect each other. The exercises emphasized the value of mutual understanding and open, nonjudgmental communication, with a focus on listening rather than persuading others.

Student C concluded that communities, like icebergs, have obvious manifestations but are strengthened by hidden factors such as shared values, a sense of belonging, safety, and common goals.

The iceberg model

The iceberg model, first introduced by sociologist Edward Hall in 1976 in the context of culture, has been since adapted for other fields, including systems thinking. In the context of this course, using the iceberg model offers a holistic approach to building our understanding of, and challenging our assumptions around, complex topics. We encouraged students to picture an iceberg. Above the waterline are the things we can easily see, such as opinions, facts, and behavior. However, beneath the surface is a whole realm of submerged, not easily identifiable factors.

The Iceberg Model argues that events and patterns (which we can observe) are caused by systemic structures and mental models, which are often hidden. Systemic structures are the organizational hierarchy; social hierarchy; interrelationships; rules and procedures; authorities and approval levels; process flows and routes; incentives, compensation, goals, and metrics; attitudes; reactions and the incentives and fears that cause them; corporate culture; feedback loops and delays in the system dynamics; and underlying forces that exist in an organization. (Monat & Gannon, 2015)

We guided students to explore the notion that when we discuss complex and often divisive topics, in many instances we focus solely on the visible differences. This can emphasize difference and create dissonance and distance between people. In taking a holistic perspective, the iceberg model is a tool for exploring beyond surface-level tensions, differences, and contradictions. By asking why something might be the way it is and placing it at the tip of the iceberg, as we work down the iceberg visualizations asking "why", we gain insight into the underlying factors at play. One outcome of the exercise is that, when we place a topic on the iceberg, it becomes detached from any individual. As such, the iceberg enables us to remove our focus from who said what, and explore the topic as an object of exploration, separate from any one individual or group. This depersonalization or shift in perspective encourages curiosity and mobilizes a desire to understand more about the issue at hand.

By acknowledging the existence of invisible factors such as values and needs beneath the surface, the iceberg model fosters an appreciation for the diversity of viewpoints and backgrounds that individuals bring to the table, that is, an inclusive mindset and intercultural competence. In depersonalizing hot-button and potentially divisive societal issues and providing a tool for creating mutual understanding and structured discussion around complex topics, the iceberg model nurtures inclusive communication and mobilization skills.

Many students noted the impact working with the iceberg model had on their awareness of the complexity of grand systemic challenges. One student, Faith, discussed how the method was critical to the development of her understanding of how essential collaboration is to leadership on sustainability challenges. She wrote:

Singapore's competitive culture was a lens through which I perceived success and achievement. This mindset was especially prevalent in my experiences with education, where individual academic achievements are often prioritized over team efforts, fostering a culture of intense competition among students. In such an environment, collaboration was not something that I naturally gravitated towards. There were two eye-opening moments that solidified the importance of collaboration over competition for me. Firstly, my exploration of the iceberg model. This model allowed us to delve beneath the surface of visible issues to understand the challenges comprehensively. During the preparation for our presentation, my team and I applied the iceberg model to the issues that our interviewees mentioned. The issue that struck me the most was regarding Scope 3 emissions, as unravelling its complexity recognized the issues that were deeply rooted within the ecosystem. Doing this elucidated that collaboration with a diverse range of stakeholders (e.g., suppliers, colleagues from different departments, sustainability reporting firms that leverage technology like EcoVadis, etc.) is imperative when trying to address grand sustainability challenges.

Reflection and takeaways for faculty and practitioners

In creating Be the Change: Exploring Systems Leadership for Sustainability, Fabio, Rachel, and Justus strived to create space for the development of a shared understanding of what it takes to lead meaningful change on sustainability challenges. In doing this, central goals were to: first, bring the knowledge and experience of students into the classroom; secondly, to engage in ongoing reflection at individual, small group, and large group levels; and finally, to tackle real-world challenges with case partners, enabling students to discover the complexity of sustainability challenges and identify levers for change in collaboration with one another, and with their practice partners.

Engaging the students in their own learning process to this extent presents both challenges and opportunities. One challenge we encountered was the co-creation of roles at the level of the three facilitators, which were comprised of one bachelor student (Fabio) and two university lecturers (Rachel and Justus). Developing a process by which Fabio was able to take ownership of the course, while still incorporating the subject-matter expertise of Rachel and Justus, was an ongoing puzzle. Similarly, a second challenge was in navigating the role of students in co-creating course content, while simultaneously empowering Fabio in the role of student co-facilitator. A third level of complexity was presented by the incorporation of case partners. To engage with dynamic and ambiguous sustainability challenges in line with systems leadership, students needed to take ownership of these partnerships. However, in practice, the schedules, needs, and priorities of students and practitioners differ widely. The result of these three dovetailing challenges was a course that was constantly in motion, where the next steps were often emergent, and where both students and faculty needed to accept uncertainty.

However, the unique opportunities of the course also lay within these uncertainties. As a central learning outcome was for students to develop self-awareness, collaborative skills, and agency to tackle complex challenges in a changing environment, the microcosm of the course provided ideal conditions in which to do so. The component of ongoing individual and group reflection gave students the opportunity to make sense of what they were experiencing and what they were taking out of these experiences. Reflections online and in papers demonstrated on multiple occasions that students were unsure of what systems leadership was at the outset of the course. However, over the journey of the semester, they made sense of it for themselves, at a personal level, in relation to their studies, and concerning their future careers. They had done this in concert with a community of co-learners, co-shaping their own knowledge of how to make decisions, what leadership can and must be in a changing era, and the central role of reflection. In essence, reflection papers indicated the reconfiguration of underlying assumptions about how these students wanted to live their lives, build their teams, and shape their careers.

For faculty and practitioners seeking to build IDG skills in the pillars of *being* and *collaborating*, we found that leveraging a style of facilitation that allows for individual and collective reflection, emergence, and co-creation to be highly effective in promoting a critically reflective space of accountability, kindness, and trust. The code of conduct exercise enabled students to consider how they wished to be treated and what they needed to feel safe in a community. This brought their attention to three areas often underexplored in the university classroom: What do I need to bring my best work to collaborations? What do I expect from others? and, What can others expect from me? In this sense, the code of conduct compels students to wrestle with connection, and to (re)connect with one another on a human, rather than subject-matter-based or functional, level. Sharing triads enabled students to focus on different roles in exchange – sharing, listening, observing – which added complexity to the previous understanding many of them had regarding the purpose, function, and practice of exchange. Making these learnings concrete in personal reflections enabled them to transfer learnings from the exercise into other areas of their lives, and to imagine the transformative implications of the simple act of listening for sustainability work. The iceberg model provided a tool for making complexity visible. In depersonalizing potentially divisive societal topics, it enabled students to collectively explore root causes of issues. In doing so, they embarked on a collective journey of discovery, rather than a debate with winners, losers, and resultant divisions of the classroom community.

Looking ahead

More than isolated experiments, the "Be the Change" courses carried out so far at the University of St. Gallen are the manifestation of a potentially growing movement towards a new and transformative learning approach that takes current global challenges into focus. If business schools are to remain relevant, they need to reinvent themselves and acknowledge society's pressing need for systemic approaches to economic, social, environmental, and cultural dynamics. During this learning journey, a new generation of future leaders will be educated with a new set of values, perspectives, and worldviews. By partnering with organizations dedicated to building a regenerative economy, we can strengthen our connection to nature and develop truly holistic practices of value creation.

We need to be ambitious about leveraging these new ways of bringing about systemic change, turning inner development into a new paradigm within business education. As a next step, we aim to develop new courses with a focus on entrepreneurship for sustainability and nature-based solutions. At the same time, we understand that to make such offerings attractive to business students on a bigger scale, we need the capacity to transform existing formats by infusing avant-garde language and knowledge bases. Navigating through a transition period requires a balanced approach as societal structures change at their own pace. We experiment with co-creative learning journeys, learn and fail forward by dancing with systems (Meadows, D., 2001). Our purpose is to provide young business students with new life and career perspectives based on global impact and systemic change, showing them that their business drive and ability to learn and cooperate can be a game changer for the planet and the future of humanity.

The close collaboration with student associations proved to be a successful strategy as it enabled bringing the entrepreneurial spirit present in those associations closer to academic theory and practice. For this to happen, lecturers must also reinvent themselves by further developing facilitation skills, and the openness to come into a horizontal dialogue with the partner student organizations as well as with the students. Hence, the expansion of the BTC concept requires working with the university´s lecturers on the development of this new mindset where the lecturers do not possess all the knowledge, but rather act as facilitators that enable collective intelligence to emerge in the classroom.

Further collaborative initiatives have already emerged from the BTC ecosystem, such as a partnership with the World Systemic Forum, an annual event organized by The System Change Foundation, and the recent launch of the IDG St. Gallen Hub, initiated by sustainability-oriented lecturers and researchers from the University of St. Gallen in collaboration with a diversity of local stakeholders.

Finally, we hope that by sharing our experiences and efforts we can inspire and encourage others to develop new and ambitious learning approaches and spaces, giving access to inner development processes and tools to future changemakers in business and society, driving positive outer change from within.

References

Bornemann, B., Förster, R., Getzin, S., Kläy, A., Sägesser, A., Schneider, F., Wäger, P.; Wilhelm, S., & Zimmermann, A. (2020). Sustainability-oriented transformative learning and teaching in higher education: Eight propositions on challenges and approaches. Swiss Academic Society for Environmental Research and Ecology (saguf). https://scnat.ch/en/id/NPcym (accessed Jan. 30, 2024).

Bristow, J., Bell, R., Wamsler, C., Bjorkman, T., Tickel, P., Kim. J., & Scharmer. O. (2024). The system within: Addressing the inner dimensions of sustainability and systems transformation. The Club of Rome. *Earth4All: Deep Dive Paper 17*. https://www.clubofrome.org/publication/earth4all-bristow-bell/.

De Witt, A., Bootsma, M. Dermody, B. J., & Rebel, K. (2023). The seven-step learning journey: A learning cycle supporting design, facilitation, and assessment of transformative learning. *Journal of Transformative Education, 22*(3) 229–250. https://doi.org/10.1177/154134462312203.

Dreier, L., Nabarro, D., & Nelson, J. (2019). Systems leadership for sustainable development: Strategies for achieving systemic change. Harvard Kennedy School.

Hall, E. (1976). *Beyond culture*. Anchor Books.

Hoffman, A. J. (2024, May 9). Business education is broken: Here are strategies to fix it. Harvard Business Publishing Education. https://hbsp.harvard.edu/inspiring-minds/business-education-is-broken (accessed May 15, 2024).

Laasch, O. (2024). Radicalising responsible management education: Why and how? *Global Focus – The EFMD Business Magazine, 18*(2), 13–18.

Meadows, D. (2001). Dancing with systems. The Donella Meadows Project. https://donellameadows.org/archives/dancing-with-systems/ (accessed Jan. 30, 2024).

Morrell, A. & O'Connor, M. A. (2002). Introduction. In E. O'Sullivan, A., Morrell, & M. A., O'Connor (eds.). *Expanding the boundaries of transformative learning: Essays on theory and praxis* (pp. xv–xx). Palgrave.

Monat, J. P. & Gannon, T. F. (2015). What is systems thinking? A review of selected literature plus recommendations. *American Journal of Systems Science, 4*(1), 11–26. doi:10.5923/j.ajss.20150401.02.

Rovelli, C. (2014). *Seven brief lessons on physics*. Riverhead Books.

Senge, P., Hamilton, H., & Kania, J. (2015). The dawn of system leadership. *Stanford Social Innovation Review, 13*(1), 27–33. https://doi.org/10.48558/YTE7-XT62.

Wamsler, C. & Brink, E. (2018). Mindsets for sustainability: Exploring the link between mindfulness and sustainable climate adaptation. *Ecological Economics, 151*, 55–61. https://doi.org/10.1016/j.ecolecon.2018.04.029.

Wamsler, C. (2020). Education for sustainability. Fostering a more conscious society and transformation towards sustainability. *International Journal of Sustainability in Higher Education, 21(*1), 112–130. https://doi.org/10.1108/ijshe-04-2019-0152.

Ella Stadler-Stuart, Niels Rot and Ivan Jovanovic

Chapter 6
What we have learned at Rflect: Catalyzing the scalable integration of the Inner Development Goals in higher education through tech

Abstract: In this chapter, co-founders Ella Stadler-Stuart, Niels Rot, and Ivan Jovanovic from Rflect, an edtech start-up in Switzerland, discuss their journey and methodologies in integrating the Inner Development Goals (IDGs) into higher education. They emphasize the increasing necessity of nurturing human competencies amid rapid technological advancements and global challenges. Rflect aims to help universities redefine their pivotal role in society and prepare their students for the future by embedding inner development into academic curricula.

The authors outline the origins of Rflect, their motivation as co-founders, and share the start-up's hypothesis that fostering reflective practice at scale leads to better outcomes for both people and the planet. It details the development of Rflect's tech platform, which includes features like guided reflection, peer coaching, self-assessment, and insight-to-action challenges. Rflect was intentionally built to make inner development accessible and scalable, addressing systemic challenges such as high costs, scalability issues, and lack of in-house expertise within universities.

The chapter illustrates Rflect's impact through a case study from George Washington University, showcasing how the app enhances experiential learning. They go on to highlight preliminary study findings indicating positive shifts in student users' self-awareness, emotional maturity, and other IDG-related skills.

Challenges in embedding IDGs in higher education are discussed, including raising awareness, systemic resistance, and resource constraints. The chapter concludes with practical recommendations for educators and institutions to facilitate the integration of IDGs and a reflection into teaching practices, online and offline.

Keywords: student inner development, lifelong learning, universities, edtech, reflection app

Introduction

As machines get better at being machines, humans have to get better at being more human.
– Andrew J. Scott, London Business School

https://doi.org/10.1515/9783111453729-007

In an era calling for educational reform, the integration of inner development into academic curricula is paramount. This need is accelerated by two significant megatrends, prompting us to ask whether our educational systems are equipping students with the skills necessary for a dramatically changing future. These trends are the rapid evolution of artificial intelligence (AI) and the ongoing global challenges highlighted by the Sustainable Development Goals (SDGs). The Inner Development Goals (IDGs), aimed at nurturing key human competencies, have captured the attention of educators eager to holistically prepare tomorrow's leaders and citizens. Yet, the challenge remains: how to implement these goals effectively and at scale within the complex ecosystem of higher education.

At Rflect, we have tackled this challenge by harnessing technology to transform theoretical frameworks into actionable strategies. This chapter shares our journey as a young edtech start-up working in the field of higher education in Switzerland and wider Europe and offers insights and open-sourced methodologies to help educators worldwide to integrate student inner development more effectively into their programs. While Rflect focuses on higher education, there are lessons here that are relevant across all stages of education. Through our experiences and the findings from our impact studies, we aim to empower educational institutions to foster environments that prioritize both personal growth and academic excellence.

> In personal communication with Rflect in 2023, Prof. Samuel T. Ledermann of George Washington University, stated that: "As our educational landscape shifts post-pandemic, Rflect sets you up for success by building inner development competencies for our next generation of leaders."

The origin story

Rflect was co-founded by Niels Rot, Ivan Jovanovic, and Ella Stadler-Stuart in Zurich, Switzerland in early 2023. As co-founders, we share a commitment to personal growth, entrepreneurship, and improving education for a better future for all. Niels, a serial-for-purpose entrepreneur and co-founder of Impact Hub Zurich, highlights the significance of cultivating essential skills that are often overlooked in conventional education settings, such as leadership, critical thinking and project management. Ella, a professional coach, facilitator, and program director, advocates for the importance of reflection in fostering both personal and academic development, emphasizing the necessity of understanding one's values and learning goals. Ivan, a software engineer previously with Microsoft, views technology as a tool to enhance human capabilities and help manage the complexities of today's world. Together, our mission is to enable universities to equip their students with a lifelong habit of inner development.

With Rflect, we started with a simple hypothesis: *If we can enable people at scale to reflect more and connect with their values, it will make the world a better place.* To put this idea into practice, we sought an environment that would allow us to engage a diverse audience – not just those who already share our views. We needed a setting where people are open to new ideas and where a sustainable business model could thrive, and higher education emerged as the ideal arena. With this in mind, our founding team embarked on a journey of iterative development and experimentation aimed at validating our core assumptions. In the European spring semester of 2023, we started with five initial pilot partners and a minimal viable product (MVP) consisting of a lecturer dashboard and a student app, and we have been seeing encouraging growth ever since. At the time of writing, Rflect had partnered with over 20 universities in six countries, including Switzerland, Germany, the Netherlands, Norway, and the USA. Rflect is enabled by the Migros Pioneer Fund.[1]

> In personal communication with Rflect in 2023, Pablo Villars, Project Lead at Migros Pioneer Fund stated that: "The claim "outer change through inner development" is compelling, but also still shaky. With its app, Rflect has a tangible and scalable plan on how to put the IDGs into practice in an impactful way. The Migros Pioneer Fund is excited to support the Rflect team on this endeavor."

The changing requirements of competence development

Echoing the insightful words of Andrew J. Scott in the introduction, a consensus is forming among industry leaders and technology pioneers: the next generation of graduates and employees must acquire distinctly different skills to achieve two key objectives: (1) keep pace with rapid technological progress; and (2) cultivate the human capabilities needed to tackle global challenges facing society. As intelligent technologies increasingly assume roles in handling physical, repetitive, and basic cognitive tasks, skills such as adaptability, flexibility, emotional intelligence, analytical judgment, creative thinking, bias recognition, and effective AI management are gaining prominence (McKinsey & Company, 2023; Microsoft WorkLab, 2023).

Universities, tasked with shaping the citizens and leaders of tomorrow, frequently assert their commitment to comprehensive educational goals in their mission statements. However, there are critical questions to be addressed: Are the "right" skills being prioritized in curricula? Is a focus on technical proficiency sufficient in a world marked by growing complexity? The necessity to integrate human-centered compe-

---

1 The Migros Pioneer Fund supports sustainable solutions for societal challenges with the goal of initiating systemic change towards a future-oriented society. The impact-oriented funding approach combines financial support with active funding and risk management. The fund is part of the social commitment of the Migros Group and has an annual budget of approximately 15 million Swiss francs. The Migros Pioneer Fund is supported by companies such as Denner, Migros Bank, Migrol, migrolino, and Ex Libris. More information: www.migros-pionierfonds.ch.

tences into all levels of education, not just confined to leadership and sustainability-focused programs, is becoming increasingly apparent.

The IDGs offer a unified framework that highlights the essential skills we should be imparting to students, bringing much-needed clarity to an intricate issue, similar to the role played by the SDGs in promoting sustainability in higher education. There is optimism that the IDGs could similarly revolutionize the focus on personal growth within academic institutions. However, the implementation of such frameworks remains a collective responsibility. The IDGs provide a shared narrative, a communicative framework; it is up to individuals, groups, and institutions – including universities and innovative enterprises like Rflect – to turn these theoretical frameworks into actionable solutions. At Rflect, our mission is to help universities redefine their pivotal role in society, and bring inner development to 200 million tertiary students worldwide.

Challenges universities face around inner development

Universities today recognize the urgent need to evolve, addressing the changing requirements of students and society by offering a broader array of skills beyond traditional academic disciplines. Yet, integrating inner development systematically into higher education presents significant barriers.

The cost challenge

Commonly employed methods for personal development, such as coaching, mentoring, learning diaries, retreats, and seminars, are notably time- and labor-intensive. This not only drives up costs but also limits the frequency and reach of these programs within the university setting.

Scalability issues

While personalized approaches like coaching and retreats are effective for individual growth, scaling these methods to accommodate the needs of thousands of students at a single university is not only challenging but also prohibitively expensive. The infrastructure and resources required to implement these programs on a large scale are immense.

Lack of in-house expertise

Another significant barrier is the pervasive lack of in-house expertise on inner development competencies within university faculties. This often necessitates the involvement of external experts, coaches, and guest lecturers to lead these developmental tracks. Not only does this approach incur high costs, but it also results in a fragmentation of knowledge, with valuable insights and methodologies remaining confined within certain departments or external entities, rather than being disseminated throughout the institution.

Challenges students face for their inner development

The university experience varies greatly among students, yet there are common hurdles that many encounter during their learning journeys. These challenges can significantly impact a student's learning experience and future career prospects.

Lack of orientation

The educational path in higher education, particularly in programs spanning multiple years, often feels fragmented and very "one size fits all". Many students that we speak with struggle with decisions about course selection, thesis topics, and career paths post-graduation. This confusion is often compounded by a lack of structure to explore personal strengths and learning objectives, leading to stress and disengagement among students who find themselves passively moving through their coursework without clear direction.

Employability and skill gaps

While many students attend university to gain the skills necessary for employment, there is a growing disconnect between the skills taught and those needed in the modern workforce. As automation and intelligent technologies take over routine tasks, competencies like adaptability, emotional intelligence, analytical thinking, and creative problem solving are becoming even more important. However, these are not consistently integrated into the university curriculum, leaving students underprepared for future challenges.

Purpose and well-being

The recent emphasis on mental health, accelerated by the COVID-19 pandemic, has brought well-being and psychological safety to the forefront of academic discussions. Students are increasingly seeking not only academic success but also a meaningful educational experience that aligns with their values and contributes positively to their overall well-being. Universities are thus challenged to create environments that prioritize these aspects, fostering a sense of purpose and community among their students.

Development of Rflect's methodology

In an answer to the above challenges, we built Rflect. The foundation of Rflect's methodology is built on well-established principles of vertical development and Gibbs' reflective learning cycle, as well as our founding and advising team's extensive experience in teaching, coaching, and adult development. Additionally, we draw on the IDGs as a unifying narrative that outlines essential human competences for students.

Vertical development

This concept is best understood in contrast to horizontal development. Whereas horizontal development focuses on adding specific skills within particular fields – like programming, accounting, or social media marketing – vertical development centers around broadening how individuals think, instigating a shift in how they perceive the world, themselves, and others. This can also mean "unlearning" and challenging long-held beliefs about themselves and how the world works. This form of development is aimed at improving adaptability, self-awareness, collaborative capabilities, and proficiency in managing complexities – skills that align with the objectives of the IDGs. *Reflective practice serves as a gateway to vertical development*. When students reflect on their identity, values, and mental models, they embark on a journey of profound personal growth. This is why guided reflection is a foundational aspect of Rflect's approach.

Gibbs' reflective learning cycle

The reflective learning cycle was founded by Graham Gibbs in 1988 to help students give structure to learning from experiences (University of Edinburgh, 2024). Its cyclical nature emphasizes that a student has not completed the learning loop until reflection has taken place, as noted by renowned American philosopher John Dewey: "We do not learn from experience . . . we learn from reflecting on experience" (Dewey, 1933). By evaluating a situation through the six stages, a learner is encouraged to think about what happened (description), how they felt (feelings), evaluate what worked and what did not (evaluation), why that is (analysis), and what they want to take forward with them in terms of a lesson or action (conclusion) and (action plan) (CrowJack, 2024). Rflect's methodology draws inspiration from Gibbs' cycle and this can be seen in its features, from guided reflection exercises to insight-to-action challenges.

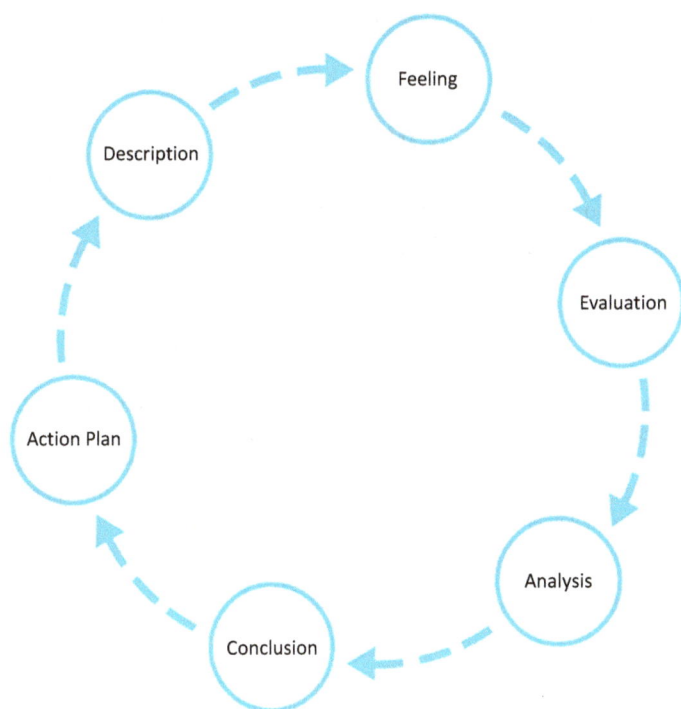

Figure 6.1: Gibbs' Reflective Cycle. Adapted from *Reflectors' Toolkit: Reflecting on Experience*, University of Edinburgh, 2024.

The Inner Development Goals (IDGs)

Universities have long discussed the importance of teaching "future skills", or skills for sustainable development, using various frameworks to guide their curricula. However, their implementation is fragmented, and can be very expensive and difficult to scale (see "Challenges universities face around inner development"). We believe the IDGs have the potential to unify fragmented frameworks into a robust global movement. What's more, the skills outlined in the IDGs align well with many of the competencies identified in other future skills frameworks.

While no framework is flawless and the IDGs are not without their limitations, they are fostering a "common narrative" that is rapidly gaining international traction. The IDGs are positioned to do for inner development what the SDGs achieved for sustainability in 2015 in terms of alignment and momentum.

At Rflect, we utilize the IDGs to enrich our reflection question library, allowing lecturers to prompt their students to reflect on all or selected IDG skills throughout their learning journey. Notably, there has been a growing acknowledgment and adoption of the IDG framework at Swiss universities, especially in, but not limited to, programs and courses with a focus on sustainability or leadership development.

Understanding and implementing Rflect

Rflect is an intuitive tech platform with a lecturer dashboard and a mobile-friendly app for students. This section delves into the current features of Rflect,[2] crafted to nurture students' journeys toward self-awareness and help them build a lifelong habit of reflection. We have also added implementation tips for how to apply these interventions in an offline setting, so that educators and learners from all stages can benefit.

> In personal communication with Rflect in 2023, Marino Sampayo, a student user shared that: "For me, inner development is a creative way of delving into oneself. It involves opening your mind to rational reflection and allowing your body to feel the positive aspects of this self-learning process. Rflect serves as a reminder in a "busy life" to take time to think and feel, to better understand yourself, and to facilitate the implementation of the changes you wish to achieve."

Guided reflection

At the core of Rflect is the guided reflection feature. Lecturers can tap into an extensive library of reflection questions and strategically schedule these to send to students in alignment with key moments in their learning journey, e.g., program start, first experiences, group work, and exam preparation, among others. This timely interaction allows students to contemplate course content deeply, making abstract concepts more tangible and personalized. Students can also set personal learning goals and reflect on their skills development, inspired by the IDG framework, e.g., self-awareness, sensemaking, critical thinking, and collaborating. This process functions akin to an in-app journal that accompanies students throughout their academic journey, like a "coach" in their pocket. Each reflection entry is categorized as either private or

---

2 Visit our website for an up-to-date feature overview: www.rflect.ch.

shared with lecturers, cultivating a secure environment that bolsters student trust and encourages them to go deeper in their reflections. In Rflect, students have their reflections all in one place, and can export them for future reference.

Implementation tip: Allocate 8–10 minutes for your students to reflect and write down their key takeaways at the end of a lecture or course day. You do not have to do this after every learning unit, you can always start with the first day of a course and ask students to give feedback on the approach.

Peer coaching

Recognizing that significant personal growth often occurs through interaction, the peer-coaching feature facilitates tried-and-tested peer-to-peer exercises. This aspect of Rflect is instrumental in honing critical leadership abilities such as active listening, effective feedback delivery, and asking the right questions. By engaging in these structured interactions, students not only learn from each other but also build a supportive network, enhancing their educational experience and developing key interpersonal skills. Via the lecturer dashboard in Rflect, lecturers can assign students into small groups, set them a peer-coaching topic and give them Rflect's coaching script. Students then meet in real life, hold the peer-coaching session, and reflect on what they learned into Rflect afterwards, helping them to cement their insights.

Implementation tip: Reflecting together can be powerful and, in our experience, peer coaching can work really well even with inexperienced students. There are lots of open-source scripts for peer-coaching exercises online that you can print and give your students in groups of two to three. Give it a try, our users love it![3]

Self-assessment

The self-assessment feature is another foundational aspect of Rflect. Students independently assess their skills development at the start and end of their learning program in Rflect. This self-evaluation employs evidence-based scales and meta-reflection questions, inspired by the IDG framework, ensuring thorough and thoughtful self-examination. While individual assessments remain confidential, aggregate data is accessible to lecturers. This feature enables educators to monitor overall class progress. Preliminary studies indicate significant positive shifts in students' skills development, in particular on self-awareness, emotional maturity, and resilience, underscoring the practical bene-

---

3 Try this one from Rflect: https://www.linkedin.com/pulse/power-peer-coaching-education-free-script-ella-stadler-stuart-74z4f/?trackingId=EFOH%2B7EVShWc74U8934Log%3D%3D.

fits and motivational impact of their commitment to personal growth (refer to the section "What we have learned" for detailed insights).

> Implementation tip: Ask your students to set one to three personal learning goals at the start of the learning program and put them somewhere visible to them. At the middle of the program, ask students to check in with their learning goals and make any necessary adjustments, and if they need any support. At the end, ask students to reflect on if they achieved their learning goals, or if completely new ones arose in the process. This can also be a good topic for group discussion.

Insight-to-action

Reflection at its best leads to meaningful insights, and Rflect offers a structured approach for turning personal insights into action. By encouraging students to take action based on insights from their guided reflections, Rflect inspires students to transform knowledge into changes in their thinking and behavior, thus closing the learning loop. In every reflection field there is a "Take Action" button which students can click to write a new action and, if desired, set a daily reminder for 21 days, as it takes time to establish a new habit.

> Implementation tip: Ask your students to reflect on an "aha" moment they recently had about themselves or what they are learning and want to remember in one year's time. Next, ask them to write down a concrete action they could start taking tomorrow for 21 days that will help them remember this insight and implement it in their day-to-day lives. You can also ask them to share their action with a peer and put it somewhere visible to remember it.

> In personal communication with Rflect in 2023, Dorota Sokół-Wach, a student user shared that: "Rflect provided a framework that guided my thoughts, preparation, and focus, enriching my learning process and helping me deal with everyday challenges. It allowed me to engage more deeply with the content and interact more effectively with the teachers during sessions. This tool not only structured my time but also broadened my perspective, enabling me to ask better questions and get more from the lectures."

Rflect in use: Experiential learning in Malawi with insights from Prof. Samuel T. Ledermann

Prof. Ledermann, assistant professor of the practice of international affairs and director of the global capstone at George Washington University's Elliott School of International Affairs, has innovatively incorporated Rflect into his curriculum,[4] enhancing

---

4 Prof. Ledermann made the use of Rflect mandatory and part of the exam criteria (pass/no pass) in a three-month, three-credit course.

experiential learning for graduate students focusing on sustainable development. Prior to Rflect, inner development components were notably absent from his courses. This changed when Prof. Ledermann designed a new short-term course that takes students to Malawi for hands-on fieldwork.

> In personal communication with Rflect in 2023, Prof. Samuel T. Ledermann stated that: "We used Rflect to guide their preparation, enhance team building, and help them reflect on their experience in Malawi, as well as debrief what they can take away from their experience for themselves and their future career."

The integration of Rflect has brought significant benefits to both the students and Prof. Ledermann himself. Prof. Ledermann ascertained that by facilitating a deeper connection with their personal experiences in the field, students showed improved capacity to internalize and apply their learnings. "Rflect increases students' awareness of the importance of the inner dimensions for sustainability," Prof. Ledermann notes. For him, when managing 17 graduate students, Rflect's seamless operation and easy adoption were invaluable. It provided "tremendous value without a steep learning curve", he adds.

Looking ahead, Prof. Ledermann sees potential for broader integration of Rflect within the international development studies graduate program. He believes that a systematic, long-term engagement with Rflect could profoundly impact students' development and prepare them as the next generation of ethical leaders.

This case study underlines the transformative potential of integrating inner development tools into academic curricula, and that Rflect can be adapted to a diverse range of learning contexts, from project-based learning to longer programs like bachelor's and master's degrees.

Practicing reflection as a team

Building a start-up can be hard and incredibly fast-paced. That is why it is important to us as a team to "practice what we preach" and take time to reflect. We ourselves use the guided reflection feature in Rflect to have regular individual and team check-ins, reflecting, for example, on our team goals and values before a team retreat, brainstorming new ideas and improvements, and doing retros on significant product releases (What went well? What challenges did we face? What specific actions do we want to take to enhance our collaboration and productivity?), among other things. This regular time to reflect helps us to check in with ourselves as entrepreneurs, prepare individually before team meetings, and to test our own product and capture insights that might have otherwise gone unnoticed. We also make an effort to look after our own well-being as best as we can, prioritizing family and health over business, and making time for a team badminton session once a month. It is not always easy to keep everything in balance, but it is worth it.

Using our app as a team has demonstrated that Rflect effectively enhances various team activities, such as important meetings, retreats, and feedback sessions. This highlights Rflect's potential to support reflective learning journeys across diverse contexts, including corporate teams.

We frequently receive inquiries from interested parties about applying Rflect in different sectors. We appreciate this interest and recognize the potential for broader applications. However, as a start-up, it is crucial for us to maintain a clear focus. Currently, our primary goal is to assist universities and their students, ensuring we provide the best possible support for their reflective learning needs.

Best practices and limitations

To maximize the effectiveness of Rflect, it is important to engage in an open discussion about its best practices and its limitations. Some examples:
- Rflect is optimally integrated within structured educational contexts, such as bachelor's or master's programs, or specific courses. Rflect also works very well with project-based and experiential learning programs.
- It is beneficial to make Rflect a mandatory, credit-earning component of the curriculum.[5] This approach not only emphasizes the importance of reflective practice to students but also helps in allocating budget resources. Completion rate as well as total characters and time reflected can be measured in the lecturer dashboard.
- Like any tool, the success of Rflect can be impacted by the facilitator's motivation and experience. Lecturers who are inherently motivated to use the Rflect dashboard typically foster more impactful reflection journeys. Recognizing the challenges that may arise in environments lacking specialized expertise, we offer a comprehensive solution that includes both the tool and facilitation support. An experienced Rflect coach can manage the reflection program tailored to the learning objectives of the program, ensuring an effective integration.
- It is essential to understand that Rflect alone is not a comprehensive substitute for student psychological support. While the tool may help in identifying students who are struggling early on, institutions should adhere to their established intervention protocols for mental health issues.
- We acknowledge that learners have diverse reflective and learning styles. Currently, Rflect is primarily text-based. We are exploring options to make the tool more accessible to visual and auditory learners (e.g., image and audio upload), as

---

5 E.g. pass/no pass based on percentage of reflections completed.

well as to expand our question library with meaningful exercises for deeper student personal growth.

Our commitment to openness and transparency is paramount. We aim to tailor our approach to meet the unique needs and contexts of each university, ensuring that every student can derive the maximum benefit from their Rflect experience.[6]

What we have learned

Overview of preliminary study

In the autumn of 2023, we underwent a nonscientific preliminary study to evaluate the perceived improvement in skills development among student users of the Rflect app (Stadler-Stuart et al., n.d.). This was done for our own learning and product development, as well as for reporting our impact to our supporters. The analysis involved assessing the mean average score changes between pre- and post-assessment surveys across five dimensions inspired by the IDGs, as well as examining qualitative responses using a multi-stage qualitative content analysis.

Survey respondents

Respondents included 39 students enrolled in seven different higher education programs in German-speaking Switzerland during the autumn semester of 2023. These programs included various further education certificate programs, such as certificates of advanced studies, as well as modules within bachelor's degree programs.

Approach

Student users of Rflect were invited to complete pre- and post-surveys starting with quantitative questions based on the IDGs, using a 1–10 scale. Each survey took approximately 20 minutes to complete. Between the pre- and post-surveys, students engaged in their regular curricula while using Rflect to reflect on and learn from their experiences. Upon completing the post-survey, they were then asked to write meta-reflections on their comparative results from the two surveys, which are displayed in-app.

---

6 If you have any questions about this, please do not hesitate to contact us at info@rflect.ch.

Example questions

– Quantitative examples from pre-survey where students were asked to give themselves a score of 1–10 where 1 = not at all, 5 = OK/solid, and 10 = very confident:
  – How confident are you in your ability to set goals? (from Self-Awareness and Goal Setting [IDG: Being])
  – How confident are you in your ability to collaborate with others in a team/group work setting? (from Social and Communication Skills [IDG: Collaborating])
– Qualitative examples from post-survey, after students have seen comparative results from pre- and post-surveys:
  – To what extent do the results fit with where you feel you are in your personal development? Were there any surprises or unexpected insights?
  – What aspects or skills are you eager to explore or enhance going forward?
  – In what aspects or specific skills do you personally feel you have grown or changed the most since your pre-assessment? Give 1–3 examples. Is this visible in your results?

Key findings from quantitative results

The quantitative results show that students using Rflect reported a *positive mean improvement across all five tested dimensions*, thus exceeding our initial hypothesis. We expected to see notable improvements in Category 1: Self-Awareness and Goal Setting (IDG: Being), Category 3: Social and Communication Skills (IDG: Collaborating), and Category 5: The World Around Me (IDG: Relating).[7] The most notable changes were observed in Category 4: Emotional Maturity (IDG: Being) (+0.90) and Category 1: Self-Awareness and Goal Setting (IDG: Being) (+0.60). See Figure 6.2 for mean improvement scores by competence dimension.

We believe that reflective practice enhances self-awareness, and both the quantitative and qualitative analysis confirmed this. In terms of emotional maturity, for many students, this was one of the first times they were asked to reflect on their emotions and emotional responses to key experiences during their learning journey. For Rflect, it will be interesting to explore what further input could help students to grow further in these and other dimensions.

These results provide a foundation for making Rflect a more evidence-based tool, with plans to continue this research with an academic rigor study (and control group) using evidence-based scales in the spring semester of 2024.

---

7 The decision was made during autumn semester 2023 to align more deeply with the IDG framework, which is why some labels from the report vary from the five dimensions listed in the IDG framework.

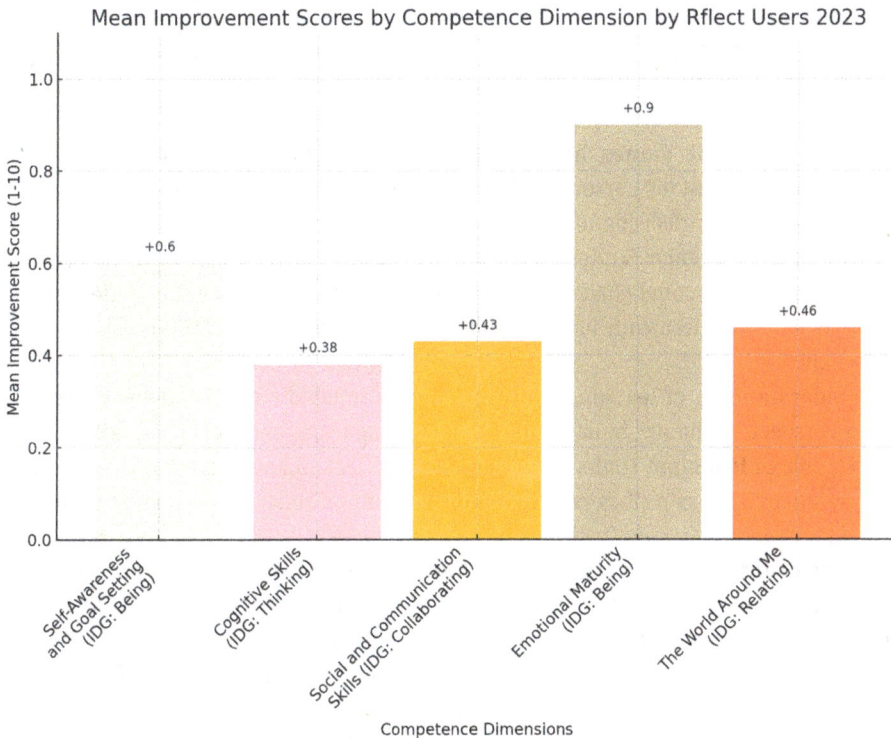

Figure 6.2: Mean Improvement Scores by Competence Dimension by Rflect Users 2023. Adapted from *Preliminary Insights into Student Skills Development*, by E. Stadler-Stuart et al. (n.d.).

Key findings and thematic insights from qualitative results

> In personal communication with Rflect in 2023, one anonymous student user stated: "It's fascinating to watch the growth of my answers over time. Seeing this transition reflects the improvement in my personal development journey."

Students self-reported improvements across several key competencies and gave insight into where they felt further improvement and support was needed. These findings will guide Rflect's product development for future improvements.

– **Increased self-awareness**: Students reported enhanced self-awareness, a direct outcome of regular reflective practices facilitated by the app. This is where we also expected the most positive change.
– **Self-confidence and compassion**: By reflecting on personal progress and learning goals, students noted an increase in self-confidence, attributing it to the recognition of their own personal growth.

- **Emotional maturity**: For many, the app provided a first opportunity to intro-spect on emotional responses and conflict management, marking significant growth in emotional maturity. We see a lot of potential here for future interventions.
- **Importance of values and sustainability (in decision making)**: Regular prompts to consider personal values led students to report greater consideration of these in their decision-making processes.
- **Building resilience**: Students acknowledged an enhanced capacity to manage academic and personal challenges. Having the space to recognize this, reflecting on how to deal better with future challenges, and practicing self-compassion builds resilience.
- **Understanding of learning**: This was an area in which many students expressed a perspective change, in particular that learning transcends technical skills.
- **Future of learning**: Students were asked to reflect on key skill areas they wanted to improve on, as well as reported improvement on reflection as a meta-cognition skill.
- **Insight into action (transforming knowledge into behavioral change)**: Connecting theoretical knowledge with practical application was identified as a critical learning outcome, essential for real-world impact.
- **Building metacognition (Livingston, 2003) as a skill**: We observed a range from beginners to daily practitioners in reflection, indicating varied levels of proficiency and engagement with this meta-skill. We see a lot of potential here for future interventions.

Conclusions on study results

The initial results indicate promising progress in students' personal and interpersonal skills across the tested dimensions. These findings underscore the potential of interventions like Rflect in fostering holistic inner development among students, while also highlighting areas for continued exploration and refinement. As a self-study, these results should nonetheless be interpreted with cautious optimism.

Looking ahead, the upcoming academic rigor study in spring 2024, led by Dr. Prof. Anna Jasinenko and incorporating a control group, aims to provide more robust evidence for the effectiveness of Rflect. This study will build on the insights from our initial research, further substantiating Rflect's impact. We are committed to transparency and will share updates on our progress via the Rflect website as we continue our journey towards educational innovation.

Hurdles practitioners face integrating IDGs into higher education

Raising awareness

The first substantial challenge in integrating the IDGs or any new framework into higher education is the effort required to raise awareness among key stakeholders, predominantly faculty staff and university leadership. Despite the recognized value of fostering personal growth and emotional intelligence in students, inner competences such as those bundled in the IDGs are often seen as secondary to academic, or "hard", learning objectives. This is why engaging with intrinsically motivated lecturers, as well as honing your storytelling and mobilization skills, is important when bringing the IDGs to higher education institutions (see "Practical recommendations for integrating IDGs into higher education").

System change takes time and persistence

Another significant hurdle is the systemic nature of educational institutions, which are typically resistant to rapid changes. Educational reforms can take years to implement, with curricula often set one year in advance. To effectively embed the IDGs, they should be mandatory and for-credit, linking their inclusion directly to allocated budgets and underscoring their importance. Assessing inner development then becomes a pivotal issue, necessitating a reevaluation of traditional assessment methods. Options such as graded reflective essays, pass/no-pass personal reflections, and peer coaching could be explored to measure personal growth alongside academic achievement. As AI continues to challenge the way students learn and are assessed, developing innovative, effective assessment methods that can keep pace with both academic and inner development metrics is becoming increasingly urgent.

Limited resources

Lastly, the challenge of limited resources – both time and money – cannot be overstated. Integrating IDGs into higher education in the traditional sense (coaching, seminars, retreats) requires significant investment in training educators, developing new materials, and creating support systems for students and staff. Financial constraints are a common barrier, particularly in institutions with already allocated or tight budgets (another reason why making inner development for-credit is crucial). Additionally, the time required for training and curriculum development is substantial. The current academic structures, filled with packed schedules and stringent curriculum requirements, leave little room for the incorporation of extensive IDG-focused programs without sacrificing other academic components.

Overall, while the integration of IDGs into higher education presents multiple benefits, the path is a challenging one that requires strategic planning, resource allocation, and rethinking educational practices. No doubt, enabling change requires courage, creativity, optimism, and persistence, as we know from Dimension 5: Acting.

Practical recommendations for integrating IDGs into higher education

As a for-purpose start-up, we have benefited from the generously shared knowledge and experiences of a growing community of partners, advisors, and stakeholders. We want to pay it forward as best we can. Here are some practical recommendations for integrating the IDGs and reflection into higher education.

- **Integrate a reflection component in your teaching:** Adding a reflective practice to your learning program, be it on- or offline, does not have to be complicated. Consider allocating time to your students to reflect on their key takeaways at the end of a class, or ask them to set their own learning goals and share these with their peers. Focus the reflections on specific skills, for example from the IDG framework, to create awareness and tools around developing these competences. Another tip: Normalize taking "cognitive breaks" and lead your students through some simple breathing exercises or stretching between learning units. You might be surprised by how little this is being done in education, considering how effective and helpful it is.

- **Engage students and listen to their needs:** We can learn a lot from successful start-up practices and product-led organizations and place the needs and desires of our users at the forefront. Spend time understanding your students' specific challenges and aspirations when it comes to their own inner development. Students are often an untapped source of innovative ideas and genuine insights, and getting them involved can help unlock motivation and engagement!

- **Engage intrinsically motivated educators as early adopters:** Seek out educators, researchers, and decision makers within higher education who are not only passionate about student inner development but also understand the necessity for systemic support. These people often have their own "hacks" or innovative solutions but lack the means to scale them. By identifying and engaging with these change agents, their ideas and energy can potentially influence broader institutional strategies. The IDG Global Practitioners' Network is a good place to start.

- **Leverage technology for scale:** Utilize technology to transition time-tested offline solutions to more scalable online platforms, reaching hundreds of students simultaneously. As technology evolves, particularly at the intersection of AI and educational tools, it is crucial to stay abreast of how these advancements can enhance inner development training.

– **Cultivate early co-creation partnerships:** Follow the entrepreneurial principle of involving a diverse mix of collaborators early in the development process. This diversity fosters rich dialogue and innovation, which is crucial to learning and creating meaningful educational solutions. Early engagement with varied stakeholders allows for a broader perspective and accelerates the learning curve.

– **Master storytelling and mobilization skills:** Storytelling is an essential skill in leadership, also in academia. Develop and refine your ability to communicate your vision in ways that resonate with different audiences. A compelling narrative that addresses the specific needs and goals of your audience can significantly enhance engagement and support for your initiatives.

– **Practice what you preach:** If you advocate for the IDGs, it is vital to embody these principles in your own work and daily practices. Regular self-awareness and reflective practices should be part of your routine, serving as a model for the values you promote. Share your personal development journey and the lessons learned along the way, embracing both successes and setbacks with grace and resilience.

While endeavoring to integrate inner development in higher education you will likely face many challenges and some closed doors. However, we hope that by sharing these recommendations, which have helped us on our journey, you can enable change and help foster learning environments that nurture both the personal and professional growth of students.

A word on the IDGs and impact entrepreneurship

Building a start-up is hard enough already. Finding a true customer problem, building a solution that addresses that issue, and setting up a business model that actually works can by itself feel like a miracle. Yet, in the area of impact entrepreneurship, there is an additional difficulty: the risk of mission drift when you grow. This is why an impact start-up should not just think about their purpose (the "why"), their product (the "what"), but also about the company setup (the "how"). We are closely looking at the model of steward ownership (Purpose Economy, n.d.) for the future and have decided to follow the "deep design of business" (Doughnut Economics Action Lab, n.d.) principles of Kate Raworth's "doughnut economics" (Raworth, n.d.) in our setup, keeping in mind how Rflect's business design can both unlock or block transformative action. In order to create a model where the beneficiaries of our activities (students and universities) are not "dependent" on us, we are inviting them in as co-creators and involve them at governance, finance, and ownership level. Inner development needs the right systemic setup to flourish.

Conclusion

We envision a world where every student cultivates a lifelong habit of inner development, making it as commonplace as writing a thesis is today. Our mission is to enable universities to equip their students with this essential habit, as we believe that inner development leads to better outcomes for both people and the planet, and that students simply deserve better. We are working tirelessly towards this vision, aiming to reach 200 million students globally and supporting universities in redefining their pivotal role in society.

We hope this chapter has illuminated ways through which you too can contribute to and participate in this transformative educational movement.

References

CrowJack. (n.d.). Gibbs' reflective cycle: A complete guide. CrowJack. Retrieved April 21, 2024, from https://crowjack.com/blog/strategy/reflection-models/gibbs-reflective-cycle.

Dewey, J. (1933). How we think: A restatement of the relation of reflective thinking to the educative process. D.C. Heath and Company.

Doughnut Economics Action Lab. (n.d.). Doughnut design for business core tool. Doughnut Economics Action Lab. Retrieved April 21, 2024, from https://doughnuteconomics.org/tools/doughnut-design-for-business-core-tool.

Gill, G. (2014). The nature of reflective practice and emotional intelligence in tutorial settings. *Journal of Education and Learning, 3*(1), 86–100. https://doi.org/10.5539/jel.v3n1p86.

Livingston, J. A. (2003). Metacognition: An overview. Retrieved April 21, 2024, from https://www.research gate.net/profile/Jennifer-Livingston-5/publication/234755498_Metacognition_An_Overview/links/0fcfd5112609b7ced5000000/Metacognition-An-Overview.pdf.

McKinsey & Company. (2023, October 6). Five Fifty: Soft skills for a hard world. McKinsey & Company. Retrieved November 14, 2024, from https://www.mckinsey.com/featured-insights/future-of-work/five-fifty-soft-skills-for-a-hard-world.

Microsoft WorkLab. (2023, October 6). Will AI fix work? Microsoft WorkLab. Retrieved November 14, 2024, from https://www.microsoft.com/en-us/worklab/work-trend-index/will-ai-fix-work/.

Purpose Economy. (n.d.). What is steward-ownership? Purpose Economy. Retrieved April 21, 2024, from https://purpose-economy.org/en/whats-steward-ownership/.

Raworth, K. (n.d.). Doughnut economics. Retrieved April 21, 2024, from https://www.kateraworth.com/doughnut/.

Stadler-Stuart, E., Blume, D., Jasinenko, A., & Barroso, M. (n.d.). Preliminary Insights into Student Skills Development. Rflect. Retrieved April 21, 2024, from https://rflect.ch/2024/08/12/white-paper.

University of Edinburgh. (n.d.). Gibbs' reflective cycle. University of Edinburgh. Retrieved April 21, 2024, from https://www.ed.ac.uk/reflection/reflectors-toolkit/reflecting-on-experience/gibbs-reflective-cycle.

Section 2: **Interventions for organizations**

Ana Gabriela Mata Carrera and Mauricio Campos Suarez
Chapter 7
Prelude

This section explores how inner qualities can transform organizational practices, leading to more conscious and sustainable outcomes. It presents a cohesive narrative, guiding you through the interconnected aspects of inner development and its profound impact on organizational success and sustainability.

The connecting thread across this section is the progressive integration of inner development into organizational practices, highlighting the significance of fostering inner qualities for both individual and collective growth. Each chapter contributes uniquely to this overarching theme, offering insights, practical tools, and real-world examples to support the evolution of more conscious and sustainable organizations.

We begin with the World Civility Index, implemented in 19 countries, that encourages the development of soft skills and qualities such as empathy, communication, and intercultural awareness through an index that has been part of the UN Sustainable Development Goals since 2019. This index demonstrates how fostering civility and inner qualities can positively impact societal behavior.

Building on the importance of soft skills, the next chapter delves into practical methods for measuring and training inner development. The meaning, awareness, and purpose (MAP) model provides tangible tools for fostering intrinsic motivation and purpose. Through these instruments, organizations can cultivate a personal connection to global challenges, empowering individuals to become sustainability leaders.

With the foundation of measuring and training established, we explore the practical application of these concepts in organizational settings. This chapter examines the transformative journey of ten23 health, a pharmaceutical service provider that adopts a holacratic approach. By focusing on self-management, transparency, and purpose-driven work, ten23 health demonstrates the power of unlearning ingrained behaviors and fostering inner development for personal and organizational growth. The chapter emphasizes the relevance of IDGs in driving sustainable transformations, showcasing how innovative organizational structures can thrive through inner development.

The final chapter introduces an integrated framework and roadmap to enhance leader and leadership capacity in addressing sustainability challenges. It begins by critically examining the underlying assumptions within the neoliberal paradigm that often undermine sustainability efforts and describes the types of leadership that emerge from this system. From this analysis, the chapter provides a novel perspective that aims to reconstruct these fundamental assumptions. It then outlines a practical roadmap for implementing this novel perspective, featuring an integrated framework which incorporates the Inner Development Goals into a model of global leadership for sustainability (GLfS).

https://doi.org/10.1515/9783111453729-008

As you immerse yourself in this section, may you find inspiration and practical insights to support the evolution of more conscious and sustainable organizations.

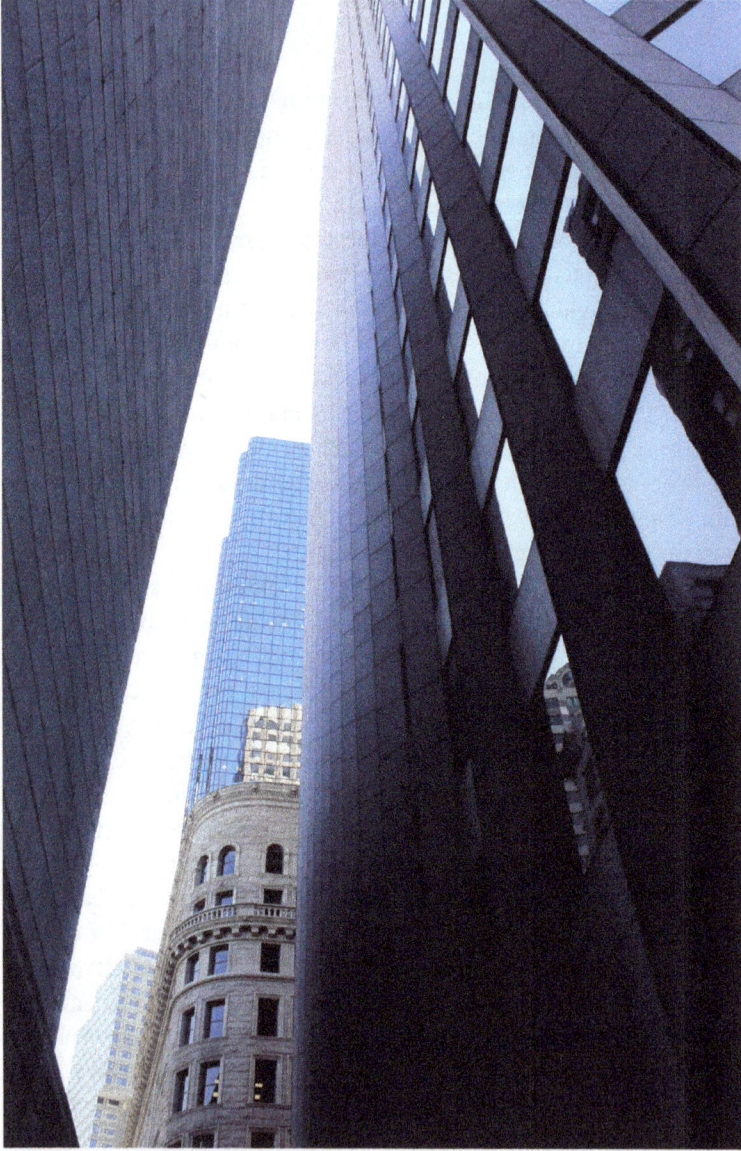

Figure 7.1: Embracing Light (2010).
Photograph by A. G. Mata Carrera, Boston, Massachusetts, USA.
"The light struggles to penetrate the dark concrete of the skyscraper, emblematic of organizations not designed for a human scale. Yet, it's within the gaps between these buildings where light emerges, illuminating pathways for new organizations to prioritize both people and the planet, fostering a more sustainable and compassionate approach to business and society."

Pachamama Seat

Mother Earth has a seat at the table.
Pachamama has many things to share.
Are we able to listen?

The empty chair of Pachamama is full.
Full of stories of joy and sorrow
Full of hope and wisdom
Full of dreams and realities
Are we able to listen?

Yes, we are,
we have to listen.
listening with our heart
deep listening

Let's bring Pachamama to our debates,
into our plans, ROI, and projects
Let's dance with her.
Preserving human life
and helping this beautiful planet to heal
Dancing close together through the night

M. Campos Suarez (2022)

Author's note. Pachamama is a term from the indigenous cultures of the Andes that refers to "Mother Earth." It represents the goddess of fertility, agriculture, and the earth itself, embodying the natural world and its life-giving aspects. This poem emerged after a workshop with a country leadership team of a large multinational company. During the workshop, an empty chair symbolized the need to listen to the voices of absent stakeholders. Pachamama was one of those voices, reminding participants of the importance of environmental stewardship and the interconnectedness of all life.

Patrick Chun
Chapter 8
World Civility Index and Inner Development Goals: Connecting inner development to mainstream success

Abstract: This article introduces the World Civility Index (WCI), a pioneering initiative by the International Soft Skills Standards & Testing (IITTI) that integrates the principles of the Inner Development Goals (IDGs) framework, aiming to quantify and elevate the importance of soft skills in both the workplace and broader society. In an era where technical skills have traditionally dominated educational and corporate landscapes, the increasing significance of soft skills like empathy, communication, and intercultural awareness is becoming undeniable. Yet, formal recognition and measurable standards for these skills have been notably absent. The WCI emerges as a solution, offering a universal metric for evaluating and credentialing soft skills, akin to a personal credit rating in finance. Developed through a collaborative effort involving soft skills trainers and technology experts, the WCI promotes a micro-learning model, encouraging daily engagement with inner development qualities and providing tangible proof of personal growth. This novel approach not only enhances employability and company culture but also aligns with the United Nations Sustainable Development Goals (SDGs), particularly SDG 8 emphasizing decent jobs and economic growth. Deployed across 19 countries and embraced by diverse organizations, the WCI represents a significant step toward integrating essential human values into global business practices, thereby fostering a more civil, empathetic, and interconnected world.

Keywords: World Civility Index, Inner Development Goals, soft skills measurement, Sustainable Development Goals, micro-learning

Section 1: The introduction

Background and introduction

When people talk about education, they frequently meant hard skills such as chemistry or finance. But for the twenty-first century, increasingly it is the soft skills such as empathy, communication, and intercultural awareness that are the most sought-after, highly transferable skills that every business would ask for. Yet most schools and com-

https://doi.org/10.1515/9783111453729-009

panies would not have formal courses that "count" – with a proper credentialing – in helping students and employees in these inner development topics.

Some people could argue that such soft skills should have been picked up "along the way". But in modern life, families no longer sit around the dining table during dinner where valuable life skills are passed on from parents to children. Sadly, our social fabric, for this reason and many others, has been slowly torn apart for the last 50 years. One does not have to look far to read about the increasing mental issues and drug overdoses as proof.

The good news is that things are changing. In 2011, a group of soft skills trainers and tech experts asked the question:

> How can we "connect the dots" in bringing inner development from a niche discipline into the mainstream; a wide-scale deployment that every company and job seeker can use?

The answer turned out to be that there was no common standard in measuring such skills; a universal measurement that can be used globally, where employees, HR, and trainers can all be "on the same page". The group further stipulated that such a standard would be an open standard (everyone can access) and open source (free for trainers around the world).

After four years of work, the group introduced a soft skills standard measurement called the World Civility Index (WCI).

The aim is to align people's personal interests to that of businesses, and also what is advocated for by the Inner Development Goals (IDGs) so as to affect real behavioral improvement for the betterment of humanity as a whole, particularly as that defined by the United Nations Sustainable Development Goals (SDGs).

In particular, with respect to the IDG framework, we focus on:
- Dimension 3: Relating (appreciation, connectedness, humility, empathy, compassion);
- Dimension 4: Collaborating (communication skills, inclusion/intercultural competency); and
- Dimension 5: Acting (perseverance),

which we will collectively refer to as our IDG dimensions, a particular set of soft skills that we will focus on. (There are five IDG dimensions but the other two are outside the scope of discussion.)

What exactly is World Civility Index?

This index is somewhat similar to a person's credit rating, but instead of measuring how well a person can pay their bills, it measures a person's soft skills. Qualities like communication skills, empathy, intercultural competency.

It is based on field-tested evidences that individuals who engage in consistent training over the long term on average exhibit more civility (Ariely, 2009).

Instead of relying on subjective surveys or assessments, the index takes an objective, data-driven approach that involves various indicators, such as the number of articles read, videos watched, webinars attended, and formal written exams taken.

The concept is that job seekers can get the credential based on the WCI, as proof, to show to employers.

From an employer's point of view, they can raise company culture in terms of better people interactions by requesting job applicants to have this credential before coming on board. HR can also use such credentials for internal performance evaluation, a new kind of KPI (key performance indicator) that historically had been difficult to do.

In addition, having a neutral, third-party measurement for a company's social impact, such as human capital and cultural development within the company, can not only have a ripple effect to the larger society, but also help eliminate suspicions of "greenwashing" and positively affect their ESG (environmental, social, and governance) ratings. (That is, the social impact or "S" in ESG. ESG ratings are important to financial analysts and investors in deciding which company to invest in.)

The WCI became a part of UN Sustainable Development in 2019 to help young people gain meaningful employment, i.e., jobs that provide a sense of purpose for the person. It focuses on SDG 8: Decent work and economic growth, which emphasizes jobs that provide productive, inclusive employment to directly promote sustainable economic growth. Without such standardized measurement, employers can only judge a job applicant's soft skills based on expensive interviews.

As IDGs emphasize essential human values like empathy, humility, and compassion, vital for personal and professional growth, the WCI quantifies these values, enabling businesses to embed IDG principles into their culture and performance evaluations, and by doing so, raising the awareness of the importance of inner development.

Operation model

The operation model is based on bite-sized lessons (aka micro-learning): participants could develop inner development qualities such as humility, empathy, and intercultural awareness on a daily basis at the participant's convenient time by reading an article or watching a video for an average of 5 minutes and earn WCI "points" as tangible proof of their commitment to personal growth.

Minimizing bias

The International Soft Skills Standards & Testing (IITTI) team established an international vetting committee to minimize implicit bias, with members from different continents with different cultural background, and so far has vetted educational materials from sources such as *Harvard Business Review* and *Psychology Today*, as well as from academia and trainers.

Connection between IDGs and World Civility Index

The WCI serves as a tool to quantify intrinsic values promoted by the IDGs, including humility, empathy, and intercultural competency, into a universally recognizable metric for the business sector. Since IDG enthusiasts consist of coaches, trainers, academic professionals, "leaders" of public and private organizations, as well as NGOs, the WCI enables these members to enhance their training programs by awarding WCI points as a form of credential. This approach not only makes students of such training programs more appealing to potential employers, but also helps the IDGs in communicating with the business world how purposeful, sustainable, and productive living can be integrated into their corporate values with a measurable benchmark.

Impact, conclusions

In the bigger picture of the many issues society faces, the root cause can frequently be traced to human behavior, or more concisely, the lack of inner qualities, such as empathy and compassion. These are the "little things". Without such social constructs to make citizens feel safe and respected, they would have little mental space to think about the "bigger things", such as climate change. And they would not have the awareness to vote for the right politicians to be in office to put in the needed environmental policies.

Without the little things, it would be hard to build the big things.

But what is even more important, when employees are feeling respected, the ripple effect can propagate to their families, customers, and business partners. By extension, communities become more civil. Crime rate goes down (Sampson, Raudenbush, & Earls, 1997). Policing fees can be used elsewhere more productively.

Social fabric that has been slowly torn apart can now be rebuilt.

What gets measured gets done!

Section 2: The details

Methodology: Crafting a universal civility metric

The methodology behind crafting a universal civility metric, such as the World Civility Index, emphasizes the importance of daily micro-learning and frequent activities as central components. For the real "keeners", there are also the more traditional classroom instructions followed by written exams. This approach recognizes that the development of soft skills is most effective when integrated into everyday activities and frequent reminders, rather than through infrequent, formal training sessions alone.

Path 1: Reading program & activities

The reading program involves breaking down soft skill development into small, manageable segments that can be easily understood and applied. These bite-sized learning modules of articles and videos are designed to be engaging and accessible, fitting into the busy schedules of individuals. Micro-learning leverages the principle of spaced immersion, where short learning sessions are spread out over time, aiding in better retention and application.

The application of soft skills in frequent interactions is crucial for development. As activities, the methodology encourages individuals to practice these skills in action scenarios, anything from attending seminars, workshops, and lectures to field trips.

Path 2: Written exams

Certain topics in soft skills are actually quite "hard", as in hard skills! These are subject matters that have definite right/wrong answers, such as dining etiquette. And they can easily be learned in a classroom setting with practice in order to gain the needed muscle memory. The follow-on written exams are multiple-choice questions with definite correct/incorrect answers.

By focusing on the reading program and activities (Path 1) and written exams (Path 2), the methodology supports the gradual and continuous improvement of soft skills, making the development of civility an ongoing process. This approach promotes a culture of learning and growth that is both practical and sustainable.

How IDGs are implemented by the World Civility Index

We focus on three of the dimensions of the IDGs (3, 4, 5). They are, at this stage, implemented under different applications: business, travel, and youth. The reason for the three areas is that somewhat different skill sets are required for different situations, and each area represents a context with the most frequent need for people to have high inner qualities.

For example, in business settings, working with co-workers and external interfaces requires a high level of inclusiveness and empathy skills. In travel and tourism, a good knowledge of international social etiquette and respect for location cultures would bode well for tourists to be welcomed by a destination's local citizens. In youth, a certain level of self-reflection and resilience would help fend off mental illness and feelings of loneliness.

However, as inner qualities are sometimes difficult to train on their own, some IDG skills take a different form of implementation. For instance, empathy is indirectly cultivated through social etiquette, teaching the art of making others feel comfortable, which helps students to gradually develop empathy (Schonert-Reichl & Hymel, 2007).

In other words, external behavioral training can subtly instill inner qualities such as empathy. See Figure 8.1 below.

Each component of the World Civility Index is designed to be measurable, providing clear criteria and benchmarks for evaluation. The index established an international vetting committee to ensure a comprehensive and objective measurement. The ultimate goal is to offer actionable insights that individuals and organizations can use to enhance their civility quotient, contributing to a more respectful and productive society.

Difference between World Civility Index and predecessors

The biggest breakthrough of the World Civility Index is that it is not just a measurement of accuracy, like math (in our case, business etiquette, professional dress code, for example), but also a measurement of raising awareness; that is, how much a person is exposed to experiences that foster empathy, patience, resilience, etc.

IITTI recognized early on that hard skills such as math and science are an education of the brain, while soft skills such as empathy and resilience are an education of the heart! That's why they measure awareness, not just accuracy.

For example, to measure empathy, IITTI will count the number of articles read, videos watched, and seminars attended that are related to empathy. Say each article, video, or seminar is worth one point. So, if a person has read 20 articles, watched ten videos, and attended three seminars, this person would have earned 33 World Civility Index points.

Having 33 points may not be conducive to a person being more empathetic, one could argue. Very true. That is why many predecessors with snapshot measurements don't work. That is, they don't improve empathy. But over a long period with such frequent reminders, measured in months or years, and the person has 300 points, it will have an effect (Ariely, 2009).

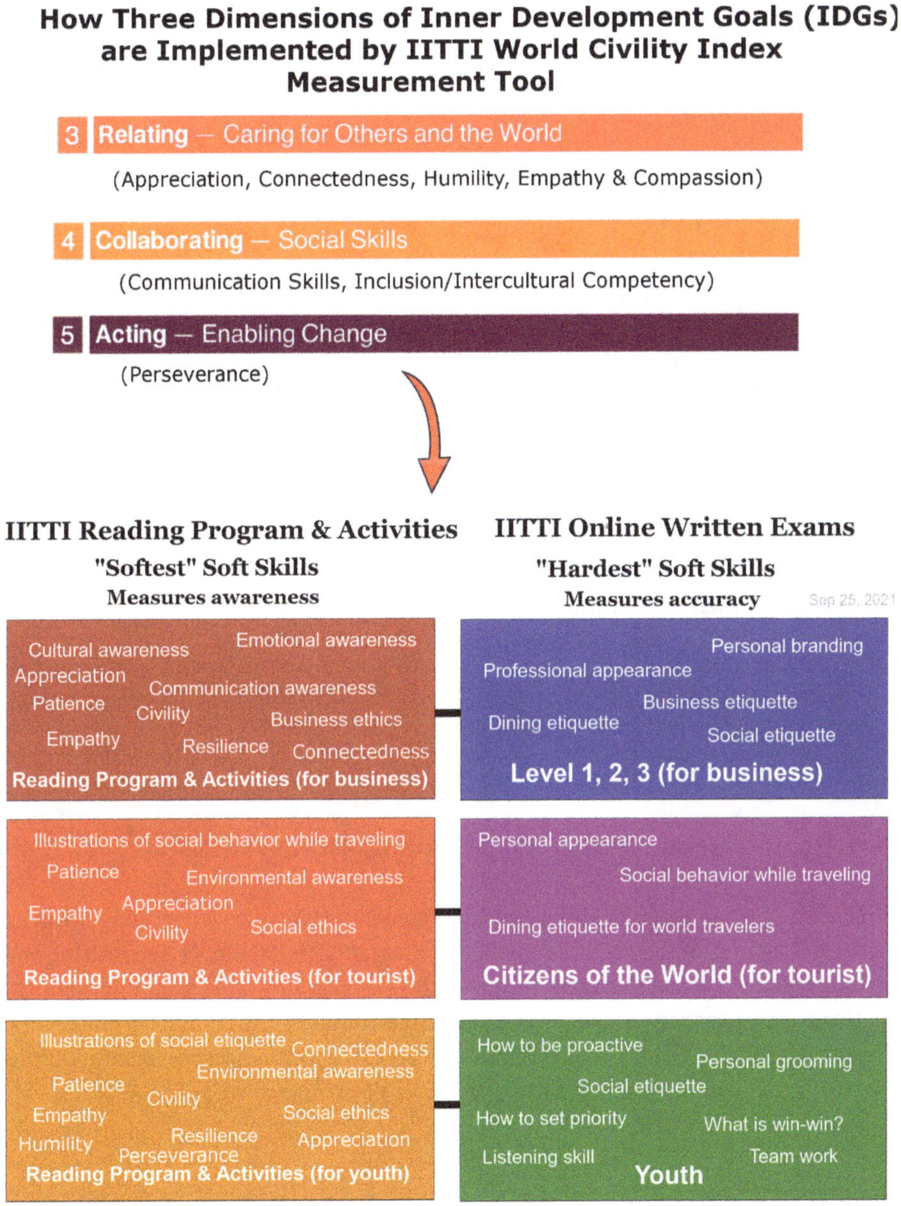

How Three Dimensions of Inner Development Goals (IDGs) are Implemented by IITTI World Civility Index Measurement Tool

3 Relating — Caring for Others and the World

(Appreciation, Connectedness, Humility, Empathy & Compassion)

4 Collaborating — Social Skills

(Communication Skills, Inclusion/Intercultural Competency)

5 Acting — Enabling Change

(Perseverance)

IITTI Reading Program & Activities
"Softest" Soft Skills
Measures awareness

IITTI Online Written Exams
"Hardest" Soft Skills
Measures accuracy   Sep 25, 2021

Cultural awareness   Emotional awareness
Appreciation   Communication awareness
Patience   Civility
        Business ethics
Empathy   Resilience   Connectedness
Reading Program & Activities (for business)

        Personal branding
Professional appearance
        Business etiquette
Dining etiquette   Social etiquette
Level 1, 2, 3 (for business)

Illustrations of social behavior while traveling
Patience   Environmental awareness
Empathy   Appreciation
    Civility   Social ethics
Reading Program & Activities (for tourist)

Personal appearance
        Social behavior while traveling
Dining etiquette for world travelers
Citizens of the World (for tourist)

Illustrations of social etiquette   Connectedness
        Environmental awareness
Patience   Civility
Empathy   Social ethics
Humility   Resilience   Appreciation
    Perseverance
Reading Program & Activities (for youth)

How to be proactive
        Personal grooming
    Social etiquette
How to set priority   What is win-win?
Listening skill   Team work
Youth

Figure 8.1: IDG skills as implemented by IITTI under the "Softest" Soft Skills (highlighted on left).
Source: IITTI (www.iitti.org).

The key is frequent exposures.

(How much exposure is "frequent" enough? It depends on many factors such as the background of the participant, the current stage of life, the people and culture surrounding the person, etc. Current state of research can only validate that the more exposures, the more likely a person is to develop such skills. Future development could use new technologies, such as AI, to help map the exact cause and effect of specific lessons to specific outcomes.)

For individuals: Enhancing upward mobility

For individuals, a strong civility credential could enhance upward mobility and employability, signaling to potential employers their proficiency in soft skills crucial for effective teamwork and leadership in multicultural environments.

In every job market, regardless of the industry, the ability to communicate effectively, collaborate, and navigate interpersonal relationships is crucial. The WCI provides a standardized metric to evaluate these essential soft skills, making it relevant across various sectors. From technology to service industries, the principles of civility underpinning the index are fundamental to professional success and organizational effectiveness.

I frequently tell my story to our team:

> As an engineer many years ago, I thought the way to better myself for promotion was by my technical know-hows. It was only after many years in the industry, and then starting my own company did I realized the other half of the equation was in people's relationships. That is, the soft skills. The higher up you go in the corporate world, or in business, it is the soft skills that matter most!

For companies: Enhancing company culture through civility credentials

Enhancing company culture through civility credentials involves integrating the principles and metrics of the WCI into the fabric of organizational life. By recognizing and valuing civility as a measurable asset, companies can foster a workplace environment that prioritizes respect, empathy, and effective communication among employees. This shift towards a civility-centric culture can have profound effects on organizational dynamics, employee satisfaction, and overall performance.

Integration into core values

Embedding civility credentials into the company's core values and mission statement signals a commitment to fostering a positive and inclusive work environment. It aligns employees with a shared understanding of what constitutes acceptable and desired behaviors, guiding interactions and decision-making processes.

Performance evaluation

Incorporating civility credentials as a new KPI for HR in internal performance evaluations provides a tangible measure of an employee's interpersonal effectiveness. This encourages employees to develop behaviors that contribute to a collaborative and respectful workplace, knowing that these aspects are valued alongside traditional performance metrics.

Recognition and rewards

Establishing recognition programs that celebrate individuals and teams who exemplify outstanding collaboration can further reinforce the importance of these behaviors. Rewards and acknowledgments for demonstrating high civility credentials can motivate employees to consistently engage in positive interactions.

Training and development

Offering training programs focused on developing the competencies measured by the WCI ensures that employees have the resources and support to improve their civility credentials. This can include workshops, seminars, and ongoing learning opportunities, such as the IITTI Reading Program and Activities, that address communication, empathy, conflict resolution, and cultural sensitivity.

Impact on recruitment

By promoting civility credentials as a cornerstone of the company culture, organizations can attract talent that excels in soft skills, further enhancing the work environment and team dynamics. This allows rapid enhancement of corporate culture when "new blood" already have the education before onboarding.

In summary, enhancing company culture through civility credentials creates a more productive workplace. It emphasizes the importance of interpersonal relationships in achieving organizational success, fostering an environment where employees feel respected and motivated to contribute their best. In a way, credentialing quantifies company culture.

Broader implications: ESG ratings and social impact

Eliminating misrepresentation

The World Civility Index plays a pivotal role in addressing the issue of greenwashing, a practice where organizations misleadingly tout their environmental and social efforts to appear more sustainable than they truly are. By providing an independent, third-party, standardized measure of civility, administered by the neutral IITTI NGO (similar to the International Organization for Standardization [ISO]), it eliminates conflicts of interests where a company does its own measurement, and the suspicion of misrepresentation. The WCI helps stakeholders in evaluating the transparency of a company's ESG initiatives, thus contributing to a more accountable approach to sustainability.

Ethical conduct

At its core, the WCI embodies principles of ethical conduct. The way to integrate these values into their operations and decision-making processes is through a long-term, systematic "reminder" on a daily basis, such as the micro-learning discussed above. We are not alone in this, but with Dr. Richard Thaler, who won the Nobel Prize for his "nudge theory", a concept in behavioral science which proposes small prompts can have big influences on behavior.

Stakeholder engagement

The WCI fosters a culture of active listening and empathy, enhancing stakeholder engagement. This can lead to more meaningful collaboration with environmental groups, communities, and consumers, ensuring that sustainability efforts are grounded in real, measurable actions and impacts, rather than just promotional rhetoric.

Employee involvement

By embedding soft skills into the organizational culture, the WCI can empower employees to become advocates for genuine sustainability practices. Engaged and informed employees in a safe and respectful workplace allow them to have the "mental space" to think about the "bigger things" such as climate change, and are thus more likely to hold their employers accountable to authentic ESG initiatives.

Comprehensive ESG assessment

Integrating civility metrics into ESG evaluations provides a more holistic view of a company's corporate responsibility, complementing traditional ESG metrics (which frequently treat the "S" in ESG as a second-class citizen!) by adding a layer of independent, quantitative assessment that highlights the company's commitment to ethical, transparent, and responsible behavior.

Enhancing reputation

In the long term, adherence to the principles measured by the WCI can enhance a company's reputation, making it more attractive to consumers, investors, and partners who prioritize sustainability and ethical conduct. This reputational boost can serve as a deterrent against greenwashing, as mentioned, as the risks of being exposed for misleading claims outweigh the potential benefits. The key is to have a neutral third party, such as the IITTI World Civility Index, in doing the "heavy lifting" in measurement so the numbers are real and believable.

In conclusion, the WCI's emphasis on ethical behavior, transparency, and accountability makes it a valuable tool in the fight against greenwashing. By promoting integrity in all aspects of business conduct, the index helps ensure that companies' sustainability claims are not only heard but also reflected in their true actions and impacts on the environment and society.

The world needs more than a GDP measurement for progress

The gross domestic product (GDP) has traditionally served as a metric for quantifying the total value of goods and services produced within a country. However, it does not adequately capture the well-being and quality of life experienced by its citizens, including aspects such as safety, respect, and overall life satisfaction. In certain instances, GDP can actually be a misleading indicator of societal progress. For example, during wartime, GDP may actually increase due to heightened production in the defense sector, such as the manufacturing of ammunition, despite the adverse effects on societal well-being. In this context, the World Civility Index emerges as a valuable supplementary metric, offering a more nuanced understanding of what truly contributes to human fulfillment and societal health.

For example, in 2022 the IITTI embarked on a wide-scale measurement of civility efforts in some selected countries. The results are quite different compared to a GDP measurement, as shown in Figure 8.2.

World Civility Index

The World Civility Index Country Average is calculated based on citizens' individual World Civility Index points, and a country's gross domestic product (GDP), Gini coefficient measuring wealth inequality, and human development index (HDI).

The derived mathematical formula allows the Country Average to reflect the effort taken by a country in terms of soft skills development. Rich countries are expected to do more in absolute terms, while less affluent ones can still earn respectable standing (as seen in the bar graph) if tangible, objective, measurable efforts are shown.

World Civility Index Country Average

Dec 30, 2022

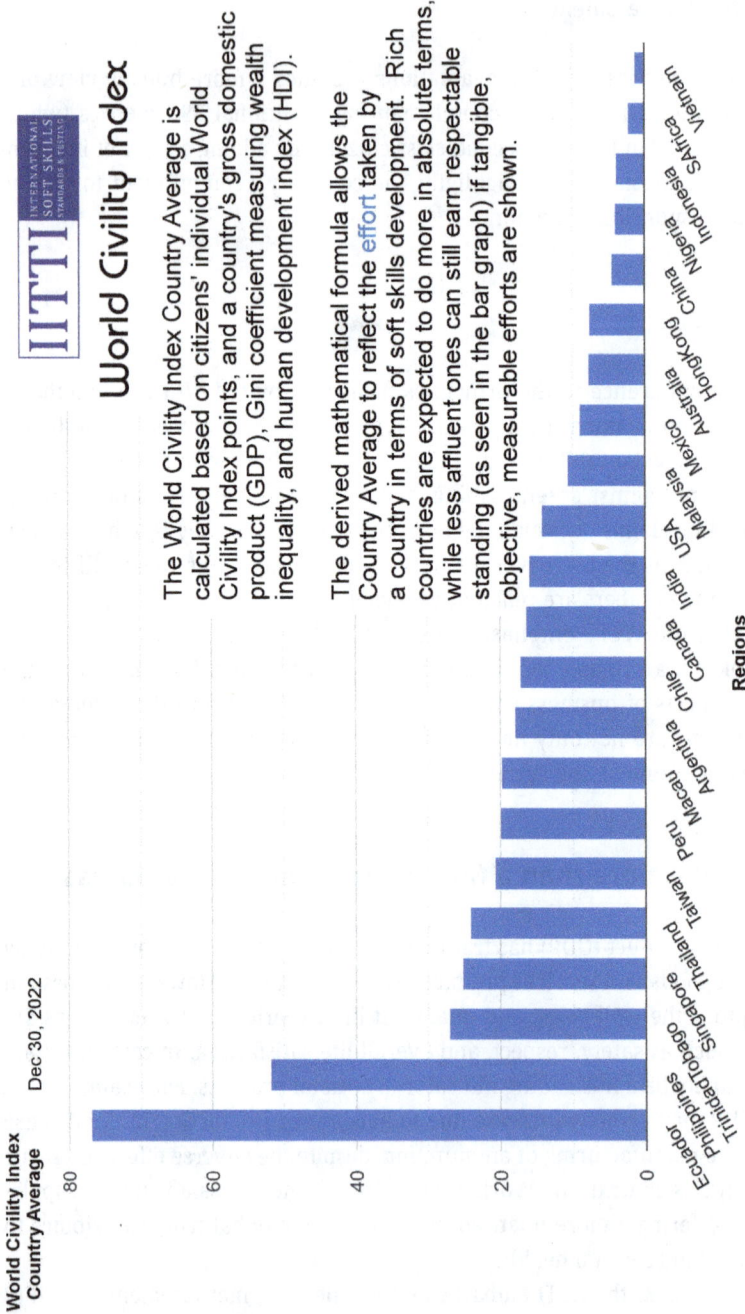

Bar graph generated via rapidtables.com and forms part of the IITTI World Civility Index whitepaper

Figure 8.2: Country average World Civility Index. Source: IITTI.

Real-world adoption and impact

The spread of the World Civility Index across 19 countries

The spread of the World Civility Index across 19 countries signifies its growing recognition and adoption as a valuable tool for enhancing soft skills globally. The IITTI group started out in 2011 writing a "Business Etiquette 101" standard, naively thinking it would take three weeks to finish. In reality, this 50-page document took four years before the group reached consensus and agreed that the standard was ready for publishing! But once published, there were overwhelming cheers among the many HR managers, as then there was an international authoritative standard on subject matters such as professional dress code that a company would like employees to follow but historically difficult to justify as there were no standard.

Why is topic such as professional attires relevant to inner qualities and IDGs? It is a non-verbal communication to show respect for others. It is a way to make others feel comfortable around you.

Collaboration and partnerships

The spread of the WCI has been facilitated by collaborations with local organizations, businesses, and civic groups. Particularly innovative are collaborations between historically distinct business categories in having synergy in driving its implementation and integration into existing training and development programs (e.g., case study 3 in the following section).

Case studies

We will highlight three case studies: (1) Tecnológico Universitario Espíritu Santo in Ecuador; (2) Asia United Bank in the Philippines; and (3) Daji Image (大吉形象) Boutique in China.

Case study 1: Fostering soft skills in higher education at Tecnológico Universitario Espíritu Santo in Ecuador

Background
In the evolving landscape of global education, the imperative to integrate soft skills into academic curricula has become increasingly recognized. Tecnológico Universitario Espíritu Santo in Ecuador, under the guidance of Viviana Aguayo Maruri, MBA, and president of the Association of Image Consultants International (AICI) Ecuador, has taken innovative steps to address this need among their MBA students.

Initiative

Viviana Aguayo Maruri has spearheaded an initiative leveraging the IITTI Reading Program to instill a habit of daily engagement with soft skills articles among her students. This program forms a cornerstone of her pedagogical approach, aiming to complement traditional academic learning with essential soft skills development.

Implementation

For example, over 300 students have actively participated in this program in 2021, engaging with a diverse range of articles curated by Viviana as well as other experts and publications vetted by the IITTI. Topics span social etiquette, professional image, business ethics, empathy, and intercultural awareness, all centered around the theme of what it takes to be a contributing, civil citizen for the twenty-first century.

Students were introduced to the IITTI Reading Program where a daily read on business etiquette, empathy, intercultural awareness earns them one point per day.

Outcomes

1. **Civility credentialing**: Each participating student has the opportunity to earn one World Civility Index point daily, accumulating tangible evidence of their commitment to soft skills development.
2. **Enhanced employability**: The initiative addresses the increasing demand among employers for proof of soft skills. Esteemed companies like Google, Apple, and Starbucks now consider such competencies as pivotal, often turning to the World Civility Index as a benchmark.
3. **Leadership and differentiation**: Students equipped with World Civility Index points not only stand out in the job market but also demonstrate leadership by introducing potential employers to the index. This proactive approach can reflect highly on a student.

Benefits for trainers

This case study also highlights how professional trainers can integrate the WCI into their training programs, elevating their professionalism and offering an independent, unbiased measurement of student progress. By adopting IITTI standards, trainers can validate their effectiveness through an internationally recognized framework.

Conclusion

The collaboration between Viviana Aguayo Maruri and Tecnológico Universitario Espíritu Santo exemplifies the transformative potential of integrating soft skills into higher education. Through the IITTI Reading Program, students are not only better prepared academically but also equipped with the interpersonal skills essential for success in the modern global economy. This case study serves as a model for educational institutions worldwide, showcasing the tangible benefits of prioritizing soft skills alongside traditional academic pursuits.

Case study 2: Enhancing corporate image and soft skills at Asia United Bank in the Philippines

Background

In the dynamic landscape of the banking sector, Asia United Bank (AUB), a prominent financial institution in the Philippines, recognized the necessity of enhancing its corporate image and the soft skills of its employees to maintain a competitive edge via exceptional customer service.

Initiative

AUB embarked on a comprehensive training program spearheaded by Carolina Tan, AICI CIP, a licensed IITTI Master Instructor renowned for her expertise in professional image consultancy. The collaboration aimed to elevate the bank's corporate image and equip its employees with essential soft skills, aligning with the principles of the WCI.

Implementation

Carolina Tan designed and executed a tailor-made training curriculum for AUB employees, focusing on key areas such as professional demeanor, business etiquette, and emotional intelligence. The program was structured to integrate with AUB's existing training frameworks, ensuring a holistic approach to employee development.

All participants earn two World Civility Index points as proof for HR internal performance measurement. The bank can also receive a "company average", a single number to put in their ESG report for investors, business partners, and customers.

Outcomes

1. **Elevated corporate image**: The training program resulted in a noticeable enhancement of AUB's corporate image, with employees projecting a more professional and confident demeanor that resonated positively with clients and stakeholders.
2. **Improved soft skills**: Employees benefited from a deeper understanding of soft skills on an on-going basis, leading to more effective communication, better conflict resolution, and enhanced teamwork within the bank.
3. **Increased customer satisfaction**: The emphasis on professionalism and soft skills translated into a gradually higher levels of customer satisfaction, as clients experienced a more attentive and empathetic service.
4. **Competitive advantage**: AUB's investment in soft skills and corporate image training provided the bank with a competitive advantage, distinguishing it in a crowded market and reinforcing its reputation as a customer-centric institution.
5. **Enhance confidence in ESG reporting**: By engaging an independent non-profit like IITTI to measure soft skills, AUB can report its social impact in their annual ESG reports with confidence. This is achieved through a concrete World Civility

Index number that provides a company-wide average. Such an annual, singular figure offers investors a clear view of changes and progress over the years.

Conclusion

Corporate culture is hard to come by. It not only takes effort, but it also takes time. It is something money cannot buy instantly! When a company starts early, it is just that much harder for competitors to catch up. AUB understands this, and their proactive approach not only enhances its corporate image and employee competencies, but also contributes to a more satisfying customer experience, underscoring the value of such initiatives in the banking sector.

Case study 3: Daji Image Boutique – blending professional image consulting with fashion retail in Guangzhou, China

Introduction

In the bustling cities of Guangzhou and Shenzhen, China, an innovative approach to boutique retail has emerged through Daji Image Boutique. Spearheaded by Amy Leung, a licensed IITTI Master Instructor, and her two business partners, both veteran boutique operators, Daji Image Boutique has redefined the shopping experience by integrating professional image consulting into the retail space.

Background

Amy Leung brought her expertise in professional image training to the venture, combining it with her partners' extensive experience in boutique management. This unique collaboration led to the creation of a boutique that not only sells clothing but also educates customers on professional image and attire suitable for various business contexts.

The concept

Dubbed the "IKEA effect" by yours truly, Daji Image Boutique operates on the principle that customers are drawn in by the value-added service of professional image consulting, which in turn influences their purchasing decisions. Similar to how IKEA customers are inspired by showroom designs to buy furniture, Daji customers receive personalized advice on professional dressing, which motivates them to purchase attire that aligns with their image goals.

Expansion

Starting from a single store, Daji has expanded to eight locations across Guangzhou and Shenzhen, areas known for their dynamic business environments and as manufacturing hubs, notably for electronics such as iPhones. This expansion reflects the strong market demand for a holistic approach to professional attire.

Services offered
Daji Image Boutique offers a range of services, including:
– Personalized image consulting sessions that guide customers on dressing for various business occasions.
– Workshops and seminars on professional image and etiquette, enhancing the boutique's role as an educational hub, where customers can earn World Civility Index points to show employers.
– A curated selection of clothing and accessories designed to meet the professional image needs of business professionals.

Customer experience
The synergy between professional image consulting and boutique retail has significantly enhanced the customer experience. Shoppers not only leave with high-quality attire but also with a deeper understanding of how to present themselves in professional settings, adding intangible value to their purchases.

Business model
The boutique's business model, which merges retail with service, has proven to be a key differentiator in the competitive fashion industry. By offering expert advice alongside clothing, Daji Image Boutique has established a loyal customer base that values the dual benefits of style and substance.

Impact
The success of Daji illustrates the growing recognition of professional image as a critical aspect of business success. It also highlights the potential for retail businesses to innovate by offering services that complement their products, thereby creating a more enriching shopping experience.

Conclusion
Daji Image Boutique's innovative approach, combining Amy Leung's expertise in professional image consulting with traditional boutique retail, has set a new standard in the industry. By focusing on the holistic needs of their clientele, Daji has not only achieved business success but has also empowered individuals to enhance their professional presence, demonstrating the transformative power of integrating service and retail in the fashion industry.

All three case studies demonstrate the tangible benefits of incorporating the WCI into organizational practices. By prioritizing soft skills, Tecnológico Universitario Espíritu Santo, Asia United Bank, and Daji Image Boutique not only enhanced their internal cultures, but also positively impacted their stakeholder relationships and competitive positioning, showcasing the broad applicability and value of the WCI in diverse industries.

Again, how do all these help promote the essence of IDGs?

As discussed, training in outward behavior can gradually develop internal traits like empathy.

Contribution to social cohesion

Beyond the corporate world, the adoption of the WCI in various countries contributes to broader social cohesion by promoting values of respect, empathy, and understanding. We don't have to go far but to turn on the TV and listen to the nowadays rhetoric from politicians to feel the toxic dialog.

In November 2023, breaking from tradition, the new Canadian Speaker of the House of Commons, requested politicians to exercise decorum and show respect for each other!

Greg Fergus was elected Speaker of the House of Commons on October 3, 2023, and, in an unprecedented move, wasted no time in criticizing fellow parliamentarians for being too disrespectful with each other, and pointed to the dysfunctional consequences where *"very little gets done!"*

Simply advocating for such qualities is half the equation. The other half is to have a common measurement so citizens can see value in getting such credentials as a personal interest for employment and promotion, yet such actions would be very much aligned with what the business and political world needs for better culture, and equally much needed for humanity as a whole to mend a deteriorating social fabric.

Perhaps election candidates should be required to earn some points on the World Civility Index before being qualified!

In an increasingly interconnected and digital world, these values are more important than ever for fostering harmonious and productive communities. In the next section, we will explore why a common measurement of inner qualities is crucial. This is significant not only because it promotes personal well-being and benefits corporate bottom lines, or polite politicians to get things done, but because the survival of humanity may very well depend on it!

Existential AI threats and the need for inner qualities standards

In the digital age, where interactions often occur online, the imperative for a standardized measure of civility has grown. The anonymity and distance provided by digital platforms can sometimes lead to a breakdown in social norms and respectful communication. A standardized measure of civility, such as the World Civility Index, aims to provide a clear pathway for evaluating and encouraging positive, respectful interactions in both personal and professional settings. This is crucial for fostering a healthy digital culture and ensuring that technological advancements are accompanied by a corresponding growth in respectful human interactions.

What is more urgent, and perhaps even an existential threat to humanity, is the advent of artificial intelligence (AI).

Recently, the IITTI team wrote about their thoughts on the World Economic Forum's "360° on AI Regulations" discussion held at Davos 2024 (WEF 2024):

> Like experts in AI, such as the 'Father of AI' Geoffrey Hinton (Nobel prize winner who quit Google as VP and engineering fellow), and Mo Gawdat (who quit Google as Chief Business Officer) warned about AI and suggested the only way is for humans to be role models and act as 'good parents' so we can build AI with good genes.
>
> But simply wishing humans would act with civility is tough! They won't do it! Unless there is a reason to do so.
>
> The strategy is to align the interests of individuals to the interests of humanity.
>
> The solution is to have an incentive, a reward system so that individuals are rewarded for good behavior. A 'report card' of sorts, measuring soft skills such as social etiquette, empathy, and intercultural awareness.
>
> We call it the 'World Civility Index' where people can get preferential treatment for employment, school admissions, airport lounge use, housing rental discount, better seats at restaurants, or more importantly, better pay when some kind of universal basic income (UBI) kicks in not too far in the future in our AI-dominated, post-work world.
>
> Let this world be no longer measured just by money, but also by your refinement!

How the World Civility Index quantifies IDG values for the world

Bridging Inner Development Goals with the World Civility Index involves translating the qualitative aspects of personal growth and development into quantifiable metrics that can be applied in business, politics, and communities. The IDGs focus on fostering core human values and skills such as empathy, mindfulness, resilience, and ethical awareness, which are crucial for both personal well-being and professional effectiveness. The WCI serves as a tool to measure these values in a structured manner, making it possible for businesses to integrate IDG principles into their corporate culture and performance evaluations. If we see that businesses drive society, what employers demand, the workforce will comply, and by extension, society will follow.

As the World Civility Index quantifies the IDGs inner qualities, IDGs, in a very direct way, help save the world! IDGs set the framework, the index charts the path.

The future of the World Civility Index lies in being adopted by IDG members, so that much more awareness can be realized by companies and employees. One possibility is a collaboration with other organizations such as the UN Global Compact (UNGC), which is made up of 10,000 companies committed to the UN SDGs.

Section 3: Going full circle: A personal transformation

We talked about how inner qualities, as quantified by a simple measurement called World Civility Index, could help businesses in improving corporate culture. And what companies demand, the workforce will comply, and by extension, society will also follow. We also talked about the very recent existential threat of AI and how this simple measurement of civility could incentivize citizens to refine their manners and inner self in order to be good role models for AI to learn from. Now we will go full circle to back to a personal journey of transformation.

This story spans some 30 years, comparing myself in a self-reflection when I was a young "hot shot" engineer, believing technical skills trump everything else, and fast forward to an older version of myself within the last few years, and how my mindset has changed. It illustrates the transformative power of the IDGs, not only in theory but in the tangible realities of life.

A personal journey of Patrick Chun

In the winter frost of January 2019, I embarked on a journey that would etch itself into the canvas of my heart. From the vibrant streets of Guangzhou, China, where I lived for four years to learn the language and culture, I traveled with the CFO of a partnering company, Alan Cheung, to the neighboring city of Shenzhen. Our spirits were high, fueled by the productive echoes of a marketing meeting that promised new horizons.

As we arrived at the bustling high-speed train station in Shenzhen, we were greeted by an unexpected spectacle – a throng of humanity, a living, breathing mosaic of lives in transit. The station, designed to cradle a modest congregation of perhaps a few thousands, was now awash with a wave of souls that seemed to stretch into infinity, perhaps 20,000 strong.

At that moment, Alan, as a Chinese national, with a gentle tone tinged with apology, revealed the heart of the matter – it was Chinese New Year's Eve. The air was electric with the pulse of anticipation, as countless individuals were caught in the tender grip of tradition, each seeking passage on the last train home to reunite with their kin for the cherished family gathering that marks the Lunar New Year.

Alan's apologies hung in the air, a testament to his concern that I, a visitor from the vast expanses of Canada, might find the dense tapestry of people overwhelming, a stark contrast to the open spaces I knew. He worried that the unforeseen swell of the crowd might fray the fabric of our meticulously planned schedule.

There was a time, in the days of my youth, when such a twist of fate would have sparked a storm within me, igniting the fires of frustration and discontent. But as I stood there, amidst the symphony of hurried footsteps whispered by each passerby, a profound realization dawned upon me.

Before me was not merely a crowd, but a living narrative of human connection, each individual a bearer of hope, love, and the timeless yearning to return to a place of distanced land. The air was thick with the scent of anticipation, each person a vessel of stories untold, carrying the weight of gifts and the promise of shared meals, a beacon of light calling them home.

And in that moment of clarity, as I gazed upon the sea of souls before me, a sense of awe washed over me, and I found myself uttering in hushed reverence, "Wow! 20,000 love stories!"

Conclusion

In this chapter, we highlighted how the framework of IDGs is quantified by the World Civility Index, enabling organizations to use it for internal performance measurements. This coupling of IDGs and the WCI serves, in some sense, as a breakthrough in human capital development, offering a way to gauge progress. In the corporate world, there is a saying: *You are flying blind without measurement!*

We discussed how we arrived at the conclusion that in order to help solve world problems, be it climate change, equity, or the threat of AI, the root cause is often humans' inability to make good choices due to a lack of inner qualities such as communication skills, empathy, and intercultural competency.

I invite you to join in an exercise of self-reflection on this critical revelation by examining and asking:

> *What exceptions are there to current and past events in history that were not caused by our own inability to make a wiser decision? Isn't it all in our heads?*

As previously stated, the World Civility Index quantifies IDGs inner qualities, IDGs, in a very direct way, help save the world! IDGs set the framework, the index charts the path.

We have highlighted three case studies to show the range of possible applications. Each being a success story achieved through the significant efforts of believers who risked time, energy, and perhaps most precious of all, professional reputation, to see it to fruition. It is like what Nelson Mandela once said:

> *It always seems impossible until it is done!*

References

Ariely, D. (2009). Dan Ariely on our buggy moral code (2009) [Video uploaded by JANE72427, Apr. 26, 2011]. YouTube. https://www.youtube.com/watch?v=MNFXuJLZcwY.

Sampson, R. J., Raudenbush, S. W., & Earls, F. (1997). Neighborhoods and violent crime: A multilevel study of collective efficacy. *Science*, 277 (5328), 918–924. https://doi.org/10.1126/science.277.5328.918.

Schonert-Reichl, K. A., & Hymel, S. (2007). Educating the heart as well as the mind: Social and emotional learning for school and life success. *Education Canada*, 47(2), 20–25. https://eric.ed.gov/?id=EJ771005.

WEF (World Economic Forum) Davos 2024. https://www.weforum.org/events/world-economic-forum-annual-meeting-2024/sessions/360-on-ai-regulations/.

Jonathan Rhodes, Jaime Blakeley-Glover, Andy Miller and Alan Taylor

Chapter 9
Measuring and training Inner Development Goals: Developing inner drivers for achieving sustainability goals

Abstract: Organizations worldwide are pledging ambitious climate action, but translating these commitments into meaningful progress remains a significant challenge. This chapter introduces an approach focused on Inner Development Goals (IDGs) – measuring and training the critical inner capacities that enable individuals to become effective agents of environmental change within their own lives and within organizations. Through an insightful narrative, the chapter chronicles the journey of developing the Inner Development Goals – Adapted (IDG-A) scale to rigorously assess 29 personal skills, qualities, and mindsets across six key dimensions: self-awareness, cognitive skills, caring for others and the world, social skills, driving change, and feelings of organizational belonging. Research validates the IDG-A in evaluating employees' readiness for climate action. Moreover, the chapter presents the meaning, awareness, and purpose (MAP) model – an experiential coaching process designed to activate teams by connecting them deeply to the meaning behind sustainability efforts, fostering collective awareness, instilling a shared sense of purpose, and translating their inner work into consistent outward impact. Findings show the MAP model's benefits in elevating IDG-A scores and catalyzing measurable climate initiatives compared to conventional training approaches. When focusing on human inner drivers as the catalyst for organizational outer change, this chapter offers a framework for addressing a critical impediment: the intrinsic motivation required from employees to fully embrace their role in achieving an organization's environmental goals.

Keywords: climate change, sustainability, Inner Development Goals, organizational change, MAP

Introduction

As the reality of climate change becomes increasingly dire, organizations around the world are under immense pressure to take substantive action. Ambitious sustainability goals and public commitments to reduce carbon footprints and achieve net-zero emissions are becoming the norm. However, a critical gap remains: successfully translating these laudable pledges into meaningful behavioral changes and progress on the ground that breaks the inertia of business as usual.

https://doi.org/10.1515/9783111453729-010

Despite having the technical knowledge, resources, and strategic plans in place, a report by Accenture (2022) found that 93% of companies struggle to inspire their employees to fully embrace and drive climate initiatives forward with consistent effort. A fundamental disconnect exists between the high-level goals set by leadership and the intrinsic motivation required from individual employees to proactively adapt their mindsets and behaviors in service of those goals.

This chapter explores an innovative approach aimed at bridging this divide between intention and action on climate change within organizations. Focusing on the concept of Inner Development Goals (IDGs) and rigorously measuring the personal skills, qualities, and mindsets required for individuals to become effective agents of environmental change. This work equips organizations and coaches working to support businesses, with powerful tools to motivate and activate their workforces.

Through rich narratives, empirical research findings, and the development of novel assessment frameworks like the Inner Development Goals – Adapted (IDG-A) scale, this chapter focuses on a human-centric pathway towards developing the intrinsic motivation, self-awareness, and sense of purpose necessary for employees to fully commit to their organization's sustainability efforts.

Motivation

Sarah Miller was no ordinary British professional. She grew up in a working-class family in the southwest of England, and despite humble beginnings, she excelled academically and became the first member of her family to go to university. After graduating with first-class honors, Sarah began her corporate career in the finance industry in London. Her meteoric rise was fueled by a relentless work ethic, analytical brilliance, and unwavering determination to succeed – traits that were somewhat unconventional for a young woman in the male-dominated finance world at the time.

Sarah's journey through the corporate trenches included pivotal roles as a data analyst at two prominent insurance firms and later at a hedge fund. In these capacities, she emerged as the linchpin for the financial growth and success of these businesses. If we were to liken those organizations to a basketball team, they would undoubtedly have been the '96 Chicago Bulls, with Sarah standing as the Michael Jordan of the corporate court. She not only led but also inspired, worked tirelessly, and consistently demanded and delivered results.

Yet, as the narrative of every great individual within a world-class team unfolds, there comes a juncture when a new direction beckons; a choice point, and the pursuit of a fresh challenge becomes inevitable.

Sarah's quest for a new challenge led her to identify the most formidable role within her current finance organization: environmental, social, and governance (ESG) leadership. The mere contemplation of this ambitious undertaking amplified a creative fire within her, culminating in a meticulously crafted pitch after 16 hours of dedicated effort. The result? A ground-breaking role as the head of thought leadership and net-zero.

Undeterred by the inherent challenges, Sarah orchestrated an informal conversation with the ever-busy chief executive officer (CEO), strategically planting the seeds of this novel role over a cup of coffee. Three days later, a new chapter unfolded as Sarah assumed her position, tasked with shaping a team poised to undertake a challenging net-zero goal.

Her first order of business? A pragmatic dive into the realm of data. Armed with an arsenal of spreadsheets, Sarah immersed herself in a comprehensive fact-finding mission. Reports, academic papers, and government policies became her literary companions, while conferences provided dynamic classrooms for gaining insights into the complex struggles of ESG within the industry. With each endeavor, she enriched her expanding datasheets with best practices, navigating the terrain with strategic finesse.

Over the initial months, Sarah not only discovered what worked but also gained profound insights into the less traveled paths that proved less effective. As her understanding of the sustainability impacts of the finance industry grew, so did her education. She looked beyond conventional boundaries, encompassing United Nations initiatives, global directives, government projects, organizational pledges, and ambitious targets. Fueled by this wealth of knowledge and her eye for detail, she felt equipped with the requisite skills and tools to enlighten others on the path to achieving net-zero targets.

The culmination of her efforts occurred six months into her role when the executive team, on this occasion led by Sarah, made their climate pledge public – a commitment to work towards three scopes, and achieve net-zero by 2030. The seeds of change had sprouted, and Sarah found herself at the forefront of a collective endeavor towards a sustainable future.

Drawing upon her comprehensive assessment of the company's carbon footprint, Sarah charted a course toward the ambitious goal of achieving net-zero. The objectives, as meticulously outlined, appeared not only feasible but grounded in a pragmatic approach: localize supply chains where possible, curtail energy consumption (particularly in business travel), enforce waste reduction measures, and elevate employee awareness regarding sustainability practices. With a specific goal and a meticulously detailed plan, Sarah set the stage for an organizational change. However, amidst the precision of her strategies and the clarity of her objectives, there lingered a factor that had eluded Sarah's initial considerations: human motivation.

In this dynamic equation of corporate evolution, the variable of human behavior emerged as an unforeseen challenge. The attitudes, perceptions, and the inertia of routine posed a barrier, one that was not captured on spreadsheets and strategic plans. It was a realization that prompted Sarah to reevaluate her approach and seek solutions that would bridge the gap between intention and action.

To Sarah's astonishment, an intriguing paradox unfolded within the organization. Despite being well-versed in the various avenues leading to the net-zero target, employees exhibited a surprising ambivalence toward altering their existing behaviors. A disconnect from the net-zero goal presented itself, and a sense of stagnation permeated the workplace, as if the gears of change were rusted in place. It was not merely a matter of awareness; it was a poignant realization that a personal connection to the overarching goal was lacking.

The workforce, it seemed, was entangled in the vines of habitual routines, exhibiting a resistance to change that mirrored an unwillingness to untangle from the familiar. More than just a lack of motivation, there was a conspicuous absence of the skills and qualities required to activate both themselves and their peers. The workplace had become an environment of inertia, a paradox where knowledge coexisted with a resistance to change.

Puzzled by this apparent motivational vacuum, Sarah assumed the role of an organizational detective, driven by an unwavering determination to decipher this enigma. It was a challenge that resonated with her go-getter spirit, prompting her to embark on a search for a solution that would untangle the knots of complacency and set the stage for a harmonious convergence of intention and action.

Developing a research team and shaping the project

While Sarah Miller delved into the labyrinth of motivational challenges, a parallel convergence of minds was underway in the digital realm: over a hundred executive coaches, business executives, psychologists, and researchers, all committed to the cause of climate change, gathered in a virtual rendezvous hosted by the Climate Coaching Alliance (CCA). The focal point of this virtual gathering was nothing less than ambitious: activating teams for climate change.

After the formalities and initial introductions, conversations evolved and shifted as participants seamlessly transitioned into breakout rooms, each dedicated to delving into specific areas of the overarching theme. Picture 48 Zoom windows illuminating Breakout Room 3, under the able chairmanship of Dr Alyson Whybrow, a founding member of the CCA and an accomplished executive coach. The spotlight of this particular breakout room was fixed on the intriguing domain of activating teams through coaching frameworks.

Participants discussed a wealth of concepts and frameworks, battle-tested in the trenches of activating teams toward climate initiatives. Familiar models like the GROW (goal, reality, options, and will; Whitmore, 1996) model and the solution-focused coaching model (see Grant, 2022) took center stage, creating a series of tried-and-tested methodologies. But an underlying issue began to surface: while these frameworks proved effective in the realm of individual coaching, their utility within the complex systemic dynamics of sustainability and team change remained elusive.

Beyond the subjective views voiced on the Zoom call, broader research revealed a stark reality about the struggles organizations face in driving impactful climate action. Bain & Company's comprehensive survey and interviews involving 300 organizations uncovered a disheartening statistic: a staggering 98% of climate programs fail in organizations, with 81% deeming the applied frameworks and approaches to be of only moderate value (Davis-Peccoud, 2017).

The reasons behind this perceived inefficacy seem to stem from a range of factors, including the ability to form a robust business case, communications, and an inability to embed sustainability in the way the business runs on a day-to-day basis. The impact of this in many organizations is a culture that creates a misalignment between the personal motivations of individual employees and the organizational/team objectives related to sustainability. Many climate initiatives fail to create an emotional resonance or sense of deeper purpose that connects people's core values and intrinsic drives to the environmental goals being set. Without this internalized commitment from individuals, organizational climate efforts risk becoming merely compliance-driven box-ticking exercises devoid of passion, stamina, and what it takes to identify and drive through the changes required. Even employees who intellectually understand the importance of sustainability can remain unmotivated if the initiatives feel disconnected from their own "why" – the personal reasons that give an issue spiritual or existential significance. Furthermore, a lack of frameworks that firstly bridge the gap between personal concern and professional action and secondly that bridge team and organizational divides around shared purpose seemed to undermine climate initiatives. Differing motivations, perspectives, and accountabilities across levels created a dysfunctional siloed environment rather than an aligned collective force.

The consensus from this data emerged like an unwavering verdict: the prevailing approach by most organizations was failing to truly activate their human capital and tap into the intrinsic drivers required to power authentic, sustained climate action from the ground up. Clearly, a fundamentally new paradigm for engaging the human factor was desperately needed. This sobering diagnosis of ineffectiveness provided the platform for the novel solution proposed by this research.

In response, a compact but determined research interest group coalesced during the call. Based in the United Kingdom were Dr Alyson Whybrow, Tabitha Jayne, Jaime Blakeley-Glover, and Dr Jonathan Rhodes, with additional expertise contributed by Alan Taylor in Australia and Andy Miller from Canada. Their mission: to delve into the specifics of personal characteristics relevant to climate change, paving the way to construct a comprehensive method that other coaches could wield as a blueprint for their coaching endeavors.

As the group grappled with their first question – what aspects should be measured to gauge effectiveness? – the IDG framework stepped into the spotlight. This framework held the promise of offering a perspective on personal characteristics crucial for climate change engagement. The second question, equally pivotal, revolved around identifying individuals who could serve as test pilots for the measurements and interventions crafted by the group.

As a segment of the research team set out on the journey to pinpoint willing organizations for their research, Jonathan, based at the University of Plymouth and cofounder of Imagery Coaching, adopted a distinctive strategy. He cast a wide net within his academic domain, advertising the project "Measuring Inner Development Goals" among his undergraduate and master's students. Isabelle Rochmankowsk, an astute undergraduate, eagerly joined forces with Jonathan, forming a dynamic partnership as they delved into uncharted territories, intent on deciphering how to measure skills and qualities for inner development.

Their goal centered around the construction of a robust assessment tool, a process that required collaboration with focus groups composed of individuals with extensive experience within organizational settings and as climate coaches.

Focus groups: Crafting a blueprint for Inner Development Goals assessment

The objective was clear: orchestrate open discussions through focus groups to curate a collection of items that could seamlessly integrate into any organization's toolkit. The goal was to create a robust evaluation mechanism for inner goals, underpinned by personal skills and qualities of the IDG framework. This, in turn, would catalyze meaningful climate dialogues and pave the way for proactive measures. Armed with the five originally identified dimensions – relationship to self, cognitive skills, caring for others and the world, social skills, and driving change – alongside the collection of 23 skills and qualities (Inner Development Goals, 2022), the research team convened two distinct focus groups.

In the first group, comprising six CEOs, the emphasis lay on leveraging their high-level perspectives to scrutinize and refine the five dimensions and their related sub-themes. Simultaneously, the second group, comprising five executive coaches external to the research team, brought a meticulous and specialized viewpoint to the table. Their collective mission, again to dissect each of the five dimensions including the associated 23 skills and qualities and map out how these could seamlessly interlace to form a comprehensive questionnaire. In this collaborative forum, the fusion of executive leadership wisdom and coaching acumen became the mixture in which the foundation for assessing IDGs took shape.

In the realm of research, one quickly learns that plans rarely unfold as anticipated. The journey of our focus groups, each conducted online with a duration of approximately 1.5 hours, was no exception. In the CEO focus group, a consensus swiftly emerged on the appropriateness of the identified five dimensions. However, an astute observation highlighted a missing link: a gap in the IDG framework. In response, the CEOs introduced a sixth dimension named "organizational belonging". One CEO eloquently voiced the sentiment that the IDG framework "misses the link between the individual and their working environment, which is where the change is set to occur".

Meanwhile, the discussions within the executive coaching focus group unfolded independently, shielded from the insights of the CEOs. Surprisingly, the executive coaches delved into an additional dimension, labeling it "culture connection". Their focus encompassed crucial aspects such as "aligning personal values to the organization", "role clarity", and "feeling heard during team meetings".

Harnessing the wealth of insights gleaned from these distinct discussions, a separate group of students, not privy to the original focus group deliberations but using transcripts, embarked on the meticulous task of refining a set of questions. These questions were designed to align with the 23 skills and qualities identified in the original IDG framework (refer to Table 9.1, items 1–23). Additionally, an extra set of six questions (Table 9.1, items 24–29) was tailored to capture the essence of the newly introduced sixth dimension. This amalgamation of perspectives and dimensions culminated in the birth of the Inner Development Goals – Adapted (IDG-A) questionnaire. Much like the pioneers of the IDG framework, the research group embraced openness in science, freely sharing the scale to foster collaborative advancement in the field.

Table 9.1: Inner Development Goals – Adapted (IDG-A).

Please circle one per row	Strongly disagree	Disagree	Neutral	Agree	Strongly agree
1 I am aware of my values and purpose and am committed to my goals.	1	2	3	4	5
2 I act with sincerity, honesty, and integrity.	1	2	3	4	5
3 I have a willingness to be vulnerable and embrace change and consistently develop.	1	2	3	4	5
4 I am reflective with my own thoughts, feelings, and desires.	1	2	3	4	5
5 I can live in the here and now, without judgment and in a state of open-ended presence.	1	2	3	4	5
6 I critically review others' views, evidence, and plans without bias.	1	2	3	4	5
7 I have an understanding of, and skills in, working with complex and systemic conditions and causalities.	1	2	3	4	5

Table 9.1 (continued)

Please circle one per row	Strongly disagree	Disagree	Neutral	Agree	Strongly agree
8 I understand and actively make use of insights from differing perspectives.	1	2	3	4	5
9 I can make sense out of complex stories and patterns.	1	2	3	4	5
10 I have a long-term vision and can formulate goals and sustain commitment.	1	2	3	4	5
11 I relate to others and to the world with a basic sense of appreciation, gratitude, and joy.	1	2	3	4	5
12 I have a keen sense of being connected with and/ or being a part of a larger whole, such as a community, humanity, or global ecosystem.	1	2	3	4	5
13 I act in accordance with the needs of the situation without concern for my own importance.	1	2	3	4	5
14 I relate to others, myself, and nature with kindness, empathy, and compassion and address related suffering.	1	2	3	4	5
15 I really listen to others to: foster genuine dialogue, manage conflicts constructively, and to adapt communication to suit diverse groups.	1	2	3	4	5
16 I motivate others and help facilitate collaborative relationships with diverse individuals, characterized by psychological safety and genuine co-creation.	1	2	3	4	5
17 I am willing and competent to embrace diversity and include people and collectives with different views and backgrounds.	1	2	3	4	5
18 I show trust, create, and maintain trusting relationships.	1	2	3	4	5
19 I inspire and mobilize others to engage in shared purposes.	1	2	3	4	5
20 I stand up for values, make decisions, take decisive action and, if need be, challenge and disrupt existing structures and views.	1	2	3	4	5
21 I generate and develop original ideas, innovate, and am willing to disrupt conventional patterns.	1	2	3	4	5

Table 9.1 (continued)

Please circle one per row	Strongly disagree	Disagree	Neutral	Agree	Strongly agree
22 I sustain and communicate a sense of hope, positive attitude, and confidence in the possibility of meaningful change.	1	2	3	4	5
23 I stay engaged and remain determined and patient even when efforts take a long time to bear fruit.	1	2	3	4	5
24 My values and goals align to my organizations' and teams'.	1	2	3	4	5
25 I have detailed role clarity, autonomy, and feel accountable.	1	2	3	4	5
26 Stressful situations are dealt with as a collective team and there is a culture of support, compassion, and learning.	1	2	3	4	5
27 It is easy to contribute and feel heard and valued in meetings.	1	2	3	4	5
28 Strategy is discussed and disseminated, and I have a sense of team belonging.	1	2	3	4	5
29 I contribute to the collective vision, have clear targets, and can track progress of myself and team.	1	2	3	4	5

Source: Reproduced with permission from the authors (Rhodes et al., 2023).

Subsequent to the formulation of the questionnaire, the research group proactively sought validation by sharing it with the two focus groups, inviting their critical assessment and feedback. The response was resoundingly positive, with both focus groups unanimously endorsing the suitability of the questionnaire, affirming that the instrument effectively assessed the skills and qualities crucial for individuals engaged in change initiatives. However, one potential issue raised was the possibility of self-reporting bias, where respondents may respond in a way that presents themselves in an overly positive light rather than being fully objective. To address this, the IDG-A employed three strategies. First, the phrasing of questions avoided leading or prescriptive language that could prime respondents. Additionally, the anonymity of responses was ensured to reduce socially desirable responding. Finally, before delivering the IDG-A we informed participants that the responses, although confidential, require honesty as scores will shape future research. With robustness a key focus, the next step was to test-drive the IDG-A in the field.

Test-driving the IDG-A and beyond

As the IDG-A was being shaped, the main portion of the research group had recruited four global organizations to test the measure. A pilot study, involving 39 participants, ranging from those highly engaged with climate issues to those more ambivalent, was conducted. Participants were chosen by the organizations (not the research team), selected based on their roles, which involved sustainability in some capacity. This pilot study served as a test-drive for the IDG-A. The participants, comprising 14 females and 25 males, with a mean age of 31 (SD = 10.5), completed the test twice, then had a debrief interview. The retest window was available a week after the initial test and remained open for six weeks. Initially, only seven respondents completed the questionnaire in time for their data to be included in the original publication, however, since then, a commendable 31 out of the original 39 participants have participated in the retest. To gauge the reliability of the IDG-A, a correlation score above 0.8 is considered strong, with a score of 1 indicating perfect reliability. Impressively, the reliability of the IDG-A stands at 0.89, signifying that the IDG-A questionnaire demonstrates strong reliability.

Moving forward, exploration extended to the six domains, aiming to unveil any potential relationships. The initial assumption was that each dimension possesses a unique quality, leading us to expect minimal, if any, significantly strong correlations. However, as is often the case when developing questionnaires, findings diverged from this expectation. Contrary to the initial hypothesis, most domains and the combined average score exhibited noteworthy relationships with each distinct domain. This intriguing revelation suggests that the total score serves as a robust indicator of inner development. It appears that the domains, far from being mutually exclusive, intricately link to one another, forming a cohesive framework that collectively contributes to the assessment of inner development.

Delving beyond the mere statistical relationships and probability values, the questionnaire's intriguing items unfolded as a catalyst for deep conversations about climate and personal growth. In debrief sessions with participants, the majority shared instances where the questions not only ignited engaging discussions with colleagues but also penetrated into essential topics such as values and communication. What materialized surpassed the boundaries of a conventional questionnaire; it organically morphed into an intervention. The IDG-A actively shaped dialogues and, in the process, evoked a profound inquisitiveness regarding individual motivations rooted in collective values within organizational contexts. During debrief conversations with participants, the outcome seemed to be an activation of teams through enhanced self-awareness, paving the way for more cohesive and purpose-driven collaboration.

Upon reflection, the research team recognized that they had acquired a significant measure of personal skills and qualities seamlessly intertwined with organizational actions. However, eight months into the project, a setback emerged with the departure of two crucial members who had played instrumental roles in shaping our collective thinking – their absence attributed to workload and illness. This unforeseen turn of events entrusted the responsibility to Andy, Alan, Jaime, and Jonathan to navigate the final phase of the research. Their focus shifted towards investigating whether a meticulously designed climate intervention could not only influence the elevation of IDG scores but also trigger meaningful net-zero behaviors. This critical juncture refocused the team's unwavering determination to stretch the boundaries of their research and delve into the practical implications of their findings within the realms of climate action and individual well-being.

Adverts went out on social media platforms and phone calls were made in the hope to recruit participants for a small study investigating "measuring and training Inner Development Goals". In this buzzing arena of outreach, Sarah Miller's eyes caught wind of the advert, and a flicker of recognition danced across her thoughts: "Inner Development Goals . . . where have I heard that before?" she pondered. The answer lay within the recesses of her conference notes, a topic that had sparked her interest in a bygone event. Driven by her penchant for data, research, and empirically grounded interventions, she followed the link and swiftly coordinated a meeting with the research team.

Sarah Miller, known for her efficiency and aversion to time-wasting, prefers straight talk and direct answers. Her initial encounter was with Jaime, a seasoned professional with over two decades immersed in sustainability and ESG, possessing the adaptability to ensure Sarah felt heard and understood. In the first few minutes of their interaction, the alignment became apparent to Sarah – this was a project she envisioned within the corridors of her company.

With no time to spare, Sarah cut to the chase, questioning Jaime on the starting point. "Do we begin with our organizational goal?" she inquired. Jaime's response was a strategic redirection. "No," he asserted, "we commence with 'Why should you personally care?' We firmly believe that motivation, particularly intrinsic motivation, is the cornerstone for goal setting. Setting targets without individual buy-in, without understanding the 'why', turns the endeavor into an uphill battle." Music to Sarah's ears.

Sarah continued to question Jaime: "Okay, so you start with the why, then what happens next?"

"Imagery," Jaime responded.

Training Inner Development Goals

At the project's inception, our research team operated devoid of a specific method or framework; instead, the research group navigated through a cacophony of ideas, theories, and a diverse array of approaches each team member brought to the table. Amidst this noise, a foundational belief emerged: they wouldn't focus on teaching methods to achieve net-zero. The stumbling block, as people often express, lies not in the lack of knowledge but in the motivation to act. It's akin to understanding the importance of daily fruit and vegetable intake for health or committing to 30 minutes of daily exercise: knowledge exists, action falters. In tune with two of the IDG domains – relationship to self and cognitive skills – they aimed to commence with personal meaning. This commenced discussions surrounding personal values, fostering self-awareness. Simultaneously, they delved into cognitive skills through the exploration and coaching of imagery, an immersive experience that you are invited to trial now.

Wherever you find yourself, take a moment to pause. In the theater of your mind, in a moment we are going to ask you to transport yourself into the future as if a time machine has been unveiled and you've harnessed its power for time travel. So, let's propel ourselves 25 years into the future. Before you embark on this mental journey, allow us to provide some scaffolding.

Imagine this: goals have been achieved, climate pledges have been steadfastly kept, and the clean air resonates with motivation evident in the vibrant ambiance surrounding you. Achievement manifests in conversations and expressions. Even the wildlife contributes to the melody of a thriving environment. This is the optimistic future, one that you and others have diligently worked towards.

Take a moment to immerse yourself in this imagined scene – layering the sounds, the scents, sensations of the air, the visual elements, how you move, and how you feel being in this vivid landscape.

Such positive imagery is a rarity in our mental repertoire, often overshadowed by bleak narratives and tales of impending doom. Attempts to think positively frequently revert to negative probabilities, limiting the expansiveness of our imagination, a crucial cognitive skill to solving any challenge. Consequently, the training of our thought processes must be personalized and anchored in positive outcomes.

But why does this personalization matter? Its significance lies in aligning an issue with individual emotions, values, and behaviors, thereby transforming change from a mere aspiration into an essential imperative. At the core of our approach lies the articulation of a crystal-clear message: Why is this important to me? In a quest for meaning, the research team painstakingly crafted a well-defined program, seamlessly weaving together personal emotions, values, mindsets, attitudes, cognitions, and behaviors. This detailed flow, a choreography aptly termed the meaning, awareness, and purpose (MAP) model, endeavors to reveal the interconnected layers propelling meaningful change that links you to your team and your organization.

Partnering with two major corporations grappling with motivational challenges akin to those faced by Sarah Miller, she watched our study unfold, eager for her company to start the project if the results suited her needs. Using the IDG-A, baseline scores were assessed, and no discernible differences were discovered between the organizations, highlighting the similarities in their employees' skills and qualities.

To test the MAP model, a control group organization was needed, who would receive the well-known and highly successful approach of carbon literacy training, while the other received the MAP model. Carbon literacy training lasted for 15 hours over 10 weeks, dissecting strategies for climate action and resulted in an organizational project. On the other hand, the MAP group, which had a total of 9 hours over 10 weeks, delved into intrinsic motivation headed by Andy and Jaime, explored imaginative solutions for change with Jonathan, and triggered a shift towards purpose (How do my actions impact others?), aligned with the IDG framework domains: caring for others and the world, social skills, and enabling change.

While the carbon literacy training group received a conventional top-down approach with goals set by leadership, the MAP group took an employee-driven path. Forming this group proved challenging initially, as individual participants arrived with widely varying levels of motivation, personal meanings attached to climate change, and comfort exploring inner drivers. Some were highly passionate environmental activists, while others were relatively disconnected from the issue. Through the early MAP workshops on self-discovery and visioning, these divergent individual "MAPs" initially occurred as conflicts and barriers to team-wide cohesion. Vocal activists could come across as preachy, while the disengaged seemed apathetic. However, as the group delved deeper into mutual understanding, perspective taking, and caring for each other's journeys, a team MAP emerged organically.

The diverse composition – a microcosm of the broader organizational workforce – became a strength rather than an obstacle. Safety was built for the disengaged to become curious, and the activists learned to inspire through listening. Collectively, they crafted an authentic, employee-led sustainability goal that resonated personally while promoting the new organizational belonging dimension. Specific systems thinking workshops under the guidance of Alan and Jaime enabled this group to turn their individual epiphanies into real-world projects and accountability partnerships across differences. A common "language" took root, fueled by renewed openness to others' experiences. While conflicts still arose, the team's shared investment in crafting and sharing their goal created a cascading effect, with the blueprint of the journey shown on Figure 9.1. The MAP model shows the coaching process which progresses from discussing individual meaning through to personal action, then on to team meaning and team action. After one cycle, the individual and the team operate together, thus making the numbers and direction of the process moot.

In contrast, carbon literacy participants reported gaining valuable climate education, but often perceived it as an obligatory exercise divorced from their inner world. Some found the MAP model's self-work more uncomfortable initially but described it as catalyzing deeper personal breakthroughs. The contrasting outcomes highlighted the power of the MAP model for activating teams in a grassroots way – bridging individual inner work to collective outer impact.

In a surprising twist, IDG-A scores soared in the MAP group whilst the carbon literacy training group remained static, showing a significant difference between the two groups – a resounding testament to the impact of personal inner development within the realm of climate coaching.

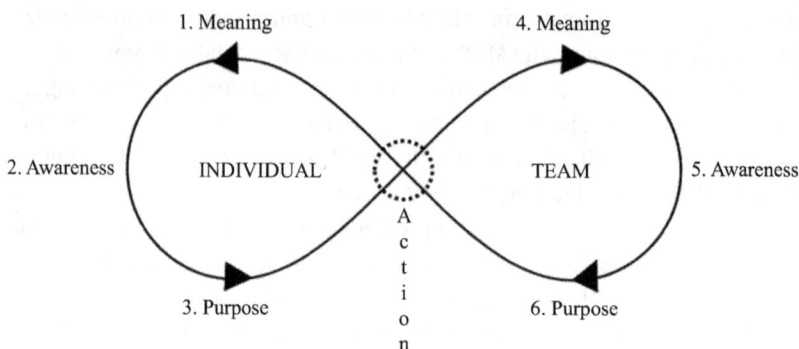

Figure 9.1: The MAP model. Source: Reproduced with permission from the authors (Rhodes et al., 2023).

As the results trickled in, Sarah Miller eagerly delved into the findings, keen to uncover the impact on the two organizations. Her expectations ran high, tempered only by a touch of cautious optimism. The question lingered: Could this research, even if it successfully activated other teams and organizations and improved inner development, evoke a similar response from hers?

To her delight, the results didn't just meet but exceeded her expectations.

Two months later, Sarah's team underwent the MAP model intervention and exhibited a remarkable change. Energized by the process, the team seamlessly transitioned from theoretical understanding to practical application. Encouraged by the newfound clarity on personal values and motivations, they initiated a small-scale climate action project within the organization. This initial endeavor not only bolstered their confidence but also served as a catalyst for broader engagement.

The success of this additional project laid the foundation for more ambitious ventures. Empowered by the MAP model, Sarah's team formulated a series of net-zero goals that intricately connected personal targets, team aspirations, and community initiatives. The collaborative spirit fostered by the MAP intervention not only propelled the team towards their climate action goals but also fostered a sense of shared purpose and togetherness. What began as a tentative exploration had evolved into a robust framework guiding Sarah's team towards meaningful contributions to both organizational and environmental well-being.

Beyond the research

This research has sparked extensive global discussions among government and business leaders across diverse industries and sectors. While we cannot disclose the names of specific organizations, the IDG-A measure has been downloaded and utilized thousands of times by entities around the world, indicating its widespread adoption and appeal.

Some broader trends have emerged: the approach seems to resonate particularly well in larger, multinational organizations with globally distributed workforces and operations. The challenges of aligning employee mindsets and channeling passionate but scattered sustainability efforts into cohesive action appear magnified in these complex environments. The MAP model has proven valuable in these situations for unifying disconnected "green champions" under a shared purpose and vision.

Interestingly, the framework has also gained traction in more hierarchical, traditional industries like manufacturing, energy, and natural resources extraction. Here, the ability to inspire grassroots-level commitment to environmental goals, rather than mere top-down compliance, has been a key driver of adoption. Regardless of industry, size, or structure, organizations seem to gravitate towards the IDG-A and MAP model when seeking human-centric solutions – tools that tap into the innate psychological and emotional drivers required to fully activate their workforces as agents of sustainability and positive climate impact.

For Sarah Miller, who has left her ESG role and is now a CEO, this journey has taken on a personal passion, and the solutions generated have proven to be innovative. In her current team, she is actively engaged in the pursuit of sustainable goals and shared leadership, effectively bridging the gap between individual awareness, collective team action, and global sustainability goals.

The impact of this research, shaped by a handful of coaches with diverse backgrounds, extends beyond coaching boundaries and has fundamental implications for how organizations approach climate and sustainability. The research calls into question the accepted wisdom that the path to catalyze employee action on these critical issues is more technical training and information. It points to the need for wider skill sets for sustainability leaders and an expanded role for human development professionals. Sarah Miller didn't need more information to layer on top of what she already knew. She needed a more human-centric approach, one that helped her connect with the power of her and her team's "why" and feel part of a community committed to change. It was only by unlocking the potential of this "latent" motivation that she could truly start to embed sustainability in the DNA of the organization and bring about the human-centric change required to shift business as usual.

These coaches initially connected through the CCA, a charitable organization dedicated to supporting coaches and psychologists involved in climate change initiatives within organizations. Following this research, we've conducted workshops hosted by the CCA, participated in national and international conferences, and worked diligently to elevate the profile of our findings, further administering the IDG-A and MAP to industry leaders globally. However, we must remain cognizant that the neoliberal paradigm pervading modern capitalist societies could influence the positive impacts observed. The prioritization of profit motives, market competitiveness and individualism intrinsic to neoliberalism may drive sustainability efforts into reputation management and greenwashing rhetoric rather than genuine organizational change. Nurturing personal meaning and human connectedness, as the IDG-A and MAP model advocate, could inadvertently reinforce consumerist and self-actualization narratives that paradoxically drive unsustainable overconsumption. Nurturing a "why" that places the health of our planet at the heart of any intervention has to be a non-negotiable. To counterbalance such insidious undercurrents, we are actively expanding our approach as a team and in our own networks.

Jaime is spearheading the development of the Most Sustainable Workplace Index (MSWI) measure, already administered to thousands of employees worldwide. This tool assesses the degree to which sustainability is intrinsically embedded into an organization's culture and decision-making processes beyond just the level of individual employees. Initial results accurately indicate where the motivational gap exists in organizations, and therefore where to focus time and effort in promoting sustainability action.

Meanwhile, Jonathan is playing a dual role: supporting cutting-edge net-zero research projects in collaboration with the University of Plymouth, while also translating the lessons from the IDG-A and MAP model into innovative coaching practices. On the research front, a key focus is on building self-awareness and leveraging the power of motivational imagery through an approach called functional imagery training. This research has shown to be five times more effective than traditional methods at motivating individuals when working towards challenging goals. Complementing the research is Jonathan's work at Imagery Coaching, the consultancy he runs with US-based business partner Joanna Grover, integrating scientific inquiry with cutting-edge applied coaching practices. Here, they deliver unique coaching (and courses) that break the status quo by formally assessing clients' motivations, imagery and imagination capacities. This reveals unique insights that allow them to refine personal and team performance, while developing tailor-made frameworks for operationalizing the identified opportunities.

Alan, based in Australia, is developing comprehensive coaching packages centered around utilizing the MAP model, combined with systems thinking principles, to equip organizations and communities with strategies for sustainable transformation. And Andy, operating out of Canada, is actively working alongside diverse communities to co-create localized approaches that amalgamate the IDG-A/MAP model with indigenous wisdom and cultural perspectives to reach net-zero targets in a holistic, inclusive manner.

Conclusion

Ultimately, what our findings reinforce is the indispensable role of fostering genuine interpersonal connection, shared commitment to a mutual higher purpose, and institutionalizing sustainability as a collective way of being rather than just an extrinsic obligation – teams create sustainability norms. While challenging prevalent paradigms, this pathway highlights how global issues can overcome being perceived as remote, instead becoming deeply relatable and intrinsically motivating for both individuals and organizations alike. Holistically integrating the intrapersonal, interpersonal, and cultural dimensions, our expanded work strives to catalyze transformative change that is authentically embraced and collectively reinforced from the inside out – igniting a dynamic force that can propel consistent, impactful climate action that endures.

References

Accenture (2022). *Nearly All Companies Will Miss Net Zero Goals Without At Least Doubling Rate of Carbon Emissions Reductions by 2030, Accenture Report Finds*. Available online: https://newsroom.accenture. com/news/2022/nearly-all-companies-will-miss-net-zero-goals-without-at-least-doubling-rate-of-carbon-emissions-reductions-by-2030-accenture-report-finds#:~:text=1%2C%202022%20–%20While%20more%20than,Accenture%20(NYSE%3A%20ACN).

Davis-Peccoud, J. (2017). *98% of Corporate Sustainability Programs Fail. 4 Proven Ways to Boost the Success Rate*. Retrieved from https://www.bain.com/about/media-center/bain-in-the-news/2017/corporate-sustainability-programs-fail-ways-to-boost-the-success-rate/.

Grant, A. M. (2022). Solution-focused coaching: The basics for advanced practitioners.*Coaching Practiced*, 311–322.

Inner Development Goals. (2022). The 5 Dimensions with the 23 Skills and Qualities. Retrieved from: https://www.innerdevelopmentgoals.org/frameworkInner.

Rhodes, J., Blakeley-Glover, J., Miller, A., Taylor, A., & Rochmankowski, I. (2023). Inner Development Goals and the Meaning, Awareness and Purpose (MAP) Model for Climate Coaching. *Journal of Mental Health and Climate Change*, 1(1), 101–119.

Whitmore, J. (1996). *Coaching for performance*. N. Brealey Pub.

Hanns-Christian Mahler and Felicia Werk

Chapter 10
How to get rid of old habits: The relevance of unlearning and inner development in self-organization – experiences of a pharmaceutical service provider journey

Abstract: In this chapter, we describe the journey of ten23 health®, a pharmaceutical service provider, as a human-centric and sustainable organization, founded on the basis of the Loop approach in 2021 and committed to "patients, people and planet". Our approach is a focus on purpose, inherent motivation, stakeholder thinking and leverages concepts from the Loop approach, including role and tension based work, strengths and proposal based work and integrated decision making. The four spaces model is a great framework to differentiate between the operational and governance space ("rolational" space, typically in focus of traditional companies) and the individual and tribal space ("relational", inner and relationship space). The chapter discusses challenges we encountered during our journey, and learnings we had along the way – change must come from the inside, and in order to meet the challenges of 21st century, we must unlearn prior habits and start to self-reflect, collaborate, and act. The Inner Development Goals (IDGs) provide the basis for such societal change, yet starting by individual transformations and are hence an important framework for individual, collective and organizational (company) reflections to ensure sustainable transformation.

Keywords: teal, holacracy, self-organization, Loop Approach, purpose, unlearning, inner development

Introduction to ten23 health

ten23 health® is a pharmaceutical service provider (contract development, manufacturing, and testing organization [CDTMO]): we develop, manufacture, and test sterile medicines in partnership with our customers, those being pharmaceutical companies or biotech start-ups. The company was founded in April 2023 in Basel, Switzerland, with funding from the private equity group 3i. ten23 health was launched in September 2023 with offices and laboratories in Basel and soon acquired the company Swissfillon in Visp, Valais, Switzerland at the end of October 2023 as a 100% daughter company of ten23 health (holding) and Swissfillon was meanwhile renamed ten23 health Valais.

https://doi.org/10.1515/9783111453729-011

To date, ten23 health® has been growing to about 200 employees at our two sites in Basel ("BASE®") and Visp ("VIVA1®"). The company has been growing in customer-base and revenues and is investing into further expansions, building an additional facility and building manufacturing capacity and microbiological laboratories in Visp ("VIVA2"®) and quality control laboratories at BASE®.

ten23 health's purpose and ambitions

Why do we want to build a company where people are working differently? The answer goes down to the very personal journey and purpose of the founder of ten23 and the people he started to gather around him. Most colleagues shared the experience of working in global organizations for decades. Besides the advantages and opportunities, things we did not appreciate in these environments were usually:
- unhealthy working rhythm;
- bureaucracy and (micro)management and control mechanisms vs. decision making at the right level, distributed responsibility and leadership, empowerment, and trust;
- company politics and hierarchy-related communication issues and power games;
- performance conversations that focus to feed into Excel sheets and focus on weaknesses vs. true learning and development, honest feedback with good intention, and focus on strengths;
- "professionalism" vs. authenticity, inclusion, and true contact;
- regular reorganizations/restructurings vs. being an evolutionary organization;
- "window dressing" vs. true values;
- lack of transparency – possibly intentional (management by access to more information);
- traditional approaches, for example of performance and rewarding; with focus on "time spent" and "in office" (not output) and (only) financial recognition (vs. individual appreciation – based on needs);
- how often did we truly understand the "why" behind?

Therefore, our journey aimed to have a shared purpose and ambition: working as a team that shares the same values; working based on trust and also sharing the responsibility.

When starting the company, the concept of "patients, people, and planet" as fundamental commitments was conceived. The idea was, building on many things read about in different books including *Reinventing Organizations* by Frederic Laloux (2016), to build a new company in the field of pharmaceutical services and the pharma sector that is different and can serve as a seed to disrupt traditional beliefs and approaches. A company where employees like to work, are motivated and have fun, can be their real selves and authentic (rather than putting on any "masks" at work), where trust and collaboration are the basis of company/employee and employee/employee interactions (rather than "command and control"), where the organizational setup is evolutionary from within (rather than running through major reorganizations with support from consultants every two to three years). A company where the output (developing and manufacturing sterile medicines to benefit patients) matters most, and where the "how" matters, both from a human/human perspective, as well as from a planet/sustainability perspective. Businesses are and need to be a force for good and need to act and think sustainably and long-term – for any of its stakeholders, including employees, the planet, customers, patients (our customers' customers), investors, etc. (rather than having a sole short-term financial focus only for shareholders' benefit). "Stakeholder thinking" vs. pure "shareholder thinking" is a key component of running a business towards a triple bottom line.

Our sustainability agenda at ten23 is a key element of our DNA. It touches all aspects of our organization, from sourcing to operations and invoicing. ten23 concluded the Swiss Triple Impact (STI) certification, which helped us identify our five priority Sustainable Development Goals (SDGs) and formulate our ambition and goals. We track our sustainability KPIs, both absolute and relative, and have been decreasing energy use and emissions per FTE significantly (data: ten23 internal, 2023/Q3 vs. 2022/Q2, and published in our 2023 sustainability report on the ten23 website). The way ten23 approaches sustainability is beyond traditional environmental, social, and governance (ESG) measures. As an example, we implemented a compost heap for any organic waste at our Basel facility.

What is the benefit of all this? There are multiple examples in literature where companies that deliver on growth, profit margin, and sustainability generate the best returns McKinsey & Company (2023). Businesses that operate sustainably show more resilience, better risk mitigation, can be a trustful and trusted brand, BLab (2023) and are reported to better attract and retain employees and serve as market differentiator (Whelan & Fink, 2016).

The purpose of business should be in our view to solve the problems of people and planet profitably, and not profit from causing problems Collier, Coyle, Mayer & Wolf (2021)

Early on, we chose the "Loop Approach" ((Klein &Hughes 2019) as the organizational design template, acknowledging that we would have individualized its components to a certain degree. Our organization is hence based on holacratic principles: ten23 health is organized in roles and circles. We believe in self-management and self-responsibility and purpose-driven work. Colleagues are typically working in a main role and circle, but have the opportunity to work – based on their interests, strengths, or development needs and wishes – in any other role or team as well. As an example, a colleague from our customer delivery circle (operations) is working there as "laboratory bee" (technician) but is at the same time also coordinating ten23's activities for biosafety as well as our LGBTQ+ agenda as Diversity lead. Another colleague has changed roles from the business/sales circle to our people and culture (P&C) circle, given the wonderful fit of skills and motivation for this other role.

Our meetings per circle are organized as "tactical" (synch meetings to share), "governance" (meetings to evolve, clarify, or change accountabilities, roles and/or circles), or "focus" meetings (for specific deep-dive topics). All meeting notes and organizational details, including accountabilities, roles, and circle are available for everyone in the organization.

Such an organizational design by definition provides better clarity and transparency for its employees. If something is unclear for any colleague, they are invited to bring up their tension for clarification in the respective forum.

Decision making is done per accountability and relevant role, based on the integrative decision-making (IDM) process. Decisions are taken when "safe enough to try" (SETT), not looking for a perfect decision, for example one that had no risks involved.

As an organization, we don't want to operate with traditional "command and control" management tools. We embrace trusted work time and work-from-anywhere. But one experience was that too general a guiding principle, such as, "Please use the company money as it were your own money" or "Please give each other feedback regularly and proactively", was not enough; people were insecure about what was okay and what was not, so they rather did not want to do something wrong and withdraw from taking decisions or action. An interesting study we came across during our discussions on how to solve this was a study on the behavior of kindergarten kids on the playground (Hampton 2017). Interestingly, on playgrounds without any fences, the children tended to gather around the teacher (feeling insecure), whereas on playgrounds with fences (some boundaries), the children utilized the entire playground, feeling more free to explore. Whilst such a study may not be directly translatable from children to adults, its concept is interesting. In fact, adults that were previously used to boundaries and limitations from any prior workplace or from school days even, may not have the psychological safety, but also not the courage (IDG 5: Acting) or trust (IDG 4: Collaborating) into a new environment that provides larger boundaries or even no rules at all. We took away as organizational learning, that whilst our company does not want to police any colleagues since we are working based on trust and empowering colleagues to work self-responsibly, self-empowered, and taking ownership, we still needed to generate "frameworks" – assuming that giving a frame will unleash the same intrinsic motivation and confidence as kids with a fence in kindergarten.

These frameworks (intentionally not called "corporate policies") should provide a context and guidance for specific topics that may be required for decision making, equality, and to prevent chaos, anarchy, and unfairness. These frameworks aim to serve as reference points to increase trust and allow courage for colleagues entering as yet unknown territory. Topics addressed here include work time, holidays, general work terms and conditions, work-from-anywhere, learning and development, and feedback. Of course, these frameworks were carefully designed in compliance with legal considerations and requirements.

The four spaces – relational and rolational spaces

The Loop Approach is defining four relevant spaces for tensions at ten23: the "relational space" with (a) the individual room and (b) the relationship room; and the "rolational space" with (c) the operative room and (d) the governance/structure room see fig. 10.1. Hence, we leverage these four squared. However, most companies focus on the operational and governance rooms, typically defined by other individuals or groups than the individual employee. The relationship space has typically not received lots of attention in many organizations.

At ten23, we aim to address tensions or unclarities in the operative and governance rooms with our roles, circles, and meeting structures, aiming to support the self-evolution of our organization and enabling the individual to clarify their tensions and unclarities.

The relationship space is addressed by workshops and feedback – either self-driven or supported by a mediator/facilitator. In critical situations, concepts like "clear-the-air meetings" may be an approach to address potential relational challenges.

For the individual space, we invite and support our colleagues for a journey towards self-reflection. Helpful tools may include our onboarding sheets where we invite each new colleague to think about their personal purpose, our (360) feedbacks utilizing Profile Dynamics, or other tools.

Challenges during our journey – how are we doing?

After one year of self-management, we have done a "retrospective" to assess how we are doing. Generally, employees felt more valued and happier compared to their prior experience in workplaces.

We also had further learnings and challenges along our journey so far:

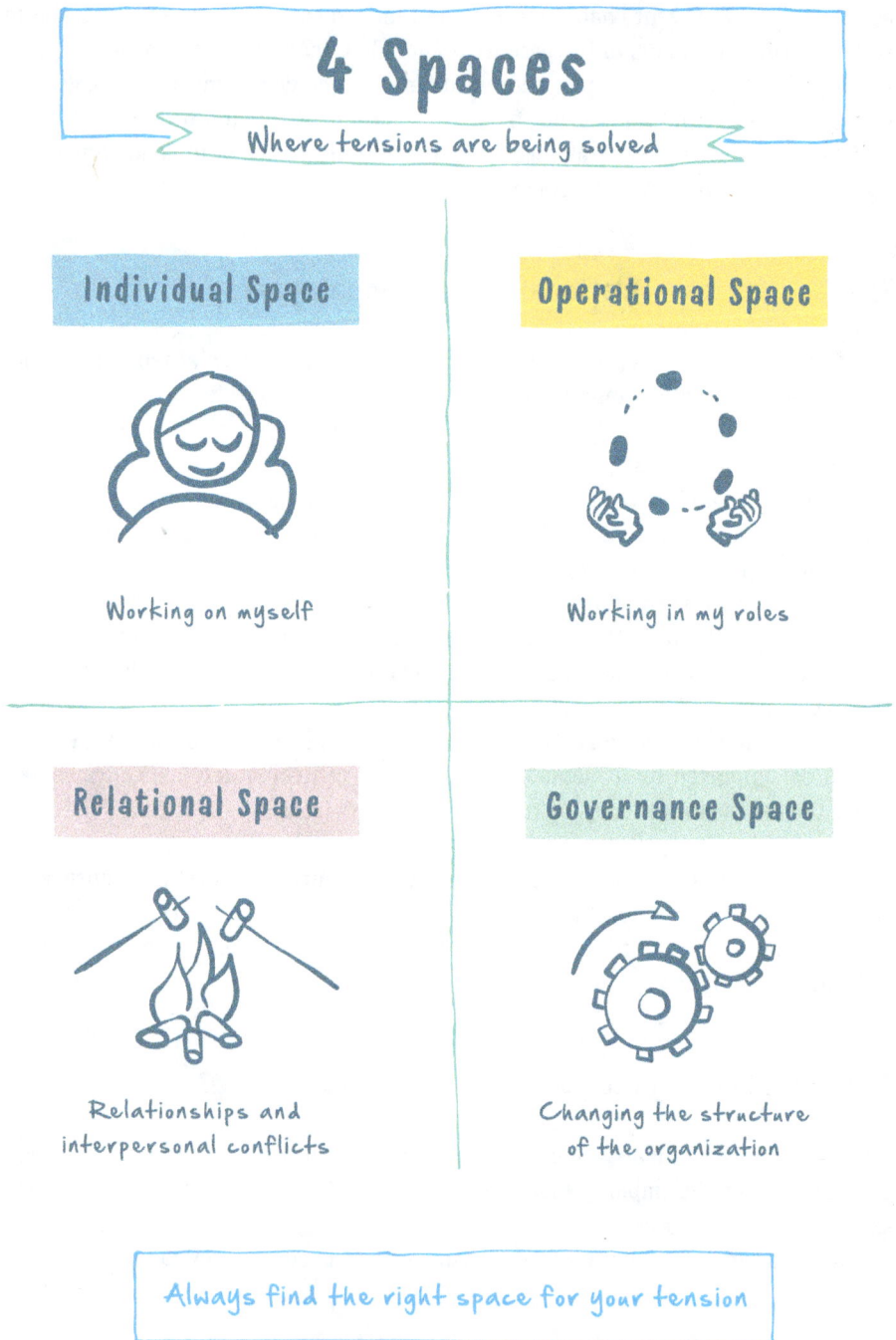

4 Spaces

Where tensions are being solved

Individual Space

Working on myself

Operational Space

Working in my roles

Relational Space

Relationships and interpersonal conflicts

Governance Space

Changing the structure of the organization

Always find the right space for your tension

Figure 10.1: The Four Spaces of Tensions.
Source: The Loop Approach Handbook by The Dive GmbH, licensed under CC BY-SA 4.0. (p.1, module 2, chapter 2)

Circle lead = manager?

During the change of organizational setup, especially when transforming the previously acquired company, traditional line management roles were made obsolete and replaced with "roles". Some colleagues were assigned a "circle lead" role, which is one of the three templated roles we have per circle (next to "facilitator" and "transparency master"). Interestingly, there seemed to be a perception that "circle lead" equals a "managerial role" and despite the many training sessions, that perception seemed to have partly survived, both with circle lead incumbents but also other colleagues. To note, our circle leads are not determining any performance rating, nor determining other employee's salaries, hence, do not include some of the "traditional management" tasks. Being consistent in the approach and use of the circle lead role has helped to clarify any thoughts or perceptions related to this role. We also had cases where colleagues working in a "circle lead" role previously did change to other (non-circle-lead) roles that matched their strengths more. We found the possibility of such changes within an organization as liberating, as they allow focusing on one's strengths and allowing changes in role assignments. In a traditional organization, such a change may have been perceived a demotion and may not have been pursued by the employee, but also not from the company's side either. Such a change also requires self-awareness, courage, and trust.

Changing employment agreements

When we changed employment agreements for the previously acquired organization, we moved from a 12-page document to a two-pager. The process was, of course, accompanied by legal expert support. We reduced formal working time (from 41 to 40 hours), changed from "mandatory time recording" to "trusted work time and facilitated time recording" and eliminated all job titles, using "fellow" in every employment contract. Interestingly, many questions and concerns were raised during this process: "*Who am I*, if I don't have a job title anymore?" Well, we responded that we believe that titles don't make humans any better or worse. We have a "choose your title" policy, so if anyone would feel better being "VP" or something, they can choose to. With regard to trusted work time, concerns were brought forward that related to how other people (colleagues) may react when the employee chooses to leave work earlier and work from home on a given day, or a concern that the company may consider the work not being done. Interestingly, it seems there is still significant peer pressure in many workplaces, assuming that "performance" (work done well) is a (linear) function of time, which obviously is not true. We observed "What's in it for me?" questions – which focus on individual improvement (e.g., financially) – without any context or worry being framed.

Decision making is hard

Making decisions is not an easy task – especially not in the workplace. Have you experienced in any workplace that any request required multiple management layers of approval for a seemingly simple decision? Have you ever experienced in any (prior) workplace that your decision did not lead to the intended outcome and/or that you were approached by your line manager (or anyone else) on that decision? Have you been blamed for any wrong decision?

When having done a company event in early 2022, one of the most common questions was on travel: "Which train ticket am I allowed to buy?" We intentionally do not had any travel regulations in the beginning, as we wanted the colleagues to take decisions themselves. We do have a section related to decision making in our company handbook (we call it ten23.operating system, or ten23.OS), and a good guiding principle are questions like: "What would you decide in your private life?", "What would the planet say about your decision?", "Is it reversible?", "Is it safe enough to try (SETT)?", "Is the decision potentially risking patient/human/planet safety?"

Keeping the good from the old way of working

Often we found the good intention behind things in the "old world" and try to reactivate this positive core. For instance, for sure we did not want to have performance ratings in our ways of working. But, when discussing it with our internal "cultural soundboard", it was emphasized that to sit down at least once a year and reflect on what went well and what did not is a pretty important habit that we should keep. Therefore, we implemented self-evaluations: Once a year, everyone needs to reflect on what makes them proud, what they want to do differently, on which of their IDGs they want to work, etc. Everybody needs to discuss this with at least a sounding partner of their choice to get feedback on their contribution to our purpose.

Unlearning and self-development

Many of the challenges we observed on our company journey, including the ones mentioned above, are often based on prior experience. Experiences start from early childhood – kindergarten, school, other workplaces. Focus is often on compliance to rules and conformity and "normalizing" people. However, the world is volatile, uncertain, complex, and ambiguous (VUCA) and brittle, anxious, nonlinear, and incomprehensible (BANI).

How did that make you feel, when someone at a prior workplace made a bad comment when you were leaving work a little earlier? When you tried to book a trip asking for multiple levels of signatures and approvals (and being rejected the 50 Swiss franc train ticket)? We all have our experiences and small traumas, leading to specific behaviors. These behaviors may become hard-wired in our brains and hence a "default", without thinking about the root cause or impact or relevance in a new context.

Isn't it clear that looking at the twenty-first century challenges ahead for human-kind, humankind rather needs to have skills in complexity management, communication, ownership, and initiative? Isn't it time to focus on inner development? Moving from "ego" to "eco"? We need an inner compass, a true north and purpose, acting with a learning mindset, being able to think critically and drive long-term orientation for a broad being, being able to connect to others with empathy, and collaborate and be inclusive rather than competing, normalizing, and focusing on ourselves. We need an environment to learn and try things, supporting our continued journey of learning and growth. The ability to unlearn things, to try again and trust again is required. All in all, we need inner development, self-awareness, and self-reflection. Change must come from the inside.

This is where the Inner Development Goals (IDGs) also resonated very well with us: *being, thinking, relating, collaborating,* and *acting* are key themes and well-framed from the start.

Our next stage at ten23 includes self-reflection on the various IDGs and under-standing how our relationship to self and relations with others (the so-called relational space) will help enable the much required change – change for a volatile world that requires that change; change in order for our children to still live on a planet that is worth living on.

Our takeaways and recommendations

We believe that modern workplaces need to focus on all its stakeholders. Businesses can be (and should be) a force for good. This is also true for companies in regulated environments and, as Nelson Mandela once said, "Things are only impossible, until they are done."

A company with a focus on its employees and the planet will be better for humans, and have higher employee motivation and retention. When employees have (and know) their personal purpose, and that purpose aligns with the (real) purpose of an organization, magic happens! When employees are happy, customers are happy and the company prospers financially.

The SDGs provide a great framework for organizations (and individuals) to reflect on where action and improvements are required in order for business to do good. However, change must come from the inside, and in order to meet the challenges of the twenty-first century, we must unlearn prior habits and start to self-reflect, collaborate, and act. The IDGs provide the basis for such societal change starting with individual transformations and are hence an important framework for individual, collective, and organizational (company) reflections to ensure sustainable transformation.

Practical application of the IDGs at ten23

We see the whole IDG framework as a compass for our organization and the people within our organization that helps us in developing the skills needed to work sustainably. Working sustainably means for us not only supporting the SDGs, it also means a sustainable self-development, and the IDGs give a useful framework for this. It gives our employees inspiration in which areas to set goals for personal development. In the section below it is described what we do in terms of individual, team, and organizational development with regard to the IDG dimensions and skillset.

Being – relation to self

"Being", according to the IDG framework, is: "Cultivating our inner life and developing and deepening our relationship to our thoughts, feelings and body help us be present, intentional and non-reactive when we face complexity." (IDG Framework: https://innerdevelopmentgoals.org/framework/). Being aware of yourself, including strengths, needs, and triggers, is of utmost importance in self-organization. We work tensions-based – which means that we see any tension somebody has as something positive since it implicates the possibility to improve something. One magic question in our meetings is "What do you need?". Therefore, one needs to be aware of his or her their needs and also to be able to apply nonviolent communication (NVC), which is a cornerstone of our feedback culture. But as recommended by Simone Sinek, let's start with the why (Sinek 2011) – the inner compass.

Inner compass

The IDG definition here is: "Having a deeply felt sense of responsibility and commitment to values and purposes relating to the good of the whole." (IDG Framework: https://innerdevelopmentgoals.org/framework/). This relates very well with our company purpose of collaborating for a healthy life and planet – patients, people, and planet. To ensure a fit between individual, role, and company purpose, we integrate purpose-related questions into our recruitment and onboarding process. For example, every employee has a "Who I am" sheet that is filled out and shared with the organization during the onboarding (see Figure 10.2). This sheet is asking for the individual purpose as well as for strengths, triggers, and values. For the future, we plan a deeper dive into the questions of "What is my source?" in the onboarding as well as other workshop formats.

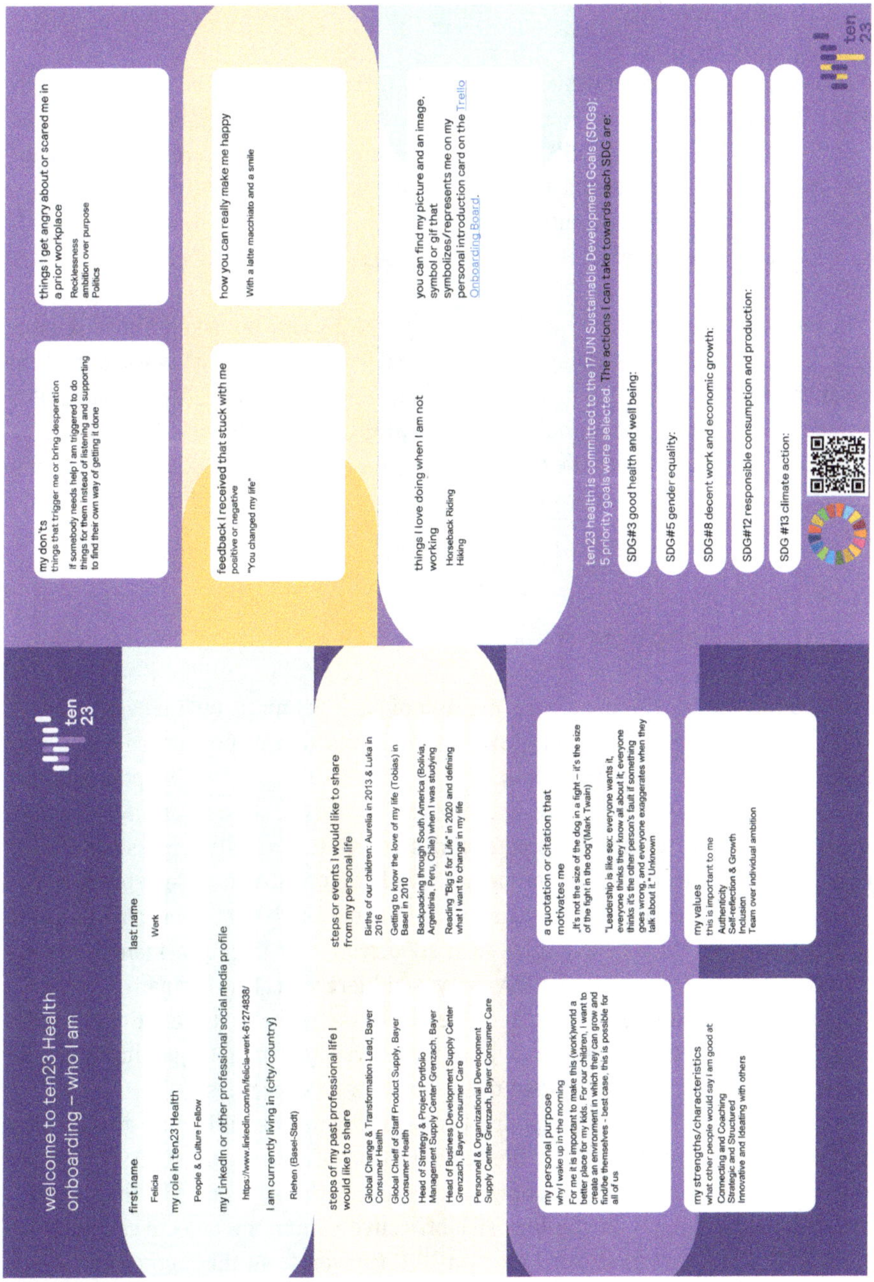

Figure 10.2: Onboarding sheet at ten23.
Source: ten23 internal Sharepoint.

Integrity and authenticity

The IDG definition, "A commitment and ability to act with sincerity, honesty and integrity." It is fundamental for a culture of inclusiveness and psychological safety. We have a "transparency per default" mindset in our company. Therefore, all meeting minutes, objectives and key results (OKRs), roles, and accountabilities (including changes in terms of organizational evolution) are transparently shared in Holaspirit – a software accessible by every employee. Here all circles and their members are visualized (see Figure 10.3).

In our "Ask Me Anything" sessions, all questions can be asked and discussed openly. Also, workshop results are openly shared, e.g., after the last workshop of the general circle (GC), the results of session on OKRs and the team profile regarding Profile Dynamics (a profiling tool based on the Spiral Dynamics theory (Beck & Cowan, 1996)) have been shared with the organization, supporting our idea of everybody having the freedom of being vulnerable and authentic, role-modeled by the leaders of the organization.

Openness and learning mindset

The IDG definition is: "Having a basic mindset of curiosity and a willingness to be vulnerable and embrace change and grow." (IDG Framework: https://innerdevelopment goals.org/framework/) We foster this kind of mindset through self-responsibility in self-development. At ten23, we are working role-based. So, we do not have positions with a wide range of tasks and responsibilities, where it is usually impossible that everything fits with the profile of one person; we have roles with a clear purpose and accountabilities. An employeehas usually several roles and sometimes also in different circles. We also do not have titles such as "director" or "vice president" – we are all "fellows". Therefore, we do not have a typical hierarchical career path. Everybody needs to define for themself what career means for them; for us it is about developing yourself, inner growth, and developing into roles that foster that – getting into your sweet spot, where your strengths and needs match with your roles.

We developed a process to support this journey with the individual growth plan. The process is usually initiated by the person themself (see Figure 10.4). The person choses a mentor to support them in the process and is also supported by the "learning and development fellow". In the first kick-off conversation, the objectives and needs are clarified and a first feedback based on NVC is given from the mentor to the person. Then the Profile Dynamics is conducted and a one-to-one report discussion and coaching is conducted with the learning and development fellow. Step 3 is again a conversation between the person, the mentor, and the learning and development fellow with the aim of exchanging insights and developing the individual growth plan on these grounds. One question in the individual growth plan template is asking for

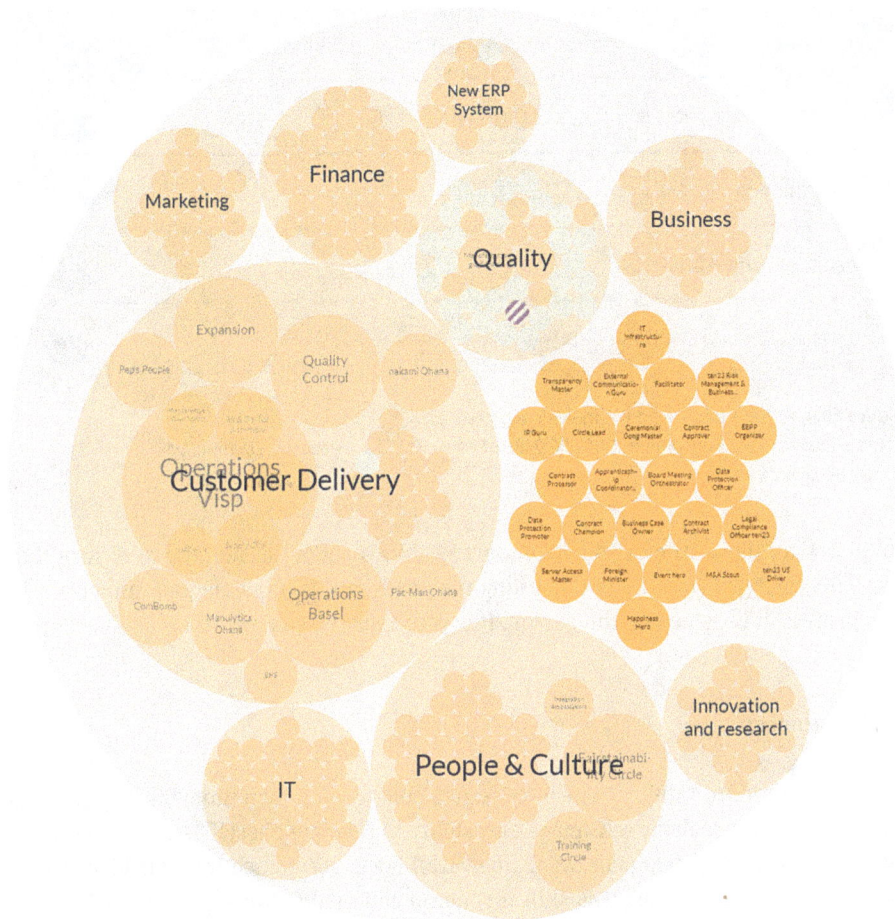

Figure 10.3: Organizational setup of ten23 based on circles and visualized in Holaspirit.
Source: ten23 internal Holaspirit Software.

individual growth goals; we shared the IDGs with the organization for inspiration in this regard. IDGs were introduced during the launch of the framework to the organization and are mentioned in our template of the individual growth plan as a source for individual development goals.

If there is a gap between growths goals and current competencies, ideas are exchanged on how to close the gap. Every fellow can spend a fixed amount of money annually on their training externally without any approval process as long as an individual growth plan is in place. But we experience that, when digging deeper into the question of what is really needed, it is seldomly about external training and titles such as MBA, PMP, etc. Usually, it is more about experience, on-the-job training and growth through feedback and coaching.

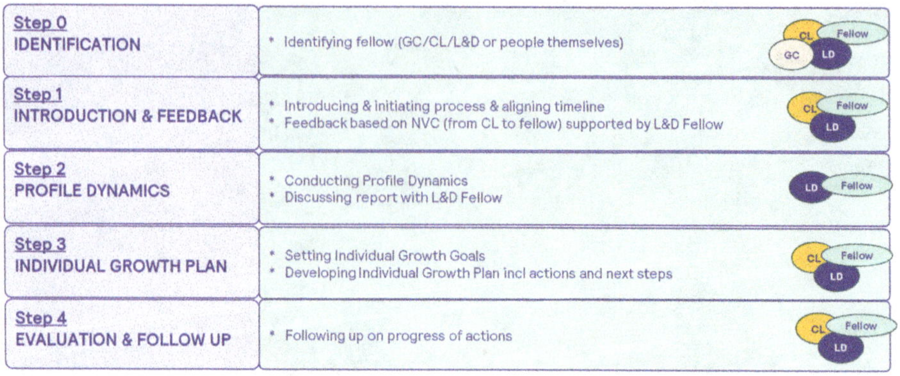
Step 0
IDENTIFICATION
• Identifying fellow (GC/CL/L&D or people themselves)
CL
Fellow
GC
LD
Step 1
INTRODUCTION & FEEDBACK
• Introducing & initiating process & aligning timeline
• Feedback based on NVC (from CL to fellow) supported by L&D Fellow
CL
Fellow
LD
Step 2
PROFILE DYNAMICS
• Conducting Profile Dynamics
• Discussing report with L&D Fellow
LD
Fellow
Step 3
INDIVIDUAL GROWTH PLAN
• Setting Individual Growth Goals
• Developing Individual Growth Plan incl actions and next steps
CL
Fellow
LD
Step 4
EVALUATION & FOLLOW UP
• Following up on progress of actions
CL
Fellow
LD

Figure 10.4: Process to develop the individual growth plan.
Source: Internal ten23 document. *COR FPC 0007_01 Framework for "Feedback, Contribution & Development", p.13.*

In Step 4, a follow-up meeting is conducted after a couple of months to ensure that the individual growth plan is still fitting the needs and is implemented. Important in this process: it is owned by the person. It is your tension, you own it.

Self-awareness

The IDG definition, "Ability to be in reflective contact with own thoughts, feelings and desires; having a realistic self-image and ability to regulate oneself," (IDG Framework: https://innerdevelopmentgoals.org/framework/) feeds very much into our idea of self-development. We support this skill through a self-evaluation (see Figures 10.5 and 10.6). We do not believe in performance ratings by line managers; at the same time,

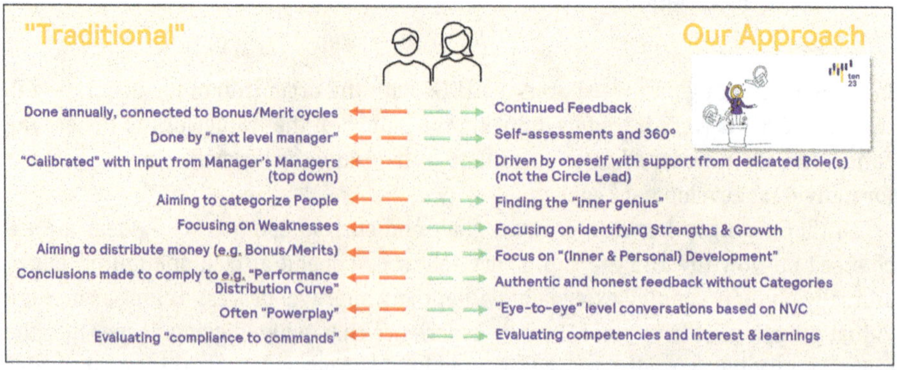
"Traditional"
Our Approach
ten 23
Done annually, connected to Bonus/Merit cycles
Continued Feedback
Done by "next level manager"
Self-assessments and 360°
"Calibrated" with input from Manager's Managers (top down)
Driven by oneself with support from dedicated Role(s) (not the Circle Lead)
Aiming to categorize People
Finding the "inner genius"
Focusing on Weaknesses
Focusing on identifying Strengths & Growth
Aiming to distribute money (e.g. Bonus/Merits)
Focus on "(Inner & Personal) Development"
Conclusions made to comply to e.g. "Performance Distribution Curve"
Authentic and honest feedback without Categories
Often "Powerplay"
"Eye-to-eye" level conversations based on NVC
Evaluating "compliance to commands"
Evaluating competencies and interest & learnings

Figure 10.5: Traditional performance approach vs. contribution approach at ten23.
Source: Internal presentation of ten23 on Self Evaluation.

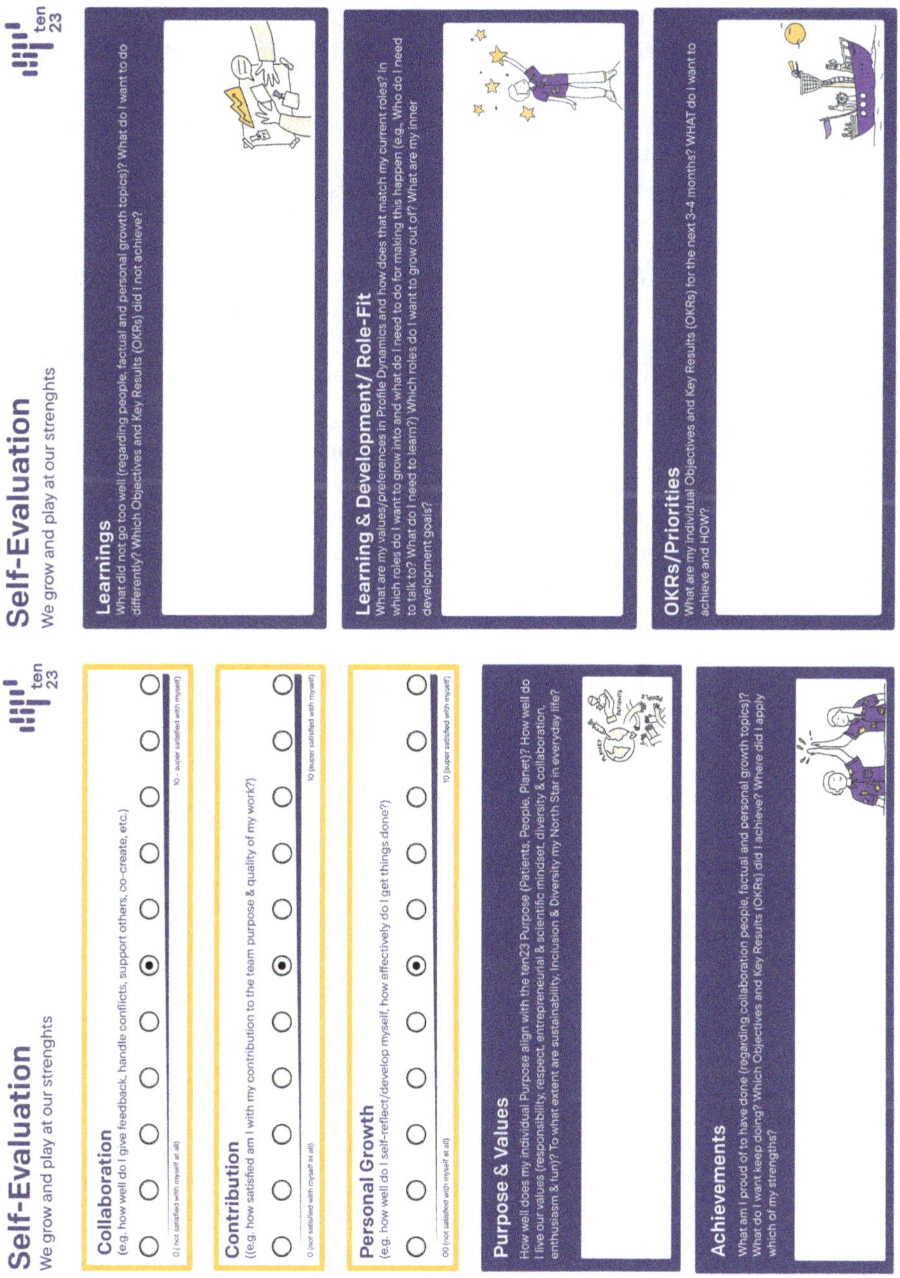

ten23

Self-Evaluation
We grow and play at our strengths

Learnings
What did not go too well (regarding people, factual and personal growth topics)? What do I want to do differently? Which Objectives and Key Results (OKRs) did I not achieve?

Learning & Development/ Role-Fit
What are my values/preferences in Profile Dynamics and how does that match my current roles? In which roles do I want to grow into and what do I need to do for making this happen (e.g., Who do I need to talk to? What do I need to learn?) Which roles do I want to grow out of? What are my inner development goals?

OKRs/Priorities
What are my individual Objectives and Key Results (OKRs) for the next 3–4 months? WHAT do I want to achieve and HOW?

ten23

Self-Evaluation
We grow and play at our strenghts

Collaboration
(e.g. how well do I give feedback, handle conflicts, support others, co-create, etc.)

0 (not satisfied with myself at all)   10 – super satisfied with myself)

Contribution
((e.g. how satisfied am I with my contribution to the team purpose & quality of my work?)

0 (not satisfied with myself at all)   10 (super satisfied with myself)

Personal Growth
(e.g. how well do I self-reflect/develop myself, how effectively do I get things done?)

00 (not satisfied with myself at all)   10 (super satisfied with myself)

Purpose & Values
How well does my individual Purpose align with the ten23 Purpose (Patients, People, Planet)? How well do I live our values (responsibility, respect, entrepreneurial & scientific mindset, diversity & collaboration, enthusiasm & fun)? To what extent are sustainability, inclusion & Diversity my North Star in everyday life?

Achievements
What am I proud of to have done (regarding collaboration people, factual and personal growth topics)? What do I want keep doing? Which Objectives and Key Results (OKRs) did I achieve? Where did I apply which of my strengths?

Figure 10.6: Self-evaluation template.
Source: Internal ten23 document. *COR FPC 0007_01 Framework for "Feedback, Contribution & Development"*, p.5.

we would like to keep the useful habit to regularly self-reflect our individual contribution to team performance, company success, our collaboration, individual growth, etc. and discuss this with a sounding partner of our choice. Therefore, everybody has to fill out the self-evaluation at least once a year and discuss it with at least two people who can give insightful feedback.

Below are two pieces of feedback from our fellows on this process:

In the current situation, with a huge workload, cultural changes in progress, set up of new systems and sites, the tendency is to feel overwhelmed by the topics and work to do. In this situation it is important to look at what was already achieved and to see which work was already done. For me, it is important to look in the rear-view mirror to recognize the progress we made. I think it was a quite honest way to recap as I have not done this as preparation for an evaluation with a manager or team lead to discuss bonus payments or salary increase. My main reflection was the role fit. Am I working in my strength, can I fill the roles, can I fulfill purpose and gain energy. Do I need to change anything? Grow in new topics or leave something behind?

Having a clear understanding of myself, the next key point was the feedback round. It was super helpful to get feedback on my own evaluation from different perspectives of the daily work. Seeing the appreciation and space to improve in different situations really helps to classify the points of self-expectation. (**Patrick S.**)

The self-evaluation was time-consuming for me, but it showed me what has worked well so far and in which areas I would like to develop further. It was very motivating to share my thoughts with my sounding partners and to realize that my self-assessment matched their impressions and that I was shown other positive perspectives that I hadn't thought of. I can definitely highly recommend it if you really want to take a self-critical look at yourself and develop further and choose suitable sounding partners. *(Ariane S.)*

Presence

To foster the "Ability to be in the here and now, without judgment and in a state of open-ended presence", we established check-ins at the beginning of meetings. With the simple question of "How are you here today?" we encourage people to land in the here and now, to listen to yourself and breath a second before starting the meeting. Sometimes it is just good to know the simple things, e.g., that somebody is tired today. Sometimes even bigger topics are shared in these rounds as the trust is increasing in the teams through this exercise. Meetings are also closed with a "check-out" asking the question of what needs to be said to leave the meeting in a good way or what is your takeaway from this meeting. Again, inviting introspection and reflection.

Thinking – cognitive skills

The idea of "developing our cognitive skills by taking different perspectives, evaluating information and making sense of the world as an interconnected whole is essential for wise decision-making" (IDG Framework: https://innerdevelopmentgoals.org/framework/) and fits with the approach of leveraging the potential of every individual in our organization to its full extent.

Critical thinking

"Critically reviewing the validity of views, evidence and plans" (IDG Framework: https://innerdevelopmentgoals.org/framework/) is essential for integrated decision making. At ten23 we work tension-based and proposal-oriented. That means that you need to bring your tensions and a proposal for improvement. In an integrative decision-making process this is critically reviewed and enriched by the ideas and viewpoints of others.

Complexity awareness

We foster "understanding of and skills in working with complex and systemic conditions and causalities" (IDG Framework: https://innerdevelopmentgoals.org/framework/) through our transparency per default philosophy. Almost all information is available to almost everybody – but as usual freedom comes with responsibility and it is in every individual's responsibility to filter so as to not be overwhelmed and ensure that you get what you need. In our cultural onboarding training, we train our fellows in "personal effectiveness" on the basis of *Getting Things Done* by David Allen (Allen 2015).

Perspective skills

"Skills in seeking, understanding and actively making use of insights from contrasting perspectives" (IDG Framework: https://innerdevelopmentgoals.org/framework/) are trained in our nonviolent communication and feedback training. This is already part of our onboarding training, but we plan to have another deep dive into these topics with all our circles in 2025 since we realized how valuable these skills are in collaboration, but that perspective taking and being able to "put yourself in the shoes of others" needs training to become habit.

Before facilitating "clear the air" meetings, we share a template with the participants to prepare the conversation that encourages to first become aware of your own emotions and needs but then also of those of the other conflict party (see Figure 10.7).

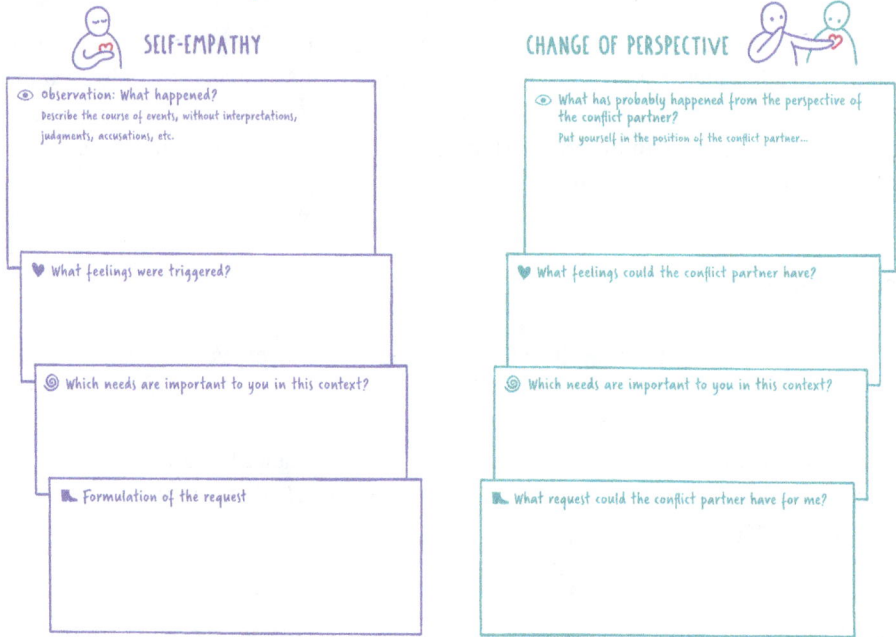

Figure 10.7: Template for "clear the air" meetings according to the Loop Approach.
Source: The Loop Approach Handbook by The Dive GmbH, licensed under CC BY-SA 4.0. (p.26, module chapter 3)

Sensemaking

The skill of "seeing patterns, structuring the unknown and being able to consciously create stories" (IDG Framework: https://innerdevelopmentgoals.org/framework/) is reflected in the development of our roles. We are working role-based at ten23 and every role needs a catchy title that makes it easy for others to understand what the role is about as well as its purpose. This is fundamental in a purpose-driven and self-organized company: your individual purpose should be aligned with your role purpose; your role purpose pays into your circle purpose and the circle purpose contributes to the overall company purpose. Through this, we can work in a purpose hierarchy instead of a person or power hierarchy. In our experience, work becomes tremendously more meaningful and energizing when this purpose hierarchy from individual to company purpose is aligned.

Long-term orientation and visioning

The "long-term orientation and ability to formulate and sustain commitment to visions relating to the larger context" (IDG Framework: https://innerdevelopmentgoals.

org/framework/) is deeply anchored in our culture and manifested in our ten23 Health Operating system (OS). The OS is a document that describes our organizational culture, values, and commitments regarding sustainability and LGBTQ+ agenda. Here a brief excerpt:

> The **why**, hence the ultimate goal of all we do is to contribute to a net positive economy: ten23 health shall have a material positive impact on society and the environment, taken as a whole, through its business and operations. A business that considers and puts people in its focus, such as ourselves as employees with the goal of people being healthy (physically and mentally); and considers the planet in everything we do (sustainability focus), in line with the UN Sustainable Development Goals.
>
> Our ultimate customers are patients, aiming to improve their health.
>
> Of course, our business also aims in making profit, in order to pay our costs, our salaries and to benefit our shareholders. Our business however should at any time not generate any damage, but create a positive impact.
>
> Internal Document of ten23: Ten23 Operating System (COR_POL_0001, effective Jan. 1, 2023).

Every employee needs to read and sign this document when joining the company. The implications for everyday decision making are described in our frameworks. For instance, we take public transportation over individual car travel and all our employees get a Swiss Half Fare Card (Halbtax), which enables them to buy tickets with 50% off for business trips, but also for private journeys.

Relating – caring for others and the world

As cited above, we aim to have a "material positive impact on society and the environment", therefore, "appreciating, caring for and feeling connected to others, such as neighbors, future generations or the biosphere, helps us create more just and sustainable systems and societies for everyone" (IDG Framework: https://innerdevelopment goals.org/framework/) is fundamental at ten23.

Appreciation

"Relating to others and to the world with a basic sense of appreciation, gratitude and joy" (IDG Framework: https://innerdevelopmentgoals.org/framework/) is reflected in many ways at ten23. We embrace fun at work – our meeting rooms have a beautiful decor, giving the feeling of being in Hawaii, and regular get-togethers such as movie nights, team events, etc. let us connect on a deeper level. Among our fellows at ten23, 80% agreed to the item "I have fun at work", which is 10 percentage points above the benchmark.

In our "kudos" channel on Slack, appreciation and successes are shared widely in the organization giving a positive vibe for everyone.

Connectedness

The "sense of being connected with and/or being a part of a larger whole, such as a community, humanity or global ecosystem" (IDG Framework: https://innerdevelop mentgoals.org/framework/) is fostered through our purpose and several events in the relations space. From organized waste collection events to workshops in the relations space, connection is where the magic happens.

One structured process at ten23 to connect with others is our "fellow feedback". We offer to every fellow the possibility to receive written feedback supported through a Profile Dynamics(R) 360-degree feedback process. This process is facilitated by our P&C circle but is driven individually. It has been a wonderful basis to discuss why sometimes intention did not equal impact and has brought more connectedness to many fellows.

Humility

We decided to not have titles at ten23 to inspire "being able to act in accordance with the needs of the situation without concern for one's own importance" (IDG Framework: https://innerdevelopmentgoals.org/framework/). Since most of us have been trained in hierarchical systems (schools, companies, etc.), it is not easy for many of us to let go off these traditional symbols of power. Interestingly, after a first phase of irritation, we received very positive feedback in this regard since it encourages us to think about why we would like to have such a title and what would it give us that we cannot give ourselves.

Self-organization does not work without leadership – to the contrary self-leadership is of even greater importance. We also have a templated role called "circle lead" but made sure to carefully describe the accountabilities of this role and not to bundle too much power in one role. Leadership in our culture is about connectedness and not power or management.

Empathy and compassion

The "ability to relate to others, oneself and nature with kindness, empathy and compassion and address related suffering" is addressed in many ways at ten23, but we try to not only establish this mindset in our company, we also encourage and support suppliers and even competitors to join us on this journey. Recently, we shared several documents from our "fairstainability" (fairness and sustainability) circle with our competitors and gave an "impulse talk" at an event of one of our customers to encourage people-centric ways of working. This is not a zero-sum game for us and we believe that spreading these ideas will be for the greater good of all of us.

Collaborating – social skills

As pointed out above, we strongly believe in a joint approach in sustainability: "To make progress on shared concerns, we need to develop our abilities to include, hold space and communicate with stakeholders with different values, skills and competencies."(IDG Framework: https://innerdevelopmentgoals.org/framework/).

Communication skills

Defined as the "ability to really listen to others, to foster genuine dialogue, to advocate own views skillfully, to manage conflicts constructively and to adapt communication to diverse groups" (IDG Framework: https://innerdevelopmentgoals.org/framework/), we believe that nonviolent communication[1] lays out the basis for this skill. NVC has four steps, with observations, feelings, needs, and requests see fig 10.8. By focusing on the observation, it automatically decouples the person from jumping to conclusions or using assumptions. It allows perspective and critical thinking. By framing the feelings and needs from the individual perspective, it ensures the tension remains with the self, and hence, would not be confrontative. Hence, NVC supports various elements also captured in the IDG framework, from being and self-awareness (understanding your emotions and needs), to empathy and communication with others, and with courageously framing the requests, providing mobilization and inviting a trust-based collaboration.

To take over responsibility for your emotional reactions and the fulfillment of your needs is the basic step in being able to constructively leverage conflicts in life and in organizations. Therefore, nonviolent communication is not only four-step tool of giving feedback, it is a "life philosophy" and deeply embedded in our company culture.

Co-creation skills

The skills needed "to build, develop and facilitate collaborative relationships with diverse stakeholders, characterized by psychological safety and genuine co-creation"

---

1 Nonviolent Communication: A Language of Life: Life-Changing Tools for Healthy Relationships (Nonviolent Communication Guides) (English Edition) eBook: Rosenberg, Marshall B., Chopra, Deepak.

Why the four steps?

Understanding each other is simple

UNDERSTANDING MYSELF

UNDERSTANDING YOU

👁 Observation

♥ Feeling / Emotion

◎ Need

🥾 Request

EXPRESSING MYSELF

To understand does not mean to agree

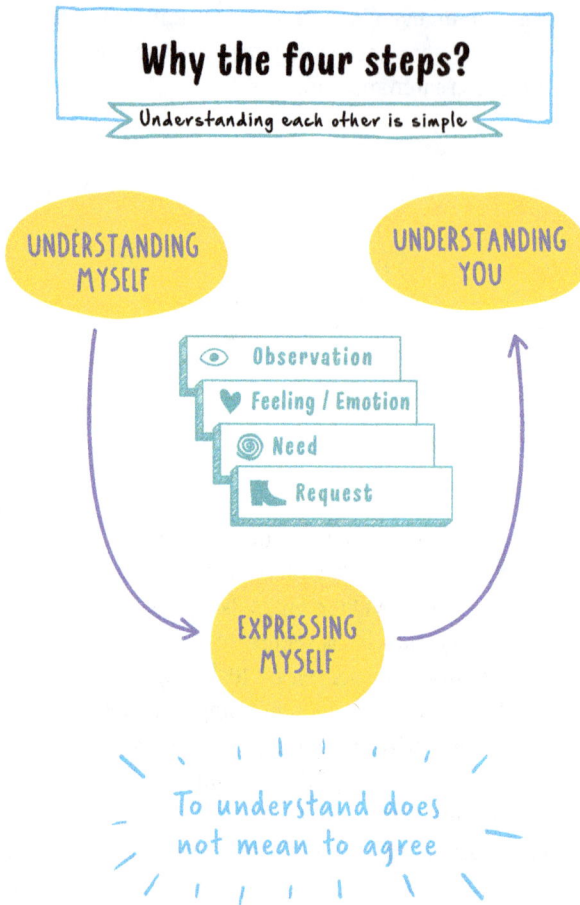

Figure 10.8: Why the 4 steps of nonviolent communication?
Source: The Loop Approach Handbook by The Dive GmbH, licensed under CC BY-SA 4.0 p.25, module chapter 3)

(IDG Framework: https://innerdevelopmentgoals.org/framework/) are of utmost importance in a connected world and in organizations. As mentioned in the section on critical thinking, we work tension- and proposal-based, and through an integrative decision-making process co-creation is ensured. It is the responsibility of the tension owner to collect the input of important stakeholders before a decision is taken. The basis for this is "consent vs. consensus" and a "safe enough to try" mindset. Failure in these processes is important for learning and we are aiming to build a psychologically safe culture in which true learning from failure is enabled.

Inclusive mindset and intercultural competence

Our fairstainability circle supports bringing this mindset of "willingness and competence to embrace diversity and include people and collectives with different views and backgrounds" into action. Here follows some highlights from our fairstainability report (ten23 Health AG, 2023).

In regard to fairness:
- 48% women employees
- 31% women in "management"
- no gender pay gap
- no serious injury or fatality
- 84% employee satisfaction score
- PRIDE Champion gold award
- 2nd place in Swiss HR Award
- 3rd place in Modern Work Award

At ten23, we currently have 200 employees with 24 different nationalities and ensure through our inclusive culture that this diversity is leveraged in our idea creation and innovation. Inclusion starts for us in every meeting with a check-in so that every voice is heard and is continued through integrated decision-making processes and so forth. We also celebrate the "different colors" of our personalities in team development workshops with Profile Dynamics®. Profile Dynamics® is a personality profile based on a motive theory of Clare W. Graves. Every employee at ten23 is invited to conduct this profiling, including an individual coaching.

Trust

The "ability to show trust and to create and maintain trusting relationships" (IDG Framework: https://innerdevelopmentgoals.org/framework/) is mainly reflected in our frameworks. Our frameworks are not "policies", they are guidelines for decision making that are based on trust. We have trusted work time as well as trusted holidays, which is described in our work-from-anywhere framework.

From our experience, trust grows when it is given and people are treated as trustworthy adults. We trust our people to spend the company's money as wisely as their own when it comes to business trips or external training. In cases where behavior seems not to be matching our company values, we give feedback and ask for the reasons.

Mobilization skills

"Skills in inspiring and mobilizing others to engage in shared purposes" (IDG Framework: https://innerdevelopmentgoals.org/framework/) are precious. Experience shows that being purpose-driven yourself very much inspires others to follow. That is one of the reasons why we work so much on the "why".

As a company, we grow significantly and it is important to recruit people that are inspired by our ways of working. In our recommendation program, our fellows inspire others to join us if it feels right for them and as a reward they can chose between a financial bonus or trees being planted for them. This real net promoter score is a sign for us that the mobilization skills of our fellows are already great – and surely driven by their purpose.

Acting – enabling change

"Qualities such as courage and optimism help us acquire true agency, break old patterns, generate original ideas and act with persistence in uncertain times." (IDG Framework: https://innerdevelopmentgoals.org/framework/) Unlearning old patterns is specifically important at ten23. Most of us have been trained for years in different hierarchical institutions and to now work self-organized is a journey of unlearning. For instance, we learn in school only to speak when we are asked; at ten23 we expect people to speak up whenever they have a tension. One example of the required unlearning is the "escalation" to a circle lead of any inter-personal conflict (relational space), whereas such interaction should be handled by direct feedback based on NVC.

Courage

Unlearning needs courage – the "ability to stand up for values, make decisions, take decisive action and, if need be, challenge and disrupt existing structures and views" (IDG Framework: https://innerdevelopmentgoals.org/framework/). Trusted work time and holidays, no titles, etc.: Many people tell us that these are crazy ideas and that it is impossible that we can be successful with this. Our learning so far is that it is hard to let go of some old patterns – but that it is so worth it to take courage and try.

Creativity

We strongly believe that everybody has the "ability to generate and develop original ideas, innovate and being willing to disrupt conventional patterns" (IDG Framework: https://innerdevelopmentgoals.org/framework/) – it is just often blocked by negative beliefs derived from negative experiences. Our workplace fosters creativity: sit down in a well-filled library or take a break in our break room with a hammock. Our role names range from "framework fanatic" to "mediation angel" and we encourage people to embrace creativity in roles names, office decor, innovative solutions for tensions, etc.

Optimism

The "ability to sustain and communicate a sense of hope, positive attitude and confidence in the possibility of meaningful change" (IDG Framework: https://innerdevelop mentgoals.org/framework/) is embraced by our cultural ambassadors. This is a circle that is responsible for driving the change towards our new ways of working.

The purpose of the role of an Cultural Ambassador is: To remain our culture at its core, and at the same time continuesly develop it through, tensions and exchange.

accountabilitiesof a Cultural Ambassador are:
–   being a role model and exemplifying our culture;
–   supporting the conception of P&C topics – be a critical sounding board;
–   supporting the rollout of P&C topics;
–   supporting in facilitation requests as help for self-help (without preparation and follow-up effort);
–   giving and receiving feedback and asking colleagues to address tensions themselves (being a loudspeaker/amplifier);
–   regularly exchanging regarding topics in the organization with the GC;
–   addressing when colleagues are not behaving in the spirit of our culture – being a mirror.

Perseverance

We are on a journey towards sustainability that needs the "ability to sustain engagement and remain determined and patient even when efforts take a long time to bear fruit" (IDG Framework: https://innerdevelopmentgoals.org/framework/). Therefore, we celebrate our successes on this journey to nurture perseverance. Here some highlights from our fairstainability report (ten23 Health AG, 2023):

In regard to sustainability:
–   100% renewable electricity
–   6% absolute reduction in total energy consumption
–   44% reduction in Scope 1 and Scope 2 GHG emissions/revenue
–   43% waste diverted from disposal (up from 34% in 2022)
–   150% offsets of our plastic waste sent to incineration

- 104% compensation of our total operational GHG emissions[2]
- silver medal from EcoVadis for our first participation (top 13% in our industry category)

Conclusion

We started our journey with the vision of a human-centric organization, and with the learnings and traumas of years and possibly decades of work experience in larger organizations. Our motivation and purpose is to create a human-centric and sustainable workplace, providing inspiration for other organizations, and aiming to contribute to a societal change, for which businesses do play a vital role as well.

We at ten23 are on a journey towards a new way of working based on self-organization, people-centricity and sustainability. We perceive the Inner Development Goals as a useful framework in developing the skills and mindset needed to fulfill our purpose of collaborating for a healthy life and planet. In the spirit of this purpose, we believe that we can provide something for our employees that will hopefully change not only their work life but their life as well.

IDGs help in identifying gaps and providing focus. Its five dimensions and 23 skills touch a variety of considerations for individual development that relate well to required twenty-first century skills – skills that are urgently needed to solve environmental and societal problems of today and tomorrow. We believe in inherent motivation, purpose, self-awareness, the need for critical thinking and complexity management, relating, collaborating, trust, courage, and creativity as key skills required in our organization. We support the growth of these skills by the application of the tools described in this chapter; ranging from recruitment to onboarding, to working and learning, to communication and conflict resolution, feedback.

In many of the skills, we did only the first step and often did not yet cover individual, team, and organizational levels with our approaches – but we will continue our journey and keep sharing our learnings.

We hope that with this chapter we can provide an inspiration for others and are open to further exchange, since we do not believe in a "zero-sum game" in that sense – in any kind of competition regarding company culture. What do you think about leadership in your organization? What is needed to drive sustainability and how could IDGs serve this purpose? What could the application of IDGs in the workplace do for you as an employee? Let us co create the future of work together!

---

2 GHG emissions from Sc1, Sc2 market-based, and Sc3 from fuel- and energy-related activities, waste generated in operations, business travel, and employee commuting.

References

Allen, D. (2015). *Getting Things Done: The Art of Stress-free Productivity*. Piatkus.

Beck, E. & Cowan, C. (1996). *Spiral Dynamics: Mastering Values, Leadership, and Change*. Blackwell Publishers 1. April 1996).

BLab (2023). Insights Series: Financial Performance and Resilience of B Corps – Infogram (accessed Jun. 3, 2024).

Collier, P., Coyle, D., Mayer C., Wolf M. (2021).*Capitalism*: *what has gone wrong, what needs to change, and how it can be fixed*, Oxford Review of Economic Policy, Volume 37, Issue 4, Winter 2021, Pages 637–649, https://doi.org/10.1093/oxrep/grab035.

Hampton, M. (2017). Fenced-in playgrounds: how boundaries can encourage greater creativity. https://uxdesign.cc/fenced-in-playgrounds-d5f9371f8414, accessed Jun. 3, 2024.

Inner development Goals. *Framework*. https://innerdevelopmentgoals.org/framework/.

Klein, S. & Hughes, B. (2020). *The Loop Approach: How to Transform Your Organization from the Inside Out*. Campus Verlag (August 1, 2020).

Laloux, F. (2016). *Reinventing organizations. A guide to creating organizations inspired by the next stage of human consciousness*. Nelson Parker.

McKinsey & Company. (2023, August 9). *The triple play: growth, profit and sustainability*. www.mckinsey.com/capabilities/strategy-and-corporate-finance/our-insights/the-triple-play-growth-profit-and-sustainability (accessed Mar. 23, 2024).

Sinek, S. (2011). *Start with the Why*. Penguin Publishing Group; Reprint Edition (27. Dezember 2011).

Ten23 Health AG (2022). *Fairstainability Report 2022*. https://www.ten23.health/introducing/knowledge-center.

Ten23 Health AG (2023). *Fairstainability Report 2023*. https://www.ten23.health/introducing/knowledge-center.

The Dive (2022). *The Loop Approach. How to transform your Organization – Handbook*. The Dive.

Whelan, T. & Fink, C. (2016). *The Comprehensive Business Case for Sustainability*. Harvard business Review, The Comprehensive Business Case for Sustainability (hbr.org) (accessed Jun. 3, 2024).

Eleftheria Egel, Louis W.(Jody) Fry and Mauricio Campos Suarez

Chapter 11
Global leadership for sustainability (GLfS) and Inner Development Goals (IDGs): An integrated framework and roadmap to enhance leader and leadership development

Abstract: This chapter proposes an integrated framework and roadmap to enhance leader and leadership capacity in addressing sustainability challenges. By employing the first principles thinking approach, it delves into the fundamental assumptions that underpin sustainability solutions within the neoliberal paradigm, aiming to deconstruct and comprehend holistically how the system conditions leaders. Second, it reconceptualizes these building blocks to offer a novel, coherent perspective able to tackle the root causes of the sustainability crisis and identifies the leadership qualities necessary to shift this system. Third, it provides an integrated framework which integrates the Inner Development Goals (IDGs) within a model of global leadership for sustainability (GLfS) (Fry & Egel, 2021). The chapter concludes with reflections and questions regarding the shifting perspectives on sustainability, the evolving roles and responsibilities of leaders in this context, and the feasibility and implications of the suggested roadmap.

Keywords: GLfS, IDGs, first principles thinking, sustainability, triple bottom line, levels of being

Introduction

> Trying to change the world without changing our mind is like trying to clean the dirty face we see in the mirror by rubbing the glass. However vigorously we clean it, our reflection will not improve. Only by washing our own face and combing our own unkempt hair can we alter the image. Similarly, if we want to help create conditions that foster peace and well-being in the world, we first need to reflect those qualities ourselves. (Chagdud Tulku Rinpoche, 2003)

Most organizations, despite advocating for the triple bottom line (TBL), craft their main strategies solely around profit, relegating considerations for people and the planet to secondary operational roles. This profit-centric focus renders any real transformation towards genuine sustainability difficult, if not impossible. To be able as leaders and organizations to generate innovative solutions that enhance social and

https://doi.org/10.1515/9783111453729-012

environmental flourishing, it is essential to gain a deeper understanding of the complex phenomenon of sustainability. The first principles thinking approach used in innovation helps address current complex challenges, such as sustainability (Thiel & Masters, 2014). It is attributed to ancient Greek philosophers Aristotle and Socrates but, in our days, has been popularized by successful entrepreneurs like Peter Thiel and Elon Musk. It involves three stages of intervention. The first stage involves breaking down abstract concepts into their simplest forms, while eliminating unnecessary preconceptions and biases. Doing so allows one to delve into the essence of matters, avoiding superficial interpretations; to identify core truths and reveal hidden connections and dependencies. The second stage takes place once one returns to fundamentals. It encompasses reassembling insights into holistic understandings, synthesizing pieces into a coherent perspective. Ultimately, the third stage involves inventive approaches to solving a problem.

We followed the first principles thinking approach in our webinar held online via the Swiss IDG Hub on 25 January 2024. We began by examining the underlying assumptions underpinning sustainability solutions within the neoliberal paradigm and the types of leadership that emerge from this system (Stage A). We called this operational system Sustainability 1.0. To guide our analysis, we utilized a conceptualization of leadership by levels of being, as described by Fry and Kriger (2009). Then, we critically reconstructed these assumptions toward a holistic perspective (Stage B), which we called Sustainability 2.0. Finally, we provided a novel solution: a framework to implement this fresh perspective within organizations to foster leader and leadership capacity for sustainability. The integrated framework comprises the global leadership for sustainability (GLfS; Fry & Egel, 2021) and skills of the Inner Development Goals (IDGs) inherent in the GLfS. Together, they offer a synergistic, comprehensive approach towards leadership for sustainability (Stage C; see Figure 11.5).

Below we provide a detailed explanation of how we applied the three stages of the first principles thinking approach in our webinar to explore the necessary narrative shift to enable organizations to innovate to enhance social well-being and environmental sustainability. We examine the inner shift from the perspective of individual leaders, focusing on mindset and narrative, as well as from a cultural and collective standpoint in terms of leadership development.

First principles thinking

Stage A

Utilizing analytical thinking, we looked into the root causes behind the sustainability challenge (sometimes called primary drivers, fundamental principles, or basic blocks) in order to achieve a holistic understanding of the entire predicament. Our aim was

to comprehend how the basic assumptions of the system (the neoliberal paradigm) impact both sustainability efforts and leaders' personal and organizational decision making regarding sustainability issues (see Table 11.1).

Central to our query was the question: *Why do leaders struggle to implement the TBL even though they are passionate to do so?*

Stage B

After synthesizing our findings, we started searching for a solution from scratch. Our aim was to reshape the foundational assumptions of the system in order to legitimize the choice of sustainability over profit-driven alternatives as well as envision the leadership qualities required to realize this transformation.

During our quest we pondered: *How can we reshape and rearrange the basic blocks in order to provide a novel, coherent perspective conducive for sustainability?*

Stage C

Having devised a blueprint, we proposed a tailored toolkit intended to help implement this coherent perspective. Our aim was to provide a roadmap of transformation; a new system along with new attributes that can boost leader and leadership capacity for sustainability.

Considering our path forward, we asked ourselves: *How can we act on this novel, coherent perspective?*

Finally, we invited our participants to a collective exchange and deep reflection. Our aim was to provoke critical thinking and discussion about the future direction of sustainability efforts.

In the following sections we will look into each one of the three stages and will close with a discussion on the reflections and questions by the webinar participants.

Table 11.1: First principles thinking approach applied in the webinar.

First principles thinking	Core question	Modus operandi
Stage A	Why do leaders struggle to implement the TBL even though they are passionate to do so?	Sustainability 1.0
Stage B	How can we reshape and rearrange the basic blocks in order to provide a novel, coherent perspective conducive for sustainability?	Sustainability 2.0
Stage C	How can we act on this novel, coherent perspective?	Transition

Sustainability 1.0

First principles thinking – Stage A

At this stage we examined the root causes behind the sustainability challenge by analyzing the fundamental assumptions that underpin the system, including our worldview and the economy, as well as the leadership qualities that the system promotes and rewards. The core question we aimed to answer was: *Why do leaders struggle to implement the TBL even though they are passionate to do so?*

We live in an era where we acknowledge the volatile, uncertain, complex, and ambiguous (VUCA) nature of our world. In academic literature, over 3,000 papers including "sustainable" or "sustainability" in their titles or abstracts are published annually (Kajikawa et al., 2007). Furthermore, the asset value of European sustainability funds exceeds 5.5 trillion euros in 2024 (Mitra, 2024), while US-domiciled assets under management surpassed 8.4 trillion US dollars in 2021 (US SIF Foundation, 2022). Despite the engagement and resources committed, we have not made significant progress towards achieving the Sustainable Development Goals (SDGs), except for transitioning from a VUCA to a BANI (brittle, anxious, nonlinear, incomprehensible) (Zakharov, 2022) understanding of the current global environment, which in addition to the fragility and unpredictability of modern systems, acknowledges their emotional and cognitive impacts of the world.

Our incapacity to find solutions despite our best intentions and willingness prompted us to examine the systemic barriers and leadership limitations that prevent leaders from effectively implementing the TBL within their organizations. In this pursuit, we used a widely accepted definition of sustainability which describes sustainability as a prerequisite for attaining the sustainability goals and as a constraint on sustainable development. This perspective views sustainable development as development that "meets the needs of the present generation without compromising the ability of future generations to meet their own needs" (Brundtland, 1987, p.54).

The system

We define our current phase as Sustainability 1.0. This phase is largely shaped by the neoliberal economic paradigm, which emphasizes market-driven approaches, individualism, and short-term profits. The neoliberal economic paradigm, central to Sustainability 1.0, prioritizes economic growth and efficiency over environmental and social considerations. This approach often leads to superficial sustainability efforts that do not address the root causes of environmental degradation and social inequality (see Figure 11.1).

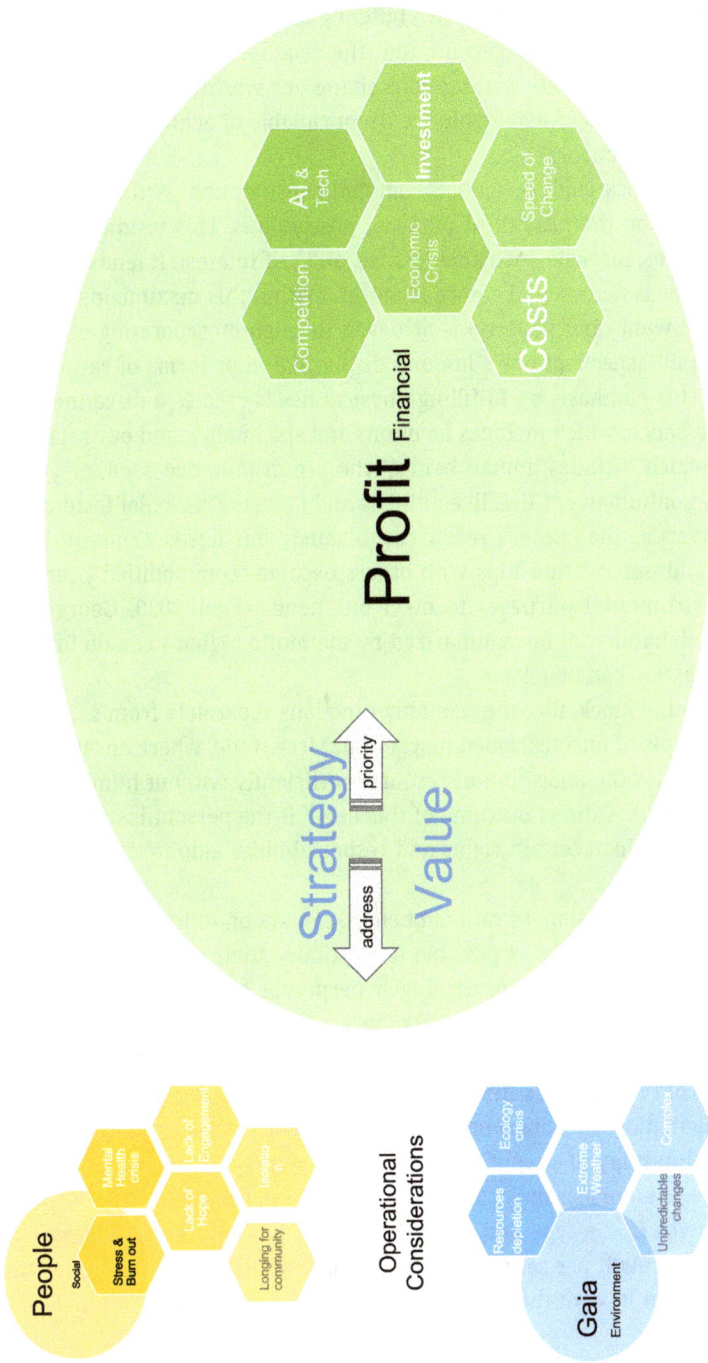

Figure 11.1: The Triple Bottom Line at Sustainability 1.0 (Source: Authors' own).

The Sustainability 1.0 context operates on two building blocks. First, that the physical world is the prevailing reality, and second, that the economy functions separately from society (see Table 11.2). These assumptions shape our worldview, the decisions we make, as well as the types of leadership we deem capable of achieving our vision both individually and collectively.

The first building block leads to materialism and consumption. Within this reality, our vision focuses on the pursuit of material possessions. This vision wants to maximize profit, desires, markets, instrumental use, and self-interest. It tends to build a world where "bigger is better" and "more is more". Within this maximizing framework, freedom from want (and poverty) is achieved through incorporating effective market behavior in all aspects of one's life and displacing other forms of rationality (McMurtry, 2009). This emphasis on fulfilling physical needs creates a disconnection between our own essence, which includes emotions and spirituality, and our relationship with others, which includes human beings who are distant, deceased, or yet to be born, as well as nonhuman entities, like animals and nature. This belief fosters our right to use and overuse the planet's resources to satisfy our needs. Consequently, both our identity and our relationships with others become "commodified", serving functional and instrumental purposes to meet our needs (Egel, 2020; Georgescu-Roegen, 1971). This dynamic can be summarized by the motto "What I can do for you in exchange for what you can do for me".

The second building block, that the economy functions separately from society, is reflected in the concepts of unconstrained markets and free trade, where an "invisible hand" supposedly guides the allocation of resources efficiently without human intervention (Swedberg, 2009). A direct outcome of this belief is the personification of corporations, which grants them certain rights and responsibilities akin to those of natural persons.

Within this reality, our vision, as rational beings, centers on utility maximization: allocating resources as efficiently as possible to maximize their utility. The scarcity mindset fuels relentless competition, driving a perpetual quest for development where success is measured by outperforming others, often at their expense. Technological innovation and resource substitution are viewed as the means to disassociate economic growth from the planet's limited capacity (Fligstein, 2018). It is worth noting, that in cost calculations, products or goods have no inherent value; their price is determined by the interplay of supply and demand (Hayek & Stelzer, 1960). Alternative development (e.g., emphasis on local efforts, promotion of community autonomy, etc.) proposes changes in the type and scope of growth, but does not challenge the concept of economic growth per se. Another trait of paternalism is arrogance, as the Global North decides on its own the means and ends of the assistance it offers to the Global South.

Table 11.2: Sustainability 1.0 First Principles Thinking – Stage A (Source: Authors' own).

BUILDING BLOCK 1	BUILDING BLOCK 2
The prevailing reality is the physical world	Economy is separate from society
IMPORTANT IMPLICATIONS	**IMPORTANT IMPLICATIONS**
Human identity and relations	Homo lupus and neoliberalism
Vision based on consumption leads to constant pursuit of material possessions and the constant desire for newer and better product (secularism)	There is an "invisible hand" that efficiently guides the allocation of resources without human intervention
Physical human needs are more important than other needs (e.g., emotional, spiritual). Focus on satisfying physical needs first (fragmented approach to human needs)	Human role is utility maximization. It is justified by utilitarian ethics
Our well-being (happiness and success) is an outcome of satisfying our physical needs (materiality/consumerism)	Competition is the driving force

Leadership within Sustainability 1.0

To explore how leaders perceive and respond to sustainability challenges, make decisions, and interact with others, we examine how their state of consciousness, reflected in their "being" (personal identity, beliefs, values, emotions, and subjective experiences) and their "knowing" (the cognitive process of acquiring, understanding, and applying information) shapes their reality and results in specific leadership actions and outcomes. We use as our guide Fry and Kriger's (2009) seminal work "Towards a theory of being-centered leadership: Multiple levels of being as context for effective leadership".

Being-centered leadership

The being-centered leadership (BCL) theory (see Figure 11.2; Fry & Kriger, 2009; Kriger & Seng, 2005) is based on the world's major wisdom traditions. It illustrates a spiritual journey of transformation of leaders from ego-centered to other-centered states of knowing and being to guide leaders, facilitate clear vision, consciousness from moment to moment, and the ability to engage and enlist others. The levels of being are different states of consciousness, marked by the lower-order systems of knowledge and moving to progressively higher-order systems. When at a particular level of being, a person tends to experience psychological states and states of self-awareness that are appropriate to that level. In addition, an individual's feelings, motivations, ethics, values, learning system, and personal theories of what constitutes happiness are consistent with and appropriate to that level of being.

Each higher level is holonic in that it transcends and includes each of the lower levels. Moreover, each lower level can be activated or reactivated as individuals progress and then fall back to a lower level, even in a single day. Thus, each level can manifest in any particular activity depending on the level of self-awareness and spiritual development of the individual at that time. More important still, every individual has all of these levels potentially available, independent of their current stage of development. At each level, leaders find themselves concerned with questions such as: What is knowledge? What are the processes by which knowledge is acquired? What do people seek to know? How do we become more aware of both ourselves and the world around us?

Nondual Leadership
(leadership based on Oneness and & Unity with True Nature or Divine Essence)

Global Leadership for Sustainability
(leadership based on self -transcendent love and service of others)

Conscious Leadership
(leadership based on being aware in the now from moment -to-moment)

Leadership from Vision & Values
(Leadership based on social construction of reality)

Leadership from Having & Doing
(Leadership based on leader traits & behavior appropriate to the context)

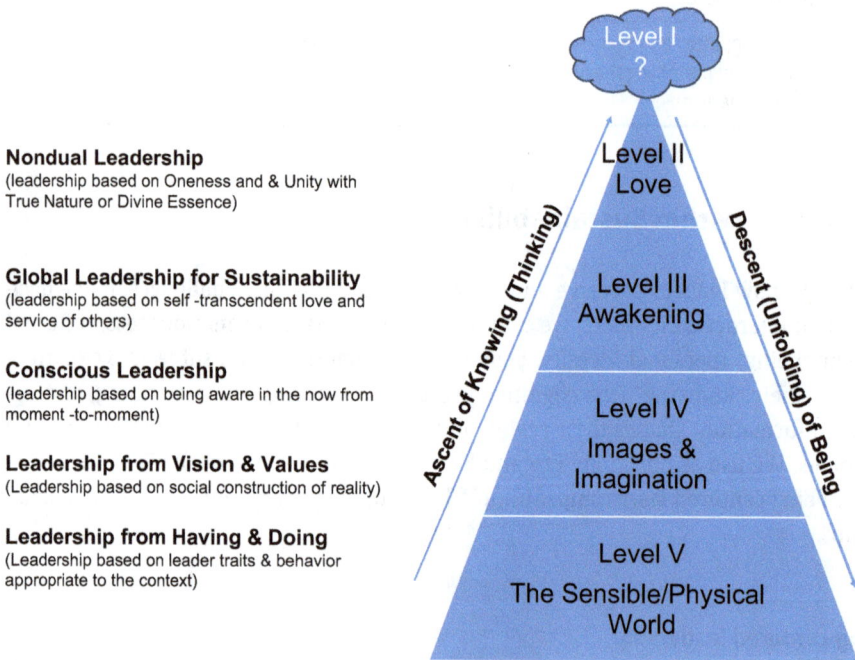

Figure 11.2: Levels of being (Source: Fry and Kriger, 2009).

Sustainability 1.0 argues for "heroic" leadership types. Leadership qualities promoted and valued include rationality, instrumentality, individualism, control, assertiveness, advocacy skills, domination, and a preference for hierarchical relationships. In Sustainability 1.0, leaders function at Levels V and IV. Below is a brief overview of Levels V and IV (see Table 11.4).

Level V way of knowing and being

The fifth level comprises the physical observable world which is based in the five senses, wherein a leader creates and transfers knowledge through an active engagement in worldly affairs. As a state of being, it is composed of individuals that are born into and still live within a social world where the major view of reality is based on the sensible/physical world. Effective leadership in the sensible/physical world requires developing appropriate diagnostic skills to discern the characteristics of tasks, subordinates, and the organization and then being flexible enough in one's leadership behavior to increase the likelihood of desired effectiveness outcomes. Leadership theories at this level include trait, behavior, and contingency theories of leadership (Bass, 1990; Kirkpatric & Locke, 1991; House, 1996).

Level IV way of knowing and being

The fourth level of being is where reality is socially constructed through the creation and maintenance of vision, cultural values, and images. At this level, leadership involves the use of images and imagination, the process of creating a compelling vision, and establishing strong cultural values. The main goal of leadership at this level is to create agreement on a socially constructed reality which motivates followers to high levels of organizational commitment and performance. The primary focus at this level is on the subjective experience of individuals and groups as they relate to the development of awareness and knowledge. Out of this level arises the legitimacy and appropriateness of a leader's vision, as well as the ethical and cultural values which individuals and groups should embrace or reject. Here the vision and values of the leader may be either self- or other-centered (e.g., Hitler vs. Mahatma Gandi). Charismatic and transformational leadership theories characterize this level (DeGroot, Kiker, & Cross, 2000; Judge & Piccolo, 2004).

Sustainability 2.0

First principles thinking – Stage B

At this stage, we reshaped and reorganized the foundational assumptions that underpin the system, including our worldview, the economy, as well as the leadership qualities that the system promotes and rewards. We provided a novel, coherent perspective conducive for sustainability. The core question that guided our inquiry was: *How can we reshape and rearrange the basic blocks in order to provide a novel, coherent perspective conducive for sustainability?*

The system

We define this phase as Sustainability 2.0. It is largely shaped by a shift from a dualistic to a holistic understanding of the relationship of people with people and people with nature. This shift is also described as "spiritual transformation" (Coates, 2003). Specifically, the two building blocks of Sustainability 1.0 as well as the type of leadership at the system are redefined (see Figure 11.3). First, the world is no longer seen primarily as a collection of physical matter to be exploited, but as a life-enhancing ecology which recognizes the interconnectedness and intrinsic value of all life forms and nature. Second, the economy is not viewed as an independent system operating separately from social concerns, but as one embedded within the broader context of society (see Table 11.3). As far as leadership is concerned, Sustainability 2.0 advocates leadership types that are at Levels III and II (see Table 11.4).

The first building block – that the world is a life-enhancing ecology which recognizes the interconnectedness and intrinsic value of all life forms and nature – calls humans to a new role in "solidarity with all other creatures of the earth" and to seek what Lyons et al. (2016) identifies as "mutually enhancing human-earth relationships" (p. 13). The consciousness of unity and interdependence can manifest itself in our reasoning, our personal attributes, and our ethics. At that level, human fulfillment is not limited to our own self-actualization (though this is indeed part of the process). It expands beyond self to incorporate compassion for the needs of all people and species on Earth, a willingness to act for the common good, and assuming responsibility for our conduct. Relationships are not egocentric and commodified; they become personal, egalitarian, and dialogic.

The second building block – that the economy is integrated in society – means that politics and culture are not external to the economic dynamic (Carruthers, 1999). From this perspective, social forces are crucial to the functioning of markets as the development of new markets requires extensive social organization (Podolny, 1993). The focus has shifted from "alternative development" to "alternatives to development", where the economy respects planetary boundaries and promotes the harmonious coexistence of all lifeforms. Breaching these boundaries would mean destabilizing Earth's systems on a planetary scale, threatening most life on earth. This approach emphasizes local efforts, community autonomy, grassroots movements, collaboration, local knowledge, and popular power to transform development. It rejects the former supremacy of global culture over local cultures and paternalism, promoting equity and collaboration. It also considers multiple types of rational action, including value rationality. Within the value rationality logic, social and ecological costs are not "externalities". Instead, they are integral costs that must be included in the sale price (Stiglitz & Charlton, 2006).

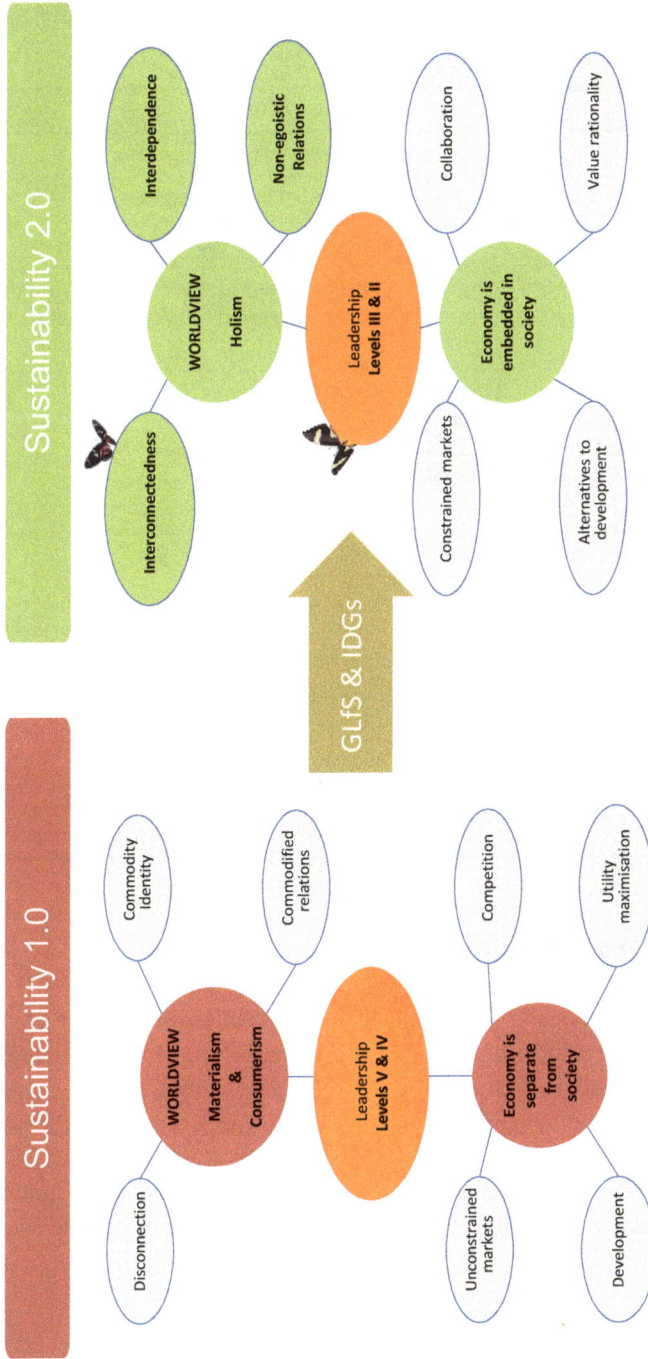

Figure 11.3: Shifting from Sustainability 1.0 to Sustainability 2.0 (Source: Authors' own, based on Egel, 2015).

Table 11.3: Sustainability 2.0 First Principles Thinking – Stage B (Source: Authors' own, based on Egel, 2015).

BUILDING BLOCK 1	BUILDING BLOCK 2
The prevailing reality is life-enhancing ecology	Economy is embedded in society
IMPORTANT IMPLICATIONS	**IMPORTANT IMPLICATIONS**
Human identity and relations	**Homo socius and social economy**
Holistic vision of flourishing based on ecological awareness of our relationship with the full depth and mystery of the universe	Economy is there to solve societal problems. The allocation of resources is decided on ethical principles of equity
Nonphysical human needs (emotional, spiritual) and also the needs of nature and other living creatures are equally important. Material possessions are a means for meeting human needs and not a goal per se	Human role is stewardship
Our well-being is tied to the well-being of all (interconnectedness)	Collaboration is the driving force
We go beyond our illusion of taking our own environment of being the world itself (self-transcendence)	The price of a product has an innate value which includes social and ecological costs
Human relations are personal, egalitarian, and dialogic	No economic growth per se. Respect for planetary boundaries
	Equal power relations: emphasis is on local efforts, community autonomy, grassroots movements

Leadership at Sustainability 2.0

Sustainability 2.0 promotes and values leadership qualities that include empathy, helpfulness, caring, and nurturance, as well as a focus on community, vulnerability, and interpersonal sensitivity. Leaders are attentive to and accepting of others, responsive to their needs and motivations, and orientated towards collective interests and integrative goals such as group cohesiveness and stability. They prefer open, egalitarian, and collaborative relationships. In this paradigm, leaders primarily function at Level III, occasionally at Level II, and aspire to reach Level I. Below is a brief overview of Levels III, II, and I (see Table 11.4).

Level III way of knowing and being

This level of being is foundational for Sustainability 2.0. At this level, self-awareness and self-transcendence begin to emerge and become more dominant. To awaken or become conscious at Level III involves the capacity to be aware from moment to moment of all of our experiences, thoughts, feelings, and bodily sensations. Without this felt experience in the current moment, a leader's thinking will tend to become focused on past memories based in anger and resentment, as well as future imaginings that produce worry and fear.

By committing to an inner life practice (e.g., meditation, prayer, yoga, journaling, walking in nature, etc.), a leader's individual and social identity are redefined through a discipline of constantly observing one's thought patterns and what one pays attention to in order to get the self-centered ego out of the way. It allows one to explore the often crippling emotional programs for happiness that are developed in early childhood based on needs for survival, security, affection, esteem, power, and control (Keating, 1999). It also requires exploring the over attachment or over identification with any particular group or culture to which one belongs. In doing so, questions or issues are addressed, such as: What is my agenda? What is my predisposition? What are my prejudices? What are my fears? What are my angers? Answering these questions requires one to develop the ability to stand away from themselves, listen and look with a calm, nonjudgmental objectivity.

Level II way of knowing and being

Level II builds upon the commitment to Level III to more consistently be able to love and serve others through self-transcendence and deepening connectedness with all things in the universe. Once one accepts the possibility that their view of the world is just one of many alternative interpretations of reality and can more consistently remain present in the now, which is devoid of feelings, thoughts, and emotions, one's ways of experiencing (existential being), knowing (cognitive), and behaving changes.

At Level II, leaders more readily and consistently seek to understand and empathize stakeholders' perspectives and respect their opinions and dignity as human beings. At this level, the focus is on leadership based on loving and serving others. Recognized examples of leadership at Level II include Mother Teresa, Gandhi, Martin Luther King, and Nelson Mandela. Very few organizational leaders are consistently at Level II, though they can often lead from this level temporarily.

Level I way of knowing and being

Level I is the most inclusive level of being, characterized by a transcendent unity. Underlying this level is a central theme: the transcendence of all opposites and the realization of self-actualization. Level I thus incorporates all of the previous levels of being and is beyond all distinctions, including that of leader and follower. Level I leadership is an ideal stage of being that is more aspirational, rather than a current reality within human or organizational settings.

The awakening that occurs at Level III and above enables us to shift from the limited leadership types found at Levels IV and V, which are inherent in Sustainability 1.0, to the more evolved and integrated leadership types found at Levels III and II that are essential for achieving Sustainability 2.0 (Egel, 2020).

Table 11.4: Leadership at levels of being ((Source: Authors' own, based on Fry & Kriger, 2009).

Level of being	Leadership types	Key attributes of leadership	State of consciousness (being & knowing)	Goal of organizational leadership
Level V	Trait, situational, transactional Path-goal and contingency	Having and doing	It is shaped by the five senses	Acquire resources, be efficient and effective
Level IV	Charismatic/ narcissistic, transformational	Compelling vision and strong cultural values	It is shaped by the social and cultural context in which we live	Foster inclusive environments, effectively navigate complex social dynamics, achieve shared goals, promote organizational success
Level III	Conscious, responsible, ethical, authentic, relational	Self and other-awareness	It is rooted in our subjective felt experience of the present	Awaken leaders' capacity to lead more wisely and more lovingly
Level II	Spiritual, servant, global leadership for sustainability (GLfS)	Self-transcendence and interconnectedness	It is shaped by our connection to a deeper, more expansive self and our holistic understanding of the systemic, relational, and contextual aspects of reality	Make decisions that prioritize ethical considerations and long-term sustainability, and foster a culture of compassion, collaboration, and continuous improvement.
Level I	Non-dual	Oneness	It is rooted in inclusion of both pure emptiness and pure completeness	–

Paving the pathway from Sustainability 1.0 to Sustainability 2.0

First principles thinking – Stage C

At this stage, the core question we wanted to answer is: How can we act on this novel, coherent perspective? Referencing Figure 11.3, we proposed shifting successfully from Sustainability 1.0 to Sustainability 2.0 by employing the GLfS framework, supported at every step by the IDG framework. The skills outlined in the IDG framework are crucial for cultivating leaders and leadership that effectively support sustainability. These skills are also inherent in the GLfS. Highlighting them (see Figure 11.5) aids in the successful implementation of the GLfS.

An important element in this process is to remember that we are dealing with two levels of intervention. Based on Day et al.'s (2000) distinction between "leader and leadership development" (2014) we are targeting individual leaders and leadership which includes influencing others to achieve a shared goal. "Leader development" focuses on supporting individual leaders to overcome their industrial meaning making (see Table 11.2). In this category, leaders are defined as all change agents who seek sustainable change, regardless of role or position (Ferdig, 2007). Leadership development aims to create a comprehensive process that inherently involves multiple individuals (e.g., leaders and followers or among peers in a self-managed work team) and legitimizes the choice of sustainability over profit making. These two levels of intervention inform each other in an iterative way. If leaders do not expand their consciousness from Levels V and IV to Level III and beyond, they cannot effectively interact with others or make decisions at the level of Sustainability 2.0. Conversely, when leaders operate at Sustainability 2.0, they support the evolution of individual leaders.

In the following sections we will briefly introduce the GLfS and IDG frameworks. We will then present an integrated framework for sustainability that incorporates the IDG dimensions and skills within the GLfS (see Figure 11.5).

The global leadership for sustainability (GLfS) framework

GLfS is a model for organizational transformation to a learning organization designed to facilitate vision and value congruence across the individual, empowered team, organization, and stakeholder ecosystem levels. GLfS (see Figure 11.4) is grounded in being-centered leadership theory, spiritual leadership theory, and the spiritual leadership model, which has seen extensive research, validation, and application (Benefiel, Fry, & Geigle, 2014; Fry & Nisiewicz, 2020). GLfS requires the cultivation of a global mindset for sustainability (GMS), which fosters leadership for sustainability (LfS) through hope/faith in a vision for sustainability and sustainable development and an

Leadership for Sustainability

Spiritual Well-Being

Triple Bottom Line

HOPE/ FAITH

Vision for Sustainability

PURPOSE

Calling for sustainability
Life has meaning / Makes a difference

Organizational Commitment & Productivity
Life satisfaction
Triple Bottom Line (TBL)

ALTRUISTIC LOVE

COMMUNITY

Membership/belonging for sustainability

GLOBAL MINDSET
Presencing Practice

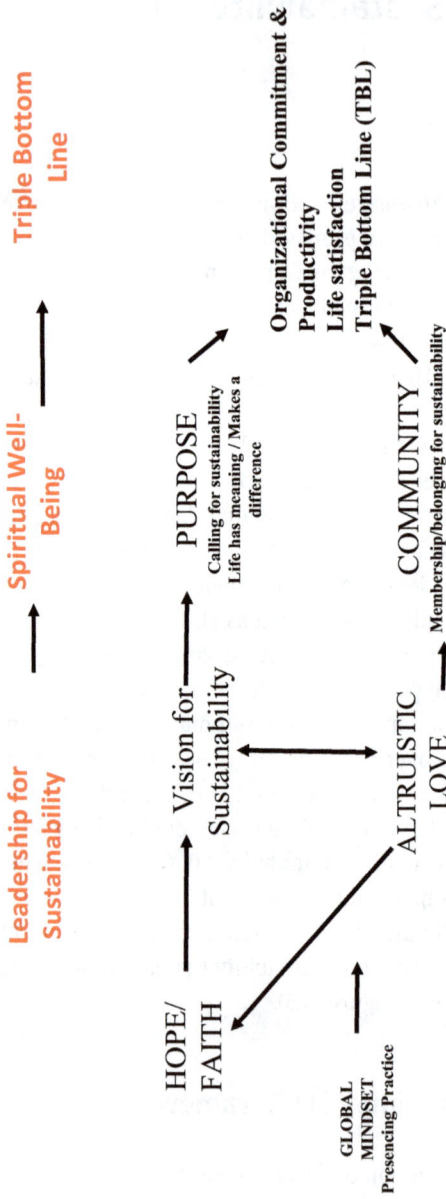

Figure 11.4: Global leadership for sustainability (GLfS) framework Source: Fry & Egel 2021.

organizational culture based on the values of altruistic love. LfS, then, satisfies the fundamental needs of both leaders and followers for spiritual well-being through a sense of (1) calling/purpose to be change agents for sustainability and (2) belonging or membership in a loving, supportive community for sustainable development. In turn, spiritual well-being positively influences the economic, social, and environmental outcomes for sustainability that are inherently represented through triple bottom line key performance indicators.

A global mindset for sustainability is the foundation for leader development and global leadership for sustainability. This mindset involves committing to the cultivation of Levels III and II of the levels of being, developing self-awareness and presence through an inner life practice, and moving beyond the stress-reduction focus of typical corporate mindfulness programs to a deeper consciousness. This interconnectedness and awareness enable leaders to have a more transparent lens through which to make better sense of the global world within which they operate (Rhinesmith, 1996), helping them build more meaningful relationships and realize the futility of Levels V and IV inherent to Sustainability 1.0. GMS fosters communication based on universal values that are common to the world's spiritual and religious traditions, transcending cultural and religious differences.

The Inner Development Goals (IDGs) framework

The IDGs offer a scientifically informed approach to cultivate the inner qualities critical for developing leaders and leadership for sustainability. The IDG framework encompasses five key dimensions and 23 skills (Stålne & Greca, 2022). These skills are abilities that people can learn and improve over time through training, practice, and exposure to challenges, and they can be useful in both personal and professional life.

Below we will briefly describe the five dimensions and how the skills and qualities within each dimension relate.

Being dimension

This refers to our relationship with ourselves. Leaders cultivate self-awareness by being present (*self-awareness and presence*). This cultivation fosters curiosity and a willingness to be vulnerable and embrace change and grow (*openness and a learning mindset*). Greater self-awareness leads to a clearer "inner-standing" of our motivations, values, and purpose (*integrity and authenticity*) and encourages action from that deeper state of being (*inner compass*).

Thinking dimension

This emphasizes systems thinking, which enables leaders to understand root causes and craft solutions that address the entire system, not just isolated symptoms (Meadows, 2008). Systems thinking involves analyzing and evaluating different components of a system and how they interact (*critical thinking*), considering the long-term implications and sustainability of actions within the system (*long-term orientation and visioning*), integrating knowledge and perspectives from various disciplines to better understand complex systems (*perspective skills*), gaining a comprehensive view of the system's overall dynamics (*sensemaking*), and identifying the interconnections and interdependencies within the system (*complexity awareness*).

Relating dimension

This pertains to our ability to care for others and the broader world. It involves valuing the worth of others (*appreciation*), recognizing and fostering the link between individuals and the interconnectedness of all life (*connectedness*), maintaining a grounded sense of self (*humility*), understanding the feelings of others and responding with kindness and support (*empathy and compassion*).

Collaborating dimension

This focuses on how we work together effectively. It is built on a foundation of psychological safety where individuals feel secure, valued, and respected (*trust*) and an appreciation of diversity (*inclusive mindset and intercultural competence*). It informs conveying ideas clearly and listening actively (*communication skills*) leading to generating innovative solutions and achieving common goals (*co-creation skills*) as well as activating others to collectively act (*mobilization skills*).

Action dimension

To drive meaningful change we need to generate novel solutions and approaches (*creativity*) and confront and overcome obstacles with bravery (*courage*). In case difficulties persist, we need to maintain positivity (*optimism*) and continue striving towards our goal (*perseverance*).

In the following section, we will examine how the IDG dimensions and skills are integrated within the GLfS framework. We will explore the synergistic approach of this integrated framework for global leadership for sustainability for leader and leadership development, designed to facilitate the transition from Sustainability 1.0 to Sustainability 2.0, ultimately aiming to achieve the triple bottom line (TBL; see Figure 11.5).

The integrated framework for global leadership for sustainability

Figure 11.5 provides a framework for leader and leadership development, which represents a synergistic approach to achieving the TBL. This integrated framework, which includes both theoretical and conceptual elements as well as practical implementation components, serves as a comprehensive roadmap for developing leader and leadership capacity for sustainability.

Global mindset for sustainability and "being" dimension

Leaders cultivate a GMS when they commit to the spiritual journey of self-transcendence and interconnectedness and have developed the ability to more consistently lead from Levels III and II of being (Fry & Egel, 2021). One of the key things for leaders is to develop self-awareness through practices that help them stay focused and mindful moment to moment. This helps ensure that they can better discern their strengths and weaknesses and thus not be overly influenced by negative emotions and not fall blindly or unconsciously into selfish actions that are inappropriate, destructive, or self-contradictory (Mackey et al., 2021.

The *being* dimension of the IDGs supports leaders to develop and sustain a GMS by emphasizing personal growth and self-awareness as fundamental for driving sustainable development and positive societal change. When *being* skills, such as presence, inner compass, integrity, and self-awareness are cultivated, they enable individuals to navigate complexities with clarity and authenticity. This dimension advocates for mindfulness, emotional regulation, and a profound connection to one's values and purpose, fostering a sense of responsibility and resilience.

Leadership for sustainability and "thinking", "relating" and "acting" dimensions

A GMS is the source of leadership for sustainability(LfS), and fosters it through hope/faith in a vision for sustainability and an organizational culture based on the values of altruistic love. The *acting, thinking,* and *relating* IDG skills are particularly important for developing leadership for sustainability.

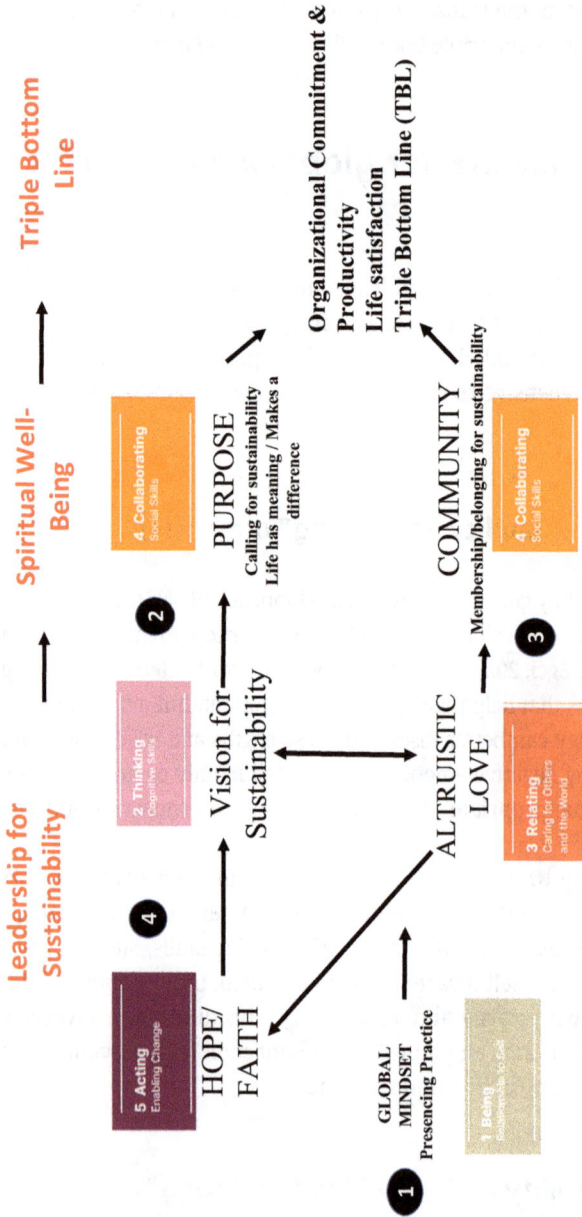

Figure 11.5: Integrated framework for global leadership for sustainability (Source: Authors' own).

Hope/faith and "acting" dimension

Hope/faith in the context of LfS involves inspiring trust in an organization's vision and aligning this vision with broader sustainable development goals (Fry, 2003; Fry & Egel, 2021). Furthermore, hope/faith facilitates a leader's capacity to inspire trust and confidence in a shared vision, motivating individuals to persevere through challenges and remain committed to their goals. This conviction fosters trust in the vision's pursuit. MacArthur's (1998) "vision quest" metaphor aptly compares this faith to preparing for and running a race, driven by hope for victory and the joy of the journey itself.

Similarly, the *acting* dimension of the IDGs focuses on the ability to initiate and drive change by translating intentions into concrete actions for sustainability. Like hope/faith, *acting* is based on the conviction that the vision holds value and requires proactive effort. Leaders must inspire trust and motivate change agents within the organization, even when immediate success is not evident. This dimension equips leaders and changemakers with essential skills – such as courage, creativity, optimism, and perseverance – that empower them to embody and convey hope/faith, effectively moving from intention to action. These skills support the development of true agency, the disruption of outdated patterns, the generation of original ideas, and the ability to persist in uncertain times.

Vision and "thinking" dimension

A compelling vision fuels organizational success by defining its aspirations and rallying leaders and followers (Collins & Porras, 1996. For a vision to mobilize effectively, it must be broadly appealing, chart a defined journey, inspire hope, uphold high ideals, and set a high benchmark for performance excellence. Collaborating with all partners actively in developing an inspiring and compelling vision for sustainability becomes essential, as it fosters a shared sense of purpose for sustainable development.

The *thinking* dimension of IDGs aids in developing such a clear and compelling vision by equipping leaders with the cognitive skills and mental models necessary for navigating uncertainties and aligning efforts with sustainable development goals. This dimension emphasizes the development of critical thinking, systems thinking, and long-term orientation, which are essential for understanding interdependencies and the broader context of challenges. By fostering a shared understanding of root causes and potential solutions to societal and environmental challenges, it encourages collaborative problem solving and the formulation of well-informed strategies and effective solutions.

Altruistic love and "relating" dimension

Altruistic love in LfS fosters a strong sense of community and shared purpose for sustainability, which is critical for achieving sustainable organizational success. Altruistic love is "a sense of wholeness, harmony, and well-being produced through care, concern, and appreciation for both self and others" (Fry, 2003, p. 712). The practice of integrity, compassion, and kindness leads to developing a feeling of interconnectedness among those involved. It promotes a culture where employees feel genuinely valued and supported, increasing intrinsic motivation and engagement.

The *relating* dimension of the IDGs is rooted in the values of altruistic love, which prioritize caring for others and the broader world. Sourced from the heart, a humble leader appreciates the inner worth of others, listens empathetically, and acts compassionately to their concerns in a way that only those who feel the connectedness of all life can. Leaders who have developed a GMS through self-transcendence and interconnectedness are able to function with the *relating* skills and create a culture of acceptance which promotes genuine communication, fun, collaborative action, and bonding.

Spiritual well-being and "collaborating" dimension

Leadership for sustainability positively impacts spiritual well-being as leaders for sustainability exemplify altruistic love, fostering hope/faith in a shared vision for sustainability. Spiritual well-being comprises two aspects (Fry & Nisiewicz, 2020: (1) a sense of purpose and calling as a change agent for sustainability, providing meaning and impact; and (2) a sense of belonging to a loving community, where leaders and followers feel appreciated and supported in their commitment to the partnership.

Purpose and community

Inherent to the human experience is the universal yearning for a purpose or calling that makes a difference in the world. A strong purpose combats doubts and distractions, elevating one's focus beyond personal circumstances (Fairholm, 1997). In sustainability, this purpose fosters intrinsic motivation, drawing on internal strength to serve others. Through it, leaders can influence the meaningfulness experienced by their followers, serving as a transformative force, driving individuals to channel their efforts toward positively impacting the world.

Membership embodies the universal need for belonging and community, where one is understood, appreciated, and accepted. This sense of membership is crucial as it nurtures compassionate identification with others, personal ethics, and conduct codes that recognize the universality of shared pain and suffering. In an organizational setting, it enhances employees' sense of importance, value, and belonging, leading to enhanced collaboration and performance through open dialogue, increased engagement, and team cohesion.

The *collaborating* dimension is vital for both creating and sustaining a sense of purpose and community in GLfS. An inclusive mindset involves actively listening to diverse viewpoints and bridging cultural gaps. By encouraging open communication and fostering a safe environment where all team members can share their ideas and perspectives without judgment, it enhances cooperation, resilience, and the capacity to address complex challenges together.

In the following section, we provide a detailed process for implementing the integrated framework (see Figure 11.6) within an organization. This process is designed to enhance both leader and leadership capacity for sustainability, ensuring that they can effectively drive meaningful change and promote sustainable practices throughout the organization.

The journey of implementation

The first step in our method focuses on aligning a leader's inner capacity with the outer complexity. To develop the essential *being* and *relating* skills, we introduce what we call the **Leader Orientation Canvas**, a workshop designed to bridge this gap. Here, leaders from diverse backgrounds explore the core principles of IDGs and GLfS, fostering a common language for understanding the qualities of a sustainability champion. They grapple with questions like: How can I embody Sustainability 2.0 principles – collaboration, global mindset, and care – in my daily actions?

The next phase involves introspection through the **Leader Assessment,** a tool designed for purposeful self-reflection, developing the essential *thinking* skills. Aligned with the GLfS competencies, this assessment prompts leaders to reevaluate their impact, exploring their values, motivations, and the ripple effects of their actions within the organization and the wider world. They consider questions such as whether their decisions reflect a long-term perspective on systemic change (Meadows, 2008) and if their leadership practices foster a culture of shared responsibility and psychological safety within their teams (Goleman, 2006).

This introspection informs the creation of a personalized **Leader Action Plan**. Bridging the gap between self-discovery and action and enabling the essential *collaborating* skills, this plan outlines specific areas for growth aligned with both IDGs and GLfS dimensions. It includes concrete goals, targeted actions, and timelines for improvement. However, this development journey doesn't happen in isolation; the **Leadership Assessment** brings the broader organizational context into play. Leaders consider team dynamics and culture when designing their action plan, ensuring their efforts translate effectively within the team.

Empowered by this inner work, leaders are now prepared to co-create a shared vision for a sustainable future. Sustainability 2.0, with its emphasis on collaboration

Implement IDG through GLFS lenses

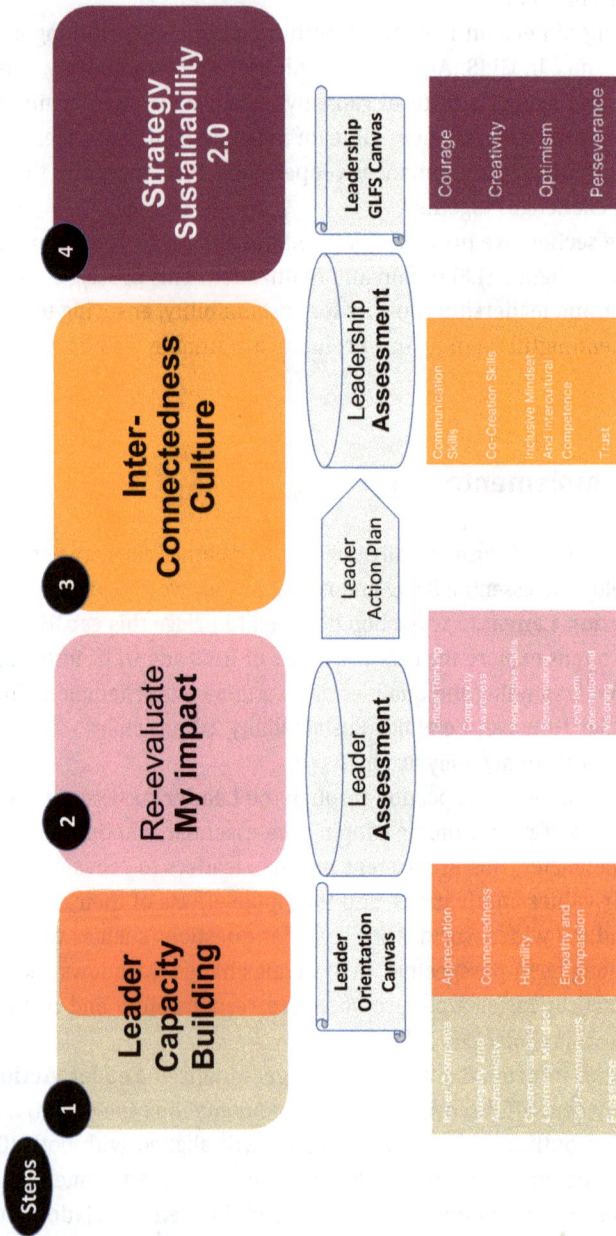

Figure 11.6: Steps to implement GLFS through IDG lenses (Source Authors' own).

and long-term vision, becomes the guiding light. The **Leadership GLfS Canvas** serves as a valuable tool in this stage. Rooted in the core qualities of courage, creativity, optimism, and perseverance, this canvas helps leaders translate their vision into actionable plans while fostering a spirit of innovation and resilience within the team.

Continuous learning and improvement

This journey is not linear but rather a continuous cycle of learning and improvement. Regular collective reflection and action sessions create a space for open dialogue and the sharing of experiences. These sessions, crucial for fostering a culture of continuous learning, allow teams to celebrate successes, identify challenges, and refine strategies for moving forward.

The narrative doesn't end here. The co-created vision must be translated into concrete action. Through a process of implementation of strategy changes, leaders identify necessary adjustments within the organization's strategy to embed the principles of sustainability, including the triple bottom line – people, planet, and profit.

Monitoring, evaluation, and ongoing development

Monitoring and evaluation is the compass that ensures the organization stays on track. Data and feedback from various stakeholders are used to continuously monitor progress towards goals and make adjustments as needed.

The journey within requires ongoing investment in capacity building and training. Leaders and teams are offered workshops, coaching programs, and access to resources that support their development in areas like self-awareness, relating well, and systems thinking (van der Waldt, 2020). Finally, the importance of celebration and recognition cannot be overstated. Acknowledging successes and milestones achieved along the sustainability journey motivates ongoing commitment and reinforces positive behaviors.

This narrative underscores the transformative potential of integrating IDGs and GLfS frameworks. By cultivating the inner qualities of leaders and providing a structured framework for action, this approach empowers organizations to bridge the gap between intention and action, ultimately contributing to a more sustainable future.

Discussion

Our discussion with the webinar participants centered on three main topics. First, we focused on a conceptual refinement and connection of some of the terms we used;

namely, leader and leadership development, social sustainability, and triple bottom line. Second, we discussed the existing overload of leadership frameworks and tools for sustainability and their deficiencies. Finally, we explored how the integrated framework of GLfS and IDGs addresses these deficiencies.

To start with, one of the participants commented that there is a lack of consensus on the definitions and scope of key terms such as leader development, leadership development, sustainability, and personal growth. These terms are frequently used in various contexts without a clear shared understanding, which can lead to miscommunication and misalignment in goals and strategies. To address this issue, we provided explicit definitions and scope (see Figure 11.3 and Table 11.4). We defined "leader development" as the process of guiding leaders from Levels IV and V of consciousness and cognition to Levels III and II. The desired outcome is for individual leaders to embody the qualities inherent in Levels III and II: self-awareness and self-transcendence. These qualities foster humility, recognition of the dignity of all human beings, acceptance of diverse perspectives, love, a vision to serve others, and a deepening connectedness with all things in the universe. These qualities, as illustrated in the integrated framework (see Figure 11.5), are also reflected in the skills included in the *being*, *thinking*, and *relating* dimensions of the IDGs.

We defined "leadership development" as a comprehensive process that inherently involves multiple team members with various degrees of decision-making power within an organization. The process aims to enhance collective leadership capacity while fostering a culture of collaboration. It involves embracing a broader and more advanced worldview termed Sustainability 2.0. Detailed in Figure 11.3 and Table 11.3, this concept outlines the conditions a system needs to meet to achieve a desired level of sustainability. Specifically, it promotes a collective vision that fosters a life-enhancing ecology recognizing the interconnectedness of human life with nature and other living beings, and emphasizes relationships based on collaboration. This new vision, as showcased in the integrated framework (see Figure 11.5), is also reflected in the skills included in the *collaborating* and *acting* dimensions of the IDGs.

Furthermore, this conceptualization underscores the critical role of social sustainability in achieving tangible sustainability outcomes and supporting long-term environmental impact and social well-being. Currently, sustainability interventions primarily focus on measurable outcomes, reflecting a Sustainability 1.0 mindset (see Table 11.2), where only quantifiable results are considered significant to drive action. This approach often leads to interventions that prioritize measured metrics, potentially overlooking vital social dimensions, such as community well-being, equity, and social cohesion. Our holistic approach highlights the importance of integrating social sustainability into sustainability interventions to address the root cause of the issues and consider the dynamic and context-specific nature of sustainability challenges.

As many of the participants were HR and leadership development professionals, they raised the second topic. Specifically, they talked about a prevalent issue in their organizations: leaders are increasingly overwhelmed by a proliferation of frameworks and self-leadership tools. These tools and frameworks, although numerous and varied, often fail to deliver the anticipated impact. This disconnect stems from their introduction within existing paradigms and mindsets that do not support meaningful integration or application. Participants also shared that many of these frameworks and tools are implemented without sufficient consideration of the organizational culture or the specific challenges faced by leaders. As a result, these interventions often fall short of their intended outcomes. Leaders frequently find themselves grappling with a fragmented approach to development, where the tools and frameworks appear disconnected from their daily realities and strategic goals.

A key insight from the discussion was the recognition that to effectively address sustainability challenges, a more coherent and integrated approach is required. This approach should transcend the superficial application of disparate tools and instead focus on cultivating a mindset and culture that supports sustainable practices.

The third topic emerged as a natural continuation of the previous key insight. The question raised was: How does the integrated global leadership for sustainability framework offer a more coherent and integrated approach than those existing?

The GLfS fosters a leadership culture grounded in altruism, community purpose aligned with an organizational clear vision for sustainability, and a global perspective. It aids organizations to better equip their leaders to address the multifaceted challenges of sustainability and lead with greater effectiveness and coherence. By emphasizing these qualities, organizations can create a fertile environment for leaders to connect the dots and make sense of sustainability as a complex and evolving issue. A shift towards these values facilitates a more holistic understanding of sustainability, enabling leaders to integrate various frameworks and tools into a cohesive strategy. This alignment helps leaders not only to navigate the complexity of their roles but also to drive meaningful and impactful change within their organizations.

The five IDG dimensions organize and support the development of 23 specific skills essential for personal and collective growth (Stålne & Greca, 2022). These dimensions provide a structure that helps individuals and organizations cultivate the inner capacities necessary to address complex global challenges and contribute to sustainable development. Each dimension serves as a guide for organizing and developing the 23 specific skills within the IDGs, helping individuals and organizations identify areas for growth, set goals for personal and collective development, and align their actions with the broader aim of contributing to sustainable and meaningful change.

As such, the five dimension and 23 skills add richness and focus to the GLfS framework as a model for leader and leadership development focused on sustainability and sustainable development. They provide examples of methods, practices, and activities that focus on the "how" of leader and leadership development necessary for the practice of GLfS. Taken together, these skills offer an integrated combination of knowledge, abilities, behaviors, and personal attributes necessary to perform tasks for each of the components of the GLfS model in order to achieve desired outcomes. They go beyond mere technical proficiency. This includes not only the capability to execute tasks with precision but also the judgment, adaptability, and interpersonal effectiveness required to succeed in diverse situations.

Conclusion

This chapter looks into the type and qualities of leadership necessary for sustainability. Using a first principles thinking approach, it first deconstructs and understands how the current neoliberal system conditions leaders and leadership for sustainability. It then offers a new perspective that addresses the root causes of the sustainability crisis while identifying necessary leadership qualities. Finally, it provides an integrated framework that incorporates the Inner Development Goals (IDGs) within a model of global leadership for sustainability (GLfS). The chapter concludes with a discussion on the future of sustainability leadership and the practical application of the proposed ideas.

References

Avolio, B. E., Zhu, F., Kohut, M. F., & Sosik, B. S. (1999). Longitudinal effects of authentic leadership on follower outcomes. *The Leadership Quarterly, 10*(2), 245–292.

Bass, B. M. (1990). From transactional to transformational leadership: Learning to share the vision. *Organizational dynamics, 18*(3), 19–31. DOI: https://doi.org/10.1016/0090-2616(90)90061-S.

Benefiel, M.; Fry, L.; Geigle, D. Spirituality and religion in the workplace: History, theory, and research. *Psychol. Relig. Spirit.* 2014, *6*, 175–187. https://doi.org/10.1037/a0036597.

Brundtland, G. H., (1987). What is sustainable development? *Our common future, 8*(9), 1–40.

Coates, J. (2003). Exploring the roots of the environmental crisis: Opportunity for social transformation. *Critical Social Work, 4*(1), 1–15.

Collins, J. C. & Porras, J. I. (1996). Building your company's vision. *Harvard Business Review, 74*, 65–78.

Carruthers, B. G. (1999). *City of capital: Politics and markets in the English financial revolution.* Princeton University Press.

Day, D. V. (2000). Leadership development:: A review in context. *The leadership quarterly, 11*(4), 581–613. DOI: https://doi.org/10.1016/S1048-9843(00)00061-8.

Day, D. V., Fleenor, J. W., Atwater, L. E., Sturm, R. E., & McKee, R. A. (2014). Advances in leader and leadership development: A review of 25 years of research and theory. *The leadership quarterly, 25*(1), 63–82. DOI: https://doi.org/10.1016/j.leaqua.2013.11.004.

DeGroot, T., Kiker, D. S., & Cross, T. C. (2000). A meta-analysis to review organizational outcomes related to charismatic leadership. *Canadian Journal of Administrative Sciences/Revue Canadienne des Sciences de l'Administration, 17*(4), 356–372.

Drolma, L. S. (2003). *Change of heart: The Bodhisattva peace training of Chagdud Tulku.* BookBaby.

Egel, E. (2015). *Spiritual leadership: Expressions in diverse organizational environments* [Unpublished doctoral dissertation]. Nice, University of Nice Sophia-Antipolis.

Egel, E. (2020). From "I" to "we" through "female" leadership: Bringing inclusion and inclusiveness to the next level. In J. Marques (ed.), *The Routledge Companion to Inclusive Leadership* (pp. 288–298). Routledge.

Egel, E., & Fry, L. W. (2017). Cultivating a global mindset through "being-centered" leadership. In J. Neal (ed.), *Handbook of Personal and Organizational Transformation. Springer International Publishing.*

Elkington, J. (1997). *Cannibals with forks: The triple bottom line of 21st century business.* Capstone.

Fairholm, G. W. (1997). *Capturing the heart of leadership: Spirituality and community in the new American workplace.* Bloomsbury Publishing USA.

Ferdig, M. A. (2007). Sustainability leadership: Co-creating a sustainable future. *Journal of Change Management, 7*(1), 25–35. DOI: https://doi.org/10.1080/14697010701233809.

Fligstein, N. (2018). *The architecture of markets: An economic sociology of twenty-first-century capitalist societies.* Princeton University Press.

Fry, L. W. & Egel, E. (2021). Global leadership for sustainability. *Sustainability, 13*(11), 6360.

Fry, L. & Kriger, M. (2009). Towards a theory of being-centered leadership: Multiple levels of being as context for effective leadership. *Human Relations, 62*(11), 1667–1696. DOI: https://doi.org/10.3390/su13116360.

Fry, L.W.; Nisiewicz, M.S. *Maximizing the Triple Bottom Line through Spiritual Leadership*; Stanford University Press: Redwood City, CA, USA, 2020.

Fry, L. W. (2003). Toward a theory of spiritual leadership. *The leadership quarterly, 14*(6), 693–727.

Georgescu-Roegen, N. (1971). *The entropy law and the economic process.* Harvard University Press.

Goleman, D. (2006). The socially intelligent. *Educational leadership, 64*(1), 76–81.

Hayek, F. A. & Stelzer, I. M. (1960). *The constitution of liberty (vol. 311).* University of Chicago Press.

House, R. J. (1996). Path-goal theory of leadership: Lessons, legacy, and a reformulated theory. *The Leadership Quarterly, 7*(3), 323–352. DOI: https://doi.org/10.1016/S1048-9843(96)90024-7.

Judge, T. A. & Piccolo, R. F. (2004). Transformational and transactional leadership: A meta-analytic test of their relative validity. *Journal of Applied Psychology, 89*(5), 755–768. DOI: https://doi.org/10.1037/0021-9010.89.5.755.

Kajikawa, Y., Ohno, J., Takeda, Y., Matsushima, K., & Komiyama, H. (2007). Creating an academic landscape of sustainability science: An analysis of the citation network. *Sustainability Science, 2*, 221–231. DOI: https://doi.org/10.1007/s11625-007-0027-8.

Keating, T. (1999). *The human condition: Contemplation and transformation.* Paulist Press.

Kirkpatrick, S. A. & Locke, E. A. (1991). Leadership: Do traits matter? *Academy of Management Perspectives, 5*(2), 48–60. DOI: https://doi.org/10.2307/4165007.

Kriger, M., & Seng, Y. (2005). Leadership with inner meaning: A contingency theory of leadership based on the worldviews of five religions. *The leadership quarterly, 16*(5), 771–806.

Lyons, C. O., Berry, T., Hanh, T. N., Bwoya, C. T., Stanley, J., Loy, D. R., ... & Johnston, L. J. (2016). *Spiritual ecology: The cry of the earth.* The Golden Sufi Center.

MacArthur, J. F. (1998). *In the footsteps of faith.* Wheaton, Illinois: Crossway Books.

Mackey, J. D., Ellen III, B. P., McAllister, C. P., & Alexander, K. C. (2021). The dark side of leadership: A systematic literature review and meta-analysis of destructive leadership research. *Journal of Business Research, 132*, 705–718.

McMurtry, J. J. (2009). Ethical value-added: Fair trade and the case of Café Femenino. *Journal of Business Ethics, 86*, 27–49. DOI: https://doi.org/10.1007/s10551-008-9760-x.

Meadows, D. H. (2008). *Thinking in systems: A primer.* Chelsea Green Publishing.

Mitra, P. (2024, May 17). Sustainability focused funds see 20% growth with assets exceeding €5tn. Funds Europe. https://www.funds-europe.com/sustainability-focused-funds-see-20-growth-with-assets-exceeding-e5tn/ (Accessed Jul. 5, 2024).

Oh, J.; Wang, J. Spiritual leadership: Current status and agenda for future research and practice. *J. Manag. Spiritual. Relig.* 2020, *17*, 223–248. https://doi.org/10.1080/14766086.2020.1728568.

Podolny, J. M. (1993). A status-based model of market competition. *American Journal of Sociology, 98*(4), 829–872.

Rhinesmith, S. H. (1996). *A manager's guide to globalization: Six skills for success in a changing world (2nd edn).* McGraw-Hill.

Samul, J. (2019). Spiritual leadership: Meaning in the sustainable workplace. *Sustainability, 12*(1), 267. DOI: https://doi.org/10.3390/su12010267.

Samul, J. Spiritual Leadership: Meaning in the sustainable workplace. *Sustainability* 2020, *12*, 267. https://doi.org/10.3390/su12010267.

Scharmer, C. O. (2018). *Theory U: Leading from the future as it emerges.* Berrett-Koehler Publishers.

Stålne, K. & Greca, S. (2022). *Inner Development Goals: Phase 2 research report.* Inner Development Goals. https://idg.tools/assets/221215_IDG_Toolkit_v1.pdf.

Stiglitz, J. E., & Charlton, A. H. (2006). Aid for Trade: a report for the Commonwealth Secretariat.

Swedberg, R. (2009). *Principles of economic sociology.* Princeton University Press.

Tackney, C. T., Chappell, S., Harris, D., Pavlovich, K., Egel, E., Major, R., Finney, R. & Stoner, J. (2017). Management, spirituality, and religion (MSR) ways and means: A paper to encourage quality research. *Journal of Management, Spirituality & Religion, 14*(3), 245–254. DOI: https://10.1080/14766086.2017.1316764.

Thiel, P. & Masters, B. (2014). *Zero to one: Notes on startups, or how to build the future.* Crown Business.

US SIF Foundation. (2022). *2022 report on US sustainable investing trends.* US SIF Foundation. https://www.ussif.org/trends (Accessed Jul. 5, 2024).

Van der Waldt, G. (2020). Constructing conceptual frameworks in social science research. *TD: The Journal for Transdisciplinary Research in Southern Africa, 16*(1), 1–9.

Zakharov, Y. (2022). Comparative analysis of approaches to world concepts: SPOD society, VUCA society and BANI society. *Social economics, 64*, 149–158. DOI: https://doi.org/10.26565/2524-2547-2022-64-13.

Section 3: **Systems change**

Xuan Dung Burckhardt and Rosanna Rippel
Chapter 12
Prelude

Throughout history, humanity has grappled with the complexities of life. For much of our modern era, a mechanistic worldview has dominated, shaping our approach to complexity and change. However, the limitations of the classical linear problem-solving mindset have become increasingly evident over the past century, especially in dealing with complex systems and wicked problems. In seeking systemic change, we advocate not only for localized fixes but also for enhancing the relationships between elements within the systems we aim to transform.

In this section, you will explore the need for new narratives and holistic strategies that foster resilience, collaboration, and sustainable solutions. You will explore a global tapestry of chapters from different continents addressing current challenges with a focus on improving relationships and advocating for a narrative shift through inner development.

Your journey begins with a critical examination of the prevailing narrative, where you delve into the relationship between self and the world, and examine the narratives and beliefs you've internalized from capitalism. This exploration highlights the need for a new narrative and mindset that can pave the way toward a more sustainable future.

Next, your journey takes you to Thailand, where you witness the transformative power of mindset and empathy in action. Here, changemakers are combating student dropout rates by adopting systemic perspectives that address the root causes of this issue.

Transitioning from education to political science, you explore integral politics – a paradigm that integrates profound inner development with political action for the collective good.

Continuing your journey, you travel to Colombia, where you confront the profound impacts of intergenerational trauma on well-being and flourishing.

Finally, you embark on a Theory U journey in southern Switzerland, where a community leverages IDGs to catalyze dialogue and implement conscious systemic actions. This initiative shapes a future grounded in collective wisdom and sustainable practices, demonstrating the transformative potential of integrating inner development with community empowerment.

United by the pursuit of systemic change and informed by the principles of inner development, these chapters offer you practical insights and transformative possibilities for navigating complex global challenges.

https://doi.org/10.1515/9783111453729-013

Figure 12.1: *Painting a Sustainable Future (2019).*
Drip paintings by X. D. Burckhardt, Basel, Switzerland.
"These two drip paintings were created using the same materials, colors, and techniques but at different times, resulting in distinct pieces. The left panel evokes tranquility with its calm, flowing lines, while the right panel bursts with vitality, capturing a moment of excitement and creative energy. Together, they highlight the interconnectedness of emotions and artistic expression, symbolizing the need for systemic change that embraces the interdependence of economic, social, environmental, and political systems for meaningful transformation."

Hold
When you choose to meet the world today.
Openheartedly.
It is, a lot, to hold.

Shutting your eyes can feel like a savior but most of us know it's a behavior
that won't shield.

Ignorance is not bliss. It's rejecting what is.
And when you stop denying what is real, and the truth you locked inside you is
unsealed, you're forced to feel. Suddenly showering in this overpowering task.
Of holding the hurt.

Who taught you how to be in pain? Have you learned how to be in pain?

How to acknowledge. How to stay in it. How to grieve. Then accepting, and
from that presence, connecting.

To response ability. Our capacity to cope with hope and teach ourselves to be
energetically lit enough, psychologically fit enough, have grit enough so that
when shit that's tough hits the fan, we can – change.

We don't have more time for hurrying.
No more energy to spend on worrying.
Because when we fight against violence or scream that we need silence, we
defeat ourselves. It is a reification of despair. A broadcasted scare.

Rather, we need beacons that are not strobe lights but fireplaces. A higher-
places kind of voice that pierces the noise with compassion and calm. People
who stopped pointing in a direction and became the goal themselves.

Playing that unique part of the picture, like we all have to do.
Not going towards, but going through
The process of discovering the motive of yourself as a jigsaw puzzle piece.
The process of starting to "know thyself", in the words of Socrates
The ruthless rewiring of your brain.

And it's for these points in history we train.
It's hard to be brave in paradise.
We don't get wise from surfing highs.
It's when we know how to cruise the low
That we can rise and grow.

When we learn to love the challenge, look straight into its eyes, and go:

Hello. Welcome. We are team humans. We want this planet to be habitable for
our children. We fucked up. We know we need to do things differently. We
know the world will change. We know we will have to change. But we will do it

together. And we will do it with the joy of doing it together. Because we are a
team. Thinking and moving as a stream.

We are the flock who forgot that it is a flock. Heading towards a cliff many of
us can see. Those who are trying to stop are starting to sense the speed and
force of the motion. A greedily stampeding ocean. With the course of the race
set straight off the face of the earth.

So what do you do in a situation like that?

I don't know. I don't know if anybody knows.

It's a hard question. Ill structured, wicked, wet problem. With an undefined but
definite deadline.

There is this mouthful of uncertainty.
A lot we need to hold, since
You can't know a story
That's never been told.
The outcome can't be predicted
Nor controlled.
You can't push evolution
It has to unfold.

And the least we can do is pay attention. To what is being played out.
Focus with intention. As we're watching something unmade sprout.

For humanity. And the world they dream about.
I choose to believe in the team we won't survive without.

Rosanna Rippel (2023)

Author's note. This poem was written for the IDG Global Summit 2023 in Stockholm.
The process of writing this piece impacted me deeply. It fiercely forced me to face
facts and feelings that I hid under a heavy lid since I got depressed by them as a teenager. Because I wasn't able to hold them.

I also learned. I studied the IDG goals, listened to podcasts about the state of our
world, read research about murmurations and did an inner journey of inquiry; What
is it like for me to try to hold everything that is going on? What do I want to say
about that?

Sharing the very personal text that came out of this process on stage during the
yearly IDG summit made me feel more connected to humanity as my species. Even
months after the performance, I have felt more connected to strangers on the train,
people I buy secondhand clothes from, even ancestors and kids. It's such a precious
experience; something I truly wish for more people to have more often.

I feel like it doesn't make sense how little we talk with each other about what it's like to be alive in this world in its current state. One of the speakers before me at the summit shared that 56% of youth globally thinks that humanity is doomed. Pretty heavy stuff. Stuff that I believe we have to learn to hold together.

I want to thank the IDG crew for the trust and for all the work that they do. Thank you also to the audience for receiving me and to everyone who shared their resonance afterwards. It feels like connecting the flock.

Laura Hartley

Chapter 13
Getting free from internalized capitalism: Inner Development Goals and narrative shift

Abstract: This chapter explores the mirrored relationship between self and world, the stories and beliefs underpinning capitalism, and ways in which the reader may have internalized capitalism. Unpacking capitalism's narrative, the chapter suggests it is built on three components: the pursuit of infinite growth, scarcity, and the devaluation of living systems to lifeless resources. It then offers a reflection for the reader to examine the way in which capitalism's narrative intersects with the climate crisis and extractivism, and how this narrative can be internalized, shaping the reader's beliefs and values about labor, success, time, and self-worth. The chapter suggests that a tool of system change is narrative change and offers practices to support the reader in getting free, unlearning the story of capitalism, and developing the skills and qualities of the Inner Development Goals.

Keywords: internalized capitalism, capitalism, unlearning, Inner Development Goals, climate crisis

Introduction

In 2005, David Foster Wallace opened a college commencement speech sharing a story of two young fish swimming along, when they happen to meet an older fish swimming the other way. The older fish nods toward them and says, "Morning, boys. How's the water?" The two young fish swim on for a bit, until eventually one of them looks over at the other and goes, "What the hell is water?"

The water of capitalism can be difficult to see, but it is water we're all swimming in, and the currents of which drift us toward burnout and our burning planet.

The intention of this chapter is to empower you to see, feel, and sense into the mirrors of self and world, to examine the stories that shape us, to ask what happens when a system or story lives within you. How might it influence the ways you think, relate, collaborate, and act? And how might developing the skills and qualities of the Inner Development Goals (IDGs) reshape a system in response?

Although this chapter will focus on the system and story of capitalism, the intention here is not to proselytize for one economic system over another, but to provide an entry point for self-reflection. Bridging story with self-reflection allows us to approach the problems we face from a new perspective, and to work with the root conditions to facilitate change – personally and collectively.

https://doi.org/10.1515/9783111453729-014

This work has never been more necessary.

We live in a world that is rapidly destabilizing. In the last 50 years, we've lost almost 70% of the Earth's wildlife (WWF, 2022), we've passed six out of nine safe planetary boundaries (Richardson et al., 2023) and 2023 was designated the hottest year on record (NOAA, 2024).

In a world with a myriad of urgent demands and challenges, each crisis intersects with the other – a feedback loop of possibility and potential. The call of this time is that we shift from the narrow lens of solo tweaks and individual solutions to widespread, collective system change. System change, however, requires more than just a policy or political shift, and more than innovation, business, or technology can traditionally offer.

Instead, it requires we work with story; with the beliefs, values, and mindsets that uphold a system and shape it. Changing a story asks that we expand our goals beyond new policies, products, or figureheads, and into a deep inquiry of the structures – political, cultural, and economic – that underpin our lives.

Imagine for a moment that you are growing a tomato plant in your garden. Perhaps you had hoped for a healthy plant when you sowed the seeds, but instead it's small and scraggly, producing only a few small tomatoes at a time.

What would your first course of action be?

In most likelihood, it wouldn't be to blame the plant, or give it a pep talk filled with messages of endurance, pushing through, or how strong it could be after this experience. It's also unlikely that you would judge or criticize the plant, condemning it for not thriving like the kale you planted nearby.

Instead, you would likely look at the plant's conditions: the soil, sunlight, rain, or quality of the nutrients.

Stories are the soil of our shared world, shaping our mindset and values. They're assumptions, stated and unstated, that play out in our thoughts, words, and actions. They form the conditions that inform how we be, think, relate, collaborate, and act in this world.

Stories determine the shared reality of a culture, they define the limits of what is commonly believed to be possible or impossible, normal or abnormal, wise or reckless, desired or undesirable, and they're cemented into our world through systems – cultural, economic, and political. They create the playing field, setting the rules of the game, the players and power structures, the expectations and goals.

Stories, it is no exaggeration to say, make our world. In today's interconnected age however, many of the stories underpinning our systems do not serve us.

The story of scarcity that says there's not enough to go around, and that we must hoard, control, or dominate to ensure there's enough.

The story of supremacy that says one race, gender, or body is superior to another. That bodies of a certain size, color, or ability are either undesirable or less valuable.

The story of separation that says humans are separate from the natural world. That our well-being is not tied with that of our nonhuman kin.

And the story of modern capitalism, with its insatiable need for growth on a beautiful, but finite, planet. It's this story that impacts development in almost every dimension of the IDGs, shaping the way we perceive and interact in each of the five dimensions – *being, thinking, relating, collaborating*, and *acting*.

Stories, however, no matter how entrenched in culture, are never static, and they have the potential to be changed. Through deepening our presence, engaging in critical thinking, and connecting to our inner compass we can unlearn the stories we carry, and sense into more just and regenerative possibilities.

The offer contained herein is to embrace the work of slowing down, unlearning capitalism's messages of scarcity and urgency. With space to notice your body and the natural world, the language with which they speak, and the unfiltered honesty of your inner compass, we can truly start to inhabit a more regenerative way of being, and we can sense into new stories.

Together, we can create the inner conditions necessary for deep outer change.

The story of capitalism

Author Rebecca Solnit writes:

> We think we tell stories, but stories often tell us, tell us to love or to hate, to see or to be blind. Often, too often, stories saddle us, ride us, whip us onward, tell us what to do, and we do it without questioning. The task of learning to be free requires learning to hear them, to question them, to pause and hear silence, to name them and then to become the storyteller. (Solnit, 2013, p. 259)

The invitation extended to you now is to explore the story of capitalism, to consider how it shapes the world, and to ask what messages a person may receive and interpret when they live within a system built on these messages.

Because systems are never just outside of us. Created, upheld, and perpetuated by humans, systems live *in us, as us, and through us.* Every system contains a story, a narrative that plays out in our beliefs, mindsets, and values. This narrative is both shaped by the system, but also in turn upholds the system, maintaining its stasis and status quo.

Capitalism, as this chapter will explore it, is both an economic system and an ideology. It's the dominant system that shapes the economies and labor markets of the Global North, and that underpins many of our collective and political decisions.

Capitalism's story contains three main components worth examining, both at the level of system and self (see Figure 13.1).

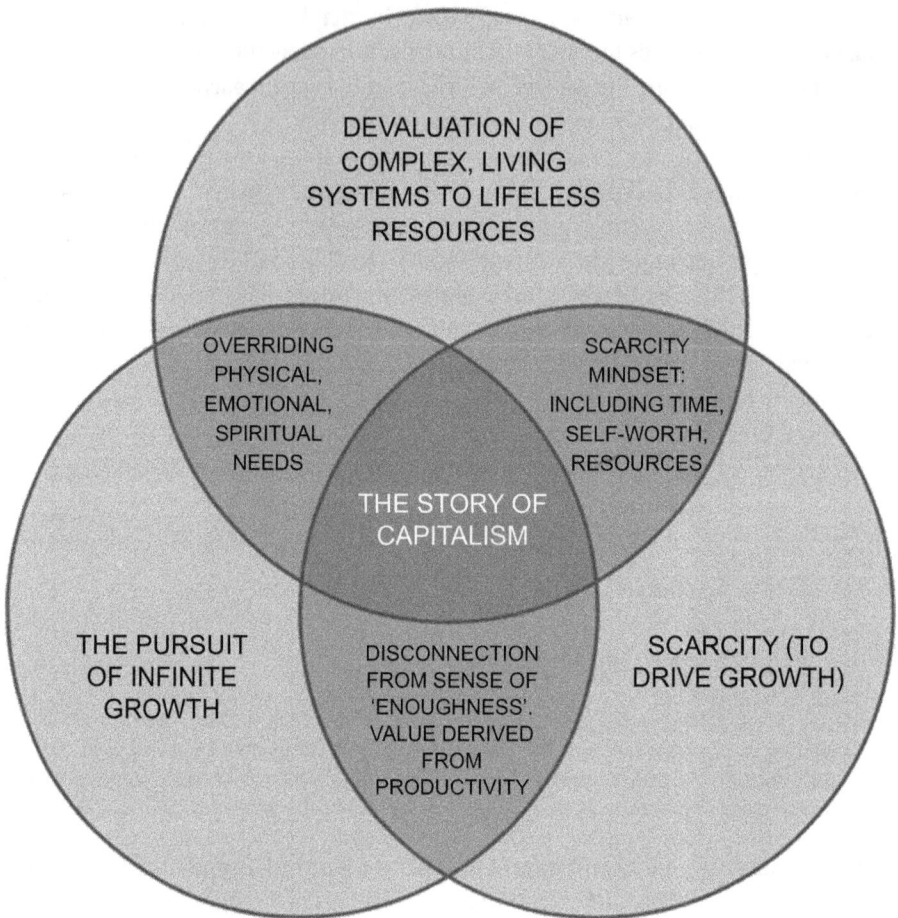

Figure 13.1: The story of capitalism.
Source: Author's own

Growth

First is capitalism's definition of success: growth – the endless pursuit of "more" with value derived from size or quantity, more than quality. Whether it's gross domestic product (GDP), share values, or company profit margins, growth, upward mobility, and the need for more are the ever-present goals of capitalism.

The difficulty is when ecology conflicts with economy, and the pursuit of infinite, ever-expanding growth on a finite planet contains a cost the biosphere cannot pay.

Despite overfishing (Jackson et al., 2001) and ecosystem collapse (Tebbett et al., 2021), and in a world where human-made material (Elhacham et al., 2020) now out-weighs all living beings on Earth, the equation of growth as success still holds strong,

even as it is limited in what it can offer. After all, growth, in its purest form, is not a synonym for well-being.

Systems and stories, however – including capitalism – never exist just outside of us. They live in us, as us, and through us.

Internalized capitalism is the inner dimension of a story and system obsessed with growth. It manifests as feeling guilty with rest or time off, the inner compulsion to continue working when sick, either from the office or at home – because if the only metric of success is growth, output, and productivity, rest can be interpreted as without value (or alternatively, rest's value lies only in *enhancing* productivity).

Internalized capitalism often shows up as that feeling of "not enough". Never doing enough, being enough, giving enough, having enough. *Never enough.* Within the story of capitalism's endless quest for growth is also the presence of insatiability. "Enoughness" must lie in a future destination, in order to encourage the pursuit of growth.

This can manifest as a disconnection from the feelings of satiety and satisfaction; rest or pleasure becoming treats to be earned rather than inherent needs. If growth is all that matters, our care for ourselves can become conditional on our actions and achievement.

With internalized capitalism, even fitness or inner work can become hijacked into the ideology of growth at all costs, limiting inner development; a message focused on "bettering" or "levelling up" as opposed to our liberation, well-being or thriving. Mindfulness becomes a tool not just of insight and harmony, but of productivity and performance; presence measured by its results, rather than the experience of being.

If, from a zoomed-out perspective, you were to view the whole of a person's life, you would undoubtedly see a cyclical rhythm: periods of time for rest and recovery, moments of action and energy; emotions of grief and loss, met with joy and anticipation; a robust wholeness to the experience of being human.

But when a linear, limitless upward direction is all that is considered desirable or successful, perspective is limited, and the wisdom that comes from presence and our inner compass can be viewed only through the story they're contained in.

Scarcity

The second component to the story of capitalism is the necessity, and manufactured creation, of scarcity. If growth is the goal and metric of success, there must be a motivator to drive that growth. From this perspective, satiety, satisfaction, and abundance are poor drivers of the need to consume, but scarcity provides a valid incentive.

Scarcity is built into capitalism in a myriad ways. One of the most visible aspects can be seen through the marketing that underpins consumerism: "Buy now or miss out", countdown timers, "limited spots left", or the online message "someone else is looking" are all designed to invoke scarcity. Urgency and FOMO (fear of missing out) become leverage points, encouraging quick decisions and bypassing our normal decision-making routines.

Planned obsolescence, the practice of designing products to be non-repairable or single-use to drive consumption, is another example. From mobile phones to blenders, batteries are often rendered inaccessible or small parts difficult to purchase, making it easier to buy something new.

Scarcity can also be seen in luxury goods deliberately designed and marketed to be "exclusive"; their desire and selling point based in the idea that most people will not possess them, but a small minority can.

Jason Hickel, in his article Degrowth: A Theory of Radical Abundance, wrote:

> We can also see the logic of artificial scarcity at work in the realm of consumption. Industrialists who fear that people's existing needs are too limited to absorb capitalism's immense productive output must seek to create new needs, or else the juggernaut will grind to a halt. (Hickel, 2019, p. 62)

Within the story of capitalism, scarcity is a necessary driver for growth.

What messages might we internalize when we live inside a system and story where scarcity is not only expected, but made? How might it influence the ways we think, collaborate, relate, and act? How might it influence our ability to feel safe and present?

One of the most common internalizations of scarcity is in our experience of time. Throughout the English language, the expressions of time scarcity are everywhere: "I wish I had *more* time!", "I *wasted* so many hours", "I can *squeeze* that in my diary."

A common answer to the "How was your weekend?" question is "Not long enough" or "Crazy busy". A scarcity of time, the experience of busyness, has become both normalized and a common benchmark in ideas of success.

Time, from the perspective of internalized capitalism, is often viewed as linear and extractible, something that we race against. It's an experience producing stress, activating the fight-flight-freeze response of our bodies.

With internalized capitalism, urgency becomes equated to a rejection of needs. You need to *do more, be more, faster, quickly*; whatever needs you have – physical, emotional, spiritual – can wait. Output and productivity drive growth, and so urgency becomes more likely to require a response of speed rather than a pause, break, or change of tact.

This story of scarcity inhibits our presence, our connection to our inner compass, and our creativity. Flow states, those feelings of energized focus and timelessness, that allow for deep work and creativity, are built on the foundations of presence and joy, but when we live in a story that says there is never enough time, our access to these states becomes limited.

In a story where scarcity is the default, internalized capitalism can even shape the way in which we relate and collaborate with others; the value we give to other people or groups based on what they can bring or produce, rather than their intrinsic worth, or the depth and quality of relationships.

Scarcity is what keeps the growth treadmill moving, even when growth is no longer what is needed.

Living systems to lifeless resources

The third component of capitalism's story is the devaluation of beautiful, living, complex systems to lifeless resources; jungles, oceans, and forests only have value when we can take or use something from them. This might be timber, or it might be tourism, but in this story their value is only in our relationship to them, not inherently tied to their existence.

This devaluation of living systems is where extractivism and capitalism collide. Extractivism at its essence (though by no means fullness) speaks to the extraction of minerals and resources from the Earth, with little care for the well-being of the surrounding people and environment, and usually with inequitable power dynamics between the Global North and Global South.

It's a process that allows for the pursuit of infinite growth on a finite planet, the commodifying of life and natural systems to sellable resources.

What messages might we internalize from a story that devalues living systems? How might it affect our relationship with the beautiful, living, complex system that is the human body?

When we internalize the story of capitalism, labor can be viewed as more important and more necessary than pleasure, than enjoying the moment we have right now, enjoying our bodies and world (unless it's "guilty pleasure", tinged with the "forbidden" and often able to be bought).

It's not uncommon to treat our inner resources – our creativity, energy, attention – in much the same way we treat the Earth's: with the expectation that they will always be there, available on demand, with little regard for their renewal or the surrounding environment, which in this case is our body or nervous system.

Resilience becomes equated with endurance, pushing through our inner limits and capacities because *growth, productivity, output* are the primary measurements of meaning and success.

This way of working – this belief that we always need to be extracting more from ourselves – becomes a form of physical and psychic violence against ourselves. Its banality is seen in the English language, shaping the ways we relate and communicate: "You're making a killing", "You nailed it", "It's a tight deadline", "It's a minefield", "You'll knock them out."

Internalized capitalism – the message internalized from a system built on the above principles – becomes the equation of self-worth with productivity or what we produce. It's a belief system that influences our thoughts and actions, that mirrors the story of capitalism, and hinders our inner development.

These three aspects in the story of capitalism – the pursuit of never-ending growth, scarcity to drive said growth, and the commodification of living systems – shape the world that we live in, and in turn shape us through overriding the needs and limits of the beautiful, living complex system that is the human body; the sense of time scarcity, needing to do more, quickly; feeling guilty when you stop producing, even when it's just to rest.

Within the story of capitalism, the IDGs can become markers to be achieved, more than qualities to be embodied. Our approach to inner work is shaped by the need to "grow" or "do better", rather than to deepen, embody, learn, or heal.

The work of this time is to challenge this story, to unlearn it from the inside out, and in doing so to deepen our capacity for sensemaking and emergence. To allow new ways of operating and new relationships to arise *in us, as us, and through us.*

As we explore tools for unlearning this story, deepening the skills and qualities of the IDGs, consider the following prompts:

1. In what ways do I treat my creativity, energy, or inner resources as something I can extract, without end or consequence?
2. Where might I equate urgency to mean postponing or rejecting my needs?
3. In what ways might the *way* that I work be reflective of violence?

Getting Free: Unravelling the Narrative Within

If every system has a story, and the story lives in us, then it is through our inner development and collective unlearning that we can truly remake a system. The IDGs offer a framework for engaging with the complexity of our time, and through developing the skills of the *being* and *thinking* dimensions, we can also unlearn cultural and collective narratives, including the story of capitalism.

Because in the opposite of what you likely did with the tomato plant as we began this chapter, our culture has a tendency to individualize collective, systemic problems; to transfer the weight of change and impact to the individual's shoulders, and frame problems that belong to our stories and systems as belonging to "you" or "them".

But the impacts of capitalism we've explored – climate change, burnout, exhaustion, time scarcity, insatiability – are not individual problems. They cannot be solved by one person alone, nor can they be solved purely from an external perspective. It is only through going within, and holding the willingness to work collectively, that we can begin to shape a new response.

Unlearning internalized capitalism is a process with three parts: developing a connection to presence, the use of critical thinking and self-inquiry, and trusting the wisdom of an inner compass. The first aspect grounds us into the being dimension of the IDGs, centering us in our body as a source of wisdom and information. It is this grounding that allows us to recognize the impact that stories have in our body and being, and that connects us to a sense of integrity and authenticity. It is in our body, more than our thinking mind, that we can access a space free from the story, and presence is the doorway in.

The second aspect of unlearning deepens our skills in the IDGs' thinking dimension, using self-inquiry and critical thinking to understand how capitalism's story shapes us, and why it exists. It lets us ask new questions of the story, like who benefits and why, which gives us more perspective and insight. It's this process that gives us agency and power, and that returns the weight of "not enough" from the individual to the collective.

The third aspect of unlearning offers a path forward, because as we free ourselves from capitalism's story, we must also find a deeper, more authentic compass; a place from which to make our decisions that aligns both with our personal integrity, and our collective well-being. Listening to our inner compass returns us to the IDGs' being dimension, deepening the foundations of our inner development.

It should be said that unlearning a story – getting free – is a subversive act that at its heart is a tool of system change, a powerful leverage point in the story or mindset of a system, but it is also an act of liberation and imagination. This work is less of an "aha" moment or single strike of enlightenment than the day-by-day work of deepening our self-awareness.

It's through this work that the conditions and soil for new stories are planted, and that we develop our fullest capacity to engage with and embody the IDGs.

Presence

The story of capitalism – and its components of infinite growth, scarcity, and the devaluation of living systems – relies on a lack of presence. The story survives by ignoring the capacity and information given by the beautiful, living, complex system that is our human body. Decisions instead become made from the place of "should" or "supposed to", satisfying external or cultural expectations, more than genuine energy, capacity, or desire.

Developing the IDG skills of presence and self-awareness is foundational to unlearning this story. After all, insatiability – the prerequisite for infinite growth – can only exist in a space without presence, detached from awareness, to determine what "enough" is.

Clarissa Pinkola Estés writes in *Women Who Run with the Wolves* that:

> The body is a multilingual being. It speaks through its color and its temperature, the flush of recognition, the glow of love, the ash of pain, the heat of arousal, the coldness of non-conviction. It speaks through its constant tiny dance, sometimes swaying, sometimes a-jitter, sometimes

trembling. It speaks through the leaping of the heart, the falling of the spirit, the pit at the center, and rising hope. (Estes, 1992, p. 210)

Returning to the sensations of the body, noticing expansion or contraction, heaviness or lightness, rising intrigue or the "weight of the world", is how we listen to the body's language, and to what else might be happening within us. It is this practice of presence and increasing self-awareness through which we gain access to a space beyond the story, where its message can be released.

Although bringing present-moment awareness to our body is, in essence, a simple task, it is not always easy. If we have been disconnected from the presence and awareness of our body for some time, it can be unfamiliar and uncomfortable to attune to present sensations. Mindfulness practices that bring awareness to the body and breath are a helpful portal, and with time bring a deeper sense inquiry to what we are feeling and why.

The below exercise is designed as an entry point for unlearning internalized capitalism and deepening our skills in the being dimension of the IDGs.

Exercise: Body sensing

To begin, bring to mind a recent time that you can remember feeling stressed or scarce of time, or perhaps held a judgment that you hadn't done enough. The aim of this exercise is not to invite a memory that is too stressful or traumatic to hold – aim for something light and safe to sit with, but that has some tension attached.

If you struggle to recall a memory, you can use this example: Imagine a busy workday, one filled with looming deadlines and urgent tasks. Throughout the day you are interrupted frequently, and thoughts start to circle around how much more there is to do, how much hasn't been done. Perhaps a creeping anxiety arises, the desire to just "get on top of things".

As you bring either your memory or this example to mind, just notice your body.

What is happening in your shoulders, chest, and belly? What sensations or feelings are present?

Bring awareness to your jaw and forehead. Is there any tension or tightness? Is there a tingling or pulsing present?

Pay attention to the way your breath moves through your body, gently expanding and contracting with each inhalation.

You might want to release or relax any places of tension and you can do this, but the aim of this part of the exercise is just to notice what is happening, without judgment.

Keeping the scenario or memory in mind. What can you feel?

What sensations are present? Do they stay the same, or do they shift and change?

Can you name any emotions that are present in your body?

Any messages that arise in your mind?

As you keep your awareness on your body, noticing any sensations or feelings, consider journaling the following reflection prompts.

1. What do I need right now – physically, emotionally, and spiritually? Where might this be in conflict with the story of capitalism?
2. If I listened to my body, I would know . . .
3. Where or how does my body tell me my limits, or what is enough?

Critical thinking

Stories make the world. They underpin our systems and shape the ways in which we think, relate, collaborate, and act. Part of unlearning the story of capitalism stems from questioning the value of the story we are acting from, where and how it is playing out and whether it is actually serving us (or the wider collective we belong to).

Self-inquiry is a practice that allows us to think critically, and that helps us see the water we're swimming in. It gives us the capacity to connect with our inner compass, and to relate to ourselves, each other, and the world differently. Because when we can see a story and learn its parts, not only do we increase our sense of agency, but we create the conditions for emergence. We are no longer ruled by the story, and so can tap into something deeper that wishes to arise.

If stories play out in thoughts, words, and actions, we can look to our language to seek the origin and threads of stories. One example of this is the word "should", which acts as a throughline to stories passed down through culture, family, religion, and more. The word "should", along with other rigid words like "must", "have to", and "cannot", is often rooted in the expectations and stories of culture, more than necessarily the authenticity or inner compass of an individual.

Bringing awareness to how or when the word "should" is used allows it to be interrogated, to ask: Is it true? Why do I believe that? Who benefits from this belief? Critical thinking must always involve this two-way lens of looking both inward and outward: inward, toward the way stories live within us, whether they align with our values and inner compass; and outward, to who benefits, what system or story they uphold, and how they influence the world.

Self-inquiry is a practice that can be returned to on a regular basis, and over time our responses have the capacity to deepen, allowing wisdom to emerge.

Exercise: Self-inquiry

Before beginning the inquiries below, take a moment to center your breath and body at this moment.

Bring awareness to your whole body, feeling the way it meets the chair or ground underneath you. Notice the way your breath moves through your body, expanding your belly and chest with each inhale, collapsing as you breathe out.

Stay with this body awareness for a few breaths, just letting yourself drop into this moment, and when you feel ready, cast your mind to an experience associated with internalized capitalism. As an example, perhaps you can recall a feeling of being time scarce or overwhelmingly exhausted, but feeling the need to push through and keep going.

Keeping this memory in mind, use pen and paper to journal your answers to the following self-inquiry prompts:

1. Who benefits when I have this experience or feeling? Consider all possible answers to this question, including people, systems, stories, and power structures.
2. What goes uncreated or undone when I act from this energy?
3. Can I identify any "should" (or "supposed to", "must", etc.) influencing my decisions or actions? Is this "should" aligned with my values? E.g., I should work harder, I should have got more done, I shouldn't take much time off. "Shoulds" are often throughlines to stories of expectation and value.
4. If you can identify a "should": Is this true? Is it in alignment with the reality of your capacity or desire?
5. What would feel liberatory at this moment? The answer to this question can be big or small, but notice your body as you answer it. Can you sense a subtle opening, expansion, or release with any possibilities?

Inner compass

The story of capitalism isn't concerned with the good of the whole – it's concerned with growth, and the best way to achieve that growth. Growth, however, is not synonymous with well-being, harmony, or liberation, and while it may be an organic process we can see in nature, growth only matters to the point of maturity. What if beyond that, as Edward Abbey said, "growth for the sake of growth is the ideology of the cancer cell"? (Abbey, 1977, p. 183)

Connecting to values and purpose beyond growth is essential for unlearning the story of capitalism; to determine what it is that actually matters, and what it is we are looking to experience from the idea of "growth". This connection can also be called our inner compass, and through rooting into the IDGs' being dimension we can develop a new framework from which to take action, making decisions from our inner alignment rather than scarcity, urgency, or insatiability.

Importantly, values work always includes the dual approach of applying to both how we treat ourselves and how we treat the world. Values are verbs, not nouns; they're living, breathing, dynamic principles that we act into existence. We seed a new story through living our values in our thoughts, words, and actions.

Exercise: Values as compass

The next time you notice the story of capitalism arising within you, take a moment to notice what is happening. What thought process or "should" is driving your actions? What are you experiencing physically, in your body?

You might notice a story of scarcity ("There's not enough time!") or urgency ("We have to do this now!") that, upon reflection, is out of alignment with truth (perhaps there is time, it's just that mentality of hustle culture, or a default reaction).

Ask yourself: Is acting from this story in alignment with my values? Is it in alignment with what feels good or light or freeing in my physical sensations?

If you're not clear on your values, take this time to reflect on what they may be. What is it that you want to live in? What do you want to feel – and help other people feel – as a result of your actions? What matters to you at the deepest core of your being?

Writing a definition of three core values, what they mean, and how they work in practice, not just theory, is a helpful way for them to take dimension. You can also consider the following reflection prompts:

1. What story of the world would I like to be part of telling? What are the values – living states of action – that make that story possible?
2. What would those values look like demonstrated through thought, word, and action? Have I considered how I treat myself when I reflect on them?
3. How does living these values align with or help me develop the skills and qualities of the Inner Development Goals?

Conclusion

Internalized capitalism is strung together through the threads of scarcity and urgency, necessitating our ever-present need to grow, do, and extract more. It's not a story that is in alignment with the natural world, the rhythms of nature, or of the human body. It leaves us increasingly burnt-out and devoid of the energy, creativity, and resourcefulness we need in this time.

It's a story that upholds the world as it is, perpetuating systems and models of extraction and scarcity across the Earth, and it's one that limits our full embodiment of the Inner Development Goals.

In an age of intersecting crises, unlearning the story of capitalism and developing the skills and qualities of the IDGs holds potential not just for personal well-being, but for the collective flourishing of all life, because as we unlearn a story, we create the space and capacity for a new one to emerge through us; one written in collaboration with the energy of life, that senses possibilities from the margins, and one that fosters a more just and regenerative world.

As we close, these final reflection prompts are offered to you with the principles of emergence in mind.

1. What patterns – in yourself, others, or the world – can you see tied to the story of capitalism, as we've explored?
2. As you imagine a more just and regenerative world, what is arising within you? What can you sense in your body and heart, before it is visible to the eyes?
3. What networks of unlearning internalized capitalism – and skill building the Inner Development Goals – can you foster? What communities of practice can you join or create?

References

Abbey, E. (1977). *The journey home: Some words in defense of the American West*. Dutton.

WWF. (2022). *Living planet report 2022 – Building a nature positive society*. R.E.A. Almond, M. Grooten, D. Juffe Bignoli, & T. Petersen, T. (eds). WWF, Gland, Switzerland.

National Oceanic and Atmospheric Administration (2024). *2023 was the world's warmest year on record, by far*. https://www.noaa.gov/news/2023-was-worlds-warmest-year-on-record-by-far 24/01/2024.

Elhacham, E., Ben-Uri, L., Grozovski, J., Bar-On, Y. M., & Milo, R. (2020). Global human-made mass exceeds all living biomass. *Nature, 588*(7838), 442–444. https://doi.org/10.1038/s41586-020-3010-5.

Estes, C. P. (1992). *Women who run with the wolves: Myths and stories of the wild woman archetype* (30th anniversary edition). Penguin Random House.

Hickel, J. (2019). Degrowth: A theory of radical abundance. *Real-World Economics Review, 87*(19), 54–68. https://www.paecon.net/PAEReview/issue87/Hickel87.pdf.

Jackson, J. B., Kirby, M. X., Berger, W. H., Bjorndal, K. A., Botsford, L. W., Bourque, B. J., Bradbury, R. H., Cooke, R., Erlandson, J., Estes, J. A., Hughes, T. P., Kidwell, S., Lange, C. B., Lenihan, H. S., Pandolfi, J. M., Peterson, C. H., Steneck, R. S., Tegner, M. J., & Warner, R. R. (2001). Historical overfishing and the recent collapse of coastal ecosystems. *Science, 293*(5530), 629–637. https://doi.org/10.1126/science.1059199.

Richardson, K., Steffen, W., Lucht, W., Bendtsen, J., Cornell, S. E., Donges, J,F. Drüke, M. Fetzer, I. Bala, G. Von Bloh, W. Feulner, G. Fiedler, S. Gerten, D. Gleeson, T. Hofmann, M. Huiskamp, W. Kummu, M. Mohan, C. Nogués-Bravo, D. Petri, S. Porkka, M. Rahmstorf, S. Schaphoff S. Thonicke, K. Tobain, A. Virkki, V. Wang-Erlandsson, L. Weber, L, & Rockström, J. (2023). Earth beyond six of nine planetary boundaries. *Science advances, 9*(37), eadh2458. https://doi.org/10.1126/sciadv.adh2458.

Solnit, R. (2013). *The faraway nearby*. Penguin.

Tebbett, S. B., Morais, R. A., Goatley, C. H., & Bellwood, D. R. (2021). Collapsing ecosystem functions on an inshore coral reef. *Journal of Environmental Management, 289*, 112471. https://doi.org/10.1016/j.jenvman.2021.112471.

Wallace, D. F. (2012). *This is water* (D. Nathan, narr.; U. Blumenbach, trans.) [Audiobook]. Roof Music. https://roofmusic.de/produktkatalog/produkt/874-this-is-water-das-hier-ist-wasser (Original work published 2012).

Pacharamon Boonyanupongsa

Chapter 14
Keeping students in school with the Inner Development Goals framework and the Insights Finding program: A Thai case study

Abstract: This chapter examines how the Insights Finding program equips change-makers with the skills to address social issues, focusing on Arthit Thongkhum's fight against student dropout in Phetchaburi, Thailand. The program utilizes a structured approach to equip individuals with critical thinking and data analysis skills. In Arthit's case, this led to a deeper understanding of the dropout problem, including factors like poverty and lack of motivation. Importantly, the program fosters empathy through the Inner Development Goals (IDGs) framework, allowing Arthit to see the issue through the eyes of students and families.

This focus on empathy, alongside skills development, is highlighted as a crucial element for tackling complex social issues. Arthit's resulting solutions, such as career exposure programs and community collaboration, aimed to address the root causes of dropouts and encourage students to stay in school. This case study suggests that the Insights Finding program's emphasis on both analytical and empathetic skills empowers changemakers to develop sustainable solutions.

Keywords: Insights Finding, student dropout, empathy

Introduction

In 2019, according to a report, there were 1,276,473 dropout students in Thailand, or around 16.24% of all students, because of many reasons including poverty, inefficient government subsidies, and hardships in studying. (Thai's Out of School Children Information System, 2017) Dropout led to even worse poverty from job limitation, higher crime rates, substance abuse, reduced national economic growth, and strain on social services.

While the national dropout rate in Thailand was concerning, specific factors exacerbated the situation in Phetchaburi province, one of the central provinces of Thailand. Some of the reasons students left school in Phetchaburi include:

- **Economic hardship**: Poverty can force students to enter the workforce to contribute to their family's income. This is a significant issue in Phetchaburi, where some communities rely on agriculture or low-wage industries.

https://doi.org/10.1515/9783111453729-015

- **Lack of academic motivation**: Students who struggle academically or feel disconnected from school may lose interest and opt to drop out.
- **Limited career awareness**: Students unaware of diverse career paths might see education as irrelevant to their future and choose to leave school early.
- **Family dynamics**: Strained family relationships or negative parental communication can push students towards dropping out.

This complex situation demands innovative solutions that address the root causes of the problem. This story explores how the Insights Finding program – a program with a set of tools that were created by Insights for Change (IDG Thailand Changemaker Hub), originally to understand social issues and later was used to promote inner skills by leveraging the Inner Development Goals (IDGs) framework to solve complex problems – was applied by a changemaker to tackle dropout rates in Phetchaburi.

In this chapter, we will delve into the real case of one of our participants in the Insights Finding program, offering a comprehensive exploration of the tools and processes they employed along the way.

The problem and the changemaker: Arthit Thongkhum's journey

Arthit Thongkhum is a professional working in the education sector, and he is a changemaker. A changemaker is someone who takes the initiative to solve a social problem. Arthit is passionate about making a positive difference and is driven to find creative solutions. He joined the Insights Finding program in 2019 seeking personal growth. He chose to focus on the issue of student dropouts in his hometown, Phetchaburi.

Phetchaburi province is located in the central region, situated on the Gulf of Thailand. With a population of approximately 472,589, the province has around 52,000 students. Within this figure, in 2019 there were 7,693 dropout students, accounting for approximately 14.72% of all students. (City Population, 2015) Arthit himself nearly became a dropout when he was young, but he was fortunate enough to change his path. Meanwhile, other students, including his cousin, opted to end their educational journey for various reasons. Arthit aimed to uncover the underlying reasons behind this issue to change perceptions and encourage those considering dropping out to return to the classroom.

The initial stages of a changemaker's journey are often fraught with challenges. It typically takes a significant amount of time, approximately six to eight months, for individuals to uncover and attain a profound understanding of the complex problems they aim to address. Moreover, during this starting period, some changemakers struggle to keep up with their projects, or even give up entirely. Through in-depth interviews conducted with changemakers, four key challenges were identified at the outset of their journey:

1. **Connecting personal experiences to broader issues**: Changemakers often embark on their journey by exploring problems directly affecting them or their communities. However, this initial exploration can be overwhelming, as they confront "wicked problems" with intricate interconnected aspects. The ability to bridge personal experiences with broader issues becomes crucial.

2. **Paralysis by analysis**: Faced with the vastness of the chosen issue, many changemakers become paralyzed by the sheer multitude of potential starting points. The abundance of information and avenues creates a sense of uncertainty, hindering their ability to take that crucial first step toward change.

3. **Deficits in empathetic engagement**: Effective change-making necessitates understanding the lived experiences and perspectives of those affected by the issue. This requires not only the ability to actively listen and truly hear others but also a deep inner journey of self-awareness and presence. Some changemakers struggle to conduct user research and engage in empathetic interviews effectively, limiting their ability to gather crucial insights.

4. **Navigating the data maze**: While collecting data is crucial, many changemakers get overwhelmed by the sheer volume of information at their disposal. They often find it challenging to process, analyze, and synthesize the gathered data, hindering their ability to extract meaningful insights. This difficulty leads to struggles in identifying key patterns, trends, and root causes, ultimately impeding the formulation of well-defined design challenges that drive impactful solutions.

The Insights Finding program guided Arthit through a structured eight-week process which equipped him with the skills to understand the problem from multiple perspectives, including five main steps: exploring and scoping the problem, conducting secondary research, preparing to empathize, empathizing with stakeholders, and extracting insights.

The insights-finding journey

Arthit began his insights-finding journey in the "exploring problem" phase of the Insights Finding program. This initial step focused on comprehensively understanding the issue. He utilized two key tools: mind mapping and visual scoping. Mind mapping helped him delve into the problem by identifying stakeholders (students, parents, teachers), potential causes (low self-esteem, financial hardship), and areas of impact (family dynamics, community perception). Visual scoping then came into play. By having participants draw pictures representing the consequences of the problem, this technique further clarified its reach and impact. By examining the dropout sequence, Arthit reasons through the situation and comes up with key questions to explore further.

244 — Pacharamon Boonyanupongsa

These tools, along with the *thinking* and *relating* dimensions of the IDG frame-work, empowered Arthit as a changemaker. The critical thinking in the IDGs gleaned from this process helped him recognize the interconnectedness of various factors (e.g., poverty, lack of motivation, and social pressure) that affected the social problem and stakeholders involved, including students, parents, and teachers. Through per-spective thinking, which involves considering different viewpoints such as the main stakeholder viewpoints, the family viewpoints, and the community viewpoints, Arthit gained a holistic understanding of the student dropout problem.

In his first assumption, Grade 7–9 (or junior high school) students dropped out because of self-confusion towards their future and bad attitudes towards themselves. Arthit started to understand more about the problem from this point.

Simultaneously, he was tasked with generating a list of questions about the prob-lem's situation, causes, and effects in the visual scoping tool to be addressed later.

Following the list of questions, Arthit moved on to the "conducting secondary re-search" phase, the second step of the Insights Finding program. This phase focused on gathering and analyzing data that already existed on the topic. A specific tool, second-ary analysis based on the iceberg model, was introduced here. The iceberg model helps users categorize available information, making it easier to identify what's read-ily apparent and what lies beneath the surface.

Through this process, Arthit further honed his critical thinking skills, an aspect of the IDG framework. He learned to evaluate the credibility of sources and identify rele-vant information from secondary sources such as websites and journals. For example, Arthit searched for the dropout statistics in Thailand in the government document compared with the related research to recheck the information and find the connec-tion between each statistic. Additionally, he employed sensemaking techniques to structure the information and identify patterns of the problem. For example, he found out the pattern that people in the community always think that students drop out because they are bad and lazy without asking what happen to them. These techni-ques, aligned with the thinking dimension of the IDGs, enabled Arthit to extract valu-able insights from existing research and knowledge, which is mentioned below.

However, some information cannot be found through the previous steps and re-quires direct inquiry from stakeholders. Arthit diligently sought information from various sources, uncovering several intriguing findings:

- In 2019, 1.2 million Thai youths dropped out of school, constituting 12.87% of all youths. The repercussions include an increase in unskilled labor, low wages, pov-erty, gambling, and other related issues.
- A staggering 68.4% of dropout students reported being subjected to daily verbal abuse by parents, leading them to avoid staying at home and studying further.
- Due to generational poverty, some students opt to work instead of pursuing edu-cation, albeit earning less than their graduated counterparts. Consequently, their children often inherit poverty, hindering their ability to afford schooling.

Furthermore, numerous policies aimed at addressing dropout issues exist, yet none effectively align with the students' needs, perpetuating the problem's persistence.

To conduct the interviews with at least three stakeholders, the tools called interview guidelines and interview questions are used by changemakers to make another list of questions that they must ask from stakeholders (see Appendix 1: Interview Protocol 1). We remind users to be careful of sensitive questions and topics, especially with sensitive interviewees. The IDG framework emphasizes self-awareness as a crucial skill for changemakers. In this step, the Insights Finding program encourage changemakers to examine their biases, beliefs, and values, enabling them to approach empathetic engagement with stakeholders in a more open and unbiased manner. For example, Arthit once thought that dropping out was a choice that students made by themselves because they were lazy and this step encouraged him to ask the students the actual reasons for their decision. By developing self-awareness, changemakers foster compassion and concern for the well-being of others, which are essential qualities for effective and sustainable changemaking.

In the case of dropout students, Arthit chose to interview three of them, one of whom was his relative. The questions were carefully crafted to ensure that they would not cause damage to the interviewee's heart. Arthit mainly created the questions on what the steps of deciding to drop out of school were, what the main reason for dropping out was, how they feel after dropping out, what makes them think it is good to stop learning and start working, how their parents and community members think about their decision, and what are their needs and pains of making this decision.

When the questions were ready, Arthit was encouraged to interview the real stakeholders. Nevertheless, we emphasized that students should leave their solution, bias, opinion, or negative attitude behind. They were required to open their minds and use open-ended questions to talk with the attitude that they were eager to empathize with the stakeholders. Moreover, it is not only going there to gain the answers for the project, but students also need to observe nonverbal communication such as facial expressions, tone of voice, and expressions of eyes while the interviewee tells each story. All information will be noted down in a tool called and interview record which the users need to jot down their observations of the interviewee's nonverbal communication of how they react to each question or story they told.

The tools guide changemakers to actively listen and understand the lived experiences of stakeholders affected by the problem. Through empathetic interviews and genuine conversations, changemakers develop empathy, presence, and openness. These skills allow them to establish meaningful connections with stakeholders, gain deeper insights into their needs and aspirations, and co-create solutions that are truly impactful and sustainable.

Three dropout students in the case were interviewed with questions that allowed them to comfortably tell sensitive stories about dropping out of school. There is a lot of significant data Arthit got from that interview, which in the next step will be synthesized and analyzed to find the insights.

After the interview, he was encouraged to reflect on his feelings and thoughts towards the interview with eight questions (see Appendix 2: Interview Protocol 2).

Regarding the reflection, his mindset towards dropout students was changed. As mentioned above, one of the interviewees was Arthit's relative and, as the girl's story was related to him, it shocked and inspired him to his next journey.

After reviewing themselves, the last two steps brought Arthit to the synthesis and analysis part.

All collected data are spread out and arranged as a timeline of the stakeholders from the beginning of the problem until the end or after. This process is well known as journey mapping. Also, below the timeline, changemakers should add the feelings or thoughts of the interviewee while describing each experience. After that, it could be seen which part of the whole story the interviewee gave the most importance or had the most feelings for. The user can also synthesize from the arranged data which one is an insight that they cannot find in the secondary data, which one is a gap that should be filled, or which one is an opportunity to utilize to solve the problem. Then they can write those three categories of data in a sheet called a synthesis review to think further about what the users should do in the next step.

In Arthit's case, he figured out that there are three major insights from the field that he visited and conducted the interviews as follows:

1. Students think about dropping out since primary school because they see many examples from seniors and want to help their families make money.
2. Parents do not know how to speak well with their children.
3. Adults in the community believe that students drop out because they are lazy.

He planned further in this step that he wanted to get more data from other stakeholders such as dropout students' parents, adults in the community, and teachers. Before that, Arthit reflected on his work on journey mapping and synthesis in another set of reflection questions. The questions include:

1. How do you feel after synthesizing?
2. What did you learn about the problem, cause and effect, target people, and other stakeholders?
3. What data surprised you?
4. Do you see the pattern involving the problem? How?
5. Which gap, opportunity, or insight do you want to pick up for working on? Why?

Based on this reflection, the process carries on to the last tool. In the summary tool, he was encouraged to choose a stakeholder involved in the dropout problem that he wanted to work with or help solve the problem, which he identified as preventing primary school students from dropping out of school. Also, he was required to choose the need and gap, opportunity, or insight that he wanted to work on. Arthit found out that most of dropout students have the idea of dropping out and start to disconnect with school since they are in primary school. So, he chose this gap to work with the primary school students. Then, he could create a final problem statement and a "How might we" sentence to be a starter for the idea generation later.

In these last steps, the IDG framework equips changemakers with the critical thinking skills necessary for data analysis. The Insights Finding program enable changemakers to analyze data that they got from the secondary research and the primary interview, identify patterns from the data and trends, and synthesize information to extract meaningful insights. By formulating well-defined design challenges based on these insights, changemakers are empowered to devise actionable solutions that address the root causes of the problem and drive sustainable change. For instance, Arthit defined the above-mentioned stakeholder, pattern, and gap. So, he created the intervention based on the information. The skills of problem solving and perseverance are crucial in this dimension, as changemakers navigate the complexities of the data and remain committed to finding effective solutions.

Instead of just equipping changemakers with skills to tackle social challenges, the program cultivates self-awareness, empathy, and critical thinking – all core competencies within the IDG framework. These skills not only empower changemakers to address social issues but also foster their inner growth and well-being.

The intervention and its impact on multiple levels

Arthit repeated the interview step for many times as he had planned, before coming up with many more insights to create an intervention. He and his team created two interventions based on the insights they got. These programs addressed the issue holistically, impacting various groups, as shown in Table 14.1.

Table 14.1: The intervention and its impact on multiple levels.

Intervention	Group	Outcome
Career sharing: A session for parents who work in the community (salt pan, fishery, rice paddy, grocery) to share with primary students about their work and everyday life.	Primary students	Through exposure to diverse career paths and role-playing exercises, the program challenges romanticized notions of work held by primary students. This early intervention fosters realistic expectations and career awareness, potentially influencing future academic and professional choices.

Table 14.1 (continued)

Intervention	Group	Outcome
	Parents	By participating in activities alongside their children, parents gain valuable insights into their offspring's perspectives and challenges. This increased understanding fosters stronger parent-child relationships, potentially mitigating behavioral issues and encouraging improved communication.
Career field trip: 1. A field trip bringing primary students to work in a real working field like their parents or adults in the community do. 2. Dropped-out seniors are invited to be caretakers for students.	Dropped-out students	The program acts as a catalyst for personal growth and reengagement for at-risk youth. By developing empathy and problem-solving skills, participants gain confidence and express a renewed desire to reenter the classroom. This second chance at education can significantly impact their future trajectories.
	Community adults	The program raises awareness amongst community members about pressing social issues like dropout rates. Recognizing their potential role in addressing these challenges, adults become more engaged in finding solutions, fostering a collaborative approach to community improvement.

The Insights Finding program: A solution for efficient changemaking

The mentioned challenges faced by changemakers shed light on the critical need for efficient methods and frameworks to equip changemakers with the necessary skills for sustainable change. The Insights Finding Tools address this need by promoting the IDG framework in the process. The tools blend systems thinking and design thinking, empowering changemakers to navigate problems more effectively and drive impactful change. Let us explore how the IDG framework enhances the Insights Finding Tools and the skills it encompasses:

1. **Systems thinking**: By understanding the "big picture", changemakers can grasp the intricate web of factors impacting the issue at hand. This systemic thinking encourages them to "think big, act small" by identifying a focused entry point for change. By analyzing connections and resource limitations, changemakers define a clear and manageable

system boundary. This ensures that their data analysis and insights are targeted and impactful. The skills of critical thinking, complexity awareness, perspective thinking, and long-term vision are developed through this dimension of the IDG framework.

2. **Design thinking**: In addition to systems thinking, tools in the Insights Finding program incorporate design thinking using the Design Council's double diamond framework (see Figure 14.1) to cultivate deep empathy for those affected by the issue. The double diamond framework explained two loops of the changemaking process. The Insights Finding program emphasized the first diamond, which starts with exploring the problem and ends the loop with the synthesis step. The loop can be repeated many times before starting the steps in the second diamond. By simplifying ethnography techniques, the tools guide changemakers in conducting meaningful conversations and observations. This direct experience of the problem fosters compassion and a shift in perspective. The IDG framework encourages self-reflection exercises, enabling changemakers to examine their own biases, beliefs, and values while developing empathy for others. This introspection fosters paradigm shifts about the issue, leading to innovative insights and solutions. The skills of empathy, compassion, self-awareness, and presence are cultivated through this dimension of the IDG framework.

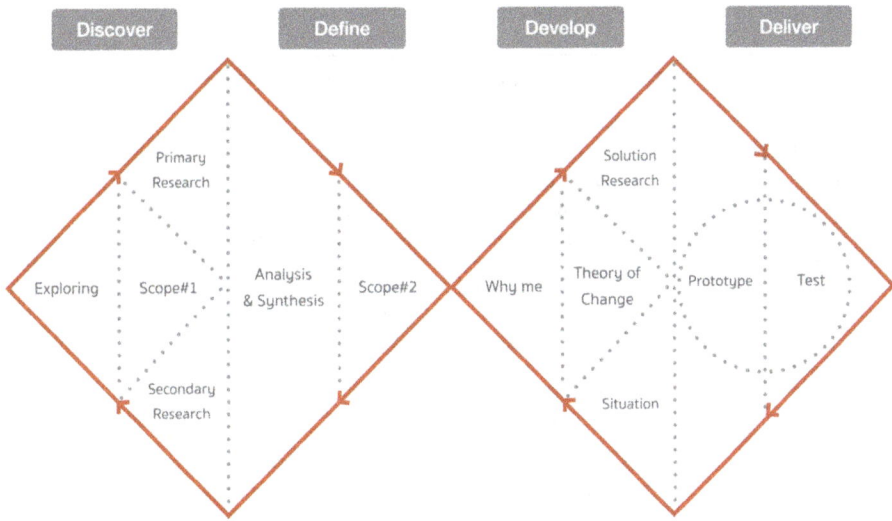

Figure 14.1: Double Diamond Framework.
Source: Insights for Change's own, based on Design Council (2003)

3. **Data analysis and synthesis**: The ability to navigate the data maze is a crucial skill for changemakers. The IDG framework equips them with the necessary tools to effectively collect, process, analyze, and synthesize data. Changemakers learn critical thinking skills to analyze data, identify patterns and trends, and derive meaningful in-

sights. They develop synthesis skills to draw connections and find meaning within the data. This analytical prowess enables them to formulate actionable solutions based on well-defined design challenges. The skills of perseverance and problem solving are also fostered through this dimension of the IDG framework.

Beyond skills: Cultivating inner development

The Insights Finding program go beyond equipping participants with just skills. They promote inner development by fostering self-awareness, empathy, and critical thinking – core competencies of the IDG framework. These skills empower changemakers to address social issues effectively while nurturing their well-being (see Table 14.2).

Beyond the structured approach and emphasis on empathy, the program offers personalized support through homework feedback from trained coaches. Throughout the eight-week journey, changemakers receive constructive feedback tailored to their progress and needs. This personalized guidance ensures deeper understanding, refines critical thinking skills, and empowers participants to confidently navigate the problem-solving process.

Table 14.2: Insights Finding program enhances Inner Development Goals.

Insights Finding program step	How Insights Finding program enhances the Inner Development Goals
Exploring and scoping the problem	**Critical thinking** (identifying subtopics, stakeholders, pains, and situations) **Complexity awareness** (recognizing interconnectedness) **Perspective thinking** (considering different viewpoints)
Conducting secondary research	**Critical thinking** (evaluating source credibility, identifying relevant information) **Sensemaking** (structuring the information and seeing the pattern)
Preparing to empathize	**Self-awareness** (examining biases, beliefs, and values) **Compassion** (developing concern for others' well-being)
Empathizing with stakeholders	**Empathy** (actively listening, understanding lived experiences) **Presence** (being fully engaged in the moment) **Openness** (remaining receptive to different perspectives)
Extracting insights	**Critical thinking** (analyzing data, identifying patterns and trends) **Synthesis** (drawing connections and finding meaning) **Problem solving** (formulating actionable solutions) **Perseverance** (being able to participate and finish the intensive journey)

By addressing the challenges faced by changemakers and nurturing essential skills, the IDG framework empowers individuals to drive sustainable change effectively. The systemic thinking and design thinking approaches embedded within the framework enable changemakers to understand complex problems, cultivate empathy, and derive meaningful insights from data. Through the acquisition of critical thinking, problem-solving, empathy, compassion, self-awareness, and presence skills, changemakers are equipped to tackle complex challenges and create sustainable impact.

As the Insights Finding program continue to evolve and be refined, they hold the intention to advance inner development goals. By emphasizing inner development and empowering changemakers with the necessary skills, these tools contribute to the collective efforts aimed at addressing societal challenges and creating a more sustainable and equitable future.

Summary and next step of the Insights Finding program

Beyond crafting solutions driven by personal perspectives, the Insights Finding program empower changemakers to gain a fresh lens on social issues. Through self-reflection, participants learn to shift their viewpoint from "me" to "we", understanding problems through the lived experiences of stakeholders. This fosters empathy, dismantling self-centered approaches and fostering holistic solutions for complex challenges. For those yearning to address social issues but feel unsure where to begin, these tools offer a structured pathway to embark on their change-making journey.

However, acknowledging the intensity of the current program, we are actively developing a youth-friendly version to make this experience more accessible. In addition, we are planning to improve the user-friendly version of the online platform. Moreover, an English version will be developed soon, while other languages are open for partnership and collaboration.

Feedback from students and audiences

The Insights Finding program and the article have received valuable feedback from students and audiences, who have experienced their usage and engaged with the accompanying story, by organizing an online session to present the article. The feedback can be categorized into two groups, highlighting both the strengths and weaknesses of the tools:

Strengths

– The tools effectively assist students in comprehending complex problems through structured thinking. They provide a framework that enhances students' understanding of intricate issues.
– In addition to offering motivation, the tools and accompanying case studies enable audiences to develop a deeper understanding of sustainable solutions for social problems. They broaden perspectives and promote awareness of impactful social change.
– The well-designed structure of the tools facilitates the inner development of students and audiences throughout the process. It fosters personal growth and cultivates essential skills and mindsets.
– The tools and case studies not only transform the mindset of changemakers regarding problem solving but also influence their perception of themselves. They inspire self-belief and confidence.

Weaknesses

– It has been observed that the tools primarily cater to those who possess a genuine desire to instigate change. However, since changemakers are relatively few in society, there is a need to simplify the tools to promote and inspire a broader range of individuals to act.
– Some users have found certain parts of the tools to have language that is difficult to understand. Simplifying the language and ensuring clarity would enhance user experience and comprehension.
– Continuous follow-up on the case studies and the progress of changemakers is recommended. Maintaining an ongoing narrative and providing updates would contribute to the users' understanding of the long-term impacts and sustainability of the changemaking efforts.

By incorporating the strengths identified, such as promoting structured thinking and facilitating inner development, and addressing the weaknesses highlighted, such as simplifying the tools and maintaining continuous follow-up, the Insights Finding program can further amplify their effectiveness and impact.

Key improvements are:
– **stronger opening sentence**: more captivating and directly addresses the main point;
– **flow and structure**: improved organization and flow of ideas;
– **clarity**: simplified and clarified sentences for better understanding;
– **removed repetition**: avoided redundancy for conciseness;
– **emphasis**: highlighted key points for greater impact;
– **positive tone**: maintained a positive and encouraging tone.

The crux of the challenge lies in shifting from self-centered solutions to those grounded in stakeholder realities and their struggles. This transformation demands dedication, time, patience, robust support systems, and an open mind. The Insights Finding program aim to streamline this process within realistic timeframes, guiding participants towards impactful solutions. Further, we believe the process cultivates and strengthens the skills and competencies aligned with the IDGs, ultimately empowering individuals to become even more effective changemakers.

Conclusion

Arthit Thongkhum's story exemplifies the power of the Insights Finding program in empowering changemakers to tackle social issues. Through the program, Arthit gained a nuanced understanding of the student dropout problem in Phetchaburi, Thailand, and developed empathy for those affected. The program equips individuals with not only critical thinking and data analysis skills, but also fosters inner development through self-awareness and compassion. This holistic approach, incorporating the Inner Development Goals framework, is essential for creating sustainable solutions to complex social problems. Arthit's resulting initiatives, including career exposure programs and community collaboration, addressed the root causes of dropouts and aimed to keep students engaged in education.

Reflection

Have you ever encountered a social issue that you felt compelled to address?
    What challenges do you think prevent people from taking action on social issues?
    How can we cultivate empathy and understanding in ourselves and others to tackle complex problems in our communities?
We encourage you to reflect on these questions and consider your role in creating positive change. The Insights Finding program offers a framework for anyone who wants to make a difference.
    Additionally, the chapter highlights some areas for improvement of the Insights Finding program:
    simplifying the language for broader accessibility;
    providing ongoing support and updates on changemaking efforts;
    making the program more youth-friendly.
If you have any thoughts or suggestions on how to improve the program, we welcome your feedback via insightsforchange.official@gmail.com.
    Together, through empathy, critical thinking, and a commitment to inner development, we can create a better future for all.

Appendices

Appendix 1: Interview Protocol 1
1. What were the steps of deciding to drop out of school?
2. What was the main reason for dropping out?
3. How do they feel after dropping out?
4. What makes them think it is good to stop learning and start working?
5. How do their parents and community members think about their decision?
6. What are their needs and pains in making this decision?

Appendix 2: Interview Protocol 2
1. How do you feel about the interview?
2. What can you relate to the interviewee?
3. After listening to the story, how do you understand the interviewee?
4. What are the similarities and differences of your thoughts and feelings towards the interviewee between before and after the interview?
5. If you were in their position, facing the same experience, being in the same context, what would you feel or need?
6. In your opinion, what are the choices the interviewee has?
7. What opportunities do you observe from the interview?
8. Who else could be stakeholders involved in the problem?

References

City Population. (2015). *Phetchaburi (Province, Thailand) – population statistics, charts, map and location*. Retrieved November 20, 2023, from https://www.citypopulation.de/en/thailand/admin/76__phetchaburi/.

Thai's Out of School Children Information System. (2017). Dropout Situation. Retrieved November 20, 2023, from https://oosc-report.firebaseapp.com/.

Elke Fein
Chapter 15
IDGs and Integral Politics: The marriage of depth and power

Abstract: This chapter explores the interrelations between the Inner Development Goals (IDGs) framework and an integral approach to politics as outlined in my/our recently published book reviewing 100 years of holistic and integral thinking about politics (Fein, 2023). In a nutshell, it argues that the two are complementary in that the IDGs help to illustrate the added value and deep transformation that Integral Politics implies in the realm of personal development. At the same time, the integral framework helps to map and specify the IDGs' role and potential contribution as part of a new paradigm of doing politics; in other words, of designing the ways in which we as a global human community organize our living together on planet Earth.

The chapter unfolds this claim by going through ten basic principles of an integral paradigm of doing politics, asking how each of them relates to, and includes, various of the IDGs' skills while adding the dimensions of culture and collective action, as well as an overall ontology and specific tools for implementing inner awareness and a growth-based approach in politics. It thereby offers a reframing of the IDGs as a crucial constitutive element of a new paradigm of politics that we currently see emerging – and that we urgently need on a global scale.

Keywords: Integral Politics, development, complexity, depth, meaning, consciousness

Introduction

The Inner Development Goals (IDGs) framework has been created to compensate for a lack of attention to the inner dimensions of human development, in particular in view of humanity's chances to achieve the Sustainable Development Goals (SDGs) within a reasonable time frame (Inner Development Goals, n.d.). Moreover, its creators rightly argue that humanity will not be able to implement the SDGs without corresponding inner, personal developments – for our human behavior originates in our thought and belief systems, worldviews, capabilities, and skills. If we don't adapt these to the global challenges that the SDGs aim to address by adopting a perspective, attitude, and worldview of interconnectedness, learning, and collective agency, no one will magically implement the SDGs for us.

Note: I thank Bettina Geiken for comments and advice.

https://doi.org/10.1515/9783111453729-016

So, if the IDGs are there to support the implementation of the SDGs, they are by definition a political project. Given their concise and easily accessible entry points into our inner dimensions, they are even a crucial contribution to a more holistic approach to systems change, in other words, to a new, integral paradigm of doing politics. The latter is urgently needed to overcome what increasingly appears as the dysfunctionalities of an old paradigm (*politics as usual*) that is no longer fit for purpose.[1]

At the same time, politics and political action is not the main focus of the IDGs. Hence, I argue that the IDGs and Integral Politics are complementary, mutually inspiring and enriching concepts on our way towards co-creating more sustainable, regenerative futures.

This chapter presents the vision of an integrally informed way of understanding and doing politics as it has been developed by a considerable number of inspirational thinkers over the last hundred years, as sketched out in my recently published book (Fein, 2023), and discusses the role that the IDG framework can play as a core pillar of this new paradigm.

The IDGs as a core ingredient of an integral paradigm of politics – the map

Assuming that most readers of this book will be more familiar with the IDG framework than with the concept of integral and Integral Politics, I will start by a short introduction of the latter and suggest a tentative overview of how the two concepts relate.

Politics based on an integral consciousness and worldview – inspirations from 100 years

Integral Politics as proposed here can be understood as a new paradigm for understanding and doing politics, based on an integral worldview. While the latter has been described by many great thinkers in different ways, in part independently of one another, using different terms and categories for describing their observations (for an overview see Fein, 2023), their overall message is astonishingly similar: Integral consciousness is the next more complex structure of thinking, perceiving, and processing the world that is emerging as its predecessors, modern (mental) and post-modern (relativistic) structures of consciousness are reaching their limits. We are witnessing

---

1 For more detail, see my presentation at the Integral Europe Conference 2023: www.youtube.com/watch?v=x_r7EoEbl9A.

today that the latter dramatically fail to adequately address and solve some of the main problems they have co-created over the last decades and centuries.

Among the typical challenges of our times are the three divides proposed by Otto Scharmer and Käufer (2013): a sense of separation from nature (ecological divide), from our fellow beings (social divide), and from ourselves and our inner sources (spiritual divide). Together, they have led to an unheard-of exploitation of planet Earth, a mass extinction of species, global warming, grave social inequalities and injustice between humans, as well as to a deep crisis of meaning in the Western world. Some of the symptoms of these developments are rising rates of burnout, loneliness, depression, and suicide, to name just a few of the increasingly visible consequences of humanity's previous and current, less-than-integral worldviews.

While Indian mystic and politician Sri Aurobindo was the first to speak about integral consciousness (Aurobindo, 1950/1999; Haldar, 1972), the Swiss-German cultural anthropologist Jean Gebser (1949/2020) first claimed that it was the next, emerging structure of consciousness on a global scale. He did so based on decades of thoroughly studying human cultural artifacts from various areas of the globe, some of them dating back several thousand years. Interestingly, Gebser's model of cultural evolution that resulted from his research largely coincides with the one developed three decades later by US psychologist Clare W. Graves based on an entirely different data set, namely clinical psychological field work and participant observation conducted over 15-plus years (Graves, 2005). While Graves[2] did not call the most complex structure he found "integral", his description of it strikingly matches that offered by Gebser, even though the two scholars were not familiar with each other's work.

Later, US philosopher Ken Wilber has done important work to integrate this previous body of research with many other streams of integrative, holistic, and consciousness studies into what he came to call the "integral model" (Wilber, 1995, 2000). All of these and six more recent streams of integral thinking, as well as their views and insights with regard to politics, social design, and governance are summarized in our book on the major foundations, inspirational resources, and principles of Integral Politics (Fein, 2023). The fact that this collection is but a choice from among a wide range of thinkers and approaches demonstrates that there is not one single definition of "integral", nor one specific model for explaining, describing, or doing politics in an integral way. Rather, the integral paradigm should be conceived as a broader vision and attractor, and hence, as an evolving entity, not a closed system or framework.

However, its essentials can be summarized by the following ten core principles which the most relevant thinkers and approaches hold to be crucial. Integral Politics:

---

2 Graves' work gained more widespread acknowledgement, especially through his students', namely, Don Beck and Christopher Cowan's Spiral Dynamics model (Beck & Cowan, 1996).

1. aims to draw on and integrate a vast range of perspectives, in particular inner dimensions (collective intelligence);
2. is based on a developmental understanding of political action logics (vertical complexity);
3. actively works with states of presence and awareness to increase quality (depth);
4. is grounded in an ontology of interconnectedness of all living beings (spirituality);
5. serves a higher goal, the common good, that transcends particularistic perspectives (purpose);
6. translates this integral understanding of the nature of human beings into corresponding structures, institutions, and politics (co-creation);
7. walks its talk, translating theory into experiential practice (coherence);
8. enacts a culture of lightness and playfulness (resonance, creativity, and flow);
9. rethinks agency on the basis of a quantum social science paradigm (power of possibility);
10. acknowledges its own limitations by offering space for not knowing and emergence (humility).

This chapter claims that the combination of these principles constitutes a new paradigm of understanding and doing politics, including both a new political culture informed by an awareness of inner qualities and a new political operating system informed by the former.

Mapping IDGs and SDGs within an integral political narrative

The above list of principles shows that inner development informs integral paradigm politics in many ways. While the first five substantial principles (1–5) immediately relate to the IDG dimensions of *being, thinking,* and *acting,* the last five principles (6–10) are more about applying the former into real life. They focus on translating them into structures, processes, and into a political culture that takes into account deeper qualities of *being, relating,* and *collaborating,* in service of transforming ourselves, societies, and systems towards more regenerative lifestyles.

To map the relation between the IDGs and Integral Politics however broadly, Ken Wilber's (1995, 2000) four-quadrant model is a helpful starting point. It distinguishes inner and outer, as well as individual and collective, perspectives on any phenomenon:

- The upper left quadrant looks at "individual interiors", i.e., the contents of a person's consciousness, including states of being, emotions, structures, habits of thinking, personal growth, and much more.
- The lower left quadrant focuses on "collective interiors", i.e., what holds a group of whatever size together in an invisible realm, e.g., shared values, norms, worldviews, shared trauma, taboos, etc.

- The upper right quadrant looks at "individual exteriors", i.e., visible behaviors, actions, and practices of individuals and social actors.
- Finally, the lower right quadrant holds a systems perspective, focusing on "collective exteriors" and their interrelations, e.g., social institutions, formalized rules and incentives, and the ways in which they structure and shape social realities.

While the SDGs have their main focus in the lower right quadrant (having been created by the rational mind and its preference for technical solutions, as Alfons Striegl [2023] put it) and aim at changing a number of parameters in the outside world, the IDGs focus primarily on the upper left quadrant, i.e., individual consciousness, attitudes, and qualities of awareness as inner personal skills.

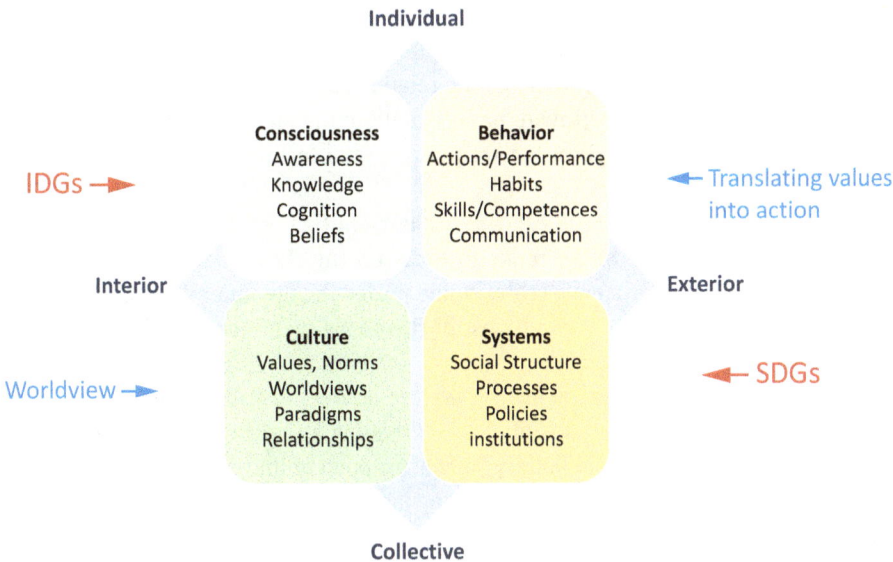

Figure 15.1: Mapping the core focus of the SDGs and the IDGs from an Integral Politics perspective. Source: Author's own

The integral model suggests that we need all four quadrants in order to bring about sustainable change. Yet, Figure 15.1 shows that, even if we take the SDGs and the IDGs together, there is less focus on both the lower left quadrant of culture, collective values, and paradigm and on the upper right quadrant of actual behaviors, habits, and concrete actions. In other words, an integral lens can offer a narrative for mapping how the IDGs and the SDGs are both complementary and potentially insufficient in themselves. At the same time, it also shows that the IDGs are a crucial contribution to a new, integral paradigm of doing politics by bringing inner dimensions to the table, all the more since they do so in an easily accessible way.

The IDGs and Integral Politics – a productive dance

Assuming that the readers of this book are more or less familiar with the IDG framework itself, my following discussion of the mutual relationship between IDGs and Integral Politics is structured based on an outline of the latter. It goes through the ten principles of Integral Politics and explores how each of them relates to the IDGs and the specific skills they are proposing, as well as what else might be needed in view of a four-quadrant, integral approach to global change.

(1) Collective intelligence: Integral Politics integrates more perspectives, in particular inner dimensions

The general ambition to "include more", or ideally "all relevant perspectives" aims at covering at least all four quadrants and the relations between them, making sure that we don't ignore/neglect or cultivate paradigmatic blind spots in or between any of them. In other words, it implies that we put a special focus on previously neglected perspectives.

As the overview in Figure 15.1 shows, our current (late) modern paradigm (which has brought forward the SDGs) tends to focus on the right quadrants of material change in the outer and systemic realm, while neglecting the inner dimensions. Moreover, this blind spot has co-created most of the above-mentioned challenges we are facing today.

Integral Politics' specific attention is therefore on the inner dimensions. This means that what is the heart of the IDGs, namely cultivating and developing our individual inner perceptions, attitudes, and skills is the starting point of Integral Politics. At the same time, the latter goes beyond this by also putting a strong focus on collective inner spaces (i.e., social norms, implicit language rules, taboos, traumas, etc.) and the ways in which they impact people's behaviors and social life.

Research shows that many of the problems we see on the outside have their roots in our ways of relating, i.e., in miscommunications, mutual injuries, and experiences of trauma that often have not been properly processed or even recognized. By creating safe enough spaces for putting a focus on these difficult aspects of our being together, we can recognize projections, silo thinking and polarization, and start to deconstruct and overcome them.

So, if Integral Politics calls for an upgrade of our political operating systems towards integral, this means to deepen our democracies by taking broader, aperspectival views, decelerating and re-focusing our communication and decision-making processes to invite the wisdom of collective intelligence, thereby transcending partisan political divides.

(2) Vertical complexity: Integral Politics is based on a developmental understanding of political action logics

This principle equally touches the core of the IDGs, namely the fact that every person's patterns of thinking, perceiving, and processing "reality" are subject to structural development, i.e., to increases in complexity as humans mature. All humans start their developmental journey at an embodied, "egocentric" place, where considering anything beyond their own personal needs is impossible. From there, they gradually develop more complex and more differentiated ways of perceiving, thinking, and problem solving, as they are going through various kinds of challenges and educational support.

This fact is so far rarely taken into account in the political realm, even though, holding true for every person, it applies to citizens, politicians, and any other societal actors alike. Moreover, the degree of complexity by which every one of us perceives, understands, and makes sense of the world has a direct influence on how we act on it, on what we perceive as "problems" in the first place, and what we assume to be (im) possible or good solutions to these.

For example, a person operating at an egocentric level will view and evaluate political events and developments through the lens and filter of their own personal interests ("[how] does it serve me?"). Someone at a conventional level will evaluate events with regard to their specific system of norms or rules ("Is it socially/morally/ legally acceptable? Will my peers or my authority X approve of it?"). In contrast, a person at a post-conventional level will likely weigh various perspectives, options, and arguments and prioritize choices based on overarching, higher principles such as "the value of human life beats specific rules".

The IDGs are based on roughly 100 years of research in structural adult development, distinguishing different realms or dimensions of development, such as being, thinking, and relating. Ken Wilber's (1995) integral theory uses the term "lines of development" for describing that these different realms within the personality can develop at different paces, and sometimes rather independently of one another (see Figure 15.2). This means that a person can be highly developed cognitively (i.e., be a professor of mathematics), while having only very poorly developed their social cognition (perspective taking skills) or their moral and ethical reasoning. And we all are examples for the uneven development of what Howard Gardner has called "multiple intelligences" (Gardner, 1987): some people are good thinkers, others are good musicians, and others still perform well in sports, while few are equally good in many areas alike.

When it comes to politics, a minimum level of cognitive complexity and perspective taking are preconditions for understanding what is at stake and, hence, for successfully acting in systems as complex as modern societies. This is especially the case in democratic societies, where many stakeholder positions – and (ideally) every citizen's voice is considered as equally valuable and important. Likewise, successful problem solving in and between social groups and even whole societies (as in foreign politics) calls for a certain capacity of empathy and taking others' perspectives into account.

THIRD TIER   **SECOND TIER**   **FIRST TIER**

Colors	Maslow Needs	Gebser Worldviews	Commons & Richards / Piaget/Aurobindo Cognitive	Graves/Spiral Dynamics / Wade Values	Kegan Orders of Consciousness	Loevinger Cook-Greuter Self-Identity
CLEAR LIGHT	Self-Transcendence		Supermind	Unity		Transpersonal
ULTRAVIOLET			Overmind			(Ego-aware)
VIOLET			Intuitive Mind, Meta-Mind	Transcendent		
INDIGO			Illumined Mind, Para-Mind			
TURQUOISE	Self-Actualization	Integral	High Vision-Logic (Cross-paradigmatic; Global Mind) — Systemic	GlobalView (Turquoise)	5th Order	Construct-aware (Integrated)
TEAL			Low Vision-Logic (Paradigmatic)	FlexFlow (Yellow)		Autonomous
GREEN	Self-Esteem	Pluralistic	Pluralistic Mind (Meta-systemic; Planetary Mind) — Relativistic	HumanBond (Green)	(4.5 Order)	Individualistic
ORANGE		Rational	Formal Operational (Rational Mind) — Multiplistic	StriveDrive (Orange)	4th Order	Conscientious
AMBER	Belongingness	Mythic	Concrete Operational (Rule/Role Mind) — Absolutistic	TruthForce (Blue)	3rd Order	Conformist
RED	Safety	Magic	Preoperational (Conceptual) — Egocentric	PowerGods (Red)	2nd Order	Self-protective
(MAGENTA)			Preoperational (Symbolic) — Magic-Animistic	KinSpirits (Purple)	1st Order	Impulsive
INFRARED	Physiological	Archaic	Sensorimotor	Survival (Beige)	0	Symbiotic

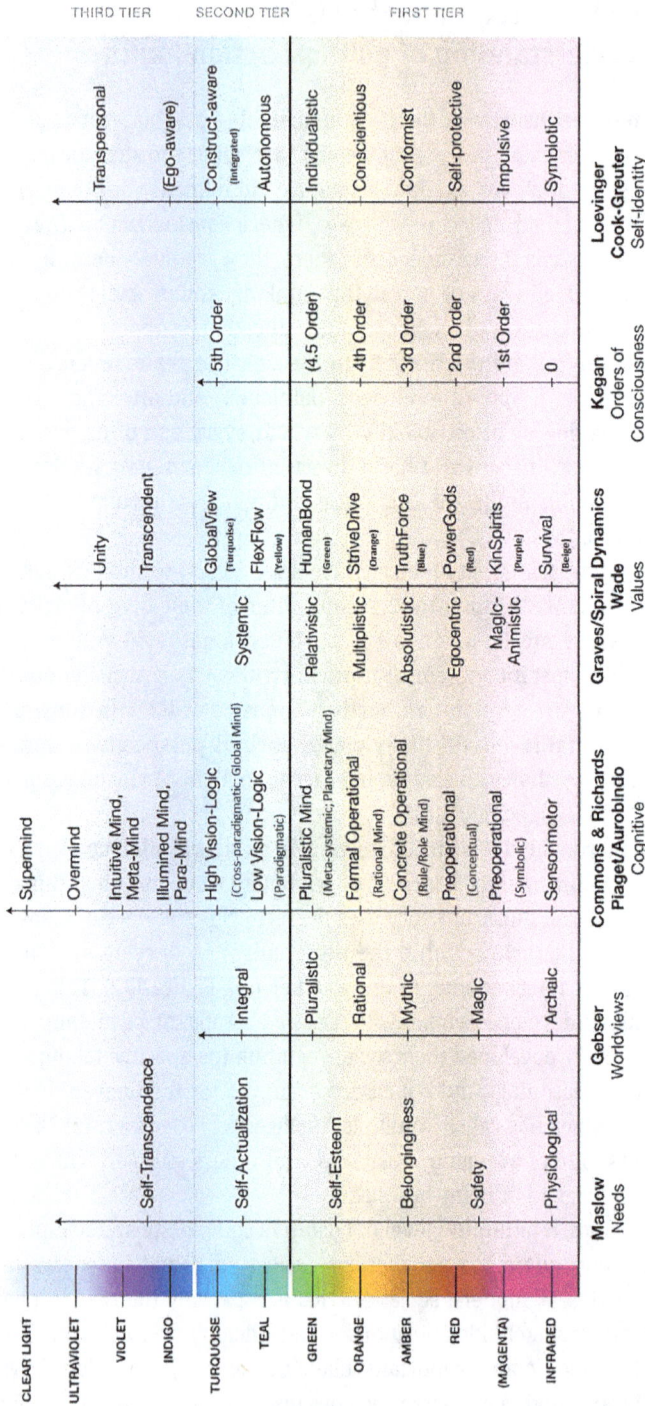

Figure 15.2: Lines of development.
Source: Wilber (1995)[3]

While the IDGs discuss and promote the development of similar skills on a personal level, the Integral Politics lens goes beyond the focus on developmental goals (offered in the form of 23 skills). Given that developing personal skills is a matter of social context, resources, opportunities, and appropriate scaffolding, the IDGs' strategy of promoting development will only generate broader impact if these goals are adopted as political goals and translated into actual policies by decision makers at the appropriate levels. And while the positive example of Costa Rica (Rodríguez, 2021) shows that such policy impact is possible, it is a long-term or at least medium-range strategy to globally develop more people's skills in more dimensions of the IDG framework.

In the meantime, a majority of people, including political leaders, are thinking, making meaning, and acting at the levels they are currently at – which, for the most part, is not the target level that the IDG framework proposes for each skill, but rather a less complex structure of consciousness. The added value of a developmentally informed politics is therefore to take into account actual developmental differences in reasoning and meaning making, and to acknowledge that political actors, groups, and even (parts of) societies display logics of thinking and action at different levels of complexity. Moreover, I would argue that similar differences are the root cause of most of the tensions, conflicts, and challenges we are facing in our societies.

A developmentally informed politics is therefore much more effective in understanding these root causes and, thereby, in understanding what can(not) be expected by specific political actors, knowing their respective thinking and action logics. This asset can hardly be overestimated, given that our "automatic" (i.e., unconscious, habitual) way of meaning making and acting likely expects others to think and behave in similar ways as we do ourselves. In contrast, taking into account actual action logics helps to prevent acting automatically, on the basis of projections, ideological agendas, or wishful thinking, rather than real life. It thus helps to prevent misunderstandings, to meet other stakeholders where they are and to find suitable partners for collaborative action. So, based on its developmentally informed understanding of thinking and behaviors, Integral Politics can come up with much more adequate and, hence, more effective solutions to socio-political challenges than conventional policy approaches.

(3) Depth: Integral Politics works with states of presence and awareness

Third, integral paradigm politics consciously works with states of presence, attention, and awareness in political, leadership, groups, and all kinds of cooperation contexts. The IDG framework touches upon this dimension by stressing and promoting several skills in three of its dimensions, in particular: presence (being dimension), connectedness and empathy (relating dimension), and communication skills (collaborating dimension) as individual competencies. As mentioned in the previous section, developing individual skills on a larger scale is indeed a crucial and important endeavor. At the same time, this process demands continuous effort on an individual level, as well as constant attention and support in various ways.

In addition to the IDGs' focus on developing the above-mentioned skills as individual capacities, Integral Politics also puts a strong focus on the "how" of our being together (lower left and upper right quadrants). More precisely, it offers a rich body of experience in view of actively shaping the qualities of our interrelations, in particular through actively working with different states and qualities of presence in groups.

One of the most prominent resources in this regard is the work by Otto Scharmer (2016) and his colleagues (Senge, Scharmer, Jaworski & Flowers, 2008) around "Theory U" and the art and skill of using state awareness to improve the quality of listening and communication. As integral theory points out, states are much more fluid and flexible phenomena than stages (or levels) of skill development. This means that whereas it usually takes years to develop structures of meaning making and reasoning by just one level, states can be modulated and changed quite easily through appropriate exercises (individual level) and skilled facilitation (in groups). This allows to modulate different state experiences in the course of just one group session, for example. In this way, groups can be guided from more conventional, superficial modes of listening and communicating into deeper and more meaningful ones in a short period of time, thereby helping them to access new perspectives and potential shadow sides of an issue which had previously been avoided. Moreover, it helps to transform shadow into potential and supports the co-creation of better, more visionary, and effective responses to socio-political challenges.

The magic of Theory U lies precisely in taking groups into deeper collective states of awareness, in which fresh perspectives arise and new solutions appear that draw on an emerging future, rather than the patterns of past thinking. By integrating similar methods and approaches into its standard repertoire, Integral Politics promotes a state-aware political culture.

(4) Spirituality: Integral Politics is grounded in an ontology of interconnectedness

Fourth, Integral Politics is grounded in spirituality, i.e., based on an ontology of (inter) connectedness with all living beings.

The IDGs do not speak of spirituality explicitly, but they do propose several related skills and capabilities like presence and integrity (being dimension), connectedness and humility (relating dimension), trust (collaborating dimension), and courage (acting dimension) as individual competencies that can and should be developed.

Drawing on Sri Aurobindo's (1999) view of the human person, Integral Politics proposes anthropology consisting of four equally important pillars: body, emotions (vital), mind, and spirit (see Figure 15.3). By adding spirituality as one of these, Integral Politics is very explicit in going beyond the modern, primarily materialistic worldview. More-

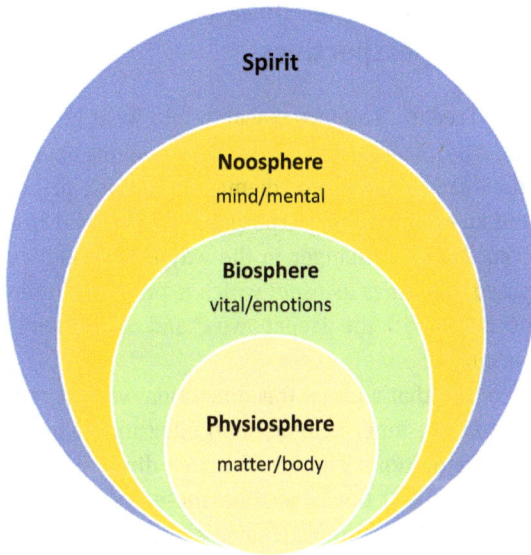

Figure 15.3: The four dimensions of integral anthropology and ontology.
Source: Author's own

over, by claiming that physical, emotional (vital), mental, and spiritual needs and capabilities are equally important, it turns this anthropology into a political statement.

In this perspective, all humans have basic needs in at least those four dimensions. Consequently, politics needs to address all four of them with equal attention and care. The integral anthropology also makes clear to what extent the current modern worldview and the *politics as usual* based on it try to compensate emotional or spiritual needs by material consumption or mental distraction, both endeavors that are bound to fail.

This spiritual foundation of interconnectedness also helps to recognize – and to ultimately heal the three "divides" identified by Scharmer and Käufer (2013): from ourselves and our inner source (spiritual), from each other (social), and from nature and the ecosystem (ecological). Counteracting these is a profoundly political project that requires an anthropology grounded in interconnectedness.

On the ecological level, it is clear that we won't heal the ecosystem by perpetuating our currently dominant mindset of exploitation. On the social level, an attitude of interbeing will put the focus on healthy relationships as a precondition of happiness and, hence, a flourishing society. On the personal level, connection with the origin/source and with one's higher self helps to relativize the ego, to transcend self-centered concerns and identities, and gives a deeper meaning to one's life and actions. It allows us to live according to our higher purpose and inner calling (see Principle 5) instead of primarily pursuing material interests.

(5) Purpose: Integral Politics serves a higher goal, the common good, transcending particularistic perspectives

This principle is essentially inspired by Frederic Laloux's research into what he calls "teal" (integral) organizations (Laloux, 2014). Laloux found that organizations operating on the basis of teal (integral) consciousness have implemented three basic principles: self-management, wholeness, and an evolutionary purpose as their *raison d'être*. For Integral Politics, the latter is a crucial game changer in the way it sees politics' very mission and legitimacy. As opposed to *politics as usual* which is primarily interest- and stakes-driven, Integral Politics starts with the deeper "why" and consequently defines its own agenda and strategy around it.

The IDG framework does offer elements that address this dimension when it calls for personal skills and characteristics like the inner compass and integrity (being dimension), sensemaking and long-term orientation/visioning (thinking dimension), or courage and perseverance (acting dimension). At the same time, these are primarily viewed as to be developed personal skills, rather than as elements of a new political agenda.

Integral/teal politics takes these ambitions to a higher level and broader scale. By turning the commitment to serve a higher, evolutionary purpose into its own reason of being, it sets clear priorities and acts based on the question "What is ultimately at stake?". By reorganizing all political action around its higher purpose of serving the larger common good, it transcends silo thinking and particularistic interests in favor of solutions that work for everyone. And based on Principle 1 (see earlier section) of taking into account much wider horizons, Integral Politics aims at including all relevant stakeholders, including nature and future generations. This allows to act on the basis of a powerful vision and sense of meaning which makes it vibrant, alive, and attractive.

Jim Rough (1996), the inventor of the wisdom circle and citizens' assemblies format, shares that his co-creative processes show over again that if you invite people into doing meaningful work in the realm of politics, they get more excited as problems get bigger, i.e., more fundamental. This is because they sense that something is at stake – and that they can do something about it. Citizens' assemblies also show that participants are very ready to make personal sacrifices for a higher cause if the decision to do so stems from a collective process they have been involved in. In contrast, our current *politics as usual* is slower and more hesitant to adequately react to current challenges, partly due to power games, partly to its ties with certain lobbies and interest groups.[4]

The next five principles deal more with implementing and enacting the vision of Integral Politics, and putting the former into practice.

---

4 In an online presentation of these ten principles, I propose some examples for putting purpose into the center of politics: www.youtube.com/watch?v=x_r7EoEbl9A.

(6) Co-creation: Integral Politics translates the integral understanding of the nature of human beings into corresponding structures, institutions, and politics

I have found no corresponding skills in the IDG framework for the principle of invit-ing integral consciousness and wholeness into politics by translating it into more spe-cific structures. This seems to illustrate the specific focus of each of these approaches. While the IDGs focus on personal skill development, Integral Politics offers an over-arching framework that aspires to join inner and outer dimensions by translating es-sential qualities, states, and capacities (left, inner quadrants), into structures, institu-tions, processes, and practical actions (right quadrants). Principle 6 is where updating the operating system of our current democracies becomes practically visible.

A lot could be said about this topic, for countless pioneering initiatives are al-ready prototyping new paradigm deliberation and dialog processes, decision-making formats, and behaviors all over the world, thereby creating and testing new struc-tures for overcoming partisanship and party bickering through cultures of nonparti-sanship. For ultimately, these new cultures must be sustained and scaffolded by also replacing incentives for competition with incentives for cooperation on the level of the political system itself (lower right quadrant).[5]

As one of the products of our LiFT Politics project, Indra Adnan and Harald Schel-lander have created an interactive Prezi-based universe of new politics called "Planet A".[6] They thereby suggest that a new planet built up of countless pioneering initiatives of a new, more Integral Politics is virtually emerging underneath our feet. You can enter the universe of Planet A through many different doors and walk your own way through your personal exploration.

Another prominent suggestion for translating the core principles of an integral worldview into policy recommendations is Hanzi Freinacht's distinction of six forms of metamodern politics (Freinacht, 2019, see figure 15.4). To name only three of them:

– *Democratization politics* enacts the idea that democracy is an evolving entity that is never fully implemented but widens and deepens as our cultures evolve and our values and ethical standards develop. In other words, deepening and further developing democracy is an ongoing political goal that should get continuous and systematic attention by political actors and public bodies.
  – Among the ideas discussed in this area are:
    – gradually replacing majority rule by formats scaffolding collective intelli-gence;

---

5 Sociological research has shown that polarization is to a large degree produced and co-created by the political parties themselves, while acting out the current system's compulsion for self-presentation at the expense of political opponents (Mau, Lux, & Westheuser, 2023).
6 The prezi can be accessed online at prezi.com/view/3cXiKo6Cvz2xpUTddcMw/.

- creating more incentives for cooperation and co-creation instead of competition (consensus- or consent-based decision making as it is practiced
  in citizens' councils); and
- creating more safe spaces for integrity in politics. Ultimately, these all re-
  volve around an invitation to parties to either become more constructive
  or ultimately superfluous.
- *Gemeinschaft politics* responds to the increasing erosion of social bonds and relationships, suggesting various public measures, spaces, and forms of scaffolding to
  build social and relating skills and to strengthen social ties. It thereby also proposes concrete responses to the dimension of basic emotional needs in Aurobindo's (1999) integral anthropology, holding that these cannot be compensated by
  money or material consumption.
- *Existential politics* responds to the dimension of the spiritual need for meaning
  and personal growth, as fundamental pillars of happiness. Like emotional needs,
  metamodern politics acknowledges that these cannot be fulfilled on a material
  level, by consumption or money transfers, even though many people seem to
  compensate unfulfilled existential needs by shopping or engaging in other addic-
  tions. Moreover, existential politics aims to scaffold processes of re-sensing and
  repurposing and makes sure that inner development is part of public education.

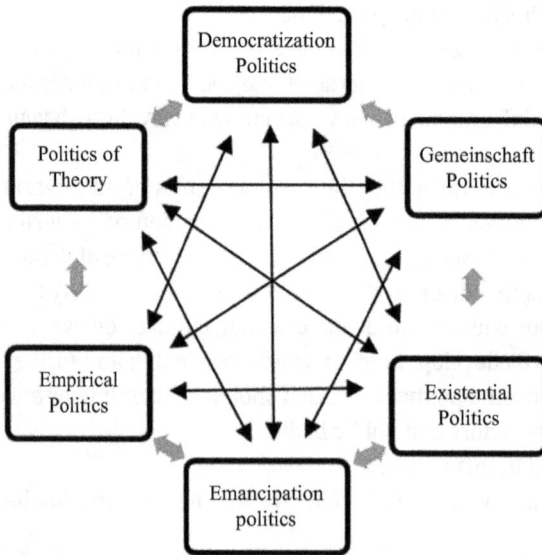

Figure 15.4: The six forms of metamodern politics.
Source: Freinacht, 2019

These are by far not the only suggestions and practical tools for translating integral
consciousness into more specific structures, processes, and policies. Moreover, this

principle is an open invitation to all of us to co-create new operating systems for the ways in which we organize our shared governance processes through the wisdom of collective intelligence.

(7) Coherence: Integral Politics walks its talk by translating theory into experiential practice

While the previous principle focused on "innovating" specific new paradigm structures, processes, policies and institutions, Principle 7 is a call for coherence across all quadrants. While many great thinkers, philosophers, and models have described integral consciousness, a new integral paradigm of understanding and doing politics will only gain traction if it can be experienced in practice by people, whether they are familiar with the "theory" or not.

As an all-quadrant approach, Integral Politics needs to be embodied and speak to people's hearts, minds, and souls alike, in a language they can hear and understand, or it is not integral.

The most straightforwardly corresponding skill in the IDGs framework for this ambition is integrity and authenticity (being dimension), calling for personal coherence across the different dimensions of the personality. Integral Politics extends this call for coherence to the wider social system, including both groups of people working together, their organizations, and the ways in which we try to shape the overall social and political systems.

While this principle appears to be a no-brainer at first sight, it is probably one of the most difficult ones to implement. Many an integral political initiative failed precisely because its members did not manage to walk their talk and to embody their vision and theory in a coherent and, thus, convincing way in "real life". This includes the willingness and openness to engage in shadow work, to get in touch with traumatic experiences, and to process and heal tensions and conflicts in oneself, one's group or organization, as well as within the larger social fabric.

Given that this ambition calls for a truly transformative attitude and approach, it implies the commitment to be radically honest and radically real – and to be willing to let go of one's favorite beliefs, opinions, and even identities, if needed.

Integral Politics thus aims to practice what Otto Scharmer (2016) calls "seeing with fresh eyes", i.e., to start with what is, rather than what should be. It values process qualities just as much as actual results. It happily makes mistakes and learns from them, keeping the overall vision in focus. It values doing over talking (walks its talk) and resists dogmatism by making sure its ideals are translated into visceral practice. Ultimately, Integral Politics' striving for integrity can be measured by how much vitality and joy it generates among those who practice and experience it. In fact, after successful meetings, participants would state that they are leaving "more alive" than they came in. Indeed, this was the most important feedback I have received from participants of my IDG and Integral Politics workshop (see section below).

(8) Resonance, creativity, and flow: Integral Politics acts with lightness and playfulness

One of the ways for achieving a degree of coherence that makes people "more alive" is to draw on all senses, the whole body, and the arts when inviting people into integral political experiences. It is well known that the mind (our mental and cognitive capabilities) – even though highly valued in Western culture – is but one among many modalities by which humans can communicate and express themselves. While we all are trained extensively in using our minds, many, if not most of us, have other talents beyond thinking – or are even more at ease in using the latter (see Principle 2).

Moreover, the integral approach to politics holds that bringing all of these together is the best strategy for not only involving a maximum number of people, but to also involving their bodies, hearts, souls, and minds alike. While we might think that "politics" is or has to be something serious, given that it deals with serious issues, experience shows that once a group of people has developed a sufficient degree of vibrational coherence, based on mutual trust and safe enough spaces, new levels of creativity, lightness, and flow emerge. These, in turn, help them to open up, let go of narrow, fear-based assumptions and perspectives, and to access collective states where out-of-the-box thinking is welcome and new ideas can emerge easily.

The IDG framework mentions some of the skills that are necessary for similar experiences, namely openness and learning mindset (being dimension), trust (collaborating dimension), as well as creativity, optimism, and perseverance (acting dimension). So, while these are important ingredients on a personal level, we can also do a lot to support their more widespread development by creating cultures of trust, playfulness, and creativity in groups and on a societal level.

In a nutshell, Integral Politics' ambition is to change our political cultures towards more collaborative, co-intelligent, and co-creative qualities, while limiting incentives for competition to areas where they don't produce losers or other forms of exclusion.

Integrating music, dance, art, and other playful, more "feminine" approaches into our ways of doing politics not only increases the level of fun and aliveness, it also helps to strengthen a sense of interconnectedness and, thus, trust in higher (collective) modalities of intelligence that allow to give up narrow ego perspectives, identities, and their desire to control outcomes.

While global problems are of course very serious, not taking ourselves too seriously helps us to remain open to new solutions, positive surprises, and to grace, coming in the form of wisdom, deeper insights, healing, and synergies of all kinds. Hanzi Freinacht has described this attitude as "sincere irony" (Freinacht, 2017, 2019), by which he means to take a critical distance towards "the hysterically pursued ideologies of the 20th century" or, in other words, to combine the lightness of postmodern irony with a sincere engagement with the world that goes beyond postmodern relativism (Freinacht, 2017a).

In short, this principle calls for dancing tango with our challenges, including our creative abilities, in view of inviting miracles that our cognitive mind might not be open to, but that start to appear once we open up all channels of our humanness.

(9) Power of possibility: Integral Politics rethinks agency on the basis of a quantum social science paradigm

The attitude described in Principle 8 prepares the ground for a new epistemology that, in turn, is grounded in a new ontology, namely quantum theory. We all know that quantum theory is about the latest "state of the art" when it comes to humanity's efforts to explain and make sense of the mechanisms governing the universe. Having emerged in the realm of physics, quantum theory has been around for over 100 years now. However, its basic insights, such as entanglement (interconnectedness), non-locality, and complementarity as described by generalized quantum theory (Walach & von Stillfried, 2011) seem to not have arrived in many other areas of everyday life, including politics, yet.

However, if we take these insights and principles seriously, this implies a completely different understanding of and perspective on the world and of our role and potential agency in it. Karen O'Brien has spelled out the consequences of what she calls a "quantum social science" perspective for politics in her contribution to our handbook (Fein, 2023). She holds that:

- Our current paradigms limit the ways in which problems are defined and approached, including what we assume to be realistic, legitimate, effective, and possible.
- A quantum lens provides an alternative perspective that challenges, provokes, and invites people to engage with politics in a profoundly different way: It sees humans as "'walking wave functions' of potentiality and possibility".
- It supports the ontology of wholeness and interconnectedness, in which we see ourselves as entangled parts of a much bigger whole, where politics is essentially about how we manage our entangled relationships.
- Quantum theory sees space, time, and matter not as given, but instead as iteratively performed and produced in every moment (nonlinearity, serendipity).
- Its fractal approach to politics calls for generating patterns that reflect integrity at all scales, which, in turn, impact each other.
- This alternative paradigm, grounded in connections, intra-actions, and values applying to all life on the planet helps us to relax fixed mindsets and to open our minds in view of making the potential for sustainability a reality. It offers a way of seeing solutions that are obscured by the current lens and provides alternative ways of responding rapidly and collectively to interrelated problems (O'Brien, 2023).

Again, while the IDG framework mentions skills like the ability to mobilize, perseverance, and courage in its *acting* dimension, Integral Politics goes beyond this focus on individual skills and capabilities by radically rethinking our agency on the basis of a quantum social science paradigm. It thereby offers a new (meta)narrative in which both personal development and political agency are (re)framed towards the power of infinite possibility.

In this metanarrative, we are profoundly interconnected. Therefore, all our actions impact everything else. Hence, we are extremely powerful. We have created the world we live in and, thus, we can also change it. Our mind and every thought held in our consciousness counts as an origin of our actions – and as the potential source of other actions. "We matter" in the double sense of being important and because of the fact that we are materializing what we hold to be true or important. In this new paradigm informed by quantum science, we are fully aware of our power. Barack Obama's slogan "Yes we can" is embodied knowledge.

Due to the power of this new paradigm, agency social scientists now speak of "positive social tipping points" (Otto et al., 2020) which can be reached if enough people start to subscribe to its ontology and start to enact it. In this case, unexpectedly positive, regenerative human action can start to constructively counteract the biophysical tipping points of our Earth's system by implementing behaviors and solutions that have been unthinkable in the current paradigm.

(10) Humility: Integral Politics offers space for not knowing and emergence

As a complementary quality to Principle 9, Integral Politics finally takes a position of humility in view of its own status, relevance, and agenda. Even though its rationale is based on the latest available science, it would never mistake the latter's insights as "the ultimate truth" about the world. From a developmental perspective, all knowledge is subject to evolution, to constant improvement through probing, testing, trial, and error. Therefore, our concept of Integral Politics self-identifies as a vision and attractor, rather than a concise program that can or should be implemented in ten (or so) well-defined steps. Moreover, as explained in the context of the first principle, in order to include "more perspectives", we always have to ask: What else do we need to include and consider, beyond what we already know is important? Metaphorically speaking, it is the politics of the additional empty chair at the table, as a symbol for the incompleteness of our knowledge and wisdom at any time.

The IDG framework acknowledges this principle in various of its dimensions. It calls for self-awareness and presence (being dimension), for critical thinking and complexity awareness (thinking dimension), for humility (relating dimension), and for trust (collaborating dimension). Again, these are primarily framed as developmental goals in the realm of personal skills, attitudes, and capacities.

In turn, Integral Politics puts the focus on tools, methods, and practices which help both individuals and groups to listen to their intuition and to the voice of wisdom that emerges from silence. Hence, it facilitates processes of tapping into the vast realms of potential that can be accessed whenever we make room for the collective intelligence beyond our individual minds, in service of the overall evolutionary purpose (Principle 5) of our doing politics together.

Table 15.1: The IDGs and Integral Politics – overview of interrelations.

Integral Politics principle	Relates to IDG dimension	IDG skills in focus
Collective intelligence	Being, thinking, collaborating	Critical thinking, complexity awareness, perspective skills, long-term orientation and visioning; communication, inclusive mindset and intercultural competence
Vertical complexity	Being, thinking, relating, collaborating	Critical thinking, complexity awareness, perspective skills, long-term orientation and visioning; empathy and compassion
Depth	Being, relating, collaborating	Inner compass, integrity and authenticity, presence, connectedness, empathy and compassion, communication, inclusive mindset and intercultural competence
Spirituality	Being, relating, collaborating, acting	Inner compass, integrity and authenticity, presence, connectedness, humility; empathy and compassion, trust; courage, optimism
Purpose	Being, thinking, acting	Inner compass, integrity and authenticity; critical thinking, long-term orientation and visioning; courage, perseverance
Co-creation	Being, relating, collaborating	(no immediate correspondence), long-term orientation and visioning; co-creation, mobilization; creativity
Coherence	Being, relating, collaborating	Inner compass, integrity and authenticity; courage, creativity, perseverance
Resonance, creativity, flow	Being, relating, collaborating, acting	Inner compass, integrity and authenticity, openness and learning mindset; humility; courage, creativity, optimism
Power of possibility	Being, relating, collaborating, acting	Openness and learning mindset; complexity awareness, long-term orientation and visioning; connectedness, trust, mobilization, creativity, courage, optimism, perseverance
Humility	Being, relating, collaborating, acting	Openness and learning mindset, self-awareness, presence; critical thinking, complexity awareness; humility; trust

Integral Politics put into practice

The feedback I received after my 4-hour-workshop on IDGs and Integral Politics at the Swiss IDG Hub in Basel in March 2024 indicates that we can give people a taste of this new paradigm even in a few hours. While most participants had heard of the IDGs, many were unfamiliar with integral thinking before.

Yet, they left "grateful and curious", "nourished, inspired, and touched" and experienced the workshop as "broadening horizons, stimulating through a wealth of ideas that need more time to integrate". One participant framed their experience as "a sip of wisdom, combined with resonance, soothing connection, and calming togetherness". This nicely illustrates another's perception that "the integral quality was already there" and could be tasted with different senses. One of the most encouraging pieces of feedback was expressed by a woman who said that her initial need to "experience, enjoy, and be" was fulfilled, and that the workshop had given her "an appetite for politics!".

Conclusion

This paper claims that the combination of the ten principles outlined above constitutes a new paradigm of understanding and doing politics, including a new operating system and political culture. It transcends the *politics as usual* we have known so far by adopting much deeper, wider, and longer horizons. Can you imagine what politics would look and feel like if this new paradigm was the "new normal"? How would this change your experience of politics and sense of agency?

The IDGs are a wonderful framework that can attract and redirect public attention to the much-neglected inner dimensions of being and (co-)developing. Not only do they spell out one of the core dimensions of Integral Politics in an easily accessible way, they also point to a wider, integral narrative and worldview that seems to be emerging more visibly now as our collective global challenges grow.

The integral paradigm can be framed as the response to these increasingly complex challenges, acknowledging Einstein's famous quote that problems can never be solved at the same level of thinking that created them. This chapter has argued that the above-sketched integral paradigm of politics is precisely this new, more holistic way of understanding and being in the world that is so miraculously different from *politics as usual*, because it includes the inner dimensions of our being (together).

Whereas the IDG framework has been developed as a comprehensive and readily available response to the lack of depth and inner growth in current, late-modern ways of struggling with today's multiple crises, Integral Politics integrates its core concerns into a completely new narrative and operating system. By including the dimensions of depth and inner development, Integral Politics not only responds to specific limitations and shortcomings of our current paradigms, but is much better prepared to actually deal with the multi-crisis times in targeted and effective ways.

At the same time, as a structurally new, and by definition, more complex mental and cultural operating system, it is less easy to grasp unless it can be experienced first-hand. This is where the IDG framework and Integral Politics can enter a productive, mutually supportive dance, a marriage of depth and power. This chapter has spelled out both sides of this marriage, arguing that:

- an exploration of inner development provides us with a much more adequate understanding of political conflicts and tensions;
- deeper qualities of being, relating, and collaborating can be purposefully designed and can lead to much more powerful and effective solutions to socio-political challenges;
- a politics that is grounded in a deeper, spiritual notion of global connectedness will set different priorities than our current-interest – or ego-driven – one, and lead to much better results for all involved;
- putting inner development at the center of politics will create a completely different political culture that will transcend polarization through active listening and deep dialog and that will start to heal the multiple individual and collective experiences of trauma that largely inform our current *politics as usual.*

A developmentally informed politics can thus help us to "bend the curve" and open up new windows of opportunity and to unlock the power of possibility and potential for more sustainable and regenerative ways of living on planet Earth.

References

Aurobindo, S. (1999). *The ideal of human unity*. Lotus Press (Original work published 1950).

Beck, D. E. & Cowan, C. (1996). *Spiral dynamics: Mastering values, leadership and change*. Wiley-Blackwell.

Fein, E. (2023). *Foundations, principles and inspirational resources of Integral Politics*. Tradition Verlag.

Freinacht, H. (2019). *Nordic ideology: A metamodern guide to politics, Book Two (Metamodern Guides)*. Metamoderna ApS.

Freinacht, H. (2017). *The listening society: A guide to metamodern politics, Book One (Metamodern Guides)*. Metamoderna Ap.

Freinacht, H. (2017a), *Metamodernism: The Conquest of a Term*, https://metamoderna.org/metamodernism-the-conquest-of-a-term/, accessed March 28, 2024.

Gardner, H. (1987). The theory of multiple intelligences. *Annals of Dyslexia, 37*, 19–35. https://doi.org/10.1007/BF02648057.

Gebser, J. (2020). *The ever-present origin*. Ohio University Press (Original title *Ursprung und Gegenwart*, originally published 1949. Deutsche Verlags-Anstalt).

Graves, C. W. (2005). *The Never Ending Quest*. C. Cowan & N. Todorovic (eds.). ECLET Publishing.

Haldar, M. K. (1972). Political thought of Aurobindo Ghosh. *Indian Literature, 15*(2), 56–67. http://www.jstor.org/stable/23333774.

Inner Development Goals (n.d.), https://innerdevelopmentgoals.org/about/, accessed March 24, 2024.

Laloux, F. (2014). *Reinventing organizations (vol. 58)*. Nelson Parker.

Mau, S., Lux, T., & Westheuser, L. (2023). *Triggerpunkte: Konsens und Konflikt in der Gegenwartsgesellschaft*. De Gruyter.

O'Brien, K. (2023). Politics through a quantum lens. In E. Fein (ed.), *Foundations, principles and inspirational resources of Integral Politics*. (pp. 345–366). Tredition.

Otto, I. M., Donges, J. F., Cremades, R., Bhowmik, A., Hewitt, R. J., Lucht, W., & Schellnhuber, H. J. (2020). Social tipping dynamics for stabilizing Earth's climate by 2050. *Proceedings of the National Academy of Sciences of the United States of America, 117*(5), 2354–2365. https://doi.org/10.1073/pnas.1900577117.

Rodríguez, J. V. T. (2021), *Why Costa Rica is the place to start co-creating the Inner Development Goals (IDGs) manifesto?* https://www.undp.org/es/costa-rica/discursos/why-costa-rica-place-start-co-creating-inner -development-goals-idgs-manifesto, accessed March 24, 2024.

Rough, J. (1996). The Wisdom Council and responsible leadership. *The Journal for Quality and Participation, 19*(7), 74.

Scharmer, C. O. (2016). *Theory U: Leading from the future as it emerges*. Berrett-Koehler Publishers.

Scharmer, C. O. & Kaufer, K. (2013). *Leading from the emerging future: From ego-system to eco-system economies*. Berrett-Koehler Publishers.

Senge, P. M., Scharmer, C. O., Jaworski, J., & Flowers, B. S. (2008). *Presence: Human purpose and the field of the future*. Crown Currency.

Striegl, A. (2023), *Presentation on the IDGs by the Pioneers of Change*, December 2023.

Walach, H. & von Stillfried, N. (2011). Generalised quantum theory – basic idea and general intuition: A background story and overview. *Axiomathes 21*(2) 185–209. https://doi.org/10.1007/s10516-010-9145-5.

Wilber, K. (2000). *Integral psychology: Consciousness, spirit, psychology, therapy*. Shambhala Publications.

Wilber, K. (1995). *Sex, ecology, spirituality: The spirit of evolution*. Shambhala Publications.

Monica Novoa-Gómez

Chapter 16
Relating, cooperating, and co-creating: The inner skills at the heart of cultural and intergenerational trauma healing and flourishing

Abstract: This chapter shows the process by which the traumatic experience of ancestors negatively affects their children by interfering with their socioemotional development and general health – a process that has been described as intergenerational trauma. This study analyzes the results in light of Inner Development Goals (IDGs) and the analysis of cultural practices within the framework of functional contextual science. Resources that promote the flourishing of individuals whose ancestors have experienced traumatic events associated with armed conflict were identified where intergenerational exchange privileges three elements in a reciprocal relationship: relating (caring for others), collaborating (social skills), and acting (driving chance) in light of the history of a lineage of Colombian women as an emblematic case. The analysis of the female lineage made it possible to identify the events historically anchored in the Colombian sociopolitical dynamics that were most clearly associated with intergenerational trauma and the experience of early adversity events. At the same time, the capacities/skills that emerged, according to the participants, have been indispensable to mitigate and heal such sequels in themselves and the following generations: relating, collaborating, and acting. Models explaining cultural trauma and intergenerational trauma have focused on three factors associated with trauma recovery: individual psychological processes, social interaction processes, and acting on social determinants. Psychotherapeutic approaches have focused on variations in exposure to traumatic events and the recovery of historical memory, as well as identifying the dynamics that select cultural practices of peace and human flourishing in these individuals and communities.

Keywords: intergenerational trauma, cultural trauma, resilience, Inner Development Goals, flourishing cycle, psychology

Introduction

Feelings of bitterness, including a sense of having been deeply wronged, righteous anger, and a desire for justice, even revenge, may be normal and not pathological in individuals and communities traumatized by extreme violence. These experiences are

https://doi.org/10.1515/9783111453729-017

deeply social and relational; they are traumas at the community and individual levels. As such, the harm caused by these experiences requires interventions at the individual and family level and responses at the community and public policy level for healing and recovery.

Is it possible for the transformation of the suffering and harm we feel to have positive consequences on the variations of pain and trauma that our lineage experiences? Can countries, communities, and families that have experienced severe trauma move healthily towards the sustainability of their own families, their descendants, and their community? How is the inner knowledge and journey empowered by cooperation and co-creation? What are the links between the flourishing of an individual and that of a whole community that has experienced deep pain?

Models have been proposed to promote this kind of restoration, ranging from the prosecution of war crimes through the United Nations to truth and reconciliation commissions to restorative justice programs that emphasize the psychosocial accompaniment of local communities. These frameworks have been linked with multilateral commitments and initiatives led by philanthropists and various foundations to understand that inner transformation is a condition for global change, as they increase our collective capacities to face and work effectively with complex challenges and to address them in a combined way with the mindset and behavioral, culture, and systems change required to make sustainable development –Sustainable Development Goals (SDGs)– possible. One such framework is the Inner Development Goals (IDGs) which supports visions such as that of Wamsler et al. (2021) with the inner-outer transformation model to trigger transformation at the individual, collective, and system levels (Ives et al., 2023).

The multiple cases of people and communities traumatized by extreme violence indicate the existence of considerable individual and local resources of resilience and healing, such as generational consciousness, practices of traditional knowers and healers, ceremonial rituals, and everyday acts of humanism, love, respect, and care that include and transcend suffering. The dialogue of knowledge has been the key to inner and outer, individual and collective movement. System-level phenomena are understood as interdependent and co-created.

As an example of this flourishing, I will describe the case of a lineage of Colombian women – Columbia being a country traversed by years and years of internal conflict – and how it can be understood and empowered by framing it within the skills of the IDGs.

Intergenerational trauma in the light of lineage

I met Maríarosa in my work as a psychotherapist; her story reflects the experiences of people from different generations of Colombians seeking help to alleviate their suffering. Maríarosa is a lawyer, a mestizo woman and native of Vaupés, an area of the Colombian Amazon. Vaupés is a department inhabited by more than ten different ethnic groups – Arapaso, Bará, Barasano, Desana, Karapana, Cubeo, Makuna, Mirita-Tapuya, Pira-Tapuya, Siriano, Tariana, Tukano, Tuyuca, Kotiria, Tatuyo, Taiwano, and Yuruti – each with its own worldview and language. These groups have their government according to their uses and customs and also conserve their cultural, social, religious, and economic heritage. In addition, there are the settlers or mestizos, people mainly from rural areas and intermediate cities in the interior of the country who were known as "whites", who settled in the area after importing nonperishable food-stuffs and various inputs from other industrialized areas in Colombia. Although they make up no more than 5% of the departmental population, the mestizos are hegemonic in commercial centers, stores, and other places where the social, political, and public life of the territory takes place. It is an area, moreover, crossed by various armed groups, guerrillas, and drug traffickers operating outside the law, making it a disputed territory with a history of armed confrontation in which the population is immersed – and, of course, suffers the consequences.

Maríarosa seeks accompaniment and psychological support for the consequences for her and her family after horrific experiences caused by drug trafficking, kidnapping, forced disappearance, and death threats that had forced her to move from her native region. Her only daughter, 18-year-old María, was starting her third unsuccessful university studies and described much suffering, significant difficulties of adaptation and emotional regulation, self-injury, and recurrent thoughts of suicide. She had recently had an episode of drug overdose. María was the only female child in a marriage that repeated a pattern of various forms of violence (intrafamilial, gender-based, and associated with psychosocial processes in Colombia).

In Colombia it is considered that hundreds of thousands of people attempt suicide, regardless of geography, culture, ethnicity, religion, or socioeconomic status, among others (Hernández et al, 2023. In the meta-analysis conducted by Xiao et al. (2022), the global prevalence and characteristics of non-suicidal self-injurious behaviors were studied, based on research published between 2010 and 2021 in an adolescent population, identifying prevalence rates of 22%.

María's self-injurious behavior with and without suicidal intent is a growing phenomenon in the population between 15 and 29 years of age, which has a significant impact at the individual, family, and social levels, making it a public health problem (Organización Panamericana de la Salud [PAHO], 2021). The worst outcome is suicide. According to figures from the National Institute of Legal Medicine and Forensic Sciences of Colombia, hundreds of cases occur in children between 5 and 17 years of age (Secretaría Distrital de Salud, 2021, 2022).

When I met them, the husband and father had not been heard from for more than ten years. María was 6 years old the last time she saw him – another victim of forced disappearance in a country where at least 80,000 people have been victims.

The figures expose paramilitary groups (52%), guerrillas (24%), state agents (8%), and multiple perpetrators (9%) as the main perpetrators (Gallego, et al, 2024).

The suffering that this woman transmitted, the narrative about the stories of intense pain that she and her parents and grandparents and her grandparents' parents had lived through because of colonization and the armed conflict in the country was moving. At least four generations had experienced intense adversity firsthand.

María described her mother as a bitter person who tended to remember events in a way that she found to be both painful and gratifying, becoming increasingly ruminant about what happened to them and their family. María also learned to continually revisit their grievances, stoking anger and helplessness. Thoughts and images related to the events that accompanied the violence inside and outside the home, the disappearance of the husband and father, the threats, and the subsequent displacement from the hometown. Feelings of anger and helplessness, a shattered belief about the justice of the world, as well as rage and desire for revenge, could be the mark of the bitterness they both described. The recurring question was "How dare they?". There were three basic fears: fear of annihilation, fear of rejection, and fear of meaninglessness.

When, as a teenager, María's mood began to change from anxious to irritable, and to self-harm, her grandmother suggested they return to the home area and take in the care of family and community. It took time and a suicide attempt before Maríarosa agreed to return. The grandmother gave María and her mother a recipe based on medicinal plants to stabilize the mood and maintain well-being, which she in turn had learned from her mother.

That was when we began to get together twice a week with the other women of the family lineage, and around weaving, singing, and pottery, to talk about pains and sorrows. There came to be four generations of women narrating how inner harmony (individual), communal harmony, and harmony with nature remained basic and interrelated dimensions that had to be recovered if they wanted to move towards recovery/healing.

The act of love and protection of the great-grandmother and grandmother, and the respectful act of María accepting the healing rituals accompanied by conversations between them, her mother, aunts, and cousins strengthened the family and their connection to the missing ancestors and the land. These women come from a cultural context in which strength is offered through generational connections in which love and support flow from earlier generations to later ones, connecting humans to nature and life. However, amid a context that remains at war, where persecution and the risk of losing one's life remain latent, coming together and talking about what happened, about the perpetrators, about dignity and resistance, is difficult, even risky. The rupture of the tradition of meeting and healing, of the symbols and rituals associated with migration to other cities, increased the damage.

Intergenerational transmission of trauma

Various social scientists have described this phenomenon as cultural or psychosocial trauma, as it pertains to a disruption within the social structure that impacts a group that has developed a certain level of unity (Lerner & Yehuda, 2018; Argenti & Schramm, 2009). As such, the impact of community-level trauma, such as war or genocide, is transmitted through community ruptures, identity shifts, and concrete socio-structural changes brought about by the traumatic historical event.

The question of whether and how the experience and consequences of surviving trauma are transmitted from one generation to the next has been the subject of a broad interdisciplinary approach. At the individual and psychological level, clinical and functional reports of the descendants of traumatized individuals emerged after World War II, as clinicians and researchers sought to understand the legacy of the Holocaust among survivors and their children. This led to an expansion of research on the intergenerational transmission of trauma in many communities and populations that have experienced war, genocide, and trauma, such as First Nations/Native American communities, survivors of the Rwandan, Croatian, and Cambodian genocides, war refugees who have been tortured, and combat veterans (Daud, Skoglund, & Rydelius, 2005; Davidson & Mellor, 2001; Dekel & Goldblatt, 2008; Evans-Campbell, 2008; Field, Muong, & Sochanvimean, 2013; for critiques, see Kirmayer, Gone, & Moses, 2014). This literature has sought to understand whether there are intergenerational effects of trauma, the nature of such effects, and the mechanisms of their transmission.

The emblematic case study has been with Holocaust descendants, and clinical reports have revealed that second-generation survivors are more vulnerable to stress and PTSD problems and mood and anxiety disorders compared to Jewish controls (Kellerman, 2001; Yehuda et al., 1998). At the same time, other nonclinical and epidemiological samples have found that offspring do not show higher rates of psychopathology than comparable control subjects (Kellerman, 2001; Levav et al., 2007; van IJzendoorn et al., 2003) and even report higher well-being (Shrira et al., 2011).

At the community level, the transmitted effects may have less to do with the event itself than with the community's resources (cultural, political, spiritual, etc.) to make sense of, respond to, and heal from the trauma. The traumatic event resonates across generations, but not with a singular outcome. Trauma can profoundly affect parenting, especially those involving the loss of family members. Children have described overprotection by parents, but also insensitivity, distance, and neglect. In the case of Maríarosa and María's lineage, maternal role reversal was characterized by mother-figure powerlessness, invalidation and incompetence, use of blame, demands for attention, seeking direction, and the relationship with the daughter as a companion. Parenting styles characterized by role reversal and maternal overprotection mediated the relationship of the mother's traumatic symptoms to depression and anxiety in the adolescent daughter.

Biological transmission of the effects of trauma

Now, it is true that research in animals and other human populations (Palma-Gudiel et al., 2015; Liu et al., 2016; Rodgers et al., 2015) has repeatedly documented the hypo-thalamic-pituitary-adrenal axis dysregulation observed in PTSD. Circadian rhythm, urinary and plasma cortisol levels, glucocorticoid sensitivity, and epigenetic regulation of the glucocorticoid receptor gene have been shown to distinguish offspring with parental PTSD from those without and from controls (Lehrner et al., 2014; Ye-huda et al., 2000; Yehuda et al., 2014; Yehuda & Bierer, 2007; Yehuda, Teicher, et al., 2007). Possible mechanisms for this transmission include in utero programming resulting from exposure to maternal stressors, postnatal adaptation to parental behavior, or direct transmission of a trauma-related epigenetic change from parent to offspring.

However, biology has no positive or negative value; trauma-related biological changes simply reflect the adaptive capacity of our species. Epigenetic adaptations could be the result of postnatal influences from upbringing and family environment, or more directly from parent to offspring. Therefore, the fact that children of traumatized parents may show differences in their stress response systems does not necessarily imply that they are impaired.

In our cases, one-third of the participants reported feeling more resilient to stress than other people their age who were not raised by direct survivors of armed conflict. Many described political activism and community volunteering as improving their lives, which they directly relate to their status as descendants. This is consistent with findings of higher levels of optimism and hope among offspring compared to controls (Shrira et al., 2011) and with research on post-traumatic growth (Lev-Wiesel & Amir, 2003; Prati & Pietrantoni, 2009). Humans are unique in our ability to make sense of things, and knowledge of ourselves and our past can help us make decisions about how to respond to the world around us.

Emphasis on resilience and flourishing vs. psychopathology

Research with survivors of armed conflict and their children identifies several mechanisms that can lead to the transmission of the effects of trauma or resilience. The degree to which the survivor has been able to overcome their traumatic experiences is critical to the functioning of their children. When survivors are unable to process their experiences and manifest psychological and somatic symptoms, communication styles are characterized by fragmentation, indirectness, silence, and keeping secrets. The repercussions for offspring include feelings of guilt, victimization, and identification with the survivor, as well as the development of a frightening view of the world.

Conversely, when survivors recovered and developed personal narratives and stories, cultural rituals, and a defense of universal values emerged, they developed communication styles characterized by openness and love and the use of humor as a symbolic resource of resilience. The evidence is consistent with cases reported in other populations exposed to threats of war, suggesting that the possible outcomes may be fewer, rather than more, mental health problems.

At the heart of psychotherapeutic work are questions about the path to optimize biological and psychological adaptation, resilience, and individual and community flourishing. Framing them within the IDGs is appropriate, as this set of five broad abilities and 23 skills captures the psychological and social processes that are supported by empirical evidence and recognized by diverse populations in more than 15 countries on all continents.[1]

For Maríarosa and her community, coming together and remembering the events and terror experienced also has a resilient value in terms of encouraging the community to maintain vigilance for their safety and survival and to stand in solidarity with other communities facing violence and injustice. However, in María, for whom this grievance was mediated through her parents, the process was slower. She resented her parents: her mother for her overprotective upbringing, for her strange behaviors and for being different from other mothers, for her fragility and neediness; her father who acted in a risky, illegal way and exposed her to violence and abuse to finally leave her abandoned. The anger and helplessness towards her parents was, for her, of course deeply conflicting, generating feelings of shame, guilt, and rage. Resentment would then be directed at herself, fueling feelings of rage and frustration at being unable to save or heal her parents, and at her own social and academic weaknesses and failures. She lingered longer in justice with the women of her lineage and resorted to other strategies to transform the meaning of grievances and flourish as a woman and as an agent of social change. María began studying art, creating designs and writings, visiting places important to her parents seeking information about what had happened, promoting forms of collective bonding, and developing social support networks.

Although my first impression of María, as well as with other recorded cases, was that the descendants of survivors of the armed conflict in Colombia showed signs of psychopathology, quickly, clinical evidence and the results of my line of research have shown that the descendants have demonstrated resilience and success and that in second- and third-generation survivors no higher rates of psychopathology or impairment are identified compared to the offspring of control groups. I have consistently recorded people in conditions of psychosocial vulnerability, adaptability, strength, and flexibility in the face of various stressors.

---

1 For more information on the Inner Development Goals framework, see www.innerdevelopment goals.org/framework.

Perhaps there is a healthy or appropriate degree of bitterness that spurs individuals or communities to action. The commemoration of traumatic events and persecutions is at the core of many Colombian fiestas. No doubt these remembrances are designed to provoke some degree of negative affect, but also to acknowledge that there is life after tragedy, triumph after adversity, and courage in the communal celebration of resistance and survival.

Relating, cooperating, and co-creating – axes of inner transformation and social strengthening

Within the framework of the five IDGs competencies – *being, thinking, relating, collaborating*, and *acting*– and the 23 skills that comprise them, relating, cooperating, and co-creating seem to be the axes of bi-directional transformation between person and community. Now, from a psychological perspective, none of the above three is activated without a transformation in the cognitive and emotional processes of being and thinking. In the first case, cultivating our inner life and developing and deepening our relationship to our thoughts, feelings, and body helps us be present, intentional, and nonreactive when we face complexity and is linked to the awareness of thinking processes as developing our cognitive skills by taking different perspectives, evaluating information, and making sense of the world as an interconnected whole is essential for wise decision making (Ankrah et al., 2023). Appreciating, caring for, and feeling connected to others – characteristics of relating – helps us create more just and sustainable systems and societies for everyone. In the same way, collaborating implies the awareness of actively developing our abilities to include, hold space, and communicate with stakeholders with different values, skills, and competencies. Without the previous four, acting seems impossible.

The useful strategies in the word circles and the knitting and weaving gatherings were shaping the blossoming of María and her family lineage and, to synthesize, I have categorized several aspects common to other cases followed in the research.

I have already mentioned that the original intervention consisted of promoting a meeting between the women of the lineage and others who met once a week to reflect on the events and pains experienced and, from there, could give thanks for the life they had lived and the things for which each one had. Each session resulted in weavings and handicrafts, as well as various recipes based on ancestral traditions, which allowed us to imagine the best possible world. They began to recognize the past and be grateful for what they had lived, to get in touch with the present and the opportunities it offered – to live tasty or savor life – and to imagine the future as women, members of surviving families, resilient and resistant communities, and as managers of social change. Recognizing what is good in the current situation, trying to increase focus and awareness of a present positive experience, and sharing or celebrating something good were the phases before the closing of each meeting.

Thus arose the association Tejido Vital, which produces handicrafts and generates income from their commercialization in various stores inside and outside the municipality. The Women's Advisory Council is part of the local government's advisory bodies on gender issues, political and civil rights, financial autonomy, and social entrepreneurship. Helping can, of course, increase well-being and make one feel more engaged, less anxious, and more connected. Such acts also often encouraged others to do similar acts of caring, and acts of kindness continue to spread in various forms of volunteering.

Volunteering was associated with improvements in various aspects of well-being. In a sense, volunteering and regular participation in various activities and organizations shows a commitment to repeated acts of cooperation directed toward an important goal in the life of the community. These women's organizations have provided a powerful sense of social connection and common purpose.

Those women who participate in this relational, cooperative, and co-creative initiative can approach life events or problems with higher levels of gratitude, as well as better feelings about life as a whole, fewer complaints of physical symptoms, and more satisfying family and community relationships. After three years, they report higher levels of well-being and lower levels of depressive symptoms.

Collective movements are therapeutic and powerfully transformative at the territorial level. An example is the village of El Congal in the municipality of Tamaná, a population center that has more than 20 families displaced and dispossessed of their lands amidst threats and massacres. At the closing of this writing, seven families have achieved the recognition and restitution of their lands. This generates a lot of satisfaction. Among these benefited families, some people had not returned to the territory for more than 21 years and are now returning and receiving symbolically and legally the return of their territories and the recognition of their ancestors and lineages. These families, and their descendants, are making productive projects a reality through cooperation and relationships.

In summary, it makes sense to close with the words of Maríarosa: *"Living well and flourishing are the best revenge"*, because it summarizes a central axis of resilience and common humanity to which the IDGs framework aims: the transformation of cultural practices always crosses the path of inner transformation, and we can move towards it decisively if we do it collectively.

References

Argenti, N. & Schramm, K. (2009). *Remembering violence: Anthropological perspectives on intergenerational transmission*. Berghahn Books.

Ankrah, D., Bristow, J., Hires, D. & Artem Henriksson, J. (2023). Inner Development Goals: From inner growth to outer change. *Field Actions Science Reports. The journal of field actions, 25*, 82–87. https://journals.openedition.org/factsreports/7326.

Davidson, A. C. & Mellor, D. J. (2001). The adjustment of children of Australian Vietnam veterans: Is there evidence for the transgenerational transmission of the effects of war-related trauma? *The Australian and New Zealand Journal of Psychiatry, 35*(3), 345–351. https://doi.org/10.1046/j.1440-1614.2001.00897.x.

Daud, A., Skoglund, E., & Rydelius, P. (2005). Children in families of torture victims: Transgenerational transmission of parents' traumatic experiences to their children. *International Journal of Social Welfare, 14*, 23–32. https://doi.org/10.1111/j.1468-2397.2005.00336.x.

Dekel, R. & Goldblatt, H. (2008). Is there intergenerational transmission of trauma? The case of combat veterans' children. *American Journal of Orthopsychiatry, 78*, 281–289. https://doi.org/10.1037/a0013955.

Evans-Campbell, T. (2008). Historical trauma in American Indian/Native Alaska communities: A multilevel framework for exploring impacts on individuals, families, and communities. *Journal of Interpersonal Violence, 23*(3), 316–338. https://doi.org/10.1177/088626050731229.

Eyerman, R. (2001). *Cultural trauma: Slavery and the formation of African American identity*. Cambridge University Press.

Field, N. P., Muong, S., & Sochanvimean, V. (2013). Parental styles in the intergenerational transmission of trauma stemming from the Khmer Rouge regime in Cambodia. *American Journal of Orthopsychiatry, 83*(4), 483–494. https://doi.org/10.1111/ajop.12057.

Hernández, F., Bastidas, M., & Gómez, F. (2023). Resilience, adverse childhood experiences, and mental health in Health Science students during the COVID-19 pandemic. Salud mental, 46(2), 111–119. https://doi.org/10.17711/SM.0185-3325.2023.015.

Kellerman, N. P. (2001). Psychopathology in children of Holocaust survivors: A review of the research literature. Israel Journal of Psychiatry and Related Sciences, 38(1), 36–46.

Gallego, M. L., Gil Osorio, J. F., Posada Herrera, C. J., & García Cuartas, M. Y. (2024). Revisión sistemática de la desaparición forzada en el contexto internacional y Colombia. *Revista Logos Ciencia & Tecnología, 16*(1), 178–192. https://doi.org/10.22335/rlct.v16i1.1864.

Ives, C.D., Schäpke, N., Woiwode, C., & Wamsler, C. (2023). IMAGINE sustainability: Integrated inner-outer transformation in research, education and practice. *Sustainability Science, 18*, 2777–2786. https://doi.org/10.1007/s11625-023-01368-3.

Lehrner, A., Bierer, L. M., Passarelli, V., Pratchett, L. C., Flory, J. D., Bader, H. N., Harris, I. R., Bedi, A., Daskalakis, N. P., Makotkine, I., & Yehuda, R (2014). Maternal PTSD associated with greater glucocorticoid sensitivity in offspring of Holocaust survivors. *Psychoneuroendocrinology, 40*, 213–220. https://doi.org/10.1016/j.psyneuen.2013.11.019.

Lehrner, A., & Yehuda, R. (2018). Trauma across generations and paths to adaptation and resilience. Psychological trauma: theory, research, practice, and policy, 10(1), 22.

Levav, I., Levinson, D., Radomislensky, I., Shemesh, A. A., & Kohn, R. (2007). Psychopathology and other health dimensions among the offspring of Holocaust survivors: Results from the Israel National Health Survey. *Israel Journal of Psychiatry and Related Sciences, 44*, 144–151.

Lev-Wiesel, R. & Amir, M. (2003). Posttraumatic growth among Holocaust child survivors. *Journal of Loss and Trauma, 8*, 229–237. https://doi.org/10.1080/15325020305884.

Kirmayer, L. J., Gone, J. P., & Moses, J., (2014). Rethinking historical trauma. *Transcultural Psychiatry*, *51*(3), 299–319. https://doi.org/10.1177/1363461514536358.

Liu, K., Ruggero, C. J., Goldstein, B., Klein, D. N., Perlman, G., Broderick, J., & Kotov, R. (2016). Elevated cortisol in healthy female adolescent offspring of mothers with posttraumatic stress disorder. *Journal of Anxiety Disorders*, *40*, 37–43. https://doi.org/10.1016/j.janxdis.2016.04.003.

Organización Panamericana de la Salud [OPS]. (2021). *Vivir la vida. Guía de aplicación para la prevención del suicidio en los países*. https://doi.org/10.37774/9789275324240.

Palma-Gudiel H., Córdova-Palomera, A., Eixarch, E., Deuschle, M., & Fañanás, L. (2015). Maternal psychosocial stress during pregnancy alters the epigenetic signature of the glucocorticoid receptor gene promoter in their offspring: a meta-analysis. *Epigenetics*, *10*(10):893–902. https://doi.org/10.1080/15592294.2015.1088630.

Prati, G. & Pietrantoni, L. (2009). Optimism, social support, and coping strategies as factors contributing to posttraumatic growth: A meta-analysis. *Journal of Loss and Trauma*, *14*, 364–388. http://dx.doi.org/10.1080/15325020902724271.

Rodgers, A. B., Morgan, C. P., Leu, N. A., & Bale, T. L. (2015). Transgenerational epigenetic programming via sperm microRNA recapitulates effects of paternal stress. *Proceedings of the National Academy of Sciences of the United States of America*, *112*, 13699–13704. http://dx.doi.org/10.1073/pnas.1508347112.

Secretaría Distrital de Salud. (2021). *Intento de suicidio en menores de 18 años en Bogotá D.C.* https://saludata.saludcapital.gov.co/osb/indicadores/conducta-suicida/.

Secretaría Distrital de Salud. (2022). *Suicidios consumados por grupo de edad y sexo*. https://saludata.salud capital.gov.co/osb/indicadores/conducta-suicida/.

Shrira, A., Palgi, Y., Ben-Ezra, M., Shmotkin, D., (2011). Transgenerational effects of trauma in midlife: evidence for resilience and vulnerability in offspring of Holocaust survivors. *Psychological Trauma: Theory, Research, Practice, and Policy*, *3*(4), 394–402. https://doi.org/10.1037/a0020608.

Wamsler, C., Osberg, G., Osika, W., Herndersson, H., & Mundaca, L. (2021). Linking internal and external transformation for sustainability and climate action: Towards a new research and policy agenda. *Global Environmental Change*, *71*,102373. https://doi.org/10.1016/j.gloenvcha.2021.102373.

Xiao, Q., Song, X., Huang, L., Hou, D., & Huang, X. (2022). Global prevalence and characteristics of non-suicidal self-injury between 2010 and 2021 among a non-clinical sample of adolescents: A meta-analysis. *Frontiers in Psychiatry*, *13*, 912441. https://doi.org/10.3389/fpsyt.2022.912441.

van IJzendoorn, M. H., Bakermans-Kranenburg, M. J., & Sagi-Schwartz, A. (2003). Are children of Holocaust survivors less well-adapted? A meta-analytic investigation of secondary traumatization. Journal of Traumatic Stress, 16, 459–469. http://dx.doi.org/10.1023/A:1025 706427300.

Yehuda, R., Bierer, L. M., Schmeidler, J., Aferiat, D. H., Breslau, I., & Dolan, S. (2000). Low cortisol and risk for PTSD in adult offspring of holocaust survivors. *American Journal of Psychiatry*, *157*(8), 1252–1259. http://dx.doi.org/10.1176/appi.ajp.157.8.1252.

Yehuda, R., Daskalakis, N. P., Lehrner, A., Desarnaud, F., Bader, H. N., Makotkine, I., Flory, J. D., Bierer, L. M., & Meaney, M. J. (2014). Influences of Maternal and Paternal PTSD on Epigenetic Regulation of the Glucocorticoid Receptor Gene in Holocaust Survivor Offspring. American Journal of Psychiatry, 171(8), 872–880. https://doi.org/10.1176/appi.ajp.2014.13121571.

Yehuda, R., Schmeidler, J., Wainberg, M., Binder-Brynes, K., & Duvdevani, T. (1998). Vulnerability to posttraumatic stress disorder in adult offspring of Holocaust survivors. *American Journal of Psychiatry*, *155*(9), 1163–1171. https://doi.org/10.1176/ajp.155.9.1163.

Yehuda R, Teicher MH, Seckl JR, Grossman RA, Morris A, Bierer LM. Parental Posttraumatic Stress Disorder as a Vulnerability Factor for Low Cortisol Trait in Offspring of Holocaust Survivors. *Arch Gen Psychiatry*.2007;64(9):1040–1048. doi:10.1001/archpsyc.64.9.1040.

Yehuda, R., & Bierer, L. M. (2007). Transgenerational transmission of cortisol and PTSD risk. Stress Hormones and Post Traumatic Stress Disorder Basic Studies and Clinical Perspectives, 121–135. https://doi.org/10.1016/s0079-6123(07)67009-5.

Yehuda, R., & Lehrner, A. (2018). Intergenerational transmission of trauma effects: putative role of epigenetic mechanisms. *World Psychiatry : Official Journal of the World Psychiatric Association (WPA)*, 17(3), 243–257. https://doi.org/10.1002/wps.20568.

Manuela Pagani Larghi and Paolo Fedi

Chapter 17
Future Dialogues: Co-creating common good and becoming a community through the IDGs

Abstract: This chapter explores a social improvement project in Novazzano, Switzerland, between June 2022 and May 2024, as a part of a national project called Future Dialogues. The purpose was to implement a social improvement through a dialogue process with the population – local stakeholders including municipal administrators.

We first guide a group of local stakeholders on a journey of self-discovery, discovery of the Novazzano "system", and co-creation of *conscious individual and collective actions and initiatives* for the *common good and the best future* that wants to emerge.

Secondly, we *transferred* to a working group *methodological principles, instruments, and skills* as anchor points of community development and innovation projects.

Thirdly, we invited these "guardians of the principles and method" to *act over time as custodians* of the validation, implementation, and evaluation of current and future initiatives, acting as catalysts between the needs of citizens and the municipality through the creation of a civic association.

The project, co-designed and co-facilitated with Theory U,[1] took shape in two distinct phases over two years, involving more than 60 citizen participants, reimagining and reshaping a new future, developing inner skills (*Inner Development Goals framework*[2]) and more conscious and systemic actions (*Theory U)* guided by some basic principles and a new awareness of our interdependency. It was truly a journey of learning and growth for everyone.

Keywords: immunity to change, collective intelligence, Theory U, iceberg model, citizens' awareness

---

1 For more information, see https://www.u-school.org/ (accessed Mar. 28, 2024).
2 For more information, see https://www.innerdevelopmentgoals.org/ (accessed Mar. 28, 2024).

https://doi.org/10.1515/9783111453729-018

The project

The context and the common intent

Novazzano is a small commune of approximately 2,400 inhabitants, located in the south of Switzerland (approximately 9 million inhabitants) and borders Italy to the south. Switzerland is a confederation of states, groups 26 cantons, and is known because, although small, it groups four different languages and cultures that coexist peacefully. Switzerland is considered "neutral" and is one of the richest countries in the world.

Nevertheless, over the past two decades, the canton Ticino where Novazzano is located, has undergone profound changes, particularly related to Italy's entry into the EU in 2003, resulting in Italy's relinquishment of monetary policy sovereignty, and the abandonment of banking secrecy in Switzerland.

Border business activities, based on the sale of fuel, chocolate, and cigarettes, have shrunk enormously, while banking and financial activities have undergone a technological transformation that has caused the loss of a high percentage of jobs, particularly in border areas. All these transformations have been "silent". The gradual aging of the population and low birth rate have accentuated immigration. The border location feeds a steadily increasing flow of border labor, with consequences for traffic, the labor market, and the types of businesses setting up in the area.

Historically and culturally, geographically shrouded by the Alps and mountain ranges, the canton of Ticino tends to be closed in on itself, disinclined to change. The population, particularly the entrenched population, has a strong tendency toward immunity to change, perceiving the other and the new as threats to an already changing reality. As a linguistic minority, with a strong dependence on Italy for labor and one of the most disadvantaged cantonal financial situations, Ticino is perceived by both Ticinesi and other Swiss as the "unlucky" canton, except for the weather (compared to the rest of Switzerland, it is warmer and sunnier, being south of the Alps). There is often an unconscious attitude to complaining, and there is a preference for the status quo over the risk that a change may bring. There is a perceived strong tendency to cling to privileges that, looking at them more objectively, are slowly weakening.

To date, in the municipality of Novazzano, there are three bars and a football pitch as meeting places. There are no grocery shops, no shops selling clothes or other goods, only services.

There are many small and medium-sized enterprises active in the municipality, mostly involving labor from the border; this makes frontier workers have little or no presence in the social life of the city, so much so that we were unable to involve them in the project.

On the contrary, there are many associations in the municipality that are highly active in the social sphere, mostly offering moments of conviviality (village festivals, bingo, carnival, Christmas markets, sports activities, etc.).

The project arrived in Novazzano shortly after the COVID-19 period and after a rupture within the town related to an initiative promoted by the city hall, linked to the construction of apartment buildings for self-sufficient elderly people. The rupture was related to financial and environmental/ecological reasons.

Against a backdrop then of "forced" change, blockage and caesura made its appearance the Future Dialogues project, with the stated intent of *co-creating common good and becoming community.* What a challenge, what a journey!

SELF-REFLECTION
What are the obstacles and potentials of where you live to adopt a project to co-create common good and become a community?
Who are the key stakeholders?
Could they be involved? How?

The authors involved almost all the stakeholders of the city to create a community and to be able to see the system through the eyes, thoughts, and expectations of all its actors. They collaborated with political authorities and the citizenry to overcome the dichotomy between top-down and bottom-up approaches, integrating them into a transformative journey toward a paradigm: from "ego- to ecosystem". The goal was to become aware of the deep roots of the ecological, social, and spiritual crises we have caused and continue to perpetuate, to develop a systematic and conscious vision to transform ourselves and our organizations, creating collective actions and solutions based on a new awareness: awareness-based collective action (ABC; Scharmer 2018).

A key "success" factor that allowed the project to get off the ground was the previous participation of the mayor of Novazzano in one of the Theory U u-lab 1x workshops the authors organized during the pandemic. This – ex post – created fertile ground to informally present the Future Dialogues project to the mayor in May 2022, sparking curiosity and interest within the entire city hall, which then formally accepted it unanimously, despite some skeptical voices in the background (the same of the rupture mentioned above in the context).

During the project's journey, the authors had to confront *"immunity to change"* attitudes and mindsets from citizens (thoughts like: "We've seen these things before, they don't work", "They don't serve any purpose", "We're fine as we are", "There's nothing to change", "There's no alternative", "I don't have time", "My contribution doesn't change things", etc.), a local cultural element that can hinder the transformation process and that instills fear in anyone who sets out to promote change. It is as if they live in a kind of "counter U", characterized by the closure of mind, heart, and will, which prevents from embracing the emerging future based on fear.

SELF-REFLECTION
What would be the common intent to enable the city-system in which you live to address global challenges (eco, social, and spiritual)?

The "heart" of the project

The project was born involving Manuela as a representative of the canton Ticino thanks to the invitation of Collaboratio Helvetica and Daniel Gut. Its path has been troubled, and it was not until March 2021 that we were able to restart the initiative with a new working group of four people, of which Manuela represents the canton Ticino.

The focus is on Future Dialogues, with the intention of spreading them to other Swiss communities to collectively address the challenges that have emerged from the COVID-19 crisis and to inspire political and civic action. The authors want to overcome the collective torpor and sense of helplessness by consciously processing the trauma caused by the polycrisis we still experience, actively involving citizens in creating regenerative solutions for the future.

Manuela chose to *collaborate* with Paolo Fedi, practitioner and Theory U expert, to use this methodology to facilitate the project and the citizens' collaboration, turning our private approach into a public action.

The choice to realize the project in Novazzano was based on two elements the authors thought could "make it easier!": the mayor's knowledge of the methodology, and the fact that Manuela is a resident of Novazzano and knows its history and part of the population. These two factors facilitated the mobilization of local stakeholders, but at the same time it also required a lot of inner work on Manuela's part to overcome local cultural resistance to change.

As for the financial aspects, setting a budget was difficult. On the one hand, the authors had to remain open to the emerging future without being rigid in the plans, considering the Theory U methodology they were adopting. On the other hand, they had to come to terms with the need to make an "acceptable" proposal while knowing that considerable effort would be required to manage relationships within and outside the group, especially for Manuela living in the municipality.

The project could be realized thanks to the financial support of two foundations (3FO and UNESCO), the municipality, to the partly paid and partly donated work of the authors, and more than 1,300 voluntary citizens' hours.

Despite the *financial challenges*, it was always clear that the real value of the trip offered by Future Dialogues lay in the opportunity to use Theory U in a complex participatory project, which more than repaid the time and resources invested even at no cost.

The initial project's design, as presented to city hall, provided for a single phase. As you will see below (Figure 17.1), the use of Theory U allowed to remain open to what emerged as the project progressed. After the celebration of the completion of the first phase, which provided for the sharing with the citizens of the 14 initiatives with the greatest impact on the common good, the city hall requested that a second phase be launched to investigate and carry out the five initiatives considered a priority by the population.

The entire project was therefore implemented in *two phases*.

Co-creating the transition process in municipalities

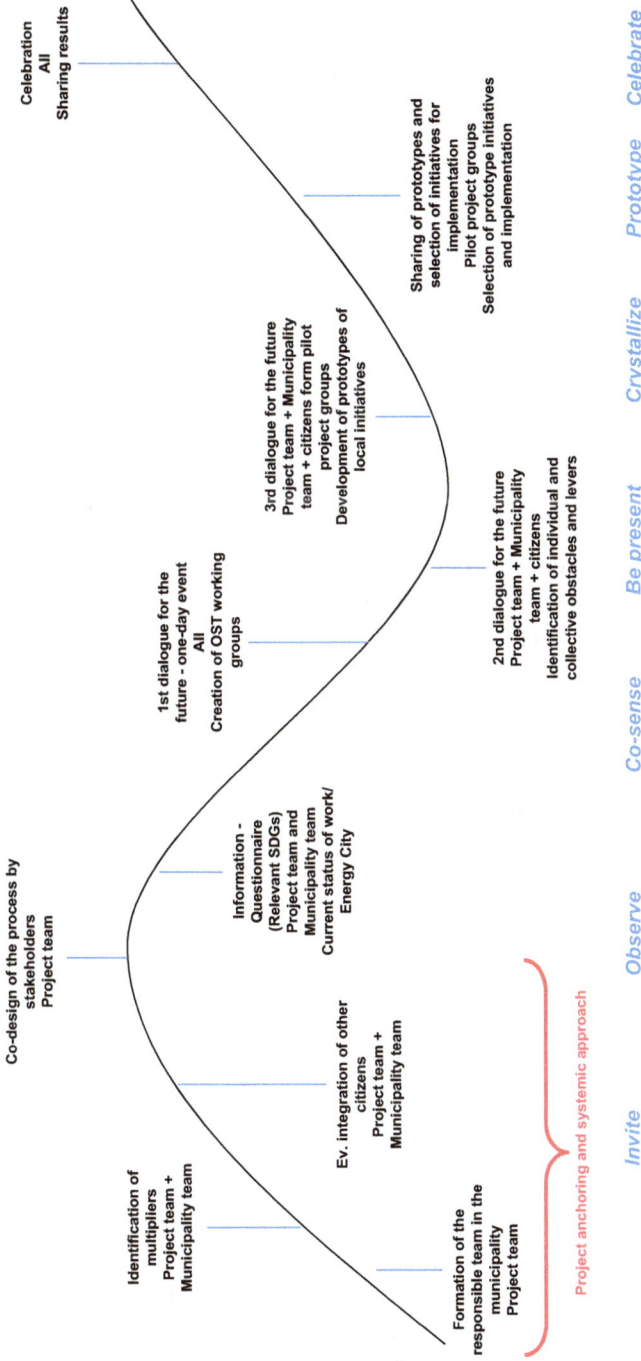

Identification of multipliers
Project team + Municipality team

Co-design of the process by stakeholders
Project team

Information - Questionnaire (Relevant SDGs)
Project team and Municipality team
Current status of work/ Energy City

1st dialogue for the future - one-day event
All
Creation of OST working groups

3rd dialogue for the future
Project team + Municipality team + citizens form pilot project groups
Development of prototypes of local initiatives

Celebration
All
Sharing results

Sharing of prototypes and selection of initiatives for implementation
Pilot project groups
Selection of prototype initiatives and implementation

2nd dialogue for the future
Project team + Municipality team + citizens
Identification of individual and collective obstacles and levers

Ev. integration of other citizens
Project team + Municipality team

Formation of the responsible team in the municipality
Project team

Project anchoring and systemic approach

Invite *Observe* *Co-sense* *Be present* *Crystallize* *Prototype* *Celebrate*

Figure 17.1: The initial project's design as defined by the authors.
Source: Novazzano Future Dialogues

Phase 1

During the initial phase that began in May 2022, the first goal was to *heal a still open conflict and wound* by building and facilitating an empathetic and generative dialogue among various local stakeholders.

To conduct the project, the authors had a clear idea to create two teams: a "core" team of more cohesive and committed people and an "extended" team of people who could collaborate on the multiple activities planned in the project.

Establishment of the core team

For methodological reasons, it was decided that the core team would consist of three to a maximum of eight people, representing the most relevant stakeholders, when possible, while the extended team would be the expression of the voices of all citizens.

The role of the core team was to be a guarantor for the citizens, collaborate with the facilitators, and offer insight of:
- the most important and pressing issues;
- current internal and external challenges and opportunities;
- the actual resources available;
- inform, motivate, and involve as many citizens as possible.

It was attended by eight representatives of:
- public institutions through one representative per party;
- schools;
- the business world;
- the world of associational life;
- a voice from outside the field of representatives of the "Referendum Committee", welcomed to regenerate a climate of welcoming and trust among the people of Novazzano.

Establishment of the extended team

Creating an extended team was one of the main challenges. To change the system, the authors had to allow the system to see and sense itself. Although it would not be possible *to involve enterprises*, this absence provided valuable information about the system itself. With the help of trusted people and perseverance, an extended team of about 17 people was formed – a great achievement for a small municipality.

Vision setting (best possible future) for each root of the common good

To get an overall picture of the "Novazzano system", the entire population was involved through a questionnaire. The survey addressed four macro areas (economy, climate change, security, and justice) and culture by delving into certain areas and their possible trends for each, gathering comments on the potential personal and collective needs that might have arisen. At the end of the answers collection, the authors realized from the feedback gathered that it was too challenging. From the responses and the work of the extended team, *six priority areas emerged for Novazzano: the quality of relationships and awareness, education and culture, nature, sustainability, initiatives and meeting spaces, and the territory.*

Thanks to one participant's drawing, the following image of the tree of the common good (with its roots, see Figure 17.2) accompanied us through the journey.

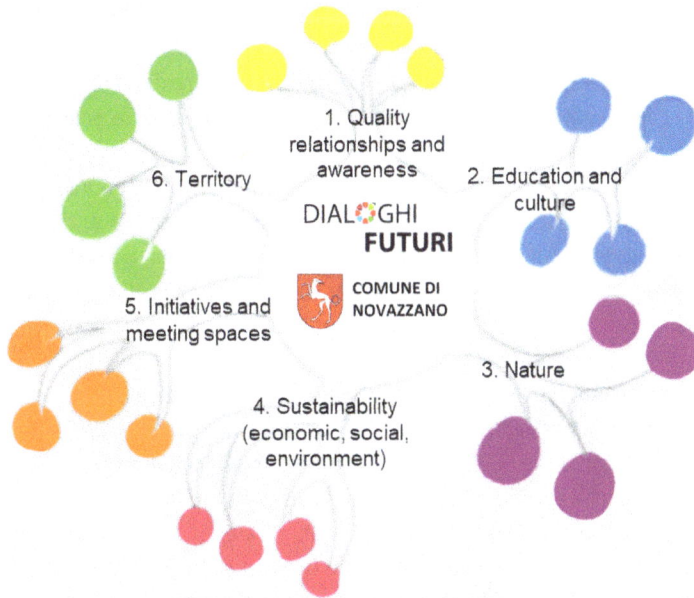

Figure 17.2: Roots of the common good as designed by the working team.
Source: Novazzano Future Dialogues

So, there were six roots to work on, but what fruits would want to grow from cultivating those six "plants"?

The extended team worked on two fronts:
- *developing inner skills* and a systemic approach to promote *"expanded collective intelligence"*[3];
- *co-creating initiatives* that can realize a better future for each root of the common good.

At the end of November 2022, it was decided the time was right to share the results of the work done with citizens and collect their feedback and contributions to continue on.

First Future Dialogue: Resounding event of November 26, 2022

The design of the day also followed a U-shaped path, integrating the Inner Development Goals (IDGs) framework, with a collective collection of the expectations of a better Novazzano (through drawings), the development of a collective awareness on the roots of the common good on the initiatives necessary for the creation of a better future and to the internal abilities (superpowers) necessary for the realization of that expected future, and finally gathering the availability to collaborate on the project in its subsequent activities.

On November 26, 2022, the "stunning event" was organized by the elementary school in Novazzano, inviting the entire population to participate in a full day of workshops. To embody the theme of "community", citizens were engaged in a comprehensive *art experiment,* exploring through drawing (see Figure 17.3) "the meaning of life" in the municipality of Novazzano. It was a deeply inspiring moment, and the drawings collected were shared with the international community of *Viva la Vida,*[4] making the project feel part of an even greater sense of community purpose.

From the drawings, *paradoxes emerged* that highlighted how reality can be interpreted in different ways, depending on the observer and their subjective experiences.

Participants in the extended team had the opportunity to evaluate themselves with more than 80 participants and apply the leadership skills they had acquired, while the authors worked to bring out and solidify the link between the development of the inner skills and the ability to empathetically lead people through a participatory process.

---

3 By "expanded collective intelligence" we mean the contributions of a collective of people who not only share and co-generate ideas by engaging the mind, but at the same time bring to bear the ability to see the system in its entirety, their feelings, compassion, suspension of judgment, curiosity, their senses, and their courage, i.e., their willingness to enact change.
4 Viva la vida is a worldwide collective project that asks people to express through a drawing the sens of life in their community. Drawings collection from Novazzano Future Dialog event VIVA×ZU-KUNFTS (vivalavida.today) (accessed Mar. 28, 2024).

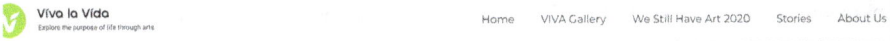

VIVA × NOVAZZANO

(PROGETTO DIALOGHI FUTURI)

Figure 17.3: Some drawings of Viva la Vida.
Source: Novazzano Future Dialogues

Major challenges

Facing *pressing demands for pragmatism and tangible results* from some members of the group, the main challenge was to make them understand the overriding importance of embarking on an inner journey, both individually and collectively. This journey would enable everyone to serve the community not only with the mind but also with the heart, opening to letting go of personal judgments, attachments, and preconceptions, learning to relate empathetically even to those with differing opinions, and accepting to embrace the unknown and relinquish control.

Paolo clearly expressed that we have become too often accustomed to "going from one side of the U to the other" instead of immersing ourselves in reflection and awareness. More time would need to be spent on bringing out the value of the outcomes achieved through the U path and placing a magnifying glass on the different personal and collective impacts of both approaches (linear and U-shaped).

After the event, the inclusion of new people in the group added additional challenges, especially when a person involved in the community division caused by the referendum joined. Despite criticism of this person, the authors chose not to exclude him from the group, welcoming all voices and establishing rules of behavior and empathetic listening. This decision led to some participants leaving the group.

There was a critical moment in which the facilitators intervened to quell a verbal conflict in the group which was breaking the principles of Theory U and absorbing energy and time while not being constructive. The debate was heated on positions of harsh comparison between one person and the rest of the group. It just seemed like the discussion could not be stopped. What allowed to return to a calmer session and an observation of quarrelsome and dysfunctional behaviors was the request for a minute of silence, during which the team could observe what was happening in the field and understand how each role could improve the situation and by avoiding conflict and facilitating a collective perception of the topic under discussion.

SELF-REFLECTION
Have you ever been in such a situation, either as a facilitator or as a participant? How was the conflict resolved?
What thoughts and emotions do you experience in bringing that memory back to mind?

Second Future Dialogue: Celebratory event of March 31, 2023

From December 2022 to March 2023, the team worked to refine the visions and initiatives that emerged during the first event, with the goal of meeting again with citizens and the municipality in a second Future Dialogues event, sharing the results and the choices on the initiatives with the greatest impact for the population.

During the U-shaped second Future Dialogue, with the participation of about 80 people, 14 co-created initiatives were presented, and citizens participated in the selection of initiatives deemed most valuable.

The final verdict, which surprised the authors, included the following chosen initiatives:

1. **Casa Nova**: Create a space to sell local products, involving producers from the municipality (40 points).
2. **Qua la zampa Novazzano**: Create a dog park (31 points).
3. **Repaired swap**: Create a place and activities to repair objects and give them a second life, educate on circular economy (31 points).
4. **Monthly conscious market**: Create community, offer visibility to village associations, reflect together with workshop proposals, local food, etc. (30 points).

5. **NOVA Welcomes**: Improving the municipality's website to make it easier to welcome those arriving from outside and to make information clearer and more efficient (23 points).

All the initiatives presented aim *to promote the common good and become community,* as well as *foster systemic awareness.* The authors accepted with openness and surprise the choices made, trying to abstract from "personal judgment", accepting that these decisions reflected the free expressions of the community.

The unexpected birth of phase two of the Future Dialogues project

As the subgroups proceeded working partially asynchronously, it became clear the need of making full sense of the collective work done. It was clear that ending the project with only the identification of prioritized initiatives would probably not translate into concrete actions, as *city hall did not have the human resources to conduct the remaining work.*

Therefore, Phase 2 was proposed to implement the initiatives with greater impact, considering the available budget. Among the goals there was the formation of a "reference group" of citizen volunteers to guard and pass on civic leadership skills, serving as a liaison between the city council and the people.

City hall welcomed the proposal.

Having to plan Phase 2, the lack of funds from UNESCO and the limitation of the funds available from the municipality, the authors nevertheless decided to present a continuation proposal being fully aware of having to commit a large part of our time as civic volunteers to be able to complete the project as expected.

Phase 2

Phase 2 of the project began and went through some aftershocks along the way. After expanding the group by bringing in new stakeholders, including the detachment of the municipalities to avoid influences on operational aspects (at least officially), some people left the group because they did not find the level of working concreteness they expected.

Despite moments of fatigue and exhaustion, especially during the project validation phase, the group recognized the importance and value of their work.

The value of validating the initiatives, through site visits and interviews, became apparent. In fact, there was a realization that some ideas created by the working groups were not shared by the population and that others, if modified, would have attracted more interest from users. The ability of the working groups to adapt the design due to the added information acquired demonstrated the value of the methodology followed in developing personal and collective capacity for leadership for change.

In November 2023, the group presented the results to the city hall, surprising them with the quality, depth of the analyses and evaluations carried out with so much commitment and dedication, prompting a moment of revelation for all.

Project summary

The highlights of the two phases are summarized in the Table 17.1:

Table 17.1: Future Dialogue project summary.

Project summary		
Characteristics	**Phase 1**	**Phase 2**
Conception period	March – April 2022	March – April 2023
Implementation period	May 2022 – March 2023	April 2023 – May 2024
Objectives	– Involve citizens/stakeholders in the working group – Transfer Theory U principles and tools – Transfer IDG framework and identify primary capabilities for the project – Identify common good tree roots for Novazzano – Identify possible initiatives to carry out for the common good – Verify with population and municipality interest on initiatives	– Working group for Phase 2 – Selected initiatives validation – Selected initiatives design and feasibility – Initiatives deployment plan – Initiatives municipality "Go to realize" – "Saturday Market in the town square" deployment – Supernova Civic Association founded – Workgroup mindset change and capabilities developed
Activities	– 10 months of work – > 15 working meetings of Future Dialogues in the community – 3 public events for sharing the project plan and results with the citizens – Overall activity of more than 1,300 hours	– 10 months of work – 16 working meetings – Several public moments during which we carried out validation activities, interviews and learning journeys – 1 press conference and 5 written articles published – 1 public event celebrating the end of the project, the birth of Supernova Civic Association and the first "Saturday Market in the town square" – Overall activity of more than 1,200 hours

Table 17.1 (continued)

Project summary		
Characteristics	**Phase 1**	**Phase 2**
Tools	Theory U principles, process, techniques, IDG framework	Theory U principles, process, techniques, IDG framework
Outputs	– > 30 citizens involved in working group (8 in the core team, 23 in the extended team, representing political authorities, stakeholders, and the citizenry) – > 80 citizens attending first Future Dialogue public event – 6 Novazzano common good tree roots (CGTRs) – Visions and initiatives for each one of 6 CGTRs – Population validation for six roots vision and prioritization of 20 initiatives – 22 volunteers for the second phase – Municipality acceptance of 5 main initiatives follow-up and deeper analysis – Future Dialogues project mention in Presencing Institute annual report – 1 interview published on Presencing Institute blog – 8 articles in local newspapers	– > 20 citizens involved in working group (12 co-founder of Supernova Civic Association) – > 60 citizens attending second Future Dialogues public event – > 200 citizens and >30 merchants and exhibitors attending the first "Saturday Market" – > 20 children participating in the bartering initiative – Theory U & IDG principles and contents people skilled – 5 initiatives designed and validated – 1 Initiative fully deployed (Saturday Market) – 1 initiative almost deployed (Novazzano city website welcome info) – 1 initiative defined to be deployed within the year (Novazzano dog park) – 1 press conference – 1 video news published on Ticino TV – 5 articles published in local newspapers – Supernova Civic Association which will: 　– serve as the guardian of the principles and methodology of Theory U 　– serve as a catalyst for present and future city initiatives 　– be responsible for the implementation of the initiatives in collaboration with the municipality and associations in the area and new volunteers

Table 17.1 (continued)

Project summary		
Characteristics	**Phase 1**	**Phase 2**

Qualitative results	– Acquisition of new skills:
	  – systemic vision
	  – "in-depth" vision (iceberg model)
	  – recognizing the quality of one's own listening
	  – greater awareness of oneself in relation to others and the local and global system (interdependence)
	  – development of empathic skills, greater sense of responsibility, and ability to influence the future.
	– Personal and collective transformations:
	  – more empathetic behaviors
	  – change in level of listening/conversation and more generative relationships
	  – more open-minded in accepting different points of view, particularly on political issues
	  – more collaborative attitudes and greater sense of belonging and social responsibility
	  – new awareness about superpowers (IDGs) as inner qualities to be cultivated to realize true change
		– Sharing of the principles and experience of protected space, deep listening, "feeling and seeing the social field" through the body and learning journeys with open mind, heart, and will
		– Experiencing the systemic approach, co-creation, presencing, and absencing together
		– Stimulating awareness about superpowers (IDGs) as inner qualities to be cultivated to realize true change
		– Strengthening the feeling of belonging and community and inaugurated new collaborations among existing and operating city associations in the municipality, also involving new citizens as volunteers
		– Embodiment of the emerging future through the unforeseen Phase 2 and the birth of the Supernova Civic Association

Impacts	– Increased sense of belonging – Development of aggregation initiatives – Creation of meeting spaces and attendance at them – Creation of a "steward" association that nurtures values and method, serves as a catalyst for present and future town initiatives, is open to welcoming new volunteers, and promotes effective and generative collaboration among town associations	

In summary, the project generated, in addition to the personal growth of the participants who acquired both technical leadership skills for change projects and developed some of their internal skills, tangible results: *five social innovation initiatives* and a *new city association* (Supernova Civic Association) responsible both for their implementation and management and for ensuring the application of Theory U principles and the development of IDGs for the common good in the collection and implementation of future projects.

The quantum measurement of project impact

The idea of exploring the impact of the Future Dialogues project through a "quantum measurement" of inner change came about during meetings of the IDGs Global Practicioners' Network Core Team of which Manuela is a member. During a morning session, Mark Vandeneijnde, co-founder of Being at Full Potential, shared reflections on the appropriateness of measuring IDGs.

In a world based on the *Newtonian* model, we try to predict the future and maintain control over events. However, in the *quantum* model, we open ourselves to the idea *of unpredictability and relinquish control.* This perspective prompted to consider the quantum approach as a more suitable way to understand and evaluate the inner changes of both the facilitators and the group and community system involved in the Future Dialogues project.

> *The early explorers of the quantum realm discovered that each time they asked a question of this new realm, the answer came as a paradox, and the more they strove for clarity, the stronger the paradoxes became. They finally had to accept that paradox is a part of the intrinsic nature of quantum physics.* (Seale, 2010, p. 6)

In this paper, the authors have chosen to explore the inner change generated by the Future Dialogues project, rather than adopting traditional tools to measure impact in numerical terms. They wanted to go beyond conventional measurement and grasp the potential generated through awareness of the change experienced, reflecting on the project's milestones and observing the changes in ourselves, participants, and the community.

The approach is based on ex-post self-observation, allowing to become aware of change as we embody it. Preferring this method to the Newtonian measurement process that reduces complex reality into numbers allowed to observe change from the internal perspective of the system.

SELF-REFLECTION
How often do you use introspective retrospective work to assess and crystallize the value of a path, journey, or experience you have made? What are the key questions you ask yourself? What are the answers to be able to say "I have changed; I am not what I was before. I feel better"?

The project tools: The U journey and the IDG framework

The project represented a wonderful opportunity to involve citizens in a journey designed and facilitated with Theory U, a methodology the authors have been passionate about for years, used in smaller contexts, which allowed them to experience *true personal and systemic transformation*. The recurring problem, which emerged on various occasions, consisted in the *difficulty of communicating* the type of work that would take place. This in fact involved a willingness (even an inner willingness) to change the path and open up to an uncertain future, guided by a common intent rather than by precise and fixed objectives, following a U-shape instead of a straight line. This problem was reduced using the IDG framework, which is easier to communicate and understand in its versatility.

Theory U is a leadership methodology, based on "collective system awareness", to drive personal, collective and systemic change for a better future.

Among the cornerstones of the methodology is "presencing" – being present to oneself and aware of the inner place from which change decisions are pursued; change that requires developing thoughts and actions from the emerging future of the system, for the good of all, instead of getting trapped in egocentric thinking and old patterns of the past; letting go of what no longer works and embracing the new with an open mind (curiosity), open heart (compassion and empathy), and open will (courage to change).

The U journey (see Figure 17.4) is accomplished through *five movements*:
1. Co-initiate: defining the common intent you want to pursue in the change project.
2. Co-knowing: observing with new eyes, opening the mind, suspending judgment, observing the system and oneself in the system.
3. Presencing: developing an awareness of self, what to let go of and what to accept of the emerging new, from what inner place decisions are made.
4. Co-creating: crystallizing the emerging future, rapidly prototyping desired changes.
5. Co-evolve: bringing changes to the system by listening to the whole.

Figures 17.5 and 17.6 report on the U-shaped journey drawn for each of the two phases, with the various movements that guided each of the many meetings.

Phase 1

The description of the five movements of the first phase was as follows:

Downloading
past patterns

suspending

Seeing
with fresh eyes

redirecting

Sensing
from the field

letting go

*Open
Mind*

*Open
Heart*

*Open
Will*

Presencing

Performing by
operating from the whole

embodying

Prototyping the new by
linking head, heart, hand

enacting

Crystallising
vision and intention

letting come

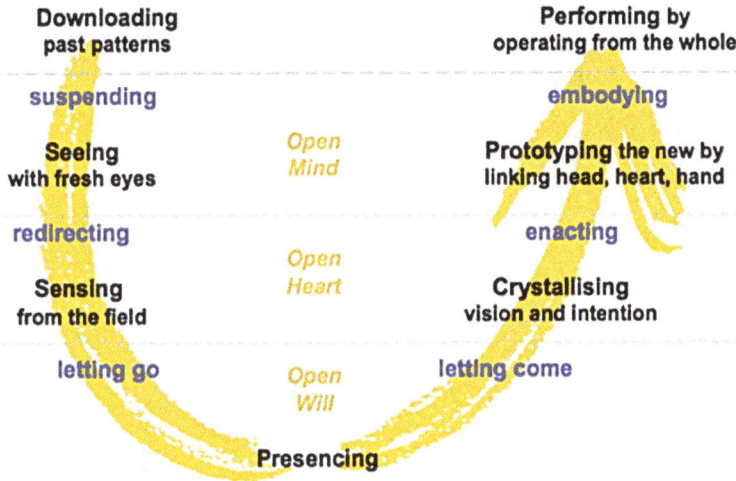

Figure 17.4: Theory U inflection points – Theory U Leading from the Future as It Emerges.
Source: Scharmer, 2021.

PHASE 1 JOURNEY

Presentation of the Future Dialogues
project to City Hall and the population

1. Co-setting: mobilizing and involving City Hall and
stakeholders in the creation of the Central Team and
Extended Team. Submitting questionnaires to the
population, setting up of the website.

5- Celebration and co-evolution: opening
the Extended Team to new participants

2. Common intent: defining together the best
future for Novazzano (6 roots of the Common Good,
keywords, Visions)

4. Crystallizing: refining the raw initiatives co-
generated during the First Future Dialogue

3. First Future Dialogue: shaping the Common Good
together, letting go of individual preferences, welcoming
the good of Communities

Figure 17.5: Phase 1 journey. U shape from Presencing Institute, Phase 1 journey as defined by authors.
Source: Scharmer 2021 and Novazzano Fututre Dialogues

Phase 2

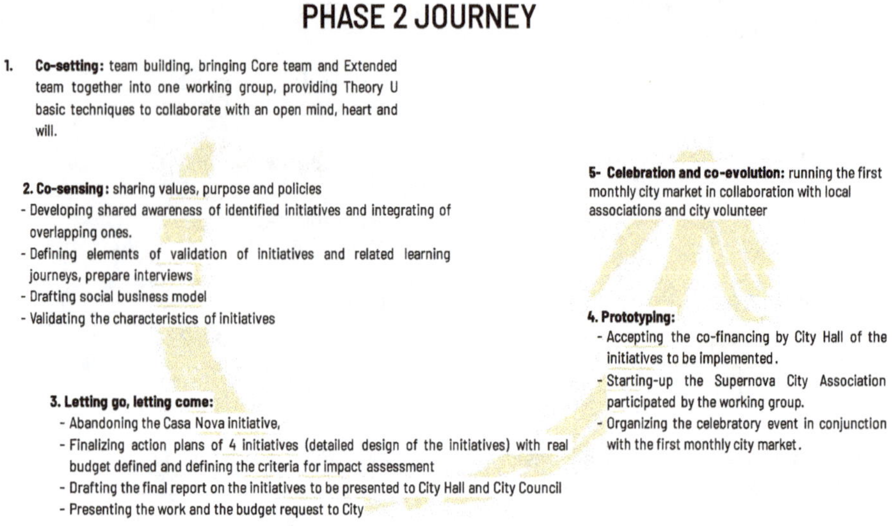

PHASE 2 JOURNEY

1. **Co-setting:** team building, bringing Core team and Extended team together into one working group, providing Theory U basic techniques to collaborate with an open mind, heart and will.

5- Celebration and co-evolution: running the first monthly city market in collaboration with local associations and city volunteer

2. **Co-sensing:** sharing values, purpose and policies
- Developing shared awareness of identified initiatives and integrating of overlapping ones.
- Defining elements of validation of initiatives and related learning journeys, prepare interviews
- Drafting social business model
- Validating the characteristics of initiatives

4. **Prototyping:**
- Accepting the co-financing by City Hall of the initiatives to be implemented.
- Starting-up the Supernova City Association participated by the working group.
- Organizing the celebratory event in conjunction with the first monthly city market.

3. **Letting go, letting come:**
- Abandoning the Casa Nova initiative,
- Finalizing action plans of 4 initiatives (detailed design of the initiatives) with real budget defined and defining the criteria for impact assessment
- Drafting the final report on the initiatives to be presented to City Hall and City Council
- Presenting the work and the budget request to City

Figure 17.6: Phase 2 journey, U shape from Presencing Institute, Phase 2 journey as defined by authors. Source: Novazzano Future Dialogues

Each meeting delivered with the working group (about 40 in the two phases) was designed to follow the U-shaped process (Theory U), driving from awareness of current system conditions to prototyping and implementing meliorative solutions. In this way, by practicing a U-shaped process at each meeting, we made the participants internalize the process.

Theory U and the Iceberg model

Following insistent requests from many people in the group to take immediate action, which were creating a feeling of impatience and distrust in the process, the iceberg model was introduced. The purpose was to not work only on the visible effects, but to understand that it was necessary to listen deeply to the system to be able to identify the causes of the visible behaviors that one wanted to change, to realize the best possible future.

The iceberg model (see Figure 17.7), an integral part of Theory U, is used to deepen the analysis of the system (left side of the U) by identifying its "deeper" elements that give rise to the current situation; the same is used to "draw" the expected elements to determine the "best possible future" object on the right side of the U (ascending). It allows to analyze the systemic root causes that give rise to events and behaviors that are visible to all. While these visible system behaviors are overt, the root causes that give rise to them are more difficult to detect, following a depth scale as below.

ICEBERG MODEL

Current reality   Vision of the Future

BEHAVIOURS

PROCESSES AND STRUCTURES
What relationships between the parts?

BELIEFS AND MENTAL MODELS
What values determine the system?

SOURCE OF INSPIRATION

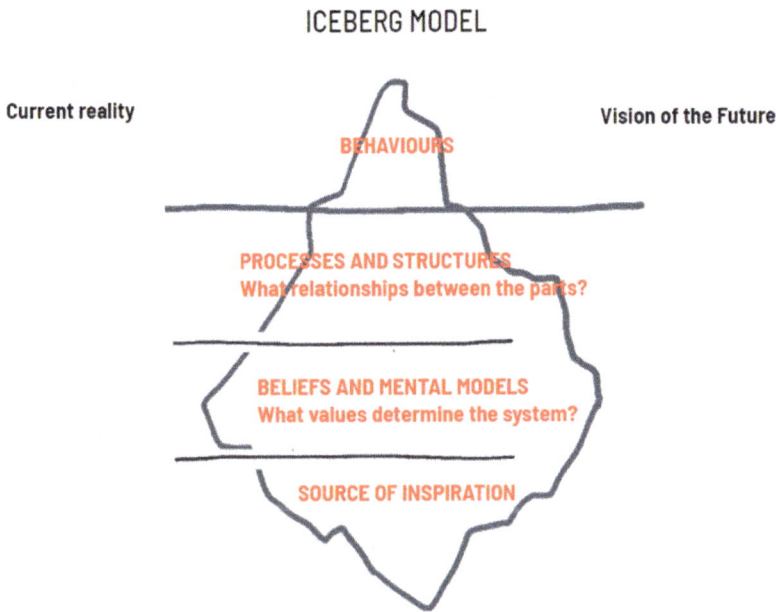

Figure 17.7: Iceberg model.
Source: Senge 1990, 1994; Sterman, 2000.

The iceberg model made it possible to look at the obvious effects and understand the causes and motivations (Figure 17.8) of the current reality. Starting from what is observed and evident in the behaviors of people and the system. It then goes on to ask what are the processes and structures that generate such evident behaviors. One then proceeds by identifying the mental models that determine the previously defined processes and structures, to arrive at identifying what personal inspirations induce those mental paradigms.

Vision of the desired future
In the process of "rising up," to "build" a system that makes virtuous behaviors evident (the visible tip of the iceberg) starting from the sources of inspiration that can determine virtuous mental paradigms which in turn generate processes and structures that facilitate the desired behaviors of people and the system.

Going up the iceberg from the right side (see Figure 17.9), the model allowed to identify similar elements to see new behaviors expressed.
6. What sources of inspiration do we need to operate from?
7. What beliefs and mental paradigms can support this change?
8. What processes and structures are needed?
9. What behaviors and events do we want to see in the new system?

ICEBERG MODEL NOVAZZANO MUNICIPALITY

Current reality

1. What behaviors and events are we seeing?

Factions and divisions are perceived in the municipality despite the fact that the perceived quality of life remains high. Absence of participation of businesses and the majority of the citizenry in choices for well-being in the municipality.

2. What are the processes and structures that shape these behaviors and events? What relationships between the parts?

Decision-making processes in the municipality occur in silos: politics, schools, associations...each operates individually. No one stimulates a systemic vision (DF role)

3. What beliefs and mental paradigms shape these structures? What values determine the system?

Politicians think they make decisions for the good of everyone. Citizens think they cannot change things. Businesses are business oriented and are detached from the local area.

4. What sources of inspiration are shaping these mental paradigms?

TINA There Is No Alternative), ego-system, individualism

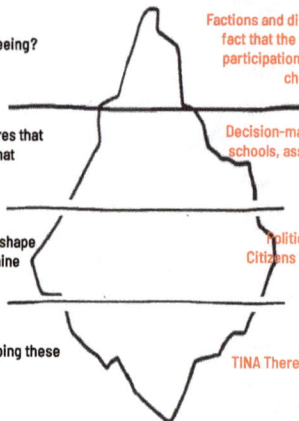

8

Figure 17.8: Iceberg model elaboration by the authors: Novazzano current reality.
Source: Novazzano Future Dialogues

ICEBERG MODEL NOVAZZANO MUNICIPALITY

Vision of the Future

Citizens and organizations (structures) collaborate, actively contribute and relate harmoniously, overcoming egocentrism in favor of eco-systemic behavior, that is, guided by harmonious relationships with others, nature, and the land. It becomes community.

8. What behaviors and events would we like to see as results?

We need organizations (school, policy, business, associations, citizens) that collaborate through people who relate with curiosity in an empathetic way, without fear and with a growth mindset. Collaboration should be cultivated and facilitated through principles, processes, methodologies, and techniques that promote it (e.g. Theory U, IDGs, etc.)

7. What processes and structures are needed?

By collaborating, value can be generated for all, thanks in part to a systemic view. Change is possible and can only happen starting with our own inner work and everyone's involvement. It takes time and commitment, effort.

6. What beliefs and mental paradigms can support this change?

Recognize our interdependence within the territory and with the outside world. Cultivate a systems approach. Feel with an open heart. There are infinite emerging futures we can co-create, starting with us!

5. From what sources of inspiration do we need to operate?

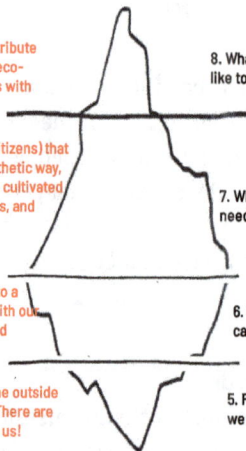

9

Figure 17.9: Iceberg model elaboration by the authors: Novazzano Future vision.
Source: Novazzano Future Dialogues

Why not use the iceberg model to test its effectiveness? Think about your current personal and/or professional life. Follow the eight steps (starting from the left side, going down and up – Mamma mia! we are making a U!). What does it take to go from current reality to realizing the best future? From which source of inspiration are you acting, fear or love? From which would you like to act? What inner qualities would you like to develop in order to access the source of your true essence, which answers the question, Who am I? What work and mission does life ask me to accomplish?

The IDGs framework

To support the journey in change, the authors used the IDG model (see Figure 17.10) to assess the most relevant capacities needed for the project, focusing the attention on those less developed in the group, thus developing a self-awareness of the inner collective "tools" needed to successfully progress in change.

The IDG model, which originated from another international movement, can also be read as walking through a U. Starting from *being* and *thinking* (co-initiating) to *relating* (understanding others) to communicating (sharing the expected change) to complete the U with *acting*, bringing to fruition what is needed for the best possible future. This allows the focus to be on people and inner functional capacities to lead and act on change.

Compared to the original framework, the authors integrated (see Figure 17.11) "Connecting the five areas: Emergence of the future that wants to be born", *feeling the need to make visible what happens when operating by integrating the above five dimensions*. The result is the realization of the Ư journey, in which expanded collective intelligence co-creates the emerging future, inhabits it, and shapes it.

The IDG framework was used in two specific moments:
1. Defining the capabilities necessary for the realization of the community change project (opening to the common good tree with the six roots – and the concept of community – see Figure 17.12)
2. Gathering the capabilities necessary for the implementation of the initiatives proposed (see Figure 17.13).

During the first Future Dialogue, the people visiting the roots' rooms were asked to reason about the "superpowers" (inner capacities) needed to conduct the initiatives. In a second round (see Figure 17.13), participants were invited to place an initiatives/superpowers Post-it in the right box on the IDG template. At the end of the event, both the proposed initiatives for each root and the capacities needed to implement them (Figure 17.14) were collected. In addition, the citizens - facilitated by the root team-co-leaders- were able to learn about the IDGs model and experience its effectiveness (see Figure 17.15).

After the initiatives were presented and voted on, people were asked what inner capacity they needed to improve, thus again stimulating to think about IDGs and gathering some personal commitments to their development (Figure 17.16).

At the end of the journey, the IDGs model was used again to do a self-assessment by participants to evaluate the change occurred during the journey.

The following summary (Table 17.2) helps to make connections between the project's achieved milestones and the tools used.

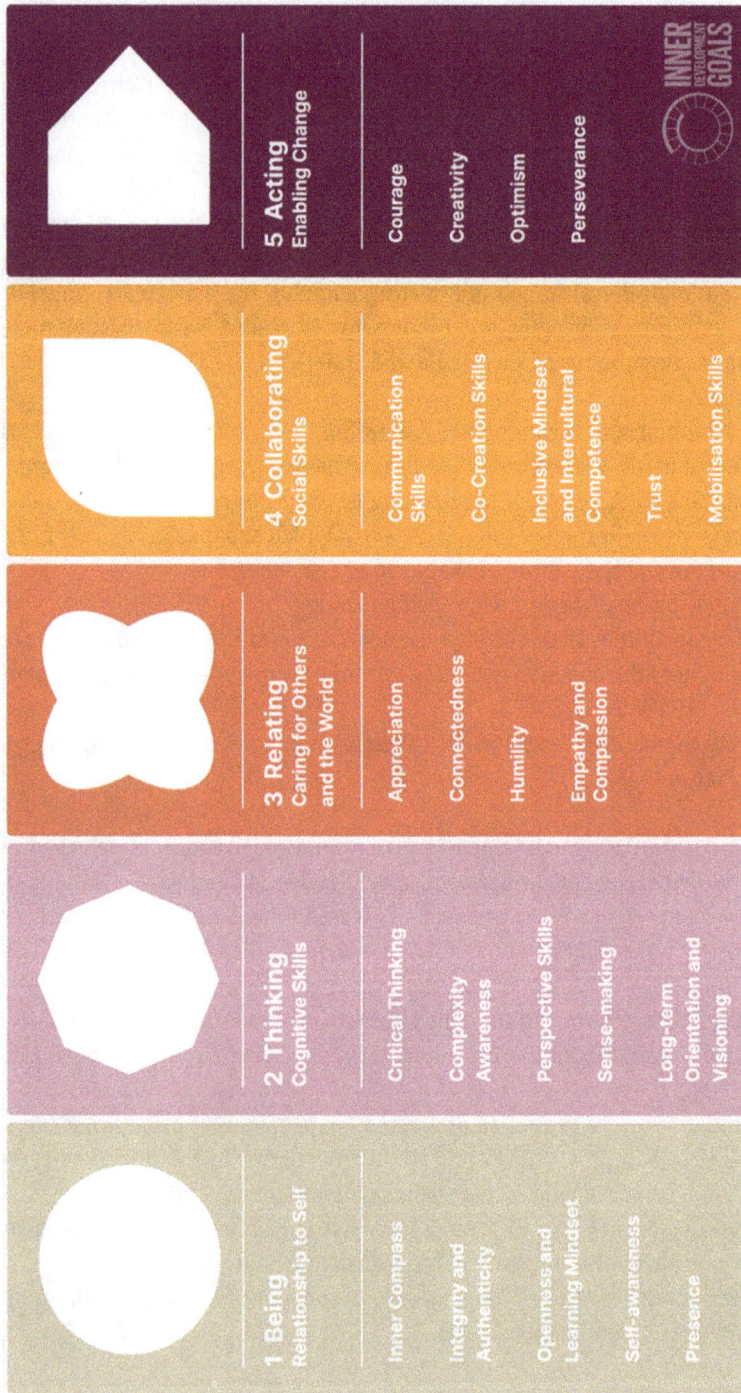

Figure 17.10: IDG framework, Source: Inner Development Goals (n.d.).

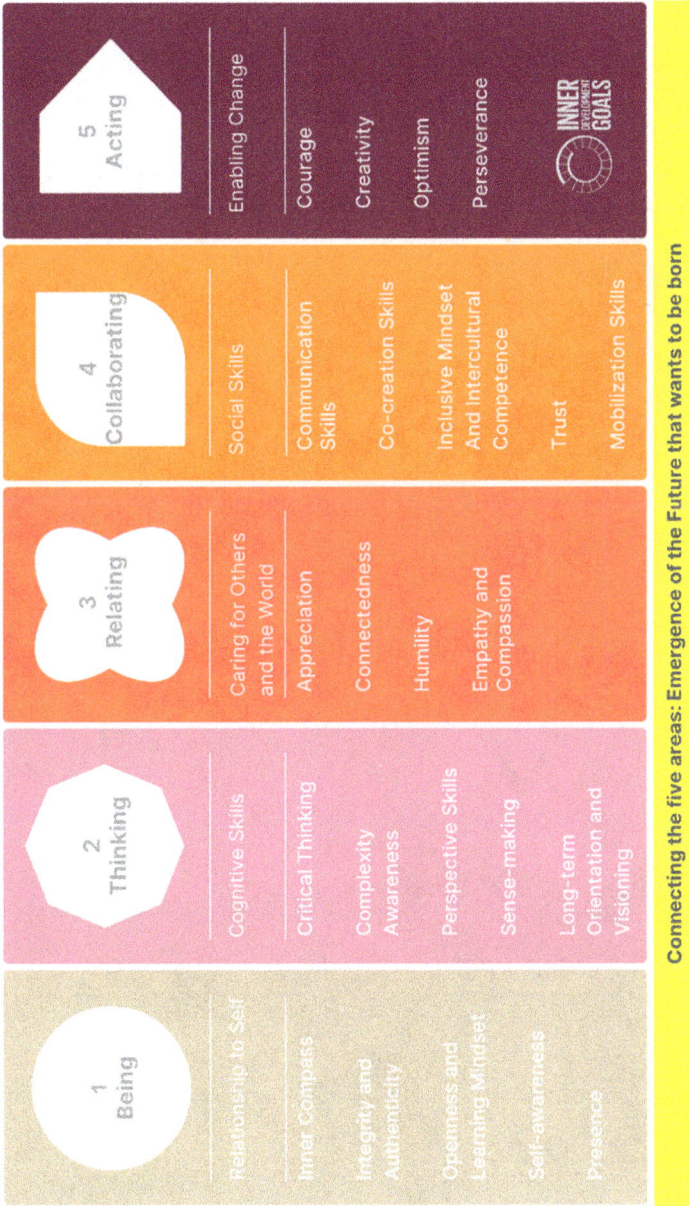

1 Being	2 Thinking	3 Relating	4 Collaborating	5 Acting
Relationship to Self	Cognitive Skills	Caring for Others and the World	Social Skills	Enabling Change
Inner Compass	Critical Thinking	Appreciation	Communication Skills	Courage
Integrity and Authenticity	Complexity Awareness	Connectedness	Co-creation Skills	Creativity
Openness and Learning Mindset	Perspective Skills	Humility	Inclusive Mindset And Intercultural Competence	Optimism
Self-awareness	Sense-making	Empathy and Compassion	Trust	Perseverance
Presence	Long-term Orientation and Visioning		Mobilization Skills	

Connecting the five areas: Emergence of the Future that wants to be born

Figure 17.11: IDG framework with additional element connecting the five areas, Source: Inner Development Goals and authors connecting elements.[5]

─────────

5 The addition of the horizontal yellow "emergence of the future" stripe to the original figure was made by the authors.

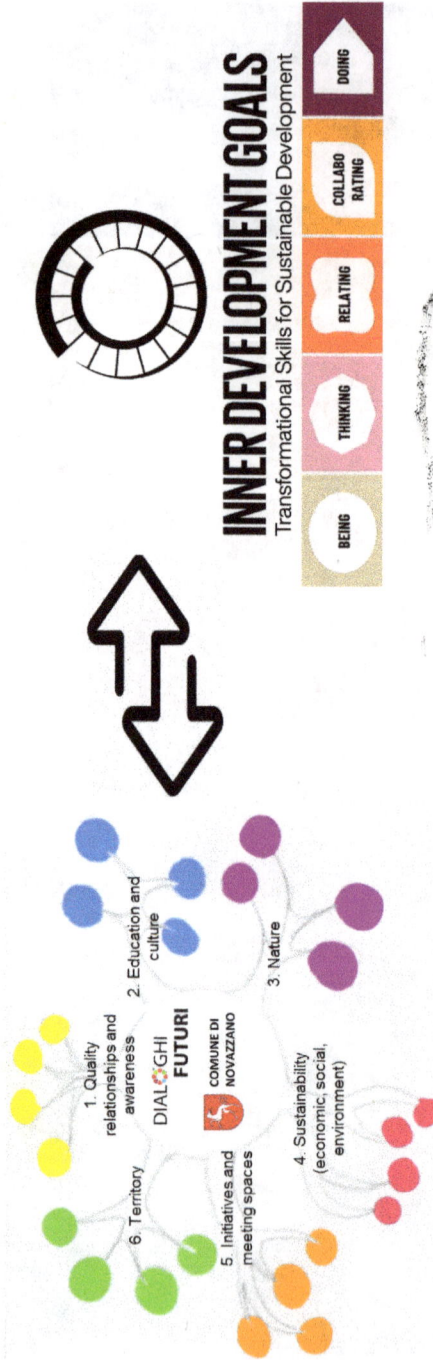

Figure 17.12: The inner roots of the common good as developed during the Future Dialogue project.
Source: Novazzano Future Dialogues and IDGs logos

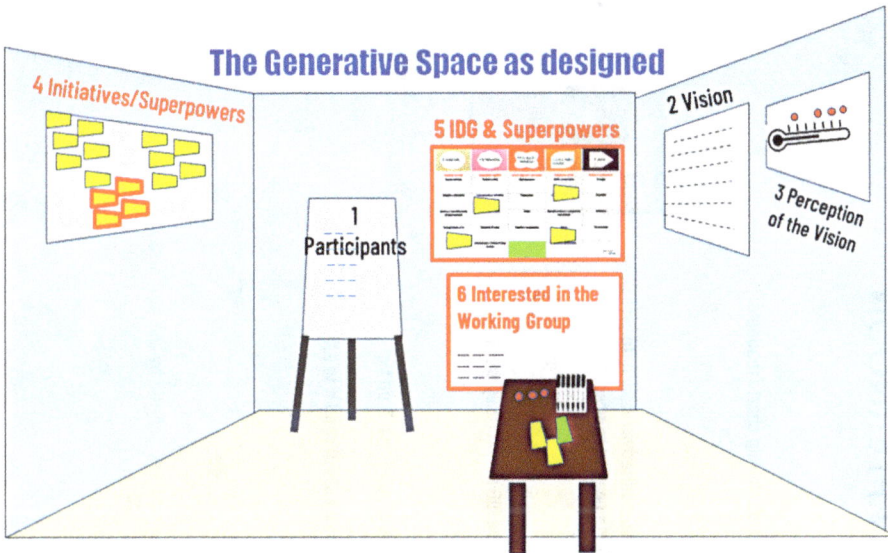

Figure 17.13: The generative space as designed and IDG framework during first Future Dialogue.
Source: Novazzano Future Dialogues

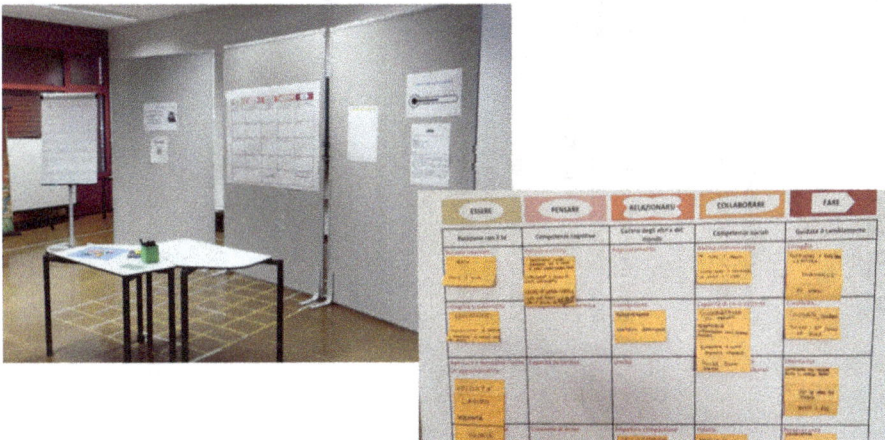

Figure 17.14: The Generative Space and IDGs Framework during First Dialogue as realized.
Source: Novazzano Future Dialogues

ROLE OF THE CO-LEADERS - AFTERNOON

IMPORTANT TO STICK TO THE SCHEDULE!

Have participants write their first and last names in block letters on the flip chart (readable!). Vision narrative, key words, place of reference (5')

Have the Post-its divided horizontally (folding). At the bottom write initiative/activity to be accomplished, at the top write superpower (qualities, aptitude needed to accomplish the activity). Hang it on the board (10')

5': Brief introduction by co-facilitators on the IDG model.
5': Participants are asked to move post-its from the board to the IDG model (they work silently, if they have questions ask).

5': Spokesperson is chosen. What emerges?
5': People are asked who is interested in participating inworking groups – pin it on flip chart.
co-leaders take a picture of the IDG model with Post-it notes attached and send it to XXX

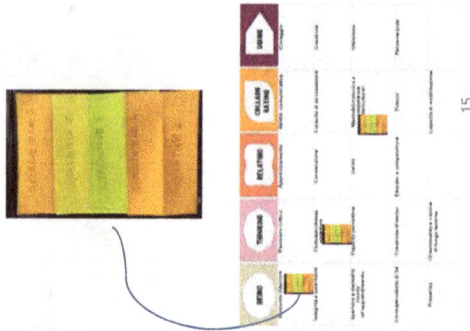

Root explanation

Superpowers & dialog

Back to plenary

Figure 17.15: Co-leader facilitate citizens in placing initiatives and superpowers in the IDG framework (as defined by the authors).
Source: Novazzano Future Dialogues

2nd FUTURE DIALOGUE
Gathering personal commitments for inner capacity development

Figure 17.16: Second Future Dialogue event: Charts for gathering personal commitments IDGs for inner capacity development.
Source: Novazzano Future Dialogues

Table 17.2: Future Dialogues project: Phases, milestones, and tools.

Phase/ activities	Period	Milestones	Tools
Phase 0 – Presentation of the project to the city hall	May 2022	– Project presentation to city hall and citizenship	– Theory U: 3 disconnects, systemic vision
Phase 0 – Presentation of the project to the population			
Phase 1	Jun. 2022–Mar. 2023		

Table 17.2 (continued)

Phase/ activities	Period	Milestones	Tools
Website creation Survey on the future in Novazzano	Jun. 2022–Sep. 2022	– Website and questionnaire addressed to citizenship to map primary needs and define the common good – Creation of core and extended teams, involving municipalities and stakeholders	– IDGs: mobilization, growth mindset, empathic listening, co-creation, long-term vision
Core team constitution meeting 1st operational meeting 2nd operational meeting	Sep. 2022–Oct. 2022	– Co-definition of the common good, the six roots of the common good and related visions	– Theory U principles: levels of listening and self-assessment, presencing and absencing, journaling on collective responses to common good questionnaire, SPT (social presencing theater) – Iceberg model – Practices of "embodiment": sensory experience with DUDUUM (pure cocoa)
3rd operational meeting 4th activist meeting 5th activist meeting 6th meeting learning journeys			– Theory U: learning journeys – IDGs: turns of phrase (sociocratic assent), inclusive thinking, collaboration
7th operational meeting 8th operational meeting 9th operational meeting First Future Dialogue with the population	Oct. 2022–Nov. 2022	Preparation and implementation of the first Future Dialogue open to the whole population: sharing results, gathering and integrating new perspectives on the roots of the common good and rough co-definition of initiatives to realize it	– Theory U: learning journeys, journaling, integration systemic vision – IDGs: mobilization, long-term vision, superpowers to realize vision and initiatives for the common good – Iceberg model

Table 17.2 (continued)

Phase/ activities	Period	Milestones	Tools
1st working group meeting	Dec. 2022–Mar. 2023	– Crystallization and refinement of the raw initiatives co-generated – Deepening, optimizing, validating and revising initiatives, reinforcing Theory U principles, assessing costs and resources for initiative implementation, evaluating initiatives and prioritizing them	– Theory U: levels of listening, presencing/ absencing, learning journey, stakeholder interview, systemic vision integration – IDGs: mobilization, long-term vision, superpowers to realize vision – Iceberg model – Initiatives prioritization model – Initiatives validation model
2nd working group operational meeting			
2nd extended team meeting online			
3rd extended team meeting online			
3rd working group meeting			
Second Future Dialogue with the population		– Celebration and co-evolution: presentation to the population and evaluation of initiatives to be implemented, stimulation of assessment of one's inner capacities, openness of the working group to new participation	– Theory U in the day design – IDGs
Phase 2	Apr. 2023–Apr. 2024		

Table 17.2 (continued)

Phase/ activities	Period	Milestones	Tools
F2 1st meeting	Apr. 2023–Nov. 2023	– Establishment of the governance and operational groups to develop the selected initiatives – Training to the governance group on the principles of change leadership – Validation, optimization, and cost evaluation of initiatives – Activation of relationships with other territorial associations and ATTE (Associazione Ticinese Terza Età) – Co-design and planning of the Prima-Vera festival – Establishment of the Supernova Civic Association – Co-design and preparation of the first Saturday in the Square	– Theory U: levels of listening, presencing/ absencing, learning journey, stakeholder interview, systemic vision integration – IDGs: superpowers to realize vision, initiatives for the common good, steps in the process of generating initiatives – Initiatives validation model
F2 2nd meeting			
F2 3rd meeting			
F2 4th meeting			
F2 5th meeting			
F2 6th meeting			
F2 7th meeting			
F2 8th meeting			
F2 9th meeting			
F2 10th meeting	Nov. 2023	– City hall approval for the implementation of 5 initiatives	

Table 17.2 (continued)

Phase/ activities	Period	Milestones	Tools
F2 11th meeting F2 12th meeting F2 13th meeting F2 14th meeting F2 15th meeting F2 16th meeting Press conference	Jan. 2024–May 2024	– Finalization of the design of the initiatives for their implementation – Design of the Prima-Vera festival. – Design of the first Saturday in the Square – Establishment of the Supernova Civic Association – Involvement of other associations in the territory – Involvement of ATTE (Associazione Ticinese Terza Età) – Press conference and outreach to local media	– Theory U: levels of listening, presencing/ absencing, learning journey, stakeholder interview, systemic vision integration – IDGs – Initiatives validation model
3rd Future Dialogue: Prima-Vera Market		– Realization of the First-True Party for the conclusion of the Future Dialogues project, presentation of the Supernova Civic Association to the citizenship, realization of the first Saturday in the Square – Collection of feedback – Collection of memberships in the association – Collection of volunteer applications	– Theory U and IDGs: reflective survey through posters with four guiding questions and "communal sunrise" that allowed us to collect feedback from the day with respect to the feeling of community and call for citizen mobilization and activation in collaboration with Supernova Civic Association.

Conclusion and insights

Manuela

From my perspective, the collaboration with Paolo was crucial to the success of the project. Deep mutual trust and empathy allowed me to lead the group through the unknown with confidence and courage, combining my knowledge of the Novazzano system with Paolo's objectivity to generate creative insights and generative visions.

Being two allowed me to feel supported, with open minds and hearts, ensuring that the project flow remained connected to the emerging future instead of retracing the past, driven by fear and old ways of thinking and operating.

With the approval of budgets to implement all the initiatives proposed during the second phase of the Future Dialogues project, the group was *imbued with a new energy and enthusiasm*. I sensed with Paolo a nascent need and gave it a voice, encouraging the group to create the Supernova Civic Association, which could continue to generate value even after the project ended.

With Supernova's birth, me and Paolo experienced a double role as *parents of Future Dialogues and grandparents of Supernova*, a magnificent and unexpected experience that allowed a positive future to emerge in the present.

This project allowed me to meet and relate in depth with people in the country I did not know or knew little about and to observe the system from the inside out, to feel it. I witnessed transformations in the system that occurred during the journey, in particular: new collaborations between participants outside of Future Dialogues, the school used the vision of one of the roots as a long-term goal for its program, more trust between the municipal technical office and the population, collaboration between village associations, more desire to engage. In general, more curiosity and empathy: a waxing nascent community.

On a more intimate level, I felt I was "growing" by becoming more aware of my inner work and refining my skills as a facilitator, thanks to the "coaching" work that Paolo indirectly conducted for me during the work of co-leadership.

Paolo

For me, this project was a fantastic journey into the world of Ticino, in a small border town with its rhythms, its habits, its needs and fears, with the relationships between families and people who have known each other for years. It was a journey of personal, professional, and human growth; the closeness of Manuela, who passed on to me her points of view, her skills, her polite and at the same time strong way of relating to people and situations.

Furthermore, in this project we knew and were able to experience the power of the IDG model, and how people, if made aware, can exercise those internal capacities in which they can grow. The same thing was true for me.

I feel like I have grown in many ways, and this is thanks to have been able to interact with Manuela and also thanks to the mutual commitments we have made to improve. It was a demanding project, each meeting meant two days of travel, evening meetings with the working groups from 7:45 p.m. to 10:15 p.m., as well as preparations and debriefings. There was no shortage of moments of strong emotion as we delved into the personal aspects of ourselves and the participants, having co-built a safe environment in which to interact. A perfect test field in which to measure and practice Theory U and the IDGs in a real context of daily life and future life.

We are grateful to life, our work together, Theory U, and the IDGs, the people in the groups, city hall, Daniel, Eric, and our families for making this wonderful journey possible.

SELF-REFLECTION
What are the biggest insights you take home from this reading? What resonated? What could you "make yours" starting tomorrow?

References

Inner Development Goals. (n.d). https://innerdevelopmentgoals.org/. (Accessed Mar. 28, 2024.

Scharmer, C. Otto. (2018). "Teoria U I fondamentali". Guerini NEXT.

Scharmer, C. Otto. (2021). "Theory U Leading from the Future as It Emerges". Second edition. Berrett Koehler.

Seale, Alan. (2010). "The View From the Field A Fundamental Understanding of Basic Principles of Quantum Physics as Related to Transformational Presence". Center for Transformational Presence. https://transformationalpresence.org/downloads/misc/The-View-From-the-Field.pdf. (Accessed Mar. 28, 2024).

Senge, Peter. (1990). "The Fifth Discipline: The Art and Practice of the Learning Organization". Doubleday.

Senge, Peter. (1994). "The Fifth Discipline Fieldbook: Strategies and Tools for Building a Learning Organization." Crown Currency.

Sterman, John D. (2000). "Business Dynamics: System Thinking and Modeling for a Complex World". McGraw-Hill Europe.

U-School for Transformation. (n.d.). https://www.u-school.org/. (Accessed Mar. 28, 2024).

Section 4: **IDG Movement**

Ana Gabriela Mata Carrera and Harrison Wavell
Chapter 18
Prelude

This section explores the Inner Development Goals (IDG) movement, a decentralized, open-source, and non-profit initiative that illuminates its profound impact on sustainability leadership, community building, and personal transformation.

The journey begins in Switzerland, where a community dedicated to conscious leadership for sustainable social entrepreneurship blossoms like a lotus flower. In "Lotus Gardening: CoCreation of Inner Development Goals Switzerland," we explore how the IDG framework guides this community from introspective "mud" to a purposeful "bloom." This metaphorical journey underscores the importance of inner development in supporting global sustainability goals and sets the stage for understanding how individual growth can catalyze collective action.

Next, "How to Unravel the IDGs' Skills in Practice" transports us to Colombia, where the IDGs are implemented in business and educational settings. This chapter showcases success stories and the effective use of the IDG Toolkit, revealing how these skills address modern leadership challenges and foster transformative change. Through ongoing dialogue and collaboration, we see how the IDG movement creates a ripple effect, influencing management practices and educational outcomes.

We then shift our focus to the IDG Global Practitioners Network in "Using the IDGs to Accelerate Mindset Shifts Towards Achieving the Sustainable Development Goals (SDGs)." This narrative delves into how the IDGs serve as a catalyst for individual and collective transformation, emphasizing the role of mindset shifts in driving sustainable development. This chapter highlights practical applications and key learnings from the global practitioners' experiences, illustrating the power of a co-creative approach.

Following this, you'll find an insightful interview with the Head of IDG Research. As the initiative advances its co-creation efforts, the interview reveals how collaboration among diverse global stakeholders is shaping a more inclusive and comprehensive framework. The chapter emphasizes the importance of interdisciplinary collaboration, global representation, and the integration of diverse knowledge systems, all of which are key to building an IDG framework that is both adaptable and transformative.

Next, you'll explore how the Global Leadership for Sustainable Development (GLSD) program is pioneering the integration of the IDGs into leadership development. This international capacity-building initiative equips leaders with transformational skills and integrates these capacities into organizational strategies, policies, and operations to drive action toward the SDGs. The chapter describes the pilot program launched in 2023, which involved high-level decision-makers from Albania, Colombia,

https://doi.org/10.1515/9783111453729-019

Costa Rica, India, Rwanda, and Zambia—key players in SDG implementation. It details how the program was developed, evaluated, and its outcomes, offering key insights into how sustainability leadership can catalyze cultural and systemic transformation. By shifting the focus from individual development to systemic change, the authors demonstrate how personal growth, when combined with the right principles, can empower leaders to challenge unsustainable paradigms and embed inner development into organizational mechanisms and structures for lasting impact.

The journey concludes with "Deepcasting the IDGs: Exploring the Cross-Dimensional Quality of Coherence," a collective contribution from the EU-funded Cohere+ project team. This chapter emphasizes coherence as a crucial element within the IDG framework, exploring its role across the five dimensions of inner development. Through action research and personal stories, we uncover how coherence enhances the IDGs' impact, fostering a deeper sense of interconnectedness and alignment in various contexts.

As you immerse yourself in this section, you will uncover the intricate tapestry of the IDG movement. Each chapter builds on the previous one, weaving together the themes of inner growth, leadership, practical application, and coherence. Through these narratives, you will gain insights and practical tools to support the evolution of more conscious and sustainable organizations. The journey within these pages is a testament to the transformative power of inner development, illustrating that true change begins within and radiates outward to create a more sustainable and conscious world.

Figure 18.1: *Unica* (2023) Photograph by A.G. Mata Carrera, Ho Chi Minh, Vietnam.
"The lotus flower finds its roots in the nutrient-rich mud, drawing sustenance from the intricate ecosystem that flourishes around it. Rather than criticizing the muddy waters, it thrives and blossoms, symbolizing resilience and growth amidst adversity. The mud represents the challenges inherent in every community, while the flower embodies the value and beauty of the ecosystem."

This is Us

Only a revival of the sacred can save us now.
Only the love of the great mystery can return our hearts
to their rightful home.
Only the slowing down to notice
what is
here and now
can break the tyranny of thought
that leads to thoughtlessness.

Beware the false God of Mind, for the minds of many
have spoken:
who needs the earth, the sky, the rain or sea
to bless us with life?
We have life by the throat. We're in control, nothing
and no one can tell us what to do
or how to be.
Throw away the good books, do away with creed,
we have no need
for faith, for soul, pure superstition,
out of date.
In the name of unfettered freedom we shall
TAKE TAKE TAKE.

We are lost in the wilderness with no guide, no love,
nothing but distrust, stuff, lust,
power, money, more stuff,
buy the lot, have it all.
This is it.
Is it any wonder we're sick, disengaged, unmoved,
afraid,
unable to live or to listen when everything calling us
is cancer to the soul?

Don't believe the lie that you've been told—
that you're just a body, a mind, a mould
to fit the system and
CONSUME CONSUME CONSUME.

You are the eternal formless finding form,
a star through which divine light pours,
here to shine in the great constellation of life.
It is love that bodies you into being—
nothing more, nothing less. We are miraculous.
Miraculous somethings born out of the nothing
of everything. Like words we emerge from silence
and return; do not fear—
burn brightly, my friends, burn brightly.

Let unsuppressed love shatter your illusions,
break old habits, end delusion.
May you breathe in every breath the joys of loving tenderness
and be a friend to Earth,
this hurt and loving mother of ours.
Let stars beam
with celestial meaning,
the sea silence you with song,
let us dream and touch the gold and laugh
at how wrong we've been,
for trying so hard to find what was always hiding
in us.
Let us lay down our weapons, our hurts, our hates,
the kingdom of heaven is within us,
open your heart, open the gates.
Let us love our neighbour as ourselves
not because we should but because it's true;
after all, what happens to you happens to me
we are all in this together— sisters, brothers, each and every
one of us.

A time will come
when the truth of our oneness
shines like the sun,
when the broken pieces of our yesterdays are swept up
and we are lovingly made
into a new mosaic of different colours, sizes, shapes. . .
each unique and perfectly placed,
a thing to marvel at and say:

This is us
This is us

H. Wavell (2023)

Author's Note. Anger compelled me to write This is Us. The kind of anger that is a form of blessing, for it moves us to speak out against injustice, oppression and exploitation of all kinds. I was reading about industrial farming practices when it struck me. Indignant at the suffering we inflict on our fellow creatures (not to mention the ensuing ecological devastation), I put pen to paper in an attempt to express the pain of violating that which is sacred. I wanted to explore what lies at the root of the disharmony within us, between us and with our relationship to the natural world. It is a poem of two halves — of darkness giving way to light — that embraces suffering yet defiantly resists despair in favor of hope.

Mauricio Campos Suarez, Lutz Hempel and Eleftheria Egel

Chapter 19
Lotus gardening with presence, wisdom, and inner freedom: Co-creation of the Inner Development Goals Switzerland Center

Abstract: In a world increasingly driven by technology and external accomplishments, the Inner Development Goals (IDGs) framework invites us to turn our focus inward, promoting actions grounded in deeper meaning and purpose. Amid ongoing planetary crises, how can we cultivate hope and foster resilient communities? This chapter explores how collective leadership emerges from individual inner growth, highlighting the community-building journey of IDG Switzerland – a network committed to conscious leadership in sustainable social entrepreneurship. Using the metaphor of a lotus flower's growth, from the introspective "mud" to the purposeful "bloom", we describe our collaborative evolution. This narrative illustrates how inner development can reinforce global sustainability efforts, empowering communities to drive positive change.

Keywords: community building, Switzerland, IDG movement, collaboration, collective intelligence

Introduction

Amid rapid technological advancements, a material-growth mindset, and an external-achievement focus, the pursuit of inner growth and development often takes a back seat. However, we, a group of passionate volunteers in Basel, Switzerland – a city with a rich cultural diversity – recognized the need for an inner shift in our narrative to enable a more sustainable future for our children. For many years, we understood the significance of cultivating qualities for conscious leadership (Dethmer, Chapman, & Klemp, 2015) to promote sustainability, but we lacked a structured approach to communicate with organizations and collaborate effectively.

Conscious leadership involves leading with awareness and intention, fostering a supportive environment that prioritizes the well-being of individuals and the organization as a whole. It encourages leaders to reflect on their actions and decisions, ensuring they align with their values and contribute positively to their teams and communities. However, many organizations struggle to fully grasp the essence of conscious leadership or recognize its potential benefits. Resistance to change and a lack of commitment are common, as conscious leadership challenges existing power

https://doi.org/10.1515/9783111453729-020

structures and ways of thinking. Conscious leadership requires leaders to be more open, authentic, and vulnerable, which can be uncomfortable for those accustomed to projecting an image of constant strength and certainty. Additionally, some organizational cultures may not be conducive to the principles of conscious leadership, such as open communication, emotional intelligence, and shared responsibility. The emphasis many organizations place on measurable outcomes and the prioritization of short-term results and profits over long-term sustainability and employee well-being further hinders the adoption of conscious leadership. Embracing this approach requires a shift towards long-term thinking and investment in people development.

The Inner Development Goals (IDGs) movement changed all of that. It offered us the IDG framework, which uses purposefully simple language that is easy to understand and implement, making it an effective tool in our communication with organizations. The IDG framework is memorable due to its simple and clear visual design. The five dimensions are distinctly organized, each represented by different colors and icons, helping users quickly identify and differentiate between the various areas of inner development. The accompanying IDG toolkit includes methods, practices, and activities that are visually aligned with the framework's design, ensuring consistency and ease of use. The framework's open-source and flexible nature allows for global applicability and customization, while its collaborative design process ensures inclusivity and diverse representation. Finally, by adding the "being" dimension, it incorporated the importance of cultivating conscious leadership as a step toward collective change.

In this chapter, we share the path we took at IDG Switzerland to reshape perspectives and nurture intrinsic capacities at both individual and collective levels. We created spaces for many to come together and contribute to something greater than the sum of its parts, allowing meaningful change to occur. We also explore what we observe as the essence of our movement. Lastly, we highlight the transformative power of collective leadership in action and awareness-based systems change, guided by our aspirations, plans, and dreams for the future.

As you read on, imagine yourself in our gatherings, sitting in the circle, sharing our hopes and challenges, and enjoying moments of fun. Picture the vibrant discussions, the warmth of community gatherings, and the quiet moments of reflection that shaped our journey. This is not just a story of an organization; it is a story of a collective awakening to our shared humanity and the realization of our responsibility to the world we are crafting for the generations to come.

Where everything started

The Swiss IDG Hub's journey began in late 2021 when Mauricio first encountered the IDG framework. This concept deeply resonated with his desire to articulate the profound connection between personal growth and societal change.

Inspired by the potential of the IDG framework, he envisioned hosting the first IDG summit broadcast and workshop in Basel in early 2022. This idea took shape during a conversation after his meeting in a mindfulness-based strengths practice course led by Lutz. His enthusiasm, combined with Lutz's immediate and positive response, sparked our collaboration. Drawing on our combined two decades of experience in mindfulness, executive education, capacity building, and adult development, we recognized the importance of integrating diverse perspectives and breaking down the silos that often separate various approaches to inner development. We saw that the IDG framework encapsulated essential qualities like presence, wisdom, and inner freedom – qualities long explored by ancient traditions such as Buddhism and deeply connected to both individual and collective well-being.

Our shared aim was to cultivate self-awareness, compassion, systemic awareness, and the capacity to let go and unlearn, thus facilitating the discovery of new perspectives and advancing our Sustainable Development Goals (SDGs). Above all, we strongly believed that the only way forward was through community and cross-sector collaboration. Fostering a broad base of connections facilitates resource mobilization, enhances problem solving, sustains collaboration, amplifies impact, and helps navigate complex environments.

Securing support was crucial, and Mauricio successfully brought Impact Hub Basel on board through a connection within his university alumni community. The shared vision of IDGs and Impact Hub, which revolves around fostering sustainable development, social innovation, and community-driven impact, made the partnership possible and set the stage for what was to come. The emerging Swiss IDG Hub found a home and support at the Impact Hub Basel.

The initial plan was straightforward: to host a one-off local event that would coincide with the IDG Global Summit 2022. April 29, 2022, was set as the date for the event. It included a two-hour broadcast and a half-day workshop. However, that day became the inception of something much larger than we had anticipated. Little did we know that this event was merely the first step on a path toward building a thriving, interconnected community. Over the next 20 months, our impact exceeded our initial expectations. We organized more than 30 gatherings, welcomed more than 500 members, and engaged more than 50 organizations, all eager to contribute to our mission.

Simultaneously, our initial efforts attracted a group of enthusiastic volunteers who rallied around our vision to foster sustainable development, social innovation, and community-driven impact. Their support helped strengthen the broad ecosystem we were building across Switzerland from the initial seeds we had planted. Our gatherings attracted a diverse audience, but one attendee stood out: Eleftheria, the third co-author of this chapter and third member of our core team. She attended one of our first events, and from that moment, our journey of co-creation began. Together, we laid the foundation for what we now envision as the IDG Switzerland Center – an organization dedicated to catalyzing sustainable development across Switzerland by activating individual potential and building collective capacity through inner development.

The path forward

We began our journey in Basel, but from the inception of our work, we envisioned an IDG organization that could complement and amplify the impact of the multiple decentralized IDG hubs in Switzerland. This perspective guided our actions as we embarked on establishing the IDG Switzerland network. Our goal from the beginning was to move beyond the city boundaries of the IDG hubs, creating a strong national ecosystem that could support one another and the movement. By fostering collaboration and mutual support, we aimed to build a cohesive and dynamic network dedicated to sustainable development and inner growth across the entire country.

As the Swiss IDG Hub gained momentum, we realized that these gatherings generated a wealth of collective wisdom that we wanted to share with the broader IDG global community. Driven by this strong motivation, we decided to publish a book on the IDGs to collect the wisdom of the global IDG community and to develop educational programs in the form of leadership courses to support various organizations. These programs, tailored for young leaders and changemakers in corporate, nongovernmental organization (NGO), and start-up settings, provided a platform for exploring and integrating inner work into their professional journeys. These programs became the foundation for our Swiss IDG Academy and our core program, the IDG Learning Lab.

Over the past two years, our initial concept of a national hub has evolved into the vision of an IDG country center – "the IDG Switzerland Center"– built around four pillars: capacity building, research, ecosystem building, and policy advocacy (see Figure 19.1).

In the final section of this chapter, we will share more about our center and our vision for the future.

Next, we want to share our story through a metaphor, in order to transport some essence and insight of it in deeper ways. To connect to the power of our metaphoric sharing, we invite you to pause for a moment, connecting with your breathing and body, and to picture a beautiful, peaceful pond with lotus flowers blooming in it.

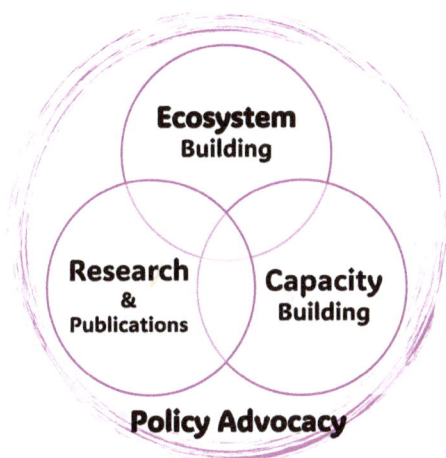

Figure 19.1: IDG Switzerland focus areas (Source: Authors' own).

No mud, no lotus

Our journey unfolds across four interconnected components, each metaphorically mirroring the stages of a lotus flower's evolution. Just as a lotus emerges from the mud to bloom with exquisite beauty, our journey begins with the "guiding questions" (Kabat-Zinn, 1990; Tolle, 2004, akin to the mud that nurtures growth. These questions serve as the foundation, challenging us to delve deep into self-discovery and the shared purpose of our community (See Figure 19.2).

The next stage represents the unfolding of individual potential, like the petals of a lotus flower. Here, we witness the blossoming of qualities such as presence, wisdom, and inner freedom – referred to as mindfulness, insight, and liberation by Thích Nhất Hạnh (2014). These qualities, rooted in the *being* and *thinking* dimensions of the IDGs, begin to manifest within us, shaping our interactions and aspirations as we support each other in discovering what is emerging.

The analogy extends further to the pond, symbolizing our collaborative space. Just as the pond holds water, our space embraces the collective ecosystem that nurtures growth. The "we" space reflects the interconnectedness, with the waters of collective energy and intention rippling outward.

Finally, like the radiant bloom of the lotus, we venture into the realm of action. Our commitment to inner energy and unwavering dedication mirrors the lotus's steadfast growth. This stage manifests through transformative actions and trust in the dynamics of emergence, nurtured by a unified purpose and a shared commitment to inner and outer change (Kegan & Lahey, 2009).

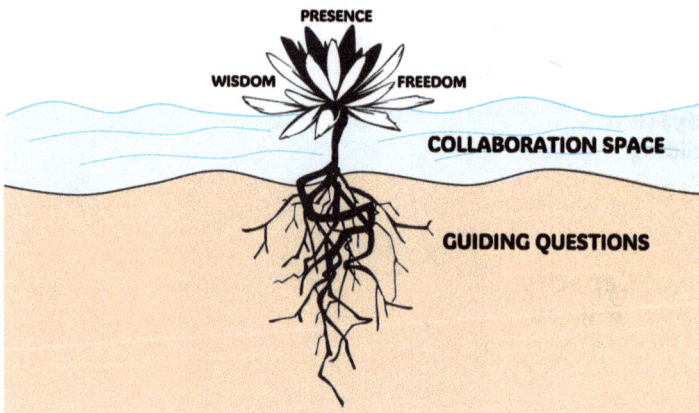

Figure 19.2: Our development journey as a lotus flower metaphor (Source: Authors' own).
Both suffering and happiness are organic, which means they are both transitory; they are always changing. The flower, when it wilts, becomes compost. The compost can help grow a flower again. Happiness is also organic and impermanent by nature. It can become suffering and suffering can become happiness again. (Thích Nhất Hạnh, 2014, p. 2).

Guiding questions: The mud of individual and collective unfolding

The community is more than the sum of its parts if the members of the community embrace the inner work required for their individual "unfolding" and contribute to the collective one (Senge, 1990; Wheatley, 2006).

At the core of this work, we found powerful questions that, through the content and practices shared, enable and direct the growth.

Guiding questions for unfolding at the individual level:

1. **Who am I?** (source[1]): Reflecting on your journey, what experiences, values, and influences have shaped your identity? How have your past experiences informed your current perspective on leadership and personal growth?

2. **Why do I care?** (present): What drives your passion and commitment toward sustainability, conscious leadership, and inner development? How do your current beliefs and aspirations align with the qualities of presence, wisdom, and freedom?

3. **How do I show up?** (future): Envisioning your future self, how do you see yourself embodying the qualities of presence, wisdom, and freedom? How will your evolving understanding of these qualities influence your actions, decisions, and interactions?

---

1 "Source" refers to the foundational elements of our identity, values, and "higher" self – the origins that influence our current and future self.

Guiding questions for unfolding at the collective level:

1. **Why are we here?** (source): As a collective, what is the overarching purpose that unites us in our journey toward conscious leadership? How do our shared goals resonate with the cultivation of presence, wisdom, and freedom in ourselves and our community?

2. **Where is our energy?** (present): Sensing the current state of our collective efforts, where are we directing our energy and focus? How are we nurturing an environment where individuals can contribute their strengths and perspectives to our shared mission?

3. **What is about to emerge?** (future): What does "life" need from us? How might our commitment to presence, wisdom, and freedom lead to new insights, collaborations, and transformative outcomes in our "system"?

These guiding questions serve as beacons of introspection and direction, guiding our individual and collective journeys toward a deeper understanding of ourselves, and our purpose, encouraging taking action from a meaningful place.

The lotus of being and thinking: Core qualities of our individual unfolding

At the heart of this movement is a shared vision: to create environments where individuals, teams, organizations, and society can explore and cultivate qualities that go beyond mere external skills.

Central to our collective transformation is the concept of "the self", grounded in individual purpose and embodied by the *being* and *thinking* dimensions of the IDG framework. The framework presents ten inner qualities in those dimensions: inner compass, integrity and authenticity, openness and learning mindset, self-awareness, presence, critical thinking, complexity awareness, perspective skills, sensemaking, and long-term orientation and visioning. These qualities form the foundation of our initiatives and inner work, distilled into three fundamental themes: presence, wisdom, and inner freedom (see Figure 19.3).

Presence: The foundation of self and systems awareness

Our journey at IDG Switzerland began with exploring presence as the foundation of both self-awareness and systems awareness, supporting our complete immersion in the current moment. We are actively engaged in these practices during our gatherings and beyond.

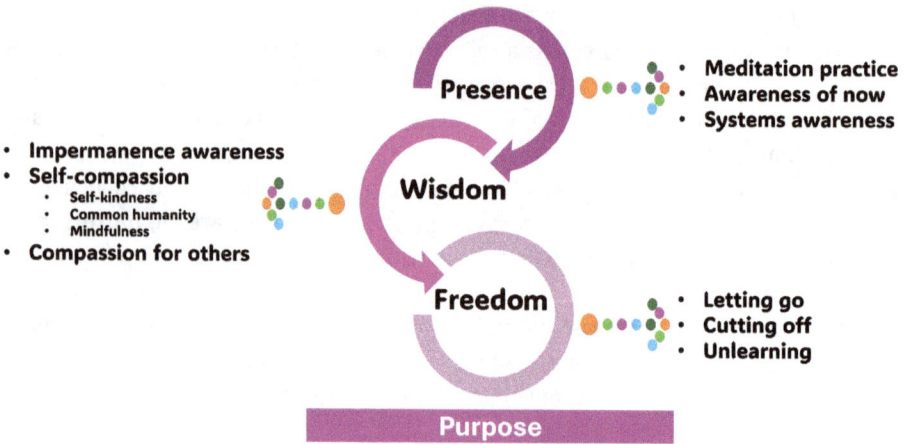

Figure 19.3: Core qualities of our individual unfolding (Authors' own).
Figure 19.3 A diagram of three interconnected circles representing the core qualities of individual growth and transformation. The uppermost circle embodies Presence, with its key attributes: Meditation Practice, Awareness of the Now, and Systems Awareness. Below it, the second circle signifies Wisdom, characterized by qualities of Awareness of Impermanence, Self-Compassion, and Compassion for Others. The base circle represents Freedom, encompassing the core practices of Letting Go, Cutting Off, and Unlearning.

We use meditation practices as a powerful tool in our pursuit of presence (Kabat-Zinn, 1990). During our gatherings, trainings, presentations, and meetings we encourage individuals to focus their attention on their breath, bodily sensations, or a specific object, sharpening their awareness of the present moment. Through regular meditation practice, participants cultivate the ability to observe their thoughts and emotions without judgment, which is integral to self-awareness (Brown & Ryan, 2003).

Additionally, we employ visualization techniques to cultivate presence and self-awareness. In our sessions, we use guided imagery to help individuals create vivid mental images of their goals, desires, and inner landscapes (Hudetz, 2012). These exercises offer profound insights into participants' aspirations, fears, and motivations, thus enhancing self-awareness.

This heightened self-awareness extends to systems awareness, fostering an understanding of how individuals are interconnected with their environment and society. Through these practices, we realize the power of being fully present, not only in our personal lives but also within the systems we interact with. We continue to integrate these methods into our work, helping individuals and groups connect deeply with themselves and hopefully enabling them to act more sustainably.

Wisdom: Nurturing compassion and impermanence awareness

Wisdom, the second pillar, is a profound exploration into the nature of compassion. At IDG Switzerland, we practice generating compassion, which involves facing our fear of pain. This practice is daring; it requires us to relax and move gently toward what scares us. The key is to stay with emotional distress without tightening into aversion, allowing fear to soften us rather than harden into resistance (Chödrön, 2001).

Our approach to self-compassion, based on the work of Kristin Neff (2015), encompasses:
– Self-kindness: Being warm and understanding towards ourselves when we suffer.
– Common humanity: Recognizing that suffering and setbacks are part of the shared human experience.
– Mindfulness: Maintaining a nonjudgmental, receptive mindset where we observe thoughts and feelings as they are, without trying to suppress, deny, or change them.

In addition, we emphasize and practice compassion for others, based on the work of Brown (2021). This encompasses the daily practice of recognizing and accepting our shared humanity, treating ourselves and others with loving-kindness, and taking action in the face of suffering.

Through discussions, workshops, and contemplative exercises, participants learn to embrace impermanence – the idea that everything is in a state of constant change. This understanding leads to greater compassion for oneself and others and provides insight into our unconscious assumptions and competing commitments that no longer serve a purpose. Competing commitments are a form of self-protection, shielding us from deeply rooted beliefs about ourselves and the world (Kegan & Lahey, 2009).

The transformational journey toward greater compassion unfolds as an opening process of our hearts, minds, and will to a new level of wisdom and deeper acceptance of life's impermanent nature (Cosley, McCoy, & Saslow, 2010). Through our continuous efforts at IDG Switzerland, we help individuals integrate these practices, fostering a more compassionate and wise approach to life.

Freedom: Embracing letting go, cutting off, and unlearning

Letting go of attachment, particularly attachment to the outcomes of our actions, helps us find stability within chaos. This stability allows us to look deeply into our essence to find freedom and, consequently, happiness (Freeman & Taylor, 2020).

Participants explored their conditioned beliefs, societal constructs, and personal limitations. This process of deconditioning paved the way for authentic self-expression and a sense of liberation. We found ourselves shedding layers of preconceived notions, making space for new perspectives and a profound sense of inner freedom.

This journey toward freedom is intrinsically linked to sustainability. As we let go of limiting beliefs and attachments, we become more mindful of our actions and their impacts on the world around us. By embracing a mindset of freedom, we foster a deeper connection with nature and a commitment to sustainable living. Unlearning harmful habits and societal constructs enables us to adopt practices that support the well-being of the planet and future generations.

Through this journey, we embrace the process of unlearning, which is crucial for true freedom and sustainability. By letting go of ingrained habits and thoughts, we open ourselves to new possibilities and a deeper understanding of ourselves and our potential. This continuous practice at IDG Switzerland fosters a liberated mindset, enabling us to navigate life with a renewed sense of clarity and purpose while contributing to a more sustainable and equitable world.

The pond of relating, collaborating, and acting: Me, us, and the action

The organization of the Swiss IDG Hub transcends traditional hierarchical models, emphasizing shared responsibility, deep connection, and a shared purpose. Anchored in our commitment to embodying the qualities of presence, wisdom, and freedom, they ignite a shared vision of relating, collaborating, and acting together.

In this dynamic approach, leadership is distributed across the group, allowing for the harnessing of collective intelligence, creativity, and decision making. Through active engagement, open dialogue, and a commitment to our common goal, we have a sense of ownership and empowerment among all participants, resulting in a stronger, more cohesive community.

Crafting our collaborative space

Central to collective leadership is the idea of establishing a space for collaboration. This idea revolves around setting up a space that encourages open conversations, values diverse perspectives, and empowers individuals to share their unique thoughts and ideas (Isaacs, 1999).

This collaborative space serves as a fertile ground for numerous positive outcomes. It's akin to a garden where the flowers of creativity and teamwork flourish (Block, 2009). When individuals feel comfortable expressing themselves and are motivated to listen to one another, it becomes much easier to generate innovative solutions to complex challenges. Additionally, this shared space fosters a sense of belonging and purpose among participants, creating a shared identity that transcends individual contributions.

Our approach to crafting this collaborative space revolves around several fundamental principles. First and foremost, we prioritize the authenticity of each person. We believe that staying true to oneself is a crucial aspect of effective collaboration. Furthermore, we place a strong emphasis on active and empathetic listening. By truly understanding different perspectives, we can work collaboratively and effectively. Additionally, we encourage spontaneous and unrestrained expression of thoughts, unburdened by preconceived notions or rigid guidelines (Brown & Isaacs, 2005).

Another essential element is the practice of staying present in the moment. This helps prevent getting bogged down in past experiences or future uncertainties, allowing us to engage more constructively in discussions. Simultaneously, we recognize the importance of collective unity (Senge, 1990). By acknowledging our shared purpose and common goals, we harness the power of synergy to drive meaningful change.

Transitioning from discussions to actions, we bring our collective energy and focus to the task at hand. We establish clear objectives and remain dedicated even when faced with challenges. To ensure inclusivity and equal participation, we adopt a circular seating arrangement during discussions. The symbolism of the "empty chair" encourages fresh perspectives and open dialogue. Incorporating nature into our meetings also contributes to a sense of tranquility and interconnectedness (Wheatley, 2006).

In essence, creating a collaborative space serves as the cornerstone of our collective leadership approach. It's within this space that ideas are transformed into actionable plans, and where individuals work in harmony to create positive impacts. Much like tending to a garden, this space nurtures the seeds of cooperation and understanding, enabling them to grow into strong, vibrant contributions that benefit the entire collective.

The core elements of our collective space in summary (see Figure 19.4):

1. The **self**: grounded in the qualities of presence, wisdom, and freedom, as explained earlier.
   a. **Deep listening**: actively and empathetically engaging in conversations, understanding others' perspectives without interrupting or judging.
   b. **No pre-cooked thoughts**: encouraging spontaneous, original ideas rather than relying on predetermined notions.
   c. **Stay with what is present**: focusing on the current moment, avoiding getting lost in past experiences or future uncertainties during discussions.
2. The **we**: acknowledging the collective identity and unity of the group, transcending individual contributions.
   a. **Connection**: establishing and nurturing meaningful relationships and bonds among participants.
   b. **Intention**: approaching discussions and actions with clear purpose and objectives in mind.
   c. **Reflection**: taking time to contemplate and evaluate experiences, discussions, and outcomes to facilitate continuous improvement.

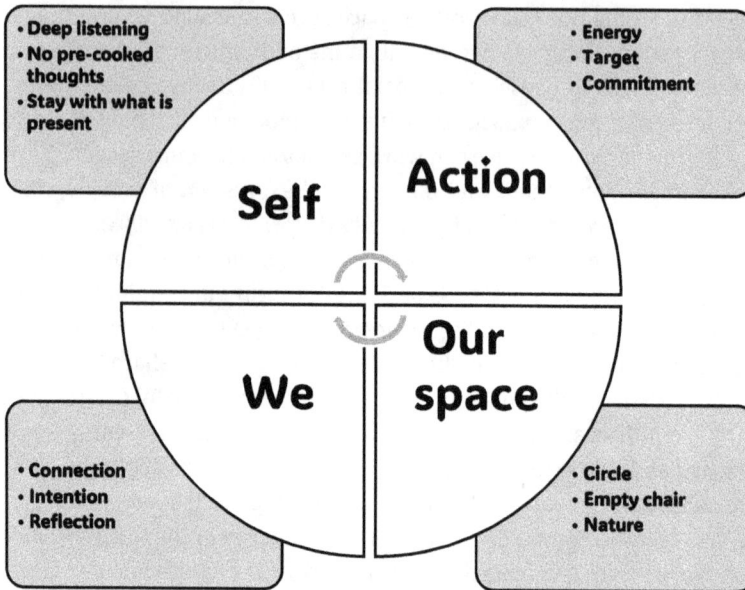

Figure 19.4: Core elements of our collaborative space (Source: Authors' own).

3. The **action**: shifting from discussions to tangible efforts, implementing plans to bring about change.

   a. **Energy**: infusing passion, enthusiasm, and commitment into the collective efforts.

   b. **Target**: connecting with our purpose as a flame that is up to the collective to keep alive.

   c. **Commitment**: "Energy flows where attention goes." To play on our strengths and to boost the collective energy of each individual.

4. Our **space**: the environment in which interactions occur, both physically and energetically.

   a. **Circle**: arranging seating in a circular format to promote inclusivity, equal participation, and open communication.

   b. **Empty chair**: symbolizing the welcome for fresh perspectives and the acknowledgment of voices yet to be heard.

   c. **Nature**: incorporating natural elements into the space, such as plants or natural lighting, to foster tranquility and connection with the environment.

In essence, crafting a collaborative space is the cornerstone of our collective leadership approach. It is within this space that ideas metamorphose into actionable plans, and where individuals engage in an emergent, dynamic flow, catalyzing positive impacts.

In brief: Our vision and future

Our journey has led us to adopt the institutionalization strategy (see figure 19.5) of IDG Global in order to pursue the IDG Switzerland Centre, a vision we have held since the inception of the Swiss IDG Hub. This strategy focuses on creating a coalition, defining a strategic plan based on ecosystem, upskilling, research, and policy advocacy, and seeking funders to ensure sustainability. Our aim is to democratize transformation literacy for sustainable development in Switzerland, working in collaboration with partners across sectors and the Swiss IDG community.

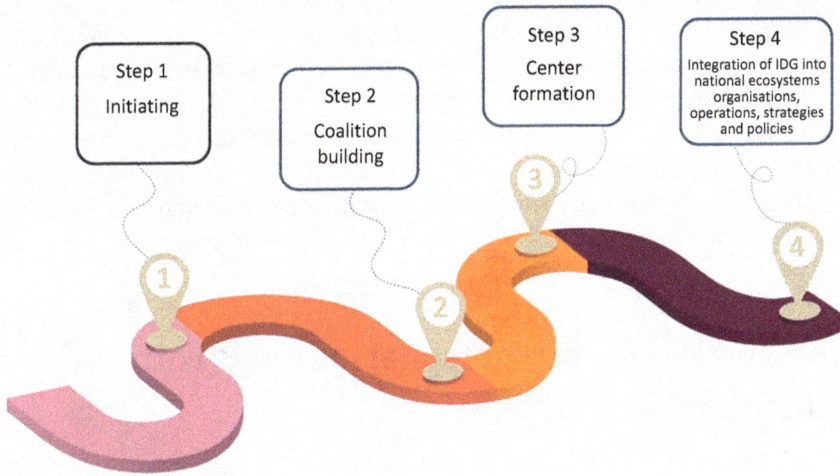

Figure 19.5: IDG Global's institutionalization strategy of minimal viable ecosystems for inner development and human flourishing. Source: Inner Development Goals. (Retrieved from www.innerdevelopmentgoals. org).

The problem we are solving

Despite its wealth and technological advancement, Switzerland struggles to meet the United Nations Sustainable Development Goals (SDGs). Systemic conformity, outdated economic paradigms, reactive response patterns, extrinsic and non-holistic perspectives, and a lack of eco-systemic consciousness hinder progress. While a mindset shift towards more conscious and relational ways of being, thinking, communicating, collaborating, and acting is emerging at the individual level, organizations and systems lag behind, impeding the necessary reshaping of narratives and actions for sustainable development.

The challenging road to funding

Since our inception in 2021, we have closely aligned our efforts with IDG Global's institutionalization strategy, particularly focusing on the minimal viable ecosystems for inner development and human flourishing approach. Over several months, we developed and meticulously refined a robust concept, which we submitted to a major Swiss philanthropic fund – a potential key partner – in July 2024.

The evaluation process was rigorous, with each step bringing us closer to realizing our vision. We successfully navigated the first three phases, and although the funder expressed appreciation for our concept, experience, and dedication, they ultimately decided not to move forward with our proposal.

While the outcome wasn't what we had hoped for, we look back on our progress with a sense of gratitude, recognizing the valuable lessons learned and the opportunities that have emerged. As we move forward, we remain hopeful and deeply committed to advancing the mission of IDG Switzerland, now equipped with new insights and a clearer vision for the future.

In the following sections, we will share our personal impressions of the country center concept, our key learnings, and our vision for the road ahead.

Mud and lotus – our personal journeys with IDG Switzerland

Mauricio

The first time I learned about the IDGs in the summer of 2021, I was very excited. Here was a powerful framework that connected various insights I had gained through adult development, supported by academics I admired, to address sustainability, the major challenge of our time. The idea of integrating personal growth with societal change through IDGs felt incredibly promising and aligned with my aspirations. At the time, I was part of a large pharmaceutical multinational, feeling disconnected from my purpose and my community. The movement emerged as an exciting part of my discovery journey, and I jumped at the opportunity.

Setting up IDG Switzerland has been a journey of deep personal growth and incredible connection. From the outset, I found myself growing alongside our community. As I navigated the complexities of building a self-managed, grassroots movement in Switzerland, I embarked on a parallel journey of self-discovery. Our core team developed and evolved, embracing increasing complexity in our work. Each of us navigated this complexity in unique ways, contributing our strengths and learning from each other.

One of the biggest questions that emerged was whether we should move forward with more intention or allow the natural emergence of opportunities, ideas, and direction to guide us. This tension between structured planning and organic growth became a central theme of our collective journey. Our core team grew rapidly, but this also led some to feel they could no longer contribute. Bridging the initial excitement of new volunteers into real commitment to drive action proved more complex than I had anticipated. On the other hand, navigating the decentralized and self-organized hubs within a global movement presented its own set of challenges. Despite these challenges, the support from our partners, particularly Impact Hub Basel, has been invaluable. They believed in us from the very beginning, providing infrastructure, support, and ideas that have been crucial to our progress.

Balancing the demands of a nascent movement with my personal and professional life brought both complexity and growth. The blurred lines between volunteer work and personal time tested my limits and highlighted the importance of setting clear boundaries. Although financial instability was a reality after leaving corporate life, the drive and passion I found through my work with IDG Switzerland has been deeply rewarding. This journey has taught me resilience, the value of maintaining focus amidst evolving challenges, and the importance of trusting the unfolding process.

Throughout this journey, I have learned the importance of radical transparency and setting clear boundaries for my personal commitment. It has been essential to understand how far my volunteer work can go and what I need to sustain it both energetically and economically. Balancing these aspects has been a continuous learning process.

Reflecting on this journey, I am deeply grateful. Establishing IDG Switzerland and contributing to the IDG movement globally has become an integral part of my self-discovery journey, providing invaluable lessons and experiences. It has taught me the importance of community and the need for both intention and flexibility in pursuing our goals.

As we continue to advance the mission of the IDGs globally and in Switzerland, I remain hopeful, committed, and driven by the mission of the movement. I am excited to see how our efforts will continue to shape a more sustainable and conscious world.

Lutz

I am absolutely amazed by the richness of my IDG Switzerland journey! So much connection and energy, respect and appreciation, inspiration and creativity, co-creation and collaboration, passion and spirituality, so many memorable encounters and gatherings with people caring about and for more sustainable lives, collectives, and societies – I am deeply grateful for the experience.

Purpose, emergence, co-creation, co-leadership, connection, and mindfulness stand out for me in the inner process of creating IDG Switzerland together with Mauricio and Eleftheria, but also with the other team members at earlier stages whom I dearly thank for their presence, passionate engagement, professionalism, honesty, and friendship.

I find it stunning that a group of people inspired by and committed to a big idea (the IDG vision, i.e., catalyzing SDG achievement with the IDGs) can build such a positive groove and resonance! The purpose, even though it differed a bit from person to person, was so strong that it ignited passion and energy in us over and over again. Purposeful communication and news from IDG Global was a significant support, not to mention the actual existence of the IDGs, the emerging global movement around them, and the development of the whole.

Emergence became a principle we soon acted upon, and it helped us a lot to take action. Like professional improvisers, we were open to ideas, opportunities, and energies that showed up in us, trusting and following them (although rather raw) to keep the momentum, refining what needed to be refined on the go. Quite creative, rewarding, and fun. This powerful approach isn't suitable for everyone though, and it caused difficulties in the team.

Co-creation and co-leadership were further guiding principles and energies. In the core team, we reached an amazingly high level of it, creating and leading upon our individual competencies as the various situations or projects at hand required, deeply respecting and trusting each other, and letting each other shine (as the professional improviser would on stage). Self-leadership and self-organization were important parts of it.

Finally, connection and mindfulness. Our individual and collective practices in the team, but also with our community (in gatherings, events, etc.), made a true difference – when you start meeting with a sequence of appreciation, caring, sharing, or silence, for example, whatever follows happens in a more connected and mindful space and energy, leading to better experiences and results.

Eleftheria

Who am I, or rather, who was I when I first joined the IDG hub in Basel and who have I become 15 months later?

I am someone who mainly works online, spending long hours in front of my computer. As my life has largely been shared between my home office and various assignments abroad, I had never really cultivated a network of friends and acquaintances locally. When I joined the IDG hub in Basel, I was seeking a community – people with whom I could do nice things, share ideas, and simply enjoy lunch together. As my academic background is in spirituality in management, I jumped at the opportunity to attend my first IDG workshop at Impact Hub Basel. I loved the framework, particularly because it included the "being" dimension. By acknowledging the existence of a deeper sense of being – which may not be easily visible or measurable – it placed *being* to the limelight and made it an essential component of impact and systemic transformation. I felt a sense of relief being around other people to whom I didn't have to explain that spirituality, while inherent in religion, is not synonymous with it; and that spirituality is far from being a "spooky term" linked to supernatural powers.

During the first community gathering, I was amazed by the diversity of the personalities who were there. All very interesting, with their own story and, like me, seemed to be seeking a refuge where they could express themselves freely and take a break from the pressures of their professional lives, their materialistic goals, or their mind chatter. I also felt this deep inner *freedom*. I didn't need to explain anything. I was there, curious to listen, learn, and exchange, and looking forward to our common lunch. No expectations, no performance indicators hanging over me.

As time went by, a few of us decided to get more closely involved in the IDG hub. This marked the beginning of a new phase; that of a social start-up aspiring to function as a self-managed organization, even though our mission wasn't fully clarified. This phase was markedly different from the initial one. We now needed to bring our diverse skills together, collaborate harmoniously, and co-create. Easier said than done! This was a moment of truth as challenges with time management, use of digital tools, commitment and accountability, resource constraints, and diverse personal aspirations emerged. We were all passionate about the IDGs; we believed in the potential of the movement to realize the SDGs and we all wanted to create tangible impact. Yet, we found ourselves grappling with coordination issues and decision-making inefficiencies. At times, it felt like we were chasing our tails. This stage was the most challenging for me but also the most enriching. It taught me *wisdom*. I learned to listen with intention, practice non-judgement, and accept different perspectives and values. I became less fixated on goals and more willing to simply be present in our meetings, open to whatever might emerge from our interactions. I learned to navigate ambiguity with equanimity.

The third stage began when Mauricio, Lutz, and I decided to move on with the idea of an IDG country center. Why did I decide to join forces with them? What guided me? At this stage in my life, I am driven by purpose. The idea of a country center resonated with me deeply. Establishing an IDG country center would be a unique opportunity to make an impact on a scale we had never experienced before, both as individuals and as professionals working with others. It would enable us to influence the larger discourse and decision-making processes across broader systems and structures; to shift the narrative from above. The entire process demanded self-discipline, dedication, and countless hours of work. Filling out a business model canvas proved challenging. Although I have helped many entrepreneurs and start-up founders complete their business model canvas and refine their value proposition, I found this one particularly difficult. I suppose it was because I was so closely involved that I couldn't be detached from it. The language each of us used was so different that I feared we would get lost in translation. However, through this exercise, I learned to appreciate the diverse talents of Mauricio and Lutz. They focused on aspects I never would have and asked questions I never would have thought to ask. All I had to do was to *be present* – listening and trying to understand, communicating and trying to be understood. In our collaboration, Mauricio proved to be an indefatigable, agile innovator, with an incredible capacity to use his left and right brain simultaneously at high speed. Lutz, much like a master chess player, demonstrated a refined capacity to put himself in others' shoes, sensing their feelings and perspectives, and addressing their questions before they were even voiced.

Who have I become? Going through this transformative journey, I have gained greater clarity about who I am, the skillsets I bring, and the qualities I value in others. I have also become more open to express vulnerability and imperfection and more empowered by witnessing the grace with which many of our team members navigated their personal challenges. What has left the deepest mark on me, though, is the realization that there are many people around me who, like me, burn to do good and that by joining forces we can truly make a difference.

I feel fortunate to have embarked on this adventure with these beautiful human beings and I look forward to continuing our journey of co-creation with the IDGs in Switzerland!

Conclusion

Through the lens of the lotus flower, our collective journey unfolds. We began amidst the metaphorical mud of probing questions as individuals, coalescing through deep introspection to unearth our shared purpose. Gradually, we unfurled our individual petals, delving into the realms of presence, wisdom, and freedom. These qualities, amalgamating both being and thinking, formed the bedrock of our collective leadership ethos.

Within our collaborative space, we embodied the principles of open dialogue, diverse perspectives, and authentic self-expression. This is never easy and we faced many challenging moments where some community members had decided to step down. The key to keep going was our hope and connection to the principles of presence, wisdom, and freedom. Here, the seeds of creativity and teamwork found fertile ground, yielding effortless action and a sense of belonging that surpassed individual contributions.

As we reflect upon our journey, besides the difficulties, we recognize the pivotal role of inner development in harmonizing our values, actions, and aspirations with global sustainability objectives, and our dedication to nurturing self-awareness, compassion, systemic understanding, and the audacity to unlearn and navigate the unknown and setbacks. This approach empowers each of us to engage and keep contributing with our passion, time, and energy towards impactful changes in systems, organizations, communities, and individuals, contributing to a more sustainable future (see Figure 19.6).

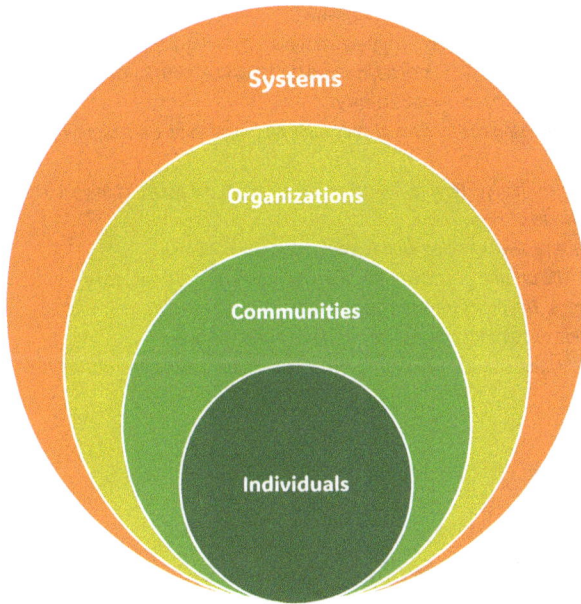

Figure 19.6: Four different levels of impact (Source: Authors' own).

As we continue our own journey with resiliency and optimism, we encourage you to join your IDG country center, if it exists. Otherwise, connect with other passionate individuals by joining or creating an IDG hub where you live. Start building a cross-sector coalition and work towards clarifying your strategy to gain broad support and eventually establish a center. What's stopping you from getting started?

References

Block, P. (2009). *Community: The structure of belonging*. Berrett-Koehler Publishers.

Brown, B. (2021). *Atlas of the heart*. Random House.

Brown, P. & Isaacs, D. (2005). *The world café: Shaping our futures through conversations that matter*. Berrett-Koehler Publishers.

Brown, K. W. & Ryan, R. M. (2003). The benefits of being present: Mindfulness and its role in psychological well-being. *Journal of Personality and Social Psychology, 84*(4), 822–848. https://doi.org/10.1037/0022-3514.84.4.822

Chödrön, P. (2001). *The places that scare you: A guide to fearlessness*. Shambhala Publications.

Cosley, B., McCoy, S., & Saslow, S. (2010). Is compassion for others stress buffering? Consequences of compassion and social support for physiological reactivity to stress. *Journal of Experimental Social Psychology, 46*(5), 816–823. https://doi.org/10.1016/j.jesp.2010.04.008

Dethmer, J., Chapman, D., & Klemp, K. (2015). *The 15 commitments of conscious leadership: A new paradigm for sustainable success.* Conscious Leadership Group.

Freeman, R. & Taylor, M. (2020). *When love comes to light.* Self-published.

Hudetz, J. A. (2012). Anesthetic-induced unconsciousness: Insights from a study of intracranial electrophysiology. *Anesthesiology, 116*(2), 253–255. https://doi.org/10.1097/ALN.0b013e318242a0c5

Isaacs, W. (1999). *Dialogue and the art of thinking together.* Currency.

Kabat-Zinn, J. (1990). *Full catastrophe living: Using the wisdom of your body and mind to face stress, pain, and illness.* Bantam.

Kegan, R. & Lahey, L. L. (2009). *Immunity to change: How to overcome it and unlock the potential in yourself and your organization.* Harvard Business Press.

Neff, K. (2015). *Self-compassion: The proven power of being kind to yourself.* HarperCollins.

Senge, P. M. (1990). *The Fifth Discipline: The art and practice of the learning organization.* Doubleday.

Thích Nhất Hạnh. (2014). *No mud, no lotus: The art of transforming suffering.* Parallax Press.

Tolle, E. (2004). *The power of now: A guide to spiritual enlightenment.* New World Library.

Wheatley, M. J. (2006). *Leadership and the new science: Discovering order in a chaotic world.* Berrett-Koehler Publishers.

Carlos Largacha-Martinez

Chapter 20
How to unravel the IDGs' skills in practice: Making the IDGs work in Colombia

Abstract: The Inner Development Goals (IDGs) global movement operates in a diverse world with varying worldviews, cultures, and traditions, presenting a significant challenge in managing this diversity. This challenge is particularly pronounced in Colombia, where a unique paradigm of nonlinearity and hybridity exists, differing from the more linear and scientific viewpoints prevalent in the Global North. Understanding Colombia's cultural landscape is vital for better assimilating and implementing the IDGs. However, cultural differences often intersect with institutional realities, making it challenging to discern the nature of the business one is dealing with. Tools such as the Lewis triangle or Hofstede's country comparison tool can offer a preliminary understanding of where organizations stand culturally and historically. Additionally, assessing an organization's stage of development necessitates methods such as the B Impact Assessment, the Humanistic Management Center's three stepped approach, or Laloux's Reinventing Organizations approach – to name just a few. The IDG Colombia Centre, established in 2021, comprises six thematic hubs representing collective efforts to drive meaningful actions. Soft skills play a critical role in humanistic management, enabling leaders to inspire and guide effectively while understanding the IDGs through Colombia's distinctive worldview. In this chapter, we propose a reverse engineering approach that could help navigate into these challenges and give light to understand better the 23 IDG skills and the 29 IDG methodologies present at the IDG Toolkit. Instead of asking the two-phase question process done by the IDGs, we asked directly to two acclaimed Colombian companies – the future we want after using the IDGs – how they perceived and internalized their skills/methodologies. What skills they had or had developed to achieve such a humane company? And which methodologies they used or developed to make it real? We hope this will provide valuable insights and inspiration for other IDG hubs worldwide.

Keywords: humanistic management, intercultural leadership, Colombia, diversity, culture

Introduction

The IDG global movement faces a compelling challenge in managing its diversity, encompassing a myriad of people, worldviews, and cultures. This diversity is particularly evident in Colombia, reflecting the intricate tapestry of global perspectives

The original version of this chapter was revised. Unfortunately, the author Carlos Largacha-Martinez was misspelled in the original publication. This has been corrected. We apologize for the mistake.
https://doi.org/10.1515/9783111453729-021

within the movement. This chapter aims to explore ideas, experiences, and cultural-historical realities that can shape the future trajectory of the IDG Colombia Centre, both internally and in its interactions beyond borders.

As we navigate this discourse, it becomes apparent that Colombia and Latin America embody a unique paradigm characterized by nonlinearity and hybridity, in contrast to the more linear and scientific worldview prevalent in the Global North. Thus, this chapter serves as a platform for deliberation on how to infuse the IDGs with a hybrid approach tailored to the context of Colombia and Latin America. It proposes fostering dialogue between nations such as Sweden and Colombia to analyze and adapt each of the 23 skills, as advocated by Garcia-Canclini (1995), to the realities of our organizational landscapes. Despite the pervasive influence of capitalism, which has permeated businesses worldwide, there remains ample room for embracing diversity and nurturing distinct perspectives.

This chapter unfolds in three parts. Firstly, it delves into Colombia's cultural reality and offers insights into understanding the IDGs through our unique worldview. It underscores the challenges and significance of cultivating soft skills, essential for humanistic managers seeking to inspire and lead effectively. Secondly, it examines an ongoing research initiative exploring how acclaimed Colombian companies perceive and could internalize the IDGs. Finally, it reflects on the evolution of the IDG Colombia Centre since its inception in 2021, highlighting the culmination of two years' worth of discussions aimed at leveraging volunteer energy for positive change. As of 2024, the center boasts six thematic hubs, which serve as testaments to our collective efforts in driving impactful actions. It is our aspiration that the experiences, insights, and developments documented herein will not only benefit the IDG Colombia Centre but also inspire and inform other IDG hubs worldwide.

Colombia and its IDG context

From a sociological perspective, it is difficult to define a culture, since there will be always so-called subcultures from that *thing* being analyzed; be it a country, a nation, a workplace, and so forth. Then, trying to understand Colombia culturally and historically in order to better interiorize and implement the IDGs is a conundrum – in any country or nation in the world, it is a global reality. Clearly there are marked differences between a Colombian and a Swedish person, like there are differences between a Colombian from the capital than from the Atlantic coast, or the Pacific coast, or the flatlands. Hence, we have to acknowledge them. A good start could be using the Lewis triangle[1] or Hofstede's country comparison tool.[2] Those will give a first glimpse of where we are located, culturally and historically. However, there is another big challenge for the IDGs. The majority of those differences are crisscrossed with the institutional reality – the organization. And as Jim Collins (2001) stated, 95% of the organizations continue to manage themselves using Theory X (traditional management). You have organizational differences all over the world, but traditional management is a strong force of *homogenization*. Thus, we need to deal with the cultural reality from the country or region, plus the cultural realities of the organizations of that cultural reality. Both ought to be taken into account to have a better assessment of what kind of *business* we are dealing with. And within the corporate culture, we need to assess in which "stage" they are. Either using the B Impact Assessment (BIA),[3] the Humanistic Management Center's three stepped approach,[4] or Laloux's Reinventing Organizations approach,[5] we need to better understand the organization/business/corporation before starting implementing the IDGs. And we could go more specific, analyzing the size of the organization, the clients, etc.

This being said, how are we, Colombians? Is there anything specific about us that it is important to be taken into account *before* spreading the word of the IDGs? Although Colombia is different from other Latin American countries, starting from there is a good strategy. Fuentes (2000), DaMatta (1991), Garcia-Canclini (1995), and Fals-Borda (1968) can help us in these endeavors. For example, Carlos Fuentes captured it in the early pages of his journey through the history of America when he wrote, *far too often, we have sought or imposed models of development with little connection to our cultural reality* (2000, p. 15). In *The Buried Mirror*, Fuentes (2000) portrays numerous facets of the history of Latin America that are clear examples of the ineffectiveness of such "importation". Additionally, the writings of Roberto DaMatta help to further understand this reality. In excerpts from his famous *Você sabe com quem está falando? (Do you know who you're talking to?)*, DaMatta (1991) presents a dialectical approach to describe the differences between individual and person. DaMatta considers that for Western scholars, the individual is a "thing", natural and life-

---

1 For more on the Lewis Triangle, visit: https://en.empowerment-coaching.com/post/cultural-types-the-lewis-model

2 For more on the Hoefstede country comparison, the reader can visit this link, and compare up to four countries per view: www.hofstede-insights.com/country-comparison-tool

3 This is a free tool developed by the B-Lab. You can visit this link, and make sure before using the B-Evaluation to select the proper language, since questions vary depending on the region: www.bcorporation.net/en-us/programs-and-tools/b-impact-assessment/

4 The HMN developed this framework which is the one in order to select the best business cases in the world, in their books 'Humanistic Management in Practice', vol 1 and 2. You can learn more about this framework in this link: http://www.humanisticmanagement.org/cgi-bin/adframe/about_humanistic_management/the_three_stepped_approach_to_humanistic_management/index.html

5 As an interesting analysis of 12 business cases in the world, you can learn more in this link: https://www.reinventingorganizations.com/resources.html

less, while for Brazilians, the individual cannot be separated from the person, or what he calls the socio-individual phenomenon. Although his ideas are framed within the Brazilian reality, one could venture to think that they might be applicable to many countries and Latin American realities. There is then a process of social construction of the individual, which DaMatta calls "person", that occurs when cultures, values, and rituals "penetrate" the individual, turning them into something socially significant. We are dealing here with persons, not individuals, with multi-active persons, not with linear-active individuals – using Lewis' approach, for example. Then, the IDG Colombia Centre must be knowledgeable of this reality.

For DaMatta (1991), when it comes to the individual, "the part is more important than the whole", which tacitly implies a subordination of the individual to the system. In the case of the person, however, the whole can only exist, and can only be constituted by the complementarity of the parts. Thus, instead of society encompassing the individual, as is the case in the Western world, here in Latin America and the Caribbean, the person encompasses society (DaMatta, 1991). This approach to the reality of the human being allows us to visualize the capacity that we, as individuals, have to create, recreate, and renegotiate our existence, which continuously shapes and changes the Latin American societies in which we live. It is clear that the individual bases their reality and their lived world on functionalist positions, while the person does so on postmodern positions. However, the assimilation and acculturation of Latin American and Caribbean peoples by Western cultures is a reality, but it will never be total or complete, and it seems that even we ourselves do not fully understand or grasp this concept.

That is why human beings from the "Third World" begin to be unreadable and nebulous for modernist prisms (Escobar, 1995), implying serious problems for proposing solutions. Additionally, assuming a narrow view of development, that is, without addressing it as a social process (Cardoso & Faletto, 1979), it is thought that not understanding people is not so serious since development will be primarily implemented in institutions composed of "individuals". These institutions are understood as universal and natural. This is part of the aforementioned challenge for the IDGs as a global institution. How to avoid acting in a *universalistic* manner? How to avoid any sort of *neocolonialism* from Europe on the Global South? It should not be surprising, then, that processes directed towards a predefined development do not yield comprehensive results. Therefore, development, nationality, identity, and "being Latin American" must be redefined, and furthermore, they must be complemented with activities that promote the cultural integrity of the human being. The challenge is twofold: first, how to acknowledge these factors at the IDG Colombia Centre, and second, how to navigate the homogenizing influence of traditional management structures on Colombian organizations and businesses.

In this Latin American process of including the whole "persona" into the IDGs, the work by Nobel Laureate Amartya Sen complements the arguments here exposed. In his book *Development as Freedom*, Sen (2000) argues that *[An] integrated approach*

[to development, that is,] one that includes economic, social, and political considera-
tions . . . allows recognizing the role of social values and prevailing customs, which can
influence the freedoms individuals enjoy and have reasons to value[6] (p. 26). To effectively incorporate the social values and customs that Colombians identify with into
the IDG Colombia Centre, there are several options worth considering. Firstly, establishing a dedicated space in Colombia for a culturally sensitive translation of the English version would ensure that terms like "sensemaking" and "inner compass" resonate with the Colombian audience and align with their cultural identity. Another
possibility involves integrating one, two, or three related skills into a single concept
that aligns better with Colombian culture, thereby creating a more cohesive understanding for learners. Furthermore, incorporating additional skills that better reflect
Colombian values and customs can foster stronger connections, whether they complement or replace existing ones. A reverse engineering strategy focused on identifying
emerging skills within the Colombian context could also yield valuable insights.

However, a crucial aspect lies in conducting extensive qualitative research to explore how businesspeople and organizations perceive and interpret the 23 skills.
Focus groups and similar methodologies provide an opportunity to deeply understand
these perspectives and tailor adaptations accordingly, ensuring relevance and appropriateness in the Colombian context. Once the skills have been adapted and translated, facilitating an easy and manageable interiorization process for businesses and
organizations becomes essential, promoting gradual adoption and practice to help
users fully embrace the new skill set and apply it meaningfully within their unique
cultural context. Legitimizing what was presented, Gabriel García Márquez (1998)
once remarked, *Five centuries later, the descendants of Indigenous and Spaniards still*
do not know who we are. The next paragraph will help the reader better understand
this statement. While addressing Latin-Americans, his words resonate with a distinct
Colombian flavor. Simultaneously, the eminent Colombian sociologist Orlando (1968) -
Borda (1968) delved into the Latin American reality, contending that, "To navigate the
chaos of such a society while preserving one's conscience and investigative role, one
must relinquish narrow perspectives and be prepared to confront what may initially
appear illogical" (p. 191). For instance, concerning the perception of time, Latin-
Americans hold a circular/elliptic view, diverging from the prevailing linear perspective found in many cultures of the Global North (Paz, 2000; Prigogine, 1997). Octavio
Paz (2000) therefore contends that for us, "Time no longer unfolds as a mere succes-
sion but reverts to its original essence—a present wherein the past and future find
ultimate reconciliation" (p. 52).

This elucidates why Garcia-Canclini (1995) discusses "hybrid cultures" and Paz
delves into the concept of the "double influence", both alluding to our intricate Indige-
nous/Hispanic reality and heritage. Thus, we embody a state of non-logic, nonlinear-

---

6 Translated from the Spanish version by the author of this chapter.

ity, and hybridity. Paz (2000) eloquently expresses, "Similar to how an Aztec pyramid may at times conceal an older structure, religious unification merely touched the surface of consciousness, leaving primitive beliefs unaltered" (p. 102). Perhaps this insight clarifies why the distinguished historian David Bushnell (1993) subtitled his book on Colombia as *A Nation in Spite of Itself*. Perhaps what we require in Latin America, specifically at the IDG Colombia Centre, is a hybrid IDG toolkit. One that integrates the perspective of inner development from the Global North, harmonized/hybridized with the vision of *transformación del ser*[7] from Colombia – acknowledging that addressing the Global South as a whole is a task that the IDG, as a global movement, should undertake in the future.

Before delving into the discoveries from studying two humanistically managed companies and interviewing three top executives about the skills they applied to achieve outstanding results, and subsequently comparing them to the IDG 23 skills, let's quickly review Latin American leadership styles. This will provide insights for the development of a future *hybridized* IDG toolkit tailored to Colombia. Enrique Ogliastri stands out as one of the foremost scholars in this field. It is noteworthy that he conducted two investigations at different points in time, one in 1999 and the other in 2015, both based on the GLOBE studies. These studies revealed enduring commonalities in Latin American values concerning leadership styles (Ogliastri et al., 1999), indicating minimal change by 2015 (Castano et al., 2015). The findings consistently point to three prevalent patterns rooted in our historical reality: paternalistic leadership, hierarchical leadership, autocratic styles, legalistic imageries, and social bonds (Castano et al., 2015). A significant part of these patterns can be traced back to the Spanish *hacienda* inheritance, as well as the worldview brought by invaders regarding kingship and elitism. Additionally, they are linked to the importance placed on social relations and family, partly explained by our Catholic milieu (Castano et ál., 2015).

An important structural aspect that poses a challenge to any discourse on management is the prevalence of informal firms, where informality refers to businesses lacking all legal and social benefits for employees. This phenomenon accounts for 40–50% of businesses (as cited by Castano et al., 2015). In some newly developed regions in Colombia, this figure rises to 70–80%.[8] The GLOBE analysis conducted by the Castano-Ogliastri team revealed that "several attributes reflecting inspirational and visionary leadership (first-order CLTs) were identified as contributing to outstanding

---

7 At the IDG Colombia Centre, within the steering committee, where two to three people represent one of the six IDG Colombia hubs, we did a survey about the best way to translate IDG. More than 50% voted for ODIs, Objetivos de Desarrollo Interior. However, the "other 50%" talk about other options that, for me, were more "culturally sensitive" like "transformación del ser", which ChatGPT translated as *'transformation of the self'* vis-a-vis inner development. There is a lot of debate about the use of "development", either from the neocolonialist scholars, but also from the psychologists, against a Jungian view of child development.

8 This is an empirical data based on research done by the author in the Uraba region in Colombia.

leadership in all Latin American countries" (Castano et al., 2015, p. 588). Given that these traits remained consistent over the 15 years between both studies, it is pertinent to reference the findings from the 1999 study where Ogliastri et al. discovered:

> *Both the description of their culture and the preference for certain values were measured. Latin American managers expressed the following cultural values: a) Latin America lives in a situation of high uncertainty with very little control over unexpected events, but it is one of the regions of the world that would most prefer to avoid uncertainty; b) they are societies with elitist values, but very strongly would like this to decrease; c) the values of family collectivism and loyalty to the group are among the highest in the world, and also the preference for it to remain so; d) they are individualistic societies, but there is a great desire for the common good to prevail over individual advantages; e) from companies that are only moderately oriented towards performance, they would like companies that are predominantly oriented towards the achievement of high objectives; f) from societies that discriminate against women, would strongly prefer gender equality; g) from present-oriented societies, they would like cultures more focused on the future; h) they would like to have a society that is a little more humane than the current one, generally located below the international average; i) Latin Americans want to maintain a culture of gentle interpersonal treatment. (1999:29)[9]*

With this Colombian contextualization and some connections to the IDGs, let's delve into an ongoing exploratory research[10] endeavor examining the correlation between successful Colombian business cases and the IDGs. The exploratory hypothesis posits that a purpose-driven organization – whether cognizant of the 23 IDG skills or not – should inherently embody and adopt several of these skills. Essentially, we are engaging in a "reverse process", akin to the initial inquiry of the IDG process.[11] Instead of asking what are the skills to expedite the SDGs, we are questioning *whether encountering an honest, transparent, purpose-driven organization managed with a humanistic approach and conscious capitalist principles would entail the manifestation of several IDG skills in their management practices.* Failure to observe such skills would prompt a reevaluation of the 23 skills, indicating a need for adjustment or enhancement.

IDGs' global challenges

A January 2024 article by *Forbes* declared, "Emotional Intelligence No. 1 Leadership Skill for 2024" (Wells, 2024), citing a World Economic Forum (WEF) report. According to the WEF's *Future of Jobs Report 2023*, qualities associated with emotional intelligence, such as resilience, curiosity, lifelong learning, motivation, and self-awareness,

---

9 Translation from Spanish done by the author of this chapter.
10 A first publication of this ongoing research was made in Largacha-Martinez (2024).
11 For more information about the history of the development of the IDG framework, visit: https://innerdevelopmentgoals.org/about/

are highly valued by businesses and will continue to be crucial for the next few years. Interestingly, this WEF list aligns closely with the IDG 23-plus skills.

The IDGs work in an area with a lot of scientific developments and empirical evidence, however, with a very low interiorization from people and organizations. As appears at the Social Impact Lab website, refering to the IDG, *We lack the inner capacity to deal with our increasingly complex environment and challenges.* With so much knowledge, why this happens, why we agree, like with the SDGs, that there is a *vision of what needs to happen,* but at the same time *progress along this vision has so far been disappointing.*[12] Maybe by reviewing other social aspects a possible answer will emerge. Let's review the "family" and "leadership" topics. The family, as a research topic, has a lot of evidence and theories. However, the results from the family as a social institution are insufficient, to say the least. Divorce rate, bullying, family violence to name just a few, exemplifies this reality. The same could be said about leadership as a research topic. More than 40 years of research in this area has not shown any real improvement in the engagement of workers. Gallup's *State of the Global Workplace* (2024) continues – after more than a decade of research – to show a stagnating picture of only two workers out of ten being engaged at the workplace, worldwide, where "in 2023, global employee engagement stagnated, and overall employee wellbeing declined".[13] A complete failure of traditional management. The list is longer, including the SDGs as well. It seems from this quick review that the challenges are not new, and not only for the IDGs as a social movement. If we had created the FDGs and the LDGs (Family Development Goals; Leadership Development Goals) very likely we would be writing today that *progress along these social topics have so far been disappointing.*

More scientific research or empirical knowledge does not automatically mean a more humane society. We have a misunderstanding between "development" and "being civilized". We think that having driverless cars, quantum computing, and ChatGPT means we are a highly developed society. We have a problem – a social crisis – founded on the myopic and defensive vision, attitudes, and beliefs that society have/apply when dealing with our social challenges. This reality was perfectly captured by *Edward O. Wilson when he said the real problem of humanity is the following: We have Paleolithic emotions, medieval institutions and godlike technology. And it is terrifically dangerous, and it is now approaching a point of crisis overall.* Not to mention that we become highly defensive when the conversation is about emotions, about our *inner self.* Be it in the family, with friends, or with colleagues, we don't want to feel vulnerable. Society – on average – doesn't know how to embrace their vulnerabilities; we live on the Paleolithic inner self with godlike apps, and we have this stance –

---

12 In this link, you can find more information: https://www.socialimpactlab.no/innerdevelopment goals

13 For more detailed information, you can visit Gallup's website: https://www.gallup.com/workplace/349484/state-of-the-global-workplace.aspx

over and over – to solve global warming, poverty, exclusion, middle-school bullying, or disengagement at the workplace, to name just a few.

Here lies one of the biggest challenges for the IDG global movement. Internally and externally, the IDGs have to balance *emotions, institutions, and technology*. We cannot repeat the vicious circle of trying to solve or advance in some social goal with an unharmonious *Paleolithic–godlike* marriage. Where does the solution reside? One approach: within the IDGs itself. By applying intentionally and intensively the 23-plus skills and the 29-plus methodologies – plus all the empirical and culturally inclusive evidence – to the IDG social movement, internally and externally. We don't have to be superwomen to solve this. Let's start with deeply listening to the other, without a defensive attitude, and open to embrace our vulnerabilities. From there, and based on the context, culture, and circumstances, some of the 23-plus skills and 29-plus methodologies will surely help to strengthen the inner growth and group transformation needed. Deeply listening, or *dialogue*, is across a lot of the skills and methodologies. As we know, the IDG framework is holistic and quantic, so it cannot be isolated or clearly measured. That is another challenge, but because of space, we will leave it for another book.

But the IDGs should have started from someplace, and that is great about the 23 skills, as a portfolio to start with. As you will notice later, when the three top executives interviewed for this chapter were presented with the 23 skills, they didn't take to them immediately, neither did they accept each one 100%. It was a mixture and redefinition of the skills based on their experience. In a similar fashion, in a workshop done on a beautiful island in Rwanda in 2022 – as part of the strengthening of the six IDG Global South centers by IDG headquarters – we sat down with three entrepreneurs from Africa and showed them the 23 skills. We were not able to advance a lot, since their personal definitions about any skill didn't match between themselves, neither with the one presented on FieldKit. Hence, as a proposal, the "fourth phase"[14] of the IDG will be to expand the short definitions of the 23 skills and make it more culturally sensitive and context-dependent to each nation-state.

With the Colombian context explained and some "food for thought" about the challenges for the IDGs as a global movement, the next section is about two awarded Colombian companies, and how they relate to the 23-plus skills and methodologies. This will help understand how top executives understand and have interiorized the IDGs, before knowing about them. It is like a reverse social engineering process for the IDGs. Interesting results emerged.

---

14 Here I am referring to the three stages that IDG headquarters defined for the whole process. First stage, answering about the skills to change. Second stage, answering about the methodologies for how to change. Third stage, the global one-question survey. Visit the IDG website and read the FieldKit for a deeper presentation, on these links: https://innerdevelopmentgoals.org/framework/, and https://inner developmentgoals.org/about/resources/

Three Colombian top executives and their reflections on the IDGs

The Humanistic Management Network (HMN) has published two books about great business cases in the world (von Kimakowitz et.al., 2011, 2021). The Management Innovation eXchange (MIX) initiative did some global challenges, and you can find the winners on their Web 2.0 free repositories.[15] These are two good places to search for the kind of business this research needs. Two companies were selected: Views Corp., a Latin American multinational marketing research company, headquarters in Colombia, with more than 15 years of existence, and 150-plus workers in seven countries. This case was published in the Spanish version of the HMN book *Tendencias Gerenciales* (Largacha-Martinez et.al., 2014). The other was Energeticos, a Colombian filial of the Scottish firm Wood, an engineering service firm for the mining and oil industry, with more than 20 years in Colombia, and 40 globally. This case won the Leaders Everywhere Challenge by McKinsey & Harvard Business Review[16] – within eight more inspiring cases. Later on, this case was published in the HMN *Humanistic Management in Practice, Vol. II* book[17] (von Kimakowitz et.al., 2021).

Three top executives were interviewed from these two companies: Daniel Perez, CEO and co-founder of Views Corp., and from Energeticos, Peter King, former CEO, and Juana Cardozo, former engagement and diversity leader. The interviews were conducted via virtual calls, each lasting approximately one hour. The interviews comprised two main parts. Initially, four open-ended questions were posed to gain insights into the "soft skills"[18] perceived by the executives as instrumental in achieving their companies' top-tier, global-class business status. Occasionally, an answer to one question would encompass another, prompting the omission of redundant inquiries. This segment aimed to comprehend the soft skills perceived within themselves and their organizations that contributed to their exemplary business cases.

Subsequently, the second section introduced the IDG framework, allowing the interviewees 1–2 minutes to review the 23 skills without accompanying definitions or descriptions. These interviews took place during the first trimester of 2023, utilizing the English version of the IDG skills as the Spanish version was unavailable at that

---

15 Use the search option on the top-right part of this link if the reader wants to explore more successful *avant-garde* business cases: https://www.managementexchange.com

16 The MIX initiative was created by Gary Hamel from the London Business School, with the support of McKinsey and Management Lab. They created several business challenges. You can find more than 5,000 entries that can help you improve your management practices. For the winners, visit: www.managementexchange.com/blog/announcing-winners-leaders-everywhere-challenge

17 See https://link.springer.com/book/10.1007/978-3-030-51545-4

18 The concept soft skills was used as a proxy for the IDG skills. Further research is needed to understand better this connection. At the IDG Colombia Research HUB we are using three categories: hard skills, soft skills, and inner skills.

time. Notably, all interviews were conducted bilingually. None of the interviewees were previously acquainted with the IDGs, although some introductory information had been provided. Three additional open-ended questions were prepared to explore any potential correlations between the executives' personal/company skills and the IDG skills. As you can see, the fourth question of the first part addresses the systemic part of the organizational success. Achieving a humanistic management approach relies significantly on top-level leadership; however, its long-term success hinges on embedding these principles within the entire workforce – a systemic approach. Without this integration, overall success remains elusive. The questions were:

First part
1. What soft skills do you possess that contributed to the success of the company?
2. How did you acquire these soft skills?
3. Do you have any special methodology to enhance such skills within yourself?
4. Have you developed or structured any methodology to train employees of your company in these skills?

Second part
1. What is your opinion of this model?
2. What correlation do you see with your work life and your skills?
3. What recommendations and ideas do you have regarding this model and its strategy?

While the comprehensive analysis is available in the HMN book, here we offer a brief overview. It's important to note that this is not an attempt at generalization or a scientific study but rather an ongoing qualitative exploration. Firstly, all participants find it challenging to pinpoint how they acquired these soft skills. Interestingly, they are averse to the term "soft skills" and prefer not to be labeled at all. This aversion might stem from their humility regarding their achievements. Peter said, "Honestly, I don't know why [I am the way I am]". Juana stated, "I don't know why Peter hired me, a clinical psychologist . . . . Later, Peter mentioned that what he needed was someone who thinks very differently. He sought diverse perspectives." There are moments in their life that they can relate to, but none of them have one single – *epiphany-like* – moment in their life that can explain why they are the way they are, and why they did what they did. Daniel feels that he wants to positively impact a lot of people, so for him being an entrepreneur was the best path.

What could be seen as a pattern – including other business cases also – is that the context matters a lot. Juana couldn't have done it if it wasn't for Peter, and the corporate culture he created. Peter felt a lot of "freedom" at Energeticos – mainly because he was achieving great financial returns – so he could do "trial and error", his management *mantra*. In his former company, Peter was not even close to his behavior at Energeticos; he sees himself as a barbarian at that time compared at Energeticos –

although he has been always against any human workplace mistreatment. Daniel answers as "it is obvious that I have to do it this way, isn't it?". Daniel wants to show it as "simple", however, he highlights that he learned what not to do in his previous job experiences – not everything, though.

Several thoughts emerge from this short previous analysis. First, there is not a specific, linear, causal model that we can apply to any organization and their top managers, so the end result is a sustainable/humble/transparent IDG-founded company. Big challenge. On the other hand, there are a lot of *IDG ambassadors* out there, already working, but they don't have the "freedom" or the possibility – several reasons – to make the changes needed to instill the IDG skills and consequently make a traditional company into a sustainable, world-class, humanistic one. Another big challenge.

Although Daniel had a difficult experience since one out of four of his employees were stealing, he deeply believed before that *forgiveness* must be on the IDG list. The thieve-workers created a parallel company, and during their formal time, they processed the marketing research, at Views' computers. Daniel and his partner decided to forgive them, and restore their full rights, since they accepted and regretted it. After that, Daniel argues, "communication is key", and always avoiding vengeance. In a short fashion, Daniel states about himself, "I am self-motivated, with internal conviction [resilient, perseverant]. I am centered on values. I am non-vindictive. I am a team player. I am forgiving of others – I deeply resonate with forgiveness." After showing the 23 IDG skills, Daniel commented, "In a way, I mentioned many. I could have used all 23 skills, replacing: *inner compass* is my self-motivation; forgiveness closely aligns with *relating* and all its components. *Thinking* and *acting* is akin to problem solving . . . teaching forgiveness."

The case of Juana is very interesting and enlightening, since Peter was the one making the decisions, but Juana's goal was to achieve them – Juana started without an office, neither a job description nor job title. When asked about how she did it, she commented that her first goal was to observe, just that. How they communicate at Energeticos. Learn. Summarizing the whole process, she commented, "Developing autonomy, freedom in decision making (no hierarchy), and empowering work teams to self-manage. Collective thinking. Interdependence. Adaptation to change, stemming from conviction rather than obligation. Giving myself the opportunity. Listening skills." And when asked about her soft skills, she commented:

- "Observation skills. We're not accustomed to observing, and at first, it saved me. Without judgment. Observing to contribute. Being a therapist helped me."
- "I realized that I struggled to listen. I thought I knew how to listen. I realized this with a manager whom I didn't listen to. I had to understand organizational realities much more."
- "Not judging when different generations of managers expressed themselves."
- "Facilitating conversations between different generations in terms of age and experiences. I developed this skill."

- "Developed the ability to open up possibilities in conversations so that agreements could be reached."
- "Holistic/systemic thinking, not individualistic."
- "Connection of relationship, of context, a way of seeing life."
- "Patience."

We can observe several IDG skills embedded in that list, however, with different names, contexts, and connotations. The pattern after all the interviews is that each one has a particular name for something, and that the 23 IDG skills list becomes a "straightjacket" in the way that I showed. For future interviews, I have to show them as a portfolio for a dialogue, not a comparison, or a correlation, since that made them uneasy. However, they just commented in a very constructive manner. This is even clearer with Juana, that after showing the list to her, she presented in a very personal manner. Similar do Daniel, and the same, shown below, with Peter. To discern overarching systemic patterns from the responses and reflections at Energéticos, I inquired of Juana whether a single term might encapsulate the holistic/systemic nature of the process. She proposed, "Dialogue indeed represents the systemic emergent pattern." This realization brought about significant positive change within the organization. It is important to note that this does not imply every employee at Energéticos possesses a "dialogue-skilled mindset". Rather, fostering such a mentality across the workforce presents an ongoing challenge for management and the IDGs, yet offers substantial potential benefits.

The challenge that we have, then, is that it seems that each leader has their own definition of what the inner development capabilities are. Not only that, when shown to them, at the start, they had different opinions of each skill.[19] Hence, Juana commented:

- "Self-awareness."
- "The cognitive aspect, from where I relate."
- "Relationships, all the time, caring for others as a way of being in the world."
- "Coexistence with others, collaborating. Fritjof Capra's book *The Web of Life*, changed my thinking and values."
- "Acting, creativity we call innovation. Allowing spaces, experiences for others."

As stated, when invited to choose specifically from the list, with that specific name/ label – in her personal Spanish translation – she picked:

- *Apertura y mentalidad de aprendizaje* (Openness and a learning mindset)
- *Integridad y autenticidad* (Integrity and authenticity)

---

19 This is a finding that first emerged during a small workshop done with four African entrepreneurs, done in 2022 in Rwanda. This finding, thus, emerged as well during these three interviews in Colombia.

- *Búsqueda de sentido* (Search for meaning)
- *Empatía y compasión* (Empathy and compassion)
- *Habilidades de cocreación* (Co-creation skills)
- *Valentía* (Courage)

With Peter, as with all: very insightful. His first reaction about which methodology did you use to achieve greatness, he commented, "Getting rid of the crap [bureaucracy]. Stupid things. Why are we spending time on expense reports? It is all bureaucracy." And this has been his thought since he was a young worker at a big oil company in the UK. It is a global epidemic, as was shown by Gary Hamel and Michele Zanini (2016), stating that bureaucracy cost $3 trillion dollars to US economy in 2016.[20] That was his first thought. Since this is a sin of traditional management, at the IDGs we should be thinking why this continues to happen, and which skills are the best to allow people to change bureaucracy and bureaucratic behavior.

When pushing a little bit for Peter to label some soft skills, he commented, "I don't think that I started with a plan." His approach was *trial and error* for three months every time he, Juana, or somebody else present had a "crazy" idea. He had read the book *Maverick*, by Ricardo Semler, and Peter stated that it inspired him a lot. However, when comparing both companies – Semco vis-a-vis Energeticos – you can't find a precise correlation. Again, context, clients, culture, people really matter. Every organization is unique if we want the IDGs to fully emerge. It is really interesting that he just recalled *"horse therapy"* as a key element. Horses do not appear on the IDG FieldKit.[21] Do we need scientific research to put it in, or with all the experiential results should we advise companies to do it? Another challenge for the IDGs as a global movement. Peter joyfully commented, "Horses react to body language, they don't react to emails!"

The second "top of mind" thought for Peter was *justice*. Interestingly enough, it is not a skill from the 23 IDG skills, and it is not easy to put as a causal outcome of the 23, or as part of it, kind of a 24th-ish skill. He recalled himself as an activist during his college years. He stated this way "I am always on the side of the little guy". And he continues with challenging ideas. Continuing with his so-called methodology for organizational change, he added, "Creating chaos to make change. Throwing the *manual* into the bin." This could be a pattern from the great cases at MIX, HMN, and Corporate Rebels: that there is no "to-do-list", no manual, no model, no precise patterns to design a purpose-driven, humanistically managed business. When asked about the IDG 23-skill toolkit, his reactions/comments were:

---

20 Visit Gary Hamel's blog: www.garyhamel.com/blog/3-trillion
21 Visit the IDG Resources to find more: https://innerdevelopmentgoals.org/about/resources/. Visit also: https://drive.google.com/file/d/13fcf9xmYrX9wrsh3PC3aeRDs0rWsWCpA/edit

- *"Integrity.* Because of what is happening in the UK, which you don't expect in leaders. It goes with justice as well. 'Acting on what you said.'"
- *"Critical thinking.* I don't know what it is."
- *"Complexity awareness.* I always try to simplify things."
- *"Appreciation* is important. Appreciating the work that a waiter does at your table. You see too many people look down on some work."
- *"Empathy* is important I think. Again, what is happening in the UK with the new law of refugees. Horrendous, totally horrendous, Against UN declaration, human rights."
- *"Intercultural competence.* Maybe of a lot of places that I have worked."
- *"Trust,* very important: 99.9% all want to do a good job, that is my thought. But the majority of managers think the other way around."
- *"Creativity* more than the others."
- *"Listening* and *communication* are important and linked to *openness* and a learning *mindset."*

Finally, his last words during the interview were also enlightening. Very close to what happened to Henry Mintzberg when he researched all the MBAs in the world – the best ones, Ivy Leagues, and that staff – and he concluded, "Managers not MBAs", which is the title of his great book. So, Peter, in his words, stated:

> I don't have an MBA. Every MBA course that I have looked at, it is too technical. Maybe some about communication. How much of the IDG skills do you see in MBAs? So we should send this [the IDG toolkit] to universities to change the curriculum.

If we want to summarize the three top executives' views about the IDG toolkit, Table 20.1 does just that:

It is not easy to conclude this part of the chapter. The three interviews were very interesting and insightful. However, being ongoing qualitative research, first, it is not over yet, and secondly, it cannot be generalizable. Connecting with real humanistic organizations and understanding how they did it is another way to understand better how to escalate the IDGs globally. An important question that should be raised is: *Are there any insights about how Juana, Peter, and Daniel leveraging their inner skills in service of the collective?* Human development and organizational transformation have been central concerns for over three decades. Among the emerging patterns is the combination of experience and exploration with surrender and openness – a seemingly straightforward yet challenging approach. Allowing ample time for the cultivation and internalization of inner skills among employees is crucial, acknowledging that not everyone will adopt these new competencies. However, the majority often does, as evidenced by the experiences of Juana, Daniel, and Peter. Creating a conducive environment for error is vital, as it encourages genuine exploration and growth. Moreover, fostering openness and addressing one of the most formidable IDG challenges – letting go, surrender, or unlearning – is essential for meaningful change.

Table 20.1: Inner skills from top-executives.

Daniel	Juana	Peter
Inner compass	Integrity and authenticity	Integrity and authenticity
Self-awareness	Self-awareness	Appreciation
Long-term orientation and visioning	Sensemaking	Inclusive mindset and intercultural competence
Humility	Empathy and compassion	Empathy and compassion
Openness and learning mindset	Openness and learning mindset	Openness and learning mindset
Optimism	Co-creation skills	Trust
	Courage	Creativity
		Complexity awareness
		Communication skills
All of third category, related to forgiveness: application, connectedness, humility, empathy, and compassion.	From her vision: coexistence with the other, caring for the other, innovation exploration, cognitive interaction with the other	

Source: Largacha-Martinez (2024).

When attempting to instill new behaviors in individuals, it is imperative that they release outdated habits and derogatory beliefs, as only then can true progress towards embracing IDGs be achieved.

To finish this chapter, by way of a conclusion, I offer a short description of the structure of the IDG Colombia Centre, with its six hubs.

Conclusion: The IDG Colombia Centre's development

Over the course of two years since the establishment of the IDG Colombia Hub in 2021, we have engaged in numerous discussions about harnessing volunteer energy and becoming a force for positive change. With the dedicated support of over 15 enthusiastic volunteers, we have successfully structured an ecosystem, giving rise to the IDG Colombia Centre, accompanied by six IDG Colombia Hubs. And we have an expanded group of more than 100 volunteers that are connected to the activities we do. Here is a list of ideas/accomplishments at the end of 2023.[22]

- *Government Hub*: continuous follow up on the BIC Law to include the IDGs.
- *Education Hub*: inclusion of the IDGs in primary school, where kids will help their parents and teachers behave using the IDGs' skills, changing their old unsustainable beliefs.
- *Community Development Hub*: indigenous communities in La Guajira region, Wayuus, in a dialogue with the IDGs and their cosmovisions; continuous follow up on the human trafficking victims to use the IDGs for their healing, co-lead by Andrea Avella (Ibague, Tolima).
- *Research Hub*: Six-year, €9 million ERC Synergy Grant uploaded, using our methodology 'Situational Analysis Social Tool-SAST' for deep organizational transformation in synergy with the IDGs—based on the previous work from Chris Argyris.
- *Corporations and Organizations Hub*: we presented the Global Leadership for Sustainable Development (GLSD) 2.0, funded by the Templeton World Charity Foundation, to more than 100 corporations.
- *Arts, Dance, & Culture Hub*: we are happy that last year we launched this new hub, co-lead by Timbalé, where they will include the IDGs in their artistic practices towards soft skills and leadership.

In 2024[23] we are very happy that Colombia was included on the Global Leadership for Sustainable Development (GLSD) 2.0. It will start in June 2024, specially tailored for organizations. As presented, we contacted more than 100 corporations/organizations. Out of those 100, at the end 50 sent the registration. That is a really good number, since registering required a letter signed by a team within the organization. As this chapter is being printed, the final decision is being made since only 20 will receive the grant. However, the IDG Colombia Centre already created an ambassador program, where we will support those that registered and didn't receive the grant. We don't want to reduce the impact we see 2024 can make for us. Also, the ambassadors will contact those organizations that are interested but didn't want to send the letter of commitment now. For sure, there is growing interest in the IDGs in Colombia. For example, the minister of equality, led by our vice-president, Francia Marquez, registered. The letter was signed by herself.

---

22 An expanded version can be seen on our webpage, www.quantichumanism.org/idg-colombia/alia dos/.

23 During the work done to publish this book, the IDG Colombia Centre was launched officially in August 27th, 2024, at the Universidad Militar de Colombia, with the visit of Asa Jarksog from the Global IDG Team. You can visit this link (in Spanish): https://www.linkedin.com/posts/inner-develop ment-goals-colombia-summit_idgcolombiacentre-desarrollointerior-ods-activity-7234387744079114241-v8iU?utm_source=share&utm_medium=member_desktop

The 100 businesses/organizations contacted were using a personal networking approach. From each hub, the one to three co-leads contacted the organizations or businesses that they had in their contact list. Either as a former client, a relative, or any connection done before. We just wanted to know their reaction. It was better than expected. We have to be patient, though, since the IDGs are difficult to measure, and the mindset from top executives is around KPIs and performance indicators. This is a global challenge, not only in Colombia.

Another concern that we heard from companies is that they already had something being developed around similar lines as the IDGs, so they don't want it to "put more pressure" on the HR department. Also, they stated that they liked the IDGs, but they felt they were not ready to embrace it now. Maybe in 2025.

We are working now to have a lot of media attention on the outcomes of the GLSD 2.0 in Colombia, since it will help leverage our efforts and have more organizations curious about the IDGs and how they can use them. In this process, as all over the world, we are challenged by the financial sustainability of the IDG Colombia Centre. We hope that with the government and the big corporations that registered, we can have that support. The other strategy is grants, so we made an alliance with B Corps Colombia, and sent a proposal to the EU's Erasmus+. We will know in September.

And they lived happily ever after . . .. Well, that is not how this story ends. It is highly challenging, but highly rewarding, since all of the hub co-leads believe that the IDGs can really make a difference and change the world!

References

Bushnell, D. (1993). *The making of modern Colombia: A nation in spite of itself.* University of California Press.

Cardoso, F. H. & Faletto, E. (1979). *Dependency and development in Latin America* (M. M. Urquidi trans.). University of California Press.

Castaño, N., Sully de Luque, M. F., Wernsing, T., Ogliastri, E., Gabel Shemueli, R., Fuchs, R. M., & Robles-Flores, J. A. (2015). El Jefe: Differences in expected leadership behaviors across Latin American countries. *Journal of World Business, 50*(3), 584–597. https://doi.org/10.1016/j.jwb.2014.12.002.

Collins, J. (2001). *Good to Great: Why Some Companies Make the Leap . . . And Others Don't.* Harper Business; First Edition.

Escobar, A. (1995). *Encountering development: The making and unmaking of the Third World.* Princeton University Press.

DaMatta, R. (1991). *Carnival, rogues, and heroes: An interpretation of the Brazilian dilemma* (J. Drury trans.). University of Notre Dame Press.

Fals-Borda, O. (1968). *Subversion y cambio social* (2nd ed.). Ediciones Tercer Mundo.

Fuentes, C. (2000). *El Espejo Enterrado.* Taurus Bolsillo. Revised edition. Orginal work published 1992.

García Márquez, G. (1998). *A country for children.* Villegas Editores.

García-Canclini, N. (1995). *Hybrid cultures: Strategies for entering and leaving modernity.* University of Minnesota Press.

Hamel, G.; Zanini, M. (2016). *The $3 Trillion Prize for Busting Bureaucracy.* www.garyhamel.com/blog/3-trillion. Read also: https://www.garyhamel.com/sites/default/files/uploads/three-trillion-dollars.pdf.

Largacha.Martínez, C.; von Kimakowitz, E.; Pirson, M.; Spitzeck, H.; Dirksmeier, C.; Amann, W. (eds.) (2014). *Tendencias gerenciales. Gerencia humanista aplicada: 12 casos empresariales exitosos en el mundo.*–1a. ed. en español.–Bogotá: Ecoe Ediciones.

Largacha-Martinez, C. (2024). *Organizational Flourishing Through the Lens of Three Top Executives in Colombia: How They Relate to the Inner Development Goals-IDGs*. In: Fu, P. (eds) Humanistic Leadership Practices. Humanism in Business Series. Palgrave Macmillan, Cham. https://doi.org/10.1007/978-3-031-34366-7_9.

Ogliastri, E., McMillen, C., Arias, M. E., de Bustamante, C., Dávila, C., Dorfman, P., Fimmen, C., Ickis, J., & Martínez, S. (1999). Cultura y liderazgo organizacional en 10 países de América Latina. El estudio Globe. *Academia Revista Latinoamericana de Administración, 22*, 29–57. https://www.redalyc.org/pdf/716/71602203.pdf.

Paz, O. (2000). *El Laberinto de la Soledad*. Fondo de Cultura Económica.

Prigogine, I. (1997). *The end of certainty*. Free Press. Original work published 1996.

Sen, A. (2000). *Desarrollo y Libertad*. Editorial Planeta.Second version.

von Kimakowitz, E., Pirson, M., Spitzeck, H., Dierksmeier, C., Amann, W. (eds) (2011*). Humanistic Management in Practice*. Humanism in Business Series. Palgrave Macmillan, London. https://doi.org/10.1057/9780230306585.

von Kimakowitz, E., Schirovsky, H., Largacha-Martínez, C., Dierksmeier, C., eds. (2021). *Humanistic Management in Practice, Vol. II*. Palgrave Macmillan, London. Humanism in Business Series. https://doi.org/10.1007/978-3-030-51545-4.

Wells, R. (2024). *Emotional Intelligence No.1 Leadership Skill For 2024, Says Research*, on Forbes, January digital version. Visit: https://www.forbes.com/sites/rachelwells/2024/01/05/emotional-intelligence-no1-leadership-skill-for-2024-says-research/?sh=47f9e692888e.

Sibylle Breiner, Nadene Canning and Juergen Nagler

Chapter 21
Transforming tomorrow: The IDG Global Practitioners' Network's journey towards sustainable development – harnessing collective wisdom for global impact and personal growth

Abstract: The Inner Development Goals Global Practitioners' Network (IDG GPN), launched in October 2022, is a dynamic community of over 800 practitioners from more than 50 countries dedicated to fostering collective leadership and achieving the Sustainable Development Goals (SDGs). By modeling the five pillars of the Inner Development Goals (IDGs) in virtual sessions, the network encourages members to integrate these goals into their contexts, promoting global transformation. Monthly meetings focus on practical application, personal growth, and systemic change, creating a dynamic highly participative space for experimentation, reflection, and mutual support. Themes range from leadership development and mindset shifts to practical tools and methods. Participants, driven by a desire to contribute to a better world, engage in deep, meaningful dialogues that foster connection, learning, community, and shared humanity. Sessions, accessible and free, are designed to be inclusive, creating trust and motivation among diverse global members. The IDG GPN emphasizes inner development as a catalyst for systemic change, supporting members in their personal and professional journeys. Feedback indicates that the network's applied learning approach and intentional gatherings significantly enhance participants' ability to implement the IDGs effectively. Through co-creative collaborations and continuous learning, the IDG GPN aims to bridge the gap between inner personal development and outer societal change, driving progress towards the SDGs. The network's success is attributed to its experiential hosting framework, the passionate commitment of its members, and its holistic view of the interconnected nature of the IDGs. The IDG GPN continues to inspire and empower practitioners to build a better future collectively.

Keywords: mindset, community, relationship, peer-to-peer-learning, connection, learning, collective intelligence

https://doi.org/10.1515/9783111453729-022

Part 1: The Inner Development Goals Global Practitioners' Network – a co-creative space for change agents

Established in October 2022, the IDG Global Practitioners' Network (IDG GPN) is a global community of more than 1.000 IDG practitioners from over 50 countries (as of October 2024) and the community is steadily growing.

By purposefully modeling the five pillars of the Inner Development Goals (IDGs) in all of our virtual sessions, we support the development of IDG habits within our member community, inciting them to apply the goals in their own contexts, thus contributing to a global transformation shift through collective leadership. The IDG GPN explores and experiments new ways to put the IDGs into action and from the outset has intentionally aimed to demonstrate the 23 skills of the IDGs in the monthly online meetings. We also share our learnings with the larger IDG community of over 600 hubs, affiliated partners, private sector industry, and organizations, thereby contributing to growing awareness and knowledge around their relevance and importance.

In this chapter, we highlight key insights into our unique approach which takes a holistic and multidimensional view on the IDG framework towards achieving the Sustainable Development Goals (SDGs), while supporting participants to develop and pursue their own individual IDG journey by deepening our personal development and leadership in working towards achieving the SDGs.

Driven by a core team of volunteers, the IDG GPN embodies and models five main principles:

- We support each other with respect and acknowledge that we are all learners.
- We share our knowledge and experience to contribute in a concrete way to a larger purpose.
- We welcome the chaos and complexity that is a part of everyday challenges.
- We pay close attention to the context of our individual and collective challenges.
- We listen to everything that emerges, with curiosity and without judgment.

People feel called to the IDG GPN by a desire to "*do something to make the world a better place*", as one participant of the very first gathering commented. People do feel a sense of finding *home* when they first become acquainted with the IDG GPN community. When starting to apply the framework, they feel a deep need for connection to others, sharing and empowering each other. A safe learning space is created in order to enable practice and prototyping of ideas, explore challenges and projects in small groups, and dive deep in coaching circles with a global community. That safe space is a place to reflect, practice, and fail; a place to learn, deepen our self-knowledge, and grow as a collective in action-driven sessions.

The IDG GPN hosts two monthly gatherings, both on the same day but at different times to enable the practitioners from different time zones to participate. Every month between 15–20% of the IDG GPN members sign up and join this virtual space. Early and late sessions usually host from 35 to 80 participants who often are meeting for the first time online. Sessions are designed to be practical, experiential, and ensure that a safe learning container is created. This recipe has proven to create ease, trust, motivation, and innovation. Newcomers to the IDGs are welcome to participate in open exploration sessions for a first hands-on experience of what application of the framework with a holistic perspective is all about.

Table 21.1: A selection of GPN themes discussed during the monthly practitioner sessions.

IDGs through the lens of human design	Creating a leadership development program for an organization
Co-creating space with the IDGs and Theory U for the paradox: back to the past or embrace the emerging future	Understanding the needs of an organization through the IDG lens
Exploring inner development through a quantum lens	Shifting mindsets: creating conditions for systems change
Living the IDG values	How to get practical with methods and tools
A path to profound connection	Unleashing the power of the IDGs with an interconnected perspective
IDGs and "aha" moments	Unleashing the power of the IDGs in conflict
	Exploring play to spark the IDGs

The power of the IDG GPN meeting experience

"This is THE space", as one practitioner commented on his experience. Deep listening, caring, and curiosity are applied by the practitioners as a method for bonding and connecting with strangers. A deeply felt sense of shared humanity is created through powerful questions and the common language provided by the IDG framework.

At the heart of the IDG GPN lies a profound commitment to fostering connections, collaboration, and community across geographical boundaries. Central to this endeavor are the regular online gatherings, which serve as vibrant hubs of exchange and learning for practitioners worldwide.

These monthly 90-minute sessions accommodate different time zones, with two offerings scheduled at 8 a.m. CET and 5:30 p.m. CET providing a platform for global practitioners to exchange ideas and learn from one another.

Each session is designed and hosted by a core team of dedicated IDG learning designers and facilitators who volunteer their time and expertise.

Sessions are accessible to everyone and are free of charge. Each meeting provides a dedicated, focused, intentional space for them to connect with each other and to engage in a community of practice.

Each gathering focuses on:
- creating a safe learning environment;
- building a community;
- sharing knowledge;
- expressing a diversity of thinking;
- asking questions;
- challenging ideas.

Practitioners come from a wide range of backgrounds and cultures, creating a diverse tapestry of perspectives that serves to enrich our discourse and foster meaningful dialogue. Individuals know that they can take interpersonal risks, share their authentic thoughts, fears, and opinions, and openly express their emotions without fear of retribution, shame, or judgment.

Practitioners are passionate about inner development as a means to driving collective change. Gaining transformative individual and collective insights, in a space of deep listening, community practice, and mutual support.

The IDG GPN has a very broad definition of practitioner, and people join the IDG GPN for many different reasons. Some participants are using the IDG framework for their own personal transformation. Others work as coaches or consultants. They want to use the IDGs with and for their clients to deepen their leadership capacities. There are also a number of practitioners in education who are embedding the IDGs when designing their curricula. Still others are looking for inspiration as they are called to initiate IDG hubs in their communities.

Inner personal development as a driver to join the network

When we speak of systemic change, some practitioners look at the self as a system and understand intuitively that the first step in any kind of transformation begins with a change in our inner system. Seeking to support their own personal transformation is central to why they choose to join the IDG GPN. People find themselves at the intersection of wanting and achieving, while struggling with a palpable sense of frustration and lack of motivation leading to personal dissatisfaction. They have a desire to contribute to the creation of a better common future, but yet hold within themselves a deep sense of unfulfillment. In spite of their sincere efforts at personal growth, there is still a persistent void in their journey. It feels like the progress they make with each step highlights their evolution, but a hidden barrier is preventing further progress – a resistance to embracing the next transformative phase.

For some participants, attendance at monthly IDG GPN meetings has been a real source of motivation for change. These meetings provide the ideal space for peer-to-peer connection. They realize during the in-depth discussion in breakout sessions that their experiences are often shared by others, which gives them a sense of validation and empowerment. These interactions help members build their confidence, gaining a clearer perspective on their own personal development journey.

Encouraged by the discussion in the monthly IDG GPN sessions, one participant understood that a change in mindset was essential, especially in the way she perceived personal responsibility. She also noticed that old thinking, doing, and behavioral patterns were dominating the way she perceived learning, change, and transformation.

Sometimes inner and outer changes occur simultaneously. Because reflection is an important part of the process, people begin to reflect during the sessions and continue their reflection, writing about the insights that surface during and after the breakout sessions. One member shares how he was emotionally triggered during a breakout session, which led him to discovering an inner belief that was hindering his ability to collaborate and co-create. By reaching out to another participant, he was able to quickly overcome this belief and improve his behavior as he co-created an online session. He claims that the mindset and system transformation loop was very helpful in helping him to visualize these changes. Surprisingly, he noticed positive changes in the external world regarding issues he had been working on for a long time shortly after this realization. This experience is a reaffirmation that inner development is a continuous journey, and sometimes transformation can be rapid.

Using an inclusive hosting framework, the IDG GPN deliberately aims to foster a sense of belonging and generative inspiration that drives co-creation and meaningful change. As one practitioner aptly put it, *"This is a testament to our 'community for a community' ethos."*

For practitioners, the allure lies in the hosting and facilitation process which models a practical application of the five pillars of the IDGs. Each gathering serves as a powerful springboard to explore and exchange ideas that can then be translated into meaningful action within their local hubs and communities.

Feedback tells us that participants aspire to develop the skills that will enable them to effectively implement IDGs and integrate these principles into their daily lives, organizations, and local communities. During monthly practitioner sessions, they witness, observe, and practice how they can cultivate the 23 skills. In order to be better equipped to navigate the complexities of implementing change in their hubs, organizations, and local communities, practitioners first need to ensure they continue to learn how to model the behaviors related to the five IDG pillars (being, relating, collaborating, thinking, and acting).

Each IDG GPN gathering focuses on modeling and promoting meaningful conversations, embodied experiences, and more purposeful, deliberate choices and actions with respect to putting the IDGs into practice within our respective ecosystems. Our work here mirrors what Otto Scharmer (Scharmer, 2024) so aptly explains as "the knowing of the field":

> *[T]o navigate these deeper territories of not-knowing, risk, fear, and ambiguity, we need to access a deeper form of knowledge: the knowing of the field (a deepened sense of collective self-knowing). That type of knowledge is different from the conventional concepts of first-person (subjective), second-person (inter-subjective), and third-person knowing (objective) knowledge. In an article published yesterday, my colleague Eva Pomeroy and I refer to this deeper transformative layer of knowing as Fourth Person: The Knowing of the Field.*

Hosting framework

Sessions are usually organized around one topic; this may be a challenge that the members have brought to the table or a topic that the members have expressed an interest in exploring. While topics vary, each session follows a similar structure. The secret to our success is attested to by the high number of practitioners who return monthly knowing that each meeting will be a welcoming, caring learning environment. This intentionality has served to create and build trust over time.

Group coherence is created through a facilitated mindful sequence of checking in, deep listening, and grounding exercises.

Once the group has a felt sense of a caring space, the next step is to begin a conversation about the topic at hand in a designed series of short sequences, small breakout groups for deeper discussion, and generative plenary dialogue.

The initial sensation of deep connection usually happens in the breakout sessions when three to four people gather, inspired by carefully crafted questions which lead to exchanges and discussions which often dive into people's inner lives, reaching into the hearts and minds of attendees. Here the difference is clear; all emotions like thoughts, when shared, are welcomed.

All breakout sessions are always followed by a plenary session, which is a time for reflection and sharing of insights with the larger group. Sessions end on time after 90 minutes with a checkout to give each participant an opportunity to summarize the experience in one or a few words. The checkout process is usually done in writing by using the chat feature.

Practitioners view the global gatherings as an effective means to fostering greater understanding of the IDG projects being developed and implemented around the world. Hearing these stories of IDG integration into projects, programs, education, institutions, and organizations incites deeper curiosity, sharing, and connection that inspires and empowers their own work. They express feeling energized and motivated by the discussions in the breakout sessions, as well as the generative dialogues in the plenary. After the meetings, they feel activated and encouraged to apply the insights to their local context, whether it is an organization, a program they are developing for their clients, or a local IDG hub they are hosting.

Over the past 12 months, the network of practitioners has doubled, and we attribute this success to three factors: (1) the intentionality of practitioner gatherings; (2) a deep inner collective desire to drive purposeful change; and (3) the power of an applied learning community.

Our applied learning approach has led to a number of co-creative cooperations. One that we will discuss in the next section was with Jürgen Nagler, an experienced development practitioner and mindset researcher. Several years ago, he embarked on investigating the key role mindsets play in holistic human development, and therefore for the IDGs and SDGs. The major insights from his research are covered in the following section.

Part 2: Looking at the relevance of integrating mindset research into IDG GPN gatherings

A series of three GPN sessions to explore the latest mindset research and its applicability to the IDG practitioners' work

As mentioned in Table 21.1, one of the topics explored during the IDG GPN concerned mindset and the important role it plays in shifting our thinking.

The first session on mindset, in November 2023, was titled "Shifting mindsets: creating conditions for systems change" and was designed as an introduction to the topic. Here Jürgen Nagler distilled several years of research into a 15-minute presentation.

After a round of questions and answers in the plenary, groups of five participants were sent to breakout sessions to discuss the following questions:
–   What have you discovered?
–   How can you see using what you heard in your practice?

A month later, the second session used the energy of the end of the year to help participants reflect on their journey with the IDGs in 2023 and to begin to sense into what would emerge for them in the new year. Both of these reflections were linked to the shift in mindset that the participants would like to see in their own lives.

This second session was designed to delve deeper into the left side of the mindset and system transformation loop (see Annex 1) and focused on the left side of the loop, beginning with *awareness and intention, beliefs and attitudes change,* and *thinking, feeling, and behavior change.*

The breakout sessions were facilitated with the following questions:

- Reflecting on the year for you and the world, what have you observed? How are you an actor in the system?
- Which IDGs have been important for you this year?
- Which mindset shifts would you like to create in you in 2024?
- What is the seed that you want to observe, sow, allow?

In January 2024, for the final session specifically dedicated to mindset shift, we focused on the outside world and the systems in which we operate. This aspect is represented by the right side of the loop by looking at *collective awareness, worldview and paradigm shift,* as well as *co-creating development.* This was an ideal opportunity for participants to prepare for the start of a new year by sensing into the possibilities of what lies ahead for each of them.

Breakout sessions were moderated with these questions:
- Which of the systems you are in, are you most called to shift?
- What is the discomfort you are feeling currently in that system that leads you to want to see a shift?
- How are you an actor in that system?
- How are you catalyzing system transformation?

Participants came away from these sessions with powerful insights into the importance of the complexity involved in shifting mindsets to change systems. More importantly, they experienced a sense of connection, belonging, and trust within the group. These sessions have led to many more questions, such as how to motivate the actors to actually make change and how to unblock motivation.

Practitioners understand that it takes time to change systems and that the tasks at hand are complex and difficult. Practitioners sometimes leave feeling the weight of having to change the entire world population for anything to shift. However, the butterfly effect in a global world means that we need 13% of people in all sectors to tip the system. One participant summed up his insights with, *"We can help to build a better future",* and we will do it by continuing to learn and be in dialogue together.

See Annex 1 for a summary of the research findings presented by Jürgen Nagler.

Part 3: GPN fosters learning, nurtures communities, and inspires change

Many global practitioners are working within IDG hubs. The IDG movement is very much driven and powered by local hubs. Hubs are groups of people and/or organizations supporting the IDG initiative. People are driven by the intention of contributing to collective change in their local region. No two hubs are alike. This is what makes the movement so diverse and so special.

In the following subsection we share insights of global practitioners who are drivers of IDG hubs, delving into what they have learned and sharing their discoveries.

Paz Garcia Fernandez, an active IDG GPN practitioner from Chile, was in search of topics that would deepen her knowledge of inner leadership when she came across the IDGs. Already an advocate for women in leadership and an active contributor to the advancement of senior women on boards of directors, the IDG framework has been the missing link in her activities. The IDGs have given her a "language" and a way to express herself in formal words.

For Paz, the importance of the monthly IDG GPN meetings lies in the community of practice. She has also gained valuable ideas from interacting with other practitioners and has incorporated these ideas into her hub.

An example of another IDG activator comes from the Netherlands. Here the creation of a hub was inspired by a conversation among friends and their curiosity to lean into the IDGs in their community to connect them to the sustainable development projects being developed as well as those being implemented.

Erno Hannink is an entrepreneur who lives in the Netherlands and was surprised to see how much SDG activity was already happening in his rural area.

Erno's drive is the wonderful energy in the IDG GPN facilitation team that encourages discussions over topics. Even though we all have different energies and ideas, he loves how willing everyone is to look at things from different points of view and investigate together.

Awake was founded by Camilla Elise Berg (CEO) and Marte Alstad Hansen (creative director). Together they are on a mission to create a compelling future, with an overarching vision to contribute to raise the frequency of humanity.

In November 2022, Awake became an official IDG hub, the first one in Norway. Through this hub, they built a network of over 300 individuals, including business leaders, professors, inner work experts, curious minds, students, political figures, and senior citizens. Awake utilizes the hub as a platform for experimentation; every month they gather approximately 50 people to come together and practice the IDGs. Intuitively Camilla and Marte select themes for each gathering and develop complementary tools and exercises.

Their events feature guest speakers, performances, and even a nature spiritual teacher leading impactful drum journeys. Through partnerships with Epicenter Oslo and PwC, Awake has been able to have their hub gatherings in a variety of office spaces.

Awake has recently launched their inner program "Awaken Your Business", aimed at integrating the IDGs in organizations. Drawing on all their experience with bridging the gap between inner and outer sustainability, they are seeking clients who want to be frontrunners and embark on this transformational journey with them.

Part 4: Outlook and future ahead

The IDG GPNs journey to drive systems and mindset change with the IDG framework has only just begun. Over the last months, it has become very clear that we see the IDGs not only as skills that can be learned but as qualities that need to be experienced. Our approach and main focus do not involve a deep dive into a single IDG. It is important to note that none of the IDGs are new to the world, and there are well-proven methods and tools available to explore them in depth.

We therefore take a holistic view and see the need to strengthen the interdependent nature of the IDGs. This interconnected nature of its skills and qualities is the true strength and the real power of the IDG framework.

The path ahead is only slowly and gradually emerging. Further work will focus on the explicit link between the IDGs and the SDGs as one key objective. It will be the community of practitioners that will drive the topics and the direction of the journey ahead. The participation of the practitioners in the monthly meetings is another area of focus, as our co-creation inquiry continues to go deeper. The key to the IDG GPN is to stay relevant and address the most important aspects of the community's day-to-day concerns.

As practitioners, we have the responsibility and the power to build the bridge that will lead society from where it is today towards the desirable future we want to create by achieving the SDGs. We believe that by working together and acknowledging different perspectives we can make a positive impact on the world. Providing a safe learning space to connect and empower them as change agents has become one of the most sought-after aspects of the IDG GPN.

The IDGs are an exciting opportunity to achieve outer change by transforming individuals from within. The purpose of inner development is not only for personal growth. The primary purpose is to align with the 17 UN Sustainable Development Goals. By strengthening our abilities to shift our mindsets, we can take the crucial first step towards a better future. But we can't stop there – ultimately, we must align our behavior. People from all walks of life around the world have the power to adjust their habits and behaviors to work towards meeting these 17 UN SDGs.

The IDG movement and the IDG GPN can absolutely help more people meet the exciting challenge of living with the paradox of building a bridge from today's world to a better tomorrow. With our inclusive and supportive community, we can continue to work together to create a brighter future for all. Let's embrace this opportunity with confidence and enthusiasm, knowing that we have the power to make a real difference. Together, we can build a bridge to a better tomorrow.

"The world calls us to shift our mindsets and values from outdated ways of being and doing rooted in dominance, hierarchy, and harmful systems, to new ways rooted in relationship, collaboration, and innovation." (Fraser, 2023).

We believe in the importance of slow, steady, and contextually rooted work in deepening relationships and healing. The Systems Sanctuary calls this *"scaling deep"*

(Fraser, 2023) and is understood as the deep personal and broad cultural transformational work that is required to create durable systems change. Our view was there was much more to learn, question, and understand about how it contributes to change.

If you are interested in joining the IDG GPN, you can register online[1] or reach out to the authors.[2]

Annex 1: Mindset research insights

Having worked for over 25 years in the United Nations, business, and civil society, and having undergone a personal transformation, Jürgen Nagler embarked on a multiyear research quest. He was intrigued to answer the curious question *What role do mindsets play in human development?* and interviewed people from all around the world. This chapter is one of the first publications sharing key research insights and practical guidance on how to catalyze inner and outer transformation towards achieving the Inner Development Goals (IDGs) and Sustainable Development Goals (SDGs).

The SDGs are the only global development framework that all UN countries have signed up to. These global goals were adopted by world leaders in 2015 as part of the 2030 Agenda for Sustainable Development, and they are a universal framework applicable to all countries. Nonetheless, despite the urgency to move towards greater sustainability, the world is unfortunately largely off track to achieve these important goals.

It is obvious that the SGDs cannot be achieved by business as usual, and much remains to be done to bring about the necessary inner and outer transformations. Therefore, the IDGs have been positioned as a catalyst to realizing the SDGs, due to the recognition that achieving the SDGs requires not only external actions and policies but also significant inner development of individuals and organizations. The IDGs were created in response to this slow progress, aiming to enhance human capacity, including cognitive, emotional, and social skills to meet the SDGs' challenges (Inner Development Goals, n.d.).

Calls for a more holistic human development paradigm have also been recognized by the UN (United Nations, 2024, 2011) and are supported by various movements such as the IDGs and others calling for transforming the economic paradigm. For instance, Degrowth, Doughnut Economics, the Presencing Institute, and the Wellbeing Economy Alliance invite us to rethink conventional notions of progress and prosperity, taking into account planetary boundaries and societal well-being (Dixson-Decleve, 2022). These alternative models demand a paradigm shift going beyond endlessly

---

1 https://idg-global-practitioners-network.in.howspace.com/welcome.
2 Dr. Sibylle Breiner – sibylle@sibyllebreiner.com or Nadene Canning – nadene@allsystemsgo.ch.

growing gross domestic product (GDP) towards more equitable, sustainable, and well-being-centric development frameworks (Stiglitz, 2019).

Mindsets matter

The UN Secretary-General Antonio Guterres referred to the crucial role of mindsets when he stated: *"We cannot solve our biggest problems if we do not come together. It is not only about institutions or processes. It is in the first instance about our mindsets"* (Guterres, 2021). While the word mindset is increasingly used in the development field, little research has been done on the role of mindsets in human development and how to practically utilize mindset shifts for creating a better future.

Mindsets are defined as our deep beliefs, attitudes, and values. They frame our thinking, and therefore determine our worldview, behavior, and life experiences (Wamsler, 2022). They influence how people lead their lives, how they vote, what personal, educational, and professional opportunities they pursue, and what they make out of crises, challenges, and opportunities. Through shifting our mindset, we can change how we see the world and give our life a new positive direction.

Findings suggest that mindsets are the missing leverage point to be included in a new holistic human development paradigm of well-being for people and the planet. While we are largely unaware of mindsets due to their intangible nature, we can in fact change them. Collective and global mindsets are very similar to paradigms in that they are the source of manifesting systems, such as economic, social, and political.

Important questions

Why is it important to understand the role of mindsets in development and transformation? We are in the middle of multiple human crises, from conflict to environmental destruction and looming climate collapse. While outer events get most of the attention, it is our inner dimensions and mindsets which are our own blind spot. Based on the described need to rethink human development, the reader is invited to reflect on the following key questions:

– How can we shift towards a mindset that advances physical, emotional, mental, and spiritual well-being?
– Are we willing to leapfrog to an enlightened paradigm that recognizes and develops humans in a holistic manner?
– How can we harmoniously advance the well-being of both people and the planet?

We protect and develop what we cherish, what we feel part of and connected with. So:

– How can we nurture three essential connections: with our inner being, with our communities, and with nature?

– The opportunity to create a new paradigm for the twenty-first century comes from combining current science with timeless wisdom. Could the root causes and transformative power for well-being be within us?

The six key insights

The multiyear research conducted by Jürgen Nagler reviewed relevant literature and interviewed over 50 development experts, change makers, and thought leaders from around the world between 2017 and 2024. Based on his decade-long experience in the development field, including the United Nations, he embarked on a PhD with the Viadrina University in Germany entitled *The Power of Mindset: Inside-Out Development and Systems Transformation towards a Global Wellbeing Paradigm.*

Building upon the identified research gap – that mindsets are an important blind spot in theory and practice of human development – his dissertation pursued the question *What role do mindsets play in human development?* It employed a qualitative, inductive approach using grounded theory and the Gioia method to explore the role of mindsets in human development at the individual, collective, and global levels.[3]

This allows for gaining groundbreaking insights which are synthesized in the following six key points:

1. True transformation happens from the inside out.
2. Mindsets matter. They play a crucial role in human development and well-being at the individual, collective, and global level.
3. Mindsets can be shifted by increasing awareness and fostering self-reflection and self-responsibility.
4. Development needs to be co-created, which requires a mindset shift of social, political, and economic actors.
5. The current development paradigm is materialistic and unsustainable; therefore, a paradigm shift is needed to move beyond the obsession with GDP and economic growth.
6. A new holistic development paradigm should include inner, collective, and planetary well-being.

In the following section we will weave together these mindset insights with the IDGs and the SDGs, i.e., inner and outer development dimensions. This much resonates with other leading research illuminating the key role of inner dimensions for sustainability and system transformation such as the Earth4All deep-dive paper, commis-

---

3 Participants include development practitioners, mindset researchers, policy makers, change agents, environmental activists, and social entrepreneurs from 23 countries in five continents. For a more detailed description of the findings, insights, and recommendations please see the forethcoming full research report which will be published, inter alia, at www.wellbeingmindset.org.

sioned by the Club of Rome, entitled *The System Within: Addressing the Inner Dimensions of Sustainability and Systems Transformation* (Bristow et al., 2024).

Inside-out development: Linking the IDGs and SDGs

The most radical research finding is that human development happens inside out, meaning that we have to go inside, often into our subconscious, to shift our mindset and to bring forth inner and outer transformation. Our inner states of being, thinking, and feeling attract outer circumstances and shape our thinking, feeling, and decisions and actions. Through shifting our inner dimensions, worldview, and behavior, we are better able to co-create with others a brighter future, one that fosters the well-being of people and planet, as illustrated in the following *inside-out flow* (see Figure 21.1).

The inside-out flow

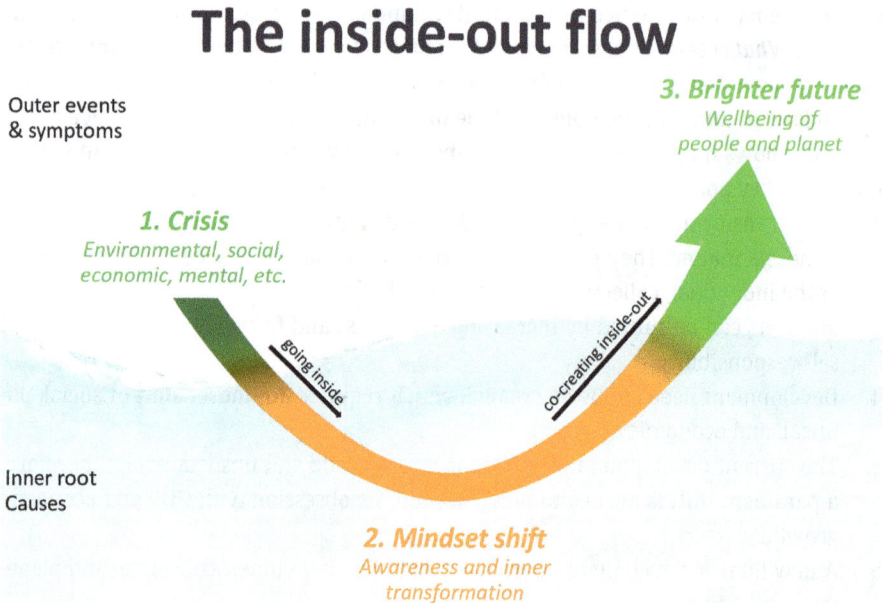

3. Brighter future
Wellbeing of people and planet

Outer events & symptoms

1. Crisis
Environmental, social, economic, mental, etc.

going inside

co-creating inside-out

Inner root Causes

2. Mindset shift
Awareness and inner transformation

Figure 21.1: The inside-out flow **(Nagler; forthcoming).**

The inside-out flow has three key steps: (1) realizing the crisis; (2) shifting mindset; and (3) co-creating a brighter future. Often significant change transformation is preceded by a crisis which shakes people out of their "business as usual" comfort zone. As humanity, we are realizing that we are faced with existential crises, such as environmental, social, economic, and mental (Step 1). In cases where crises are met with realism and wisdom, they can act as a catalyst of transformation when a new, positive intention and vision is created. Then, when people increase their awareness and change their deep attitudes and beliefs, a mindset shift occurs through inner transformation (Step 2). A shift in mindset followed by courageous action allows the realization of a higher potential and the inside-out co-creation of a new, brighter future (Step 3).

How does this all relate to the IDGs and SDGs? How are inner shifts (mindsets) and outer changes (systems) connected? In fact, they are two sides of the same coin – holistic development. According to the research findings, mindsets play key roles for both the IDGs and SDGs, and have root causal power in creating human development, well-being, and systems. In fact, shifting mindsets is considered to be the highest leverage point in systems change (Meadows, 1999).

Mindset shifts transform systems

Mindset shifts, sometimes triggered by catalytic crises, play a crucial role in transformations, individually and collectively. We manifest our individual lives as per our inner dimensions, that is, thinking, relating, and feeling. Our collective systems – social, economic, and political – reflect our collective inner dimensions. "Collective" refers to what is shared by a group of people emphasizing the group or whole over its individual parts.

Without a substantive shift in these inner dimensions, the various crises that humanity faces will fundamentally remain unchanged, or, put differently: transformative change requires profound shifts in mindsets and a new development paradigm. People have self-responsibility and agency over their inner and outer development, and collectively over systems. History is full of change makers and social leaders who have overcome adversity and changed their external circumstances and structures, and therefore written history.

The following *mindset and system transformation loop* demonstrates how inner transformative steps of mindset shifts build onto each other to catalyze systems transformation (see Figure 21.2).

This mindset and system transformation loop sheds light onto the relationships between mindsets (inner) and systems (outer) which allows a formulation of a flow of causal steps of mindset shifts and how these can catalyze wider systems transformations. The model is, of course, a simplification, as in reality stages are not that clearly separated. Moreover, there is a dynamic dance between inner and outer dimensions, mindsets and systems, and individuals and collectives. Therefore, an eternity loop visualizes these intertwined dynamics.

The loop consists of two sides: shifting mindsets on the left side (orange), and transforming systems on the right side (green), each with three steps. The shifting mindset elements are *awareness and intention, beliefs and attitudes change*, and *thinking, feeling, and behavior change*. As for systems transformation, the steps are *collective awareness, worldview and paradigm shift*, and *co-creating development*.

The mindset & system transformation loop
toward wellbeing of people and planet

Awareness & intention

Collective awareness

Beliefs & attitudes change

Shifting mindsets

Wellbeing
of people and planet

Transforming systems

Worldview & paradigm shift

Thinking, feeling & behaviour change

Co-creating development

Figure 21.2: The mindset and system transformation loop (Nagler, forthcoming).

How can this model illustrate the needed transformations towards a paradigm of well-being of people and planet, therefore achieving the IDGs and SDGs? Firstly, every human transformation begins with awareness and an intention for change, which creates an opening for new possibilities. The awareness is growing that business as usual is a dead end and that we need to change course. More and more people are practicing mindfulness and are changing their beliefs and attitudes.

When new beliefs and attitudes are confirmed by new experiences, people no longer fall back into the old thinking and behavior patterns, but actually have sustainably transformed relevant inner elements. For instance, an increasing number of people critically examine and opt out of standard education and economic systems, others choose to consume differently or to run their business in sustainable, regenerative ways. Profound behavioral change comes from within, i.e., when people expand their awareness, formulate intentions, and change their mindset. Consequently, their thinking, feeling, and behavior changes fundamentally. There are myriad ways how a shifted mindset manifests in different lives, careers, and lifestyles.

While this description sounds easy to follow, for most people, it often takes years of practice, external support, and/or a catalytic event or crisis for such a mindset shift to happen. The reason for this is that an estimated 90% of these processes happen in our subconscious, meaning that taking self-responsibility of one's mindset and dedicated inner work is required to connect with the heart and the planet.

Let us now have a closer look at systems transformation, the right side of the illustration. Individual and collective mindset shifts are promoters of systems transformation along three steps: collective awareness, paradigm shift, and co-creating development. Similar to increased awareness as the starting point for mindset shifts, increased collective awareness is the foundation for consciously transforming human systems, such as social, economic, or political. Collective awareness refers to the shared understanding among a group of people about certain issues, values, or phenomena.

Therefore, expanding collective awareness is the key leverage point for transforming systems. There can be a virtuous cycle where individual awareness influences collective awareness, and vice versa, where individuals benefit from the awareness of communities. A shift of collective awareness from an ego to eco focus, from an egocentric to a more holistic approach, is needed to foster the well-being of people and the planet. As transpersonal psychologist Stanislav Grof (2000) stated:

> A radical inner transformation and rise to a new level of consciousness might be the only real hope we have in the current global crisis brought on by the dominance of the Western mechanistic paradigm.

Building upon shifts of collective awareness and mindsets can lead to profound shifts of worldviews and paradigms, which will fundamentally transform a system. This research finds that a paradigm shift is needed: away from mechanistic, materialistic, and economic growth, based on viciously extracting resources from nature, to more holistic development of the well-being of people and planet. This also requires combining indigenous and traditional knowledge, with its timeless wisdom about sustainability and spirituality, with modern sciences.

There are several promising initiatives underway to shift the economic system towards prioritizing well-being, such as the Wellbeing Economy Alliance. An inspiring example of a more holistic development approach is also Bhutan's gross national happiness approach, which utilizes economic growth not as the end goal but as only one pillar, together with others, towards fostering a higher objective – the well-being of people and nature (Center of Bhutan Studies and GNH, 2017). We should take inspiration from these initiatives to effectively and profoundly transform the mainstream development paradigm.

Shifts in awareness, worldviews, and paradigms transform systems with their structures, goals, and policies, and help to create different systemic outcomes. A practical application of a transformation loop is multi-stakeholder dialogues that aim to co-create profound change. For instance, Theory U is an impactful awareness-based transformational methodology deployed to solve adaptive challenges at a systemic level (Scharmer, 2018). This and other awareness-based methods are, for instance, piloted by the United Nations Development Programme (UNDP; see following section).

Dialoguing and co-creating development by multi-stakeholders is at the heart of a new well-being paradigm. This involves collaborative problem solving by stakeholders, including indigenous perspectives and marginalized voices, to benefit everyone and the common good. Rather than discussing symptoms at the surface level, co-creative inquiries go deeper, i.e., to the root causal levels of mindsets, by creating safe spaces for deep reflection, and through active listening with empathy and trust.

More holistic policies and goals, as main pillars of transformed systems, will foster and lead towards a sustainable and regenerative economy, meaning that Mother Earth is no longer treated as a separate, infinite resource for exploitation, but as humanity's home which is alive, offering precious finite resources to be respectfully used and regenerated.

United Nations example of awareness-based change

United Nations agencies have increasingly applied behavioral sciences and awareness-based approaches. For instance, the UN Development Programme (UNDP) has initiated the Conscious Food Systems Alliance (CoFSA), a globally active movement of food, agriculture, and consciousness practitioners. It builds on the UNDP's many years' work around sustainability challenges of agricultural commodities and realizes that to achieve different results one has to go beyond technical interventions to catalyze inner transformation (UNDP, 2024). It does so by cultivating the inner capacities for systemic change and regeneration, and connecting members to share expertise and to cooperate in action groups (see Figure 21.3).

As of 2023, the alliance has over 150 members, over a thousand individuals have been introduced to these principles, a community of practice has been built, and an agenda for further action has been formulated. For instance, one of the alliance's members is the civil society organization World Vision which has been actively involved in promoting mindset change through their Empowered World View training program. It has helped thousands of refugees and farmers in East Africa to overcome relying on hand-outs by growing in self-reliance and resilience (World Vision, 2024).

The World Vision faith-based program involves training sessions that encourage participants to adopt an empowered worldview, leading to increased empowerment levels and the ability to become agents of change within their own lives, families, and communities. An example from Zambia: Reese Machola, 45, has been a sole provider and caregiver for her five children since she got separated from her husband a few years ago. As a single parent she greatly struggled to support her family financially and was lacking a sustainable income.

The training program provided practical skills, entrepreneurial mentorship, and helped to transform certain beliefs and cultures that tend to keep people in the cycle of poverty. After completing the training, Reese joined a local savings group and was able to start her own business venture. She summarizes the positive impact as follows: "It is through this business that I can fend for my children and sponsor them to school without any challenges. We do not lack any home necessities, and my children are doing well in school" (World Vision, 2024).

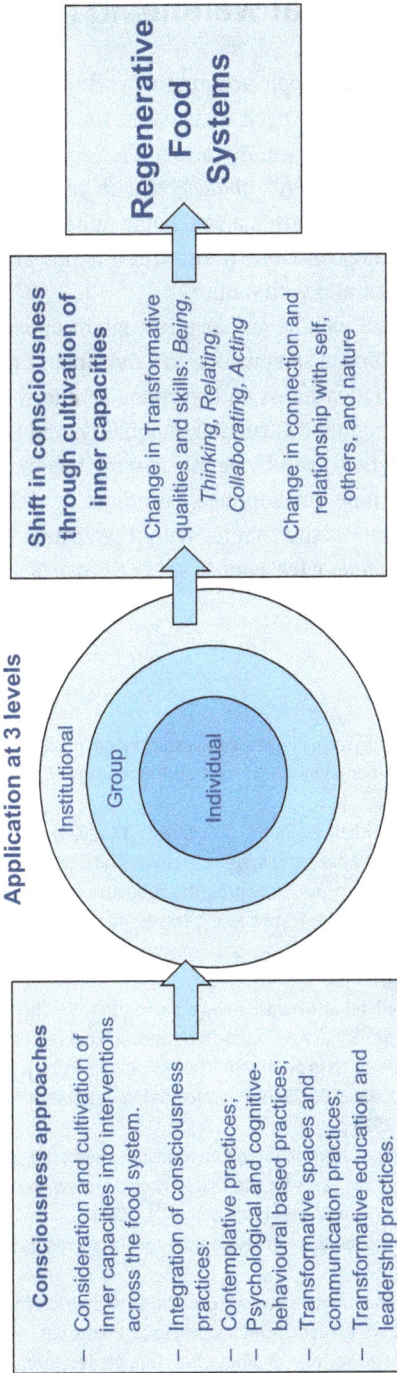

The Conscious Food Systems Alliance
Cultivating inner capacities for regenerative food systems

Consciousness approaches

– Consideration and cultivation of inner capacities into interventions across the food system.
– Integration of consciousness practices:
 – Contemplative practices;
 – Psychological and cognitive-behavioural based practices;
 – Transformative spaces and communication practices;
 – Transformative education and leadership practices.

Application at 3 levels

Institutional
Group
Individual

Shift in consciousness through cultivation of inner capacities

Change in Transformative qualities and skills: *Being, Thinking, Relating, Collaborating, Acting*

Change in connection and relationship with self, others, and nature

Regenerative Food Systems

Figure 21.3: The Conscious Food Systems Alliance **(UNDP, 2022).**

Conclusion: Towards a global well-being mindset

In conclusion, with increasing suffering of people around the world due to multiple crises, we cannot afford to despair. Instead, we need to actualize the required paradigm shift with urgency, optimism, and perseverance. As former UN Secretary-General Ban Ki-moon (2016) stated: *"We can't address today's challenges with yesterday's mindset."* Therefore, Jürgen's work proposes a new mindset: a well-being mindset which involves increasingly thinking, feeling, and acting consciously, fostering a happy and healthy life in harmony within oneself, with others, and with nature.

A paradigm shift towards a global well-being paradigm might appear utopian to some. However, we no longer can afford to sleepwalk into a dystopian future. Humanity needs to wake up to a new level of awareness and co-create solutions for the pressing challenges of our times. Environmental destruction, inequality, and unsustainability are man-made and therefore can be solved by people coming together with a new collaborative mindset that enacts a new development paradigm of well-being of all people and our planet. Closing this part of the chapter with a sentiment paraphrasing Mahatma Gandhi: *We have to be the change we want to see in the world.*

References

Ban, K. M. (2016, Apr. 11). We can't address today's challenges with yesterday's mindset. International Peace Institute. www.ipinst.org/2016/04/ban-ki-moon-we-cant-address-todays-challenges-with-yesterdays-mindset (accessed Jul. 1, 2024).

Bristow, J., Bell, R., Wamsler, C., Björkman, T., Tickell, P., Kim, J., & Scharmer, O. (2024). The system within: addressing the inner dimensions of sustainability and systems change. The Club of Rome. Earth4All: deep-dive paper. https://www.clubofrome.org/publication/earth4all-bristow-bell/

Center of Bhutan Studies and GNH. (2017). Happiness: Transforming the development landscape. http://www.bhutanstudies.org.bt/publicationFiles/OccasionalPublications/Transforming%20Happiness/Happiness-transform_Final_with-cover.pdf

Dixson-Decleve, S. (2022), From growth to well being: Why we need a paradigm shift. The Club of Rome. www.giz.de/expertise/downloads/Keynote-Sandrine-Dixson-Decleve%20(1).pdf (accessed Jul. 1, 2024).

Fraser, T. (2023), The Art of Scaling Deep – Research in Summary. The Systems Sanctuary. https://static1.squarespace.com/static/5a0b2bbb80bd5e8ae706c73c/t/650e01c6fba1ac5ee2d1ae74/1695416781894/The+Art+of+Scaling+Deep+September+2023.pdf

Grof, S. (2000), Psychology of the Future: Lessons from Modern Consciousness Research, SUNY Press

Guterres, A. (2021). Vision statement: The next five years for the United Nations. www.un.org/pga/75/wp-content/uploads/sites/100/2021/03/Letter-PGA-VS.pdf (accessed Jul. 1, 2024)

Inner Development Goals. (n.d.). IDG Resources. www.innerdevelopmentgoals.org/resources (accessed Jul. 1, 2024).

Meadows, D. (1999). Leverage points: Places to intervene in a system. The Sustainability Institute. https://1a0c26.p3cdn2.secureserver.net/wp-content/userfiles/Leverage_Points.pdf

Nagler, J. (2020). We become what we think: The key role of mindsets in human development. International Science Council. https://council.science/human-development/latest-contributions/we-become-what-we-think-the-key-role-of-mindsets-in-human-development/ (accessed Jul. 1, 2024).

Nagler, J. (Forthcoming). The power of mindset: Inside-out development and systems transformation towards a global wellbeing paradigm [Doctoral dissertation, Viadrina University].

Scharmer, O. (2018). *The essentials of Theory U: Core principles and applications*. Berrett-Koehler Publishers.

Scharmer, O. (2024). The number one problem facing humanity today is not climate change, inequality, AI or war. LinkedIn. https://www.linkedin.com/feed/update/urn:li:activity:7202607133501104128/

Stiglitz, J. E. (2019). *Measuring what counts: The global movement for well-being*. The New Press.

United Nations. (2011). Happiness: Towards a holistic approach to development. Resolution/adopted by the General Assembly. 25 August 2011. A_RES_65_309-EN. https://digitallibrary.un.org/record/715187

United Nations. (2024). Pact for the future: Zero draft. https://www.un.org/sites/un2.un.org/files/sotf-co-facilitators-zero-draft_pact-for-the-future.pdf

United Nations Development Programme (UNDP) (2022). Cultivating Inner Capacities for Regenerative Food Systems: Rationale for Action. www.undp.org/sites/g/files/zskgke326/files/2022-09/CoFSA%20Rationale%20Report.pdf (accessed Nov. 1, 2024).

United Nations Development Programme (UNDP) (2024). The Conscious Food Systems Alliance. www.undp.org/facs/conscious-food-systems-alliance (accessed Jul. 1, 2024).

Wamsler, C. & Bristow, J. (2022). At the intersection of mind and climate change: Integrating inner dimensions of climate change into policymaking and practice. *Climatic Change, 173*(7). https://doi.org/10.1007/s10584-022-03398-9

World Vision (2024). Transforming Lives through Empowered Worldview, www.wvi.org/stories/zambia/world-vision-transforming-lives-through-empowered-worldview (accessed Nov. 1, 2024).

Fredrik Lindencrona

Chapter 22
Research as co-creation: Creating a space in between for academia in the Inner Development Goals ecosystem

Abstract: This text explores the Inner Development Goals (IDGs) initiative, its research efforts, and its role in facilitating global sustainable development. The IDG framework aims to identify and cultivate human capabilities essential for driving transformative change towards sustainability. The initiative has evolved through three phases, focusing on developing a framework, reviewing evidence, and expanding global engagement. The current phase emphasizes research co-creation, involving diverse stakeholders worldwide to create a more inclusive and comprehensive framework. This text highlights the importance of interdisciplinary collaboration, global representation, and the integration of various knowledge systems. It also addresses critiques of the IDG approach and discusses future directions for advancing inner to outer transformation action.

Keywords: Inner Development Goals (IDGs), sustainable development, research co-creation, global collaboration, human capabilities, systems leadership, interdisciplinary research, transformative change, lifelong learning, UN Agenda 2030

Who are you and what is your role in the IDGs?

My name is Fredrik Lindencrona. I am a father of three living in Stockholm, Sweden. I have been leading research co-creation for the Inner Development Goals since the beginning of 2023. I was also one of the initiators of the IDG initiative. Since we started in January 2020, I've been able to follow the work and be engaged along the two previous phases of our work and now I am very proud and excited to lead our research co-creation. I cannot think of anything better than to be engaged with so many fantastic people around the globe in so many areas of expertise and I am trying to do what I can to bring us all together and bring research to all of our work and have all of our work connected to research.

My background is as a psychologist with a broad spectrum of studies and research in business and public administration. During my own PhD I looked at how different stakeholders from the public, business, and civil society could best come together to support the agency and other psychological capacities of newly arrived refugees to Sweden through building the right kind of support for these groups to resettle

https://doi.org/10.1515/9783111453729-023

well. Through this and my last decade of work in the wider well-being policy sphere I have been able to learn much more about such human qualities and abilities, the right kinds of conditions for people to flourish in their work and living environment, and how organizations could engage to build such conditions. So I guess for me this provided a golden thread to what we're trying to do in the IDG initiative.

My own engagement in the IDG initiative came out of my work leading the development of a regional strategic plan for the longer run for the Regional Authority of Stockholm, the capital region of Sweden. In this whole-of-society plan, we realized that we really needed to find a vocabulary to speak about the human capabilities and well-being of all ages throughout the life course. Such a language would be critically important to helping all sectors to think and act on building a successful, inclusive, sustainable region in collaboration between all different stakeholder categories. Those kinds of strategies work on timescales of maybe ten years and they look further into the longer-term future. We have learned that to get real transformative capacity we need time and systematic efforts to make all public administrations, the business sectors, civil society, and academia able to put psychological capabilities front and center, to become the new normal in how society works. That's my starting point and I am passionate about bringing this expertise to our work at the IDGs.

> *The sustainability revolution will be organic. It will arise from the visions, insights, experiments and actions of billions of people. The burden of making it happen is not on the shoulders of any one person or group. No one will get the credit, but everyone can contribute.*

> Donella Meadows (2004)

How does the IDG initiative engage with research?

First of all, what is relevant research about inner development and why do we need it? The way we understand research is critical to respond to that question. To me, research is an ethically grounded approach to systematically explore what we want to understand and bring our knowledge together to understand this better. For this we use some systematic methodologies and approaches.

The research we need to understand and develop the inner capabilities to drive outer sustainable development impact require widely different disciplines of research – everything from practice-based evidence to qualitative, analytical, phenomenological, deep understandings of the issues. From evidence for different ways of working, to understanding conditions at individual, inter-personal, team, organizational, ecosystem, and societal levels to how to define and assess the effects we can get, to name just a few. So, it's a wide variety of questions demanding a variety of approaches. This breadth has to be grounded in a shared understanding and acceptance that there are many ways of knowing and many ways of approaching this challenge. We also need research, policy, and practice to help build capacity across a wide variety of areas of application. I believe that the many people who are engaged in our research circle – there are now around 700 people that follow us on our LinkedIn IDG researchers and higher education group and many who join our regular meeting – come here because they believe this can help make the change they are passionate about and see as necessary.

How have the research efforts within IDGs developed over time?

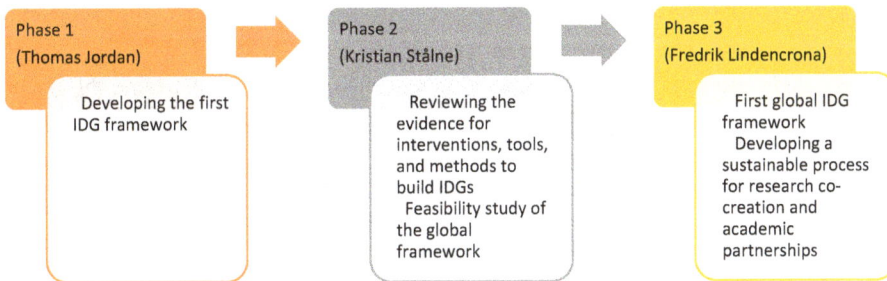

Figure 22.1: The timeline of IDG research.
Source: Author's own

Figure 22.1 shows a timeline to describe how our work has developed through two previous phases. Currently we are in Phase 3. Phase 1 was led by associate professor Thomas Jordan at the University of Gothenburg together with Maria Booth. Here we were able to engage our senior scientific advisors and some colleagues engaged in relevant areas such as adult development psychology, leadership, and organizational learning and change. The process helped us define the question and research methods used to gather data and to build agreement on the formulations used to construct the first framework. One key process here was bringing the research experts together with our global experts in communication within the IDG initiative, where board members and original initiators Jakob Trollbäck and Hannah Boman, leads for The New Division, the agency that was supporting the UN in text formulation and graphic design for Agenda 2030 and the Sustainable Development Goals (SDGs), were key critical friends. The process led to the presentation of the five dimensions and the 23 skills in the current IDG framework (Inner Development Goals, 2021) in May 2021.

After this process, Kristian Stålne, a widely recognized expert in adult development theories from Malmö University, took the steering wheel for the next step, Phase 2. Here one key focus was on identifying interventions, methods, and approaches that could help build the identified dimensions and skills in the IDG framework. Kristian also continued to engage researchers; some continued their engagement from Phase 1 and others engaged for the first time, as the new initiative grew in Phase 2 (Inner Development Goals, 2022). Kristian also collaborated with our first cohort of the Global Leadership for Sustainable Development participants led by our director for global collaboration, Åsa Jarskog. This led to the feasibility study where six academic colleagues from different countries, namely Albania, Colombia and Costa Rica, India, Rwanda, and Zambia developed a process to identify skills and abilities between diverse countries that made use of the same question used for the first framework but in widely different contexts.

I am very thankful for being able to draw a lot of learning from the previous phases and want to thank the excellent Thomas, Maria, Kristian, Stephanie, and all others engaged in helping us to be prepared for our daunting task in Phase 3. In Phase 3, which I lead and have done since its inception, one aim is to develop the global understanding around the core IDG question and to build a new framework that is able to capture the breadth of experience and understanding around the globe. I have been particularly keen to bring the research efforts closer to the wider IDG team for this and coming phases so I have continued to work to integrate research co-creation into most of what we do, making my role and responsibility more firmly integrated in the IDG team. A key aim for me is to build the bridges for co-creation so that research is able to support everything we do and to make sure that everything we do informs the research we engage in. For us, co-creation means building the bridges on at least three distinct fronts: disciplinary, globally, and between researchers and those who use research in their decision making. We look at how to continue to build further and strengthen the collaboration between our first 15 formal academic partnerships, in most continents and between our many individuals and teams of research colleagues. A core strategic enterprise for us to enable the IDG ecosystem to continuously improve how they can drive change is to make boundaries permeable to increase the flow between people outside and inside the research circle.

Can you unpack how you see how the IDG initiative can work to facilitate research co-creation?

We see co-creation as both between disciplinary areas of research and academic interest, between different parts of our beautiful world, as well as between researchers and all other stakeholders. We call it research co-creation to underline that we understand that research in this context is most valuable when it helps progress the necessary transformations towards sustainable development for all. We ask ourselves and others how this way of systematically experiencing, describing, and innovating can help us to progress the decisions of a wide set of leaders within business, public sector, civil society organizations, and academia itself can help drive new ways to approach and act together on the challenges of sustainable development. We believe that we need to bring these sectors together and to make them able to apply the most appropriate approaches to bridge inner development and transformation impact – and research has to be able to find and help describe all these experiments in practice and in policy. I think what unites all is that we are all very passionate to find ways to bring what we know to help bring about progress. It's not research only for the researchers or research itself.

We rely on our disciplinary experts from different parts of the world having a deep connection to their particular discipline. Our role is more to focus on building the best possible convening space to create interdependence and learning between areas to respond to real-world challenges. We're seeing that this development is actually paying off.

So far we can count about 100-plus publications in academic journals since 2021 that use IDGs in the abstract, title, or keywords. We have several books on the way with different book chapters on IDGs as well as full volumes only on IDGs such as this one. These span issues very widely from management to philosophy and ethics to legal studies, from environmental sciences to biomedical, clinical, and health sciences. Newer areas, such as urban planning and architecture, that focus on the places we are designing for ourselves and how we govern these together are also appearing. So, the IDG principles and framework are really widely explored across a lot of different disciplines, ecosystem levels, and areas of application.

And rest assured, IDGs have never claimed to bring some totally new approach. Rather, it's a way of finding a common ground around areas that have been very active for a very long time across subjects and fields. Bringing IDGs as a concept together is a bit of a synthesis across all diversity that exists in all areas of relevance for the inner to outer transformational change and all societal levels. So, we're really trying hard to explore the intersection between these different areas of discipline and how it really functions in the context of people's lives, where they live their life, where they work, love, and develop to make sure to ascertain a focus on global sustainable development for all. It means that IDGs is not a bubble. Instead, it should be seen as a lens that will help people to bring their knowledge together to support our capability to navigate and direct ourselves towards the necessary transformations required to build a sustainable future for people and the planet.

How do we get the process and community that spans the whole globe regarding the inner to outer transformation?

Since its inception, the IDG community has always tried to keep an openness to learn about what was going on around the globe as well as what has been going on for thousands and thousands of years through the wisdom of indigenous people, the wisdom of everyone who has been living before. We recognize and explore other ways to speak about it.

Still, in Phase 1 we realized that we had to rely on our own networks and resources which we knew weren't fully reaching the whole globe. We wanted to get started and to be able to present something early on, and that led to the current IDG framework with its five dimensions and 23 skills already being published in 2021 – in fact not much more than a year after our first early ideas for the IDG initiative were sketched out.

Through our processes so far, we have learned that the five core IDG dimensions identified in the first framework – being, thinking, relating, collaborating, and acting – seem to be a good and helpful description of these dimensions across all contexts around the globe. Our current hypothesis is that those five dimensions will also be organizing the next iteration of the framework. While their interdependence may be looking slightly different here and there, and they may not be that linear in relation to each other, they are five core dimensions that we will continue unless data we gather now will prove us wrong.

Now our dream to reach into Asia, Africa, and South America to understand and listen to all the wisdom that we can encounter in these massive world continents starts to be much more achievable. This helps us to understand that, yes, there is a lot in the current framework that seems to resonate with everyone across the globe. But it's also elements of experience that may be missed due to the lives lived in different parts of the globe related to sustainability issues such as peace and non-peace, severe economic distress, different fundamental ways of understanding people's place in relation to nature, different symbolic systems people relate to, and so on. So, one major ambition right now is trying to bring all people from all parts of the globe together in what we call our process to elucidate "the wisdom in all of us". We want to offer the opportunity to join in the global conversations around how people understand what qualities, abilities, and skills that they see are necessary to build a sustainable future for people and the planet.

Our fast mobilization around the world during Phase 1 and 2 and the continually wider reach acquired during Phase 3 have led us to connect academics from all continents; we have a close relationship with the continuously evolving network of hubs (now in about 100 countries with more than 500 hubs in total). We engage with partners from businesses and institutional funders and strengthen our relationships to philanthropy in many, many parts of the world. With this ecosystem we are now able to explore questions regarding IDG-related issues in very different contexts around the globe. During Phase 3 we have invested a lot of time to build relationships with everyone. This investment in time and energy has paid off with this amazing wide and rich network of researchers engaged across the globe and with more than 10,000 people from more than 100 countries already bringing their wisdom to the input for the new IDG framework.

We have often been asked why we do not start with the current framework and simply ask people to give their input on this. The reason is quite simple: we do not think it would be inclusive enough to prompt people around the current framework; instead we should rather try to give everyone the best possible opportunity to bring their own understanding and their own experience from different parts of the world.

Right now we use a few different ways to gather data, and this data will be worked on by research groups in all countries we can engage and then researchers and other categories of wisdom leaders such as indigenous wisdom keepers will work on this data together in order to develop an enriched and widely discussed and deeply experienced framework. The updated framework will be presented at the IDG Summit 2025. We believe this new framework will capture more of the diversity around the IDGs from around the globe.

Our approach to gathering data has focused on two aspects: volume, i.e., getting as many people from as many countries as possible to respond to a simple survey; and diversity, i.e., where the width of unique experience, such as in local communities and indigenous groups, is in focus. We realize that we have to be responsive and inclusive when it comes to the methodologies that we're using. Thus, we use methods focused on volume, like a survey where we are applying the best of technology to reach widely and handle data from many thousands of people securely. And we use other methods that capture people's own words and ideas more fully through, for example, interviews, particularly in contexts where we have found it harder to reach people through the survey approach.

We also experiment with other approaches to systematically exploring ways to understand the inner development dimensions. One such method is to engage researchers with a deep cultural understanding to work on their own cultural artefacts. We help researchers from that particular culture to deeply analyze what's been written or communicated in other ways, about our inner capacities for transformation towards sustainability. We believe that to unpack those things from the lenses of that specific culture can help us identify the wisdom that's been there for many, many thousands of years.

All of these methods are systematically brought together into a large pool of input that we can use to systematically develop a shared framework. This process helps us to understand how to build large-scale capability to further these kinds of processes together, making us able to reach a growing understanding of life changing from place to place and from time to time. The speed of change is high so a lot happens in people's lives across the globe, thus we plan for returning to this process maybe every fifth year to review again what is the right way to frame the IDGs. We have to accept that this is the first iteration at this global scale, and there will be more to learn as a lot is happening around the globe and in academic research, and in the practical and policy integration examples when we're applying IDGs to transform towards sustainable development.

Critiquing the IDGs

For IDGs to deliver, we need to be open to learning from all interesting reflections and criticisms that are raised regarding the IDG initiative. One such criticism concerns what we discussed at some length above – the first framework process not including all parts of the world. If we truly want this to be a global conversation we need to engage much more widely.

One example comes from our work on global collaboration, and the program on global leadership for sustainable development specifically. Here the conversations led us to realize that the first framework, as we would have imagined, was not necessarily fully capturing people's experiences in widely different contexts around the globe. The process at the moment is the first time we are truly able to reach as widely as we would have wanted to be able to, and we have so far (as of November 2024) around 18,000–20,000 responses. We are trying to get further fast, so we'll see where we end up at the end of 2024. Having responses from 100-plus countries is good, and we are proud to have at least one country per continent on our top ten list of responses per country. But we are not content yet. We still need to work together to reach wider, particularly in the different countries and regions in Africa.

Another critique is that inner development cannot be the only lever necessary for sustainable development impact. I have recognized that, particularly in our earlier phases, people may have misinterpreted us and believed that we wanted the IDGs to replace the SDGs. This has never been our argument. We have always argued that inner development is not the only part of what needs to happen to get sustainable development impact. Of course, there are many other kinds of resources and levers that need to be addressed simultaneously.

However, the traditional levers that we have recognized for a long time are themselves also often human-made. The inner development of all those decision-making humans is also, of course, impacted by their inner development skills and capabilities. So, we recognize an interdependence between inner development and all other levers. We need resources and commitments and funding and policy and so on, but all those are also decisions that are going to be happening based on something. And, of course, such resources and mandates are in turn crucial for building the right conditions for inner development.

I also think there has been a relevant discussion regarding what we mean by a framework. Let me unpack how I understand the concept of framework. To me, the framework that we presented (the five dimensions and 23 skills) serves to create a way to present core dimensions that people have found to be important to reflect upon and strengthen our individual and joint efforts towards driving sustainable development transitions forward.

That neither means that these skills are the only possible ones, nor that each and every one of us would be able to master all of them. It actually would be completely impossible to do so. It would not only be far too demanding for one human to master, but there might also be in-built incompatibilities at the level of an individual human being. Being strong in one particular area almost invariably leads to having some more struggles in another. At the individual level you can identify areas you want to build yourself and where you should make sure to build fruitful interpersonal relationships with those with other strengths that may help you overcome and balance your shadow sides. Perhaps the IDG framework in full is probably more appropriate at a team level. Here it can guide a team and its leadership in how to combine and bring people with different strengths and weaknesses together to jointly work on complex adaptive challenges such as sustainable development challenges. I believe that the IDG capabilities and competencies are maybe the most well-described set of such competencies for leaders to master, but we also need to keep attention on how the team and organization create the right conditions to further these capabilities.

Moreover, I believe that one key position for the framework is to guide how we can lead organizations working together horizontally. Here the IDGs provide a very unique element which we can call systems leadership, critical to most transformation processes. As we usually drive transformation processes between different kinds of stakeholder categories, between different organizations, IDGs can be very useful when we want larger sets of organizations to be moving in synergy.

What ideas do you have about how to move the needle on inner to outer transformation action?

The core IDG questions about inner development for outer transformation is moving more and more into the core of large-scale global policy processes. One example is the UN-appointed independent research panel tasked with assessing progress on UN Agenda 2030 every fourth year. These important panels of scientists from very different backgrounds come up with a shared reflection on what progress has been identified and the priorities laying ahead for us. The first independent panel delivered their report called *The Future Is Now* in 2019 to the UN secretary general, and they had many different and interesting points to bring (Independent Group of Scientists appointed by the Secretary General, 2019). For the IDG ecosystem, they made one especially poignant conclusion, namely that human capabilities and well-being must be considered the most important factor for successful sustainable development.

The next independent panel delivered their report four years later, in 2023 (Independent Group of Scientists appointed by the Secretary General, 2023). They choose to focus on the necessary transitions that we require to get to a more sustainable future for all people and the whole planet. We need to actively engage now to be able to drive these transitions together, as fast and as consistently as we can muster, to be able to turn the tide on our unsustainable development. Getting it right requires that we shift our attention to how we can navigate this process and establish such collaborative advantages that we need to make words and commitments become a reality.

In their summary, they are looking at three main strategies. First, we've got to consider all different securities and elements of sustainability to be deeply interdependent. We cannot just continue to act separately between the 17 different SDGs as they all are all so deeply intertwined; success in one part may develop at the expense of success in some of the others. So, we have to consider them integrated. Here, the overarching five elements of sustainable development in UN Agenda 2030, i.e., people, planet, prosperity, partnership, and peace, and the intersection of fundamental dimensions of ecological, economic, and social sustainability could help us see just how indivisible these are and make us able to address their synergy front and center.

Second, this requires the most significant collaborative effort that humans have ever organized. So, it's a massive approach where everyone needs to get on board, and we have to find the direction to travel together, much in line with the Donella Meadows quote earlier in this chapter. Billions of people need to take their own necessary steps, experimenting and learning how to work their way. No singular person is going to be the hero, but everyone needs to do their job. And that leads also to the third idea of this 2023 report, which really and truly asks us to consider hope and agency as key critical resources.

There they are, the three strategic transformations written in plain text. But how do we make them become our way of leading our lives, driving our organizations together, and making our societies thrive? Here, I think, is where the IDGs can really help. They provide a shared language to help us pinpoint some elements of the necessary human capabilities – core capabilities for navigating our process forward in all kinds of different situations. Through the IDGs we've learned that we have got to get to acting and that action is driven by our being and thinking. By relating well and coming together, we are ready to engage other collaborators. Through this we are able to bring the diversity of competencies and experience in a team, in an organization, and between organizations for the betterment of our societies, for our children, their children, and for generations to come. After all, now it's time to decide what ancestor we want to be!

Everywhere around the globe we are starting to see living examples of people, organizations, and local, regional, and national communities coming together trying to practically build the inner development conditions to make such sustainable development transformation possible. I am a firm believer that how this should be done will vary. I think that the path towards the future will be guided both by experience and research. At the core is how people are able to relate to each other, the place, and the living animals and nature where we live and how we make others able to do the same.

For me, having spent most of my career bringing different stakeholders together to drive transformative processes with their specific experience and their specific competence and mandate, this experience has led me to consider that maybe one of the absolute central dimensions could be something we can call systems leadership. This means that it's a leadership position for one or many that jointly is able to hold a shared ambition at the front and center, helping to bring each organization and each and every person in those organizations to act together towards that shared aim. I see it in different kinds of processes, such as those that Mariana Mazzucato calls missions (Mazzucato, 2022) and in other similar concerted efforts to orchestrate change. These form the core of joint social movements of different sorts, but I think we also must recognize that we transform quickly and well without accessing resources and helpful levers from business, policy, civil society, academia, and grassroots processes all together. In essence, we need to respectfully look at how all these can add their specific piece to the giant shared jigsaw puzzle that we need to build in a synergetic fashion.

This requires far more action, not just words. IDGs can help us be guided in how to invite others, how to find our own motivation, how to be able to withstand pressures and dare to challenge the traditional way of functioning. If I'm reaching out a hand to someone else, we could possibly build that core, that team that can take on the process. We are making active choices to act with the agency we need to take necessary decisions and often challenge ourselves and others. We must build a thick layer of trust so that we are able to experiment and thus learn from our mistakes. We will make mistakes, particularly when we're trying to formulate and try out new approaches. Our best bet is therefore to build a culture of learning between previously polarized structures. Our way forward must start with a positive view of humankind. So, we really need IDGs to help us recognize how to build the right conditions for each other. We should stay away from simplistic, competitive, win-lose dynamics because they are just not able to help us to get to decisions; they can often lock in our opportunities for shared development. So, the more we can respect what we bring as persons and see that these capabilities, together with someone else's complementary resources, is what we need to reach our shared aim. The more we can do that, the better we are able to take on the sustainable development challenges.

But we also have to make sense of what makes us able to see the world in that way. Our lenses must be sharpened so we can access and embody our inner compass, the values, worldviews, and perspectives we bring and be curious about how our different approaches to ourselves affect our willingness to see the strength in someone else. We can map out many different things together when we apply solid perspective taking, allowing for a strong analytical complexity awareness.

Donella Meadows once said that a good leader sets the right goals and gets the right thing moving, but more than that, they help us discover that we already know what to do (Meadows, 1991). So, we have a lot of these capabilities, but they have just not been prioritized. They have not been valued in organizations or societies where a lot has been focused on competitive dynamics. I think that certainly must change. Success for everyone is the only way; we cannot ethically and acceptably leave anyone behind. The principle that everyone must be included in this process must become a core foundation to reach our shared agenda.

If you had a magic wand, what would be your wish?

I would wish that the strength of this diverse ecosystem around the globe – what we call the IDG initiative – would become visible to everyone. We would start to see how people respect each other across the globe, across different stakeholder categories, and see the value of bringing others along. However, we still, to be sure, have a lot more to do when it comes to reaching out widely and becoming more inclusive. We need to be able to build the right kinds of bridges for everyone across different kinds of economic, social, and cultural diversities around the world. For example, I certainly would want us to be able to substantiate the engagement from different parts of the world.

Another important promising development is our work on lifelong learning, engaging with age groups before and after our active work life. I think taking a life-course approach is very, very helpful. Understanding better what the different phases of life would look like if they were designed with inner to outer transformation at the core would be very important. Inner development for outer transformation is naturally a life-wide and lifelong process, so we need to start in early years both in formal and informal settings of learning and proceed into elementary school and further into student inner development at university. I am also interested in bringing the intergenerational learning connecting young with people at older ages in our societies. There are a lot of experiments addressing lifelong learning opportunities. The steps taken in many different parts of the world in this area are trying to tap into and accelerate transformation together between academic, global civil society, and other stakeholders, including, of course, young people themselves.

We also must address the factors that may be hindering us – the barriers driving us away from where we need to be. I think one such barrier is that we culturally, at least in western and northern countries, rely on a very strong, simplistic, rationalistic, productivity-oriented view of what humans are and what humans can be. If humans are allowed to flourish and bring their best selves to solving problems together, we are able to make brilliant things happen. How we value humans at the highest level of business and policy and really, truly, live up to what we otherwise often just express in words, is central to success in our efforts. At a time of AI and other technological shifts, we've got to be better at being humans and value our own unique human capabilities to master this force in the best possible way.

The last element, of course, is that all these kinds of global movements – and rest assured that the IDG initiative is still very young as a movement – always struggle with their funding.

So, finding innovative ways to bring inspired funders to really work together to build a longer time frame with us to substantiate all the good things we have is, I think, a very important priority to stabilize and make all the voluntary engagement that we're seeing across the global IDG ecosystem more solid. This is true within our researcher co-creation circles but also in the hubs and elsewhere in our ecosystem.

Just imagine what we could do if we got some more stable structures and funding opportunities. This would make it possible for many more to shift even more of their time and attention to working together in the IDG ecosystem.

References

Independent Group of Scientists appointed by the Secretary General. (2019). Global sustainable development report 2019: The future is now – science for achieving sustainable development. United Nations.

Independent Group of Scientists appointed by the Secretary General. (2023). Global sustainable development report 2023: Times of crisis, times of change: Science for accelerating transformations to sustainable development. United Nations.

Inner Development Goals. (2021). Inner Development Goals: Background, method and the IDG framework. https://innerdevelopmentgoals.org/about/resources/ [Accessed on Sep. 10, 2024].

Inner Development Goals. (2022). Inner Development Goals Phase 2 Research Report. https://innerdevelopmentgoals.org/about/resources/ [Accessed on Sep. 10, 2024].

Mazzucato, Mariana. (2021). Mission Economy: A Moonshot Guide to Changing Capitalism. London: Allen Lane-Penguin. ISBN 978–0-241-41973-1. OCLC 1222804339.

Meadows, Donella. (2021). The Question Of Leadership: A good leader sets the right goals, gets things moving, and helps us discover that we already know what to do. The Donella Meadows Project. Retrieved from the web https://donellameadows.org/archives/the-question-of-leadership-a-good-leader-sets-the-right-goals-gets-things-moving-and-helps-us-discover-that-we-already-know-what-to-do/.

Meadows, Donella, Randers, Jorgen and Meadows, Dennis. (2004). *Limits to Growth: The 30-Year Update*. Chelsea Green Publishing.

Christine Wamsler and Jeroen Janss

Chapter 23
Towards an increasing institutionalization of inner development goals: From individual to culture and system transformation

Abstract: The Global Leadership for Sustainable Development (GLSD) is the first international capacity-building program based on the Inner Development Goals (IDGs) framework. It supports leaders in developing transformative capacities and skills, and integrating the IDGs into their organizational processes, policies, strategies, and operations, with the ultimate aim to accelerate action towards the Sustainable Development Goals (SDGs) and build vital networks for culture and system transformation. The first pilot capacity-building program was implemented in 2023; it included high-level decision makers from government, the private sector, civil society, and academia involved in implementing the SDGs in Albania, Colombia, Costa Rica, India, Rwanda, and Zambia. In this chapter, we: (1) present how the pilot capacity-building program came about; (2) describe its evaluation process and outcomes; and (3) summarize related key learnings regarding how sustainability leadership and education can become a vehicle for transformation. Based on our results, we provide guidance for designing and assessing sustainability leadership and education programs, which have also guided the second round of GLSD capacity development. We highlight how personal development can support culture and system change, if certain principles are in place. The focus needs to shift from individual education, towards empowering participants to jointly challenge unsustainable social paradigms and systematically mainstream the consideration of inner dimensions and capacities into existing cultures, organizational mechanisms, and structures.

Keywords: capacity building, capacity development, climate leadership, transformational learning, leadership education, sustainability education, transformative capacities, transformative skills, institutionalization, mainstreaming, policy integration, culture change, systems transformation, mindsets, paradigms, worldviews, monitoring and evaluation

Introduction

Little progress has been made since the UN Sustainable Development Goals (SDGs) were launched in 2015. The dominant policy approaches have failed to generate action at anywhere near the rate, scale, or depth that is needed (IPCC, 2022a, 2022b). This is

https://doi.org/10.1515/9783111453729-024

largely due to the fact that sustainability challenges have generally been framed as external threats or crises (Leichenko & O'Brien, 2020). Hence, we try to address them with external, primarily technical measures, simply because how we define problems automatically determines our responses (Wamsler & Bristow, 2022). This approach has, in turn, narrowed opportunities for deeper change that tackles the root causes of today's polycrisis (Filho & McCrea, 2018; Wamsler et al., 2021).

A crucial dimension is thus missing from current policy approaches: our inner lives and inner capacities (Ives et al., 2023; Wamsler et al., 2020a, 2021). We have missed asking how we can address the root causes of today's polycrisis and nurture the inner capacities and skills necessary to work effectively together to respond to increasing societal threats (Ives et al., 2023; Wamsler et al., 2020a, 2021).

The Inner Development Goals (IDGs) framework was a response to this insight. The IDGs are a communication tool that advocates for increased consideration of inner, transformative capacities and skills to help accelerate work towards sustainability and regeneration. The framework was co-designed by thousands of experts, practitioners, and scientists (IDGs, 2021) and is linked to other scientific models, such as the inner-outer transformation model (Wamsler et al., 2021).

Global Leadership for Sustainable Development (GLSD) is the first capacity-building program that is based on the IDG framework. It was developed under the IDG initiative and with a range of partners. The program aims to support leaders to accelerate progress towards the SDGs. More specifically, it helps leaders to build vital networks for culture and system transformation through developing inner capacities and skills, and integrate the IDGs into organizational processes, policies, strategies, and operations. A pilot program was launched in 2023. It included high-level decision makers from government, the private sector, civil society, and academia who were involved in implementing the SDGs in Albania, Colombia, Costa Rica, India, Rwanda, and Zambia.

A mixed-methods analysis was used to evaluate the GLSD program and its effects on participants' sustainability work. The findings led to the identification of a number of key learnings for future programs that aim to support integrative inner-outer transformation (Rupprecht & Wamsler, 2023; Wamsler, Janss, & Bell, 2023; see also Table 23.1 for a description of the field).

In the following section, we present the origins of the pilot capacity-building program ("The backstory: How the GLSD capacity-building program came about"). Then, we describe the evaluation process and outcomes ("The results: Evaluation process and outcomes of the GLSD"), summarize the key learnings, and describe how they have been adopted in subsequent programs ("Key learnings and essentials for accelerating culture and system change"). We show how sustainability leadership and education can become a vehicle for transformation – if certain key elements or principles are in place. Our results provide guidance for designing and assessing sustainability leadership and education programs, and set a precedent that other training institutions could follow or learn from.

The backstory: How the GLSD capacity-building program came about

Like the IDG framework, the GLSD program has been a collective effort. It has involved close cooperation between academics, leadership experts, and sustainability specialists. The aim of this collaborative effort was to translate the IDG framework, and associated tools, into an engaging and co-creative learning journey.

The story of the GLSD started in 2021, the year when the IDG framework was created, and before the development of the IDG toolkit. In the spring of 2021, the Inner Green Deal piloted a ten-week international Climate Leadership Program (CLP), which was designed, conducted, and assessed in close cooperation with Lund University Centre for Sustainability Studies (LUCSUS). The program integrated inner and outer dimensions of transformation (Wamsler et al., 2021) and was one of the first of its kind to be run internationally, within private and public institutions. The EU's training institute offered the CLP to staff working for a range of EU institutions, and in the same year it was included in their standard learning package.

CLP participants included a number of leadership experts and facilitators, notably Jan Artem Henriksson (now executive director of the IDG initiative) and Åsa Jarskog (now director for global cooperation of the IDG initiative). Both were familiar with the program through their work with LUCSUS, which had been a formal IDG partner since the very beginning. During the action lab, as part of the CLP program, Jan and Åsa decided to build on their shared leadership development experience and apply insights from the program to the IDGs and related initiatives. Their idea, the GLSD, was born.

Around the same time, other capacity-building initiatives were developed that built on the work of the Inner Green Deal and associated research. Examples include the Mindfulness-Based Sustainable Transformation course, the associated train-the-trainer program, and the first Conscious Food Systems Leadership Program, run by the UNDP and the Conscious Food Systems Alliance (Wamsler et al., 2022). These initiatives sought to integrate knowledge and learning from the previous program(s) and associated scientific assessments (e.g., Ramstetter et al., 2023; Wamsler et al., 2023). At the same time, all these programs decided to adopt the IDGs as an important communication tool and became part of the associated movement of actors who are pushing for a new, more relational narrative that challenges current unsustainable views, practices, and structures.

At the end of 2022, the GLSD program was launched with the support of the Templeton World Charity Foundation. The foundation fully funded the participation of over 100 sustainability leaders from six countries, and an in-person kick-off event in Rwanda, with representatives from all countries. The online program was first run between February and April 2023, facilitated by Åsa Jarskog (from the IDGs) and Jeroen Janss (from the Inner Green Deal). It was the first of its kind, and scientifically supported and evaluated by Professor Christine Wamsler, LUCSUS.

The close collaboration between the IDG initiative, LUCSUS, and the Inner Green Deal led to important scientific advancements in the field of inner-outer transformation, which has continuously enriched diverse courses and educational programs worldwide. Progress has included, amongst other things: the use of the inner-outer transformation model for designing, monitoring, and evaluation (Wamsler et al., 2021); the identification of key elements and principles to ensure transformation across individual, collective, and systems levels (Wamsler et al., 2024); and the development of ways to systematically institutionalize the consideration of integrative measures that link inner and outer dimensions.

The pilot GLSD program was completed in 2023, and results were presented at the IDG summit in October 2023 (Rupprecht & Wamsler, 2023; Wamsler, Janss, & Bell, 2023). The successful completion of the pilot enabled the launch of a second GLSD in March 2024 (as we write this article), with a greater focus on institutionalization at organizational and inter-organizational levels.

The results: Evaluation process and outcomes of the GLSD

The results of the analysis of the first GLSD found high levels of impact and satisfaction among leaders from government, the private sector, civil society, and academia. The five key results are summarized below.[1]

Key Result 1: Integration of inner and outer transformation for sustainability

The IDG framework proved highly relevant in supporting human flourishing and sustainability work across individual, collective, and systems levels. Participants demonstrated a significant increase in action taking for sustainability. Following the program, 95% of participants reported actively engaging in more SDGs and related actions. In particular, the "Partnerships" goal, relevant to all of the other SDGs, received a significant boost from participation in the program (+22%). The same applied to "Good Health and Wellbeing" and "Sustainable Cities and Communities" (both +22%).

Encouragingly, the results showed a large, post-training increase in the integration of inner dimensions into sustainability-related work processes. By the end of the program, on average, 63% of participants had initiated some, or substantial changes

---

[1] This section presents adapted text extracts from Rupprecht and Wamsler (2023) and Wamsler, Janss, and Bell (2023).

in, for example, their organization's strategic priorities, learning and development activities, and stakeholder and project management approaches (see Figure 23.1).

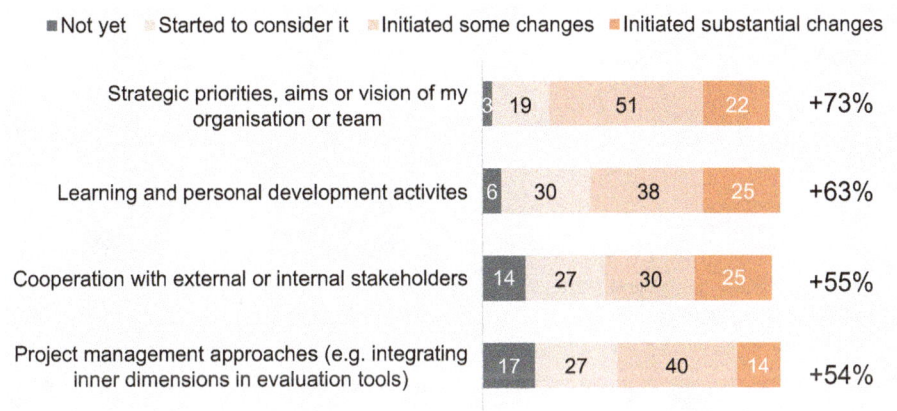

Figure 23.1: Change in integrating inner dimensions into organizational work processes that supported human flourishing and sustainability work across individual, collective, and systems levels. Source: Wamsler et al. (2023).

Key Result 2: Strengthening of inner capacities and skills

All learning activities were found to be impactful, and all of the 23 capacities and skills (e.g., self-awareness, connectedness, and inner compass) were reported as strengthened by some participants (nine each, on average; see Figure 23.2). Participants also expressed strengthened feelings of hope and collective agency, which are crucial to sustaining action.

In addition, the analyses showed that changes in IDGs were highly interrelated: improvements in certain qualities were consistently accompanied by improvements in others.

Key Result 3: Nurturing a foundational mindset of connection for sustainability

The roots of today's sustainability crises lie in a culturally entrenched mindset of separation from others and from nature – even from ourselves (our thoughts, emotions, and bodily feelings; Ives et al., 2023; Rosa, 2021; Scott et al., 2021; Wamsler et al., 2020a; Wamsler & Bristow, 2022). Cultivating a sense of reconnection is thus a vital foundation for sustainability work, as illustrated by the inner-outer transformation model (Wamsler et al., 2021; see Figure 23.5).

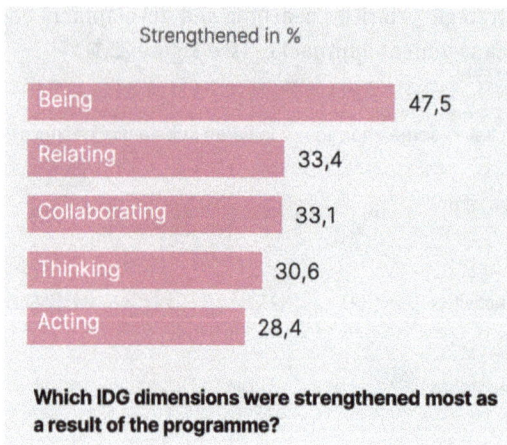

Figure 23.2: IDGs that were strengthened most as a result of the program. Source: Wamsler et al. (2023).

Against this background, the assessment of the qualitative data indicated that the GLSD program influenced participants' relationship to self, others, and nature in ways that underpin greater connectedness and action taking for sustainability across sectors and scales.

Key Result 4: Increased trust lowers eco-anxiety, unlocking sustainability action

Interestingly, the analysis also showed that increased trust in humanity, post-training, lessened the undermining effect of eco-anxiety, while in turn, lowered anxiety was related to taking increased action at work. This is a crucial outcome, since anxiety around humanity's capacity to cope with climate and other crises is on the rise (Hickman et al., 2021; Ogunbode et al., 2022; Wamsler, 2020; Wullenkord & Ojala, 2023) and a significant proportion of participants linked this worry to underperformance at work.

Key Result 5: Program quality and satisfaction

Participants also reported very high levels of satisfaction with the program and its delivery with respect to key objectives, and 97% said they would recommend it. As one participant noted: "This program should be for every human on the planet."

The success of the first GLSD program led to support for further programs, and the inclusion of new countries (the 2024 GLSD 2.0 was split in two: a Spanish-language program for Latin America, and an English-language program for Europe, Africa, and Asia).

The opportunity to extend the program was also used to reflect on the evaluation's outcomes, possible improvements, and what, ultimately, should be the focus of programs that link inner and outer transformation for sustainability. Discussions with participants and the GLSD program team (facilitators, donors, and researchers) highlighted that out of all of the outcomes, the most valuable and impactful one was Key Result 1. Key Result 1 refers to the integration and institutionalization of inner and outer change for sustainability, and related changes that were initiated across individual, collective, and systems levels. Emergent research on inner-outer transformation had been increasingly calling for more attention to be paid to these aspects (IPBES, 2024; IPCC, 2022a, 2022b; Ives et al., 2023; Wamsler et al., 2020a, 2021; Wamsler & Osberg, 2022).

GLSD 2.0 was launched in March 2024 and incorporated the outcomes and new understanding presented above. Accordingly, in GLSD 2.0 participants are asked to join the program in teams with colleagues, and work and experiment from the very start of the program with integrating inner and outer change in their organizations, and advancing the ecosystem of relevant organizations to create a field of change.

Key learnings and essentials for accelerating culture and system change

Findings from the GLSD and Inner Green Deal programs (Mindfulness-Based Sustainable Transformation, CLP, those for the EU and UNDP), have advanced knowledge on the complex intersection between sustainability, inner development, and transformation, from the individual to the global level. In addition, they provide insights that can be used to design leadership and education programs to accelerate work towards the SDGs. They can be summarized as follows:[2]

Leadership courses that aim to accelerate sustainability transformation must support participants in addressing the impacts, drivers, and causes of today's polycrisis through integrative approaches that link inner and outer dimensions of transformation across sectors and levels. This, in turn, requires providing: (1) a comprehensive understanding of the nature of today's polycrisis in a complex, constantly changing world, and one's role in it; (2) safe spaces and holistic methods for exploring inner dimensions and nurturing transformative capacities on a continuous basis; (3) practical guidance on how to design and implement integrative measures that address individual, behavioral, culture, and system change (and associated power structures) in

---

2 This section of the chapter is adapted from Wamsler et al. (2023), with input from Rupprecht & Wamsler (2023) and other program evaluations conducted by the Contemplative Sustainable Futures Program at LUCSUS (www.contemplative-sustainable-futures.com).

combination; and (4) ensuring quality education through the explicit consideration of ethics, the role of facilitators, and adequate monitoring and evaluation (see Figure 23.3). Together, these four essentials, or key ingredients, can support individual, collective, and planetary well-being, flourishing, and regeneration by covering all aspects of inner-outer transformation (ontology, epistemology, praxis, ethics) as identified in Ives et al. (2023). In the following, we describe the four essentials in more detail.

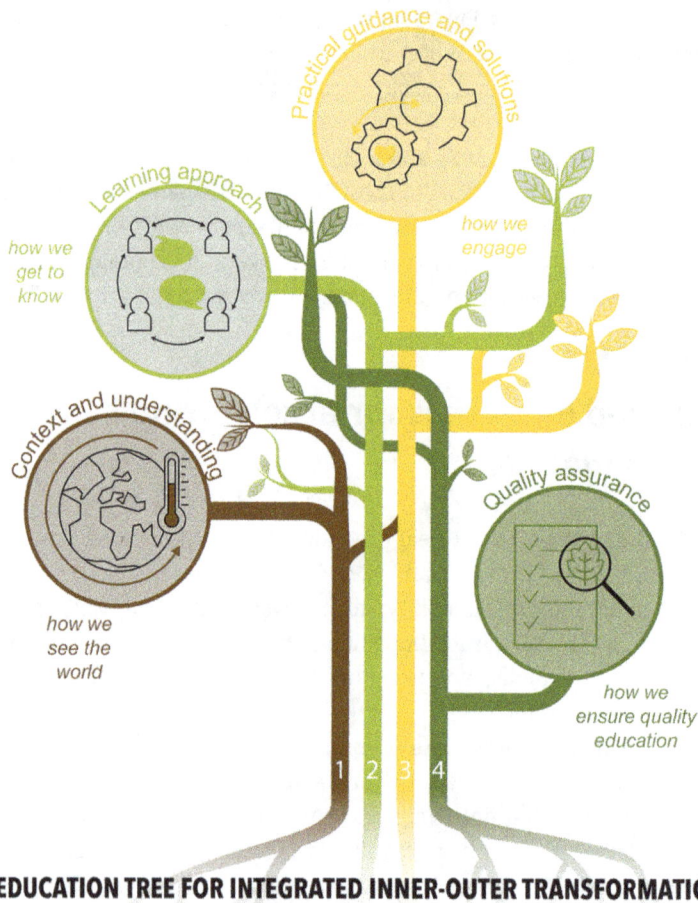

EDUCATION TREE FOR INTEGRATED INNER-OUTER TRANSFORMATION

Figure 23.3: Education tree for integrated inner-outer transformation. Adapted from Wamsler et al. (2024). The figure visualizes the four essential pieces for holistic learning and understanding to accelerate sustainability and transformation. They involve: (1) how we see the world; (2) how we get to know; (3) how we engage; and (4) how we ensure quality and equity considerations across all aspects. Together, they support well-being, flourishing, and regeneration across scales—by covering all of the key contributions of inner-outer transformation.

Essential 1: A comprehensive understanding of today's polycrisis and our role in it

Analyses of the different programs made it clear that participants' starting points, and the challenges they encounter during the courses, are often a reflection of modern society's dominant social paradigm (e.g., self-centered individualism, dualist thinking, techno-optimism, overwhelm, exhaustion, and stress; Kilbourne, Beckmann, & Thelen, 2002; Scott et al., 2021). It is crucial to make related aspects explicit if we seek to accelerate the uptake of participants' learning into their work contexts, which may operate under related norms.

Our assumptions about the nature of reality shape how problems are defined and understood, and the mental models or theories of how change comes about. They influence how we understand our own agency to support change, and how and why each of us matters in responding to global crises. Providing related information is thus crucial and requires understanding the following key aspects that relate to the ontological dimension of inner-outer transformation for sustainability:

– the nature of today's societal crises;
– the nature of the complex systems involved; and
– the associated mind-sustainability nexus.

The resultant theory of change (latent human potential, the interdependence of inner/ outer and individual/collective/system phenomena) is contrary to current mainstream thinking (Ives et al., 2023; Wamsler & Bristow, 2022). Providing related understanding is thus essential.

There is mounting evidence that today's societal crises have one common denominator, or root cause: they are a reflection of an inner human crisis of disconnection, separation, or alienation from self, others, and nature, which is itself grounded in modern society's social paradigm and associated life forms (Rosa, 2021). This paradigm is based on the understanding that our thinking mind is separate from our feelings and bodily emotions, that we are all separate from each other, that some humans are superior to others, and that we humans are separate and superior to the rest of the natural world (Scott et al., 2021). Addressing sustainability crises thus requires a shift away from these exploitative paradigms to more relational and regenerative ones (Böhme, 2023; Walsh, Böhme, & Wamsler, 2021; West et al., 2020).

The shift involves engaging in complex systems, both individually and collectively (see the second point listed above). Engaging in complex systems is, however, challenging, because they are fundamentally unlike machines (and thus contrasting modern society's dominant social narrative). Complexity research indicates that complex systems undergo a self-organization process that ultimately shapes the state they are in, and which emerges from relationship patterns within the system (Slingo et al., 2008). Consequently, system transformation concerns changing relationship patterns, and requires addressing the human, inner dimensions that influence the quality of these relationships and help people to (re)connect.

Addressing such dimensions requires, in turn, an in-depth understanding of the mind-sustainability nexus (the third aspect listed above). Related research shows that this nexus is fourfold, with the mind being: (1) a root cause, or driver of today's crises (see the first point above); (2) a victim of these crises (e.g., seen in increasing levels of eco-anxiety); and (3) a barrier for adequate action (e.g., due to cognitive biases and a related increase in polarization); which together result in (4) a vicious cycle of deteriorating individual, societal, and planetary well-being (Wamsler & Bristow, 2022; see Figure 23.4). At the same time, research reports that humans possess the innate capacity for deep conscious connection (Hunecke, 2018; Kegan & Lahey, 2009; Scott et al., 2021), which can help to reverse this vicious cycle and start a virtuous cycle that supports flourishing across all scales (Figure 23.4).

Taken together, the described aspects provide an understanding of how and why each of us matters in responding to today's polycrisis. They illustrate the need to move from an understanding of people being "agents to be changed" to being "change agents". They also show that tapping into this potential is about supporting human capacities and conditions for (re)connection. Such capacities are called transformative capacities, or Inner Development Goals, and they have been systematized in emergent research into five broad clusters (Inner Development Goals, 2021, 2022; Wamsler et al., 2020a, 2021; see Essential 2).

Essential 2: Integrative methods for exploring inner dimensions and nurturing transformative capacities

The understanding presented under Essential 1 means that change cannot be approached using the same mindsets and conceptions of knowledge that underpin it. It necessitates a different approach to epistemology (i.e., the inclusion of different kinds of knowledge systems, different approaches to knowledge development, how we come to know) and weaving together diverse perspectives (see Figure 23.3).

Sustainability leadership and education thus rely upon the following aspects that relate to the epistemological dimension of inner-outer transformation:

- a balanced mix of methods that support holistic learning and (re)connection (through cultivating cognitive, social, emotional, relational, and ethical capacities/qualities); which, in turn, requires
- the adjustment of methods for inner development to the context of sustainability;
- the consideration of the foundational role of mindfulness- and compassion-based methods; and
- a process that supports repeated, regular, and continuous practice, together with communities of practice, to foster fields of change.

IMPROVING PERSONAL AND PLANETARY WELLBEING AND FLOURISHING
CONNECTION TO SELF, OTHERS, WORLD

VIRTUOUS CYCLE

SUSTAINABILITY CRISES
• Sustainability-related risks and hazards
• Complexity, uncertainty, unpredictability
• Interrelated societal crises

Influence on individual and
collective wellbeing and
response capacities

Influence on sustainability
crises, related systems and
responses

MIND
• Victim of sustainability crises
• Barrier/driver for sustainable actions
• Root cause of sustainability crises

VICIOUS CYCLE

DISCONNECTION FROM SELF, OTHERS, WORLD
DETERIORATING PERSONAL AND PLANETARY WELLBEING AND FLOURISHING

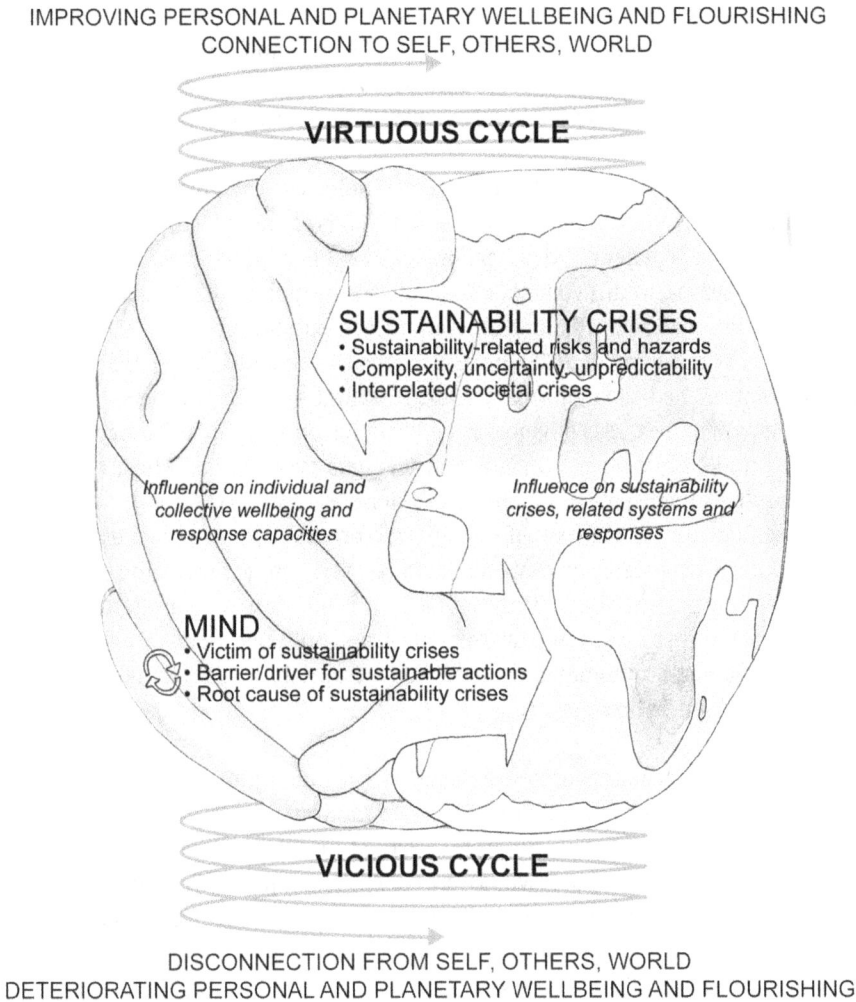

Figure 23.4: The intersection of mind and sustainability. Source: Adapted from Wamsler & Bristow (2022), cf. Janss et al. (2023), Wamsler (2022).

Based on a comprehensive understanding of how, and why, each of us matters in responding to societal crises (Essential 1), sustainability education and leadership require applying methods that, in combination, can support holistic learning (CCCE, 2019) and restore the connection to self, others, and nature in an integrative way.

Increasing scientific evidence shows that humans possess the innate capacity for deep conscious connection, and that it can be restored or strengthened through certain methods, and throughout our lifetime (CCCE, 2019; Hunecke, 2018; Scott et al., 2021; Waldinger & Schulz, 2023). In the context of sustainability, this involves nourishing all clusters of transformative capacities and addressing all facets of the mind-sustainability nexus (see Essential 1). Applied in such a way, these actions can become a vehicle for transformation across individual, collective, and systems levels. Restoring conscious connection increases not only personal resilience amid adversity, but also our chances of addressing the root causes of today's sustainability crises and mobilizing change.

Relevant methods include contemplative, psychological, cognitive-behavioral, and ethical communication and learning approaches, and creating safe (and brave) spaces to allow related engagement and reflection (Arao & Clemens, 2013; Mar et al., 2023; Wamsler et al., 2020a). In this context, our results also support other studies that indicate the foundational role of mindfulness and compassion practices (CCCE, 2019; Wamsler, 2018; Wamsler et al., 2018). If we trace the roots of the climate crisis through a culturally entrenched story of separateness (Essential 1), the relevance of mindfulness and compassion becomes obvious, as both can foster fundamental aspects of connection, and thus revert from a vicious to a virtuous cycle of individual, collective, and planetary well-being (Wamsler, 2018; Wamsler & Bristow 2022).

At the same time, our analyses of the different programs showed that engaging in inner and outer dimensions, or on IDGs and SDGs separately, misses the point, and highlights the importance of adapting methods for inner development to the context of sustainability. Other research confirms that we should not assume that methods for inner development automatically, or quickly, translate into sustainability advocacy, and action on a broader scale (Scott et al., 2021; Wamsler, 2019; Wamsler et al., 2021).

Against this background, our research shows how mindfulness-based approaches can be oriented towards sustainability. Similar to the way they have been adapted to the context of stress and depression, in the form of mindfulness-based stress reduction (MBSR; Grossman et al., 2004; Woods et al., 2021) and mindfulness-based cognitive therapy (MBCT; Segal, Williams & Teasdale, 2012), our research provided guiding principles for (developing the concept of) mindfulness-based sustainable transformation (Mindfulness-Based Sustainable Transformation). The latter involves linking mindfulness more closely to compassion, nature-based approaches, and reflection practices (such as reflective dyads) that proved to be particularly relevant in developing more relational perspectives, beliefs, and engagement (Ramstetter et al., 2023; Kok & Singer, 2017). In addition, there is a need to build (back) normative mindfulness ethics that were stripped away when the approach was popularized for the Western context, as they are crucial for the context of sustainability and associated intrinsic, universal values (Stanley, 2012; Walsh, 2016).

Finally, our research demonstrates that inner-outer transformation is a continuous process. Thus, processes must be in place to help participants engage regularly and continuously in the offered methods and practices both throughout the program and after it ends. In particular, when participants come from different organizations or communities, targeted efforts are required to sustain momentum. The establishment of communities of practice, study groups, and book circles are concrete examples of measures that can help participants to keep their practices and engagement alive (Stuckey & Smith, 2004).

Essential 3: Practical guidance on how to design and implement integrative measures for individual, behavioral, culture, and system change

The results of our research make it clear that inner-outer transformation is not a purely introspective exercise that is an alternative or complement to tangible, practical change. In fact, our research shows that understanding and experiencing how and why each of us matter, and nourishing transformative capacities through different methods and practices (Essentials 1 and 2), is insufficient to adequately translate participants' learning into concrete measures across sectors and scales. Our findings indicate that explicit guidance is required on how to design and implement integrative approaches that link inner and outer dimensions of sustainability across sectors and scales, which relates to the praxis dimension of inner-outer transformation (cf. Ives et al., 2023). It involves:

- a collaborative, action-oriented platform for the continuous application of learning to participants' organizations and wider work contexts;
- practical knowledge on how the consideration of human, inner dimensions can be systematically institutionalized/mainstreamed into organizations and organizational ecosystems; and
- the combination of solution-oriented, critical and creative approaches to sustain related engagement.

To avoid an inner-outer dichotomy and dualism, inner work has to go hand in hand with its continuous application to the work context, not only in the final program modules. This important result emerged from both the CLP and the GLSP program (e.g., Rupprecht & Wamsler, 2023), and it has been increasingly considered in subsequent programs (such as the GLSP 2.0 and the Mindfulness-Based Sustainable Transformation course). Participants are now asked to reflect on work-related needs, challenges, and potentials from the beginning of the courses.

Translating learning to participants' work contexts requires specific knowledge and skills regarding how to work with others to systematically integrate/mainstream the consideration of sustainability and associated inner dimensions within existing organizational mechanisms and structures. Whilst linking individual, behavioral, culture, and system change is crucial for supporting transformation, integrative approaches were rarely featured in participants' reported projects and engagement. Isolated changes in organizations' strategic priorities, aims or visions, working structures, communication, project management approaches, staff development, monitoring, evaluation, or human and financial resource allocation is not sufficient and, therefore, guidance on how to design and implement integrative measures across sectors and scales is essential.

Finally, methods that can support a combination of critical and problem-solving approaches (that focus on adequately responding to problems, and what has to be fixed) with more creative approaches (that focus on tapping into people's inner potential and realizing sustainability imaginaries) are, in this context, key to sustaining engagement and transformation (Fritz, 1989; IPBES, 2024; Senge, 1999, 2006; Sharma, 2017).

Essential 4: Quality education through the consideration of differences, ethics, adequate facilitation, monitoring, and evaluation

To adequately implement Essentials 1–3, it is crucial that quality and ethical considerations are taken into account. This involves the following aspects that cut across the ontological, epistemological, and praxis dimensions of inner-outer transformation:
- the embodied experience of the trainer(s) regarding, for example, relational pedagogies and ethics;
- the consideration of contextual and individual differences, fostering inclusivity and intercultural learning; and
- adequate program monitoring and evaluation (including relational, learner-focused, and collaborative approaches).

Our results support research which indicates that trainers themselves play a key role in participants' learning (Mezirow, 2018). The ability to move beyond traditional, teacher-centric pedagogy, towards relational, dialogic, human-centered methods, invite different perspectives, and give a sense of the complexity without overwhelming or confusing participants, is important. Facilitators who lack extensive experience with the offered methods, or an in-depth understanding of today's polycrisis, might do more harm than good to individual well-being and sustainability agendas. Personal burnout, reinforcing either-or propositions in inner-outer work, or preserving business as usual through "fix-it" and "fix-others" approaches that reinforce current unsustainable paradigms are concrete examples (Bentz, O'Brien, & Scoville-Simonds, 2022).

Our results also show that learning is highly personal, multifaceted, and contextual. Offering a diversity of methods and entry points for exploring inner-outer transformation is thus crucial, together with continuously improving and decolonizing pedagogy to foster inclusivity and intercultural learning.

Finally, our research studies also highlight how challenging it is to assess and evaluate leadership and education programs that involve both inner and outer transformation, and distil what contributed to the success of a program. They indicate that current monitoring and evaluation approaches must be adjusted to take account of a more comprehensive understanding of today's sustainability crises, and the associated theories of change (see Essential 1). The presented approach, based on the inner-outer transformation model and related mainstreaming theory, has proved to be valuable in shedding light on the complexities at play (Figure 23.5; Wamsler et al., 2021;

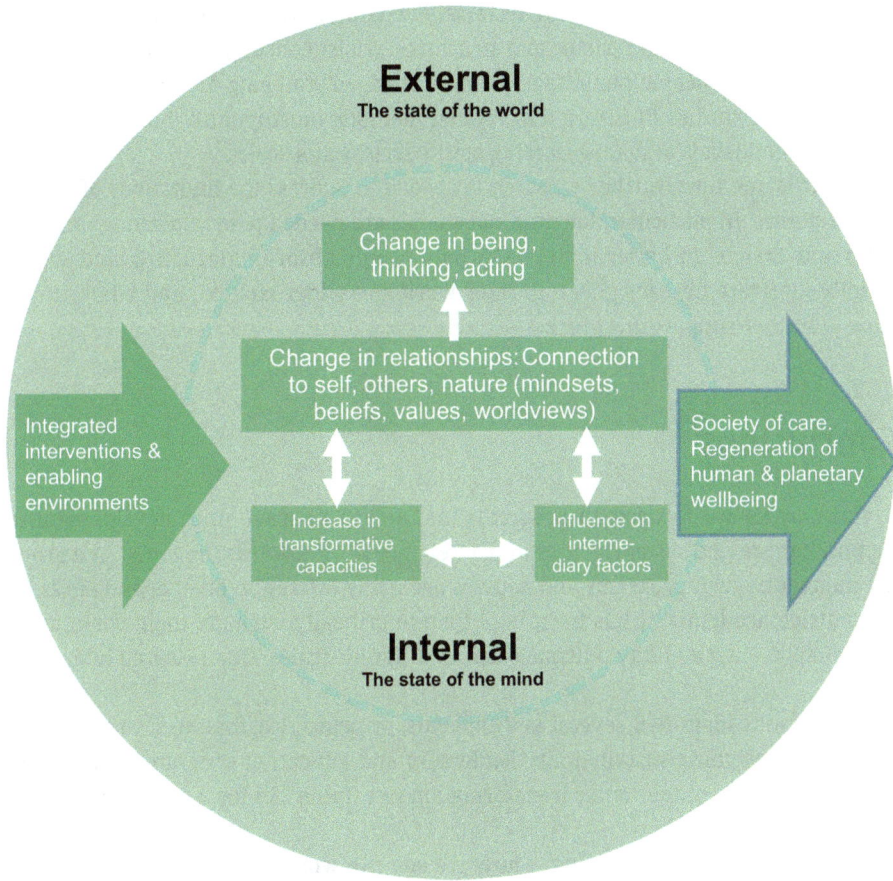

Figure 23.5: The inner-outer transformation model. It provides a roadmap for research, policy, and practice at the interface between inner development, culture, and system change. The model explains how internal and external change processes are interconnected and identifies five clusters of transformative capacities – awareness, insight, connection, purpose and agency—that can be seen as a kind of the scientific counterpart of the IDG framework. Please note that the classification into internal and external, which marks the boundary between what is "inside" (a subject) and what is "outside" (a subject) is artificial and applied for simplicity. Internal dimensions, such as our individual and collective mindsets, values, beliefs, worldviews, and paradigms are, for instance, inter-subjective (e.g., socially defined) and qualities/capacities are enacted (e.g., cultivated and expressed in relationship to other subjects and the world at large). The continuum of sustainability outcomes relates to all levels of change (mindsets/consciousness, culture, behavior, systems), and the associated spheres of transformation (practices, structures, views; cf., IPBES, 2024). Source: Simplified illustration, adapted from Wamsler et al. (2021).

Wamsler & Osberg, 2022). In fact, our analyses showed that changes in relationships were a good proxy for inner-outer transformation and action taking across scales.

Evaluation approaches need to assess what must be changed. Following on from the presented essentials and their inherent logic, the focus should thus be on assessing the quality of relationships and associated integrative approaches and initiatives (across individual, collective, and systems levels) that "rattle" unsustainable social norms, cultures, political systems and structures, whilst concurrently moving from an understanding of people being "agents to be changed" to being "change agents". Accordingly, our studies illustrate that related methods must identify both changes in narratives and levels of mainstreaming across sectors and scales.

At the same time, further research is needed to address the limitations of the reported studies. In particular, longitudinal studies are needed to monitor long-term impacts and change, to better understand how people absorb, internalize, and subsequently integrate new insights into their work and wider context, and what can be done to further support this process.

Conclusions

In this chapter we focused on programs that aim to nourish inner development to support culture and system change and accelerate work towards the SDGs. As a growing number of such programs and courses are being offered to diverse audiences, in and outside academia, it has been high time to critically evaluate their potential to contribute to sustainability outcomes across different scales. Our research addressed this gap.

Our results identified several key elements, or principles, that need to be considered when designing sustainability leadership and education programs that aim to support integrative inner-outer transformation (see Table 23.1 for a description of the field). They are:

- **Context and understanding – how we see the world**: The provision of a comprehensive understanding of the entangled nature of today's sustainability crises in a complex, constantly changing world, and one's role in it. Related transformative capacities of learners and educators include, for instance, interdependency, complexity, and systems thinking.
- **Learning approach – how we get to know**: The ongoing cultivation of safe and brave spaces, and integrative methods for exploring inner dimensions and nurturing transformative capacities. Related transformative capacities of learners and educators include, for instance, presence, self-reflection, compassion, and perspective-taking.
- **Practical guidance and solutions – how we engage**: Practical guidance on how to design and implement integrative measures that link inner and outer dimen-

sions across individual, behavioral, culture, and system change. Related transformational capacities of learners and educators include, for instance, emotional regulation, intrinsic value orientation, sense of agency, co-creation, creativity, active hope, and the courage to act.

– **Quality control – how we ensure quality and ethical considerations across all aspects**: Ensure that quality education is provided through the explicit consideration of ethics, the role of facilitators, and adequate monitoring and evaluation. Related transformational capacities of learners and educators include, for instance, humility, integrity, and equitable thinking.

Together, these four essentials or key ingredients support individual, collective, and, by extension, planetary well-being, flourishing, and regeneration, as they cover all aspects of inner-outer transformation (ontology, epistemology, praxis, ethics; cf. Ives et al., 2023). Self-awareness, personal growth, and the capacity for compassion and service on behalf of the common good become the ultimate goals.

Altogether, our research shows how sustainability leadership and learning can become a vehicle for transformation across scales. It demonstrates that this can be achieved by adapting and combining inner development methods and practices in ways that help participants to challenge current unsustainable social paradigms, and understand how they can systematically mainstream and institutionalize the consideration of human, inner dimensions of sustainability into existing cultures, mechanisms, and structures.

Our findings advance knowledge on the complex intersection between sustainability, inner development, and transformation, and set a precedent that other training institutions could follow or learn from. As we write this chapter (2024), a new edition of the GLSD program is being launched and implemented. While past years have seen important progress, broader and deeper culture and system transformation is needed.

Unfortunately, the current landscape has changed as a result of geopolitical tension and conflicts, electoral changes, and social-economic stagnation (Janss et al., 2023). At the same time, amidst the many challenges we are facing lies an opportunity for growth. Crises can serve as catalysts for transformation, prompting us to adapt and evolve. It is crucial that we capitalize on the current polycrisis to strengthen our collective sustainability efforts through inner development. We need to enhance our ability to be introspective, think critically, foster meaningful connections, collaborate effectively, and take purposeful action. By embracing inner development, and knowing how to integrate inner and outer dimensions of transformation across sectors and scales, we can navigate these turbulent times, and emerge stronger and more resilient in our pursuit of a regenerative future.

Table 23.1: Summary description of the field of inner transformation for sustainability, which can also be denominated as integrated inner-outer transformation or existential sustainability. Note that a comprehensive understanding of this field is key for adequately supporting IDGs for accelerating SDGs.

Description of the theory

Inner transformation for sustainability is an emergent field of research, education, and practice (Ives et al., 2023). The aim is to support integrative approaches that link inner and outer dimensions of transformation across sectors and levels to, consequently, enhance individual, collective, and planetary well-being, regeneration, and flourishing (Ives et al., 2023; Wamsler et al., 2021). *Inner dimensions* are defined as individual and collective mindsets, beliefs, values, worldviews, and associated inner capacities/qualities (cognitive, emotional, relational). The concept recognizes that inner and outer dimensions are never separate, but are co-created (Ives et al., 2023; Wamsler et al., 2021). On this basis, inner transformation involves changes in the sphere of human inner dimensions and refers to all kinds of actions at individual, collective, and systems levels that support integrative changes in views, structures, and practices, which address the impacts, drivers, and causes of today's polycrisis, including biodiversity loss (Ives et al., 2023; Wamsler et al., 2021).

 The field of inner transformation addresses unsustainable narratives and paradigms of separation (alienation from self, others, nature) that underlie today's polycrisis. They are an integral element of modern life forms, and they are reflected in modern societies' culture, the institutional and political landscape, and associated power structures (Ives et al., 2023; Walsh et al., 2021; Wamsler et al., 2021; Wamsler & Bristow, 2022; West et al., 2024). Inner transformation is thus about enabling intra- and inter-generational, human- and nonhuman relationships, and ways of connecting to self, others, and the world in ways that support integrative action taking across sectors and scales (Ives et al., 2023). Related research, practice, and education recognize: (1) the interdependence of inner and outer phenomena across individual, collective, and systems levels (and associated views, practices, and structures); (2) the potential that is latent within every human to enable transformative change; (3) the need to address inner dimensions across all levels; (4) the possibility to generate inner, transformative capacities/qualities through intentional practices; and (5) the need to include diverse perspectives and expand associated knowledge systems (including indigenous and local) for sustainability (Ives et al., 2023; Wamsler et al., 2021). Related key theories and conceptualizations include the IMAGINE framework, integral theory, the three spheres of transformation, the inner-outer transformation model, clusters of transformative capacities/qualities, the mind-sustainability nexus, and the framework for contemplative scientific inquiry, practice, and education (Ives et al., 2020, 2023; O'Brien & Sygna, 2013; Wamsler et al., 2021, 2022).

Summary of how intentional transformative change occurs cont.)

Inner transformation addresses deep leverage points and involves measures and methods that can support more relational and regenerative views, practices, and structures (Ives et al., 2023; Walsh et al., 2021; Wamsler et al., 2021; West et al., 2020). Change is mobilized through integrative measures that link inner and outer dimensions of transformation across sectors and levels (Ives et al., 2023; Wamsler et al., 2021). There are complementary ways to activate such integration in order to, ultimately, address mindsets, behavior, culture, and system change in combination (Ives et al., 2023; Wamsler et al., 2021, 2022; Wamsler & Bristow, 2022).

Table 23.1 (continued)

Summary of how intentional transformative change occurs cont.)

Measures at individual and collective levels include linking "outer" approaches with activities that help people tap into their inner potential, discover their internalized messages of separation, superiority, and instrumentalization, develop alternative approaches, and create fields of change (Ives et al., 2023; Wamsler et al., 2021; Wamsler & Bristow, 2022). This can, for instance, be supported through appropriate working environments, communities of practice, social movements, aesthetics, and transformative leadership and education (Wamsler et al., 2021, 2022). The latter involves holistic, contemplative, psychological, cognitive-behavioral, and ethical learning approaches (e.g., worldview journeys, mindfulness-, arts-, and nature-based methods) that nurture transformative capacities/ qualities (e.g., self-reflection, intrinsic value orientation, compassion, individual and collective agency) (Hedlund-de Witt et al., 2014; Scott et al., 2021; Wamsler, 2018; Wamsler et al., 2018, 2021, 2022; Wamsler & Bristow, 2022).

Measures at system level aim to mainstream the consideration of inner dimensions into institutional and political systems to foster more integrative approaches (Ives et al., 2023; Wamsler et al., 2021). This institutionalization entails modifying organizations' vision statements, policies, regulations, working structures, and tools for project management, resource allocation, communication, monitoring, and evaluation (Ives et al., 2023; Scott et al., 2021; Wamsler et al., 2020b, 2021; Wamsler & Bristow, 2022).

From an ethical standpoint, it is crucial to highlight that inner transformation is not about saying that we need to fix other people's views. This would turn them into objects to be changed, rather than seeing them as agents of change (Ives et al., 2023; Scott et al., 2021; Wamsler et al., 2021). Instead, it is about creating integrative measures, spaces, and conditions that nurture a culture of inner development, mutual support, and engagement. Building on a foundation of shared universal values and interconnection, the aim is, ultimately, to rattle unsustainable norms and systems (Bentz et al., 2022; Ives et al., 2023; Leichenko & O'Brien, 2020; Wamsler et al., 2020, 2021).

Inner transformation is a dynamic field. It has attracted professionals from many disciplines and domains, and is thus conceptualized using various terms (e.g., inner-outer transformation, inner transition, existential resilience, existential sustainability) (Ives et al., 2023; Wamsler et al., 2021). Actors include governmental, UN, private, nonprofit, and faith-based organizations, educational bodies, citizen groups, and local and indigenous communities (see all previous references).

Source: IPBES (2024), Annex of Chapter 3.

Reflection questions

Based on the presented chapter, we invite you to reflect on the following questions:

1. To what extent have the leadership and capacity development courses you have participated in considered the presented four essentials for integrated inner-outer transformation?
2. What has been missing, and why do you think this has been the case?
3. In your view, what are the root causes of today's polycrisis, and what does that tell you about your role for culture and system transformation?
4. What is it that we need to learn, individually and collectively, to emerge stronger and more resilient from this polycrisis?

5. Reflecting on a person who you admire and who has had a positive impact on sustainability, directly or indirectly, which inner capacities did that person embody?
6. How could you nurture these in yourself, and how could you offer conditions to nurture them collectively at your workplace?
7. To what extent does your organization implement measures that integrate inner and outer dimensions of transformation across sectors and scales?
8. Which operational mechanisms, structures, and tools would need to be modified to better institutionalize the consideration of inner dimensions, and make it a standard procedure?
9. What does moving from an understanding of people being "agents to be changed" to being "change agents" mean for the way we educate and address today's polycrisis?
10. What is the one thing from this chapter that you are most curious to explore, try out, or improve over the next weeks or months?

References

Arao, B. & Clemens, K. (2013). From safe spaces to brave spaces: A new way to frame dialogue around diversity and social justice. In L. Landreman (ed.), *The Art of Effective Facilitation* (pp. 135–150). Routledge.

Bentz, J., O'Brien, K., & Scoville-Simonds, M. (2022). Beyond "blah blah blah": Exploring the "how" of transformation. *Sustainability Science*, *17*(2), 497–506. https://doi.org/10.1007/s11625-022-01123-0.

Böhme, J. (2023). *Inner and outer transformation in the anthropocene: A relational approach* [Doctoral thesis]. Leuphana Universität Lüneburg, Universitätsbibliothek der Leuphana Universität Lüneburg.

CCCE. (2019). *The SEE learning companion: Social, emotional & ethical learning.* Center for contemplative science and compassion-based ethics (CCCE), Emory University. https://compassion.emory.edu/_includes/documents/SEE_Learning_Docs/SEE_Companion_March.pdf.

Filho, W. L. & McCrea, A. C. (eds.). (2018). *Sustainability and the humanities.* Springer.

Fritz, R. (1989). *Path of least resistance: Learning to become the creative force in your own life.* Fawcett.

Grossman, P., Niemann, L., Schmidt, S., & Walach, H. (2004). Mindfulness-based stress reduction and health benefits: A meta-analysis. *Journal of Psychosomatic Research*, *57*(1), 35–43. https://doi.org/10.1016/S0022-3999(03)00573-7.

Hedlund-de Witt, A., de Boer, J., & Boersema, J. J. (2014). Exploring inner and outer worlds: A quantitative study of worldviews, environmental attitudes, and sustainable lifestyles., *Journal of Environmental Psychology*, *37*, :40–54. https://doi.org/10.1016/j.jenvp.2013.11.005.

Hickman, C., Marks, E., Pihkala, P., Clayton, S., Lewandowski, R. E., Mayall, E. E., Wray, B., Mellor, C., & van Susteren, L. (2021). Climate anxiety in children and young people and their beliefs about government responses to climate change: A global survey. *The Lancet Planetary Health*, *5*(12), e863–e873. https://doi.org/10.1016/S2542-5196(21)00278-3.

Hunecke, M. (2018). Psychology of sustainability: Psychological resources for sustainable lifestyles. In O. Parodi & K. Tamm (eds.), *Personal sustainability: Exploring the far side of sustainable development* (pp. 33–50). Routledge.

Inner Development Goals. (2021). *Inner Development Goals (IDG): Background, method and the IDG framework* Inner Development Goals. https://drive.google.com/file/d/13fcf9xmYrX9wrsh3PC3aeRDs0rWsWCpA/edit.

Inner Development Goals. (2022). *Inner Development Goals: Phase 2 Research Report*. Inner Development Goals. https://drive.google.com/file/d/1I0ThTPl75h3M6iLzZ7KgYOsiLcrZw3Bw/edit

IPBES (2024) Transformative change assessment report - Thematic assessment report on the underlying causes of biodiversity loss and the determinants of transformative change and options for achieving the 2050 vision for biodiversity of the Intergovernmental Science-Policy Platform on Biodiversity and Ecosystem Services (IPBES). O'Brien, K., Garibaldi, L., and Agrawal, A. (eds.). IPBES secretariat, Bonn, Germany. https://doi.org/10.5281/zenodo.11382215.

IPCC. (2022a). *Climate change 2022: Impacts, adaptation, and vulnerability. Contribution of Working Group II to the Sixth Assessment Report of the Intergovernmental Panel on Climate Change.* [H.-O. Pörtner, D.C. Roberts, M. Tignor, E. S. Poloczanska, K. Mintenbeck, A. Alegría, M. Craig, S. Langsdorf, S. Löschke, V. Möller, A. Okem, B. Rama (eds.)]. Cambridge University Press. https://www.ipcc.ch/report/ar6/wg2/.

IPCC. (2022b). *Climate change 2022: Mitigation of climate change. Contribution of Working Group III to the Sixth Assessment Report of the Intergovernmental Panel on Climate Change.* [J. Skea, P. Shukla, A. Reisinger, R. Slade, M. Pathak, A. Khourdajie, R. van Diemen, A. Abdulla, K. Akimoto, M. Babiker, Q. Bai, I. Bashmakov, C. Bataille, G. Berndes, G. Blanco, K. Blok, M. Bustamante, E. Byers, L. Cabeza, K.,H. Winkler (eds.)]. Cambridge University Press. https://www.ipcc.ch/report/ar6/wg3/.

Ives, C. D., Freeth, R., & Fischer, J. (2020). Inside-out sustainability: The neglect of inner worlds. *Ambio, 49*, 208–217 (2020). https://doi.org/10.1007/s13280-019-01187-w.

Ives, C. D., Schäpke, N., Woiwode, C., & Wamsler, C. (2023). IMAGINE sustainability: Integrated inner-outer transformation in research, education and practice. *Sustainability Science, 18*, 2777–2786. https://doi.org/10.1007/s11625-023-01368-3.

Janss, J., Wamsler, C., Smith, A., & Stephan, L. (2023). *The human dimension of the green deal: How to overcome polarisation and facilitate culture & system change.* Inner Green Deal. https://www.contemplative-sustainable-futures.com/_files/ugd/4cc31e_32a45e74d07a4b179d159f0deb9f5af5.pdf.

Kegan, R. & Lahey, L. (2009). *Immunity to Change: How to overcome it and unlock potential in yourself and your organization.* Harvard Business Press.

Kilbourne, W. E., Beckmann, S. C., & Thelen, E. (2002). The role of the dominant social paradigm in environmental attitudes: A multinational examination. *Journal of Business Research, 55*(3), 193–204. https://doi.org/10.1016/S0148-2963(00)00141-7.

Kok, B. E. & Singer, T. (2017). Effects of contemplative dyads on engagement and perceived social connectedness over 9 months of mental training: A randomized clinical trial. *JAMA Psychiatry, 74*(2), 126–134. https://doi.org/10.1001/jamapsychiatry.2016.3360.

Leichenko, R. & O'Brien, K. (2020). *Climate and society: Transforming the future.* John Wiley & Sons.

Mar, K. A., Schäpke, N., Fraude, C., Bruhn, T., Wamsler, C., Stasiak, D., Schroeder, H., & Lawrence, M. G. (2023). Learning and community building in support of collective action: Toward a new climate of communication at the COP. *WIREs Climate Change, 14*(4), e832. https://doi.org/10.1002/wcc.832.

Mezirow, J. (2018). Transformative learning theory. In K. Illeris (ed.), *Contemporary theories of learning: Learning theorists . . . in their own words* (2nd edn; pp. 114–128). Routledge.

O'Brien, K. and & Sygna, L. (2013). Responding to cClimate cChange: The three spheres of transformation. *Proceedings of Transformation in Changing Climate International Conference*, Oslo, 19–21 June, 2013, 16–23.

Ogunbode, C. A., Doran, R., Hanss, D., Ojala, M., Salmela-Aro, K., van den Broek, K. L., Bhullar, N., Aquino, S. D., Marot, T., Schermer, J. A., Wlodarczyk, A., Lu, S., Jiang, F., Maran, D. A., Yadav, R., Ardi, R., Chegeni, R., Ghanbarian, E., Somayeh, Z.,. . .Karasu, M. (2022). Climate anxiety, wellbeing and pro-environmental action: Correlates of negative emotional responses to climate change in 32 countries. *Journal of Environmental Psychology, 84*, 101887. https://doi.org/10.1016/j.jenvp.2022.101887.

Ramstetter, L., Rupprecht, S., Mundaca, L., Osika, W., Stenfors, C. U. D., Klackl, J., & Wamsler, C. (2023). Fostering collective climate action and leadership: Insights from a pilot experiment involving mindfulness and compassion. *iScience, 26*(3), 106191. https://doi.org/10.1016/j.isci.2023.106191.

Rosa, H. (2021). *Resonance: A sociology of our relationship to the world*. Polity Press.

Rupprecht, S. & Wamsler, C. (2023). *The Global Leadership for Sustainable Development (GLSD) programme: Inner development for accelerating action toward the Sustainable Development Goals. Evaluation report written for the Inner Development Goals (IDGs) initiative and the Templeton World Charity Foundation.* Published by the Inner Green Deal and Lund University Centre for Sustainability Studies (LUCSUS): Lund, Sweden. https://drive.google.com/file/d/1CIjnVSroQJN4Gm6nCJRnPEIJGL5G_rOp/edit.

Scott, B., Amel, E., Koger, S., & Manning, C. (2021). *Psychology for sustainability* (5th edn). Routledge.

Segal, Z., Williams, M., & Teasdale, J. (2012). *Mindfulness-based cognitive therapy for depression: A new approach to preventing relapse*. Guilford Press.

Senge, P. (1999). *The dance of change: The challenges of sustaining momentum in learning organizations*. Bantam Doubleday Dell Publishing Group.

Senge, P. (2006). *The fifth discipline: The art & practice of the learning organization*. Crown Business.

Sharma, M. (2017). *Radical transformational leadership: Strategic action for change agents*. North Atlantic Books.

Slingo, J., Bates, K., Nikiforakis, N., Piggott, M., Roberts, M., Shaffrey, L., Stevens, I., Vidale, P. L., & Weller, H. (2008). Developing the next-generation climate system models: Challenges and achievements. *Philosophical Transactions of the Royal Society A: Mathematical, Physical and Engineering Sciences, 367*(1890), 815–831. https://doi.org/10.1098/rsta.2008.0207.

Stanley, S. (2012). Mindfulness: Towards a critical relational perspective. *Social and Personality Psychology Compass, 6*(9), 631–641. https://doi.org/10.1111/j.1751-9004.2012.00454.x.

Stuckey, B. & Smith, J. (2004). Building sustainable communities of practice. In B. Stuckey & J. Smith (eds.), *Knowledge networks: Innovation through communities of practice* (pp. 150–164). IGI Global.

Waldinger, R. & Schulz, M. (2023). *The good life: Lessons from the world's longest scientific study of happiness*. Simon & Schuster.

Walsh, Z. (2016). A meta-critique of mindfulness critiques: From McMindfulness to critical mindfulness. In R. E. Purser, D. Forbes, & A. Burke (eds.), *Handbook of mindfulness: Culture, context, and social engagement* (pp. 153–166). Springer International Publishing.

Walsh, Z., Böhme, J., & Wamsler, C. (2021). Towards a relational paradigm in sustainability research, practice, and education. *Ambio, 50*(1), 74–84. https://doi.org/10.1007/s13280-020-01322-y.

Wamsler, C. (2018). Mind the gap: The role of mindfulness in adapting to increasing risk and climate change. *Sustainability Science, 13*(4), 1121–1135. https://doi.org/10.1007/s11625-017-0524-3.

Wamsler, C. (2019). Contemplative sustainable futures: The role of individual inner dimensions and transformation in sustainability research and education. In W. Leal Filho & A. Consorte McCrea (eds.), *Sustainability and the humanities* (pp. 359–373). Springer International Publishing.

Wamsler, C. (2020). Education for sustainability: Fostering a more conscious society and transformation towards sustainability. *International Journal of Sustainability in Higher Education, 21*(1), 112–130. https://doi.org/10.1108/IJSHE-04-2019-0152.

Wamsler, C. (2022). *What the Mind has to do with the Climate Crisis: Mindfulness and compassion as pathways to a more sustainable future*. Mind & Life Institute. https://www.mindandlife.org/insight/what-the-mind-has-to-do/.

Wamsler, C. & Bristow, J. (2022). At the intersection of mind and climate change: Integrating inner dimensions of climate change into policymaking and practice. *Climatic Change, 173*(1), 7. https://doi.org/10.1007/s10584-022-03398-9.

Wamsler, C. & Osberg, G. (2022). Transformative climate policy mainstreaming – engaging the political and the personal. *Global Sustainability, 5*, e13. https://doi.org/10.1017/sus.2022.11.

Wamsler, C., Bristow, J., Cooper, K., Steidle, G., Taggart, S., Søvold, L., Bockler, L., Oliver, T. H., & Legrand, T. (2022). *Theoretical foundations report: Research and evidence for the potential of consciousness approaches and practices to unlock sustainability and systems transformation. Report of the UNDP Conscious Food Systems Alliance (CoFSA), United Nations Development Programme UNDP*. United Nations Development Programme (UNDP). https://www.contemplative-sustainable-futures.com/_files/ugd/4cc31e_143f3bc24f2c43ad94316cd50fbb8e4a.pdf.

Wamsler, C., Brossmann, J., Hendersson, H., Kristjansdottir, R., McDonald, C., & Scarampi, P. (2018). Mindfulness in sustainability science, practice, and teaching. *Sustainability Science, 13*(1), 143–162. https://doi.org/10.1007/s11625-017-0428-2.

Wamsler, C., Janss, J., & Bell, R. (2023). *Evaluation summary of the Global Leadership for Sustainable Development (GLSD) programme: An Inner Development Goals (IDGs) Initiative funded by the Templeton World Charity Foundation*. https://drive.google.com/file/d/1mb8u6izZ6AiUjbiwp_9s9msois9Pjo3E/edit.

Wamsler, C., Osberg, G., Janss, J., & Stephan, L. (2024). Revolutionising sustainability leadership and education: Addressing the human dimension to support flourishing, culture and system transformation. *Climatic Change, 177*(1), 4. https://doi.org/10.1007/s10584-023-03636-8.

Wamsler, C., Osberg, G., Osika, W., Hendersson, H., & Mundaca, L. (2021). Linking internal and external transformation for sustainability and climate action: Towards a new research and policy agenda. *Global Environmental Change, 71*, 102373. https://doi.org/10.1016/j.gloenvcha.2021.102373.

Wamsler, C., Schäpke, N., Fraude, C., Stasiak, D., Bruhn, T., Lawrence, M., Schroeder, H., & Mundaca, L. (2020a). Enabling new mindsets and transformative skills for negotiating and activating climate action: Lessons from UNFCCC conferences of the parties. *Environmental Science & Policy, 112*, 227–235. https://doi.org/10.1016/j.envsci.2020.06.005.

Wamsler, C., Wickenberg, B., Hanson, H., Alkan Olsson, J., Stålhammar, S., Björn, H., Falck, H., Gerell, D., Oskarsson, T., Simonsson, E., Torffvit, F., & Zelmerlow, F. (2020b). Environmental and climate policy integration: Targeted strategies for overcoming barriers to nature-based solutions and climate change adaptation., *Journal of Cleaner Production, 247*, (119154). https://doi.org/10.1016/j.jclepro.2019.119154

West, S., Haider, L. J., Stålhammar, S., & Woroniecki, S. (2020). A relational turn for sustainability science? Relational thinking, leverage points and transformations. *Ecosystems and People, 16*(1), 304–325. https://doi.org/10.1080/26395916.2020.1814417.

Woods, S., Rockman, P., Kabat-Zinn, J., & Reibel, D. (2021). *Mindfulness-based stress reduction: Protocol, practice, and teaching skills*. New Harbinger Publications.

Wullenkord, M. C. & Ojala, M. (2023). Climate-change worry among two cohorts of late adolescents: Exploring macro and micro worries, coping, and relations to climate engagement, pessimism, and well-being. *Journal of Environmental Psychology, 90*, 102093. https://doi.org/10.1016/j.jenvp.2023.102093.

Elke Fein, Bettina Geiken, Ivo J. Mensch, Leigh Biddlecome
and Claudine Villemot-Kienzle

Chapter 24
Deep casting the IDGs: Exploring the cross-dimensional quality of coherence

Abstract: How can the Inner Development Goals (IDGs) framework gain leverage and global impact? And how can the IDG community best position itself to communicate its message to those who need to hear it? What are the crucial factors that help to prepare it for this challenge? We argue that increasing the quality of coherence with and across the IDG field is one of them.

We see coherence both as our natural state of being, our true nature, and as a means to strengthen the collective power, focus, and impact of social change agents working towards global systems transformation.

This chapter presents and discusses a number of preliminary results of the EU-funded Cohere+ project's action research into the phenomenon and quality of coherence. More specifically, it focuses on two core questions:
1. What role does or could coherence play in each of the dimensions of the IDG framework as an overarching quality?
2. How can the IDG community be supported in increasing the degree of its own inner coherence as a precondition to fully step into its power?

Based on our deep dive into the phenomenon, we offer some insights and learnings that could benefit the IDG community.

Keywords: coherence, tension, quality, process, transformation

Introduction

This chapter is offered by members of the Cohere+ project, commencing from 2022 until 2025 and supported by Erasmus+. It focuses on the importance of coherence among inspired actors for the success of transformative systems change. It offers a *reframing* of the IDGs through the lens of coherence.

Cohere+ holds that many brilliant pioneers, visionaries, researchers, and activists around the world are working towards systemic shifts in the way the world is governed, from separate and destructive to generative and unified. But, often, they don't see themselves as part of an interconnected community, which weakens their impact.

Over the last two years, Cohere+ has explored this challenge both theoretically and practically. *First*, we aim to understand the essence of coherence. *Second*, we

https://doi.org/10.1515/9783111453729-025

argue that coherence is an implicit quality in all five dimensions of the IDG framework. For instance, the *being* dimension involves achieving inner coherence, the *thinking* dimension involves creating a coherent understanding of complex realities, and the *relating* dimension requires a minimum degree of coherence for meaningful relationships. The *collaborating* dimension needs a coherent understanding among participants, and the *acting* dimension benefits from coherence in the previous dimensions, leading to more focused and impactful actions.

Moreover, coherent action can be assumed to be more focused, powerful and, hence, have much greater impact, while acting in more mindful and present ways will require less energy and feel easier.

We will show how coherence is already implied in the IDG framework, even though not mentioned explicitly. Seeing this might sharpen our understanding of what personal growth in each dimension actually implies, and how the five dimensions are interrelated.

Additionally, Cohere+'s action research identifies factors that build or increase coherence among transformative change agents, developing practical tools and practices to enhance their learning capacity and create "communities of coherence".

As part of applying this perspective, Cohere+ has explored the IDG community and other networks of change agents. This paper presents insights from three sources.

First, a holistic SenseMaker®-based inquiry conducted at the IDG summit in Stockholm in October 2023 mapping the quality of coherence within the IDG field. Based on participants' own sensemaking of their experience in the IDG community, we start to see areas of potential improvement for strengthening the community's overall coherence, power, and impact.

Second, a series of in-depth interviews with members of the broader transformative social change field reflecting on coherence within their respective networks, challenges in this area, and tools to enable coherence.

Third, first- and second-person experiential explorations within our team to test and specify our findings.

This paper is organized in two parts. The first explores the nature of coherence and how it relates to the IDG framework. The second presents core findings of Cohere+'s empirical exploration of coherence in the field of transformative systems change, including the IDG community.

What is coherence and why is it meaningful for the IDGs?

The word coherence comes from latin *cohaerere* which means connected, consistent, harmonious. Beyond this general definition, the term and phenomenon of coherence has gained attention and relevance in many different areas.

In physics, coherence expresses the potential for two waves to interfere. Physiological coherence is seen as the degree of order, harmony, and stability in the various rhythmic activities within living systems over any given time period, while in psychology the sense of coherence is related to comprehensibility, manageability, and meaningfulness (Antonovsky, 1983). Recent research in complexity science points out that our sense of identity is determined by how we interact with others and our surroundings, and this interaction maintains coherent structures, challenging the idea that being stable means being rigid. Instead, stability actually comes from being flexible and adaptable, ensuring coherence in the group (Juarrero, 2023).

Coherence is furthermore perceived as the organizational principle of the universe, a forming, unified whole from its diverse, differentiated aspects. The fundamental aspect of our nature is coherence; it's about tuning into and aligning to it. This is a choice we can make at any moment.

While there is no agreement on one single definition across all these areas, we propose to describe coherence as suggested at the online summit "Art and Science of Cultivating Coherence", hosted by the HeartMath Institute in November 2023. On this basis, we can summarize coherence as a state of harmony and alignment when all parts of a system work in sync and in resonance in order to hold the system as whole while ensuring all parts a maximum of efficiency and a maximum of freedom (HeartMath Institute, 2023).

Personal, social, and global coherence

The HeartMath Institute is a leading organization in scientific research on coherence. It distinguishes three levels of coherence: personal, social, and global (McCraty, 2017).

Personal coherence is a harmonious state where our hearts, minds, and bodies unite, enhancing self-security, resilience, creativity, and intuition. It aligns our choices with effective responses to life's situations, allowing us to follow our creative flow effortlessly. This state activates our heart intelligence and intuitive guidance, promoting well-being and adaptability.

Social coherence involves creating harmonious connections within families, teams, groups, or organizations by aligning around shared intentions. It goes beyond collaboration, fostering creativity and a sense of safety. This state boosts collective intuition, resilience, and flow, enhancing communication and creating opportunities for harmonious outcomes. Social coherence deepens connections and fosters a more heart-connected world, facilitating better social behaviors and interactions.

Finally, *global coherence* refers to the interconnectedness of all living systems, including humanity, plants, animals, and the Earth's magnetic activity. Research in this area uses a multidisciplinary approach to explore this holistic web of interconnectedness. It aims to unite people in heart-focused love and intention, increasing collective consciousness and promoting cooperative, compassionate ways of being. By working towards global coherence, we foster a sense of unified wholeness, remembering that we are a loving, unified entity, inseparable while being unique.

Personal, social, and global coherence build upon and influence each other, creating a comprehensive framework for enhancing individual and collective well-being.

A process view: Unfolding into coherence

When exploring coherence, several questions arise: Is it a state, a way of being, an emergent property, or a precondition for developing desired capacities? The mind often imagines it as a static phenomenon.

Viewing coherence as static can lead to a desire for control, treating it as a state to preserve rather than trusting in the self-organizing intelligence of complex systems. This can create the illusion that coherence is a goal itself, rather than an enabler for achieving collective goals. It might become a hollow buzzword in the business lexicon.

In a process view, where continuous change is fundamental, we can't cling to any steady state. Instead, we follow the principle of evolving from one state to another. Coherence, then, is best understood as dynamic: a property of a system that continually adapts and optimizes to achieve its goals.

A framework like the IDGs can be seen as an evolving whole that enables coherence for communities and individuals. The metaphor of a manifold fits well, representing a multidimensional object where each part influences all others. Improved related skills enhance collaboration, and many other skills co-emerge in a symbiotic manner. What initiates coherence is often not best explained by linear protocols but by good or novel practice.

Trust, for example, is oddly tucked away under "collaborating" in the IDG framework and listed as a social skill, but might be better framed under "being", and designated a primary source and catalyst driving the emergence of many of the other elements such as *integrity and authenticity, courage, creativity*, and arguably *empathy and compassion*. Viewed through this lens, the potential for coherence of the IDG framework emerges only as a process in which cause and effect are not always clear. Coherence both emerges and enables emergence in feedback and feed-forward processes.

It has become fashionable in complexity circles to quote Ilya Prigogine, who noted that "small islands of coherence in a sea of chaos have the capacity to shift the entire system to a higher order" (Prigogine, 1984, p. 283–284).

We tend to focus on coherence as an idealized future state, aiming for a "higher order" while dismissing chaos. However, this impulse can prevent us from achieving coherence. Concentrating on a future state distracts us from the present, where potential and difficulties, often hidden, must be addressed.

Kurt Lewin's force field analysis (Lewin, 1943) frames group progress towards a goal as the interplay of driving and restraining forces. Driving forces bring us closer to the goal, while restraining ones hold us back. What looks like a steady state or "stuckness" can actually be a dynamic equilibrium.

When we face restraining forces like conflict or difference, we naturally try to amplify driving forces, often through authority and control. This can lead to more resistance, less trust, and reduced dynamism and diversity.

A process view shows any journey into coherence involves stages, including periods of dissonance and decoherence. Yvonne Agazarian, architect of systems-centered therapy, describes three phases with subphases where groups work through fight and flight responses, focus on differences, tendencies to maintain harmony by seceding agency, and presenting pseudo-independence before a trust deepens (Agazarian, 2004). Eventually the capacity to work and play arises together – making coherence happen.

Finally, the process philosopher and educator Bonnitta Roy combines her five-stages model of open group practice (which largely maps on to Agazarian's model) with an eight-part typology of social selves, which is also the name of phase one (Roy, 2016, see Figure 24.1). Here, as well as in phase two, which she calls the "groan zone", we seek to claim territory, debate, pontificate, fawn or check out – to name a few defensive postures and associated behaviors, depending on our type.

Phase	Mode	Behavior			
		Conceptual/ Power	Conceptual/ Approval	Emotional/ Power	Emotional/ Approval
Social Self	Collective Focus	Pontificate	Share Knowns	Connect	Belong
	Individual Focus	Rank	Political Games	Oblige	Obfuscate
Groan Zone	Primary Arousal	Claim Territory	Debate	Question	Dissociate
Authentic Chaos	Release Response	Release Boundaries	Release Attachment	Release Defenses	Release Anxiety
Opening Phase	Passive Mode	Seeing	Sensing	Allowing	Feeling
Emergent Phase	Active Mode	Theory Building	Imagining	Seeking	Experiencing

Figure 24.1: Bonnitta Roy's five stages of open group practice and eight social selves.
Source: Roy (2016)

During the three successive stages – "authentic chaos", the "opening phase", and the final "emergent phase" – defenses and attachments are gradually dropped, and emotions are released, allowing for the expression of differences, authenticity, and participation. From there, deeper sensing and seeing of patterns enable a free-flowing imagination, visioning, and collaboration, to name just a few other emergent possibilities that are not available in earlier stages of proto-coherence.

In other words, working through periods of "decoherence" is necessary. The lesson is that dissonance, frustration, and chaos are a natural part of a journey into coherence. What on the surface may look like coherence – harmony, for example – may in fact be the outcome of pseudo-independence and groupthink if dissenting and challenging the holy cows, or simply being creative, are not supported. Coherence easily gets confused or traded in for cohesion (see section below) if we are unwilling to stay with the trouble, limiting the potential for a community's self-actualization (Caspari & Schilling, 2016)

Unfoldment is a dynamic interplay of constraining and driving forces, which manifest as growing pains when a system continually reconfigures itself. Seen in a larger arc of unfolding, these tensions and the energies held in them, when given space for their expression, are understood as integral parts and drivers of one coherent process.

The next section takes a deeper look into the role of tensions as an instrument for measuring degrees of coherence in various contexts, including group.

Exploring the role of how tensions are dealt with as a marker of qualities of cohesion versus coherence

As argued above, "working through" occurring tensions is an essential element on the journey towards coherence. Moreover, we found the ways that tensions are dealt with (both individually and on group levels) are an important indicator and instrument for measuring degrees of coherence in various contexts, including groups.

In a nutshell, we argue that we can map possible strategies for dealing with tensions on a continuum or scale between two polar opposites, between efforts to resist tensions on the one hand, versus being open to welcome tensions as "feedback" that contains valuable information for improving the quality of cooperation on the other hand (see Figures 24.2 and 24.3). In both cases, the respective actors might subjectively be intending to do the best for what their respective group or working context needs in order to be functional. Yet, they do so on the basis of dramatically different degrees of capability when it comes to holding and dealing with complexity.

Since in both cases the challenge is keeping the group together, we suggest to describe the two poles as *cohesion* and *coherence*. The implications of these two polar strategies to deal with tensions are exemplified in politics, contrasting closed (authoritarian or dictatorial) and open (democratic) systems.

Authoritarian leaders typically handle tensions defensively, ignoring, marginalizing, or repressing critics, opposition figures, independent media, and free speech. Tension is seen as a threat to the status quo and the leaders' power. Repression becomes the primary strategy to eliminate tensions, as illustrated by Stalin's quote, "Where there is no person, there is no problem," implying that eliminating dissenters "solves" problems.

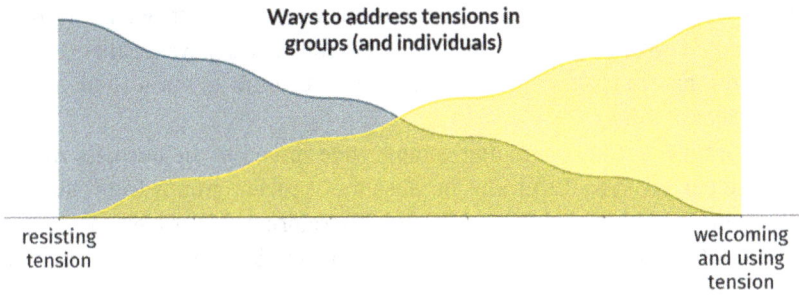

Figure 24.2: Continuum of strategies for dealing with tensions.
Source: Dr. Bettina Geiken, Cohere+

Conversely, democratic societies address tensions by facilitating agreements among all parties. This can involve majority decisions, compromises, and various deliberative processes, including as many perspectives as possible. "Liberal democracy" is a visionary ideal that guides societies in deepening their collective awareness, handling complexity, and using appropriate tools and methods. It represents a vision for ongoing improvement in democratic practices, enhancing the ability to manage tensions constructively.

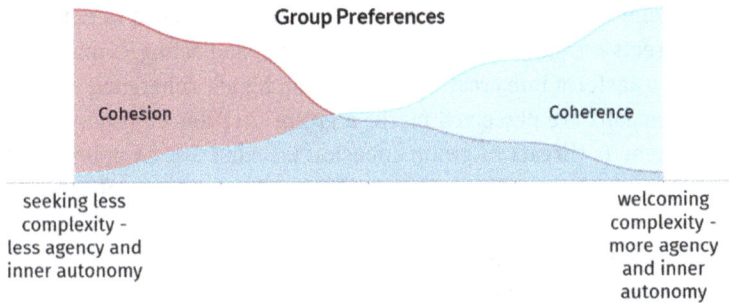

Figure 24.3: Visualization of suggested correlation between addressing tensions and states of cohesion/ coherence in groups.
Source: Dr. Bettina Geiken, Cohere+

The same dynamics also apply to the groups we have researched. If a group's dynamic is governed by the value of cohesion, tensions are usually first seen as a threat to the given situation, power structures, the status quo, agreements, group harmony, and/or a sense of belonging and safety. This discourages addressing conflicts.

Note that differences in how "cohesion" is perceived can be assumed to be a function of both individuals' and group's overall ability to hold and integrate complexity, as described by structural adult development theory, in particular ego development theory (Cook-Greuter, 2005).

If we look at it through the lens of Clare W. Graves' work (better known in the form of *Spiral Dynamics integral,* see Graves, 2005 or Beck & Cowan, 1996), we see that:

- In a conventional/traditional ("blue") value system, conflicts are a challenge to the given order of things.
- From the "orange" value system that is most wide-spread in the business world, conflicts are perceived as disturbing, because they prevent groups from "quickly reach[ing] the goals" and diminish efficiency. Therefore, profit-driven companies spend a lot of attention and money on "conflict resolution", suggesting that "we have to get rid of them".
- In the "green" value system, conflicts are perceived as threats for the harmony of the respective group, and people tend to skip or ignore them.

In contrast, the idea of interpreting conflicts as a positive force, fostering depth and coherence, only takes over with the meta-modern (integral) holistic value system (see Fein et al., 2023). Here, tensions are seen as valuable, guiding us through collective intuition to form deeper, more authentic, and more powerful relationships. This perspective is practiced in the deep democracy ecosystem (e.g., Lewis, 2013).

So, framing tensions through the lens of coherence invites us to reconsider our interactions and serve the collective field. It prompts us to ask: What has been overlooked? What is misaligned? What does the field need? Viewing tensions as potential sources rather than threats recalibrates our thinking, feeling, and acting. If mindfully explored, tensions can transform into creative frictions and higher coherence.

To sum up, how tensions are perceived marks a group's "center of gravity" on a scale from resisting them as threats to group cohesion (seeking less complexity) to welcoming them as signs of overlooked information (embracing more complexity) for greater coherence.

Appreciating tensions and conflicts could be a game changer within the IDG "acting" skills because it takes *courage, creativity, and optimism* to see the wisdom of the "no" and perseverance to enable change.

Coherence in action: Observations from the field

The Cohere+ project has so far engaged in a number of explorative methods for gathering data on degrees and qualities of coherence in groups, starting from our own team processes to other social change networks to the IDG community and similar fields. The approaches used include first-, second-, and third-person methodologies such as introspection, participant observation, in-depth interviews, SenseMaker surveys and field mapping approaches.

First- and second-person field exploration: What is coherence?

A very straightforward way to probe into the phenomenon of coherence is an introspection exercise that can be done by almost anyone and any group. The instruction is to sit down in silence for a moment and to feel what it feels like to be in a coherent (or incoherent) state/situation and describe briefly the context. We have conducted this exercise on several occasions with various groups. Here is some biofeedback by which our participants described their inner perceptions of coherence:

- sense of relaxation, peace, gut/belly, groundedness, warm;
- open perception, open mind/heart, energetic perception – am I/are we aligned or are there tensions?;
- relaxation, sinking in, rest;
- sense of equanimity, ability to make the best out of tensions;
- frequencies coming into synchronization – alignment of all personal and transpersonal elements to source, co-creating at its best.

Note that no matter which group we ask to do this exploration, the responses are almost identical. The following word cloud illustrates typical responses (see Figure 24.4):

Figure 24.4: Word cloud based on data gathered across multiple groups and movements.
Source: Cohere+, based on SenseMaker

Within the Cohere+ team, we also introspect the degree of group coherence regularly, by rating it on a scale from 0–10, and then dive deeper based on the results.

A similar exploration has been conducted in another community of practice built by change agents in the context of their participation in a transformative education program for "Social Architects" in Germany. They have been working, developing, and exchanging ideas and experiences together for almost ten years on how to operate from the "second tier perspective". (Villemot-Kienzle, 2018).

In this case, the exercise was further differentiated by a perception method that the authors call "five-sync". Participants were asked to introspect an experience of a state of coherence and incoherence/non-coherence connected to a real-life example, and to notice their inner perceptions in a more nuanced way, i.e., by distinguishing between perceptions on the physical, emotional, mental, energetic, and transpersonal levels. Besides helping participants to sharpen their individual perception skills, this exercise also produced a finer distinction of the qualities and effects involved when coherence is experienced or, in turn, is absent (see Table 24.1).

Table 24.1: Introspecting incoherence/coherence across different realms.

"Feel what it feels like"	Experience of incoherence	Experience of coherence
Physical	Physical discomfort, often in the chest area, tensions, restlessness	Calmness and lack of stress
Emotional	Helplessness, desire to escape, sense of uncertainty, anger, desperation	Experiencing causeless joy, expansiveness, acceptance, and confidence Pressure-free mindset, equanimity, and overall contentment
Cognitive/ mental	Overwhelmed by internal dialogue	Confidence in checking methods to prevent issues Clear understanding of concrete possibilities and synchronicity in planning
Energetic	Fluctuating energy levels; low energy leading to feelings of powerlessness	Feeling of inner strength and trust Confidence without the need for control, perceived as effortless by others
Transpersonal	Recognizing interconnectedness, sudden opening for more agility	Recognizes connection to a larger context Facilitates self-organization and brings out the best in individuals

Source: Cohere+ fieldwork and participant observation

Note that while most people might be able to intuitively sense and tell if a system or context they find themselves in is coherent, it takes some inner skill development to be able to refine perception in the way proposed by the five-sync method.

Results from third-person observation: Effects of coherence

Likewise, we conducted fieldwork in the form of participant observation on various occasions. One of them was the second IDG summit in Stockholm in October 2023 (including the Unconference a day before) where members of the Cohere+ team attended both the plenary conference and the five independent workshops. Table 24.2 shows a few observations we have put together during those events which we attributed to states of incoherence or coherence.

So, we can physically and energetically observe a number of behaviors and qualities that can be interpersonally recognized as expressions and effects of (in)coherence.

As to the effects of coherence, we hold the following to be particularly interesting and important, as they relate immediately to some of the IDG skills.

Table 24.2: Observations and attribution to incoherence/coherence from a third-person perspective across different realms.

Realm of observation	Incoherence was observed via:	Coherence was observed via:
Physical	fidgeting and talking; people retracting to do own work or other activities; no clapping, people on phones	no phone usage all day; not many people walking in and out; active participation by all in the room; people eager to do/participate in exercises; vivid conversations in small groups; people respecting the rules of the game
Emotional	being polite instead of naming problems more clearly; disagreement, not being in sync	feeling welcome; collective/explicit appreciation; genuine connections made; positive, open atmosphere; emotions shown openly; all emotions could come out
Cognitive/ mental	consuming attitude; people being distracted; lack of balance and red thread between sessions	asking relevant questions; curiosity
Energetic	attention fades; sense of urge for food	lack of tension (or tension mindfully held); quality of presence; focused and mindful attention over a long span of time; laughter
Transpersonal		Awe

Source: Cohere+ fieldwork and participant observation

Being dimension

In the being dimension, we see both physical and inner effects. Both relaxation and presence are psycho-physical states that have been confirmed by research and can be visualized through appropriate methods (i.e., higher heart rate variability and the relaxation of the nervous system, also conceived as elements of resilience [McCraty, 2017]).

As to the phenomenological dimension, an increased ability to focus helps to strengthen the inner compass, as well as related *thinking* qualities.

Thinking dimension

When our "being" is coherent, our thinking seems to open up and have the space and incentive to follow its natural curiosity as a precondition for unfolding creativity. Furthermore, an increased clarity of thought not only enhances a quest for meaning and purpose, but also informs clear speech and emotional composure.

Relating dimension

The main effects of coherence in the *relating* dimensions are, precisely, good relations, characterized by mutual interest, empathy, trust, and curiosity. This, in turn,
allows for seeing tensions as signposts for deepening relations, harvesting more potential and creativity, and for allowing in more diversity in a given group.

Collaborating and acting dimensions

Finally, the above qualities enhance both individual and group capacity to act and
thereby to bring about positive change in the outside world, whereby agency is based
on a sense of meaning and integrity.

First- and second-person field exploration: What brings coherence about?

Given the beneficial effects of coherence, one of the key goals and research questions
of Cohere+ is to explore how coherence arises, which conditions need to be in place
for it to emerge or to foster it, and whether or how we can actively create or support
such conditions. From available data, as well as experiential exercises on personal
and social level, we can notice such conditions in the dimensions of:
– inner state or attitude (personal qualities); and
– context and environment.

The latter can be further differentiated in terms of:
– the degree of structure and orientation that is present; and
– specific tools and practices used to foster coherence

Below is a preliminary "shortlist" of our findings thus far.

Personal qualities

Among the most important inner states or attitudes that foster coherence are openness and the absence of fear.

We understand openness[1] as the ability to engage in relationships with others naturally, practice deep listening, and communicate in a nonjudgmental way. In a more "advanced" form, it also involves the ability to access different levels of consciousness, worldviews, and mindsets a person or a group has developed so far without being identified with single ones. The resulting fluidity enables us to take many different perspectives without feeling threatened by leaving our (preferred) position.

Fearlessness or the ability to manage fear are important, because when fear takes up a lot of space in our mind – even subconsciously – certain neurobiological processes are activated. Our ability to think in a clear, complex, and differentiated way dwindles. Studies (Neurologen und Psychiater im Netz, 2017) show that our capacity for compassion is also blocked. In this state, we lose some of our inner freedom and tend to seek cohesion in order to feel safe.

Context: Safe spaces of trust and appreciation that can hold diversity

In order to reduce fear and build trust, it is crucial to create spaces[2] that are able to hold and welcome feelings of fear nonjudgmentally and with mindfulness. By becoming visible and expressible, fears often lose their power, and by translating them into needs, we can address them more easily. In turn, the experience of trust, being appreciated, and being trusted helps people to relax in a group and to disidentify with ego-driven impulses like fear.

In a very practical sense, a supportive setting is one with plenty of space to move around, practice art, and engage in other forms of self-expression or embodiment. If possible, being in nature adds another powerful context. Also, attuned and bounded formats for interacting more authentically such as an unconference design and working with the smaller intentional groups enables generating joint insight and wisdom, and thus to strengthen shared trust.

Another element of building trust and safe spaces is to actively allow and encourage the expression of difference and tension: facilitating and inviting the sharing of tension and friction, and framing these as potential for growth, allows their integration. Thus, tensions can be named without blame, vulnerability is invited, and pressure is reduced through difficult topics and emotions being voiced and held mindfully.

---

1 Participant voice from the IDG Summit 2023: "I'm touched by the quality of listening and sharing in the room in our harvesting session. It seems like there is openness to connect."

2 Participant voice from the IDG Summit 2023: "It makes a huge difference for me to share in a space I feel is safe and allows for the holding of everything that is present. Asking the group what they need to feel safe and working that out in small groups really works."

Likewise, a sense of safety and trust is supported by allowing in diversity[3] and authenticity – in other words, encouraging people to self-express beyond getting personal social needs met, like playing roles, wearing masks, claiming space, and separating by checking out. People can then speak from presence and show up as the individuals they are with their respective talents and skills. It helps coherence to manifest when each person is aware of their unique contribution in service to the whole.

Structure and orientation (internal and external)

An appropriate amount of structure and orientation creates safety and focus. This can be fostered on a personal level by striving for clarity on one's own higher purpose, and on a group level by building a common shared vision or purpose. Knowing my own "why" that extends to a purpose beyond the ego-self is a very powerful precondition for both individual and group coherence. This allows the individual to maintain the "I" in the "we" and to dance between both dimensions. To connect from that space to a shared vision and purpose enhances not only the group's coherence, but also the common purpose. It provides energy to act, to co-create in a flow state, and to shape reality accordingly.

Furthermore, orientation is supported by providing a minimal "liberating structure" that is in service to the realization of the common vision by revealing "how to be best together", i.e., that supports the embodiment of all skills, competences, and gifts that people bring to the group. The skill of creating and holding group spaces has to do with clear communication: a host team and speaker who is connected to both their purpose and the larger purpose disambiguates and gives participants an understanding of why they are there. This has the power to weave people, processes, profit, purpose, and planet in a natural, functional design.

Tools and practices

Finally, most of the above elements and conditions can be actively generated and supported through skillful meeting designs and facilitation tools. For example, we observed that short sharing or storytelling exercises in between keynote presentations brought more aliveness and energy into the field and built trust and empathy. Small conversations in pairs gives everyone the opportunity to speak, listen, and be seen, even in large group settings. A guided meditation can drop participants into sensation and deepen their embodiment, resulting in a more calm and coherent field. Various

---

3 Participant voice from the IDG Summit 2023: "I felt people were open and included everyone. I didn't feel alone even coming here alone".

forms of movement and/or nonverbal communication takes people out of their heads and allows them to let their bodies find their place in the space. Asking people to directly exchange thoughts about what brings them alive is also a good way of raising energy levels.

Conditions for coherence to manifest: Examples from our interviews

As indicated, the above list of conditions enhancing coherence is based on various forms of field exploration conducted by the Cohere+ team. As part of our ongoing work, we are also conducting interviews and observational research, and writing profiles of social changemakers working across a wide set of geographical and societal contexts. These profiles aim to bring alive how specific leaders are engaging in systems change within complex contexts, and to highlight adaptive practices and challenges to coherence within their work.

The arts as powerful drivers of coherence

As an illustration of the findings presented above, the stories of two of our interviewees provide concrete insights into how the dynamics of coherence manifest in the field. Both of them are impressive examples of the degree to which the arts – music, theater, poetry – can be vehicles for these processes.

A first example for the power of arts and music as a way to build coherence is the work of organizational psychologist, facilitator, and nonviolent communication trainer Kateryna Yasko in the extremely challenging current context in Kyiv, Ukraine. Given the sheer scale of the need to build and strengthen civic society, she has been experimenting with workshops using poetry, music, and plays to align groups around shared intention and purpose and develop empathy – ultimately enabling action and change within the civic sphere. Yasko specifically noted that group coherence – amongst participants as varied as IT company staff, school principals, and groups of teenagers and families – was enhanced thanks to a collective witnessing of a performance and the professionally facilitated discussion afterwards. Coming together around these shared experiences of the arts, with the opportunity to reflect and voice their responses "creates coherence, fosters trust, and supports emotional well-being".

It seems that these outcomes are partly due to the quality of coherence already present in their design and execution. Yasko works from a place of coherent vision and inner compass, and also engages her collaborators (musicians, directors, actors, poets, philosophers, and other trained discussion facilitators) across diverse modalities and skills. A longer-term vision of effecting change and "strengthening ties in the social fabric of the country through culture" is at the center of their work. Thus, a coherent design takes into consideration both the specific cultural and developmental needs of the participants, which results in a stronger effect on inner and interpersonal coherence for the participants.

Her experimental practices, born out of necessity, show how group processes that take into account psychological distress and trauma, as well as help participants to develop greater social coherence needed to then act in their communities. By providing safe containers for developing *relating* skills and culturally relevant emotional resonance, the arts ultimately foster transformative development for their participants (including moving towards what she refers to as Kegan's "self-authoring collective mind").

Another example is Nathan Vanderpool's work of convening the international Respond network of wisdom scholars which has developed a framework outlining domains of practice for wisdom embodiment. "I often ask: what does it mean for groups to enter into states where they can become collectively more wise?" he shares. In fact, several qualities he found in collective wisdom practice are in line with the conditions and drivers of coherence described above, such as embodiment, supportive aesthetically aligned settings, and practiced facilitation to support group trust.

Music and synchronized sensory experiences can be a uniquely effective driver of coherence and an entry point into wisdom practice, especially for those who might not otherwise have access to the more esoteric language of Respond scholars. Towards this end, Vanderpool also leads meditation and chanting sessions, open to all in a neighborhood church in Berlin three mornings a week. This is a strongly participatory, experiential practice, coherent across multiple sensory and aesthetic dimensions, including architecturally and acoustically. Thus, coherence can come about via alternative methods, in settings that do not necessarily involve discussion or verbally formulated ideas.

We therefore encourage the IDG community to consider how a "coherent sensorium" model – which includes coherent sound, visuals, and movement – could be used within facilitated workshop settings.

Creating coherence across dimensions and from experiences of tension

As observed in the case of the arts, our empirical research has also shown that coherence in one dimension flows into the others – such as from being into collaborating. Likewise, when there is palpable incoherence in one dimension, then positive impact from other dimensions is restricted.

This also holds true between different levels of coherence. One interviewee from Germany noted that, "coherence for me is that I have aligned all my inner dimensions – all elements of my complexity are aligned and working together. If we are all aligned with our purpose, then we can manifest embodied coherence between us." In this sense, inner coherence can affect relational coherence across a working team.

In our interviews with over a dozen actors in the social change field, we discovered that tensions within organizations and across movements can often be perceived as driving and/or being driven by a lack of coherence. Hence, as discussed above, ways to mindfully navigate tensions can be a powerful driver of deeper coherence.

For example, another interviewee working in the field of group process and conflict facilitation explained how any relational tensions that "naturally arise in any system" should ideally be addressed by surfacing them "gracefully and fluidly . . . internally or interpersonally, in a way that they become fuel for further refinement and improvement of the systems they are part of, rather than causing complete breakdowns". He noted that this approach can result in "flow, harmony . . . and all sorts of metrics of well-being and effectiveness".

A beautiful example of this is Vanderpool's musical metaphor for how we might transcend and include tensions within groups:

> [in a musical improvisation], say there's a note that somebody is playing or improvising, and somebody throws in something that's really strange. But that strangeness can be harmonized if we all respond to it. It might initially be out of key, but we can shift it into something where that makes sense now, where we're bringing it in. And this is the idea I have about wisdom groups – wisdom is ever-evolving, ever-changing, kind of like jazz improvisation. It's a process.

As this metaphor reminds us, coherence is brought about not by stifling or silencing a different note, but rather by carefully hearing, acknowledging, and integrating "strangeness" (or divergence) within a group into its own evolutive process.

Exploring the coherence of the IDG community as a specific field of change agents

Coming back to the core claim of this chapter, the value and power of coherence for helping communities of transformative changemakers to leverage their outreach and impact, we wish to close on our more specific case study of the IDG community itself.

In the context of the IDG Summit 2023, the Cohere+ project team conducted various forms of field work to explore the quality of coherence, as well as potential tensions and challenges to its inner coherence.

The IDG community's own sense of coherence

Similar to the "feel what it feels like to be in coherence" exercise described above, we asked about 50 participants of a workshop held by the Cohere+ team on October 13, 2023, to describe their experience of the IDG community at the summit itself. The following word cloud summarizes their stories (see Figure 24.5).

Figure 24.5: Word cloud based on data gathered at the IDG workshop on October 13, 2023. Source: Cohere+, based on SenseMaker

Two observations are worth mentioning in this regard:
1. compared to the responses from other settings, we see very similar overall patterns with "flow" being the most prominent item put forward by the IDG respondents;
2. we see a large number of items describing the high quality of the community and joint space as experienced by the participants.

Note that when asked to share their sense of what coherence is, about 30% of the participants explicitly mentioned the potential of moments of tension and "falling out of coherence" as opportunities for improvement or breakthrough towards deeper coherence, for example when describing these as:
– "disconcerting, unpleasant, risky – may unravel, but can also be a precursor to a breakthrough";
– "an opportunity for collaboration";
– "interesting – it makes me curious what is going on and what we might do next";
– "an opportunity for improvement/discussion";
– "natural, because no group is a solid construct".

Combined, these two findings support the assumption that a high degree of openness in a well-held space, as it was experienced at the IDG summit, fosters participants' willingness to welcome tensions as a means to increase group coherence. It could also be an indicator of the IDG community's high capability to hold complexity.

The role of tensions in the context of the IDG summit

As indicated above, the IDG summit participants displayed a rather high degree of openness towards tension and ambiguity. It is therefore interesting to explore how they perceived existing tensions during the meeting and the ways these were dealt with. We asked them to evaluate on a sliding scale to which extent tensions in the process (related to their own summit experience) were either "ignored or suppressed" *or* "fully addressed and integrated". Figure 24.6 below illustrates the distribution of their responses. Overall, 60% of the respondents thought that tensions were "fully addressed and integrated" (data range between 70–100), while 30% of the respondents felt that tensions were "ignored and suppressed" (data range between 10–40).

⠿ **2.3 Tension in the process were mainly...**   ⋮

Ignored or suppressed   Fully addressed and integrated

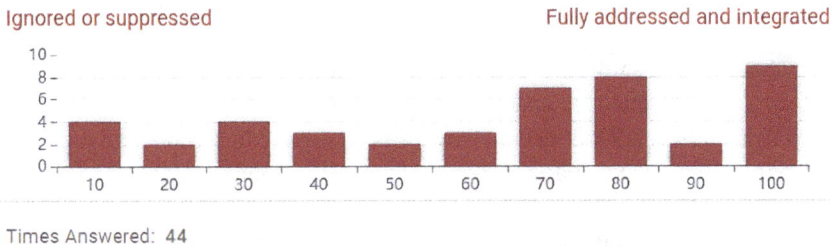

Times Answered: 44

Figure 24.6: Histogram related to "processing tensions" from Cohere+ SenseMaker® data generated during the IDG workshop on October 13, 2023.
Source: Cohere+, based on SenseMaker data

There could be different interpretations of this spectrum of perceptions. It could be due to different experiences of the respective respondents during the event, or to different degrees of awareness and sensitivity towards perceived tensions in the first place. Or, it could point to a degree of absence of fear and, hence, a certain level of coherence and tolerance towards tensions that leads to experiencing existing tensions as less of a problem. To make more specific sense of this, we would need to go into respondents' stories about their experience, which is beyond the scope of this chapter.

Data collection via the SenseMaker tool

The main tool for exploring coherence at our workshop during the IDG summit was a so-called SenseMaker capture (by Cynefin Company). This digital in-depth survey invites participants to share real-life stories, anecdotes, and experiences about a given topic and, in a second step, to evaluate these and make sense of them in a number of fields of tension between different values (for example "Does your story relate more to self – a group – or the larger system?", see Figure 24.6 above). By having respondents (and not the "experts") evaluate their own experiences, the SenseMaker software allows to generate both quantitatively relevant and meaningful qualitative data in and about complex human systems which are much better at mirroring the underlying needs, beliefs and expectations than more unidimensional, linear surveys. The collective patterns that become visible as a result of a SenseMaker survey can then be subject to joint sensemaking, enabling the respective system "to see itself".[4]

---

4 This theory-informed practice is based on several foundational sciences including complex-adaptive systems theory, and narrative and cultural anthropology. The method has been scientifically tested and applied to many different fields and topics – please see Van der Merve et al. (2019).

Challenges to coherence in the IDG community

As described in Table 24.3 above, capturing experiences and having the respondents evaluate them is only the first step. The actual process of inviting the system to see itself happens in a facilitated process of getting people together, ideally those who responded and/or others, allowing and supporting them to take in the collective patterns visualized by the software. Ideally, we would do this by having smaller groups dive into a co-creative dialogue and meaning making about these patterns. However, since the format of this book does not allow for this kind of interaction with you, dear reader, we invite you to go on an explorative journey on your own with the material presented below.

Please take a closer look at the triads in Table 24.3 (represented both as data points and heatmaps to show possible ways of displaying the data) and ask yourself the following questions:

– Which patterns do you notice?
– How do they relate to your own experience of the IDG field or, if applicable, community?
– What can we learn from the patterns showing up in the triangles?
– What do you think the patterns could tell us about the current state of cohesion or coherence within the group of respondents and/or the IDG movement as a whole?
– What challenge could this contain for the IDG community?
– If you see any challenges, what would we need to get more of or less of – and how?

Table 24.3: Triad graphs from the Cohere+ SenseMaker capture during the IDG workshop on October 13, 2023: Response patterns relating to motivation and process.

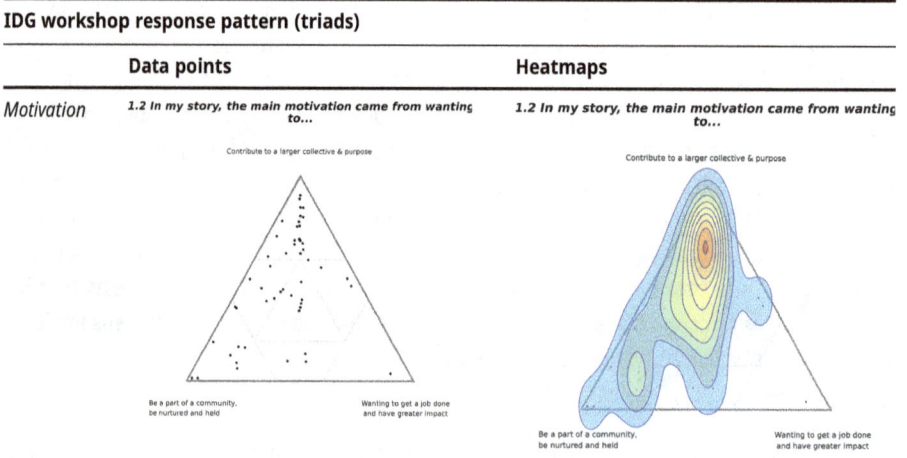

IDG workshop response pattern (triads)	
Data points	**Heatmaps**
Motivation	

1.2 In my story, the main motivation came from wanting to...

Contribute to a larger collective & purpose

Be a part of a community, be nurtured and held / Wanting to get a job done and have greater impact

Table 24.3 (continued)

IDG workshop response pattern (triads)		
	Data points	**Heatmaps**
Process	**1.4 Relating to my story, I feel we...**	**1.4 Relating to my story, I feel we...**

N = 83 n = 70 aN/A = 13 filter n = 43 %age = 61% filter N/A = 12 mu = 12 mu = L:34 T: 22 R: 45

Source: Cohere+, based on data gathered through SenseMaker

If you wish to share your insights, please get in touch with us at the following email address bettina.geiken@ifis-freiburg.de. We would love to hear from you.

Next, we invite you to explore some of the differences in the responses received from the IDG summit participants according to age. Compared to the other communities involved in our research, in the IDG group there had a significant number of participants between 26–40 years old. The following figure visualizes significant differences with respect to both the question about how tensions were addressed and about people's sense of autonomy and agency.

Again, please take a closer look at both graphs (see Table 24.4 below) and consider the following questions:
– What do you notice?
– How does it relate to your own experience?
– What sense do you make intuitively of what you see?

Again, interpreting these patterns would require taking a deeper look into the actual stories and experiences that respondents fed into the survey, which is beyond the scope of this chapter. However, the above data already raises interesting questions as to:
– What could be indications of cohesion or coherence in the group of respondents/ the IDG movement as a whole?
– For the IDGs to enable change AND involve younger people, what "more of" and "less of" would be needed?

If you wish to share any insights or ideas in this regard, please contact us!

Table 24.4: Scatter graphs from the Cohere+ SenseMaker capture during the IDG workshop on October 13, 2023: Response patterns relating to tensions and agency in different age groups.

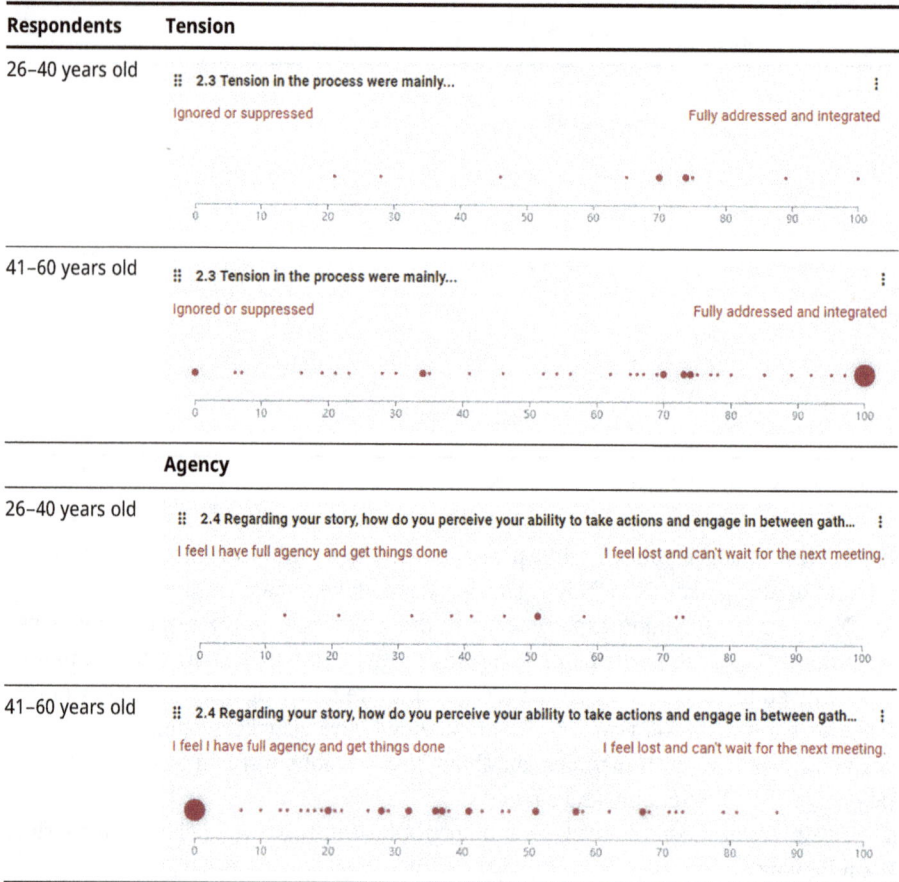

Respondents	Tension
26–40 years old	**⁝⁝ 2.3 Tension in the process were mainly...** ⁝ Ignored or suppressed · · · · · · · · Fully addressed and integrated 0 10 20 30 40 50 60 70 80 90 100
41–60 years old	**⁝⁝ 2.3 Tension in the process were mainly...** ⁝ Ignored or suppressed · · · · · · · · Fully addressed and integrated 0 10 20 30 40 50 60 70 80 90 100
	Agency
26–40 years old	**⁝⁝ 2.4 Regarding your story, how do you perceive your ability to take actions and engage in between gath...** ⁝ I feel I have full agency and get things done · · · · · · · · I feel lost and can't wait for the next meeting. 0 10 20 30 40 50 60 70 80 90 100
41–60 years old	**⁝⁝ 2.4 Regarding your story, how do you perceive your ability to take actions and engage in between gath...** ⁝ I feel I have full agency and get things done · · · · · · · · I feel lost and can't wait for the next meeting. 0 10 20 30 40 50 60 70 80 90 100

Source: Cohere+, based on data gathered through SenseMaker

However, looking at these data from a distance, these findings could point to very different hypothesis, such as:

– The IDG community is providing a nurturing hub, but does not yet support younger people to be in their own agency and capacity to act.
– Younger people seem to feel a general lack of agency in the world and therefore don't join the IDG hubs/movement.
– The cost of the conference was too high for more young people to attend.
– For older people, the IDG community seems to provide the conditions and enough sense of coherence in order to feel agency and take action.

- Older people already come with a lot more life experience supporting their sense of agency and bringing it into the community.
- The specific context of the event/movement/community does (not) create conditions for a lasting sense of agency.

Ultimately, these questions would need you/us as the IDG community to engage in collective sensemaking in its hubs and gatherings, such that the different hypotheses can be subject to deeper exploration, testing, and possibly be resolved appropriately.

Conclusion

This chapter advocates for reframing the IDG framework through the lens of coherence. It argues that enhancing coherence can expand the benefits of the IDG skills and, thus, the impact of the IDG community. By presenting evidence from various kinds of fieldwork, including within the IDG community, we argue that coherence deepens our understanding of the five dimensions and each skill within the IDG framework. The degree of coherence determines how effectively we can actualize the 23 skills, with coherence acting as an enhancer and enabler. Embodying the IDG skills, in turn, increases overall coherence.

We have proposed to distinguish between coherence and cohesion as polar opposite ways of designing interactions and group dynamics, as a function of dealing with tension. Cohesion tries to exclude tension, while coherence welcomes it as an opportunity for growth. These concepts impact our ability to handle complexity: cohesion limits perspectives and options, whereas coherence supports multiple perspectives, fostering meaningful *collaboration* and creative *action*.

Fieldwork examples show that coherence can be perceived by individuals and groups through appropriate scaffolding. They show that skills do not have to be developed one at a time, but reinforce (or, if absent, prevent) each other. In other words, in view of the IDG skills, it doesn't matter where you start.

They also show that coherence supports agency way beyond actual group meetings, and that for coherence to persist, diversity and even "productive irritation" are necessary, stimulating the system to "reshuffle" for coherence over again. Coherence can therefore be seen as a dynamic meta-stable process, that is informed and guided by enabling constraints, such as intention, purpose, authenticity, trust, "tension skills", and scaffolding structures.

We have demonstrated multiple ways to scaffold coherence, such as through art, creating safe spaces, and skilled facilitation, using specific tools and interventions. In the IDG field, we identify a few challenges to coherence that need further exploration. Our hope is that these insights will support the embodiment of the IDG skills and increase both personal and social coherence in the field.

References

Agazarian, Y. (2004). *Systems-centered therapy for groups*. Routledge.

Antonovsky, A. (1983). The sense of coherence: Development of a research instrument. *Newsletter Research Report. Schwartz Research Center for Behavioral Medicine, Tel Aviv University, 1*, 11–22.

Beck, D. E., & Cowan, C. C. (2014). *Spiral dynamics: Mastering values, leadership and change*. John Wiley & Sons.

Beck, D. E., & Cowan, C. (1996). *Spiral Dynamics: Mastering Values. Leadership and Change*. Wiley-Blackwell.

Caspari, A. & Schilling, M. (2016). A we-space process ecology. In O. Gunnlaugson & M. Brabant (eds.), *Cohering the integral we space: Engaging collective emergence, wisdom and healing in groups* (pp. 61–78). Integral Publishing House.

Cook-Greuter, S. (2005). Ego development: Nine levels of increasing embrace. *Unpublished manuscript*.

Fein, E. et al. (2023). *Foundations, principles and inspirational resources of integral politics*. Tradition.

Graves, C. W. (2005). *The never ending quest* (C. Cowan & N. Todorovic, eds.). ECLET Publishing.

HeartMath Institute. (2023). *Art and Science of Cultivating Coherence*, https://spiritualgrowthevents.com/events/art-science-of-cultivating-coherence-summit/.

HeartMath Institute's extensive collection of research studies, articles and other materials (327 Research Publications) https://www.heartmath.org/research/research-library/.

Juarrero, A. (2023). *Context changes everything: How constraints create coherence*. MIT Press.

Lewin, K. (1943). *Defining the 'field at a given time'*. Psychological Review.

Lewis, M. (2013). About Deep Democracy. *Deep Democracy-The Lewis Method. Last modified*.

McCraty, R. (2017). New frontiers in heart rate variability and social coherence research: Techniques, technologies, and implications for improving group dynamics and outcomes. *Frontiers in Public Health, 5*, 267, https://doi.org/10.3389/fpubh.2017.00267.

Neurologen und Psychiater im Netz. (2017). *Angst wirkt sich auf Immunsystem aus*, https://www.neurologen-und-psychiater-im-netz.org/psychiatrie-psychosomatik-psychotherapie/news-archiv/meldungen/article/angst-wirkt-sich-auf-immunsystem-aus/, accessed March 28, 2024.

Prigogine, I. (1984). *Order out of chaos: Man's new dialogue with nature*. Bantam Books.

Roy, B. (2016, Oct. 19). *Excerpt: Open group practice: Eight social selves*. Kosmos Journal. https://www.kosmosjournal.org/article/open-group-practice-eight-social-selves/.

Social Architect Curriculum. *Building capacity for change agents in the metamodern age*. https://socialarchitect.de/.

Van der Merwe, S. E., Biggs, R., Preiser, R., Cunningham, C., Snowden, D. J., O'Brien, K., Jenal, M., Vosloo, M., Blignaut, S., & Goh, Z. (2019). Making sense of complexity: Using SenseMaker as a research tool. *Systems, 7*(2), 25. https://doi.org/10.3390/systems7020025.

Villemot-Kienzle, C. (2018). Designing the "Social Architect" Ecosystem – Exploring factors that promote emergence, resilience and evolution of an ecosystem for transformative social innovation, https://medium.com/@claudinevillemotkienzle/designing-the-social-architect-ecosystem-exploring-factors-that-promote-emergence-resilience-a5a233432b5c, accessed October 23rd, 2024.

List of figures

https://doi.org/10.1515/9783111453729-026

List of tables

https://doi.org/10.1515/9783111453729-027

Index

https://doi.org/10.1515/9783111453729-028

Contributor Biographies

Volume 2

Allegrini, F.
University of St. Gallen, Switzerland
Fabio Allegrini resides in St. Gallen, Switzerland, where he has pursued most of his educational path. He is working on his Bachelor's degree in Business Administration from the University of St. Gallen and has a Master's degree in Secondary Education from the Pädagogische Hochschule St. Gallen. He is leading social initiatives, notably as the project lead for step into action in St. Gallen, and his current role as Assistant Manager of Curriculum Development at the University of St. Gallen. Trying to transform the curriculum at HSG towards a more sustainable and responsible management education.

Barroso, M.
Senior Researcher, Lecturer and Project Lead and at the Sustainability Innovation Lab (Institute of Technology Management) and Head of Executive Education of the Competence Center for Social Innovation, both at the University of St. Gallen, Switzerland. She has extensive experience as a lecturer and facilitator, and in consulting organizations with respect to sustainable business models and sustainable leadership in the context of corporate social responsibility, multistakeholder management, impact-oriented organizations and systems thinking. Mônica holds a PhD in Social Policy from the London School of Economics and Political Science, and was a postdoc Kleinhans Fellow of the Rainforest Alliance leading a project on "Linking Market Intelligence and Remote Villagers" in the Brazilian Amazon, where she also facilitated a number of learning journeys for executive audiences. She was also Head of Learning and senior lecturer at The School of Life Brazil, having facilitated emotional intelligence workshops for individuals and corporations. She has additionally co-founded local hubs of the Inner Development Goals in Brazil and Switzerland, supporting business students and leaders in developing inner skills that will equip them to better lead the sustainability transition from inside out.

Biddlecome, L.
Emerge
Leigh Biddlecome is a writer, strategist, and facilitator with experience living in six countries and working across multiple contexts, from international education NGOs to academia and purpose-driven start-ups. She brings an artistic and cultural sensitivity, fluency in French and Italian, and deep curiosity for alternative perspectives to her work. With training in the humanities and social sciences from Stanford, Oxford, and EHESS (Paris), she thrives in multidisciplinary problem-solving environments. She helps CEOs transform their strategy into inspiring narratives, works with academics as an 'ideas translator', and facilitates workshops at global conferences. A published writer and translator, she is currently working on an audio documentary series on contemporary forms of spirituality in Italy.

Blakeley-Glover, J.
Orientate / Most Sustainable Workplace Index
Jaime is a sustainability leader and coach with over 20 years of experience in the property industry and human development. He advises Bristol City Leap and has guided organisations in delivering major sustainability and Net Zero strategies. Founder of the Most Sustainable Workplace Index, Jaime also co-developed the Meaning-Awareness-Purpose (M-A-P) model for climate coaching and supports sustainability leaders through executive coaching. Outside of his professional life, Jaime is passionate about the outdoors. a Mountain Leader and outdoor guide. This love for nature complements his professional commitment to sustainability, grounding his work in a deep appreciation for the natural world.

https://doi.org/10.1515/9783111453729-029

Boffelli, A.
University of Bergamo, Italy
Dr. Albachiara Boffelli is an Assistant Professor at the University of Bergamo and is responsible for the courses of Sustainable and Global Supply Management, Management of Global Enterprises and Management of Business and Logistics Systems. Since December 2021, she is a member of the board of the School of Management of the University of Bergamo. She obtained the national qualification as Associate Professor in October 2022. She has been visiting researcher at Lund University in Sweden and the University of Manchester (UK). She is a member of many academic associations, including EurOMA (European Operations Management Association), DSI (Decision Sciences Institute), AoM (Academy of Management). In 2023, she won the Gianluca Spina Innovative Teaching Award with the proposal â€œDeveloping a Sustainability Mindset in Management Engineering Studentsâ€ and was selected among the finalists of the Nigel Slack Teaching Innovation Award promoted by EurOMA (European Operations Management Association) for the same initiative. Since 2024, she is the contact person for PRME at her Department.

Boonyanupongsa, P.
Insights for Change, Thailand
Pacharamon Boonyanupongsa is a dedicated advocate for social change, committed to empowering individuals and communities to drive meaningful progress. As a supporter of Insights for Change, Pacharamon works to help others harness their inner capacity to build stronger, more inclusive communities. With a deep interest in socio-ecology, learning, and inner development, Pacharamon engages in initiatives that foster sustainable social transformation. Through Insights for Change, they contribute to guiding and supporting changemakers in Thailand, helping to turn ideas into impactful actions.

Breiner, S.
IDG Global Practitioners Network
Dr. Sibylle Breiner is an economist and transformational leader who holds a Ph.D. from the University of Hohenheim, Germany. She has spent nearly two decades in corporate management, with focus on international project management. Dr. Breiner transitioned to academia to nurture values of ethical leadership and sustainable change, teaching international management, and leadership skills. As a core team member of the IDG Global Practitioners' Network, she advocates for human-centric transformations. She is the co-founder of InnerDevelopment@Work, a community that empowers individuals to embed IDG principles into business operations, fostering thriving environments and promoting integrity, inclusivity, and purpose-driven leadership.

Brooks, R.
University of St. Gallen, Switzerland
Rachel Brooks is Head of Sustainability Curriculum Development, Program Director and Lecturer in sustainability and social innovation at the University of St.Gallen, Switzerland. Her research focuses on transformation of management education and education for sustainability, particularly teaching methods and formats that spur transformative learning. Prior, she worked for a decade in professional and leadership development for sustainability, where she focused on developing programs and teaching formats that build competencies of leaders across sectors to take action on global grand challenges in an environment of mounting complexity, uncertainty, and urgency. Rachel has worked and conducted research in several Latin American countries and Switzerland on social sustainability strategy development and cross-sector collaboration in the global food industry at the nexus of business, agricultural producers, government, and non-profit organizations.

Burckhardt, X. D

Campos Suarez M.

Co-Founder Inner Development Goals Switzerland

Xuan Dung Burckhardt is the founder of FLOW and Managing Director of Burckhardt HR Consulting GmbH. With more than 20 years of experience in various industries, particularly in the pharmaceutical sector in both established companies and start-ups, she is passionate about a people-centric approach to HR.

As an well-rounded HR leader, Dung has managed the entire employee lifecycle - from talent acquisition and development to organisational development and post-merger integration. Her ability to translate business objectives into actionable HR strategies has consistently led to improved business performance, making her a trusted advisor to senior executives and leadership teams.

Beyond her HR achievements, Dung is also a dedicated artist whose work has been exhibited in galleries since 2018. This creative passion not only fuels her artistic endeavours, but also inspires her to create FLOW, a methodology that uses art as a medium in team or individual interventions to foster collaboration and innovation. Her art can be viewed at www.xdart.ch.

Canning, N.

IDG Global Pracitioner Network & Lemanic Community Network

After 20 years working in over 45 countries managing large projects in industry and sustainable development, Nadene Canning created a boutique consultancy designing learning strategies that accelerate innovation, well-being and impact. Today alongside her consultancy she co-facilitates the IDG Global Practitioner Network. Her areas of expertise include holistic leadership, collective learning and innovation, radical collaboration, curation, hosting and facilitation and the future of work.

Chun, P.

IITTI World Civility Index, Canada

Patrick Chun, engineer, entrepreneur. Sold his first company to a multinational in the mid 2000s. In 2011, Patrick co-founded a non-profit with some of the most experienced trainers around the world to set up a soft skills standard called IITTI World Civility Index. It is somewhat similar to ISO, and in other ways, similar to standardized tests such as TOEFL, IELTS, or GMAT. It is now used in 19 countries by hundreds of thousands of people, and became an official partner of UN Sustainable Development in 2019.

Delaloye, R

Emory University – Center for Contemplative Science and Compassion-based Ethics, USA

Ryder Delaloye is the Associate Director for the SEE Learning Program. He is a practitioner of education and learning having been a teacher and administrator. His prior research and school engagement focused on whole school and district transformation, district leadership, sustainability education, civic education, and teacher and administrator development. He believes that the purpose of education is interpersonal growth and societal change. He is grounded by his wife and children, with whom he loves to play and go on adventures in the mountains. He received his Doctorate in Curriculum and Instruction from the University of Montana.

Egel, E.

NavigatingTransformation Consultancy, Germany

Dr Eleftheria Egel is a visionary business builder and a big picture thinker committed to influencing and changing the world around her. She is the co-founder and product strategist of an early-stage EdTech social startup, EOS Academy, and a business mentor for female entrepreneurs. With over a decade of entrepreneurial experience and a background in academic research on leadership, sustainability, and entrepreneurship, she empowers aspiring female entrepreneurs to turn their visions into thriving businesses through tailored strategic guidance. Eleftheria is passionate about understanding how social conditioning creates meaning-making that undermines human capacity.

Fein, E.
Institute for integral Studies, Germany
Dr Elke Fein is a political and social scientist and managing director of the Institute for Integral Studies (IFIS). Her main areas of work are trauma-informed politics, political cultural research, system change, Russian studies, adult development, and the theory and practice of integral politics. Elke Fein was the initiator and coordinator of 3 EU-Projects (Leadership for Transition) (2013–2022). She is currently establishing a school for integral politics.

Fry, L.W.
Texas A&M University-Central Texas, USA
Louis W. (Jody) Fry is Regents Professor of Management at Texas A & M University-Central Texas and coordinator of their MS Leadership for Sustainability. Presently, he is a member of the editorial review boards of Sustainability, Associate Editor for Leadership and Spirituality for the Journal of Management, Spirituality & Religion, the founder of the International Institute for Spiritual Leadership, and a commissioned spiritual director. His present research, consulting, and executive development interests are focused on maximizing the triple bottom line through spiritual leadership to co-create a conscious, sustainable world that works for everyone.

Gagliardi, L
Terre des Hommes, Switzerland

Trained in Social Anthropology and Islamic Studies at the University of Zurich, University of Leiden in Kairo and the Saint-Joseph University in Beirut I developed a strong focus on Community Based Action Research. During my time as research assistant at the Ethnographic Museum at the University of Zurich I developed my interest in human competences and skills as well as knowledge transfer. After several years in social work working with young people and migrants, I am currently working for the Swiss-based NGO terre des hommes schweiz in coaching and facilitating of co-creative transformation processes.

Geiken, B.
Institute for Integral Studies, Freiburg, Germany
Starting with a PhD in natural sciences she moved into EU-project design in international development focusing on strategies for sustainable urban development and intercultural/institutional capacity building. Extensive awareness training around inner change alongside the project work with culturally diverse stakeholders led to her current focus in adult development, complex-adaptive systems, and sensemaking applied to learning design, training, facilitation and coaching. Bettina is board member of the Institute for Integral Studies and leads there the area on "Applied Complexity". She is co-author of the book chapter "Complexity Science for New Politics in Theory and Practice", supported by the EU-Erasmus programme for adult education.

Hamschmidt, J.
University of St. Gallen, Switzerland
Dr Jost Hamschmidt holds a PhD from the University of St. Gallen and has been a visiting researcher at UC Berkeley and Harvard Business School. He has spent over 20 years in positions related to curriculum innovation and academic intrapreneurship. A passionate academic project developer, he has co-founded international academic projects such as the oikos Global Case Writing Competition, the ETH PhD Academy on Sustainability and Technology and the CEMS Model UNFCCC, a simulation of the UN climate change

negotiations. He aims to inspire collaborative leadership for sustainability and was a founding member of the Impact Hub Zurich Association, the GRONEN Association (Group for Research on Organizations and the Natural Environment) and the IDG St. Gallen Hub. He is a cyclist, lifelong learner and father of three.

Hartley, L.

Laura Hartley is a leadership coach, climate activist and founder of the Scintilla Centre - an educational platform equipping changemakers with the skills, wisdom and community to reimagine and remake the world. Fascinated by the space between inner and outer change, Laura melds systems thinking & inner work to support changemakers in finding their unique impact in this time, and to sow transformative change in their communities and organisations.

Hempel, L.

IDG Switzerland

Living outside of Basel, Switzerland, Lutz helps people and organizations become more conscious, whole, naturally agile and resonant. He brings more than 20 years of experience in management consulting. Passionate about resonant collaboration and mindfulness in work and life, Lutz works with teams and leaders to help them to connect, learn and thrive, incorporating character strengths practice, music and business improvisation. Lutz is co-founder of Inner Development Goals Switzerland, founder of Groovin' Organization, associate of ICG Integrated Consulting Group. He holds an MBA from the University of Strathclyde and is a certified mindfulness teacher (MBSP).

Jovanovic, I.

Rflect, Switzerland

Software developer by nature driven by commitment to continuous personal growth and meaningful impact in society. With experience in building complex software systems and leading teams, together with the Rflect team, we are bringing to digital reality a number of new ideas in the domain of the future of education. I believe in the power of technology to create positive change and in building software solutions that make a difference. Father, husband, friend, creator.

Janss, J.

Inner Green Deal

Jeroen is co-founder and co-director of the Inner Green Deal. He designs and facilitates leadership and inner development programmes for large systemic organisations such as the EU and the UN as well as for NGOs and local communities. He has a master's degree in International Relations and is a certified mindfulness and compassion teacher. Building on 25 years of international experience as a social entrepreneur, facilitator and advisor, Jeroen regularly speaks on the human dimension of sustainability and the role of inner development.

Klingenberg, B.

FOM School of Economics and Management, SMIndicator, LLC, Germany

Dr. Beate Klingenberg is Professor of Sustainability and Supply Chain Management at the FOM School of Economics and Management, Germany and managing partner of the Sustainability Mindset Indicator (SMI)®, LLC. She teaches operations and supply chain management, sustainability and sustainable business, and decision-sciences. Her areas of research encompass the sustainability mindset, knowledge management for sustainability, and the interface of operations management and financial performance. Her credentials include a master's in chemistry, a Ph.D. in Physical Chemistry (University of Erlangen-Nürnberg, Germany) and an MBA (Marist College, USA). She has extensive industry experience in cross-cultural technology transfer, intercultural communication and project management.

Largacha-Martinez, C.

Fundacion Universitaria del Area Andina

Social futurist and quantic humanist specialising in crafting and advancing social innovations through the marriage of quantum mechanics and artificial intelligence. Carlos asserts that societal authenticity is pivotal for heightened humanity, particularly within workplaces. At the helm of the startup 'FlourishingAi,' he pioneers the fusion of humanistic management and natural language processing (NLP), aiding businesses in embracing purpose and amplifying human well-being. Esteemed as a consultant awarded by HBR/McKinsey M-Prize, TEDx speaker, quantum coach, and B-Corps devotee. Carlos is the Colombian Director of the Swiss Humanistic Management Network, the Co-Creator for the Swedish global endeavor 'Inner Development Goals-IDG' and a researcher at the University Areandina (Colombia). Holder of dual Ph.D. degrees in International Studies and Quantum Sociology, plus a Fulbright Post-Doctoral Fellow from the University of Miami.

Lindencrona, F.

Inner Development Goals Foundation, Sweden

Dr. Fredrik Lindencrona, PhD, co-initiated the IDG initiative in 2020 and now lead IDG Research Co-Creation – a global collaboration ecosystem between a diverse set of researchers from different disciplines and higher education teachers and academic institutions. Fredrik is a licensed psychologist who has been engaged in policy and systems work focusing on human capabilities and wellbeing for driving transformation towards sustainable development during more than 20 years. Fredrik has been actively engaged in international collaboration with international entities such as OECD, WHO, EU and with several countries such as Canada and US, and cities such as New York City.

Pagani Larghi, M.

Duduum Sagl and U.Lab IDG Hub Ticino

Lucid dreamer. Evolutionary economist and counselor, I love exploring the human soul from multiple perspectives. I work on issues related to personal, collective and systemic change, focusing on Theory U and IDGs as powerful tools. I am passionate about issues related to our deep relationship with money and food. Founder of Duduum Sagl, U.Lab IDG Hub Ticino and co-founder of Impact Hub Ticino and In-Patto association.

Mahler, H.-C.

ten23 health AG

Dr. Mahler is currently CEO and Board Member at ten23 health AG, the human-centric and sustainable pharmaceutical development partner. He previously worked at Lonza, Roche and Merck. Hanns-Christian studied Pharmacy, holds a PhD and did his Habilitation in Pharmacy. He further educated himself in Economics and Marketing, Organisational Development & Effectiveness (as "Loop" Fellow) and in other topics close to his heart including Sustainability. His purpose is to making a positive impact for Patients and People and to create (fun) jobs.

Mata Carrera, A.G.

I'm a photographer with a passion for capturing the stories behind the moments and storytelling through imagery (@agabriela_m). In addition to photography, I'm also an entrepreneur, founded SurYNor Art to promote the development of true aborigine communities and create awareness in fair trade and responsible consuming especially from my country, Mexico.

Mensch, I.
Perspectiva & Emerge

Ivo J. Mensch is a dedicated to navigating cultural transitions and shifts in consciousness. As the developer of Perspectiva's Praxis strand, he designs courses and practices to address the meta-crisis. Ivo's research focuses on Time (Temporics), Imagination, and Logos as fundamental dimensions of change. An ordained Soto Zen Buddhist monk, he has practiced in the Diamond Approach wisdom school for over a decade. Ivo supports individual growth as a coach and is a published author on entrepreneurship's inner aspects. His diverse career spans journalism, communications consulting, tech, yacht carpentry, and greenhouse construction. Ivo's work aims to foster skillful navigation of societal and personal transformation.

Miller, A.
Net Zero MAP

With an MSc in the Nature of Business, Andy Miller brings a unique blend of science, business acumen, and leadership coaching to the table. My work in corporate leadership coaching is particularly influenced by the Inner Development Goals (IDGs) and the Meaning, Awareness, and Purpose (MAP) model. MAP is an academically tested and peer-review published coaching programme that expedites Net Zero by guiding corporate teams to align personal and organizational emotions, values, and beliefs with sustainable development goals, fostering a resilient, purpose-driven workforce to drive impactful climate action

Mitsotaki, A.
Co-founder & president of the World Human Forum, Greece

Alexandra Mitsotaki is co-founder & president of the World Human Forum, a global citizen initiative which has its symbolic base in Delphi, launching international initiatives from important sites such as Delos, Aristotle's Lyceum in Athens and Eleusis. In 1998 she founded ActionAid Hellas, the Greek affiliate of ActionAid, the international organisation against poverty and injustice. She chaired the organisation from 1998 to 2017. She was also a member of the Action Aid international board from 2003 to 2016. From 2009 to 2019 she was in charge of the Hellenic Cultural Centre in Paris of which she is now vice-chair. Reacting to the financial crisis in Greece, in 2014 she co-founded Action Finance Initiative, the first microcredit organisation in Greece. Before her engagement in the civil society field, she started her professional life working at the OECD in Paris, where she married French lawyer Pascal Gourdain and raised their four children.

She is a member of the High-Level Roundtable of the New European Bauhaus, an initiative of the European Commission aiming to connect the European Green Deal to our living spaces. Her interdisciplinary experience over the past years has made her a profound supporter of the importance of a holistic approach to tackle the big challenges of our time.

Novoa-Gómez, M.
Fundación Universitaria Konrad Lorenz

Suma Cum Laude in Psychological Studies. As a psychologist and psychotherapist, Monica has researched and developed comprehensive protocols with people experiencing complex trauma in contexts of political violence to promote human flourishing and mental health. She is a consultant to multilateral organisations in the fields of mental health, psychological well-being, transformation of cultural practices and clinical skills, with a special focus on clinical supervision and training of practitioners, psychotherapists and supervisors.

In Colombia, she is a member of the National Mental Health Policy Council of the Ministry of Health and Social Protection. She is also an evaluator member of the National Accreditation Council of the Ministry of National Education.

Rot, N.
Rflect, Switzerland
Niels is both an entrepreneur by coincidence, as well as as by 'calling'. Over the 15+ years co-founding Impact Hub Zürich. STRIDE unSchool and other places in sustainability-related fields, Niels has developed a fairly straightforward personal theory of change. If we can make people reflect more (deeply), they will take more sustainable decisions in the long-run. So now Niels is co-building Rflect to realize that vision.

Nagler, J.
Wellbeing Mindset
Juergen Nagler is an international advisor on systems transformation and mindset shifts with over 25 years of experience in the United Nations, international businesses, and civil society organizations. His vision is contributing to a global paradigm change from a GDP fixation to fostering the wellbeing of people and planet, therefore advancing the SDGs and IDGs. For the UN Development Programme (UNDP) in Bhutan he led multi-million-dollar initiatives in the areas of climate and environment, entrepreneurship, and governance. He also co-founded the UN Transformation Network connecting changemakers across the world and has published groundbreaking research in various publications.

Fedi, P.
In-Patto Association (Switzerland), ManagerItalia, ECOnGOO ItalyD
Graduated with honors in Statistical and Actuarial Science from "La Sapienza", led his professional life as a consultant and facilitator of teams, entrepreneur, freelancer and manager in American and European multinationals (Digital Equipment, AT&T, Schlumberger-Sema Group, hp). Expert on strategy, innovation, organization, applied creativity and change management (Theory U). Member of the Board of Directors of Manageritalia and of the Economy for Common Good in Italy, co-founded the U.Lab & IDGs Hub Rome. Engaged in the development and dissemination of Generative Interdependence Agreements (ADIG) and IDGs with "mini ADIG" aimed at multiplying positive impacts on the SDGs.

Rhodes, J.
University of Plymouth / Imagery Coaching
Dr. Jonathan Rhodes is a Chartered Psychologist specialising in performance and imagery techniques. He co-developed Functional Imagery Training to enhance resilience in Olympic athletes, military personnel, and business leaders, and is currently collaborating with world-class explorers to improve decision-making in high-stakes environments.

Rimanoczy, I.
SMIndicator LLC
Isabel is an academic, who has made it her life purpose to promote change accelerators. She developed the Sustainability Mindset by studying business leaders who championed corporate initiatives with a positive impact on the environment and the community. She created the PRME Working Group on Sustainability Mindset, an international cohort of academics on five continents promoting a sustainability mindset with their students. She authored and co-edited 30 books, including poetry and fiction; many academic book chapters and papers. Her Sustainability Mindset Indicator was awarded three Prizes in 2019 and 2021 by the Reimagine Education contest, Wharton and QS, UK.

Rippel, R.
Rosanna Rippel
Rosanna Rippel is a dancer, poet and DJ working within behavior- and experience design. With a background in philosophy, cognitive science and research, she enjoys weaving intricate narratives and thought-provoking themes together with deeply personal stories of what it means to be human.

Stadler-Stuart, E.
Rflect, Switzerland
Ella Stadler-Stuart – CPO at Rflect. Passionate about impact and inner work, Ella has previously worked at SINGA Switzerland and Impact Hub in New Zealand. Professional coach, facilitator and Director of Studies CAS Women Leading Digital at HWZ.

Taylor, A.
3P Impact
Alan Taylor is an ICF accredited executive coach and team coach who empowers leaders and teams to achieve excellent results. Over the last decade Alan has provided consulting and coaching services in leadership development, team effectiveness, and business transformation. Working in IT, L&D and marketing arenas, he has guided executives through strategic planning & execution, designed and run impactful sustainability focused leadership programs, built high-performing teams and supported organisational transformations.

His supportive, outcome-oriented approach helps clients overcome challenges and move from intent to action. He has extensive experience working in diverse organisations throughout Europe and APAC.

Tschiderer, J.
University of St. Gallen, Switzerland
Johannes Tschiderer is a lecturer at the University of St.Gallen and has been active in designing and facilitating transformative learning formats at the nexus of business and sustainability at his alma mater ever since his student days. He's also a Research & Investment Associate at the TransCap Initiative, a think-and-do-tank on a mission to develop a new investment logic for funding systems transformation. Prior to this, Johannes had led the student-run sustainability consultancy Student Impact, which works with impact-oriented start-ups and SMEs. Johannes obtained a BA in Business and an MA in Finance, both from the University of St.Gallen.

Villemot-Klenze, C.
Center for Human Emergence, D.A.CH
Social architect, author, consultant for transculturalism. She was authorized by Don Beck to be a lecturer for Spiral Dynamics integral. She co-founded the Center for Human Emergence, D.A.CH, that aims at fostering societal transformation based on a holistic approach. Inspired by the study of Conscious Evolution she has been dedicating her work to support the emergence of ecosystems embodying an integral/holistic level of consciousness. She co-developed the curriculum "Social Architects" that fosters the building of evolutionary competencies for the metamodern world. She now focuses her research and work on exploring how communities can operate in alignment with coherence and co-creation.

Wamsler, C.
Lund University Centre for Sustainability Studies (LUCSUS), Sweden
Christine Wamsler is Professor of Sustainability Science at Lund University Centre for Sustainability Studies (LUCSUS), Founder and Director of the Contemplative Sustainable Futures Program, a Mind & Life Fellow, and former Co-Director of the Societal Resilience Centre. She is an internationally-renowned expert, practitioner and educator in sustainable development and associated (inner and outer) transformation processes, with 25 years of experience. Christine has been ranked as the 8th most influential scholar worldwide for her contributions to environmental science. Her work has shaped international debates and increased knowledge on personal, collective, institutional and policy transformations in a context of climate change. She has led many international projects, and published more than 200 academic papers, book chapters, and books on these issues.

Wavell, H.

Harrison Wavell

Harrison Wavell is a purpose-driven poet, musician and educator from the Isle of Wight. His work strives to cultivate connection and kinship within and between the human and more-than-human worlds. Drawing inspiration from the Perennial Tradition, that well of universal truth and wisdom shared by all major world religions, Harrison seeks to celebrate the unity underlying our diversity.

Werk, F.

ten23 health AG, Switzerland

Felicia Werk studied Organizational Psychology in Germany and the US and as well holds an MBA of the Edinburg Business School and FHNW in Switzerland. With >18 years of experience in the pharma industry, she gained expertise as change agent, people leader and coach. She worked in local and global roles of HR, Business Development and Strategy. At ten23 Health AG, she co creates innovative concepts of new ways of working with the P&C Team. Through her company Equestria Coaching she coaches also other leaders to fulfill her purpose of "Having a positive impact on peoples`lives and their personal growth".

Endorsements

"The Sustainable Development Goals are critical if the humans living today were to be described by their future generations as 'Good ancestors!' All goals begin with individual commitment and action. The five 'Inner Development Goals' are the means to manifest this action. Unless we source learning from 'Being', think with the 'Whole' mind, build trusting relations, collaborate, and act with focus and enthusiasm, our dreams for our world would only remain at an 'intent' level. This book is much needed and timely. I congratulate all the authors for their inspired work and recommend this to every person who cares for Mother Earth."

Anil Sachdev

Founder and Chairman of SOIL- School of Inspired Leadership, India

"I am pleased to support this two-volume book on how to implement the United Nations' Inner Development Goals. While many people are aware of, and support, the United Nations' Sustainable Development Goals (SDGs), the Inner Development Goals (IDGs) are less familiar but equally crucial. The five IDGs were devised to accelerate the adoption of the SDGs by highlighting the necessary skills for individuals, teams, and organizations to achieve the SDG vision. By focusing on personal and collective growth, these important and much-needed books offer useful tools, methods, and examples to empower individuals, teams, and organizations to more effectively contribute to the realization of the SDGs. This two-volume book is an invaluable resource for anyone committed to sustainable development and inner transformation."

William J. Rothwell, Ph.D., DBA, SPHR, SHRM-SCP, RODC, FLMI, CPTD Fellow
Distinguished Professor
Workforce Education and Development
The Pennsylvania State University
University Park, PA

"The world is in crisis. We urgently need to improve our individual and collective abilities to bring about transformational change. This collection provides much needed guidance on the inner skills and qualities that will support the transition to sustainability and the means to help to broadly develop them."

Stephanie Bertels

VanDusen Professor of Sustainability | SFU Beedie School of Business
Founder & Lead Researcher, The Embedding Project

https://doi.org/10.1515/9783111453729-030

INNER DEVELOPMENT GOALS
Switzerland

The Digital Workbook enhances the book's vision, offering a dynamic platform for ongoing learning, collaboration, and personal transformation. Through exclusive resources, reflections, and community engagement, the Hub extends the journey beyond the book's pages, fostering a global exchange of insights and practices to support inner development and the SDG agenda.

The Digital Workbook serves as an evolving, interactive space where authors and readers collaborate to co-create inner development narratives. It goes beyond documenting insights from these journeys, aiming to cultivate deeper connections and collaborative learning within a supportive community. In this space, participants engage in meaningful conversations, share reflections, and contribute their unique perspectives to enrich our collective understanding of inner development.

The Digital Workbook is free for readers of the book.

Simply scan the QR code below

Use the coupon code 'IDGSTORIES' for free access

idgworkbook.sutra.co

Digital Workbook